SAN ANSELMO LIBRARY
110 TUNSTEAD AVENUE
SAN ANSELMO, CA 94960

O9-BTZ-548

DISCARDED

THE VICTORIANS

Also by A. N. Wilson

NON-FICTION
The Laird of Abbotsford
The Life of John Milton
Hilaire Belloc
How Can We Know?
Penfriends From Porlock
Tolstoy
C.S. Lewis: A Biography
Jesus
The Rise and Fall of the House of Windsor
Paul
God's Funeral

FICTION
The Sweets of Pimlico
Unguarded Hours
Kindly Light
The Healing Art
Who Was Oswald Fish?
Wise Virgin
Scandal
Gentlemen in England
Love Unknown
Stray
The Vicar of Sorrows
Dream Children

The Lampitt Chronicles:
Incline Our Hearts
A Boffle in the Smoke
Daughters of Albion
Hearing Voices
A Watch in the Night

THE VICTORIANS

A. N. WILSON

W. W. Norton & Company
New York   London

Copyright © 2003 by A. N. Wilson
First American edition 2003

All rights reserved
Printed in the United States of America

For information about permission to reproduce selections from this book,
write to Permissions, W. W. Norton & Company, Inc., 500 Fifth Avenue,
New York, NY 10110

LIBRARY OF CONGRESS CATALOGING-IN-PUBLICATION DATA

Wilson, A. N., 1950–
The Victorians / A. N. Wilson.—1st American ed.
p. cm.
Originally published: London : Hutchinson, 2002.
Includes bibliographical references and index.
ISBN 0-393-04974-4
1. Great Britain—History—Victoria, 1837-1901. 2. Great Britain—
Civilization—19th century. I. Title.
DA550.W745 2003
941.081—dc21   2002033809

W. W. Norton & Company, Inc., 500 Fifth Avenue, New York, N.Y. 10110
www.wwnorton.com

W. W. Norton & Company Ltd., Castle House, 75/76 Wells Street, London
W1T 3QT

1 2 3 4 5 6 7 8 9 0

Contents

List of illustrations   vii
Acknowledgements   x

Preface   1

Part I Early Victorian
1   The Little Old Woman Britannia   9
2   Victoria's Inheritance   24
3   The Charter   34
4   Typhoon Coming On   48
5   The Age of Peel   58
6   Famine in Ireland   74
7   The Victorians in Italy   84
8   Doubt   93
9   Mesmerism   103
10   John Stuart Mill's Boiled Egg   108
11   The Failed Revolution   113

Part II The Eighteen-Fifties
12   The Great Exhibition   123
13   Marx – Ruskin – Pre-Raphaelites   151
14   The Crimean War   175
15   India 1857–9   201
16   Clinging to Life   224

Part III The Eighteen-Sixties
17   *The Beloved* – Uncle Tom – and Governor Eyre   247
18   The World of School   273
19   Charles Kingsley and *The Water-Babies*   295
20   *Goblin Market* and the Cause   305
21   Wonderland   322
22   Some Deaths   330

Part IV The Eighteen-Seventies
23 Gladstone's First Premiership   343
24 The Side of the Angels   365
25 The End of Lord Beaconsfield   385
26 *The Devils* – Wagner – Dostoyevsky – Gilbert and Sullivan   409
27 Country Parishes – Kilvert – Barnes – Hardy   425

Part V The Eighteen-Eighties
28 A Crazy Decade   437
29 The Plight of the Poor   441
30 The Rise of Parnell   451
31 The Fourth Estate – Gordon of Khartoum –
    The Maiden Tribute of Babylon   461
32 Politics of the Late 1880s   478
33 Into Africa   486
34 Kipling's India   493
35 Jubilee – and the Munshi   502
36 The Dock Strike   508
37 The Scarlet Thread of Murder   521
38 The Fall of Parnell   530

Part VI The Eighteen-Nineties
39 The Victorian Way of Death   539
40 Appearance and Reality   548
41 Utopia: The Decline of the Aristocracy   572
42 The Boer War   597
43 *Vale*   614

Notes   621
Bibliography   659
Index   688

List of illustrations

First Section
1. Steam locomotive (© *Lambert/Hulton Archive*)
2. Tennyson (© *The Bridgeman Art Library*)
3. Chartist riots (© *The Bridgeman Art Library*)
4. Ireland in desolation (© *Hulton Archive*)
5. Prince Albert and Queen Victoria (*The Royal Archives* © *HM Queen Elizabeth II/Roger Fenton*)
6. Osborne House
7. Osborne House (entrance hall)
8. Crimean War Cookhouse (© *Hulton Archive*)
9. Florence Nightingale (© *Hulton Archive*)
10. Mary Seacole (© *Hulton Archive*)
11. Darwin (© *Hulton Archive*)
12. Zoo man and monkey (*By permission of the Zoological Society*)
13. Am I a Man and a Brother? (© *Hulton Archive*)
14. Dickens and child (© *Hulton Archive*)
15. Alice Liddell (© *Hulton Archive*)
16. The Chatsworth Stove (*By permission of the Devonshire Collection, Chatsworth House*)
17. Crystal Palace (*By permission of* The Architect's Journal)

Second Section
18. State Opening of Parliament, 1851 (*Palace of Westminster Collection*)
19. The Royal Throne in the House of Lords (*Palace of Westminster Collection*)
20. *Windsor Castle in Modern Times* (*The Royal Collection* © *HM Queen Elizabeth II*)
21. *The Remnants of an Army* (© *The Bridgeman Art Library*)
22. *The Light of the World* (© *The Bridgeman Art Library*)
23. *The Awakening Conscience* (© *Tate Gallery*)
24. *Queen Victoria at the Tomb of Napoleon* (*The Royal Collection* © *HM Queen Elizabeth II*)
25. *Work* (© *The Bridgeman Art Library*)

26. Cardinal Manning banner (*By permission of the People's History Museum, Manchester*)
27. *The Beloved* (© *Tate Gallery*)
28. *General Gordon's Last Stand* (© *The Bridgeman Art Library*)

Third Section
29. Princesses in mourning (*The Royal Collection* © *HM Queen Elizabeth II/William Bambridge*)
30. Karl and Eleanor Marx (© *Hulton Archive*)
31. Annie Besant (© *Hulton Archive*)
32. Charles Bradlaugh (© *Hulton Archive*)
33. John Ruskin (© *The Bridgeman Art Library*)
34. Benjamin Disraeli (© *Hulton Archive*)
35. W.E. Gladstone (© *Hulton Archive*)
36. Survivors of Rorke's Drift (© *Hulton Archive*)
37. Zulus (© *Hulton Archive*)
38. Lord William Beresford killing a Zulu (© *Hulton Archive*)
39. The Forth Bridge (© *Hulton Archive*)
40. *Patience* (© *Hulton Archive*)
41. Collier girls by Munby (*By permission of Trinity College, Cambridge*)
42. Collier girl by Munby (*By permission of Trinity College, Cambridge*)
43. Fanny Cornforth (© *The Bridgeman Art Library*)
44. Elizabeth Siddal
45. Newspaper vendors (© *The Bridgeman Art Library*)
46. W.H. Russell (© *Hulton Archive*)
47. W.T. Stead emanating behind the head of an archdeacon (*By permission of The British Library*)

Fourth Section
48. The Rev. William Barnes and family (*By permission of the Dorset County Museum*)
49. London slum (© *Hulton Archive*)
50. Women suspended (© *The Mistress and Fellows, Girton College, Cambridge*)
51. Oscar Wilde (© *Hulton Archive*)
52. Sir Charles Dilke (© *Hulton Archive*)
53. Charles Stewart Parnell (© *Hulton Archive*)
54. Races (© *Hulton Archive*)

55. Cup final (© *Hulton Archive*)
56. Indian tennis party (© *Hulton Archive*)
57. Jubilee (© *Hulton Archive*)
58. The Queen and the Munshi (*The Royal Archives* © *HM Queen Elizabeth II/Robert Milne*)
59. Princess Beatrice as 'India' (*The Royal Archives* © *HM Queen Elizabeth II/G.W. Wilson*)
60. Devonshire House Ball: Harty Tarty (*By permission of the Devonshire Collection, Chatsworth House*)
61. Devonshire House Ball: Arthur Balfour et al. (*By permission of the Devonshire Collection, Chatsworth House*)
62. The Cecils as Elizabethan children (© *The Marquess of Salisbury, Hatfield House*)
63. Starving children in concentration camp (*By permission of the Boer War Museum, Bloemfontein*)
64. Marie Lloyd (© *Hulton Archive*)
65. The motor-car (© *Hulton Archive*)

Every effort has been made to contact all copyright holders. The publishers will be glad to make good in future editions any errors or omissions brought to their attention.

Acknowledgements

Peter Ackroyd, Berry Chevasco and David Newsome read the book in its entirety in typescript and offered invaluable suggestions. I am so grateful to them for spotting howlers and for making suggestions. Rosemary Ashton read the 1850s chapters in the middle of a very busy academic term. John Grigg, a hero as well as a friend to me, who had helped with earlier books, offered to read the typescript. Alas, before he was able to accomplish that task, mortal illness overtook him. I owe so much to his encouragement and to conversations over the years. All those interested in Victorian and twentieth-century political history are the poorer for his death, not least because it occurred before he had finished his life's work, the monumental biography of David Lloyd George. To all these I render hearty thanks.

It is impossible to finish a large task such as this without realizing how lucky I have been in my teachers, my family and friends. One does not wish to imitate an Oscar speech by thanking everyone from Momma to the hypnotherapist, but a book such as this grows, not just from a few years of intensive research, but also from a lifetime spent in the company of people who are interested in the subject. Thanks to those unnamed teachers, domestic companions, family, friends who over many years educated me and continue to do so.

Thanks, too, to Max Hastings and Lawrence James, who at different stages made helpful suggestions for further reading, especially in the sphere of military and colonial history.

My mesmeric neighbour Jonathan Miller told me much about mesmerism, the history of Victorian medicine and much else, as well as sharing some of the insights of his late mother Betty Miller, that inspired interpreter of nineteenth-century literature and life.

The 'onlie begetter' of the book was Gillon Aitken. I owe him so much, not merely for encouraging me to start the project, but for his friendship throughout. Sue Freestone, Starling Lawrence and Steve Cox were patient midwives – Steve Cox being the most punctilious of editors, and a fund of prodigious and miscellaneous knowledge. Jill Hamilton did much useful copying for me at the Society of Psychical Research, and amused me with talk of Arthur Balfour. James

Nightingale helped the book through its final journey to publication and Tony Howard made the index.

I began a conversation about Ruskin with Tanya Ledger – now Harrod – about thirty years ago and it seems, very enjoyably to me, to have been going on ever since. Tony Quinton, in moving house and reducing his library, filled my house with such treasures as the Complete Works of Carlyle and the College Sermons of Benjamin Jowett, and my mind with many stimulating thoughts. John Martin Robinson's conversations about the nineteenth-century Church, the aristocracy and the politics of age were always stimulating.

Ruth Guilding, whom I first met in Princess Beatrice's bedroom at Osborne House, where she was the curator, gave invaluable help with the picture research, as well as many insights, over the years, into the Victorian Age.

The staff of the London Library, the British Library and the Bodleian Library – especially in the New Bodleian and in Duke Humphrey's Library – were patient with an amateur researcher whose inquiries must often have seemed foolish, and brought manuscripts 'up' with astounding speed. The staff of the Manuscript Room in the British Library were similarly solicitous. For many months, though, it was the Humanities One Reading Room in the British Library which seemed like home. The friendliness and helpfulness of the staff in this stupendously well-run library are a very bright light in life. There is an anecdote on page 193 which those editing the typescript found puzzling. Lord Ashley – best known to us as the 7th Earl of Shaftesbury – who campaigned so tirelessly for improving the lot of factory children, and poor children everywhere, wanted to enlist the help of the foreign secretary, Lord Palmerston – his mother-in-law's husband. Ashley organized a visit to Palmerston's palatial house in Carlton Gardens by a delegation of trade union leaders, Surely, said Palmerston with his breezy optimism, conditions in the factories had improved immeasurably since the early reforms? Had not the advent of machinery made things much easier for factory workers? The union leaders pushed together two heavy armchairs and asked the Foreign Secretary if he would care to trundle them round his drawing room. He was out of puff after a couple of circumambulations of the room. The children in British factories, he was told, have to push machinery of comparable weight for the equivalent of thirty miles each day. Desk editors have special minds. 'What sort of machines are these?' asked Steve Cox. I don't know, I am afraid. But I often thought of these trundling

Victorian factory workers as, a little guiltily, I ordered up yet more books in 'Humanities One'. A smiling staff heaved and carried literally hundreds of books to the Issue Desk for me. The British Library is the glory of our nation; the staff are its glory. Though we, the readers, enjoy all the seemingly magic computerized catalogues and comfortable reading rooms, the books do still have to be lifted and heaved and wheeled.

The heroine of my tale, though, is Amy Boyle, who typed the whole thing up from my handwritten version; then retyped; and then cheerfully typed again, before at last – mystery of mysteries – she put it on to disk.

Preface

The Victorians are still with us. This is not a whimsical statement, intended to suggest that the shades of the Prince Consort or Elizabeth Barrett Browning or Dan Leno are still to be discovered floating in the night air if we empathize sufficiently with their memory or purpose. Rather, the Victorians are still with us because the world they created is still here, though changed. Theirs was the period of the most radical transformation ever seen by the world. Before them major industrialization was confined to a few towns in Britain. After them, the whole world was covered with railways and factories; and the unstoppable rise and spread of technology would continue into the age of Silicon Valley. Before them, the world was a small world of nation states. East was East and West was West. Large tracts of the world, especially in Africa, were unmapped. After them, the 'Dark Continent' had been penetrated by European powers: the destiny of Africa had changed; India, parcelled out in the eighteenth century between the East India Company and its own native princes, had become the linchpin of a huge British Empire – stretching throughout Asia, Australasia, Canada. Before the Victorians, democracy was the dream of a few political theorists. After them, it became the inevitable political goal towards which all Europeans and subsequently the rest of the world strove.

The Victorian era felt like a time of peace for almost everyone in Britain. Yet for the planet as a whole, because of the Victorians, it was in fact a time of almost perpetual minor warfare. Old empires and nations, most notably the Ottoman Empire, crumbled before the technological and economic giants of modern Europe, most notably France, Germany and Britain. Thereafter, their struggle for dominance and mastery led very nearly to their mutual destruction in two world wars during the twentieth century. And yet, when the dust and rubble of battle had subsided, when the twentieth-century experiments in European dictatorship and Marxist communism had been tried and discarded, when the Berlin Wall had been demolished and a new world order proclaimed with the United States as the dominant superpower, the Victorian world, with its problems, was still there. The Balkans were still the area of Europe where trouble could flare into conflict and conflict into war – and this after the Crimean War, the 'Bulgarian Atrocities', the decline of the Sick Man of Europe, the assassination of the Archduke in Sarajevo. We are still in some ways facing the same world there as Disraeli and Gladstone faced; we puzzle over the same problems of whether or not the richer countries of the world can or should helpfully intervene in Serbia, Hercegovina, Croatia. Gladstone in young middle age felt it to be his mission to pacify Ireland. Had he and Charles Stewart Parnell succeeded in persuading the electorate to allow Irish Home Rule before the scandal of Parnell's involvement in a divorce case, British history would have been very different. But we have just been living through nearly half a century in which all the problems faced by the Irish and the British in relation to one another are still alive; many of the Victorian questions in Ireland still require an answer, in spite of the collapse of landlordism, the Ascendancy and the Union.

The post-colonial problems of Africa and Asia are cognate and comparable. Of course, we have all moved on since Cecil Rhodes authorized the disastrous Jameson Raid into the Transvaal. The world still waits with optimistic wonder to see whether the Mandela legacy will spare Southern Africa from the conflicts which were eagerly predicted by the friends of the ugly old ways and days. But no one can consider Africa in any corner of the continent from Egypt to the Cape without going back to the problems which the Victorians both discovered and created there for subsequent generations. Nor is it possible for us to feel too smugly superior to them, since many of the pious impulses which might lead us to support the Aid agencies, Oxfam or Christian Aid or the United Nations – in abolishing slavery in the West African coast, for example, in campaigning for a fairer deal for workers in the cocoa industry, in wishing to tackle and eliminate plagues and diseases – were precisely the generous impulses which led many of the Victorians to intrude into Africa in the first place, believing that the solution to African problems was to import Western values in exchange for minerals or land. Anyone who wants Western governments or the World Bank to increase assistance to Africa still retains some of this colonialist attitude. And though we might blush, if we are British, at some of the cruelties inflicted in the name of the Crown – in the Ugandan campaigns of Lugard, for example, or in the suppression of the Indian Mutiny – it would be a singularly neurotic and shame-ridden Briton who did not also acknowledge that the beneficent Anglican mind of Archbishop Tutu, or the cricketing skill of the

Pakistanis and Indians, were post-colonial legacies to set beside the horrors.

Yet while we feel that we still live in a world shaped by the Victorians, there is another sense in which they have vanished totally. We feel this most in England. I was born in 1950, and for the first two or three decades of my life I met many old people who had been alive during the reign of Victoria, or who could share the memories of their parents' generation. Mine was the last generation which had the chance to hear Sir Charles Tennyson's immortal public talks in which he recalled memories of his grandfather, the Victorian poet laureate. When I went up to Oxford in 1969 there were at least two pairs of spinster sisters, the Misses Butler and the Misses Deneke, who could remember tea parties with Lewis Carroll. I never met anyone who knew Cardinal Newman, but older dons knew Phelps of Oriel, who had been provost when Newman came back to his old college after an absence of forty years. How should an Oxford don salute a Prince of the Church? By genuflecting and kissing his ring? When Newman walked into the Oriel Common Room, the old fellow, frail in his scarlet, burst into tears. Phelps stalked forward and vigorously shook him by the hand with the words, 'Well done, Newman, well done!'

Mine is the last generation to whom such tales were told as of an almost remembered oral tradition. Mine is the last, too, of the generations which can remember the physical details of Victorian life surviving. The waiting-rooms in British Railways stations in the 1950s were still gaslit. Old ladies in my childhood still clutched reticules; their cream-jugs were still covered with slightly cheesy little beaded cloths. My eldest aunt, born in the nineteenth century, saw Forbes-Robertson perform Shakespeare; my father, born just in the twentieth century, heard Marie Lloyd. When their infant brother died before the First World War the funeral was a Victorian one, with crêpe and mutes and horses. The agonies of bereavement and lost faith which followed the experience were also of a Victorian flavour. The great manufacturing towns of the Midlands and the North were still belching smoke, and still making things which other people wished to buy. These towns were still proudly independent and local, with their statue of the local bigwig in the city square, the library or art gallery endowed by his fortune in industry. The bigwig's name was still one to conjure with. Old people in Bradford or Leeds or Stoke could remember the old days when the mill-owners, the factory magnates were still residing among their workers. And of course they could remember, too, levels of

3

poverty which to our generation's way of looking at life were almost unimaginable.

The turning of the new century has inevitably been the occasion of many new biographies of Queen Victoria, and accounts of differing aspects of her reign. I am not an academic historian, and would not consider myself qualified to write for such as were. What follows is what G.M. Young in an earlier generation, and in a masterly account of the Victorians, called a 'portrait of an age'. The book has swollen to proportions which appal its author. I felt sure that if it were any longer it would deter my readers, and this can be my only excuse for the omissions. I have tried to draw a picture of the Victorians and their age which makes sense of them to our generation, to retell some of the outstanding incidents and portray some of the outstanding figures of the period. Everyone's perspective will be different. And there is always the paradox in a book of this character, which attempts plausibly to live up to a huge portmanteau-title, that an aspect of the subject which demands more words is not necessarily more 'important' than one which can be mentioned succinctly. The Crimean War for instance is not in my view more 'important' than the growth of the railways, but it has received much more space here. Sometimes, however, I have deliberately given more time or description to incidents or figures who have in my opinion been misunderstood or underestimated. For example, it seems incomprehensible to me that Cardinal Newman is generally esteemed more highly today than Cardinal Manning.

I have relied largely on the researches and books of others, as my large bibliography shows; but I have also been lucky in living near the British Library and in being able to consult their vast manuscript collections. Sometimes one letter by, let us say, Florence Nightingale or Lady Augusta Stanley has illuminated an aspect of Victorian life for me more vividly than a shelf-full of secondary sources. All history is selective, and by implication, if not overtly, it makes judgements. A book such as this inevitably reflects my own preoccupations and those of the present age. If there has been a single shift in balance since Lytton Strachey wrote his mischievous debunking of Eminent Victorians over eighty years ago, however, it is the reversal of roles in the judicial bench. Strachey and his generation self-confidently judged and condemned the Victorians. We, while noting many things amiss about Victorian society, more often sense them judging us.

The Victorians

PART I

Early Victorian

The Little Old Woman Britannia

On 16 October 1834, two visitors arrived at the Palace of Westminster and asked to be shown the chamber of the House of Lords. Parliament was in recess: sessions were much shorter in those days than now. The Speaker of the Lords, the Clerk of the Parliament, the Gentleman Usher of Black Rod, the Sergeant-at-Arms – all those charged with the responsibility for the safety and upkeep of the Houses of Parliament – were away, in the country. The place was in the charge of a housekeeper called Mrs Wright.[1]

When, at four o'clock that afternoon, Mrs Wright showed the visitors into the chamber of the Lords, they could scarcely make out the magnificent tapestries on the walls. There was smoke everywhere. The visitors complained that the stone floor was so hot that they could feel it through the soles of their feet. The throne, the grand centrepiece of the chamber, where sat the constitutional monarch when opening and proroguing their Lordships' assemblies, was invisible because of smoke. The house was, Mrs Wright agreed, in 'a complete smother'.

The workmen in the crypt who had started the blaze had been charged, in the absence of the parliamentarians, with the task of burning the wooden tallies used by the Exchequer for centuries as a means of computing tax. These were modern times and these wooden tabs were to be replaced by figures written down in paper ledgers. It had been suggested to the Clerk of Works at Westminster, Richard Whibley, that this abundance of little sticks would make useful kindling for the fireplaces of the poor. (Then, as now, there were many poor people living within a short walk of the Houses of Parliament.)

The sticks were housed at Westminster, and it would naturally occur to any intelligent person that nothing could be easier than to allow them to be carried away for firewood, by some of the many miserable creatures in that neighbourhood. However, they never had been useful, and official routine could not endure that they ever should be useful, and so the order went forth that they were to be privately and confidentially burnt. It came to pass that they were burnt in a stove in the House of Lords. The stove over-gorged with these preposterous sticks, set fire to the panelling; the panelling set fire to the House of Lords; the House of Lords set fire to the House of Commons; the two houses were reduced to ashes; architects were called in to build two more; and we are now in the second million of the cost thereof; the national pig is not nearly over the style yet; and the little old woman, Britannia, hasn't got home tonight.[2]

The voice, unmistakably, is that of Charles Dickens (1812–70), speaking years after the fire. There was, as he half implied, a fittingness about the fire. The Reform Bill of 1832 had selfconsciously ushered in a new era; when the emperor of Russia heard of the Westminster fire he thought it was heavenly punishment for the Whiggish abolition of rotten boroughs – boroughs which, with only a handful of voters, could nevertheless return a member of Parliament. That was perhaps because he saw the passing of the Reform Bill as the first stage of the modernizing of the British political system, the first unpicking of an old-fashioned system of hierarchy, and deference, the first stage in a hand-over of political power from the aristocracy to the bourgeoisie. This, however, was hardly how it appeared at the time. Few, if any, of the Whig aristocrats who had reformed the parliamentary system were believers in democracy. All deplored the notion of universal suffrage. The extension of the suffrage, which diehards so regretted, was limited wholly to persons of property. The great Reform Act 'had defined more clearly than at any time before or since in British history, and more clearly than had been done in any other country, a qualification for the inclusion in the political institutions of the country based entirely on the possession of property, and the possession of a regular income'.[3]

Even with the abolition of rotten boroughs, the new Parliament was representative of the people only in the most notional sense. That was not how it conceived its purpose. What was new about the political classes in the so-called Age of Reform was their desire, a successful desire, to exercise control over the populace. There was no divide in the Parliament of the 1830s and 1840s between what a modern person would conceive of as Left and Right. The agitations of the Left took place then – as, very largely now – outside Parliament. The problem for the political classes – whether old Whig aristocrats, Tory squires, or the new manufacturing and industrial bigwigs whose emergence into the political scene was to change the climate so radically – was all seen as the same problem: how to control a rapidly expanding population. How to feed it, how to keep it busy, how, if it was Irish, or Scottish, to restrain it from open rebellion, how, if it was poor and discontented, to discourage it from sedition, how, if it was French, to prevent it from invading Great Britain, how, if it was Jamaican or Canadian, to stop it seceding from the British Crown. Hence the development in this era of the first police force, of tight controls over paupers, and of the workhouses in which to incarcerate those incapable of feeding their families.

These were the common problems agreed upon by almost all parliamentarians, though the Tories might be more inclined in some areas, the Radicals in others, to raise a voice of protest against the incursion, by new parliamentary measures, into the personal liberty of Englishmen.

The statistics speak for themselves. Over the previous eighty years, the population of England, Wales and Scotland had doubled – 7,250,000 in 1751, 10,943,000 in 1801, 14,392,000 in 1821; by 1831, 16,539,000 – and in Ireland 4,000,000 had become 8,000,000.[4]

Economics and politics conceived in terms of population-growth was an inevitable development in the history of human thought. If the Reverend Thomas Malthus (1766–1834) had not existed it would have been necessary to invent him and someone else would have written *An Essay on the Principle of Population*, a work which he first wrote in 1798 and constantly revised – in 1803, 1806, 1807, 1817 and 1826. The Malthusian questions have not gone away in the twenty-first century, though Western societies have a polite way of exporting them and worry more about the population of India and China than they do about that of, let us say, Britain. A recent edition of Malthus's essay has an introduction which reminds us in apocalyptic terms that 'in the 1990s the world is gaining *each year* the population equivalent of Sri Lanka, the UK, Haiti and Somalia combined . . . By 2050 we shall have a world population of *ten billion*.'[5]

Such figures would have confirmed the worst fears of the Reverend Thomas Malthus, who in the 1790s had a friendly argument with his father about the population question. Daniel Malthus believed, with such sages as Condorcet, Jean-Jacques Rousseau and William Godwin, that society was advancing towards perfection. Thomas believed that human population grows at a 'geometric' rate, as in the series, 1, 2, 4, 8, 16, whereas means of subsistence must grow at an arithmetical rate – 1, 2, 3, 4, 5. The inevitable consequence of this, he believed, was starvation – and before that the misery, belligerence and social disruption which hunger brings to human societies.

Although seen immediately as a kind of monster – Shelley called him 'a eunuch and a tyrant', Dickens makes Scrooge a mouthpiece for Malthusianism by asking why the poor don't go away and die 'to decrease the surplus population' – it was in fact with the highest altruism that Malthus wrote his *Essay*. He wanted poor people not to be poor – or if inevitably poor, at least to be well fed. Paradoxically he saw that the existent Poor Laws – what we would call Welfare – encouraged a dependency-culture. Whereas the old Poor Laws had left to the discretion of local parishes the choice of to whom charitable provision should be made, the new Poor Laws – enacted by the last Parliament before the fire of 1834 – centralized the provision of Poor Relief. Rather than extending charity to the poor in their own homes, the Commissioners had built a chain of workhouses across the country. It could be said that no one had to go to the workhouse. When the alternative, however, was to watch children go hungry, it is not surprising that the hated places began to fill up, even though most were faithful to the ideals of the Reverend H.H. Milman, writing to Edwin Chadwick, 'the workhouses should be a place of hardship, of coarse fare, of degradation and humility; it should be administered with strictness – with severity; it should be as repulsive as is consistent with humanity'.[6]

No wonder that those who found themselves taken to the workhouse should have cursed Malthus in their hearts – Malthus who advocated 'restraint' among the lower orders as the only permissible form of birth control.

One such child, born surplus to requirements in Staffordshire in the 1840s, remembered:

We went by the field road to Chell, so as to escape as much observation as possible. One child had to be carried as she was too young to walk. The morning was dull and cheerless. I had been through those fields in sunshine, and when the singing of the birds made the whole scene very pleasant. Now, when the silence was broken, it was only by deep agonizing sobs. If we could have seen what was driving us so relentlessly up that hill to the workhouse ('Bastille' as it was bitterly called then) we should have seen two stern and terrible figures – Tyranny and Starvation . . . As a child – 'the very vastness of it' [the workhouse] chilled us. Our reception was more chilling still . . . No 'softening gleam' fell upon us from any quarter. We were a part of Malthus's 'superfluous population' and our existence only tended to increase the poverty from which we suffered. 'Benevolence', he said, 'in a being so short-sighted as man, would lead to the grossest error, and soon transform the fair and cultivated soil of civilised society into a dreary scene of want and confusion'. This truly was a 'nice derangement of epitaphs' to come from the pen of a clergyman in a Christian country. I have wondered if the pen with which he wrote was a steel pen.

The author, Charles Shaw, inveighed bitterly against the 'gross selfishness and unspeakable crassness' of the 'statesmanship of England' for imposing these miseries.[7]

All of which – and much more – might have gone some way towards explaining Dickens's facetious tone in describing the Westminster fire, which MPs themselves and all those interested in the history of these magnificent old buildings, containing countless documents of historical importance, saw as 'that melancholy catastrophe'.[8] The Speaker, Charles Manners-Sutton, reckoned he had lost £9,000 worth of goods in the fire, including a valuable library.

On that fateful evening of 16 October, Mrs Wright, the housekeeper, locked the door of the House at five, feeling that she had done her duty in complaining to the workmen about the smoke and heat. Around an hour later, the doorkeeper's wife, Mrs Mullencamp, noticed flames licking the underneath of the door of the House of Lords and a few minutes later the entire building burst into flames. It was not until 7 p.m. that James Braidwood, superintendent of the London Fire Engine Establishment, heard of the fire and ordered twelve manual fire engines and sixty-four firemen to attend. By 7.30, fifty of the First Regiment of Grenadier Guards had arrived, and assisted by a strong body of the newly formed and much-hated Metropolitan Police they kept a space clear in front of both Houses.

Among the immense crowd gathered to watch the blaze was Joseph Mallord William Turner (1775–1851), who stayed up all night doing innumerable pencil sketches. Afterwards he rushed home to Queen Anne Street to do so many watercolour studies, based on immediate memory, that the leaves of his sketchbook stuck together. First he was on the Surrey bank surveying the scene from afar across the water. As the blaze died down however he came over and joined the thousands who thronged into Old Palace Yard.

'I never lose an accident,'[9] Turner once told his most articulate admirer. This particular accident, this blaze of orange and gold reflected in the inky waters of the Thames at night, must have seemed to Turner like one of his own canvases come to life. The moment when the roof of the House of Lords crashed in was 'accompanied with an immense volume of flame and smoke' emitting 'in every direction billions of sparks and flakes of fire'. It sounded, said an observer, like the report of a piece of heavy ordnance, like an explosion. In all likelihood Turner, who saw visual images as symbols, envisioned the fire as an emblem of the old world being done away with, purged and destroyed.[10] In which case he can hardly have been alone. The crowds were mostly silent as they witnessed the spectacle, but when the flames increased one man cheered and was instantly arrested.[11]

Lord Melbourne (1779–1848) himself, the prime minister, personally directed the attempts to save Westminster Hall from being engulfed.[12] Fire engines were brought inside the Hall in order to play water on the replacement hammerbeam roof which had been added to William Rufus's original building when Geoffrey Chaucer was the clerk of works. It was the only substantial medieval building in the entire rich complexity to survive the night. St Stephen's Chapel, where the Commons had sat since 1547, was burnt out, though engravings of the ruin suggest that it could have been saved had the atmosphere of the times been more minded to conserve than to rebuild.[13]

For something, unquestionably, more than a collection of much-loved old buildings was ablaze. Britain was changing, and changing more rapidly and more creatively than any other country in the world. Within three years of witnessing the destruction of the Palace of Westminster, the prime minister, Lord Melbourne, was to see the death of the old King William IV (1765–1837) and the accession of Queen Victoria (1819–1901). Melbourne was Queen Victoria's mentor, her father-figure. Together this somewhat unlikely pair, the world-weary cynical Whig peer and the plain, diminutive, teenaged monarch, gazed forward to a new world more populous, more competitive and more adaptable than the Reverend Thomas Malthus could have envisaged in his worst nightmares. His death in Bath in the very year of the New Poor Laws, and of the Westminster fire, could also be seen as emblematic.

What Malthus failed to predict, with his arithmetical versus geometric rates, was the colossal growth in wealth in the era which would be known as Victorian. The more people, the more wealth-producers there were. It was an era of paupers, pauperism, famine, disease, certainly. In this, his predictions were more than amply fulfilled in the first decade of the new reign. But it was also an era of prodigious energy, growth and expansion. Foreign observers were astounded to watch Great Britain, in 1830, producing 2,000 tons per working day of iron – that is 650,000–700,000 tons per year.[14] By 1855, the figure had risen to 1 million tons of iron per annum. The same sort of figures could be discovered for coal production, for steamships, for machine-produced cotton and woollen goods. Though life was tough in the industrial towns where all this wealth was manufactured, more, numerically, benefited than suffered. Looking back at it all, our hearts are wrung by the plight of those who profited nothing from the grind and struggle of capitalism. The fortunes of the Victorian millionaires, the mill-owners, the mine-owners, the engineers and the speculative builders, were founded on the suffering of others. Nor was this suffering accidental. The struggle, the eternal warfare between the weak and the strong, the inexorable survival of the fittest, seems by this view of things to be a law of Nature, cruelly replacing the older belief that it was love which ruled the sun and other stars.

To one observer at least – and a highly influential one – it seemed as though this was quite literally the case. While the Houses of Parliament crackled and blazed, in October 1834, HMS *Beagle*, a ten-gun brig under the command of Captain Robert Fitzroy RN, was sailing towards Tierra del Fuego. Aboard was a naturalist, then aged twenty-five, by the name of Charles Darwin (1809–82). It was during this voyage, when observing the finches of the Galapagos Islands, that Darwin's mind first directed itself towards the evolution of life on this planet. Many years would elapse before isolated observations coalesced into an overall vision, or a hunch became a theory. That, by his own account, only began to happen after 1838. The crucial moment in his intellectual development, he tells us, occurred not when observing finches, or pigeons, or apes, but when reading Malthus's *Essay on Population*. 'In October 1838,' Charles Darwin recorded in his *Autobiography*, 'that is 15 months after I had begun my systematic enquiry, I happened to read for amusement Malthus on *Population* and being well prepared to appreciate the struggle for existence which everywhere goes on . . . it at once struck me that under these circumstances favourable variations would tend to be preserved, and unfavourable ones to be destroyed. The result of this would be the formation of a new species. Here, then, I had at last got a theory by which to work.'[15]

It was at once the most creative and destructive of theories, as the unfolding years would show.

Darwin's hour was not yet come. The two writers who stand at the beginning of the Victorian Age like choruses to the drama, one in tragic, the other in comic mask, are Thomas Carlyle (1795–1881) and Charles Dickens. Carlyle's *French Revolution*, after many adventures (which included the only manuscript of volume 1 being inadvertently burnt by John Stuart Mill's housemaid), was published in book form for the first time in 1837, the year of the Queen's accession. It was also the year which saw the final instalment of the serial publication of *The Posthumous Papers of the Pickwick Club.*

When we gasp with astonishment at the undemocratic nature of government (even after the Reform Bill) in the early decades of the nineteenth century; when we deplore the gap between rich and poor; when we survey the Britain of workhouses, of coal mines worked by children, of grinding poverty and even starvation in town and country, it is a striking fact that two of the most distinctive voices of the age, two of the most literate and imaginative, should not have come from privileged backgrounds. Dickens, the son of a government clerk imprisoned in the Marshalsea Prison for debt, had only rudimentary schooling and next to no money when, as a very young man, he began to report parliamentary debates in the *Monthly Magazine*. By modern standards, the poverty of the Carlyle family in Ecclefechan, Dumfriesshire, was little above a subsistence level; but by comparison with other Scotch peasants, Carlyle's parents, enterprising and thrifty, were prosperous, even though their children went barefoot until they began school, and they lived on a diet of oatmeal, milk and potatoes.[16] Thanks to the admirable educational system in Scotland by which a clever boy could rise, however poor he was, Carlyle went to Edinburgh University and immersed himself in contemporary European literature, language and philosophy. He was the great interpreter of German poetry and philosophy to the English-speaking world.

It was to France, however, that he went at the age of twenty-nine on a visit which was of crucial importance. It is difficult to overestimate the extent to which the British, after the defeat of Napoleon, continued to feel paranoia about France. Not only did all the English military, and many of their politicians, continue to believe that the greatest political threat came from France (up to and even during the Crimean War when French and English were supposedly allies); not only did Palmerston and Wellington fear the prospect of French invasion long after the very possibility of such an event had been extinguished; but France was also seen as the very object lesson of what could happen if a society imploded. For Tories of the old school, the lesson was simple enough: start to dabble with religious freethinkers, or to question the aristocratic system, and before long you find a guillotine erected; you find kings having their heads chopped off; you find the Reign of Terror and Robespierre.

For Carlyle, the story was less simple. The drama of the French Revolution is of electrifying fascination for this Scottish genius of peasant ancestry. Carlyle was one of those who had taken leave of orthodox religious belief, and certainly would never pretend to be a Christian, although he went on reading the Bible and believing that there was something Providential in the working of history itself.

We sow what we reap, both as individuals and as societies. This is the simple and compelling message of *The French Revolution* – though it is also the most exciting and readable work of history (I should say) in the English language. To the French to this day it is largely unknown. But no English-speaker can think of the French Revolution without using Carlyle's words – 'seagreen incorruptible', 'whiff of grapeshot'. Many, without knowing they have done so, have absorbed his views, even if they have not read his book.

Carlyle demonstrates clearly and relentlessly how the *ancien régime* was bound to fall, how the relentlessly selfish aristocrats and royal family could expect nothing less than a destructive apocalypse. But he is no advocate of the Terror, and his seagreen Robespierre is one of the great monsters of literature. Carlyle's agonies in print were to become the inner torments, political, religious and philosophical, of his generation, which is why he was the greatest of its prophets in the English-speaking world. He could not believe in Christianity, but his was no Voltairean delight at having done away with the old superstitions. He mourned his absent Christ and he trembled for a society with no sense of the awesome, no reverence before the great mysteries. Above all, he feared what would happen in a society which plainly could not sustain (morally or politically) a system of oligarchic privilege but which could so easily slither into something worse – anarchy, mayhem, butchery. The notion that the spiritual and political malaise of his times could be solved by parliamentary reforms, by extending the franchise or by allowing the vote to those living in households worth more than £10 rent – the notion that this could bring the Kingdom of God to Earth was ludicrous to him.

Carlyle was perhaps one of those thinkers who was strongest when he was accentuating the negative, and weakest when proposing his alternatives. His dissection of the weakness of any alternative to aristocratic government, yet the precariousness of that system itself, made many of his contemporaries shake. Carlyle was not a detached schoolroom historian – he was a great journalist who observed 'the condition of England' and saw terrible poverty, injustice, inefficiency and spiritual hunger. He was not optimistic about the prospects of his contemporaries avoiding a revolution even worse than the French. But almost worse than this, in his view, was the horrifying effect on thousands of human lives of the industrial, capitalist revolution which made so many not merely economic slaves but dullards, incapable of seeing the sort of intellectual or spiritual truths which had been clear to his own pre-industrialized, though poverty-stricken, relations and family.

Carlyle, though a vigorously comic writer, and one of the great wits both on the acerbic page and in his own conversation, had an ultimately tragic vision of life and of the world. It would be hard to conceive of a more different temperament from that which created *The Pickwick Papers*.

Few famous novels can have had more desultory origins. A comic draughtsman by the name of Robert Seymour had recently made a success with his *Humorous Sketches*, mocking the social pretensions of tradesmen who rise in the world. Seymour was an unhappy man, of illegitimate birth and depressive temperament. Riding on the success of the *Sketches*, he offered to Chapman and Hall, publishers, a series of drawings depicting the adventures of the 'Nimrod Club', Cockney sportsmen having absurd adventures. Dickens had already attracted notice with *Sketches by Boz*, journalistic observations of London life. Hall asked if he could supply some of the same for the adventures of the Nimrod Club. So, at the age of twenty-four, Dickens obliged.

Between the first and second episode of the book being published, however, melancholy Seymour had gone into his garden in the Liverpool Road, Islington, and shot himself. It is sometimes supposed that he did so because he resented Dickens receiving all the praise for what had been originally his creation. In fact, the first number had very little notice and sold only 400 copies. Seymour's suicide was prompted by his own mental illness, not Dickens's success. One of the illustrators who applied for the job in Seymour's stead was a tall public schoolboy called William Makepeace Thackeray. But the job was given to R.W. Buss, and thereafter writer and draughtsman worked in tandem.

The story, published between 1836 and 1837 in serial parts, was a rambling picaresque; its first audiences were drawn by a Janus-like double-appeal. On the one hand it celebrates and fantasizes about the holiday-freedoms of the swelling lower middle class from which Dickens himself sprang. In this sense, it is utterly modern. On the other hand it is a nostalgic snapshot, or series of snapshots, of an England which industry and the railways were to change forever.

Pickwick revealed (and perhaps in some senses created) the existence of a new public. Before it was published, the reading public was divided. Newspapers cost sevenpence. A three-volume novel cost £1. 11s. 6d. Only the substantial middle, upper middle and upper class bought what we should call broadsheet papers or hardback novels. Beneath this class of perhaps 50,000 readers there were those who read popular fiction purveyed not in book form but in cheap periodicals, loose paperbacks sold by travelling salesmen from door to door or at street markets. Ballad-sheets, satires and popular romances would be sold in this way by vendors not unlike Silas Wegg in *Our Mutual Friend*. Some of Dickens's contemporaries, such as William Harrison Ainsworth, the popular imitator of Sir Walter Scott, believed that the young journalist was making a grave mistake in writing fiction in this popular form, the loose-covered serial; a form hitherto reserved only for low trash. But within months, the sales of *Pickwick* had risen to tens of thousands. Hereafter, many of the great novels by Dickens, Thackeray, Trollope, George Eliot and others would be published serially in one of the many periodicals of the day.

Pickwick mania seized first Britain, then abroad. (It was especially popular in Russia.) Pickwick chintzes began to appear in drapers' shops. Breeches-makers were asked to cut their products to imitate the nether garments of Mr Pickwick's Sancho Panza, the cockney servant Sam Weller. Mr Tupman, Mr Snodgrass and Mr Winkle, the esteemed members of the Pickwick Club, were all turned into Toby jugs. There were pastries called Pickwicks and sugar confections in the shape of the Fat Boy. Now, such 'marketing' tricks are invented by successful publishers to cash in on the popularity of a character in a film or a book. Pickwick mania was spontaneous, and the market tapped by Chapman and Hall – a new market, a new class of people altogether – had partially defined itself by its response to Dickens.

The political student of *The Pickwick Papers* would absorb much of the spirit of this important class – the *petite bourgeoisie* who were, successively, and throughout the period, to support Free Trade, and to cheer when the Corn Laws were abolished because such measures would bring in an era of universal peace; yet they would also cheer eight years later when Britain fought an entirely avoidable war against Russia in the Crimea. They would, like the electors at Muggleton in *The Pickwick Papers*, 'have presented at divers times no fewer than one thousand four hundred and twenty petitions against the continuance of negro slavery abroad, and an equal number against any interference with the factory system at home'. Equally, those who cheered Lord Palmerston for the bombardment of Brazilian slave-ports, and who asserted their belief in freeing the negro, would have the most bloodthirsty and vengeful views of how to put down the Indian Mutiny in 1857. Pleased with the extension of the franchise to include £10 householders, this class would support Liberal measures for education in 1870. But they it was who would keep in power the oligarchy, chiefly aristocratic, who controlled the parliamentary system. In so far as they were pro-Reform Bills (both of 1832 and 1867) you could imagine them to be progressive. But they were always anti-socialist, and though they might have been anti the early nineteenth-century Toryism of Lord Liverpool, they loved Disraeli, and they voted Lord Salisbury into office over and over again.

Part of the difficulty, for a twenty-first-century reader of Victorian life, is how to draw the political map, how to see the world in those imaginative terms which help to form a political vision. In the terms of the late twentieth and early twenty-first century, free enterprise and a belief in the market are 'right-wing' beliefs, and the desire to check the voracious energy of pure capitalism seems to us 'left-wing'. But when, in *Little Dorrit*, Dickens was to satirize government bureaucracy in the 'Circumlocution Office', it was old Tory red tape which he was mocking. Old Tite Barnacle 'wound and wound folds of white cravat round his neck, as he wound and wound folds of tape and paper round the neck of the country'. That is just the complaint which free-market capitalists made of state socialists in the closing decades of the twentieth century. But in the early to middle years of the nineteenth century a radical liberal like Dickens made the complaint of paternalistic interfering Toryism.

Pickwick is a free spirit. He is a small-time merchant who has been released from the slavery which oppresses so many of Dickens's characters in the later books – the high desk, the scratch pen, the factory gate, the suppression of true sentiment (as in Wemmick's office sentiments, contrasted with the 'Walworth' sentiments of his Aged P and home). Pickwick has achieved what all enterprising Victorians aimed for – financial independence. He and his companions set out, in 1827 – ten years before the publication of the book, and the start of the Victorian era – on a series of absurd comic adventures, beginning, significantly enough, where Dickens himself began as a child before the gate slammed on his own personal Eden and his father was ruined: near Rochester.

> Bright and pleasant was the sky, balmy the air, and beautiful the appearance of every object around, as Mr Pickwick leant over the balustrade of Rochester Bridge, contemplating nature and waiting for breakfast . . . On either side, the banks of the Medway, covered with cornfields and pastures, with here and there a windmill, or a distant church, stretched away as far as the eye could see, presenting a rich and varied landscape, rendered more beautiful by the changing shadows which passed swiftly across it, as the thin and half-formed clouds, skimmed away in the light of the morning sun.

Even as they read *The Pickwick Papers*, the first readers could indulge in instant nostalgia. The first railway terminus, Euston, was built in London in the year the book was published. The old era of the stagecoach – each with its name (*Defiance, True Blue, Wonder, Tantivy, Star of Brunswick, Isis, Irresistible, Tally Ho, Rocket, Zephyr, Ariel, Emerald, Flower of Kent, Mazeppa*) – was to give place to named steam engines, about which in later eras schoolboy enthusiasts would be no less sentimental.

The nostalgia of *Pickwick* is a large part of its appeal, and it is one of the most remarkable features of the collective Victorian consciousness. That is, while they were in every sense different from previous generations, and glad to be different, they also hankered after the past. Dickens, when he settled in a large house at Gad's Hill, had some false book-backs made for a door in his library, simulating a row of bound leather volumes. The titles, still visible today in a room which is a school office (somehow this is appropriate), come under the heading: 'The Wisdom of our Ancestors – I. Ignorance. II. Superstition. III. The Block. IV. The Stake. V. The Rack. VI. Dirt. VII. Disease.' Dickens had in common with most of his contemporaries a desire to put the old world of injustice, ignorance and disease behind him. He shared with them, too, however, a sentimentality about the past, a sense that industrialization was wrecking the world. This dichotomy, felt by all readers of *Pickwick*, is to be one of the defining features of nineteenth-century socio-political debates. It defines John Ruskin, for example, who can be claimed, and justly claimed, as the father of English socialism and the bluest of old Tories.

There is another obvious feature of *Pickwick* which makes an appeal to its admirers; and of all the qualities in its author it is perhaps both the strongest and the hardest with which to come to terms. It is benevolence. How can one talk about this quality without smugness, without being saccharine? The *Edinburgh Review* in 1838, writing of Dickens, said:

> One of the qualities we most admire in him is his comprehensive spirit of humanity. The tendency of his writings is to make us practically benevolent – to excite our sympathy in behalf of the aggrieved and suffering in all classes; and especially in those who are most removed from observation . . .

Many of the 'benevolent' characters in Dickens will strike some readers as clumsily drawn and manipulative of our tear-ducts. One thinks of the brothers Cheeryble or of Mr Brownlow or Pickwick himself. It was well said that 'their facile charity forbids censoriousness; they are too busy being happy to think'. Yet each time one reads *A Christmas Carol*, it works. The ethics of Scrooge (which are the ethics of Adam Smith and Jeremy Bentham, the ethics of the mill-owners and factory-builders who created the wealth of Victorian England) are held in check by a tremendously simplified form of Christian charity.

Dickens admired and promoted the notion of benevolence, both in his person (for example in his work at Great Ormond Street Children's Hospital) and in his writings, to the point where he must be recognized as a hugely benign force in Victorian England. He is both the cause, and a symptom, of a benevolence which is palpable.

In the pages which follow, we shall read much about the Victorians which makes us feel as harshly about them as Dickens himself did about the Wisdom of our Ancestors. Their failure to better the lives of the urban wage-slaves in factories and mills; their genocidal neglect of the Irish famine; their brutality in India and Africa are not to be overlooked or glossed over. Nor were many of these abuses alleviated until history, as it were, forced them to be: the Empire was taken from the British by the poverty caused by world wars, and socialism of a benign Northern European form was imposed upon them for a corrective five- or ten-year period at the same time and for the same reason. And yet, even in the midst of the abuses, there was a significant number of people behaving benevolently. This seems to occur at all times and in all places throughout the nineteenth century. The landlords in Ireland, even, did not *en masse* starve and neglect their tenants. Not all mill-owners were monsters. Sanitation and housing was terrible, in many British slums, up to and including the mid-twentieth century. But improvements in general had been made in other areas. And a proper guilt was felt. One must not be smug about these things; for what is being discussed is human misery on an immeasurable scale – in workhouses, factories, slums, colonies, army camps, ships. Yet Dickens, partly because he is so consistently funny a writer, and so unpompous, reminds us of the existence of another Britain, in which the harshness of life is tempered by kindliness. His belief in the power of good-heartedness to triumph over evil is expressed in terms, not of a political programme, but of personality. His world, like the world of Victorian England, is not a Marxian *mass*: it is a teeming, moving screen of hilarious characters. He was in some senses the least realistic of all great geniuses; more than most writers, he created his own world. Such was his success, however, that we can almost say that the early nineteenth century in England was the England of Dickens. The figures who emerge from its prints and caricatures seem not merely just as odd as anything he created; they seem, rather, as if he did create them, and as if they are speaking lines created for them by him.

2

Victoria's Inheritance

Old William IV, dropsical, drunken, stupid, died two days after Waterloo Day, on 20 June 1837. He had been visibly sinking for some weeks. The Duke of Wellington, in the previous week, had offered to cancel the annual banquet commemorating the victory on 18 June, twenty-two years earlier, over the French emperor. William IV had robustly insisted that the banquet go ahead. He baffled everyone by exclaiming 'The Church, The Church!' just before he died. (He had shown no great interest in the Church when alive.)

William was the father of ten children by the celebrated comic actress Dorothea Jordan (1762–1816); but none of them were legitimate, so none could inherit the throne. When his niece Princess Charlotte died in 1817 – she was the only legitimate child of the future King George IV – the race had begun to determine which of George III's surviving children could produce an heir, and so become father of the new dynasty. All the late king's daughters and daughters-in-law were past the age of childbearing. The three who remained unmarried were William (Duke of Clarence), the Duke of Kent, and the Duke of Cambridge. William's marriage to Princess Adelaide of Saxe-Meiningen produced two infant daughters who survived, and one miscarriage. It was the Duke of Kent, the fourth son of George III, who was destined to win 'Hymen's War Terrific' as contemporary gossips termed it.

He was born in 1767 and for twenty-seven years he had lived as the faithful lover of a Frenchwoman called Madame de St Laurent. They were childless, and there were fears that he was sterile. When he was an elderly fifty with a pot belly and dyed receding hair, Edward, Duke of Kent, married Victoire, Princess of Leiningen, aged thirty-two. A love match it was not, still less a meeting of minds. She spoke no English, he no German. (Queen Victoria spoke no English until she was three.) Victoire was the sister of Leopold, Prince Consort and husband of the late Princess Charlotte, and of Ernest, Duke of Saxe-Coburg, who was the father of her nephew, and future son-in-law, Prince Albert. She was of that small northern Bavarian ducal family, of Coburg, which was destined to sire Emperor Maximilian of Mexico, Queen Isabella of Brazil, King Pedro of

Portugal, the last tsar and tsarina of Russia, the kings of Spain, Bulgaria and Prussia.

There are two well-established medical and genetic facts about the British royal family. One is that George III suffered from porphyria – the almost certain cause of his madness, but whose symptoms included discoloured urine (orangey-dark red), flatulence, colic, itchy skin and constipation. There is no evidence of Queen Victoria having inherited this condition or passed it on to her descendants. The disease is prevalent in the British royal family for many generations and stops with Victoria. (It is a 'dominant' gene, so that all those who carry it display its symptoms, however mildly.)

The second demonstrable genetic fact about Queen Victoria is that she was a carrier for haemophilia. A scroll written by William Bullock and Paul Fildes and kept at the Royal Society of Medicine in London traces back the medical history of Princess Victoire, Duchess of Kent, through seventeen generations. There are no cases of haemophilia. It is therefore safe to assume that Queen Victoria's mother was not a carrier.

Two alternative explanations suggest themselves for the appearance of a haemophilia gene in Queen Victoria's DNA. Perhaps the gene was newly mutated – the chances of this happening are between 1 in 25,000 and 1 in 100,000 per generation. By far the likelier explanation – particularly when we take into account the complete absence of porphyria in any of her descendants – is that Queen Victoria was not in fact the daughter of the Duke of Kent.

The Duke of Wellington's explanation for Queen Victoria's absolute hatred of her mother's secretary Sir John Conroy, and of her very tempestuous relationship with her mother, was that he 'supposed' Conroy and the Duchess to have been lovers. 'Victoria had seen her mother and Conroy in some sort of intimate situation. What She had seen She repeated to the Baroness Spaeth and Spaeth not only could not hold her tongue, but . . . remonstrated with the Duchess on the subject. The consequence was that they [Conroy and Victoire] got rid of Spaeth and,' continued Wellington, 'they would have got rid of Lehzen' – Victoria's beloved governess – 'if they had been able.'

Whether or not Conroy was Queen Victoria's father, it seems overwhelmingly probable that Victoire, uncertain of her husband's potency or fertility, took a lover to determine that the Coburg dynasty would eventually take over the throne of England. The failure of her brother Leopold to be the father of a queen of England only increased her own desire to fulfil the same ambition. Had she not done so, the inheritance would have passed to the Duke of Cumberland, widely believed to have fathered an illegitimate child by his own sister (Princess Sophia), and certainly guilty of the attempted rape of Lady Lyndhurst, the wife of the lord chancellor. He eventually became the king of Hanover. Had he inherited the throne of England, it seems unlikely that the constitutional monarchy would have long survived. The complexion of political life in Britain during the nineteenth century would have been, to put it mildly, very different.[1]

As it was, William IV's kingdom passed to his niece Victoria. The Church! The Church! in the person of the tiny figure of Archbishop Howley, clad in a wig, rochet and chimere, knelt early next morning in Kensington Palace to tell an eighteen-year-old girl that she was now the Queen. He was accompanied by the lord chamberlain. The iconic moment had its own personal drama. Victoria who had been brought up as a semi-hermit in the palace, with few friends, was going to display her own capacity for Darwinian survival and Samuel Smilesish Self-Help by effectually dismissing her domineering mother, the Duchess of Kent, and the sinister Sir John Conroy. This pair, who had so long planned to be the powers behind the throne, were banished like demons in a fairy tale. At nine that morning, the Queen received her prime minister, 'Of COURSE *quite* ALONE as I shall *always* do all my Ministers',[2] and there began that intense and mutually enjoyable *amitié amoureuse* between the tiny, plump, plain girl of eighteen and the languid, handsome fifty-eight-year-old Whig, a relationship likened by Melbourne's biographer to that sought by 'other girls . . . in some sympathetic schoolmaster or kindly clergyman'.[3]

At the Privy Council meeting, all the old men who had been governing England for years, Whig or Tory, were charmed by their new monarch. 'She not merely filled her chair,' said the Duke of Wellington, 'she filled the room.'[4]

Charles Greville (1794–1865), the greatest diarist of the age and, as clerk to the Privy Council, afforded a unique opportunity of observing the Queen at first hand, noted, 'Everything is new and delightful to her. She is surrounded with the most exciting and interesting enjoyments, her occupations, her pleasures, her business, her Court, all present an unceasing round of gratifications.'[5]

Delight in her animation was not the same thing as finding her interesting, as the following exchange makes clear.

Q. Have you been riding today, Mr Greville?
G. No, Madam, I have not.
Q. It was a fine day.
G. Yes, Ma'am, very fine day.
Q. It was rather cold, though.
G. (like Polonius) It *was* rather cold, Madam.
Q. Your sister, Ly Francis Egerton, rides I think, does not she?
G. She does ride sometimes, Madam.
(A pause, when I took the lead though adhering to the same topic.)
G. Has your Majesty been riding today?
Q. (with animation) Oh yes, a very long ride.
G. Has your Majesty got a nice horse?
Q. O, a very nice horse.
– gracious smile and inclination of head on part of Queen, profound bow on mine.[6]

It is a curious fact that comparable, if not identical, conversations probably still take place between privy councillors and the British head of state in the twenty-first century. Cynical, worldly Lord M. amazed courtiers like Greville by the evident delight with which he gave himself up to his new sovereign lady, playing draughts with her while he explained the Constitution. The man who, within the previous decade, had scandalized London by his very public affair with a married woman, Caroline Norton, and of whom the novelist Emily Eden said, 'He bewilders me and frightens me and swears too much',[7] seems in the company of the young Queen to have discovered qualities of innocence in himself which he did not know existed.

Nevertheless, as you read of their conversations, Victoria and her beloved Lord M., the question which comes most often to mind is – why was there no revolution in Britain in the late 1830s and the 1840s? In 1848, the Year of Revolutions on the European continent, crowns and aristocracies were sent packing. How does it come about that Queen Victoria was destined to survive not only the troubles of 1848 but all the subsequent years? When she died, nominal head of the largest, wealthiest and most aggressively powerful empire the world had ever known, her prime minister was the impeccably aristocratic figure of Lord Salisbury (1830–1903). Of all her prime ministers only three were non-aristocratic – Sir Robert Peel (1788–1850), William Ewart Gladstone (1809–98) and Benjamin Disraeli (1804–81). Gladstone was a millionaire, whose father and brother owned vast family estates in Scotland; Disraeli was an aristocrat by adoption. How did they all survive not merely the tumbril and the guillotine but – when it was eventually introduced – the ballot-box? Many readers of these pages, particularly if British, might consider it axiomatic both that Victorian political institutions would adapt themselves to survive, and that they would maintain sufficient popularity not to be exchanged for some thoroughgoing form of democracy. But nothing about political history is contingent. There is an inexorability about events and their consequences.

'Why bother the poor? Leave them alone!' said Lord M.,[8] quoting Sir Walter Scott (1771–1832), when his Queen asked him about the desirability of extending education to the poor. This was the man who had personally approved the treatment of 'the Tolpuddle Martyrs' – when in spring 1834 some poverty-stricken labourers in Dorset had had the temerity to form themselves into a Friendly Society, and to say that they found it difficult to live on nine shillings a week. With shorn heads and with their hands and legs chained and manacled, George Loveless and his friends were dragged to Dorchester Assizes and condemned under the esoteric Secret Oaths Act for forming a forbidden society. There was talk of trying them for sedition – punishable by death. In the event the six labourers were sentenced to seven years' transportation.[9]

When Queen Victoria asked Lord Melbourne if he could recommend the newly published novel *Oliver Twist* (serialized 1837–8), which was attracting much fame, he replied that he did not want her to read it. 'It's all among workhouses and Coffin Makers and Pickpockets . . . I don't *like* these things; I wish to avoid them; I don't like them in reality, and therefore I don't wish to see them represented.'[10] This airy unwillingness to confront one of the more displeasing aspects of contemporary existence might have been regarded as merely self-protective if Lord Melbourne's remark had been made by any rich nobleman of the period. Coming from the lips, however, of the prime minister who brought in the New Poor Laws of 1834, who was, in direct fact, responsible for the existence of the workhouses in such dimensions and numbers, the words have a chilling amorality.

The years 1837–44 brought the worst economic depression that had ever afflicted the British people. It is estimated – and we are speaking here of the years before the Irish famine – that more than a million paupers starved from simple lack of employment.[11] Many of the nation's businesses came to a halt. The workhouses whose existence

Lord Melbourne found so distressing to contemplate could not conceivably house the influx of paupers. *Oliver Twist* had inspired shocked and indignant reactions from the public. The Poor Law Amendments initiated by Melbourne's administration were not popular with the educated middle classes. In particular *The Times*, which reprinted *Oliver Twist*, took upon itself to print innumerable horror-stories about life in the workhouses. Between 1839 and 1842 almost every edition of the paper contained some such story. Many of the stories turn out in examination to be either untrue or exaggerated.[12] Enough of them sank into the public consciousness for the ostrich attitude of Melbourne to seem unendurable.

On Christmas Day, 1840, in the Eton workhouse, Elizabeth Wyse, a married woman, was allowed the rare privilege of being allowed to comfort her two-and-a-half-year-old daughter because she had chilblains. (The separation of parents and children in the workhouses was automatic, and one of the things which even in the better-run establishments caused most bitterness.) Mrs Wyse was allowed to sleep with her child for one night, but the director of the workhouse (like many of them a former sergeant-major) refused permission for a second night. When the ex-sergeant-major, Joseph Howe, found Mrs Wyse in the nursery next day, bathing and bandaging her child's feet, he ordered her to leave the room at once. She refused. He dragged her downstairs, locked her in the workhouse cage, and left her in solitary confinement with no coat, no bedding-straw and no chamber-pot, in 20°F of frost, for twenty-four hours. The following morning she was taken to eat breakfast, which was the remains of cold gruel left by her fellow inmates, and sent back to the cage and told to clean the floor – which was inevitably soiled – but with no utensils to do so.

It would be a mistake to suppose that institutional suffering was confined to the workhouse, or that the poor alone met with cruelty in their childhoods. These were indeed hard times, for none more than the young. Only a short walk from the Eton workhouse where Elizabeth Wyse and her infant suffered so hideously was St Mary's College, Eton, where a future prime minister in the early 1840s was writing to his father, the 2nd Marquess of Salisbury, of how a boy called Troughton *major*, drunk on ten pints of beer, had held a lit candle in Robert Cecil's mouth. 'I know you do not like complaints,' the child wrote, 'and I have tried to suppress them and conceal all this, but you are the only person to whom I can safely confide these things. Really now Eton has become perfectly insupportable.' He described being regularly kicked and thumped and spat at. 'They kicked me and pulled my hair and punched me and hit me so hard as ever he could for twenty minutes; and now I am aching in every joint and hardly am able to write this.' The Marquess did not withdraw his son from the school for another eighteen months, by which time he was in a state of emotional and physical collapse.[13]

If this was the fate of an aristocrat, then the son of an archdeacon, James Anthony Froude (1818–94) – destined to become a great historian – suffered as horribly at Westminster School in the early 1830s. 'The rule in College was that we were to learn by suffering, and I had to crawl to bed with a sore skin . . .' This pathetic child – only eleven when he first went to Westminster – was thrashed soundly by his father when he came home for the holidays and it was found that the bullies had stolen his shirts and ruined his few remaining possessions.[14]

But if suffering was not the unique preserve of the poor, that was not really the point. What shocked the early Victorians was the disparity between rich and poor, the visible unfairness of it all, made all the more visible in the railway age, when communications between the big manufacturing cities became so easy. In the rural, pre-railway age many of the more prosperous strata could avoid contact with the poor. In the 1840s they became much more visible because there were so many more of them, and the question could be asked, were such gross and obvious unfairnesses avoidable by acts of charity, or were the unfairness and competitiveness actually ineradicable ingredients in the capitalistic success-story in which that society was caught up?

In Fareham, in Hampshire, the workhouse had a large school; three of its pupils, bastard boys called Withers, Cook and Warren, aged between three and a half and five, were sent for special tuition from Bishop's Warren. Eight weeks later they were returned, so weakened by diarrhoea and disease that they could barely stand. What had happened? On their arrival at Fareham they had been placed together. One of the disturbed children had wet the bed. Their punishment was a cut of 50 per cent in the weekly food ration of 2 lb 10 oz of bread, 5 oz of mutton, 1 lb potatoes, 3½ oz cheese and 12 oz of pudding. The starvation diet did not cure the bedwetting. The children were then placed in specially designed stocks – imagine being the man who designed children's stocks! – and made to watch the other children having their meals. Since they now smelt intolerable they were made to sleep in an unheated shed in the yard, in the depth of winter.

Similar cases were the almost daily diet for readers of *The Times*.

This situation continued for at least the first ten years of the Queen's reign, until a scandal too far led to the resignation, and eventual abolition, of the Poor Law Commission in London. This was the scandal of the Andover Workhouse.

Andover, in Hampshire, a small prosperous market town, must, in this period, have looked like a little paradise. The Railway Fever which made each part of Britain quickly accessible, and which connected everywhere easily and efficiently, was only just beginning by Coronation Day,[15] when a great feast was held on the Common Acre: roast beef and pudding for all who attended, organized games for 1,000 children, 'to stamp on the minds of the young and rising generation a lasting impression of being coeval with our youthful, virtuous and beloved Queen Victoria'. Most of England at this date would strike any time-traveller from the twenty-first century as a Garden of Eden into which no serpent had strayed.[16] Since almost all common land had been enclosed by the 1830s, with one small area left as the 'common field' or village green, the country had the look of a well-tended garden, particularly since, unlike continental countries, England had been almost completely stripped of native woodland; it was a land of copses, parks and plantations, neat hedges and tended fields. From the 1831 census we learn that 961,100 families, or 28 per cent of the entire population, were employed in agriculture. The reality was that at least half the population – small village traders, blacksmiths, carpenters, wheelwrights, cobblers, bricklayers, millers, shopkeepers – were employed in rural communities. At this date many of the industries were essentially rural in base – the coal mines for example were not to be found in the middle of towns but gouging out the hills and fields. 'The representative Englishman was not yet a townsman, though he soon would be.'[17]

This, as we survey the coronation festivities at Andover in 1837, is how it will strike our imaginations – how fast, and how easily, all this innocence and beauty, even in rural Hampshire, would be destroyed by the coming of agricultural machinery, tarmacadamed roads, railways – and eventually the curse of the internal combustion engine, which completed the destruction and ruination of England.

Yet this Andover, in Jane Austen's county of Hampshire, is already different from the Andover Miss Austen would have known but a decade before. It possesses its Bastille. This was becoming a necessary weapon in the government's Malthusian armoury. When the twenty-first-century time-traveller had gasped at the unpolluted beauty of rural

England in 1837, he would then have begun to notice the stench of poverty. True, it depended where you went. Cobbett (1763–1835) on his Rural Rides in 1830 found the people of Leicestershire living in mud hovels: a German traveller of 1828 said that 'outside the northern factory districts and the low quarters of London one seldom sees rags and tatters in England, and seldom broken window panes and neglected cottages'.[18] Yet in real terms the agricultural labourers were poor. The Corn Laws, subsidizing the British landowners and imposing tariff on imported grain, did not translate, in years when the price of corn went up, into higher wages for agricultural labourers, though they did push up the price of a loaf of bread. (The price of wheat was measured in quarters, i.e. 8 bushels. In 1835 wheat cost 38s. 1½d., climbing to 81s. 6d. in 1836–9 and fluctuating to 47s. 5d. and 56s. 3d. in 1846.)[19] Life in the growing industrial towns of the Midlands and the North was tough in the 1840s, but there was money to be made. (Compare the lucky Northerner in 1847 with his 11s. 6d. per week, well above a subsistence wage, with an agricultural labourer in, say, Gloucestershire, Wiltshire or Suffolk, who might be struggling on less than a subsistence wage – 7s.)[20]

So it was that idyllic Andover could have more than its share of paupers coming to the workhouse for assistance. From the very start of the New Poor Laws in 1834 the local chairman of the Board, Charles Dodson, and the pair who ran the workhouse, Mr and Mrs Colin McDougal, applied the screw, the dreaded Prohibitory Order. In this parish all relief of the poor in their own homes was stopped. Single women with bastard children were obliged, if they wished to eat, to wear the yellow stripe of shame sewn across their coarse grey workhouse gown. The boys and men were set to the smelly work of bone-grinding, making fertilizer out of the bones of dead farm animals. They were so hungry they fell to gnawing the rotten bones and putrid horseflesh which came from the slaughterhouse.

Colin McDougal, the workhouse supervisor, was a rough Scotsman, born in 1793, who had fought at Waterloo and been discharged from the service as a staff sergeant in 1836. He was a drunkard who frequently got into fights with his no less horrible wife. He regularly thrashed children as young as three for messing their beds and he kept his paupers on such short rations that some survived by eating candles. Charles Lewis of Weyhill remembered his children eating the potato peelings thrown out for Mr McDougal's chickens. The scandal broke in 1845 when Ralph Etwall, the member for Andover, rose in the

House of Commons and demanded an inquiry into the administration of the Andover Workhouse, and by implication into the Poor Law Commission. In July 1847 the Commission was finally abolished – and in the very same week John Walter (1776–1847), the editor of *The Times* who had campaigned so tirelessly against it, also died. Yet, in spite of the shaming of the Poor Law Commission, and the resolution of Parliament to improve conditions in workhouses, these institutions remained grim for many decades to come.

3

The Charter

With hunger, filth, poverty, there came, inexorably, disease. On 7 November 1837 a doctor in the poverty-stricken Limehouse district of London's East End recorded the case of Ellen Green, aged seven years, of Irish extraction, living with her parents in a miserable apartment, on the second floor of a small house, situated in Well-alley, Ropemaker's Fields, Limehouse, a low, dirty and very confined situation. In the same room resided her parents, with two more of their children, and another Irish couple, with their only child, an infant at the breast.

The doctor, Charles Johnston, observed that the squalid apartment abutted on to a pigsty and that the floor was a heap of manure and filth, 'the joint produce of the house and pigsty'. Little Ellen was attacked with her first fit of vomiting and purging on 26 October; then with cramps in her legs and thighs. Within days her features had shrunk, her eyes sunk deep into the orbits, the conjunctiva had become effused, the lips were blue, the tongue was white. These were the sure signs of cholera, which killed her about a day later.[1]

A society's attitude to disease reveals more than the state of its medical knowledge. Victorian England, destined to become so densely populous, so politically powerful throughout the world, so dirty and so rich, poured much of its paranoia and its ambivalence concerning Mammon-worship into its feelings about cholera. The disease came from India, source of so much British wealth and guilt. It did not break out of the Indian subcontinent until the nineteenth century, the first major pandemic being in 1817. The extent of the outbreak was a direct consequence of trade, of the increase of traffic between European, chiefly British, merchants in Bengal and the armies sent to protect them. In 1817 the Marquess of Hastings's army, encamped at Bundelkand near Calcutta, lost 5,000 men through cholera. In 1818 it engulfed the whole of the Indian subcontinent. By 1819 it had reached Mauritius, by 1824 it had spread to the whole of South and South-East Asia. By 1829 it was in Afghanistan and Persia. By 1831 it had spread to Moscow, Petersburg, the Baltic ports.[2] 'We have witnessed in our days the birth of a new pestilence which in the short space of fourteen years, has desolated the fairest portions of the globe, and swept off at least fifty millions of our race.'[3]

The Privy Council in London immediately addressed itself to the question of whether traded goods could be contagious. Thus, from the beginning, cholera became a metaphor for the contagion of Mammon. The society which based itself entirely on profits from trade would invent arcane hierarchies and etiquettes in which to be 'in trade' was to be untouchable. Within the questions about contagious imported goods were also fears of the foreign and the foreigner. It was noted how often cholera outbreaks occurred near docks – as in the case quoted of young Ellen Green, who was, to make matters worse, Irish.

Thomas Wakley (1795–1862) caustically remarked of the government's plans to create a *cordon sanitaire*: 'Sagacious legislators who cannot prevent the spread of cholera from traversing the ocean, yet can keep it from penetrating a hedge or crossing a field.'

Wakley is himself a fascinating person, a radical in the Cobbett mould, one of the magnificently angry men of his age. In 1823, when aged twenty-eight, he founded the medical journal *The Lancet* and was in constant trouble from the London teaching hospitals for exposing their nepotistic organization and for publishing the contents of lectures which the surgeons believed to be their property. He was a coroner who used his position to expose wrongdoing – a good example occurring in 1846. Wakley presided at the inquest over a dead soldier, Frederick John White, who died from the effects of flogging. The verdict, directed by Wakley, caused such a sensation that flogging fell almost at once into disuse. After some failures to get elected, he became the (radical) MP for Finsbury in the first session of Parliament after the fire – 10 January 1835 – and he was outspoken for the Tolpuddle Martyrs.

But it is chiefly for *The Lancet* that Wakley will be remembered. It continues to this day as the great journal of medical record. For his contemporaries, however, the medical periodical was a deadly weapon of socio-political observation. *The Lancet* was persistently attacked by politicians for publicizing cholera. Wakley knew that it suited the authorities to falsify their reports, to prevent panic spreading.[4] It was one of the reasons his work as a coroner was so vital – to establish just why people died. The government had no more wish to acknowledge cholera than to recognize that soldiers died of flogging. The 1837 outbreak which killed Ellen Green was in fact quite mild. *The Lancet* alerted its readers to twenty-one cases of Asiatic cholera on board the seaman's hospital ship *Dreadnought* which spread to the adjacent Limehouse. 'The Bills of Mortality' – what we should call death certificates – for the period October to December 1837 showed a considerable increase of deaths beyond the norm, but as Wakley bitterly noted, 'We do not find a single case of cholera mentioned.'

After 1832, there were to be three major cholera epidemics in Britain: 1848–9, 1853–4 and 1866. The first of these killed 53,000 in England and Wales, 8,000 in Scotland; the next killed 26,000 – but 10,000 in London alone; the 1866 outbreak killed 17,000 – 6,000 in London. It should not be supposed that any British government was so reckless as to use plague as a political weapon. It terrified rich and poor alike, but their responses, not merely in Britain but throughout Europe, revealed the differences in attitude between the classes which were themselves the creation of capitalism. The propertied classes half feared the foreign import of plague which came as the sting in the tail of their new-found wealth. They feared it too as the outward and visible sign of that physical contagion which social division had created in the slums. The poor in most previous ages could perhaps, as the old Tory Sir Walter Scott had urged, be 'left alone', un-'bothered'. In that lost Eden of pre-capitalism, pre-industrial Britain, pre-population explosion, pre-export and import explosion, true Tory innocents, like the poet laureate William Wordsworth (1770–1850), could even find beauty in poverty. Wordsworth's Old Cumberland Beggar, by exciting charitable impulses in the poor cottagers he visited, spread grace, not disease. (Charles Lamb (1775–1834) had comparable thoughts about the beggars of London in the reign of George IV.) But the poor such as Ellen Green of Limehouse, sharing her tiny living quarters with two families and some pigs, had partly come into existence artificially. Her poverty – so the governing classes of the 1830s and 1840s uneasily began to feel – was their responsibility, in the sense of being both their creation and their duty. The virtuous parliamentarians, journalists, civil servants, wiseacres surveyed the condition of the poor and felt duty-bound to do something; to clean up the poor, to tidy them away, to improve them. These were profoundly un-Tory sentiments and the poor resented them. That is why in so many areas the European poor saw the attempts of doctors to cure cholera as mass murder. In St Petersburg a German doctor was killed and six beaten as they attempted to minister to cholera victims. In Prussia the poor refused even to believe in the existence of cholera; noting that the eruption of disease coincided with the arrival of doctors in their slums they drew the inexorably logical conclusion that doctors had poisoned them.[5]

Doctors, like policemen, were seen by the early Victorian poor as representatives of a hated governing class, come to keep the poor from doing what in the circumstances might have seemed reasonable: erupting, rebelling, looting, destroying – not necessarily with any fixed or focused aim in view, but merely as the political equivalent of a scream. The Metropolitan Police Force was established in 1829. Comparable gendarmeries grew up on the continental mainland as a simple response to the population explosion. They had two principal tasks, to protect property (and life), and to curb liberty.[6] From its inception, the police force was seen as a Benthamite organ of social control. Radicals such as Edwin Chadwick believed that the consolidation of police forces would actually prevent crime – his *Preventive Policing* (1829) was received with rapture by his philosophical radical friends, such as James and John Stuart Mill, and was even praised by old Jeremy Bentham himself.[7]

Jeremy Bentham (1748–1832) looks an unlikely godfather of the British or any state. And when one refers to his looks, these may be verified since, ardent rationalist that he was, he specified that he should not be buried with religious ceremonial but preserved in a glass case, an everlasting reminder to nineteenth-century humankind of the non-resurrection of the body and the life, far from everlasting but terrestrial, fact-based and empirical. There he sits in the hall of University College in Gower Street, in his large wideawake hat, his cutaway coat and nankeen trousers, calling up inevitable comparison with the Lenin Mausoleum in Moscow. Whereas the Russians, however, are a devout people, never more so than in their worship of the atheist revolution, and queued religiously to see the remains (or the waxwork) of the author of their political system, the English ignore Bentham. He sits like the waxwork of some eccentric footman, with his long hair sticking from his hat, and 95 per cent of his fellow-countrymen would be unable to tell you who or what he was.

His spiritual journey from High Tory absolutist to darling of the radicals, from churchman to unbeliever, was dynamoed by high intelligence and independence of mind, lubricated by enormous inherited wealth. (It was in origin a pawnbroking fortune.) He had the leisure, time, health and money to devote laborious hours to considering the whole nature of society, what makes it function and what, in revolutionary periods, makes it break down. His 'utilitarian' doctrine – the phrase was popularized by the son, John Stuart, of

Bentham's most ardent follower, James Mill – of the greatest happiness of the greatest number led in one direction to radical libertarianism and in another to rigid notions of control. His 'Panopticon' in prisons and workhouses was the architectural expression of his political outlook – central control must depend on keeping an eye on the dissident or recalcitrant elements in a state. Because of his huge expertise in the field of what we should call sociology and economics, Bentham was in fact consulted by politicians with whom no one would expect him to be in sympathy. Robert Peel corresponded with him about the setting up of a police force. The judicial reforms of Henry Brougham, from the suppression of special pleading to the setting up of local courts, followed Bentham to the letter. Wider yet and wider – Bentham's ideas about governing India, which seemed fantastic in the 1820s when the East India Company held its sway, were all put in force by the time of Imperial Expansion in the 1860s.[8]

Bentham therefore in fact as well as in spirit may be seen as the father of Victorian realpolitik. The 'greatest happiness of greatest numbers' theory was based on the callous but realistic view that pleasing everyone is impossible. The secret of a stable society is to isolate and emasculate the miserable.

Whereas in the aristocratically dominated hierarchical world of eighteenth-century England life and property were largely protected by law, meted out with great severity from magistrates or the judicial bench, the Age of Reform substituted for the concept of law the concept of preventive policing. Eighteenth-century England got by without a police force partly because the population was so small, partly because there were, by the time of the 1820s, over 200 capital offences. England had the harshest criminal code in Europe. By 1841, only eight offences remained on the statute book for which an individual could be hanged. In effect the only capital offence was murder. These reforms were the delight of liberals, happy to escape the *Beggar's Opera* world of the gallows. But the working classes were the chief opponents of introduction of the police force. Liberalism, using the term in its loosest sense, extended certain political rights to a wider group of propertied individuals, but it sharply reduced personal liberty. The establishment of a centralized police force, abolishing the local 'watch', the Dogberrys and Elbows who had kept the peace since Tudor times, tightened the hold of the state.[9]

There was, incidentally, no noticeable reduction in crimes against property after the establishment of the Met.[10] Peel's force of 3,000 men had a very largely political function in the first twenty years of its life. Almost to a man – this in itself was a sign of the times – they were agricultural labourers, drawn to the work by poverty, but detached from the urban proletariat whom they were enlisted to control. ('I have refused to employ gentlemen', Peel explained, 'as superintendents and inspectors, because I am certain they would be above their work.')[11] Though all the talk, when they were established, was of their supposed efficacy in stemming the loss of £900,000 worth of property by theft and violence, it was not long before the Metropolitan Police were being used to put down the rising tide of Chartist agitations.[12]

It is possible to view the phenomenon of Chartism as a premature harbinger of twentieth-century leftists, though the links are tenuous and it is often hard to find much in the way of an apostolic succession being passed from surviving Chartist groups or individuals to incipient Labour-ites. Chartism is perhaps more helpfully seen as a phenomenon of its time. Its aspirations, the hopes and fears which it inspired in differing parts of the populace, its near victories and its muted defeat form the most consistently interesting backdrop to the political history of Victoria's reign in its first ten years.

Those who hoped that the Reform Bill of Lord Grey (1764–1845) and Lord John Russell (1792–1878) would usher in an era of democracy, or even of government by the bourgeoisie, were to find their hopes disappointed. Grey's Cabinet was almost entirely aristocratic; the four members of it who sat in the House of Commons were Lord Palmerston (1784–1865), an Irish viscount, Lord Althorp, heir to the Spencer earldom, Cramer, a Scottish landowner raised to the peerage, and Graham, an English baronet with huge estates. The first act of Grey's government, after the passage of the Reform Bill, was to create two dukes.[13] Fifteen years later when John Bright (1811–89), the North Country radical, spoke of the middle-class composition of the new reformed Parliament and told Parliament, in 1847, that 'the present Government is essentially of the middle classes', there was laughter in the House.[14] The reforms of 1832 perhaps extended the suffrage to some propertied persons who had hitherto been excluded, but many of the old ways persisted. 'Proprietary boroughs' still existed for example, parliamentary seats which were effectively in the possession of one patron. The borough of Calne in Wiltshire was owned by the Marquess of Lansdowne. In 1832 it returned the Earl of Kerry to Westminster as its MP – Lord Lansdowne's eldest son. He died in 1836 to be replaced by John Charles Fox Strangways, Lansdowne's brother-in-law. In 1837 the seat passed to Lord Lansdowne's surviving son, the Earl of Shelburne, who was returned to Parliament in the elections of 1841, 1847 and 1852.[15] Nor should we imagine that the extension of the franchise in 1832 affected more than a handful of the populace. In terms of actual votes cast the Reform Act made no difference at all in many regions. In Harwich, which returned two members, the electorate was 214 people, of whom 156 voted in the election of 1832, and only 123 in 1835. Totnes with 179 voters returned two members; Liverpool with its 8,000 new voters also returned two members. Very many of the smaller seats, particularly those owned by aristocrats, were uncontested at elections, and the bribing of voters was an accepted part of the procedure – not merely accepted but necessary, in order to persuade those eligible to vote at all. As for voting in secret, many perhaps would share the view of Lord Palmerston, that 'to go sneaking to the ballot-box, and poking in a piece of paper, looking round to see that no one could read it, is a course which is unconstitutional and unworthy of the character of straightforward and honest Englishmen'.[16]

At the meeting of Queen Victoria's first Parliament, Thomas Wakley, our old friend the radical member for Finsbury, had suggested extending the suffrage still further, and introducing a secret ballot to make elections less vulnerable to abuse. He provoked the acknowledged Master Craftsman of the Great Reform Bill, Lord John Russell, to make his celebrated 'Finality' speech in the House of Commons. Lord John did not rule out the possibility of Reform being taken further at some future date; but if 'the people of England did not care for Lord John's moderate reforms, they may reject me. They can prevent me from taking part either in the Legislature or in the councils of the Sovereign; they can place others there who may have wider and more extended, more enlarged, and enlightened views, but they must not expect me to entertain these views.' Quite how 'the people of England' could have any effect at all on the political fortunes of Lord John Russell when he considered 'unwise' the very notion of offering any more of them the vote, His Lordship did not on that occasion vouchsafe.

It was largely in response to this intransigent Whig mindset, at a time of unprecedented economic hardship, made worse by the Liberals' workhouses and police forces, that the movement known as Chartism came into being.

'There is verily a "rights of man" let no man doubt. An ideal of right does dwell in all men in all arrangements, actions and procedures of men: it is to this ideal of right, more and more developing itself as it is more approximated to, that human society forever tends and struggles.'[17] So affirmed the great Carlyle, and others must have felt that there was something apocalyptic in the air, a change which had to happen merely because the gross disparities between rich and poor were so glaring, and the absence of political representation for the majority of the population was in the very nature of things wrong.

In 1837 *The Northern Star*, the Chartist newspaper, was founded in Leeds, using machinery and type brought from London. The comparative cheapness and speed of producing a newspaper, and the ease of disseminating its ideas by means of newly built railways, are important features of the Chartist story. The half-starved labourer in Andover was now in touch, in a manner impossible or inconceivable in previous generations, with the radical weaver of Spitalfields in London, the potter of Staffordshire choked on china clay, the overworked miner of Nottinghamshire, loom-hand of Yorkshire, cotton-spinner of Lancashire, iron-worker of South Wales, docker of Harwich. The working classes began for the first time to have a sense of solidarity. From the beginning, though its leaders were not working-class, Chartism was essentially a working-class movement because the only 'radicals' in the House of Commons represented the interests of factory-owners and industrialists who would oppose such reforms as the Christian Tory Lord Ashley's (1801–85) – from 1851 7th Earl of Shaftesbury – attempts to protect children and women from working more than ten hours a day or in dangerous conditions. The New Poor Law, believed the Chartists, placed the labouring classes 'at the feet of the rich assassins, who rob, brutalize, and enslave the population . . . It is in the nature of things that the middle classes must be worse than any other part of the community.'[18]

Carlyle believed that for the working-class movement to succeed, it needed 'not misgovernment, but veritable government'; not democracy or 'clattering of ballot-boxes' but firm leadership. 'This at bottom is the wish and prayer of all human hearts, everywhere and at all times: "Give me a leader, a true leader, not a false sham-leader; a true leader, that he may guide me on the true way."'[19] It was the undoing of the Chartist cause that no such People's King arose. James Bronterre O'Brien (1805–64), the thirty-two-year-old son of an Irish wine merchant who read for the Bar in London, presented the first petition to the

Parliament in 1837 – 'THAT THE POOR OF ENGLAND SHALL BE HEARD BY COUNCIL AT THE BAR OF THE HOUSE OF COMMONS AGAINST THE LATE TYRANNICAL AND INHUMAN ENACTMENT MISCALLED THE POOR LAW AMENDMENT ACT.'[20] He effectually passed over the leadership of the movement – as far as its parliamentary life was concerned – to Feargus O'Connor (1794–1855), the member of Parliament for Cork.

From the beginnings, however, there was always a division among Chartists between the emphasis of O'Connor, who called, in often fiery language, for working-class resistance and if necessary the use of force against their oppressors, and those who believed with William Lovett (1800–77) that the strength of their position lay in 'moral force'. Feargus O'Connor, brought up on his father's estates in Dangan Castle, Co. Cork, educated at Trinity, Dublin, called to the Bar, belonged to the colourful and noisy tradition of radical Irish gentry – though he represented in Parliament the English seat of Oldham, vacated by the death of Cobbett. Lovett, a failed cabinet-maker who became a pastry-cook and small-time shopkeeper in London, had founded the London Working Men's Association to 'draw into one bond of unity the intelligent and influential portion of the working classes in town and country, and to seek by every legal means to place all classes of society in possession of equal political and social rights'.[21]

Whether they looked to O'Connor, who was called 'an English Marat',[22] or to the peaceable Lovett, the Chartists shared a conviction (drawn from the socialist ideas of Robert Owen) that labour, being the source of value, was a form of wealth. The labourer, therefore, just as much as the man of property, was entitled to a stake in the political life of the nation. They weren't looking, as Carlyle thought they should have been, for one dynamic figurehead who could bring justice to them. Rather they believed that if every man had the vote, as opposed to the mere 8,000 property-owners of Liverpool, or the 179 of Totnes, then it would follow automatically that the interests of justice and equality would be dispensed from the parliamentary system. Electoral systems, even when the franchise had become universal, were so designed as to moderate, if not actually to thwart, the unruly majority; and to leave as unshaken as was consistent with the principles of decency the small oligarchy who in fact governed, and govern, the nation. In Victorian times this was a largely aristocratic oligarchy, evolving in time into a system of prime ministerial patronage, Cabinet government and a tightly run Civil Service. This system still obtains, so we have no means of knowing whether the ideals of the Chartists, if put into practice, would have brought universal felicity or social anarchy.

William Lovett favoured true universal suffrage, which meant, logically, the extension of the vote to women as well as to men. Other Chartists such as John La Mont and W.J. Linton shared the ideal, but it was not made part of the original Charter – which gives the movement its name – since they did not trust the Spirit of the time. It was felt to be too 'extreme' to suggest that women could vote. Another error. It would probably have made no difference to the eventual fate of the Movement, but there was no shortage of women prepared to support Feargus O'Connor, Lovett and the others. Witness the exchange between the registrar of Manchester, Richard Webb, and a Mrs King, who came to register the birth of her newborn son in March 1841.

Webb: What is the child to be called?
King: James Feargus O'Connor King.
Webb: Is your husband a Chartist?
King: I don't know, but his wife is.
Webb: Are you the child's mother?
King: Yes.
Webb: You had better go home and consider of it again; for if the person you are naming your child after was to commit high treason and get hanged, what a thing it would be.
King: If that should be the case, I should then consider it an honour to have my child named after him, so long as the child lives for I think Feargus O'Connor a great deal honester man than those who are punishing him.
Webb: Well, if you are determined to have it named after him, I must name it; but I never met such an obstinate lady as you before.[23]

The Charter itself – The People's Charter and National Petition – was published in May 1838. It had six points, asking for annual parliaments, universal male suffrage, equal electoral districts (to iron out the disparity between Totnes and Liverpool), the removal of the property qualification for membership of Parliament, a secret ballot, and payment for members. The impressiveness of the Charter was in the purity of its political language. That is, Chartism spoke, from first to last, in political terms and for political ends. Though embracing the cause of the disadvantaged and speaking up for the poor, it wasn't a glorified trade union. It was not asking Parliament as then constituted for higher wages or shorter working hours or better housing. It was asking for what it deemed to be a just and a logical political representation, confident that these other benefits would flow inexorably therefrom. 'The Charter was a means to an end – the means was their political rights, and the end was equality.'[24]

It is important to recognize that Chartism was largely a political reaction to the Whig–Radical alliance which brought in the Reform Act, the new Poor Laws, the police and all the other paraphernalia of control which were to be necessary in a successful liberal economy. In some regards therefore, the Chartists were not so much revolutionaries, still less prototypes of later collectivist solutions to social difficulties, as they were old-fashioned libertarians. Suffrage was the only possible weapon against what felt, if you lived at the bottom end of society, like a repressive coup d'état by the Whigs. In the many riots which the movement provoked, throughout the country, during the first decade of Victoria's reign, the demonstrators usually singled out for aggressive attacks those noted in the locality for their obnoxious political views. In the riots in the Potteries, for instance, it was not so much the employers and the pot banks which were the objects of violence as the Poor Law Commissioners, the unpopular magistrates and the workhouses which were besieged. The rector of Longton, a man noted for the excellence of his wine cellar, had advised the poor to use dock leaves as a substitute for coffee.[25] He did not have many glass panes left in his windows by the time the riot was over. The mob on this occasion had been directly stirred up by O'Connor, who toured the country whipping up frenzied support for the cause. About 350 women marched to greet him, each carrying a white wand. A thousand men from Stoke joined the Potteries Political Union – the local Staffordshire branch of the Chartist cause – on the day O'Connor said, 'You have about 130 master potters who annually share about one million's worth of your labour. Now, £250,000 would be more than ample for risk and speculation, and the remaining £750,000 would make you independent of the Three Devil Kings of Somerset House.' (That is, the Poor Law Commissioners.)

The most famous master potter of all, one may note in passing, was Josiah Wedgwood (1730–95), the most successful businessman of the eighteenth century, whose unwillingness to divide his wealth with his workers along the lines suggested by O'Connor directly subsidized, in the next generation, the leisure-time required by his grandson Charles Darwin to apply the Malthusian principle to the natural world at large. The Wedgwood works at Etruria in its early nineteenth century manifestation employed more than one hundred, but it was unusual in so doing, most of the rival potteries being much smaller. Even the factory mills of Yorkshire, which caused so much distress to the hand-loom weavers at home, were found by factory inspectors in 1835 to employ an average of 44.6 persons per mill.[26] We remember that Alton Locke, the eponymous hero of Charles Kingsley's (1819–75) Chartist novel, was a tailor. In those days before the mass-production of clothes there were some 74,000 male tailors in England (you can double that number because women nearly always sewed the buttonholes – smaller fingers – and usually the waistcoats, which is a quite separate skill from cutting out a coat). At this date, the Durham and Northumberland coal mines, Britain's chief coal producers, employed 20,954 men and boys.[27] Chartism was not the first blast of the collectivist–socialist trumpet; it was a cry by those described by G.K. Chesterton (1874–1936) in another context as 'the secret people':

> We hear men speaking for us of new laws strong and sweet,
> Yet is there no man speaketh as we speak in the street . . .
> It may be we are meant to mark with our riot and our rest
> God's scorn for all men governing. It may be beer is best.
> But we are the people of England; and we have not spoken yet.
> Smile at us, pay us, pass us. But do not quite forget.

The Chartists were occasionally violent – those who favoured O'Connor more than they who read Lovett – but they remained, even when forming themselves into peaceable associations or angry mobs, committed to a belief in an individualism which the growth of industrial cities was itself to undermine. Chartism, says one of its modern historians, 'needed the small communities, the slack religious and moral supervision, the unpoliced street and meeting place. The control which such communities could exercise over shopkeepers, constables, schoolteachers, local preachers and even Poor Law guardians was greater than anything that could take place in the cities or in the rural villages.'[27]

Their real enemy, therefore, were the big capitalists. *The Northern Star* of 1838 spoke of the Corn Laws (protecting artificially the wealth of the big landed aristocrats) and the horrors of the factory system. 'All have the same end, viz the making of the working classes beasts of burden – hewers of wood and drawers of water – to the aristocracy, Jewocracy, Millocracy, Shopocracy and every other Ocracy that feeds on human vitals.'[28]

Having identified the enemy, it is not surprising to find plenty of Tory–Chartists – such figures as the Nonconformist minister the Reverend J.R. Stephens of Kensal Moor, near Manchester, who saw it as the Englishman's God-given right 'to have a good coat and hat, a good roof over his head, a good dinner upon his table'.[29]

The possibility, however, of a Tory–Chartist or Tory–Radical alliance was never really a serious one, even though, or perhaps because, it 'appealed particularly to idealists, romantics, all who harked back to a largely imaginary pre-industrial golden age, all who disliked and feared the harsher manifestations of the industrial revolution and the bleaker aspects of the Utilitarian philosophy expounded by Jeremy Bentham'.[30] Throughout the next sixty years we shall see a variety of such idealisms and romanticisms – in the Young England movement, in the Oxford Movement, in the social thinking of John Ruskin (1819–1900), in Pre-Raphaelitism, Gothic Revivalism, William Morris's (1834–96) News from Nowhere, down to the time of Chesterton himself in the early years of the twentieth century. Some of its manifestations were 'right', others 'left'-wing, others apolitical. Chartism partook of some of this Merrie England idealism, though the experiences of those brave enough to present the Charter as a public petition to Parliament in 1839 were far from merry.

By the end of 1838 the number of public meetings at which O'Connor had made threats or incitements to physical violence had grown so much that there was no hope of the Commons giving the Charter a fair hearing. On 12 July the Commons refused by 235 to 46 votes to consider the national petition, which contained 1,200,000 signatures. Sir Charles Napier (1782–1853) was appointed by Parliament to command of the North of England. Having toured Nottingham, Leeds, Newcastle and Manchester, he lost no time in assembling the Chartist leaders and telling them that he would 'maul them with cannon and musketry' at the first signs of violence.

The most violent of the outbursts in that eventful and violent year of 1839 – which saw riots in Birmingham, Lovett and O'Connor imprisoned, and the hardening of government hearts against the Charter – came in Newport, South Wales. Several thousand men from the Welsh mining and ironworking valleys marched on the town in an attempt to take it over. The leaders included a linen draper named John Frost, who was a former magistrate and mayor of Newport. The invaders were beaten off by troops firing from the Westgate Hotel, with the loss of at least twenty-two lives, and the dispersal of the workers' army was followed by a large number of arrests. Frost and other ringleaders were sentenced to death for high treason.[31]

No one who read the news from Newport or from Birmingham could doubt the resolve of the propertied classes to protect their own. This would persist, even when Lord Melbourne was voted from office in 1839 – on a matter which also had bearings on the rights of humankind, but which concerned another vital ingredient in the Victorian success story: the colonies.

4

Typhoon Coming On

Whether the British Empire grew up by accident or design or by the inexorable movement of economic force is one of the questions which the reader of these pages will have decided by the end of the Victorian period. The heyday of Imperial colonization belongs to a later generation than the one we are considering here. At the beginning of the reign the East India Company, rather than the government in Westminster, still took responsibility for the administration of 'British India'. The huge expanses of Africa which would be painted red on the Imperial map were still uncharted. The attitude in London towards the colonies was both looser and less formal than would be the case at the close of the nineteenth century.

The importance of Jamaica, the largest island in the British West Indies, was both emblematic and commercial. It had been a British colony since 1655, when the Cromwellian navy, led by Admirals Penn and Venables, had taken the island from the Spanish. Jamaica had a bloody history. Its peaceable native inhabitants, the Arawak Indians, had been systematically annihilated by the conquistadors in 1509. Thereafter, its rich and exotic harvests, primarily of sugar, but also of coffee, cocoa, pimento and ginger, were cultivated by slave labour, imported from West Africa. Thus, from the beginning of British involvement with this Caribbean island it had been a source of wealth purveyed by the hands of the oppressed.

One fact which united almost all British shades of opinion in the years after the Napoleonic wars was pride in having abolished the slave trade. But although, thanks to the philanthropic enterprise of William Wilberforce and the other campaigners, the trade had been banned in all lands that were co-signatories to the Congress of Vienna (1814–15), the *ownership* of slaves persisted for another eighteen years in British colonies such as Jamaica. In 1832, when they heard a Reform Bill had been passed in London, the Jamaican slaves believed that they were at last free, and there was a rebellion. Emancipation came two years later.

Melbourne's government took a somewhat lazy attitude towards the colonies. When the question of emancipation was debated in the Lords and Commons in 1833 there was not a single member of the Cabinet present for any speeches from the back benches. The Whig government had always felt uneasy about the anomaly of allowing slave ownership to persist after the ban on the trade. It was not persuaded by the arguments of the Tory peer Lord Wynford that the Apostles had recognized slavery, 'and he presumed they' – Melbourne's Cabinet – 'did not pretend to be better Christians than the Apostles'.[1] Slavery had to go. The former under-secretary for the colonies, Lord Howick, made a devastating attack on prevailing conditions on the sugar plantations in Demerara – 'I firmly believe the well-meant measures which have been adopted for the improvement of the condition of slaves, have not in reality tended to their good, and this belief is not a little increased by the fact that, in no colony is the mortality amongst the slave population so great as in Demerara . . . Slaves labour only because if they do not do so they are punished. Their stimulus is terror . . .'

These remarks so enraged the ambitious Tory MP for Newark, then aged twenty-three, that he rose to make his first major parliamentary speech, rebutting Lord Howick's charges. The slaves had died in such quantities on his father's estate of Vreedenhoop because they were ageing naturally. The manager of the estate, a Mr Maclean, was 'proverbial for humanity' on the island of Jamaica. There is something quite fascinating in this young man's speech – for having rejected the charges against the West Indian planters as 'wholly untenable', he then admits 'with shame and pain . . . that cases of wanton cruelty had occurred'. He even conceded, this pompous young man, that 'the time has now arrived, when a definite period must be fixed for the extinction of slavery', but he nevertheless voted against the bill to abolish it.[2]

The young man was William Ewart Gladstone, destined to bestride the political century as a Liberal prime minister, but at this stage of his fortunes mocked by Macaulay (1800–59) as a rising hope of the stern and unbending Tories.[3] In later life he would repent – 'I can now see plainly enough,' he said sixty years later, 'the sad defects, the real illiberalism of my opinions on that subject. Yet they were not illiberal as compared with the ideas of the times.'[4] True, as his loyal biographer Morley recalled, Pitt, Fox, Grenville and Grey had been anxious to abolish the trade in slaves, but rejected any notion of the emancipation of existent slaves. Wilberforce himself discouraged attempts to abolish slavery, rather than its trade. Peel rejected even a 'gradualist' approach to the question. But it is not true that the young generation to which Gladstone belonged held such unenlightened views. The truth is that it was wealth generated from the plantations in Demerara which had transformed John Gladstones (*sic*), son of a Leith corn-chandler and grandson of a small-town miller and trader, into a landed grandee, a great Liverpool merchant, with Scottish estates which placed him on a level with the aristocracy.

The leisure of William Ewart Gladstone's learned hours, studying Homer and Dante, the gentility of his marriage to the Welsh gentry family of Glynn, as of his early education at Eton and Christ Church, was all underwritten by the sweat of slaves. And he knew it. The guilty knowledge underlay much of his life, as it did those of so many of his contemporaries, such as the Lascelles family, the future Earls of Harewood, the most successful of the West Indian merchant dynasties. At the huge neo-Norman castle of Penrhyn in North Wales, designed by Thomas Hopper, only a few watercolours of Jamaica give a clue as to the origins of the great wealth that built it – the slave labour and incomes in the West Indies providing money for the self-made Pennant family to acquire vast estates in Wales, where they doubled their fortunes in slate. Few slave-owning families were as honest as Richard Watt, the Liverpool merchant who began to restore Speke Hall in 1795 and who, when he took a coat of arms, included in it three blackamoors, acknowledging the origin of his new-found money and status. (In a comparable way an African head was incorporated into the frieze on the cornice of Liverpool's town hall.) Most, like the Pennants, Gladstones and Lascelleses, preferred to forget the shameful origin of their fortune.[5]

Charles Darwin, by contrast, whose grandfather, Old Wooden Leg Wedgwood, had made his fortune in England mass-producing fine china, came from a different tradition. Wedgwood had been foremost among the abolitionists, coining the legend *Am I not a man and a brother?* to accompany the medallion of a kneeling slave in chains. It simply wasn't true, as Gladstone was to aver forty-five years on, that the 'ideas of the times' saw nothing wrong with slavery. Old Wooden Leg's grandson, during the voyage of the *Beagle*, encountered slave markets in South America. One of the finest passages in the whole of his *Voyage* is when he reflects on the ship leaving the shores of Brazil, just three years after Gladstone uttered his weasel-words in the Commons:

> I thank God, I shall never again visit a slave country. To this day, if I hear a distant scream, it recalls with painful vividness my feelings, when passing a house near Pernambuco, I heard the most pitiable moans, and could not but suspect that some poor slave was being

tortured, yet knew that I was as powerless as a child even to remonstrate . . . Near Rio de Janeiro I lived opposite to an old lady, who kept screws to crush the fingers of her female slaves. I have stayed in a house where a young household mulatto, daily and hourly, was reviled, beaten and persecuted enough to break the spirit of the lowest animal . . .

Darwin went on to say that these and similar atrocities took place in a Spanish colony where the slaves were said to be *better* treated than in Portuguese or English colonies. 'It makes one's blood boil, yet heart tremble, to think that we Englishmen and our American descendants, with their boastful cry of liberty, have been and are so guilty; but it is a consolation to reflect, that we at least, have made a greater sacrifice, than ever made by any nation, to expiate our sin.'[6]

British self-congratulation on the subject was tempered by commercial self-interest. The abolition of slavery had already, even before the emancipation of the Demerara slaves, led to a disparity in world sugar prices. The price of sugar in Great Britain was 7½*d.* per lb, while Cuban or Brazilian sugar of higher quality, harvested by slaves, sold abroad for 4¼*d.* per lb.[7] Logically, a nation which was converting itself to an out-and-out belief in Free Trade should have recognized this as the luck of the draw. The fact that the South Americans were undercutting British planters and traders, however, added a keen edge to the British moral outrage against Brazilian slavers. The foreign secretary, Lord Palmerston, who was not noted for his championship of human rights on his own Irish estates for example, had no hesitation in sending British warships into Brazilian ports and flushing out any ships they found being fitted for the slave trade.[8] Biffing the Brazilians, damaging their sugar and coffee trade while maintaining a high moral tone, was good for morale.

These half-civilized governments . . . all require a dressing down every eight or ten years to keep them in order. Their minds are too shallow to receive any impression that will last longer than some such period and warning is of little use. They care little for words and they must not only see the stick but actually feel it on their shoulders before they yield to that only argument which to them brings conviction, the *Argumentum Baculinum.*[9]

Palmerston, who would become one of Victoria's prime ministers at the age of seventy, was hugely popular with a certain type of English-man.[10] His swashbuckling, vulgar belief in British intervention in every corner of the globe – now in Egypt, now in China – was largely driven by commerce: 'The rivalship of European manufacturers is fast excluding our productions from the markets of Europe, and we must unremittingly endeavour to find in other parts of the world new rents for the produce of our industry.' Expansion abroad, which would turn into the full-scale Imperial expansion seen in the mid-1850s onwards, went hand in hand with the rapid growth of industry at home.

Meanwhile, disguising beneath a genuine moral self-belief the venality of their commercial interests, the British took on the role of global policemen. The Royal Navy went in pursuit of slave ships partly no doubt with the fervour of moral liberators, partly influenced by the fact that they could earn 'head money' for the number of slaves liberated. The slavers in turn could claim insurance for cargo – i.e. slaves – lost at sea, but not for slaves who died on board. It was therefore a common occurrence, if a Royal Navy vessel pursued a slaver, that she would cast her 'cargo' into the ocean, still in chains, as a feast for the sharks. Turner's *Slavers Throwing Overboard the Dead and Dying – Typhoon Coming On*, exhibited at the Academy in 1840, depicts just such a gruesome scene. The great sunset blaze reflects on a heaving sea. The writhing forms of slaves in the foreground could be sea-serpents. They are part of the cruelty of nature itself. There is an Homeric pitilessness about the canvas, though the fiery decline of the sun tells its own tale of endings and finishings behind the old masts of the obsolescent sailing ship. 'I believe,' wrote John Ruskin, 'if I were reduced to rest Turner's immortality upon any single work, I should choose this.' The sun is going down violently and angrily on the old world. The coming typhoon boils like the rage of Darwin as it contemplates the horror of what the ship, and the sea, contain.[11] The picture is in a sense a companion-piece to Turner's canvas of the burning of the Parliament buildings.

Florence Nightingale, summing up Palmerston's foreign policy, was to say, 'he was a humbug, and he knew it'. What could be described as humbug could also be seen as a more general gift, bestowed on three or four generations of Britons, to be 'in denial' as we should say about many an issue where a twenty-first-century observer sees clear cause for moral disapprobation. Societies as well as individuals can be Prince Hamlets, incapacitating themselves by self-questioning and honesty about the inconsistencies in their very aim and nature; or they can be thick-skinned, breezy, able to live without too much hesitation or procrastination. It was emblematic that Queen Victoria detested *Hamlet*.

Doubts there were aplenty – in individuals, in groups, in society at large – about the Condition of England question (Carlyle's phrase from *Past and Present*), about the relations between Britain and the rest of the world, about religion and science, about social justice: but we who live in a fragmented society have become like an individual addicted to psychoanalysis, struggle with our uncertainties, pick at our virtues and vices as if they were scabs. The Victorian capacity *not* to do this, to live, very often, with double standards, is what makes so many of them – individually and collectively – seem to be humbugs and hypocrites.

All these things bubbled beneath the surface when Lord Melbourne, in 1839, found himself faced with an intransigent Jamaica Assembly. Eight hundred thousand negroes on the island became fully and unconditionally free on 1 August 1838.[12] The planters were offered £15 million in compensation. The British government tried to take things further and insist upon an improvement in the conditions in Jamaican prisons. This the assembly in Kingston, Jamaica (overwhelmingly made up of white planters but containing some 'coloureds'),[13] refused to do. It became, in effect, an issue of confidence. Melbourne put it to the vote in Parliament and the Tory Party defeated the Whigs by five votes. Melbourne resigned.

Historians of the period tend, as did newspapers of the time, to turn with some relief from the trivial fate of 800,000 emancipated men and women in the Caribbean – how they should work, eat, earn their livings, how their former owners could be expected to make a living in an increasingly competitive world market – and to concentrate on the high drama of the Bedchamber Crisis. Jamaica, as far as history is concerned, can be forgotten for another quarter-century before it awakens anyone's attention when Governor Eyre (1815–1901) split British opinion by the severity with which he suppressed a negro rebellion.

Queen Victoria, in 1839, was far more troubled by the thought of being deprived of her hours of playing draughts with Lord Melbourne. Sir Robert Peel was a very different sort of man. The Queen failed to understand that it was perfectly normal for incoming prime ministers to propose new members of the royal household. As a mark of confidence, Peel asked her to replace some of the Whig ladies of the bedchamber with the wives of Tory noblemen. She refused, and Peel declined to take office. The Melbourne administration therefore hobbled on towards a disastrous election defeat in 1841 – by which time the young Queen had further demeaned the monarchy in the public eye by falsely accusing one of her ladies-in-waiting, Lady Flora Hastings, of being pregnant. (Her swollen appearance was owing to cancer.) Small wonder that the House of Commons, particularly on the Tory side, enjoyed baiting the Queen when she chose as her husband Prince Albert of Saxe-Coburg. The wedding was fixed for 10 February 1840, and Victoria clearly hoped that Parliament would admit him to the peerage, and grant him a handsome allowance as a token of their esteem.

Although, or because, it is true that Prince Albert's virtue 'was, indeed, appalling; not a single vice redeemed it',[14] his arrival in England brought qualities of seriousness and intelligence to public life which are almost without parallel. Partly to embarrass Lord Melbourne and the Whigs, partly for reasons of stupid xenophobia, the Tories opposed the idea of the Queen marrying him at all. In their favour must be admitted that previous dealings with the Duchy of Coburg had been less than happy. Leopold of Saxe-Coburg had married Princess Charlotte when she was Princess of Wales, who had then died in 1817. Turning down the dangers of becoming king of Greece, he had accepted the gentler option of becoming king of the Belgians, but continued to draw a Civil List pension from the British taxpayer of £50,000. Colonel Sibthorp reminded the House of Commons that one of the conditions for receiving this handsome sinecure was that Leopold should remain a Protestant – on remarriage to Marie-Louise of Orleans he had become a Catholic. Another was that he should pay for the upkeep of Claremont House. Not a penny had Leopold paid, though by 1840 he had received over £1 million from Britain. Leopold's sister, the Duchess of Kent, Victoria's mother, was hardly a popular figure, though she was not as dissolute as their brother Duke Ernest of Saxe-Coburg, syphilitic, promiscuous and unintelligent. His wife Louise, who had married him aged sixteen, was dead – some said of uterine cancer, others of haemorrhaging as a result of a miscarriage – by the time her son Albert was twelve. By then Albert's parents had separated and Louise – who was eighteen when he was born – had had many affairs.

The genetic statistics, as we have seen, make it unlikely that Queen Victoria was really the daughter of the Duke of Kent. Likewise, doubt hovered over the paternity of her Coburg cousin, Prince Albert. It was persistently alleged, back home in Germany, that he was actually the son of Baron von Mayern, a Jewish chamberlain at the Coburg court. Certainly, unlike his elder brother Ernst, Albert does not seem to have inherited syphilitic symptoms from his supposed father, Duke Ernest I of Saxe-Coburg. Nor did he look anything like his brother. The rumours about Albert's parentage were fuelled by his mother's disgrace, in his boyhood, when she had a very flagrant affair with another courtier. If the suspicions about both Victoria and Albert are well-grounded, this means that many of the crowned heads of Europe are descended jointly from an unscrupulous Irish soldier and a German Jew. Given this, it is surprising that these families manifested so few of the talents stereotypically attributed to the Irish and the Jews: such as wit or good looks. Albert was, however, dreamily good-looking, though tiny. His qualities of domestic loyalty, his love of family, his insatiable intellectual interest, his musicality, are all in the most astounding contrast to his own Coburg supposed relations or to his bride's sybaritic, and on the whole, stupid family.[15] With forebears and relations like Leopold, Ernst and the Duchess of Kent, Albert could not hope to endear himself to an England that did not know him. Lord Ashley, a personal friend of Queen Victoria, and stepson-in-law of Lord Palmerston, was among those who joined Sibthorp in the Commons and voted against an allowance of £50,000 p.a. for Albert. They reduced it to £30,000.

As hindsight now teaches though, the Queen was making an ideal marriage. She was furious with the Tories – and cut Ashley for years afterwards.[16] Had he but known it, Ashley's criticism of the Queen's character encapsulated the reason why Albert was such a remarkable and welcome import. Victoria, Ashley said, had a 'small and girlish mind, wholly unequal to the business of government or even of common life'. She was marginally better educated than Queen Elizabeth II, but not much, and the responsibilities she bore were much greater.

Albert, only six months short of his twenty-first birthday when he married, was a highly cultivated person, of well above average intelligence, with an impressive range of gifts and interests. Baron Stockmar's approving comment was: 'He shows not the slightest interest in politics . . . while declaring that the Augsburg *Allgemeine Zeitung* is the only paper one wants or that is worth reading, he does not even read it.'[17] Such indifference to politics made Albert an ideal consort in a constitutional monarchy. In a broader sense however, he was highly aware of politics, intelligently conscious of the enormous changes which had come about in modern society as a result of the French Revolution and its aftermath, and of industrialization. He and his brother had studied at Bonn University. Old Beethoven had not long since walked its streets – Albert was an impressive musician whose *Lieder* stand comparison with many minor composers. (He's certainly better than Parry or Vaughan Williams.) He was taught literature by A.W. von Schlegel and attended Fichte's philosophy classes, absorbing perhaps that Idealism (in the philosophical sense) which was to be a marked feature of the English intellectual scene a generation later. He was well-travelled and well-tutored in art history, and while a student he had started to buy pictures on his very slender means. (Trawling the art dealers of the Rhine towns he had found a Dürer drawing and a Van Dyck portrait.)[18] You could imagine George IV being impressed by this – though he would have been too lazy to go in quest of artworks himself. Victoria and her other obese and ungifted uncles would not have recognized a Dürer drawing if it was held under their noses.

The English, then, and their royal family were receiving a quite extraordinary bargain for their £30,000 – a consort for their monarch who, if not exactly a genius, was so impressive a product of the German educational system that by English standards he was the next best thing. He was also – thanks to the dreadful emotional chaos in which he had grown up – deeply committed to the notion of loyal family life. He was energetic. He was ardently desirous to do good. No wonder it took him some time to settle in.

Monuments to Albert's range of abilities remain visible to this day: first of which was the glorious Italianate palazzo on the Isle of Wight – Osborne, with its impressive sculpture-gallery and its collection of Winterhalter masterpieces. (The interiors were much cluttered and spoilt in the long years of Victoria's widowhood.) Then there was the Gothic baronial of Balmoral, an allusion to the beloved Schloss Rosenau where Albert had grown up. Both these residences, fascinating in themselves as tributes to the eclecticism and intelligence of Albert's taste, are also embodiments of his wise attitude to modern constitutional monarchy. He saw that as well as having official residences where they were always on display, always at the mercy of politicking, they should cultivate private lives and private virtues.

Albert's improvements at Windsor, his reordering and management of the estates and the farms, his building of a beautiful and efficient dairy, still operative to this day, are further tributes to his good taste.

His model housing in Kennington, built on the very site of the last Chartist demonstration, and the huge museum complex in Kensington which some call the Albertopolis, are further reminders of the depth and range of his contribution to English public life.

His first two gifts to the British people were more personal. Primarily and most importantly, he made Victoria a happy woman. She was highly sexed and she worshipped her husband. From the first 'gratifying and bewildering night' as she described it to Lord Melbourne, the Queen was crazy about Albert. 'YOU CANNOT IMAGINE HOW DELIGHTFUL IT IS TO BE MARRIED. I COULD NOT HAVE DREAMED THAT ANYONE COULD BE SO HAPPY IN THIS WORLD AS I AM,' she wrote in her childish capitals to her cousin Victo (Victoria Augusta Antoinetta).[19]

Albert made her value private life. Although she did take an interfering interest in political affairs, he ensured that for most of the century she was at home, a private individual – until his death she was at the centre of family life, after it she retreated into the shadows for decades. Constitutional monarchy thrives on this low-key approach.

In so far as she did take a political interest in her early married life, Albert – and this was his second great early gift to the nation – persuaded her to drop her girlish tendresse for the Whigs and to see that by far the most important and intelligent political figure of the age was not Lord M. with his charming drawing-room manners, but Sir Robert Peel.

5

The Age of Peel

Sir Robert Peel was the last prime minister of whom no photograph was ever taken.[1] Even the Duke of Wellington sat to a daguerreotypist. Though the art of photography, in common with so many other modern phenomena, developed rapidly during the five years of his premiership, Sir Robert Peel remains discreetly in the shadows of the past. It seems characteristic. He was unshowy, sensible, brilliant. He was, in what he did and in his own person, a transitional figure of crucial importance. At the beginning of his premiership England, for all the changes which had been taking place since the battle of Waterloo, was still of the old world. By the time he left office, after his dramatic volte-face over the Corn Laws, the new world had come into being. Britain had become an out-and-out free-trading nation. Partly because the tariffs were lifted, and capitalism was given a free rein, partly because the economic cycle was in any event moving into a phase of quite unprecedented and extraordinary stability, fifty or sixty years of sound money were about to be ushered in. Private investors placed their money with the disciples of expanding industry and reaped not merely unparalleled riches but unprecedented leisure. As Keynes said in a classic definition of nineteenth-century civilization:

> The system worked, throughout Europe, with an extraordinary success and facilitated the growth of wealth on an unprecedented scale. To save and to invest became at once the duty and the delight of a large class. The savings were seldom drawn on, and accumulating at compound interest, made possible the material triumphs which we now all take for granted. The morals, the politics, the literature and the religion of the age joined in a grand conspiracy for the promotion of saving. God and Mammon were reconciled. Peace on earth to men of good means. A rich man could, after all, enter into the Kingdom of Heaven – if only he saved.[2]

Peel is a Janus figure at this crucial and exciting pivot of time. On the one hand, what could be more *ancien régime* than his parliamentary career, seen solely from the position of *representation*? From 1830 he sat for his small home borough of Tamworth, which his father had earlier represented. The electorate stood at only 528 in 1832. Twenty years later, Peel himself was dead and the electorate had fallen to 307. Yet many of the innovations which we should most associate with the political progress of the nineteenth century – Catholic Emancipation for example in 1829, Free Trade in 1846 – came about because of Peel's own distinctive vision of things. The paradox of English political history is that the most radical changes are often introduced by Conservatives. Janus Peel, a very rich baronet who led a party which was in effect a coalition – one destined most dramatically to split asunder over the question of Free Trade – was the heir to fortunes made not from generations of landowning, but from capitalism. It was a cotton fortune. Peel belonged to the thriving, thrusting, Darwinian new class. His grandfather had pioneered calico-printing in Blackburn; and with the money made in this great Northern industrial enterprise Peel's father, the first Baronet, had acquired the estate of Drayton Manor in Staffordshire, near Tamworth.

> Peel always poot a question and to the last said 'woonderful' and 'woonderfully'. He guarded his aspirates with immense care. I have known him slip. The correctness was not spontaneous. He had managed his elocution like his temper: neither was originally good.[3]

Thus the thorn in Peel's side, Benjamin Disraeli. But such snobbery about the vestiges of a Lancashire accent in Peel are themselves something new, rather than old. The class system, which many people nowadays associate with the aristocratic hierarchy, was in reality something distinct from it. When his father made a fortune as a calico-printer in Lancashire, England was a political triangle – it was what Peel himself called a 'mixed monarchy', or we should perhaps call it a constitutional monarchy – controlled by an aristocratic oligarchy. It was the genius of the Victorian politicians that, with any amount of change, reform, upheaval and jiggery-pokery, they kept it an oligarchy, right down to the twentieth century. The class system – in which an upper class was merely one storey in a big bourgeois building – was an innovation. Those who hated and hate the class system saw and see it as an instrument of oppression to those at the bottom, encouraging those in its upper ranks to despise those beneath them; and those beneath to hate those above. The Victorians might have seen things differently. The new economic climate gave the chance for the meanest artisan to rise, through energy or enterprise, through the ranks. The calico-printer and cotton-master becomes within two generations the baronet and the bigwig.

Hence their gradations in a new class structure marked by such shibboleths as accent. Jane Austen was no less a lady for speaking with a strong Hampshire accent, but had she lived fifty years later her rustic burr would have been carefully eradicated by elocution lessons and 'genteel' governesses. All Wellington's officers at Waterloo were gentlemen or aristocrats – all spoke with regional accents. Disraeli's vulgar snobbery about Peel's accent is itself the innovation, not the accent itself. (If he had fun waiting for Peel to drop his aitches, what would Dizzy have made of Sir Robert Walpole, the first prime minister, who spoke with the strong accents of the Norfolk farmer he was?)

Lord Ashley, the Christian Tory philanthropist who did so much to campaign for the improvement of working conditions for the poor, hated the competitive atmosphere of factories. Visiting his ancestral seat, St Giles in the county of Dorset, he noted in his diary on 29 June 1841, 'What a picture contrasted with a factory district, a people known and cared for, a people born and trained on the estate, exhibiting towards its hereditary possessors both deference and sympathy, affectionate respect and a species of allegiance demanding protection and repaying it in duty.' To the Northern factory-owners such patronizing attitudes led only to stultification. There was no movement, no struggle, in Ashley's view of society. Cobden, the Corn Law reformer *par excellence*, hated Ashley's attempts to set limits on an employer's powers – the length of hours he could make factory hands work, or the limiting of the age of his employees. 'Mine is that masculine species of charity which would lead me to inculcate in the minds of the labouring classes the love of independence, the privilege of self respect, the disdain of being patronised or petted, the desire to accumulate and the ambition to rise.'

Henry Ashworth, a Quaker mill-owner from Rochdale in Lancashire, took a comparable anti-aristocratic view. He offered all his factory hands the chance to be educated in schools built and financed by himself – to inculcate 'a desire to enlarge their views and to teach them not to be satisfied with the condition in which they were born, but to induce them to be uneasy under it and to make them feel uncomfortable if they do not improve upon the example their parents have set before them'.

Highly Darwinian sentiments, and it would be hard to think of a greater contrast between the Tory aristocratic views of Ashley and the Liberal Radicalism, based on economic laissez-faire, of Cobden and Ashworth. It was the combined good fortune and genius of the Victorians, though, that these two elements of British life, far from tearing at one another, actually learned, like the triumphant genes in a Darwinian evolutionary progress, to live together; even to integrate. Sir Robert Peel can be seen as one of the chief architects of the new order. The very fact that his adherence to a point of principle split his party and put it out of office, effectively, for twenty years, established his legacy and influence. There is a deep paradox here which hindsight does not diminish, but it is true – more than if he had caved in to the 'Ultras', the right wing of his party, and allowed Free Trade to be the policy exclusively of the Liberals. Peel died four years after the repeal of the Corn Laws and the collapse of his party. But the England of Victoria, both free-trading and aristocratic, was the England of Peel.

Karl Marx (1818–83), as so often, made an accurate observation of the political scene and drew a false inference from it. Writing in the *Neue Oder Zeitung* of 6 March 1855 he said, 'The British Constitution is, in fact, only an antiquated and obsolete compromise made between the bourgeoisie, which rules in actual practice, although not *officially* in all the decisive spheres of bourgeois society, and the landed aristocracy which forms the official government.'

What Marx omitted in his analysis was the extent of cross-fertilization between the two supposedly different species, bourgeois and aristocrat. There was more than a whiff of romantic snobbery in Marx's nature, and so he writes as if the British aristocracy (from which his beloved wife descended) was a race apart. In some of the continental caste-systems there was no doubt a stultifying immobility. The fluidity of the English system has by contrast been identified as a key precondition for the huge commercial success known as the Industrial Revolution.[4] Younger sons of aristocrats did not inherit lands or titles from their fathers: they were sent out into the world to fend for themselves in professions where they rubbed shoulders with the upwardly mobile. 'Commerce, law, lucky marriages, office under the crown could bring the wealth to purchase a landed estate; and for the landowner as long as he owned enough, the various stages in the peerage followed almost automatically.'[5]

This was the society over which Robert Peel presided and which in some senses he epitomized. There were, however, some formidable obstacles in the path of his, and Britain's, success. They make the period of his premiership so eventful that almost every month brought some form or another of crisis. There were four fundamental factors in play. The first, broadly, was the Condition of England question, the seething discontent of the poor and in particular the apparent successes and popularity, so alarming to the ruling powers, of the Chartist movement. The second was the Irish question, a lingering political problem which all British governments, in all areas, have had a tendency to bungle, but which in Peel's day was exacerbated by a calamity of Biblical proportions – that is, the famine. The third, deeply connected to both these issues, to the position of Britain in the world, and to all the social changes we have been discussing, was the issue of Free Trade in general, the Corn Laws in particular; and the fourth, obviously consequent on these three, and other issues, was the political composition of the two Houses of Parliament, the actual men who in one House by inheritance, in the other by a very exclusive voting system, were taking their seats. For it was after all the parties within Parliament who determined the success or otherwise of Sir Robert Peel's ambitions and enterprises.[6] We shall consider them in the reverse of the order just listed, but it is important to remember how much they all interconnected.

The new Parliament building which, very slowly, was a-building during this period was satisfyingly symbolic of some of the multi-stranded themes which come together in any consideration of the period. After the fire, the Lords were squeezed into the surviving Painted Chamber at Westminster, and the Commons sat in the Court of Requests.[7] Both these magnificent rooms were destined to be demolished when Charles Barry's (1795–1860) winning designs for the new Palace of Westminster were put into effect. The very Painted Chamber where Edward the Confessor had died and Charles I's death warrant had been signed would be replaced by neo-Tudor Gothic, bright as a stage set.

Barry was a brilliant architect, the son of a modest stationer from Bridge Street, Westminster. He had grown up in a shop facing the old Parliament buildings and Westminster Abbey. He was very largely self-taught, having spent three years, from the age of twenty-two to twenty-five, travelling in Greece, Turkey, France and Italy making architectural drawings. His first great building, executed when he was thirty-three, was the Travellers' Club in London, an Italianate palazzo set down in Pall Mall, breathing the spaciousness which was always to be one of his hallmarks. He was nothing if not eclectic in style – the fruit of his own travels – and in a few years he had designed the Greek revival art gallery in Manchester and the Tudor Gothic of King Edward's School in Birmingham. In each of these buildings, Barry was able to tell his clients something about themselves which they wanted to hear. He was one of the most successful architect-hierophants, creating just that blend of serviceability and fantasy which are the hallmarks of imaginative building. The gentlemen who joined the Travellers' enjoyed feeling that they were still on the Grand Tour, stepping from the dust of Pall Mall into the echoing hall and high-ceilinged domicile of some old Roman family of aristocratic lineage. The merchants and professional families who sent their boys – one of Queen Victoria's most energetic archbishops of Canterbury among them, and some of the finest Greek Testament scholars of any age – to King Edward VI Birmingham enjoyed the feeling that this excellent grammar school for day-boys had some of the august and ancient charms of Eton or Westminster.

The committee that set the competition for the new Houses of Parliament had specified that the designs should be in a Gothic or Elizabethan style. Clearly, as one whose infant eyes had first focused on the Gothic traceries of Westminster Abbey and who was as familiar with medieval Westminster as had been the infant William Blake, Barry favoured a Gothic style.

Having won the competition in 1836, he faced a series of problems before the building could so much as begin. First, there was opposition in the Commons at the proposed expense (£800,000 over six years). Barry's unsuccessful rivals in the competition then got up a petition to change the specifications to the Greek or Roman style.

There is no doubt that the British would think of themselves differently if their parliamentary buildings resembled the Assemblée Nationale in Paris or the Senate in Washington DC. Barry's solid Tudor Gothic, embellished (one is tempted to say camped up) by the florid ornamentations of Augustus Welby Northmore Pugin (1812–52), makes, as they say, a statement. These buildings say, on the one hand, we are new as paint. We are so self-confidently new that we are prepared to pull down some of the historic old rooms which survived the fire. On the other hand they say that, like the lineage of Sir Leicester Dedlock, we are old as the hills and infinitely more respectable.

Pugin, notoriously, was a convert to Roman Catholicism. One says notoriously, because his was no quiet inner conversion but a furious public campaign. His *Contrasts*, supposedly an architectural work, but one which surely presages his incarceration in the Bedlam lunatic asylum, is a tirade of hatred against the eighteenth century, the Enlightenment, the classical. Gothic, Gothic, Gothic – Catholic Gothic as interpreted by Pugin – is the only style allowable in a Christian country. Pugin was an inspired decorator – the House of Cards effect of the Chamber of the House of Lords, particularly when filled for a State Opening with peers in scarlet robes, the Sovereign in a crown, heralds in tabards and the rest, makes the spectator gasp. Left to himself – as with the polychromatic little church of St Giles, Cheadle in Staffordshire – Pugin seems like a child playing with candies which will soon make himself and his onlookers queasy. In order to be seen at his best, he needed Barry's assured knowledge of how to use *space*.

But more than an aesthetic statement is being made by the choice of late Gothic, with many Tudor elements. Most parliamentarians, and perhaps most men and women in the Age of Peel, believed that to be British was *ipso facto* to be Protestant. (Here was one of the sticking points in the whole tragic story of failed understanding between England and Ireland.) John Ruskin, most eloquent and most knowledgeable exponent of the beauties of Gothic, grew up with parents so Protestant that – addicted as they were to foreign travel – they tried to avoid staying in Catholic cantons of Switzerland. He would come to modify these views, but as an *early* Victorian he would have echoed the prevailing view that Roman Catholicism was alien to the national spirit. As Edward White Benson helpfully explained when a Birmingham schoolboy to his fellow scholar Lightfoot, 'you must know that the Roman Church may be a true church in Italy but in England it is not only in error but in heresy and schismatical'.[8] Anthony Froude spoke for the huge majority of his compatriots when he said that the Reformation was the decisive, the key event in English history. Tennyson saw it as 'the dawning of a new age; for after the era of priestly domination comes the era of the freedom of the individual'.[9]

Barry's Parliament buildings had to suggest, therefore, not so much the monastic past of the Middle Ages as the world of new families – Horners, Cecils – who took their lands from the old monastic foundations: a world when Britain, led by a young Queen and standing independent of Europe, sent forth its adventurers on the seas to discover new territories, poised for its golden age of mercantile property, religious freedom, literary flowering. That was the world, semi-mystical, half true, that Barry had to summon up. He also had to bring to life the one element of medieval tradition of which the Parliamentary Committees who paid his fees heartily approved – the medieval peerage. His Palace of Westminster was therefore to evoke a Middle Ages gutted of its central ideological *raison d'être* – namely Catholicism. The post-1689 oligarchic system of government, the Whiggish idea of an aristocracy importing and sustaining its own constitutional monarch, could be dressed up in the fancy dress of Pugin and Barry to portray a continuity with feudal times.

To a twenty-first-century reader, such notions perhaps seem bizarre, even comic. So they did to the more facetious of Barry's contemporaries. But political realities are reflected here. Immediately opposite the swampy building site on which Barry proposed to build his political sermon in stones, on the other side of Westminster Bridge, was Astley's famous Amphitheatre, where shows which were part circus, part historical *tableaux vivants* showed to packed audiences. As well as such exciting shows as *The Storming of Seringapatam and the Death of Tippoo Sahib* or *The Conquest of Mexico* there were medieval extravaganzas – *The Battle of Agincourt* or the tournament from Sir Walter Scott's *Ivanhoe*. Wildly popular too with the public in the early years of the reign was the newly opened museum at the Tower of London, showing Queen Elizabeth I's armoury, twenty gleaming knights arranged historically in their armour from Henry VI in 1450 to James II in 1685. It so excited a group of young aristocrats in 1839 that Lord Eglinton decided to stage a tournament at his castle in Ayrshire. The young silly asses who had themselves so expensively kitted out for this piece of farce in authentic medieval armour were caricatured by Doyle and mocked by everyone in the kingdom; they never managed to joust in the lists. The rain was so torrential that the grandstand was waterlogged, the lists were flooded, and the heavily caparisoned steeds sank in the mud. But the ball which followed the fiasco, everyone in fancy dress, suggested a genuine nostalgia for some medieval fantasy-past. This in turn was reflected in Peel's Parliament with the presence of the Young England movement.[10]

They were mainly aristocrats, just down from Cambridge: George Smythe, later 7th Viscount Strangford; Lord John Manners, later 6th Duke of Rutland; Alexander Cochrane-Baillie, later ennobled as Lord Lamington. They were not perhaps very serious figures in themselves but they became the friends and allies of Benjamin Disraeli, now thirty-five years old, intensely ambitious, and not so lucky as Gladstone, whom Peel had made a junior minister. Disraeli had written to Peel begging for office, but he had been humiliatingly rebuffed. He was to have his revenge, being an incessant enemy of Peel's in the House of Commons and mobilizing that opposition which prime ministers most dread – opposition from his own ranks.

What a Parliament that was! Peel had the Earl of Aberdeen as foreign secretary, Lord Stanley as colonial secretary, and young W.E. Gladstone as his vice president of the Board of Trade and master of the Mint – that is three future prime ministers in the government, and the old Duke of Wellington still active for the Tories in the Lords. Then, just look at the benches of the House of Commons! Liberal Radicals represented by figures as various and impressive as Richard Cobden, the great apostle of Free Trade, or Henry Labouchere who (with Bradlaugh) was to have so momentous an effect on the perception of the established religion and its place in parliamentary life; the glorious eccentric 'Ultra' Tory Colonel Sibthorp in his white nankeen trousers, large white hat, and huge top-boots, thundering against every innovation, from railways to the Prince Consort; Dr Thomas Wakley, founder of *The Lancet*; Thomas Babington Macaulay, representing Edinburgh; Richard Monckton Milnes – friend of Swinburne, and keeper of Keats's flame; Lord Palmerston; Lord Ashley (better known to history as the 7th Earl of Shaftesbury), Tory champion of the poor! This isn't to mention Daniel O'Connell, representing the seats of both Meath and Cork – which must somehow be a version of the Irish electoral principle to vote early, vote often; Alexander Pringle; Sir Charles Napier.

A galaxy of stars who make our modern parliaments seem very undistinguished indeed. In this Parliament, Disraeli saw Young England as rallying the country diehards against Peel, and perhaps even attracting some of the Radicals. He reckoned that out of Peel's majority of 90 seats there were 'between 40 and 50 agricultural malcontents' – country Tories who distrusted Peel even before his volte-face on the Corn Laws, who were Protestant bigots to a man and who might have been prepared to wound or dethrone Peel on a number of issues.

Disraeli's feelings for Young England – so much younger and more nobly born than himself – have an element of romanticism, perhaps even (for all his early love affairs and his devoted marriage to a widow, Mary Anne Wyndham Lewis, years older than himself) tinged with a hint of homoeroticism, and are poured out in his trilogy of novels *Coningsby*, *Sybil* and *Tancred*. The most famous passage in the trilogy has passed into the political language of English Conservatism:

'Well, society may be in its infancy,' said Egremont slightly smiling; 'but, say what you like, our Queen reigns over the greatest nation that ever existed.'

'Which nation?' asked the younger stranger, 'for she reigns over two.'

The stranger paused, Egremont was silent, but looked inquiringly. 'Two nations; between whom there is no intercourse and no sympathy; who are as ignorant of each other's habits, thoughts and feelings, as if they were dwellers in different zones or inhabitants of different planets; who are formed by a different breeding, are fed by a different food, are ordered by different manners, and are not governed by the same laws.'

'You speak of –' said Egremont, hesitatingly.

'THE RICH AND THE POOR.'[11]

It was always the Tory contention that the Whigs ruled by a sleight of hand, holding together an unpleasant alliance of Nonconformist killjoys and big landowners. The vision of Disraeli's novels is substantially the same as in his *Vindication of the English Constitution*, where he wrote that 'the Tory party in this country is the national party; it is the really democratic party of England. It supports the institutions of the country, because they have been established for the common good, and because they secure the equality of civil rights, without which, whatever may be its name, no government can be free, and based upon which principle, every government, however it may be styled, is in fact a Democracy.'[12]

The great difficulty with the Romantic–Aristocratic point of view was a religious one. Barry could imply with an architectural sleight of hand that Catholicism did not exist. Perhaps it was even possible to do so when discussing England in the 1840s. Where Ireland was in question, however, it was less easy. So it was that while Disraeli managed in the early sessions of Peel's Parliament to persuade his young friends that he could manipulate votes ('*Most private*' – Smythe wrote to Manners in 1842 – 'Dizzy has much more parliamentary power than I had any notion of . . .'), by 1845 the Young England alliance largely came unstuck over the (by twenty-first-century standards) unlikely and arcane issue of a government grant to the Roman Catholic seminary of Maynooth. The Young Englanders who had fantasized about the recreation of a medieval past, and who had even praised a scheme (more optimistic than realistic) for the reunion of the two Churches, Rome and Canterbury, voted separate ways over Maynooth and thereafter, as a political entity, were finished.

The controversy over the Maynooth grant was one of the more striking examples provided by history of the English political classes working themselves into a fury of ignorance and prejudice over a matter which seemed trivial with hindsight. Maynooth, or to give it its full name, the Royal College of St Patrick at Maynooth, had been established when Pitt was prime minister. It was called a Royal College at the special request of George III. It was – and is – the chief training-college for priests in Ireland. The grant of £9,000 per annum which had been given it by the Irish Parliament in 1795 was annually renewed by the Westminster Parliament after the Irish one was suspended, but in 1845 it was seriously inadequate. The priests and students lived in considerable hardship there and Peel was sensible enough to see – given the influence these young men would have in Ireland when they went out to become priests or bishops – that maltreating the seminarians was not a very good way of improving Anglo–Irish relations. As a sensible pamphleteer asked, when the matter flared into controversy:

> Suppose the clergy of the English Church were, during their college life, educated and supported at the expense of the nation, and suppose that in college they had to endure every kind of discomfort and bodily privation, and that when they entered on their spiritual functions, they were habitually treated by the ruling powers and the great with misrepresentation and discourtesy bordering on contempt – would they, so ill-treated in youth and manhood – be zealous loyalists? I rather think they would not.[13]

Considerations such as this, and of simple justice, prompted Peel to propose backing up his reforms of Irish schools, to which he granted more money in his Academic Institutions (Ireland) Act with a decent annual grant to Maynooth – £26,360[14] annually, with a further £30,000 for upkeep of the buildings, and with a commitment that the grant would be steady. The college would not have to come to Parliament each year cap in hand.[15]

Peel got this measure through, but not without a tremendous fight. He admitted that he was surprised by the intensity of the hostility. The opponents, who had not mounted a campaign in any of the previous fifty years of the college's existence, behaved and spoke as if Peel had encroached upon some matter of principle. Anti-Catholic prejudice, rank and sour, rose into the public air. The Duke of Manchester told his fellow peers, 'The Roman Catholic bishops in Ireland appear to us as a political body, united in their hostility to England with, as another priest tells us, three thousand of the second order of priests united in the same antipathies and ready to carry out their plans for the severance of the empire.' The Duke spoke for many when he saw the Irish in general, the Roman Catholics in particular, as a threat to Britain itself. In the fifty years since Maynooth was founded there had been a continental war, followed by thirty years in which, through economic tariffs, Britain isolated itself from Europe. In the last decade of the eighteenth century it might have seemed reasonable that the Irish, in common with most other Europeans, were Roman Catholics. In the 1840s, when the old Duke of Wellington anxiously inspected the Channel ports, convinced of the imminent likelihood of a French invasion, when the public lapped up Harrison Ainsworth's novels about Lady Jane Grey and other Protestant heroines, Popery seemed mysteriously more dangerous. Did not the priests and bishops actively encourage criminal behaviour? The Duke of Manchester believed so.[16]

There was an atavistic aversion to the Roman Catholic religion itself, which Peel's Maynooth Bill awoke. Canon MacNeile, writing to *The Times* on 29 April 1845, was presumably regarded by many readers of that newspaper as making a reasonable point:

As the Word of God forbids the bowing down to images as expressly as it forbids theft or adultery – consequently as we could not without wilful rebellion against God's authority, approve or co-operate in the endowment of a college for instruction in theft or adultery, so neither can we approve of or co-operate in the endowment of a college for instruction in bowing down to images.[17]

'No Popery' was deep in the English psyche, but like most prejudices it was capable of selectivity. When the British annexed Corsica in 1794 they had declared that 'the Roman Catholic is the only national religion of Corsica'. Here was an island which George III had actually insisted be Catholic![18] In Malta, Mauritius and French-speaking Canada, the Crown had given money to the Church.

The Maynooth controversy exposed the peculiar nature of English attitudes to the Irish. To concede the fact that the Irish were predominantly of a different Christian denomination undermined the confidence of the British and their Church. Gladstone, full of High

Church zeal, had written a book, first published in 1839, entitled *The State in its Relations with the Church* in which he argued vehemently that it was the function of the British state to propagate the practice of the Anglican faith. Macaulay in a devastating review reduced the young Etonian bigot's arguments to a nonsense. He did so, among other means, by pointing out that if the arguments used to justify the continued existence of an established Anglican Church in Ireland were used in India, 'it would inevitably destroy our Empire'. British Orthodoxy 'it seems is more shocked by the priests of Rome than by the priests of Kalee . . . Gladstone has not proposed insisting that all the Hindoos in India belong to Anglican parishes. Why does Mr Gladstone allow to the Hindoo a privilege which he denies to the Irishmen?'[19]

Ridiculously, Gladstone resigned from Peel's government over the issue of the Maynooth Grant on a point of principle so obscure that no one understood it. Between the years 1839 and 1845 he had seen the error of his *Church and State*. He was in favour of Maynooth getting its increased grant in 1845 but, because he had written in the terms so ridiculed by Macaulay in 1839, he felt he must resign in 1845.

The granting of money to a seminary of Irish priests threw into highlight the essence of the Irish problem, the profound distrust on either side, and the deep differences, widening by the hour, between the blossoming industrial power of England on the one hand and the abject poverty of the Irish rural economy. The Reverend Sydney Smith, in his breezy Whiggish manner, dismissed all talk of Irish nationalism as essentially the result of economic privation. Long before the Maynooth controversy Smith advocated paying the Irish Catholic clergy as much as their Protestant counterparts. Such a measure would, he guessed, diminish the evil both of the Irish clergy sponging off their poor peasant congregations and of anti-British feeling.

'What is the object of all government?' he had asked. 'The object of all government is roast mutton, potatoes, claret, a stout constable, an honest justice, clear highways, a free chapel. What trash to be bawling in the streets about the Green Isle, the Isle of the Ocean! The bold anthem of *Erin go Bragh*! A far better anthem would be Erin go bread and cheese, Erin go cabins that will keep out the rain, Erin go pantaloons without holes in them!'[20] When read in the dark shade of what actually befell the people of Ireland in the autumn of the year Maynooth got its grant, these words seem less like a piece of jokey common sense than like an epitaph.

*

Sir Robert Peel's common-sense conservatism was based on such a creed as Sydney Smith's – that the object of good government was a contented, well-fed and well-behaved populace. That, quite simply, explains why he was prepared to take on his own party in Parliament, and in effect to destroy the Tories' electoral fortunes for twenty years. To his supporters Peel would always seem a fundamentally decent, sensible man, a man of principle, perhaps the last truly sensible prime minister until the rise of Salisbury. For Peel's High Tory opponents he would always be the ultimate opportunist, changing one of the cardinal doctrines of the party in order to stay in office. Parallels with modern political struggles flicker in any commentator's mind; one thinks naturally of the agonies of the Conservative Party in the last decade of the twentieth, the opening decade of the twenty-first centuries, over their membership of the European Union. The greatest historian of the Conservative Party, Lord Blake, says that it was one of those extraordinary moments in English history, such as the Abdication of Edward VIII or the Munich crisis, when the whole nation was divided. Families split over it, friendships were broken. Once Peel's decision had been made, the Tory Party, 'The party of Pitt, Perceval, Liverpool, Canning, Wellington and Peel vanished in "smoke and confusion".'[21] Afterwards, the parties reformed. The Peelites either drifted with nowhere to go, or joined up with the Liberal Party which had emerged from an alliance of Whigs and Radicals. The diehards who had persisted in wanting the price of bread to be kept artificially high were led in the Lords by Lord Stanley, in the Commons by Lord George Bentinck, with Benjamin Disraeli as his rather improbable campaigner and lieutenant.

For ten years at least, there had been an active campaign against the protectionist laws designed to subsidize the English rural economy and keep out the import of cheap foreign corn. The movement centred on Manchester, John Bright, a textile manufacturer from Rochdale being one of its leading lights, the other Richard Cobden, MP for Manchester and one of the first aldermen in the city. From the outset, the Anti-Corn Law League which they formed had aimed its sights at the political power of the aristocracy. Corn Law Repeal was much more important in this respect than the electoral reforms of 1842. 'The sooner,' said Cobden in one of his speeches, 'the sooner the power in this country is transferred from the landed oligarchy, which has so misused it, and is placed absolutely – mind I say absolutely – in the hands of the intelligent middle and industrious classes, the better for the condition and destinies of this country.'[22] Cobden believed that wars had been the sport of aristocrats, and that Free Trade would bring not merely wealth to Britain but peace to the world.

Not everyone agreed. The Chartists, on the whole, inclined to the view that British agriculture needed government aid and subsidies by means of keeping the price of wheat – hence of bread – artificially high. They suspected the Free Traders' motives, believing that Northern capitalists like Bright only wanted cheap bread so that they could lower the wages of their workers.

Peel, like his ultra-Tory backbenchers, had fought the election of 1841 as an opponent of the repeal of the Corn Laws, but he had never been an anti-Free Trade fanatic; his budgets were all in the direction of Free Trade. All the economic arguments began to pile up on the side of repealing the Corn Laws. Lord George Bentinck was unconvinced – 'I keep horses in three counties, and they tell me that I shall save £1,500 a year by free trade. I don't care for that; what I cannot bear is being sold.'[23]

Given the social, economic and political situation of England in the mid-1840s it was inevitable that at some stage protectionism would be abandoned and Free Trade would win, as the market so often does. The vast increases in productivity and manufacturing which were happening while the Corn Laws were being debated were changing the nature of England. Railway mania had struck. By 1848, around 5,000 miles of line were working in the United Kingdom – only 400 of them in Ireland, a fact of dire omen. Five railway companies had built lines to Brighton, three to Norwich. The combination of private investment and improved means of production and transport prepared for an astonishing boom which would inevitably have the long-term effect of improving the cost of living for all but agricultural labourers and those whose livelihood came solely from native-grown crops.[24] Even within agriculture itself there was some economic buoyancy, with new fertilizers – nitrate of soda and guano – now in common use, and new crops: the swede and the mangel-wurzel came to be used increasingly, an invaluable feed, far more frost-resistant than other root crops. As for the wheat harvests – they had not been good – 1842, 1843 and 1844 saw a fall in the price of corn of 14s., momentarily halting the demand to lift the tariff and bring in foreign grain at a cheaper price.

But then came 1845, a disastrously wet summer and the rains which, as it was said, washed the Corn Laws away. Peel took the ultimate risk – he waged war on his own party. Rather than resign and hand the 'poisoned chalice' of Corn Law repeal to the Liberal leader Lord John Russell, he did what he deemed honourable and proposed their repeal from his position as Conservative prime minister. So the Corn Laws were abolished. The 'Ultras', the country Tories egged on by Disraeli, took their revenge by voting Peel out of power over the Irish Coercion Bill. Wellington called the alliance against Peel – Whigs and Ultra Protectionists who in turn agreed on no matter of principle – the 'blackguard combination'.[25] Thus ended the old Tory Party and the career of the best leader that party had ever had.

By then the government was faced by a problem of much wider and more sinister significance than the breaking and mending of political alliances in Westminster. The greatest single human disaster to befall the European continent in that century had begun its mortal work.

6

Famine in Ireland

While the human population of Europe, Asia – eventually the Americas – collapsed before the imperial invasion of King Cholera, another devastation was making its way to Europe: the fungal disease *Phytophthora infestans* or potato blight. It came to the Netherlands, to Belgium and to Scotland, all countries with a population of poor agrarian workers, but also with an expanding industrial life, comparatively sophisticated road or rail networks, and the will and capacity in case of hardship to help those afflicted. Of course there was hunger and wretchedness in those countries, particularly in Scotland. But it was nothing to compare in size or scale or horror with the Great Irish Famine. To the scale of the Irish disaster itself must be added the political aftermath of distrust and hatred, with us all to this day.

James Anthony Froude, not always regarded as a friend of the Irish,[1] alludes towards the close of his monumental study of *The English in Ireland in the Eighteenth Century* (1881) to a conversation with an Irish Catholic bishop, who remarked bitterly to the English historian 'that every death lay at England's door'. England, it seemed, was expected to work a miracle, like the multiplication of the bread at the Sea of Galilee. Yet, adds Froude, the supposed Carlylean anti-Irish historian, *what the Bishop said was true after all* (my italics). 'The condition of things which made such a calamity possible was due essentially to those who had undertaken the government of Ireland and left Ireland to her own devices. The conviction fastened itself into the Irish national mind on both sides of the Atlantic; and there it rests, and will rest.'[2]

This view is largely endorsed by modern historians. No one doubts the scale of the calamity. Nor is it in question that successive British administrations were incompetent, even callous. Given the nature of Ireland in 1845, however, the actual physical, social and political situation, it is hard to see how the Famine could have been averted. The modern reader is aghast at the unfolding narratives of suffering which any account of the Famine will provide. But in the circumstances, and *at the time*, it is hard to see what a different government, even a government based in Dublin, could have done. True, good landlords (of whom there were all too few) could alleviate suffering *in some measure* on their estates. True, the continued trade in corn, when the famine was at its height, was avoidable, causes anguish to read about today, and caused worse than anguish to the starving who watched Irish corn being *exported* from Cork and elsewhere. But given the social hierarchies which existed at the time, and the political tensions which already overshadowed Anglo-Irish relations, one knows that it is as unrealistic to have expected a modern-style famine relief operation as it is to have expected Lord John Russell's government to take maize to County Kerry by helicopter. A modern historian, K. Theodore Hoppen, says, 'Although the government's response was extremely inefficient, grudging and limited, perhaps only an authoritarian state committed to the welfare of the poor at all costs could have *achieved* a great deal more.'[3]

The story of the famine is therefore truly tragic, the more so when we consider the fact that those very benefits for which the Liberals campaigned so vociferously on the British mainland were, as our historian implies, more nails in the Irish coffin. Early Victorian Liberalism was posited on the notion of less state interference, not more. Liberals like Cobden and Bright were kindly men but they saw Tory Ashley's attempts to improve factory conditions as state tyranny, socialism by the back door. The idea that states were responsible for the welfare of citizens was horrifying to laissez-faire economists. Combine the idea of laissez-faire with those of Malthus and you end up, as we have seen, with workhouses, designed specifically to encourage effort and self-help on the part of the poor.

The economic benefits, in terms of the overall enrichment of society, were already being seen in the industrialized North. By 1845, the Benthamites had influenced the political attitudes of a generation. They had a natural distrust of the idea of state aid. Create what would later be called a dependency culture and you will end up with national bankruptcy. So, when the extent of the famine came to be known, there is found an instinctive reluctance on the part of the state to do anything – either in terms of welfare, or, still less, in terms of economic protectionism. Had they not just spent ten painful years campaigning for the lifting of protection on corn? Were they to throw that away because the Irish were hungry?

And here, the darker and quite undeniable fact of anti-Irish prejudice comes into play. The atavistic and irrational feelings which were provoked by the matter of the Maynooth Grant were not going to evaporate because of the sad stories which began to reach England in the late summer of 1845. In fact, the religious prejudices unearthed by the Maynooth affair only confirmed, for many English Protestants, their Malthusian hunches about the improvident and (as they believed) superstitious population of the Other Island.

It is awful to observe how the Almighty humbles the pride of Nations. The Sword, the Pestilence and Famine are the instruments of his displeasure: the canker-worm and the locust are his armies, he gives the word: a single copy is blighted; and we see a Nation prostrate, stretching out its Hands for Bread. These are solemn warnings, and they fill me with reverence; they proclaim with a voice not to be mistaken, that 'doubtless there is a God who judgeth the Earth!'[4]

These are not the words of an Ulster demagogue preaching on a street corner, nor even of an evangelical bishop. They are the home secretary Sir James Graham writing to Sir Robert Peel. The Prime Minister broadly shared Graham's religious viewpoint. These were the *moderates* of the day. There were plenty who saw the Famine as a punishment for idolatry. Some Protestants even saw it as 'a special "mercy", calling sinners both to evangelical truth and the Dismantling of all artificial obstacles to divinely-inspired spiritual and economic order', as one pamphlet put it.[5]

What is called the Great Famine was in fact a series of calamities continuing over a number of years. The basic facts are these. The first fungus struck the Irish potato crops in the summer of 1845. Some parts of Ireland escaped altogether, but about one-third of the overall potato crop was lost. By 1846, with the blight making deeper predations, three-quarters of the crop was lost. By 1847, yields were a little better, but little had been planted by the despairing population who had eaten their seed potatoes. By 1848, crops were back to about two-thirds of the normal, though it was not until 1850 that the worst was over.

During this period, the government changed. Peel, technically defeated over an Irish Coercion Bill in the House of Commons, had in reality, as we have seen, fallen foul of his own party over the repeal of the Corn Laws. His immediate reaction, on hearing of the failure of the 1845 potato crop, was to create schemes of public works. In this way 140,000 jobs were created, and he also spent £100,000 on imported maize from America to be sold cheaply to those in need. This did provide some relief, but for the relief to be effectual, it would have been necessary to get the grain to the mouths who needed it the most. Apart from the fact that there were only 400 miles of railways in the whole of Ireland,[6] ports on the west coast were non-existent. There were almost no harbours where a grain-ship could pull in.

Peel's comparatively charitable practical help was not followed up with much enthusiasm by the Liberal government of Lord John Russell, which came to power in the summer of 1846. After a year of untold sufferings in Ireland, there was, quite unrelated, a British banking crisis in 1847. The famine had now been afflicting Ireland for two years, killing hundreds of thousands of people and forcing others to emigrate. The reaction of the chancellor of the Exchequer, Sir Charles Wood, was expressed in a letter to the Irish viceroy, the Earl of Clarendon – 'Now financially, my course is very easy. I have no more money and therefore I cannot give it . . . Where the people refused to work or sow, they must starve, as indeed I fear must be the case in many parts.'[7] There *was* relief given to famine-sufferers by the British government – perhaps £7 million from a government which believed spending to be wicked and which had convinced itself that it was strapped for cash. It is only fair to note that seven years later the British government found £70 million to finance the Crimean War.[8]

How many died – and why? It is the second question which explains the gross, the truly terrible answer to the first. Indeed one needs to answer the question *why* the famine happened in at least two ways. It is very much not a simple question of one particular fungal disease destroying one tuber, though that is where one begins.

The population of Ireland by 1845 had probably reached some 8.3 million. True, it had increased dramatically over the years, as had the populations of other European countries, but apart from isolated cases of hunger in times of bad harvest, cases which could be (and usually had been) dealt with by the charity of landlords or others in the locality, there was no obvious sense in which this was an island incapable of feeding itself. 'There is no evidence that pre-famine Ireland was overpopulated in any useful sense of that word.'[9]

The way in which this population sustained itself, however, can be seen with the eyes of hindsight to be calamitous. The potato blight might have been a nuisance, or worse than a nuisance, to those farming twenty acres or more. The evidence suggests that none of these comparatively small farmers (still less the larger landowners) died of starvation. The big divide in Irish society was not so much between landlord and tenant as between those with at least twenty acres and those with less, or none. The great majority of Irish peasants farmed little strips of land, and their only crop was the potato. Few of them it would seem ever went fishing, on the plenteous inland waters of Ireland, nor did they put to sea as the Welsh, Scotch and Cornish had done, time out of mind, returning with plentiful supplies of fish. The potato was the ideal crop for a peasant economy, an agrarian world which had been unaffected by any of the momentous changes which had come upon the English countryside. The potato needed next to no maintenance, as a crop. You simply planted it, watched it grow, harvested and ate it. In the intervening months of the year, you could play your fiddle and sing your songs. What else was there to do? The education of Catholics until the abolition of the Penal Laws in the eighteenth century had been confined to the hedge-schools – run out of doors by enterprising priests so as not to infringe the law. Burke went to a good one, evidently, but for most, educational possibilities were nil. How could an Irish Carlyle, the well-educated peasant, have ever been? Such was the hold of the Protestant Ascendancy over Ireland that four years after the Catholic Emancipation Act there were still no Catholic judges in the whole of Ireland.[10]

The big landlords owned the place, the prosperous tenant farmers did well out of the arrangement. Inevitably, there was more thieving in this type of economy than there was in England, so Irish crime figures for the period are always higher than English. To English contemporaries this proved that the Irish were feckless, dishonest, potentially violent. The reality is that if you started from scratch and invented a society such as that controlled by the Protestant Ascendancy in Ireland, in which the bottom 4 (out of 8+) million were given no educational or economic advantages or incentives, they would end up, very much as the Irish peasantry did end up, cultivating very small patches of land and doing little else besides. It was simply appalling bad luck that this very deprived and numerous group of people subsisted on one tuber alone which, since its introduction in the seventeenth century, had given no sign or indication that it would fail. It was the reliability of the spud, as well as the ease of growing it, which made it the favoured peasant food. Two million acres of Ireland were given over to potatoes. *Three million people ate nothing else.* Nothing. (Adult males consumed between twelve and fourteen pounds daily.)

All visitors to Ireland in pre-famine days were shocked by the poverty of the peasants. Froude, in 1841, saw, in Galway, 'the rags insufficient to cover the children and boys of twelve running about absolutely naked . . . The inhabitants, except where they had been taken in hand and metamorphosed into police, seemed more like tribes of squalid apes than human beings.'[11] 'Only magnificent châteaux and miserable cabins are to be seen in Ireland,' said a French observer. All noted the mud floors, peat roofs and insanitary conditions in which the rural poor were housed.[12]

Comparable scenes were perhaps to be found in England, where the wages of agricultural labourers had started to fall badly behind those of the hired industrial workers in the factories. But England, because its economy was based on industry, and on the investment of the rentier class, was immeasurably richer and stronger than Ireland. The Irish landlords varied enormously. In areas where the landlord was compassionate, starvation was often averted. In many cases, however, landlords showed no mercy or were absent. Peasants who lived on estates with absentee landlords could often expect no pity from the small prosperous tenant farmers or the estate managers. Prosperous farmers continued, through the famine years, to prosecute starving labourers caught stealing food from their fields. They refused money wages to those unable to pay in advance for their 'conacre' portions of land.[13] (It was reckoned that half an acre of conacre would support a labourer's family.)[14] Many therefore simply did not have the money to buy the cheap imported corn. 'Conacre' rent was between £12 and £14 an acre, paid not in cash but in labour. A typical family of 4–7 people in Westmeath at this time was trying to subsist on 10d. a day. To earn the 10d. on one of the government's 'job creations', the labourer would have to walk 3½ miles to work and 3½ miles back, his sole meal of the day a small ration of oatmeal. No wonder violence broke out when the hungry were able to muster up the energy for it.

By the end of September 1846 the people of Clashmore, Co. Waterford, were living on blackberries, at Rathcormack, Co. Cork, on cabbage leaves. In Leitrim, the parish of Cloone, with 22,000 inhabitants, had no bread and no baker, but at the same time Irish corn grown on neighbouring farms was harvested, bagged and taken for export. At Youghal near Cork there were riots of 'enraged' people who tried to hold up a boat laden with export oats. At Dungarvan in Co. Waterford, a crowd of the starving unemployed entered the town, plundering shops and ordering chandlers and shopkeepers not to export grain. After the police failed to clear the streets, the 1st Royal

Dragoons were called out. The crowd began to pelt them with stones. After the Riot Act had been read out, the soldiers opened fire, leaving several men wounded and two dead.

'The Almighty indeed sent the potato blight, but the English created the Famine.' These words of John Mitchel in *The Last Conquest of Ireland (Perhaps) 1860* very understandably became the unshakeable conviction of the Irish, particularly those forced into exile by hunger. The tendency of modern historians is not so much to single out individuals for blame, such as Charles Edward Trevelyan, permanent head of the Treasury, as to point to the whole attitude of mind of the governing class and the, by modern standards, gross inequalities which were taken for granted. Almost any member of the governing class would have shared *some* of Trevelyan's attitudes.

But there is more to John Mitchel's famous statement (one could almost call it a declaration of war) than mere rhetoric. Deeply ingrained with the immediate horrors of the famine was the overall structure of Irish agrarian society, which placed Irish land and wealth in the hands of English (or in effect English) aristocrats. It was the belief of a Liberal laissez-faire economist such as Lord John Russell that the hunger of Irish peasants was not the responsibility of government but of landowners. No more callous example of a political doctrine being pursued to the death – quite literally – exists in the annals of British history. But Lord John Russell's government, when considering the Irish problem, were not envisaging some faraway island in which they had no personal concern. A quarter of the peers in the House of Lords had Irish interests.[15]

Of the three leading Whig ministers in 1848, only Russell himself had no direct economic interest in Ireland. Many of the English parliamentarians owned land there. Lord Palmerston for example – British foreign secretary in Russell's Cabinet – owned many acres of County Sligo. In common with many landowners he never went near his tenants in their plight, and certainly sent no relief, preferring to export them in their hundreds to Canada. When, in November 1847, the ship *Aeolus* arrived at St John with 428 passengers, almost all of them were Lord Palmerston's tenants. The following report was made of their condition:

There are many aged persons of both sexes on board and a large population of women and children, the whole in the most abject state of destitution, with barely sufficient rags upon their persons to cover their nakedness . . . One boy, about ten years of age, was actually brought on deck stark naked.[16]

Eight passengers were dead on arrival at St John. The inhabitants of the Canadian port had nowhere to house them and demanded that the passengers of the *Aeolus* be given a free passage back to Ireland. The matter caused such scandal that Palmerston was called to make a statement in the House of Commons, blaming his agents. They in turn made the tenants write cruelly unconvincing letters to the St John newspapers expressing their deep gratitude to Lord Palmerston for rescuing them from the famine. They remained in the dockside slums there, struggling for some kind of existence. That winter the streets of St John were full of 'swarms of wretched beings going about the streets imploring every passer-by, women and children in the snow, without shoes or stockings and scarcely anything on'.[17] Many more went to New York. Some, risking the frequently violent anti-Irish feeling of the English working class, came to England, usually to work in the most menial capacities as navvies, often forcibly separated from their families. These were the survivors. In the five years of the famine the population of Ireland fell from a little over 8 million to a little over 6. About 1 million of that can be attributed to deaths by natural causes, and by (usually enforced) clearances of the land.

That leaves the eternally shaming statistic of 1.1 million deaths by starvation in Ireland between 1845 and 1850. Throughout this period, the viceroy in Dublin Castle continued to draw his salary of £20,000 per annum. (The prime minister's salary was £5,000.) While labourers in Westmeath struggled their seven miles a day to earn 10d. and while over a million died for want of anything to eat, anything at all, the viceroy kept up his lavish court. Lord Clarendon's household accounts for 1848 show £1,297 spent on wine; £1,868 on butcher's bills; £619 on poulterers, £352 on fishmongers and £562 on the butter man. Lord Clarendon as viceroy, supporting a government which had come into power on the Free Trade ticket, had done nothing to check the profiteering which went on in the worst of the famine areas.[18] (Throughout the winter of '46–7, for instance, prices rocketed and speculators made a fortune selling imported maize – '£40,000 and £800,000 were spoken of as having been made by merchants in Cork', wrote one despondent contemporary.[19]

The riot police and troops were sent to quell the angry mobs, with the cynical promise of extra provisions. Trevelyan arranged for the provisioning of 2,000 riot troops with beef, pork and biscuit, to be mobilized at short notice in order to put down food riots.

It is all so horrible that one cannot and need not exaggerate the suffering of the hungry and the callousness of their governors. That should not prompt the distorted view that no one on the English side of St George's Channel was shocked by what was going on, nor offer cause to suppose that *all* the rich and powerful were (to use Bishop Berkeley's description of Irish landlords) 'vultures with iron bowels'.[20] Towards the end of 1846 a group of 'merchant princes' in the City of London, led by Baron Lionel de Rothschild and Mr Thomas Baring, set up 'The British Association for the relief of the extreme distress in the remote parishes of Ireland and Scotland'. Trevelyan did not believe the fund would do any good, but Queen Victoria donated £2,000, Rothschilds £1,000, the Duke of Devonshire (who in addition to his various English palaces also owned the castle of Lismore in Co. Waterford) £1,000 and Sir Charles Wood £200. The British Association appointed an anglicized Pole, Count Strzelecki, to administer distribution of the funds. Evangelical Christians and Quakers helped with their work.[21]

Yet these overtures from the English side were undoubtedly made against a tide of prejudice and bitterness. The hordes of Irish poor crowding into English slums did not evoke pity – rather, fear and contempt. The Whiggish Liberal *Manchester Guardian* blamed the famine quite largely on the feckless Irish attitudes to agriculture, family, life in general. Small English farmers, said this self-righteous newspaper, don't divide farms into four which are only sufficient to feed one family. (The economic necessities which forced the Irish to do this were conveniently overlooked by the *Manchester Guardian*: indeed economic weakness, in the Darwinian jungle, is the equivalent of sin.) Why weren't the English starving? Because 'they bring up their children in habits of frugality, which qualify them for earning their own living, and then send them forth into the world to look for employment'.

We are decades away from any organized Irish Republican Movement. Nevertheless, in the midst of the famine unrest, we find innumerable ripe examples of British double standards where violence is in question. An Englishman protecting his grossly selfish way of life with a huge apparatus of police and military, prepared to gun down the starving, is maintaining law and order. An Irishman retaliating is a terrorist. John Bright, the Liberal Free Trader, hero of the campaign against the Corn Laws, blamed Irish idleness for their hunger – 'I believe it would be found on inquiry, that the population of Ireland, as compared with that of England, do not work more than two days a week.' The marked increase in homicides during the years 1846 and 1847 filled these English liberals with terror. There were 68 reported homicides in Ireland in 1846, 96 in 1847, 126 shootings in the latter year compared with 55 the year before. Rather than putting these in the context of hundreds of thousands of deaths annually by starvation, the textile manufacturer from Rochdale blames all the violence of these starving Celts on their innate idleness. 'Wherever a people are not industrious and are not employed, there is the greatest danger of crime and outrage. Ireland is idle, and therefore she starves; Ireland starves, and therefore she rebels.'

Both halves of this sentence are factually wrong. Ireland most astonishingly did *not* rebel in, or immediately after, the famine years; and we have said enough to show that though there was poverty, extreme poverty, before 1845, many Irish families survived heroically on potatoes alone. The economic structure of a society in which they could afford a quarter or half an acre of land on which to grow a spud while the Duke of Devonshire owned Lismore, Bolton (and half Yorkshire), Chatsworth (and ditto Derbyshire), the whole of Eastbourne and a huge palace in London was not of the Irish peasant's making.

By 1848/9 the attitude of Lord John Russell's government had become Malthusian, not to stay Darwinian, in the extreme. As always happens when famine takes hold, it was followed by disease. Cholera swept through Belfast and Co. Mayo in 1848, spreading to other districts. In the workhouses, crowded to capacity, dysentery, fevers and ophthalmia were endemic – 13,812 cases of ophthalmia in 1849 rose to 27,200 in 1850. Clarendon and Trevelyan now used the euphemism of 'natural causes' to describe death by starvation. The gentle Platonist–Hegelian philosopher Benjamin Jowett once said, 'I have always felt a certain horror of political economists, since I heard one of them say that he feared the famine of 1848 in Ireland would not kill more than a million people, and that would scarcely be enough to do much good.'[22] As so often Sydney Smith was right: 'The moment the very name of Ireland is mentioned, the English seem to bid adieu to common feeling, common prudence and common sense, and to act with the barbarity of tyrants and the fatuity of idiots.'[23]

7

The Victorians in Italy

Ireland drew forth the darkest, most pessimistic, and most repressive aspect of the Victorian character. Italy tapped its sunniness, its optimism, and its belief in a liberal future. Gladstone's attitude to Italy is a good yardstick, not only of his own inner journey, but that of his contemporaries; for one of the secrets of his phenomenal and long-lasting political success was that, eccentric though he was, he was also a truly Hegelian figure embodying the spirit of his age. As his liberal biographer and hero-worshipper Morley saw it, 'slowly and almost blindly heaving off his shoulders the weight of old conservative tradition, Mr Gladstone did not at first go beyond liberty with all that ordered liberty conveys'. But his visit to Italy in the autumn of 1850 drew him 'into that great European stream of liberalism which was destined to carry him so far'.[1]

He had first visited Italy as a very young man in 1832, with his brother John. Since, it had been chiefly a place in his mind, the land above all else of Dante, the writer next to Homer most revered by Gladstone. It was also, needless to say, a place associated in his mind with loose living, and in 1849 he had set out on a quasi-farcical journey to 'rescue' Lady Lincoln, the wife of an old Eton friend who had eloped to Italy with Lord Walpole.[2] He had managed to hear *Lucia di Lammermoor* and an early Verdi (*The Masnadieri*) and he saw some splendid scenery as he chased from Naples to Milan to Lecco – but he failed to bring the lady home, and it horrified him to find she was pregnant. His hamfisted chase, indeed, brought on her confinement.

The journey to Southern Italy the following year, in the autumn of 1850, was undertaken to benefit the eyesight of one of his daughters. They could not have visited Naples at a time when hopes for Italian unity and independence were lower. Mazzini, who dreamed of revolution against the Austrian occupation of Northern Italy, was in exile in London. Cavour, architect of the constitutional revolution, the creation of the kingdom of Italy, was also in exile. The revolutions of 1848 had led in the kingdom of Naples to savage reaction; three months staying at the British legation opened Gladstone's eyes to the true nature of Bourbon rule. The British minister (ambassador) there was William Temple, the younger brother of Lord Palmerston. The secretary was the Anglo-Italian Joseph Lacaita, later a professor at King's College, London, and an adviser to Gladstone about European matters in Italy and Greece. It was through Lacaita that Gladstone was able to visit the Neapolitan prisons and to see Baron Carlo Poerio, briefly a liberalizing Neapolitan minister, who had been put on trial and sentenced to twenty-four years in irons. The state of the prisons and the condition of the prisoners opened Gladstone's mind to the effects which 'stern unbending' religious absolutism could achieve. He saw the political prisoners, many of them imprisoned without trial, shackled to violent common criminals. The insanitary conditions were such as Gladstone had never seen or dreamed of. Here was displayed 'The Wisdom of Our Ancestors' – medieval systems of government and repression such as gave pause to the religious prig and Tory. 'Ignorance – Superstition – The Block – The Stake – The Rack – Dirt – Disease' – those manifestations of ancestral wisdom with which Dickens humorously adorned the spines of his library-books – were alive and well in the Naples of the 1840s.

Gladstone took the lessons to heart. How did his Anglican bigotry differ from the bigotry of the Bourbons and the Catholic Church in Naples? Why did he instinctively believe that the Italian desire for self-government was admirable and just, while turning a deaf ear to Irish aspirations for, if not self-government, then some autonomy and independence, religious and economic? The great transformation of Gladstone the Little Englander Tory to Gladstone the People's William had begun, and the great political Lost Cause to which he gave his career – the 'mission to pacify Ireland' – really may be said to have begun in the prisons of Naples.

Dickens in Italy – he went there in 1844 – merely demonstrated his ability to carry around with him his own imaginative world. The apothecaries' shops in Genoa which he described so vividly could really have been in Chancery Lane – or his version of Chancery Lane; the public execution (by guillotine) in Rome could just as well have been in Paris. He ended his *Pictures from Italy*, however, with disappointingly predictable Victorian-Liberal observations on human progress. 'Let us not remember Italy the less regardfully because, in every fragment of her fallen Temples, and every stone of her deserted palaces and prisons, she helps to inculcate the lesson that the wheel of Time is rolling for an end, and that the world is, in all great essentials, better, gentler, more forbearing and more hopeful, as it rolls!'[3] The most vivid part of his book is undoubtedly the passage which relates not to Italian culture, religion or history, but to the extraordinary phenomenon of Vesuvius, whose smouldering sulphurous heat and energy boiling beneath the very feet of Dickens and his party called forth a response in his own boiling cauldron of imaginative heat. Everything about the description is 'Dickensian', from the observation that the snow-covered mountain resembled 'an antediluvian Twelfth-cake' to the rechristening of their guide 'Mr Pickle of Portici'.

John Ruskin was a much more serious Italophile. In the eighteenth century, Italy was the grand object of aristocratic collectors and dilettanti. It is characteristic of the Victorian Age that the two great English interpreters of Italy should have been Ruskin, the son of a sherry merchant, and Robert Browning, the son of a clerk in the Bank of England. The moralities drawn from Italy were, for Ruskin, always of a much more complex variety than they had been for Gladstone or Dickens.

Ruskin's objection to Gladstone's expressions of horror in Naples was that they did not go far enough:

The common English traveller, if he can gather a black bunch of grapes with his own fingers, and have his bottle of Falernian brought him by a girl with black eyes, asks no more of this world, nor the next; and declares Naples a Paradise. But I knew, from the first moment when my foot furrowed volcanic ashes, that no mountain form or colour could exist in perfection when everything was made of scoria, and that the blue sea was to be little boasted if it broke on black sand. And I saw also, with really wise anger, the horror of neglect in the governing power, which Mr Gladstone found, forsooth, in the Neapolitan prisons! But which neither he nor any other Englishman, so far as I know, except Byron and I, saw to have made the Apennines one prison wall, and all the modern life of Italy one captivity of shame and crime; alike against the honour of her ancestors, and the kindness of her God.[4]

Ruskin's first general purpose, as a European tourist, was to record as much of it as possible in his punctilious sketches before it was destroyed by neglect, by war, and by modern industry. He believed, rightly as it turned out, that his generation would be the last to look on old Europe before the belching chimney and the railway wrecked it forever. He saw the ruins of the Forum as Gibbon had seen them. That is something subsequent generations will never do.

Ruskin hated the republican movements in Italy because he saw them as destructive. In 1845 he wrote to his father:

> I think verily the Devil is come down upon earth, having great wrath, because he knoweth that he hath but a short time. And a short time he will have if he goes on at this rate, for in ten years more there will be nothing in the world but eating-houses and gambling houses and worse ... the French condemned the Convent of San Marco where I am just going, and all the pictures of Fra Angelico were only saved by their being driven out.[5]

Italy was, moreover, for Ruskin, a series of spiritual revelations. The Campo Santo at Pisa, with its depiction in fresco of the entire saving story of Christianity, revivified his understanding of the nature of Christian tradition. Having moved from the extreme evangelicalism of his mother to a secret and arid unbelief, he now revelled in an imaginative Catholicism, accepting the *mythos* of the Catholic story which formed and shaped the imagination of Europe. In Florence, to which so many middle-class American and English tourists and expatriates flocked, 'the Newgate-like palaces were rightly hateful to me; the old shop and market-streets rightly pleasant; the inside of the Duomo a horror, the outside a Chinese puzzle'.[6]

But the Italian city with which Ruskin's name will ever be associated is Venice. On one level it would be inhuman not to sympathize with his wife Effie for the fact that when he took her, newly-wed, to Venice, he neglected her so woefully and spent his entire time obsessively inspecting the buildings with his sketchbook. Yet this is to ignore the bigger fact that Effie was never the love of his life, and Venice was. He had feared that the fighting in 1848 between Italians and Austrians would have destroyed his beloved buildings. *The Stones of Venice*, whose first volume was finished in 1850, was much more than a purely architectural handbook. It was the attempt to depict the soul of a civilization. Years later, when Ruskin was being sued by the American painter Whistler, he asked his lawyers to bring into the witness box a painting he had acquired in 1864 for £1,000. It was the depiction of the Venetian Doge Andrea Gritti, and during the libel trial Burne-Jones testified that it was evidence of what a perfectly finished painting should look like. (Unlike the work of Whistler, which Ruskin said was hurling a paint-pot in the face of the public.) Ruskin believed, as modern experts do not, that the painting was by Titian.[7] One of his reasons for wanting the portrait of a Doge, however, was not merely the beauty of this picture as an object. For Ruskin, the mercantile, sea-faring city-state and empire was an emblem of Britain. The good Doge was like Ruskin's father, John James, a merchant. Everyone in Venice was 'in trade'. The Merchant King was the symbol in fact of Ruskin's own class which now rose to prominence in Britain. Would contemporary Victorian Britain rise to the moral challenge, and be like Venice in its moral, political and commercial heyday – its Gothic days, when it built the Frari and the Doge's Palace and St Mark's, buildings which were part of Ruskin's soul? Or would Britain, like Venice, 'fall' morally – a fall symbolized for Ruskin by the building of baroque and Palladian churches in an acceptance of the post-medieval secular viewpoint?

The question could be asked in the terms of the most famous English poem set in the city – and written by Ruskin's fellow Camberwell resident, Robert Browning:

> What, they lived once thus at Venice where the
>   merchants were the kings,
> Where Saint Mark's is, where the Doges used to wed the
>   sea with rings?
>
> Ay, because the sea's the street there; and 'tis arched by
>   . . . what you call
> . . . Shylock's bridge with houses on it, where they kept
>   the carnival:
> I was never out of England – it's as if I saw it all.

The poem, 'A Toccata of Galuppi's', like Ruskin's *Stones of Venice* stares at Venice in decline – 'Dust and ashes, dead and done with, Venice spent what Venice earned'.[8] Is it a poem about the transitoriness of all earthly things or a capitalist hymn to the folly of spending your savings, which should be heaped up in consols*? No one can read Browning's vivid word-paintings of Italy without feeling that they have been there.

Mazzini himself used to read Browning's 'The Italian in England' to fellow exiles to demonstrate that an Englishman could sympathize with

---

* British Government Securities – Consolidated Annuities.

their plight.[9] It is in essence a compressed novel of espionage about an Italian freedom-fighter (clearly Mazzini) betrayed by comrades, exiled but, in spite of the continued domination of Austria, determined one day that his nation would be independent.

Robert Browning himself, and his wife, were among the best-known of those English exiles who made Italy their home. Theirs had been an astonishing courtship. She was a tiny, sofa-bound invalid; her father, a decayed gentleman, had been aged twenty when she was born. The closeness of their relationship (he fathered twelve children in all) was increased by the death of Mrs Barrett in 1828. Elizabeth was both a sickly child whom he kept as a semi-prisoner in the house (she suffered from tuberculosis) and in some ways the mistress of the household. She had to escape, and love provided the best of reasons to do so.[10] The first letter Browning wrote her (16 June 1846) proclaimed, 'I love your verses with all my heart, dear Miss Barrett – . . . and I love you too . . .'[11] They could not fail to be caught up in one another's personal dramas after an opening salvo as good as this. G.K. Chesterton was right to remind us that we should not expect the letters to provide delight to the 'ordinary sentimentalist'. They are not overtly erotic, or even especially comprehensible. He quotes, 'I ought to wait, say a week at least, having killed all your mules for you, before I shot down your dogs . . . But not being exactly Phoibus Apollon you are to know further that when I *did* think I might go modestly on . . . ὤμοι, let me get out of this slough of a simile, never mind with what dislocated ankles.' Chesterton adds, 'What our imaginary sentimentalist would make of this tender passage it is difficult indeed to imagine.'[12]

They met on 20 May 1845. On 12 September 1846, after a clandestine correspondence and even more clandestine meetings, they were married at St Marylebone parish church, with a cousin of Browning's (James Silverthorne) and Elizabeth Barrett's maid, Wilson, as witnesses. Miss Barrett returned to her father's home in Wimpole Street as if nothing had happened. On 20 September, Robert and Elizabeth Barrett Browning, clutching their dog Flush and accompanied by the faithful Wilson, stepped ashore from the Southampton boat at Le Havre. It was not surprising that they headed for Italy: first to Pisa, and then, on 20 April 1847, to Florence where, on and off, they would spend the next fifteen years.[13]

Browning was thirty-four when he was married. Elizabeth Barrett was forty, and tubercular. Neither of them expected her to live as long as she did, nor perhaps, after two miscarriages, that she would give birth to 'a fine strong boy' – Robert Wiedemann Barrett Browning, known as Pen.

Browning, next to Ruskin, was the greatest English interpreter of Italy to his fellow countrymen. When he visited the Louvre with Browning, Dante Gabriel Rossetti discovered that Browning's knowledge of early Italian art was superior to anyone that he had met, Ruskin included.[14] Yet although Browning revelled in Italy, loved its art and literature, its tastes and colours and smells, he remained to his dying day (in the Ca'Rezzonico on the Grand Canal at Venice in 1889) a tourist. Though he and Elizabeth spoke Italian (and Wilson became fluent in her version of the language), they never established any lasting friendship with an Italian.

Nor really, in spite of the radical sympathies of Elizabeth Barrett's 'Casa Guidi Windows', were they much engaged, except in a generalized feeling of liberalism, with the political changes by which Italy was convulsed in their lifetimes. True, Florence had a much milder political atmosphere than Rome or Naples. The receptions and levées given by Grand Duke Leopold II (Austrian) in the Pitti Palace, just opposite the Casa Guidi where the Brownings had their flat, were undemanding occasions. More or less anyone could secure an introduction to the Grand Duke.

As for the traditions of Florentine radicalism, the radicals of the city staged a demonstration in 1849 chanting, 'Death to the Austrians!' When one of the Austrian soldiers fell from his horse, the demonstrators gathered round him sympathetically, made sure he was unhurt and gave him a leg up to remount before resuming their good-humoured 'Death to the Austrians! Death to the Austrians!'[15] Like nearly all Englishmen, Browning was pleased when the Austrians eventually withdrew from Italy and he had wanted them to go long before they did ('Go, hated house . . .'[16]). But like the majority of English Italophiles, he left Italian politics to the natives.

Most of Browning's great poems with Italian settings – 'Pippa Passes', 'My Last Duchess', 'Fra Lippo Lippi', 'Andrea del Sarto', 'A Toccata of Galuppi's', 'The Bishop Orders His Tomb' and, the towering master-piece, *The Ring and the Book* – are set in the past. But Browning is in many respects the first modern writer – acknowledged as such by proto-modernist poets such as Ezra Pound. From the first he made no concessions to his readers. Much of his subject-matter is obscure, and his diction can be so eccentric as to be impenetrable. Tennyson declared of *Sordello* (1840) that he only understood the first and last lines –

Who will, may hear Sordello's story told.

and

Who would has heard Sordello's story told.

– and they were both lies.[17]

Sordello, the thirteenth-century poet who welcomes Virgil as a fellow Mantuan in the shades of *Purgatory*, was praised by Dante for writing in different genres and dialects.[18] For Browning he becomes the type of the modern artist, not a Wordsworthian introvert but a man of masks. The poet is one who dares

> to try the stuff
> That held the imaged thing, and let it writhe
> Never so fiercely, scarce allowed a tithe
> To reach the light – his Language.[19]

> . . . accordingly he took
> An action with its actors, quite forsook
> Himself to live in each.[20]

Browning's oeuvre is an astounding variety of monologues, dramas, impressions, in which more vividly than any English dramatist except Shakespeare he allows characters to speak for *themselves* – murderers, adulterers, tyrants, old roués, young women, musicians. It is this gift for drama which makes him one of the best writers on religion, since in such masterpieces as 'The Death in the Desert' (an old, old man dies, recalling the death in turn of the author of the Fourth Gospel) or 'Bishop Blougram's Apology' or perhaps best of all 'Caliban upon Setebos or, Natural Theology' the issues of doubt and faith which so tormented Browning's contemporaries can be seen as part of an eternal dialectic, indissoluble from the human characters who entertain or lose beliefs. Browning is the great poet of human complexity, the poet of success stories which feel like failures, of failures more interesting than success, of doubt which is more religious than faith.

> No, when the fight begins within himself,
> A man's worth something.[21]

Unburdened by membership of the Established Church, Browning was not allowed to go to Oxford. A lucky escape for anyone in the nineteenth century wishing to keep an open mind about religion. His spell at University College, Gower Street,[22] did nothing to damage his essentially independent outlook: he was able to cast an oblique and always penetrating beam of light on the religious conflicts of his time.

8

Doubt

The phenomenon of the Zoo is characteristic of the Victorian Age, providing the chance of popular scientific inquiry, entertainment, and communal self-congratulation. *The Leisure Hour* of 1849, in an article entitled 'Saturday Afternoon at the Zoological Gardens', opined that 'it shows a high state of civilization when a great and overcrowded city devotes part of its energies and space to the preservation and kindly treatment of animals, which the savage looks upon as things made solely and on purpose to be hunted and destroyed'.[1] Opinions differed about the kindness and humaneness of the Zoo. In 1836 the *Quarterly Review* found something morally questionable about the notion of forcing animals to exchange their natural habitat for cages and pens. (It was making the same point nineteen years later – 'Why do we coop these noble animals in such nutshells of cages? What a miserable sight – to see them pace backwards and forwards in their box-like dens?')[2] Mortality rates were high. But from their inception, the Zoological Gardens in London's Regent's Park were enormously popular. The Zoological Society first moved there in 1828 to enclosures and grounds laid out by Decimus Burton. The original collection of 430 animals and birds was donated from the Royal Menagerie. In its first two decades of life the Zoo was an exclusive resort, open only to fellows of the Zoological Society or their guests and those prepared to pay a shilling's entrance fee. Nevertheless, it received 30,000 visitors within its first seven months of opening.[3]

Handbooks and periodicals of those first decades meditate upon what were the Zoo's primary fascinations. On the one hand they provide a glimpse of the exotic. 'In his mind's eye, [the visitor] may track the pathless desert and sandy waste; he may climb amid the romantic solitudes, the towering peaks, and wilder crags of the Himalayan heights, and wander through the green vales of that lofty range whose lowest depths are higher than the summits of the European mountains.'[4]

Undoubtedly thrill was part of the appeal – 'we are in the presence of hundreds of ferocious and wily animals; of slimy and creeping things; these restlessly parading their cages, and savagely growling their desire to escape and dart upon their mocking visitors. Those writhing upon the earth, or toad-like, crouching within some leafy hiding-hole; we dread the bare possibility of encountering the crushing coils of the upbreathing python; we think with horror upon being given over to the mercies of a tribe of chattering and malicious apes . . .'[5] Yet it was also recognized, as it is to this day, that the proximity of other species can bring consolation to the melancholy and solace to the depressed. It was more than the jolly atmosphere and the music playing from the bandstand that visitors found cheering. 'If you visit the gardens on a Monday – a sixpenny day – you will find crowds of honest people realizing from living forms what they had hitherto known only from picture-books, and impressing on their minds facts which no engraving or verbal description, be it ever so accurate, could convey.'[6]

The Zoological Society remained in principle a scientific organization, and a part of the fun, for those savouring a day's outing at the Zoo, was the notion that it was educative. 'The establishment of the Zoological Society forms an era in the history of the science in England, as regards the higher departments of animated nature.'[7] As the clothed victors gawped at their encaged fellow creatures, and as the band played, however, it is possible that disturbing thoughts were beginning to dawn in the public mind about the nature of humanity in the scheme of things. No doubt, if you were a certain type of young woman, it gave an horrific thrill to contemplate being 'given over to the mercies of a tribe of chattering and malicious apes'. At a deeper level of metaphysical awareness, was it not even more disturbing, as one viewed the apes' fingers and hands, their attentive expressions, so reminiscent of the more contemplative type of clergymen, their humourless but compulsive grins, their fussy attention to their young offspring, that they were not as alien as one could wish?

Progress was the watchword of the age: advance, improvement, struggle and climb. Thackeray in his *Book of Snobs* had chronicled with deadly accuracy how social climbers wish to kick away the ladder from beneath their feet – how those whom financial good fortune or professional skill have advanced could bitterly resent the reminder that only a generation or two ago, the forebears of the grandee were indulging in small trade, or ploughing fields. Consider the social journeys of – to take a random sample from differing rungs of the social ladder – the Reverend Patrick Brontë (born in the meanest hovel), Herbert Spencer, the Gladstone family . . . hundreds of examples could be adduced. Was the thought that Our Race could similarly be found to connect with 'lower' species on a comparable level of collective shame? If so, was that the reason that this was the decade, the first of Victoria's reign, when the idea took wing and became popular?

The commercial success of Robert Chambers's *Vestiges of the Natural History of Creation*, published anonymously in 1844, was both a symptom of how fascinating these matters had become to the public at large, and a cause of the growing obsession. It was a book which 'everybody' read. Fanny Kemble told Erasmus Darwin, 'its conclusions are utterly revolting to me – nevertheless they may be true' – thoughts which were echoed, more or less, by the 24,000 who bought the book. (Presumably you could multiply by five the numbers who read it.)[8]*

The author of *Vestiges* was not a scientist – a fact which was noted with scorn by the scientific establishment, though they did not know who he was. (Or she: Adam Sedgwick thought the book was so bad that it might be the work of a woman.) 'If the book be true, the labours of sober induction are in vain; religion is a lie; human law a mass of folly and a base injustice; morality is moonshine; our labours for the black people of Africa were works of madmen; and men and women are only better beasts!'[10]

The author of the controversial book was Robert Chambers, who was born, the son of a Peebles cotton manufacturer, on 10 July 1802. The invention of the power-loom bankrupted his father James, compelling Chambers and his brother William to strike out on their own. Robert had set up in his own business as a bookseller by the age of sixteen; William, also a bookseller, founded *Chambers's Edinburgh Journal*, one of the innumerable new periodicals of the age catering for the ever-burgeoning inquiring classes. In the past, scholarship, book-learning and natural history had perhaps been the activities of the few. In the nineteenth century there was a tremendous growth of autodidacticism in all classes. In those days before science departments in universities, before films and 'natural history programmes' on

---

* 'Readers included Queen Victoria, Elizabeth Barrett Browning, Abraham Lincoln, William Ewart Gladstone, Arthur Schopenhauer, Francis Newman, John Stuart Mill, William Stanley Jeavons and Florence Nightingale. The co-discoverer of natural selection, Alfred Russel Wallace, began his search for a lawful explanation of species after reading *Vestiges* in 1845. The book had a profound effect on literature, most notably in the writings of Alfred Tennyson, Ralph Waldo Emerson and George Eliot.'[9]

television, men and women and children could still look at the natural world about them and see. It was the great age of amateur botany – not just in the leisurely atmosphere of parsonage houses, though obviously the gentle existence of a country parson was ideal as a background for the natural historian, but in all classes of society. There were many botanical societies founded for artisans. John Horsefield recalled fixing the names of twenty-four Latin plants to his loom-post so that he could memorize them at work. At the Prestwick Botanical Society to which he belonged, men would bring botanical specimens to the pub. The president would take a specimen 'off the table, gave it to the man on his left hand, telling him at the same time its generic and specific name; he passed it on to another, and so on round the room; and all the other specimens followed in a similar manner . . .' As can be imagined, the rowdiness and noisiness of the pub often overwhelmed the men's voices as they struggled to remember Latin names, but there were many such groups.[11]

A work such as *Vestiges* could be expected to make its appeal to a far wider circle than the scientific coteries of an earlier era. Chambers was not a professional scientist. Charles Darwin's view was that 'his geology strikes me as bad and his zoology far worse'.[12] One of the many blunders in the book is his belief that birds were the ancestors of the duck-billed platypus and the latter of mammals. He believed in botanical fables such as the possibility of converting oats into rye. But these were mere details. What Chambers did, as a fascinated layman, was to read as much as he could of evolutionary scientific literature. He read Buffon, Laplace, Monboddo, Erasmus Darwin, Lamarck. He provided the book-buying public with an image: that all life on this planet had a common origin,[13] and that life as we now observe it, and geology, had come about as a result of discernible or deducible evolutionary laws. *Vestiges*, as the great geologist Charles Lyell acknowledged, 'made the English public familiar with the leading views of Lamarck on transmutation and progression, but brought no new facts or original line of argument to support these views'.[14]

Chambers vehemently rejected atheism, though we must presume that the chief reason he chose to publish anonymously was fear of the religious backlash against his book. 'We advance from law to the cause of law, and ask, What is that? Whence have come all these beautiful regulations? Here science leaves us, but only to conclude, from other grounds, that there is a First Cause to which all others are secondary and ministrative . . .'[15] *Vestiges* takes a broadly deist view, thinking that the 'Almighty Deviser' has set in place those laws which it is the job of the scientist, not the theologian, to unearth. 'Are we to suppose the Deity adopting plans which harmonize only with the modes of procedure of the less enlightened of our race?'[16]

Evolutionary theory had been aired in scientific circles for at least a hundred years before this. Benoît de Maillet published posthumously in 1748 the theory that animal species transmuted into one another – the fish into birds, and so forth. Not only was such a notion condemned by theology (hence de Maillet waiting until dead before publishing, and then under the pseudonym of his name spelt backwards, Telliamed) – it was also ridiculed by philosophy. Voltaire wrote that if such an idea were true, one species changing into another, why, 'The Metamorphoses of Ovid would be the best textbook of science that had ever been written.'[17] Diderot, however, and Maupertuis both put forward the view that there had once been one primeval animal and 'Nature lengthened, shortened, transformed multiplied or obliterated some of its organs' – according to need. Buffon began work on the kinship of asses and horses and realized that if a common equine ancestor could be found for them there was no logical reason to discount a common ancestor for men and apes.

The grandfather of Charles Darwin, Erasmus, concluded in *Zoönomia or the Laws of Organic Life* (1794–6) that the species were mutable, but it was left to Lamarck to posit an actual genealogical tree, a theory of evolution, based on what is now universally seen as a fallacy, namely the notion that acquired characteristics can be passed on genetically. (Lyell was right to see Chambers as a popularizer of Lamarck *in general*, but *Vestiges* does in fact reject the possibility of inheriting acquired characteristics.)[18]

Vestiges did not merely popularize the developments in zoology. It recognized the pre-eminence of geologists, particularly the modern pioneers of the subject from Scotland – James Hutton, John Playfair and above all Charles Lyell, whose own *Principles of Geology*, published between 1830 and 1833 but constantly revised and updated, really laid the foundation for the destruction of 'creationist' thought in Britain, America and Northern Europe. The complexities of his arguments and the depth and range of his learning forbid any simplification or summary of its conclusions. Lyell was neither a religious unbeliever nor a controversialist, but the evidence of geology convinced him that the planet Earth, and the universe, were of infinitely greater antiquity than any simple-minded reading of the Book of Genesis might suggest.

Lyell, who was landed and affluent, also belonged very definitely to the inner circle of what passed for the early Victorian scientific establishment. They partly welcomed the success of *Vestiges*: it cleared the ground for their own work. Another part of them was wistful, frightened by the vehemence of religious prejudice and perhaps genuinely fearful that if unbelief became widespread, as in France, it would have revolutionary consequences.

Charles Darwin had already completed in outline, by the time *Vestiges* was published, his own essay *On the Origin of Species by Means of Natural Selection*. He was, as a modern biographer writes, 'forestalled by a book which would injure his own arguments unless he divorced himself completely from *Vestiges*' style of popular progressive science'.[19]

Yet he wasn't Josiah Wedgwood's grandson for nothing, and he had noted the huge sales, both of *Vestiges* and of Lyell's *Geology*. He judiciously asked his friend Lyell to approach his own publisher – John Murray, himself a keen amateur scientist – about the possibility of publishing a second edition of his *Journal of Researches*. 'I should hope for a considerable sale,' he added, thereby revealing that he was not completely above the notion of 'popular science'.[20]

The question which the historian must answer is not so much whether any of these scientific notions were true, as why they excited so much popular interest in the middle of the 1840s. Voltaire's joke about the *Metamorphoses* of Ovid being a scientific textbook if the Theory of Transmutation were true all but stopped the serious reception of 'Telliamed' in non-scientific reading circles in 1748. But the 1840s were different. Disraeli's jokey references to evolution in his novels acknowledge that it was the theory by which that generation was defining itself – 'You know, all is development. The principle is perpetually going on. First, there was nothing, then there was something; then, I forget the next. I think there were shells, then fishes; then we came, let me see, did we come next? Never mind that, we came at last.'[21]

The notion that this generation was different, that its achievements, its metaphysical self-understanding, marked it out from anything which had gone before, can be attributed to the change in economic circumstances brought about by the Industrial Revolution, to the sheer force of the market economy, driving men and women into cities, wrecking some lives and improving more; dazzling them with the range of its technological changes. Tennyson wrote his poem 'Locksley Hall' in the first year of Victoria's reign,

> When the centuries behind me like a fruitful land reposed;
> When I clung to all the present for the promise that it closed . . .[22]

More than any poet before or since, Tennyson openly exposed himself to the mood of his age, mopping up its angsts and its excitements and triumphs, and transforming them into haunting lyric forms; caught up by the peculiar disturbances to be found

> In the steamship, in the railway, in the thoughts that
>   shake mankind[23]

In none of his poems is the identification of his own person with the preoccupations of an entire generation more marked than in *In Memoriam*. 'It is rather the cry of the whole human race than mine.'[24] The event which provoked the collection of lyrics was the death of his beloved friend Arthur Hallam, budding historian, friend of Gladstone, rising hope of his generation. The lyrics were written sporadically over seventeen years. When the poem was eventually published, anonymously, in 1850, lamenting

> My Arthur, whom I shall not see
> Till all my widowed race be run;[25]

it was understandable that there were those who supposed its author to be a woman. What makes the elegy so much a phenomenon of its time is the way that this one death provokes doubts about the after-life, fears that the universe itself might be a mindless machine. Tennyson has read Lyell and *Vestiges* and been as profoundly shaken by them as many another intelligent (though not scientifically educated) person. While he falls with his weight of cares

> Upon the great world's altar-stairs
> That slope through darkness up to God,[26]

he is coldly aware that the Nature revealed by Chambers and Lyell is pitiless

From scarped cliff and quarried stone
She cries, 'A thousand types are gone:
I care for nothing, all shall go.'[27]

Men and women had watched their friends die, and their children
die, for countless generations. They might not have known, in the pre-
Lyell centuries, quite how many generations those were, but the
apparent indifference of Nature to suffering seems to have prompted
astoundingly few thinkers between, say, Lucretius and Tennyson to ask
'Are God and Nature then at strife?' This is really the core of
nineteenth-century doubt about the Creator: that the God of Scripture
and the God discernible from Nature violently diverge.[28] Geology had
only lately emerged as an independent discipline. It had to fight for its
independence against those Biblical fundamentalists who, by counting
back through the genealogies in the Old Testament to the point where
'in the beginning, God created the Heaven and the Earth', were able to
date the momentous phenomenon at 4004 BC.[29]

All but crackpots now in the twenty-first century accept that these
early to mid-nineteenth-century geologists were, if not precisely
accurate in their conclusions, broadly speaking right. Independent
scientific inquiry had taken the place of a blindly erroneous reading of
Scripture, as the criterion for determining truth. If the jury is still out
over the question of Darwin's theory of evolution, not published until
fifteen years after *Vestiges*, it is because we can see how quintessentially
it is of its time, whereas the antiquity of the Earth, hence of human
prehistory, can be debated and determined on the basis of observable,
tangible phenomena – geological specimens, strata, fossils and so forth.
The theory of transmutation of species would find no comparable
verification test until the development of electron microscopes and the
whole science of molecular biology more or less a century later.

For the historian, then, the first and immediate importance of
Vestiges and the phenomenon it represented is not whether it is true,
but whether it aptly reflected a generation to itself. Robert Chambers
read Lamarck, Buffon, Lyell and others to propound the notion that
'the whole train of animated beings, from the simplest and oldest up to
the highest and most recent are . . . to be regarded as a series of
advances of the species of development'[30] (his italics).

Many have noted that in the very months that Chambers was
applying this notion to the phenomena of the visible world, John Henry
Newman was completing *An Essay on the Development of Christian*

Doctrine. 'Developments, reactions, reforms, revolutions, and changes of various kinds are mixed together in the actual history of states, as of philosophical sects, so as to make it very difficult to exhibit them in any scientific analysis.'[31] Taken to its extreme, this could lead to the view that religion itself is best understood in its sociological perspective, as an expression of the aspirations of different generations. That is not, on the surface at least, the conclusion of Newman's *Essay on Development*, though many would question, having accepted the premise, how any other conclusion was tenable.

Newman's career up to 1844 had been largely absorbed with the sometimes esoteric ecclesiastical controversies buzzing in the heads of his fellow academics at Oxford. The rallying cry for the Oxford Movement, so called, had been a sermon on 'National Apostasy' by the saintly professor of poetry, John Keble, who, together with his conservative-minded followers, saw the policy of successive governments, Whig and Peelite, in Ireland as profoundly regrettable. The reduction of the number of Protestant bishoprics in that largely Catholic land struck the Tractarians (so called after the Tracts they wrote in defence of their High Church doctrines) as worse than heretical. A typical mouthpiece of their viewpoint was Gladstone, who in his book on Church and state argued that any true believer in Anglicanism must believe in its absolute truth. For a Parliament whose function was to defend the Church, to hand over a part of the kingdom to a schismatic erroneous sect such as the Roman Catholic Church was indeed an 'apostasy'. Macaulay's robust review of this book must have led Gladstone to think again on the Irish question – as we know he did, by the time of the Maynooth Grant. Gladstone, however, remained High Church, that is a believer in the view that the true Catholic Church in England was that by law established.

The fact that very few Anglicans in history (and few of Queen Victoria's bishops) seemed to believe in the Catholicism of the Tractarians did not deter the dreamers of Oxford from their determination to make the solidly Protestant Church of England appear like a purified continuation of medieval Catholicism. Lord Blake has likened the Young England movement to the Oxford Movement. It would be even truer to see the matter the other way about and to view the intellectual contortions of Gladstone, Newman, Keble and friends as a form of mental Eglinton Tournament in which young men of the railway age tried to adopt the mentality of medieval monks or the Fathers of the Church in Late Antiquity. Newman was the most eminent of those who eventually found too burdensome the strain of defending the indefensible. He became a Roman Catholic in 1845, during one of those dark autumn rainstorms which had swept across northern Europe for weeks, destroying the crops. While the Irish starved, he worried his mind about Augustine's controversy in the fourth century with the Donatists. But his *Essay on Development* had opened doorways into new territories of thought which he was perhaps only half ready or willing to explore.

9

Mesmerism

Many in the process of observing the Lilliputian antics of the Tractarian controversialists and weighing the awful metaphysical implications of *Vestiges* had lost faith, partially or totally. Arthur Hugh Clough's Oxford Letters are only the most articulate, not the least typical, of the time. James Anthony Froude's novel *Nemesis of Faith* added insult to injury by having a hero who did not merely lose his faith but became an adulterer. It was burned by the rector of his college, Exeter, and though he was in deacon's orders (more or less a requisite of the job if you wanted to be an academic in those days) Froude left Oxford, became a disciple of Carlyle's, married (very happily) and went to live in Wales on not much money. Once Newman had 'gone over', Oxford breathed a sigh of relief, feeling it could come to its senses again. The truly distinguished academics on both the 'arts' and 'science' side produced by that university looked back on the Tractarian episode as an era of anti-intellectual madness, though the presence in their midst of the curmudgeonly Edward Bouverie Pusey was until 1882 a reminder of old unhappy far-off things and battles long ago.

For most men and women, Tennyson was a surer guide to the crises of the age. He saw that what all this religious controversy threatened to remove (whether the Science vs Religion controversy or the esoteric tournaments played out in the Tracts) was the religion of the inner life. He had this in common with the great hymn-writers of the age, of whom Newman was one. Most Christians have never heard of *The Essay in Development*, but many have been consoled by 'Lead Kindly Light'. Even more, perhaps, have found comfort in the last verses of the Reverend H.F. Lyte, the vicar of All Saints' Church in the Devonshire fishing port of Brixham.[1] Ill health made him retire before he was fifty-two. He preached his last sermon after morning service on 4 September 1847 to a church packed with hundreds of fishermen. Then he went back to his parsonage and wrote the verses for which he will always be remembered.

He was sent abroad to cure his bronchitis and died at Nice in the autumn of 1847. He left behind one of the most haunting lyrics of the nineteenth century – 'Abide with Me'. Like Tennyson he could have claimed it was the cry of the whole human race. Intelligent people waited anxiously to see whether God Himself was to be withdrawn from the modern scheme of things and if so, how they would survive the bereavement.

I fear no foe with Thee at hand to bless

The repeated plea, throughout the hymn, that the Presence will not be removed has an undoubted pathos when we remember the date at which it was written, a time when so many, and with such heavy hearts, were taking leave of God.

The story of Victorian science is not merely the account of what men and women saw, or thought they saw, when they came to examine the physical universe outside themselves. *Vestiges*, like Lyell's *Geology* before it, surveyed Creation in such materialistic language as to make some question the very existence of a Creator – anyway a Creator with a personality. And where did that leave soul, or humanity? While some investigators formed theories of a greater or lesser convincingness about the age of rocks or the evolution of species, others turned to the phenomenon of humanity itself – the nature of human personality, the question of whether 'mind' can be separated from brain, the nature of psychology. These matters cannot be studied in isolation, any more than can the work of the geologists and biologists.

The phenomenon of phrenology, for example, will seem bizarre to some readers of the twenty-first century, but there were many in its heyday who saw it as a serious science. Its various proponents divided up the skull into areas – twenty-six in one scheme, forty-three or more in another – in which it was purported that organs could be discovered explanatory of human behaviour. Quarrelsome people were found to possess a pronounced 'organ of combativeness'. The lumps and bumps of the human cranium were seriously supposed to relate to propensities and characteristics such as amativeness, hope, wonder, wit and so on. The fact that no relation between brain functions and cranial forma-tion could be demonstrated did not prevent serious people, many of them scientists, being wholly convinced by it. Phrenological ways of viewing human nature had a profound effect on the development not just of medicine but of anthropology, hence on the growth of imperialism.

Here, for example, is one phrenologist examining two skulls of

American Indians, and comparing them with European craniology.

> The magnanimity displayed by the Indians in their endurance of torture is a well-known characteristic of these tribes . . .[2]

This 'scientist' finds 'firmness' and 'secretiveness' very marked in the native Americans. The phrenological obsession with skulls was to be inherited by anthropologists of later generations. Many were influenced by Charles Caldwell's book *Thoughts on the Unity of the Human Species* which asserted, from skull evidence again, that negroes 'are no more competent to live orderly, prosperously, and happily, in a large and separate community, *under a government of laws*, prepared and administered by themselves, than is a *similar number* of buffaloes or beaters' (emphasis in original).[3]

One of the most enthusiastic disciples of phrenology in London was the professor of medicine at University College Hospital, John Elliotson. (He is the pioneer of the widespread use of the stethoscope.)[4] He was also to become, notoriously, one of the most vociferous champions of mesmerism, a practice which, like so many others engaging inquiring minds, appeared to its proponents as a science and to its critics (of whom there were plenty in Elliotson's lifetime) chicanery of the most transparent kind.

Franz Anton Mesmer (1734–1815), the Austrian medic and sage, had discovered, so he said, that the universe was penetrated and surrounded by a superfine magnetic fluid. By means which seem very close to hypnotism, he was able to put his patients into a trance, and by means of 'animal magnetism' to connect them up with the magnetic fluid of the universe. Mesmer's own demonstrations in pre-revolutionary Paris of his skills had less in common with the laboratory than with the Wizard's Den or the Masonic rituals of Mozart's *Magic Flute*. Heavy carpets, weird astrological wall decorations and mood music played on wind instruments or harmonica all helped to put his patients in a receptive frame of mind, while Mesmer himself wore lilac taffeta robes.[5]

Professor Elliotson, when he had become convinced not merely of the truth of the animal magnetism but of his own mesmeric powers, was only marginally less hierophantic when he began his demonstrations in the wards of University College Hospital, Gower Street, in 1837. His success rate was remarkable. Elliotson himself records, among many a comparable case, hysterical epilepsy with spinal affection cured outright by mesmerism; in other epileptic cases, fits much reduced. A mesmeric doctor called William Topham in Nottingham amputated a leg at the thigh of a forty-two-year-old labourer – he felt no pain.[6] (There were several cases like this.)

It is important to realize that much more than auto-suggestion was at work, as far as the mesmerists believed. Nor is it true that only hysterical or functional illnesses could be cured by mesmerism, though the great preponderance of reported cases *are* of such disorders. At the height of its popularity in the medical profession there were claims that it could cure not only neurasthenic conditions such as asthma but also deafness – 'Before mesmerism she could not hear the ticking of a watch close to her ears; now she can hear a loud ticking clock at the distance of a second room.'[7]

Elliotson, a combative man with a tendency to consider himself hard done by, was eventually hounded out by the medical 'establishment'. He resigned his chair of medicine and retired an embittered man.[8] His career might be seen as no more than a colourful interlude in the history of medicine, but mesmerism was peculiarly in tune with the spirit of the age, one of many forces inclining to suggest to the nineteenth-century mind that there could be naturalistic explanations for phenomena which had hitherto been seen as pure mysteries. The Reverend Chauncy Hare Townshend, Dickens's friend and a keen defender of Elliotson,[9] wrote of non-human creatures being just as good subjects as humans for the gifted mesmerist. Tom tits and nightingales fell into trances and allowed themselves to be tossed about like balls. The mesmeric demonstrations had brought 'the miraculous to the test of experience'. Townshend made no bones about it: mesmerism explained 'the apparently supernatural'.

They were now able to look back at the Age of Miracles, at Christ himself, and see the supposedly implausible stories of pious legend explicable in terms of mesmeric fluid. On the other hand, as has been wisely said, the mesmeric idea encapsulates the 'classic Victorian triad – will, energy, power'.[10] Although the mesmerists claimed to be materialist through and through (and it was possible to practise even on birds or idiot children without their consciously joining their will to that of the mesmerist as he concentrated his energy upon them) it inevitably foreshadows that twentieth-century preoccupation with mind which can be seen in the psychology of Freud and Jung and the literary productions of Joyce and Proust.[11]

Townshend seems aware both of the materialistic roots of

mesmerism and of its psychological progressivism. He believed that 'we mesmerists are to science what the Liberals are to politics'. This was in many cases literally true, those who believed in mesmerism being almost invariably keen abolitionists, economic liberals, in favour of 'progress'. But Townshend had discerned in the middle of this debate a deeper truth about his time, namely that there isn't such a thing as a bare fact, inseparable from the political, social or philosophical viewpoint of the person presenting it.

> All are crying out, 'Give us facts – no theories!' Yet everybody really does theorize for himself. To reason – to deduce is the prerogative of man; and we in truth, take every fact, however mysterious, in connection with a presumed cause. A visible phenomenon forces on us the conviction that there is behind it an adequate agency, even though that agency be occult. *Every fact is a theory if we did but know it* [my italics]. The fall of the apple includes the system of the Universe.[12]

In a specific defence of mesmerism, he had written a most intelligent summary of the 1840s. If every fact was a theory, the fascination of science consisted in its ability to present us with observable, verifiable truths. But could there be a science of human nature, human society? Give us facts! had been the cry of Mr Gradgrind in Dickens's *Hard Times*, the embodiment of the Benthamite philosophy. New philosophies were in the air, asking how you knew what was and wasn't a fact, questioning the sensible utilitarian ethic that the pursuit of the good was to be identified with the pursuit of the greater happiness of all. It was left to the son of Gradgrind, the Saint of Rationalism, to set these things in rational order.

10

John Stuart Mill's Boiled Egg

So it was, that throughout this decade, of riots, famine, epidemics; of industrial advancement and economic expansion; of railways and theological controversy; of Dickens-mania and mesmerism; of parliamentary intrigue and social reform; the fragmentation of the Tories and the rising hopes of the Chartists, John Stuart Mill (1806–73) made a daily walk to his office desk in the magnificent Doric building in Leadenhall Street which housed the administrative centre of the East India Company.[1] He had been coming to work here since he started as a junior clerk, aged seventeen, in 1823. (Since 1831, from Kensington.) He started on an annual gratuity of £30. His first regular salary was £100 p.a., granted when he was twenty. He rose, in 1856, to be Chief Examiner at £2,000 p.a. We will return, at a later point, to the East India Company and the important part it played in the Victorian story. For the time being, we merely note the thin, serious, sandy-haired figure of Mill, coming to the office day by day. Every morning at 10 a.m. he walked through the huge portico, down a long passage, up two flights of stairs, through a waiting-room where message-boys were brewing tea, down a long gallery filled with clerks, nosing their quills, until he reached the large room where he worked, its three tall windows overlooking a brick courtyard.[2]

Beyond, the steeples and spires of the many City churches kept the hours. Money, by a thousand Mr Dombeys, was being made, by investment in domestic industry, by foreign trade, by insurance, by shipping. Here was the epicentre of that rentier world which, by learning to manage money, was building an economy, a political system, an empire of strength and size without parallel in the world.

Immediately, an office-boy brought in John Stuart Mill's boiled egg, tea, bread and butter. It was his first refreshment of the day, and he would eat nothing thereafter until he had walked home. (His simple dinner was at 6.)

Why are we interested in this tall figure, with his ruddy complexion and his black suit? His Indian contemporaries, no doubt, would have been interested in the paperwork which he pushed across his desk between the hours of 10 and 4. There were three divisions in the East

India Company – the Secretaries, the Military Secretaries, and the Examiners. The Examiners *examined* letters coming from India on a wide range of administrative matters and were, effectively, the Indian Civil Service. There is, no doubt, a certain oddity about the affairs of the subcontinent being determined by this array of black-coated clerks perched at their high stools in the City of London.

For Mill's European contemporaries, however, and for generations of Indians born after he quitted his office stool, the significance of this man rests less in the work he did for the East India Company than in the thoughts which passed through his head as he walked through St James's Park, up Fleet Street and past St Paul's Cathedral; or as he ate his boiled egg to the sound of a hundred scratching quill pens in the offices, a hundred church steeples chiming in the rooftops, beyond.

Mill got his job in the East India Company from his father, who before him had risen to be Chief Examiner. James Mill had been the most ardent disciple of Jeremy Bentham, the most relentless of the philosophic radicals, the fiercest of the Gradgrinds. The story of John Stuart Mill's extraordinary boyhood has passed into legend – the absence of any play or playmates, the relentless learning, the accumulation of fact, fact, fact, leading, when he was aged twenty, to the 'crisis' in which he appeared to reject his father's Benthamism. By reading Wordsworth he discovered to his indescribable joy that he was capable of feeling. Mill was an emblematic figure of his age, important for what he stood for – what he was in himself – as well as what he thought and propounded. Bertrand Russell said that 'throughout the middle portion of the nineteenth century, the influence of the Benthamites on British legislation was astonishingly great, considering their complete absence of emotional appeal',[3] a curious remark coming from the godson of J.S. Mill and the grandson of Lord John Russell himself. Bentham's ideal, as Russell saw, was 'security not liberty'.[4] John Stuart Mill's task as a political thinker was to discover how to give society liberty without risk to security.

His influence on the political and social thinking of the succeeding generations was if possible even greater than Bentham's. He reckoned that he could get through his day's work in three hours, which perhaps explains how he managed, while being in the 'full-time' employ of the East India Company, to turn out so prodigious a body of work. From 1835 he was the editor of *The London and Westminster Review*, the most influential journalistic mouthpiece of radical politics of the time. More significantly, and more astonishingly when one considers the distractions of regular (if highminded) journalism and the ceaseless flow of those Indian letters passing from IN-tray to OUT-tray, he was the pre-eminent British philosopher of the nineteenth century.

Mill, and his influence, speak volumes about nineteenth-century England. Even if you question his influence, you have to recognize that this England of canals, factories and counting-houses was fertile ground for Mill's ideas in a way that Germany and France and the nascent Italy were not. If we are trying to find an answer to the question of why Britain did not explode into the revolutionary apocalypses envisioned by his friend Carlyle, part of the answer might be found in the philosophy of John Stuart Mill.

His first important work, *A System of Logic*, was published in 1843. It is a patient, even a somewhat laborious restating of the empiricist position – though Mill disliked the term empiricist, preferring to call himself an experimentalist. As philosophical works go, it is remarkably accessible to the layman, designedly so, we may safely assume, since Mill's target was a trend in contemporary academic philosophy which he considered dangerous. His attacks on the 'intuitionist' school are of interest not only to philosophers. In *A System of Logic* his prime target was Whewell, professor of Moral Philosophy at Cambridge, and eventually master of Trinity College. The 'intuitionist' view, based on Kant, was that there were some truths too high, or too self-evident, to be examined. Mill, who had attended neither school nor university, saw that in this attitude of mind the 'intuitionist' philosophy could be used to justify reaction in politics and superstition in religion. What *A System of Logic* sets out to demonstrate is that there are not two sorts of truth or two sorts of logic. Ethical truth, for example, should be demonstrable. Airy theological assertions should be verifiable or dismissed as nonsense. Any person should be entitled to ask for reasons why things are as they are. There was an obvious connection between the fact that Oxford and Cambridge were exclusive bastions of privilege, and that the philosophy taught there was a set of truths which had merely to be accepted, unexamined, unquestioned, in the philosophical sense *necessary*. Mill's defences of deductive reasoning, and of causality, and, with modifications, of the syllogism in formal logic, are all of a piece with his embracing the progressive ideas of the French thinker Auguste Comte – and with his later championing of Liberty and of Women's Suffrage.[5]

Though the later developments of Comte's Religion of Humanity caused its detractors to smile (Comte went mad), Mill – its archpriest in England – never lost sight of its central idea: social progress.[6] How we think, as societies, and how our great ones think, does have an effect on how we live. Philosophy might be the occupation of a tiny number in any generation. How many, in the 1840s, could have read, as Carlyle had done, the great German metaphysicians – above all, Hegel? In the later years of the century, Hegel would undoubtedly come into his own in England, though in a very *anglice* form. No one could doubt, however, that there was a difference between life in a country where the statesmen and civil servants, the intellectuals and the progressives, believed themselves caught up in the Hegelian dialectic, and in one where they more modestly believed that, by the benign application of reason to human problems, the greater happiness of the greater number might, patiently and gradually, be achieved.[7]

Mill devoted the years of the Irish famine to proposing drastic reforms of Irish land tenure, the establishment of independent peasant properties, answerable to no landlords on reclaimed waste land. He urged that the famine had come about not merely because of the failure of potato crops but because the landlord system reduced the Irish to the condition of paupers. What a pity he was not made the viceroy!

As far as English politics were concerned, Mill was as radical as it was consistent to be while retaining a firm belief in free market economics.* Under the influence of his beloved Mrs Taylor, whom he eventually married, Mill became his own variety of socialist, convinced that socialism meant, not that all things are held in public ownership, 'but that production is only carried on upon the common account' – a logical conclusion in fact from the pursuit of the greater good and the greater happiness. Whether the working class in the 1840s were ready for those autonomous 'associations', without which democracy could not seriously flourish, Mill took leave to doubt. Mill believed that only an elite of the working class were ready for such experiments. They were unfit 'at present for any order of things, which would make any considerable demand on either their intellect or their virtue'.[9] Yet he remained an optimist – 'It is my belief indeed that the general tendency is, and will continue to be, saving occasional and temporary exceptions, one of improvement, a tendency towards a better and happier

---

*Conrad Russell reminds us, though, of the interesting fact that Mill saw no logical connection between free market liberty and individual liberty. See C.A. Russell (1993).

state.'[10] The evidence would suggest that, in spite of the horrors they collectively endured during the first decade of her reign, the majority of Victoria's subjects would have agreed with Mill. The apocalypse which was about to engulf the European continent, viewed with hope or dread depending on your station in society, did not happen in Victorian Britain. The Chartists caused panic in the ruling powers, but not enough enthusiasm to generate the revolution. It is to that story that we must return.

11

The Failed Revolution

There are, broadly, two responses to the question why there was no revolution in Britain and Ireland in 1848, as there was to be in so many other countries of Europe. The first is to suggest that there would have been some such uprising had not the British state learnt to exercise an iron authority over the masses, by means of law, policing, and military strength. The second is to imply that, hellish as life was for many British and Irish people in the 1840s, it could have been worse, that times of economic hardship were replaced by times of prosperity, and that, quite simply, not enough people would have been found to make a Chartist Parliament, still less a British socialist state, a viable proposition. Some historians, for either of these reasons, dismiss the so-called failure of the Chartist movement as risible, inevitable, insignificant. Yet it wasn't risible – in its own way, it could be viewed as tragic were it not for the peculiar composition and character of the English nation. Radical thinkers such as Mill were rather dismayed when, after the French plebiscite of 1848, the people of France *elected* Napoleon III in 1849.[1] The truly extraordinary lesson of 1848 in England is that, had the Chartists succeeded, and had their petition become law, with every adult male given the vote by secret ballot, it is perfectly possible that a majority of Englishmen would have voted to retain Queen Victoria as head of state, and Lord John Russell or Lord Stanley as prime minister.

Recalling those heady days of spring 1848 George Julian Harney (Chartist and deputy editor of *The Northern Star*) wrote to Friedrich Engels when they were both old men:

The *old time*! and this is the 23rd February, and tomorrow is the 24th, when seeing the news placarded at Charing Cross, I ran like a lunatic and pulled the bell at Schappers [a German revolutionary exile] like a bedlamite; at some corner on my way, knocking over an old woman's apple-basket (or it may have been oranges!) I was going too quick for her gentle cursing.[2]

One wonders how gentle the cursing was, and whether this tiny vignette of political fervour does not tell us rather a lot about the state of mind respectively of a political activist and an actual working-class woman. We know that in after years most of the fruit-sellers of London declared themselves to have been in favour of the Charter. But how many would have favoured days of street-fighting upsetting their apple-baskets? This isn't a frivolous question: it goes to the heart of the story of English leftist politics. It would be an absurdity to say that no English working-class people have ever supported either physical-force Chartism, or communism or other forms of potentially violent revolution in England. Yet it would seem from the evidence as if there had always been working-class English of a different persuasion – either gradualists or conservatives. Things might have been slightly different in Ireland, Wales or Scotland.

The newspaper placard announced that the French government (the 'July monarchy' of Louis Philippe with his arch-conservative premier the historian Guizot) had been overthrown. A provisional government was set up. On 13 March Metternich, the chancellor of the Austrian empire, was overthrown. A little while before, Harney's German friends in exile had run off the press at 46, Liverpool Street in London, yards from the epicentre of the capitalist world, an anonymous pamphlet entitled *Manifest der Kommunistischen Partei*. Its authors were Friedrich Engels and Karl Marx (who had come to London on a visit and met Harney in November 1847). Engels was already living in England – in the unlikely role of a Northern capitalist. (His father had cotton manufactories in Lancashire – like Sir Robert Peel, Engels always spoke English with a pronounced Northern accent.) Marx would come to London as a refugee, his revolutionary journalism having made him an undesirable in Germany. He would never escape it, becoming *faute de mieux* a Londoner and British Museum habitué, until his death in 1883.

> A spectre is haunting Europe – the spectre of Communism. All the Powers of old Europe have entered into a holy alliance to exorcize this spectre: Pope and Czar, Metternich and Guizot, French Radicals and German police spies . . .

The quotation is from the 'authorized' English version of 1888, hastily, too hastily, revised by Engels himself, working on the English translation of a loyal plodder called Samuel Moore.[3]

There were many who shared the communist view that England

would not be immune from the spectre's power. The 'physical force' Chartists, some of whom befriended, others of whom became, communists in late years, were to this extent at one with those – such as Macaulay, the great Whig historian – who saw antagonisms between the classes as absolutely inevitable. 'The history of all hitherto existing society is the history of class struggles.' In the mind of Macaulay, for whom the Whig Revolution of 1689 was the high point and defining moment of British history, Chartism was a disastrous idea. He saw the notion of giving the vote to the uneducated and unpropertied classes as a recipe for national suicide.

> Have I any unkind feeling towards these poor people? No more than I have to a sick friend who implores me to give him a glass of water which the physician has forbidden. No more than a humane collector in India has to those poor peasants who in a season of scarcity crowd round the granaries and beg with tears and piteous gestures that the doors may be opened and the rice distributed. I would not give the draught of water, because I know it would be poison. I would not give up the keys of the granary, because I know that, by doing so, I should turn a scarcity into a famine. And in the same way I should not yield to the importunity of multitudes who, exasperated by suffering and blinded by ignorance, demand with wild vehemence the liberty to destroy themselves.[4]

When the Chartist riots had broken out in Newport in 1839 Macaulay had seen the spectre – civil war between the propertied and the unpropertied. The result would have been the destruction of property – 'All the power of imagination fails to paint the horrors of such a contest.'[5]

Marx saw the same truth of inevitable strife, and no doubt this inspired the more belligerent Chartists. There is equally no doubt that it scared many of them away from the movement, not because they were cowards, but because as tailors, small traders and craftsmen, even as factory workers, they did not wish to form themselves into a destructive mob. The old woman selling fruit would have supported (if Mayhew is to be believed, as he surely is) the notion of having a say in the way that her country was governed. She would not have seen the need to kick over her basket of apples and oranges in the process.

Fearing that a violent revolution was on its way, however, the Whig government took no chances, and when it was announced that the

Third Chartist Petition would be presented to Parliament on 10 April 1848, both sides saw this as a day of the greatest significance, the day in which it would be determined whether the English revolution could come, or not.

The wilder radicals like Ernest Jones were optimistic, particularly since the Irish protest movements seemed prepared to join forces with the English working classes.

> Lop-sided thrones are creaking,

sang Jones in his 'March of Freedom', published in *The Northern Star*,

> For 'Loyalty' is dead;
> And common-sense is speaking
> Of honesty instead.
>
> Why weeps your sorrowing sister [i.e. Ireland]
> Still bleeding, unredressed,
> 'Neath *Russell*, England's [Tsar] Nicholas,
> The Poland of the West.
>
> Cry 'Liberty to Erin!'
> It is a debt you owe;
> Had ye not armed his hand
> He ne'er had struck a blow . . .[6]

If the insurgents could compare Lord John Russell to a particularly tyrannical Russian emperor – and more, after all, had died in Ireland than had yet died in any Russian famine – the Whig prime minister and his Cabinet could take the compliment, and respond in force. They certainly took no chances. Though there were still Chartists after 10 April 1848, the government did effectively on that date crush Chartism.[7]

Military intelligence had told the government that Irish revolutionaries had been to Paris to inspect methods of building barricades in the streets. The Whig government line on the overthrow of Guizot and Louis-Philippe was cautious in the extreme – 'I can assure the House,' Russell told Parliament, '(indeed I should hardly have thought it necessary to make the declaration) that we have no intention whatever to interfere with the form of government which the French nation may choose to adopt or in any way to meddle with the internal affairs of that country.' Russell and Palmerston had viewed the departure of the French government with equanimity, but not the method by which it was accomplished.

The Duke of Wellington was enlisted, less as an actual commander of operations than as an extremely useful piece of popular propaganda. Wellington, obsessed by the possibilities of mob violence, sent a list of proposals to Lord John suggesting provisions which should be made. He was certainly included, though or because a former Tory prime minister, in the discussions of security arrangements, but when he sent in his list of suggestions he found that Sir George Grey and the military secretary, Lord Fitzroy Somerset, had already pursued them. Nevertheless it did not do any harm to allow the potential rebels to believe that they would be fighting, if violence did break out, against the victor of Waterloo.

What had Grey and Somerset already arranged for 10 April? The royal family had been sent by train to the Isle of Wight. (Waterloo station was closed for hours beforehand and cordoned off by troops.) Wellington was afraid that Osborne House, a holiday palazzo, not a fort, was vulnerable from the Solent if the rebels got hold of a warship: this was the level of paranoia felt by the prevailing powers.

Mouchards brought word that the common soldiers, chatting to Chartist demonstrators as they began to assemble in London in the few days before the 10th, had promised to fire over the people's heads in the event of a riot.[8] The thought of the military showing class solidarity filled the Whigs with horror, but they could take comfort from the numbers who volunteered as special constables. Altogether, in London alone, Lord Fitzroy Somerset had mobilized 7,122 military, including cavalry; 1,231 military pensioners; 4,000 police, both City and metropolitan, and an astonishing 85,000 special constables. Comparable measures had been taken in all the major British cities.

The British Museum was barricaded – the director Sir Henry Ellis calculated that if invaded by 'disaffected persons it would prove to them a fortress capable of holding ten thousand men'. Somerset House in the Strand had a portcullis constructed in its entrance. The Bank of England was parapeted with sandbags, and guns mounted in every aperture. All the prisons were reinforced with heavily armed guards.[9] Comparable methods had been taken in Paris and they had not prevented the revolution. The difference between the two countries was that the presence of 100,000 troops outside Paris was resented by the petit-bourgeois downwards. In England, the urban middle and lower-middle class was proportionately far higher and they overwhelmingly supported all these measures. The sheer number of special constables is eloquent; even if we suppose a high proportion of them were domestic servants, this does not mean they did not prefer the status quo.

The show of strength undoubtedly had an enormous effect, both to boost the morale of the majority who did not want the Physical Force Chartists and the Irish revolutionaries to succeed, and on the reputation of Britain abroad, as the one nation in Europe which appeared to be immune from serious revolutionary upheaval.

On 10 April, the National Convention of Chartists assembled at 9 a.m. in John Street, just north of Gray's Inn, moved down Tottenham Court Road, passed via Holborn to Farringdon Street, crossed Blackfriars Bridge and reached Kennington Common by 11.30, where some 3,000 had congregated. Another contingent had assembled in the East End on Stepney Green, a crowd of some 2,000 with music, flags and an air of jamboree. The largest single group was in Russell Square, Bloomsbury. About 10,000 proceeded from here, down the Walworth Road, and eventually reached Kennington Green. They had hoped for hundreds of thousands: in the event, a mere 20,000 or so appeared, policed by a force nearly five times that number.

It is the first significant historical event to have been photographed, probably by police spies.[10] The daguerreotypes record a scene of drizzly pathos. In the immediate foreground you can see the special officers, mounted on horseback and silk-hatted. Above and beyond the twenty thousand hopeful heads, a factory chimney stretches a defiant arm to the sky. Possibly it is Messrs Farmer's vitriol works. It seems to say that trade and capital are stronger than human dignity. The banners unfurled in the rain – IRELAND FOR THE IRISH and POLITICS FOR THE PEOPLE – display messages whose hour has not been allowed to come.

O'Connor addressed the gathering. Many of the historians of the movement blame him for its lack of success, his firebrand dissent from Lovett and the moral force Chartists in the beginning, his essential lack of sympathy with the urban population at the end of the decade since the Charter was composed. The Chartist Land Plan – in which O'Connor tried to establish systems of independent smallholdings on commonly held land – was probably never practicable and was irrelevant to the aspirations of the Alton Lockes who were the movement's core membership. 'The Charter was a means to an end – the means was their political rights, and the end was equality' – as Harney had said at the outset.

The 10th of April appeared to demonstrate that capitalism was so powerful a machine that those who had become its cogs could not imagine things to be otherwise. Systems of universal education – like those of the communists, a Chartist dream – would not in reality come about for generations in Britain, and it is open to question whether the level of political interest required in a working democracy would ever have come to pass, Charter or no Charter. Democracy in the sense understood by O'Connor, Lovett or Ernest Jones has never been tried in Britain.

The truth is that the numbers supporting the Charter itself had been dwindling for some years before 1848. Region-by-region research shows that in 1,009 areas generally supportive of Chartism in 1839, only 207 had active Chartist organizations in 1848.[11] The aims and aspirations of the working people in these districts had been splintered. The government, as a result of pressure from the Tory Lord Ashley, had lately brought in the Ten Hours Act, limiting the hours of work in factories. Conditions in a number of places were improved, not wholly, not as much as people might wish. But they knew they had a government which no longer gave capitalism a totally free rein: children were not sent down the mines any more, mill-owners or factory-masters could not so easily exact slavishly long hours from employees. The slow, creakingly slow, improvement of working conditions could be seen, by optimists, to have begun. Meanwhile, Free Trade had begun to chug into prosperous action. Wages, with profits, were up in most manufacturing areas.

For some of us, though, the thought that the conditions of the labouring poor in 1848 were not so bad really, the claim that the Ten Hours Act and a few shillings a week destroyed the Chartist ideal, is just a little too smug. The truth is, as Marx saw very clearly, that there is a genuine difference of interest between the workers and the bourgeoisie. Any dissent from such a view – the view of Cobden and similar Manchester liberals that the urban proletariat had much chance to better themselves through evening classes and the like – is a gigantic con. In the years after they wrote the Manifesto, Marx and Engels were astounded to discover the sheer force of the British gendarmerie – Britain armed to the teeth both against the working class and against the Irish. That was the first lesson of 10 April 1848. Second, and more dispiriting, the sheer numbers of the *Kleinbürger* made any realignment of the political map impossible. The preparedness of Lord John Russell to *crush* the Chartists by force was *very popular indeed*.

We shall see clearly enough in the next decade the kind of people the Victorians en masse were, with their wild enthusiasm for the Crimean War and their violent and vindictive attitude to the Indian Mutiny. There is alas no evidence that a majority, given the chance, would have tried to build a fairer or more equitable society, giving succour to the poor Irish immigrants, the illegitimate waifs and strays in orphanages or workhouses or the mills and factories of the Midlands and the North. This was a ruthless, grabbing, competitive, male-dominated society, stamping on its victims and discarding its weaker members with all the devastating relentlessness of mutant species in Darwin's vision of Nature itself.

The presenters of the Petition were allowed into three cabs to cross the river and to present the signatures to the House of Commons. Of the hoped-for signatories, there were only 1,200,000 (less than half of the expected 3 million),[12] two-thirds of which were said to be fraudulent. Old Colonel Sibthorp's name, for example, was found among the forgeries. There is many a true word spoken in jest, however. Though of course the old country diehard had not signed the Petition there was probably some sense (as the career of John Ruskin was to show) in which the defender of the Old Ways, the upholder of Corn Laws and denouncer of railroads, had more in common with *many* of the Chartists than either the future capitalists or their Marxist opponents. Both were standing for what Marx called the *Idiotismus* of the rural. Not 'idiocy' as plodder Moore and Engels rendered it, but (Marx the Hellenist uses the word *Idiotismus* in its original Greek sense of the private self) 'the privatized isolation of rural life', or, to put it another way, independence.[13] Marx and Engels exhorted:

Proletariat aller Länder vereinigt Euch!
(Working men of all countries, unite!)

April 10 demonstrated a slightly more alarming truth. Rather than being seen as a Chartist flop, it should be seen as the united front of the *Kleinbürger* – the petit-bourgeoisie – with the governing powers, the money powers, the aristocracy.

From now on, the Victorian story becomes an alarming triumph song, Great Britain growing richer and more powerful by the decade, coarsening in the process, and leaving the historian with a sense that only in its dissentient voices is redemption found.

PART II

The Eighteen-Fifties

12

The Great Exhibition

The statement that Britain 'survived' 1848, while the rest of the European continent was convulsed in revolutions (and counter-revolutions), requires at least a footnote, if not a qualification. If we look for signs of revolutionary disturbance only on Kennington Common on 10 April, then we might conclude that Britain had a peaceful year. Radical and Catholic cantons of Switzerland had been waging a civil war throughout 1847 – a war in which Count Metternich would certainly have intervened on behalf of the absolutists had he not been toppled from his position as Austrian chancellor in March 1848. His collapse had been precipitated by the abdication of Louis-Philippe in France – he and his reactionary prime minister took refuge (as did Metternich) in London. In Berlin, Frederick William was forced to accept a constitution and a Liberal government. The poet Lamartine's manifestos in France were certainly the most 'left-wing' of any government of the time, but Palmerston, the dominant political figure of this decade, was canny enough to support them, for precisely the reason that Marx denounced them – because they were in reality a sop to the socialists and they held in check the possibilities of further revolution. In Spain the revolution was resisted, and the British minister was denounced for his liberalism. In Italy, the forces of radicalism saw the chance of throwing off the dominion on the one hand of Austria, and on the other of the Pope. King Ferdinand in Naples offered his subjects a constitution. Hungary was in turmoil – invaded by the Russians. Denmark and Prussia were at odds over the vexed question of Schleswig-Holstein.

By comparison, the conventional wisdom has suggested, Britain was tranquil. There is some truth in this, of course, else why should it, and how could it, have provided asylum for refugees both from the seats of reaction – Metternich, Guizot – and of revolution – Karl Marx?

As so often in its history, Britain appeared to be going a way which was very different from that of the rest of Europe. In fact, Britain was not so very different, but it was undergoing its problems, and solving them, very much off home territory, and this is what gives us the sometimes false impression that things were stabler than they truly were. Two factors must be borne in mind. One was the extraordinary rate of imperial expansion abroad which accompanied the growth of the industrial economy at home. This enabled British governments to export many of their political and criminal dissidents where other nations had to look after them on domestic territory. But secondly, when we view the history of the colonies themselves, we remember that things were far from tranquil, either in 1848, or in the decades preceding or succeeding it.

An extraordinary expansion of British imperialism had marked the first decade of Victoria's reign. Hong Kong in the Far East – 1843, Labuan in Indonesia – 1846, Natal – 1843, Orange River in South Africa – 1848, Gambia on the West Coast of Africa – 1843. In 1842 the British fought the first of their disastrous Afghan wars, temporarily annexing that unconquerable country. Even the Russians in the twentieth century, or the Americans in the twenty-first, did not experience quite so cruelly the brutal indomitability of the Afghan guerrilla. Sir William Hay Macnaghten, through and through an old India hand, son of an Indian judge and an employee of the East India Company from adolescence, persuaded the governor-general of India, Auckland, that if the British did not move into Afghanistan the Russians would threaten British interests in India. There followed a period in which the British (just like the Russians and the Americans in a later age) backed first one and then another bunch of cut-throats who supposedly shared the interests of the foreign occupier. In November 1841, when Macnaghten was on the point of leaving Kabul to take up the governorship of Bombay, his successor, Sir Alexander Burnes, was murdered by a mob. Macnaghten himself was then assassinated by the leader of a rival Afghan faction to the one he had been supporting. The winter had begun. There was no chance of the British troops stationed at Kandahar getting through the snowy mountains to Kabul. After a series of negotiations with Afghan leaders, the British agreed to withdraw from Afghanistan. On 6 January, the entire garrison began the retreat to Jallalabad, with a huge number of Afghan camp-followers (afraid of reprisals from their hostile compatriots) and many British women and children. Akhbar Khan, the new Afghan leader who had arranged for Macnaghten to be killed, would not give any assurance that the retreating forces would be immune from attack, though the women and children were allowed through. Sixteen thousand British troops made their last stand against the Afghans in the pass at Jagdallak. Of this number, only one, Dr Brydon, was allowed to limp his way to Jallalabad to tell the tale. When spring came, the British did send forces to occupy Kabul, but they were not there for long. They did not want to be.

The only positive result, for them, of the first Afghan war was that the East India Company greatly expanded its forces in North-West India. The conquest of Sind in 1843 was the direct consequence of the Afghan war. The Sikh wars led to the appropriation of the Punjab by 1849, as well as smaller states such as Satara (1848) and Sambalpur (1849). This was less part of some great plan than the need, here and there, to create the conditions of peace in which trade could flourish. Almost all English expansionism in India began like this, the putting down of this or that disturbance leading to the annexations of more and more territory.

The discontents which other European states experienced at home in 1848 could to a large measure be exported by Britain to the imperial territories. The Whigs knew that the key to retaining the support of the middle classes at home was to avoid tax increases. 'I believe we must keep our fingers out of the people's pockets; and try to keep down our expenditure' was what the chancellor of the Exchequer, Wood, told Grey. It had been Grey's own mission to save money on imperial troops. In India, this meant pensioning off European troops and having more and more native forces, a policy which many military observers could see to be fraught with hazard.

Sir Charles Napier is usually seen as one of the less sensitive wielders of military authority in India ('Were I Emperor of India for twelve years she should be traversed by railways and have her rivers bridged . . . No Indian Prince should exist').[1] Yet when he was sent to subdue the provinces of Northern India in the early 1840s he could easily foresee the problems which would ensue. He pointed out that the constant changes in the pay of the sepoys (native Indian soldiers) caused deep discontent. He thought the Brahmins and the Rajpoots made 'admirable soldiers', and on the whole he took a very low view of the European officers in the Indian army, 'especially those of the higher ranks'.[2] He warned from Karachi, in March 1850, that the government could 'but look with feelings of alarm, upon so large a body of armed, able bodied and mutinous soldiery, clamorous and violent if their . . . demands are not complied with'.[3]

No one in government heeded his warning. The policy of squeezing the colonies to satisfy the middle classes in England was an essential part of Sir Charles Wood's budgets.[4] In India there were two aspects of this policy. One was to ride roughshod over the religious sensibilities of the native regiments if, for example, it came cheaper to disregard caste considerations and transport Brahmin sepoys with those of a lower caste or worse of a different faith altogether. Secondly there was a parsimonious tendency to reduce the sepoys' pay, which caused simmering resentment, frequent minor mutinies, and was an undoubted factor in provoking the Great Uprising of 1857.

In other parts of the Empire, the effects of Free Trade reforms caused hardship and near ruin, particularly in those places such as British Guiana and Jamaica whose economy was only just coming to terms with the emancipation of the slaves. Incendiarism and looting were widespread in the West Indian plantations throughout 1848. Similar troubles in Jamaica – there was simply no money to pay public officials – led to a British parliamentary loan being offered – of £100,000. As for Canada, the removal of the Corn Laws in England meant that Canadian wheat farmers no longer had a guaranteed market. The French Canadians in particular took it hard, organizing themselves into armed secret societies, rioting, pelting the governor with rotten eggs and conducting a series of incendiary raids in cities, particularly Toronto. In Ceylon, the attempt to raise a European-style peasant tax in 1848 led to a riot involving 60,000 men, an attack on prisons, with prisoners set free, and planters' estates being ransacked. At the Cape, the Boer leader Andries Pretorius led a small war against the settlement of British settlers in Natal and the Xhosa and Gaika peoples rebelled against the idea of a British police force being imposed on them. There was also a mutiny of the indigenous Cape Corps regiment.

In other words, in every corner of the globe the British were experiencing their own version of the 1848 revolutions, and if the dissidents of Canada, the West Indies, the Punjab, the Cape and Ceylon could by magic all have been concentrated on Kennington Common to assist the Chartists we can imagine a very different consequence to 10 April 1848. The problems thus scattered across the globe called for a new, vigorous imperial policy which, after the calamities a decade later in India, they would receive. For the time being, though, they could be dealt with piecemeal.

And meanwhile, the colonies also supplied Britain with a useful resource, and another explanation for the fact that 1848 was a quieter year for Londoners than it was for Parisians, Berliners or Viennese. Although in 1848 only thirty declaredly *political* prisoners were transported, there was a huge increase in the numbers, especially from

Ireland, who were removed from their native soil and sent to the colonies out of harm's way. Once again, we sense here a problem deferred rather than solved forever. History does not eliminate grievances; it lays them down like landmines. Irish Fenianism and the Irish Republican movement really began among the exiles. There was a lively Irish radical press in Australia, where the campaign of non-compliance with prison authorities by Irish prisoners came to a head with the rising on the Ballarat goldfield in December 1854. Transportation as a system of punishment was actually well on the way out by then. Dickens's *Great Expectations* (1861) was set thirty years in the past. By the time the book was published the convict Magwitch would have been an anachronism. By the mid-1840s, only Bermuda, Gibraltar and Norfolk Island retained offshore prisons. But in '48 the exile of so many potential British dissidents had the effect of extinguishing 'the embers of insurrection', in the phrase of a Tasmanian historian.[5]

The modern reader, in post-colonial times, is inevitably made uneasy by the knowledge that the liberal state – and for many Europeans, England was the *ideal* liberal state – was underpinned by oppression and interference by Europeans in so many different quarters of the globe. For self-confident liberals of the time, perspectives were different. The internationalism of the Great Exhibition of 1851 was an outward and visible sign of how readily capitalism could conquer the globe, exporting its modernity to Asia, the Americas, Africa and Australia, and drawing, in turn, all nations to itself under the emblematic hothouse erected for the exotic plant of Free Trade in the very centre of Hyde Park. Not that the 'Free Trade' label was always used. The Tory weekly *John Bull* nicknamed the exhibition 'The Free Trade Festival', leading one of the organizers, none other than the apostle of Free Trade himself, Richard Cobden, to suggest avoiding the term, lest it appear the political propaganda exercise it actually was. By the time the leader of the Opposition, Lord Stanley, was selling the idea of the Exhibition in his Mansion House address, he had judiciously claimed that it would 'bring into harmonious concord the nations of the world' and 'give encouragement . . . to the industry of all nations'.[6]

In fact, as we have already seen, the imposition of Free Trade caused widespread unrest all over the globe, the expansionism which trade both fed and provoked leading to Asian wars. Cobden and Bright's belief that Free Trade, because it was bound to transcend national boundaries, would lead ineluctably to the death of war was to be severely challenged during the 1850s, which saw the first major European war for nearly forty years breaking out in 1854. For the optimistic and ingenious organizers of the Great Exhibition, however, 'the steamship and the railway and the thoughts that shape mankind' had replaced military conquest as objects worthy of study.

It was no doubt partly with a feeling of lucky escape – from the revolutions of '48, from the whole decade which had seen such volatile economic change, such alarming social unease, such disease and such famine, against a background of industrial expansion and invention – that the organizers began to plan the exhibition.

Unquestionably, the galvanic force behind the whole enterprise, the man without whom it would not have left the ground, was Henry Cole. It was Cole who saw in the exhibitions held by the Society for the Encouragement of Arts, Manufacturers and Commerce (1844) or the Society of Arts (1846) models of a much bigger exhibition, which would both encourage enterprise and invention in the sphere of industrial design and advertise its success. As the pseudonymous Felix Summerly, Cole had designed a china tea service, made by Minton and Co., for the exhibition of 1846. He was the man who had been responsible for making a cataloguing system in the Public Record Office where he worked as a civil servant. With Rowland Hill, he had pioneered the Penny Post in 1838. He had campaigned for a single railway-gauge and for reforms in the patent law. He also invented the Christmas card.

Cole had first met Prince Albert during his work in the PRO, and it was he who persuaded the organizers of the earlier, smaller exhibitions to have wider ambitions and to enlist a royal patron. He also brought in Thomas Milner Gibson, the Liberal MP from Manchester who had been vice-president of the Board of Trade, Cobden, Scott Russell – a Glaswegian industrial designer and jack of all trades – and Thomas Cubitt, the London property-developer and self-taught architect who had redeveloped Belgravia, rebuilt Buckingham Palace and built Osborne House on the Isle of Wight to Prince Albert's designs. It was Cole who persuaded the Queen's husband to appoint a Royal Commission to plan the exhibition – a committee which included the Prince himself (president), the prime minister, Lord John Russell, the leader of the Opposition, Lord Stanley, the former prime minister, Robert Peel, the Duke of Buccleuch, Mr Gladstone, Charles Lyell the geologist, Richard Westmacott the sculptor, and other persons of eminence.

Cole's first battle was won – to make the pioneers of industrial design, whose previous exhibitions had felt like muted affairs, feel that they had been adopted by the mainstream of political life to which they contributed so much wealth and energy. The commission, which was formed by 3 January 1850, had just over a year to make the thing a success: to ensure that the exhibits were of sufficiently high quality, to canvass industrial opinion not only all over Britain but all over the world, and to find a design which would house the exhibition and give it identity. There was also a site to be determined, with Regent's Park, Primrose Hill, Wormwood Scrubs and the Isle of Dogs all canvassed as possibilities.

The first design for the exhibition halls, submitted by the building committee, who had rejected 233 designs sent in by architects, resembled a brick engine-shed, surmounted with a disproportionate dome, several times larger than that of St Peter's. The committee clung to the design merely because time was not on their side and – though none of the commissioners liked it – no alternative was available.

Then transpired one of those happy chances which make one understand why so many Victorians believed in the Whiggish optimism of Macaulay. This really does seem like a society, for all the dreadful sufferings of its underclass, which is powered by ingenuity and luck, a nation with a strong wind behind it soaring from triumph to triumph. It is in such moments of good fortune uniting with sheer cleverness that the fascination of the Victorian period is found. Today we think of England as a place where nothing quite works properly, where great projects are seldom tried, and if attempted take laborious lengths of time to accomplish.

On 11 June, William Ellis MP, chairman of the Midland Railway, had a meeting at the House of Commons with Joseph Paxton, the landscape-architect of the 6th Duke of Devonshire. Paxton had been much more than that to the (heterosexual) 'bachelor' Duke, being in effect the best friend to that ingenious nobleman and the companion of his many schemes of beautification in his Derbyshire palace. Paxton, from his mid-twenties, had demonstrated extraordinary skills not only as a gardener but also as an engineer and architect. The model village of Edensor, the 'Emperor' Fountain and the 'Chatsworth Stove', a giant conservatory, were only some of the glories this working-class genius achieved for his ducal friend and patron.[7] The Stove was the largest glass building in the world. When the Queen and Prince Albert visited Chatsworth in 1843 Paxton and the Duke had lit the huge conservatory with 14,000 lamps – 'This really is wonderful – astonishing,' exclaimed the Duke of Wellington, who was one of the illustrious guests.[8]

And now, Paxton, in his fiftieth year, after a life of freelance displays of cleverness for a limitlessly rich patron, had become the sort of man who sat on the board of railway companies, and was meeting William Ellis MP at the Commons before they went on to a formal meeting of the Midland Railway. Sitting in the public gallery, Paxton could not hear the debate in progress that afternoon – Ellis complained that the acoustics in Barry's new chamber were inadequate. The two men fell to discussing other botched jobs, including the designs for the new exhibition hall.

During the meeting of the Midland Railway company that afternoon, Paxton doodled a better design on his blotter, and later that day he showed it to Ellis. What he had in mind was an even bigger version of the Chatsworth Stove, all glass and cast iron, which could, if required, be dismantled and relocated when the exhibition closed. Ellis gave the piece of blotting paper to Cole, who arranged an audience at once with Prince Albert. Within a week, Fox and Henderson, the Smethwick contracting firm, had costed the design to the nearest pound. On the very day that the building committee published (to general derision) its disastrous plan – the giant domed engine shed – Paxton showed his alternative to Lord Granville, nephew of the Duke of Devonshire, who was able to present the committee with this much more attractive alternative. There were still a number of hurdles to jump. Members of the commission offered to put up money themselves to pay for Paxton's scheme. Granville and the Radical cabinet minister Henry Labouchere offered £5,000 each and the financier Samuel Morton Peto offered £50,000 – a far cry from the committee of the Millennium Dome in 2000, who were only prepared to spend other people's money for their unpopular extravaganza. In spite of opposition, the Paxton glasshouse idea was accepted, and work began constructing the space, not in Regent's Park or the Isle of Dogs, but plumb in the middle of London – Hyde Park. This, said Sir Robert Peel – his last words to the commission on this or any subject – should be the site 'or none'.[9]

The summer of 1850 saw two deaths which not only removed from the scene two of the greatest men of the nineteenth century, but also can be seen as emblematic, closing forever a particular era of human understanding. On 23 April, the Poet Laureate William Wordsworth died aged eighty and was buried three days later in the churchyard at Grasmere. In July, his widow published the autobiographical poem which she entitled *The Prelude*. Wordsworth had hardly looked at his revisions of the poem for over a decade, and its most memorable passages had been finished in 1805, which was not merely forty-five calendar years away, but separated from the England of Railways and Free Trade, Capitalism and Empire and Religious Doubt by a vast imaginative chasm.

Robert Browning, as a good young Liberal, had seen Wordsworth as 'the Lost Leader' who had left behind the excitement of a revolutionary youth and support for the French Revolution, and become an Anglican Tory who composed 'ecclesiastical sonnets'. From the perspective of 150 years, though, we can see that the move from 'left' to right – fellow-travelling Girondin to supporter of Church and Queen – was not the definitive feature of Wordsworth's trajectory. It was what remained constant, and not what changed, which strikes a reader of *The Prelude* today, particularly when we compare the two versions, one completed before the poet's thirty-fifth birthday in 1805 and the other reworked decades later for posthumous publication.

Wordsworth's life-work was to have been a vast philosophical poem called *The Recluse*. Only the first part got written. The reason his widow gave its title to *The Prelude* can be inferred from his description of it as 'The Ante-chapel . . . to the body of a Gothic Church.' In effect, it is an autobiography, an account of how Nature became all-in-all to him. As in his other long philosophical work, *The Excursion*, city life becomes synonymous with corruption. 'Cities where the human heart is sick' (XII.204) are contrasted with those small rural communities where there is still space and time to listen to the dictates of that inner voice which prompts virtue. Apart from its bearing on the question of religious language – Wordsworth saw in Nature 'the type of a majestic intellect' (XIV.64) – there is the vital issue of humankind itself. For the generation before Wordsworth's – that of Samuel Johnson – it was axiomatic that the good life, the civilized life, was to be lived in the *civis*. But the process of industrialization, and the population explosion which accompanied it, changed not only the face of towns, but the way in which urban humanity viewed itself. By the year that Wordsworth died, half the population of England was urban.[10] A hundred miles south of Wordsworth's Grasmere, grave Engels could look at Manchester, perched on a hill of clay: 'single rows of houses or groups of streets stand here and there, like little villages on the naked, not even grass grown, clay soil. The lanes are neither paved nor supplied with sewers, but harbour numerous colonies of swine, penned in small sties or yards, or wandering unrestrained through the neighbourhood.'

It is a testimony to how far industrialization and urbanization had yet to go that this description of Manchester squalor appears almost bucolic 150 years later to the reader of the twenty-first century. The sheer struggle of city existence, the struggle to avoid disease, to fill the belly, to find somewhere to sleep, removed much chance of freedom in any meaningful sense of the term; and the bourgeoisie, which grew rich on the struggles of those who toiled, were locked in the same relentless process of 'getting and spending'. Wordsworth challenged Adam Smith's definition of the 'Wealth of Nations',

> having gained
> A more judicious knowledge of the worth
> And dignity of individual man.
>
> (XIII,79–81)

With a profound gift of foresight, he saw that the growth of the free market, far from promoting liberty, would in fact enslave. Having established the story of his own individual discovery of freedom and truth by a life communing with Nature, he asks, 'What one is, Why may not billions be?' To this question of whether the individual can survive, whether the term indeed possesses any meaning in the capitalist jungle, many of the great minds of the age were to address themselves. The old arguments of Free Will versus Determinism which had concerned theologians could exercise Marx and Darwin in different ways. Those who asserted liberty, as in the days of Theology, did so with an element of defiance. For Mill and the Utilitarians, the concept of liberty had to be worked out within the political framework, but there were always, in the nineteenth century, to be those subversives who could echo Wordsworth's

> Oh! who is he that hath his whole life long
> Preserved, enlarged this freedom in himself?
> For this alone is genuine liberty . . .
>
> (XIV,130)

This concept, of individualism asserting itself against the world that capitalism brought to birth, would surface in the more interesting nineteenth-century thinkers, ranging from Tolstoy in his Christian anarchist phase (who presumably never read Wordsworth) to Ruskin, who so surprisingly said he found Wordsworth uncongenial.

In England, the year which opened the sluices was unquestionably 1846, and the most significant brain in which the conversion occurred, from economic protectionism to laissez-faire, was that of Sir Robert Peel. If you take the view that the flood could have been contained, then the repeal of the Corn Laws could still be seen as the end of an old England in which the country would have predominance over the town, and in which some ideal – religious or aristocratic or perhaps both – other than the purely commercial could dictate the nature and structure of society. Most historians would prefer to see the repeal of the Corn Laws as an inevitability, and Peel as a brave, principled man, convinced of the rightness of his course, though it spelled ruin for his party. He accepted no honours, and he declined the Garter,[11] even though it could be said that he was the single most important political educator of his age: educator, that is, of the middle classes whom he represented, of his followers in Parliament and, significantly, of the royal family. His was the voice of moderation and common sense, not always qualities which win loud applause in political life. If the death of Wordsworth could be seen as the death of a certain type of sacred individualism, increasingly difficult in a capitalist–industrial maelstrom, the death of Peel seems like the end of a certain type of modesty and reasonableness in public life. One can't say that, because Peel died, therefore there was a Crimean War; but one can say that there was that costly and futile war because Britain forgot the quiet common sense of Peel.

Four years before that war, there was an incident which was so typical of Lord Palmerston, the foreign secretary, that it could be a parable designed to explain the phrase 'gunboat diplomacy'. A Portuguese Jewish moneylender, by name Don Pacifico, living in Athens, had his house pillaged. It happened that he had been born in Gibraltar, so he applied to the British government to intervene on his behalf with the precarious and so recently independent Greece. There is no doubt that the attack on Don Pacifico by an anti-semitic mob was very unpleasant. They manhandled his wife and children, stole his wife's jewels and set fire to his house. Many of the youths who took part in the riot were well born; one was the son of the minister for war.[12]

Failing to get satisfaction from the Greek authorities, Don Pacifico applied to Lord Palmerston, and by January 1850 Palmerston had ordered a blockade of the Greek ports. He did not consult with France or Russia, the other two international custodians of Greek freedom. Nor, when a negotiation with France had been agreed, did Palmerston bother to tell the British minister (ambassador we should say) in Athens. By summer, the French had withdrawn their ambassador from London, but Don Pacifico had in large measure been compensated. The belligerent attitude of Palmerston – by extension and implication, the attitude of Britain itself – was hugely popular with the country at large. When Lord Stanley, soon to inherit the earldom of Derby from his father, moved a parliamentary vote of censure, Palmerston mounted a grand defence in the Commons. Over 2,000 volumes of Foreign Office papers were used in preparing his statement,[13] which amounted to a statement of British foreign policy since Canning.

> While we have seen thrones shaken, shattered, levelled, institutions overthrown and destroyed; while in almost every country of Europe the conflict of civil war has deluged the land with blood, from the Adriatic to the Black Sea, from the Baltic to the Mediterranean, this country has presented a spectacle honourable to the people of England, and worthy of the admiration of mankind.

No mention of his Irish tenants, naked and sick, being shipped to Canada out of harm's way. Rather,

> We have shown that liberty is compatible with order; that individual freedom is reconcilable with obedience to the law . . .

And he asked the house to decide,

> whether, as the Roman, in days of old, held himself free from indignity when he could say *Civis Romanus sum*; so also a British subject, in whatever land he may be, shall feel confident that the watchful eye and the strong arm of England will protect him against injustice and wrong.[14]

There can have been few more technicoloured definitions of what a genius of a later generation called 'the vicarious policemanship which is the strongest emotion of Englishmen towards another man's muddle'.[15]

Nothing could have been more different from the cocksure tones of Lord Palmerston than Sir Robert Peel's polite common sense. Debating the Don Pacifico affair in the Commons, Peel said, 'What is this diplomacy? It is a costly engine for maintaining peace. It is a remarkable instrument used by civilized nations for the purpose of preventing war.'[16] They were his last words to Parliament. Next day, as he was riding up Constitution Hill, his horse grew restive and he fell. Peel was carried home to his house in Whitehall Gardens, where after three agonizing days, he died.

The Victorians had invented, and come to inhabit, the newspaper age, in which it is possible to have wildly incompatible opinions displayed with garishly raw emotion. At the very height of Palmerston's popularity the country also went into deepest mourning for Peel. Naturally, some moderate conservatives were consistent enough to regret the passing of Peel precisely because they deplored the aggression and jingoism of Palmerston's radical imperialist liberalism (or however you might define his politics). Many, however, perhaps most, of the newspaper-reading public were not concerned with logic. They were perfectly prepared to beat a drum for Palmerston when it excited them, while seeing Peel as the embodiment of quiet English tolerance, common sense, and sound monetary views.

> Alas, great Robert now is dead
> Who modified our Laws,
> Who took the duty off our Bread
> And gain'd so much applause

ran one popular street ballad, 'The Poor Man's Lamentation for the death of Sir Robert Peel'.[17] Another rhymester saw Peel's two voltes-face, over Catholic Emancipation and over the Corn Laws, as the key factors which had signalled the liberalization of England and averted a continental-style revolution:

> Glory to him who, resolutely great,
> Twice wrecked his Party and twice saved the State;
> Whose well-timed daring kept Victoria's crown
> Firm in the storm when Europe's thrones went down.[18]

Walter Bagehot was less kind. 'The word which exactly fits his oratory is – specious. He hardly ever said anything which struck you in a moment to be true; he never uttered a sentence which for a moment anybody could deny to be plausible . . .' It is a brilliant, and merciless, analysis. Bagehot traced Peel's many changes of view – from being a defender of the Peterloo Massacre to being a liberal Tory, from sympathizer with the Orange Lodge to Catholic emancipator, from opponent to advocate of Free Trade. He sees Peel as a weather-vane of middle-class opinion, an able administrator, but fundamentally boring.

> The principal measures required in his age were 'repeals'. From changing circumstances, the old legislation would no longer suit a changed community; and there was a clamour, first for the repeal of one important Act, and then of another. This was suitable to the genius of Peel.[19]

He concludes his damnation of Peel with the words, 'You have excluded the profound thinker; you must be content with what you can obtain – the business gentleman.'[20] This has the cleverness and unfairness of journalism at its best – and there was no better political journalist than Bagehot. It supposes that the realistic alternative to 'the business gentleman' was the deep thinker. Politics, though, does not attract deep minds. In the early nineteenth-century Cabinets there were plenty of clever men like Gladstone and Macaulay, but no one we would call profound. Is profundity an asset in politicians?

Anyway, as Bagehot knew perfectly well, writing six years after Peel's death, the alternatives to Peel as prime minister were not Aristotle and Hegel. They were – in succeeding order – Lord John Russell, Lord Stanley/Derby, Lord Aberdeen and Lord Palmerston. Those who saw Aberdeen trying to keep alight the flickering flame of Peelite moderation and common sense might have saluted his courage or condemned his vacillation; but they would have known who waited in the wings – not a philosopher, but the loud, ludicrous figure of 'Pam', who, as Disraeli remarked, 'really is an imposter, utterly exhausted, and at best only ginger-beer, and not champagne, and now an old painted pantaloon'.[21]

Those who criticized the Great Exhibition – Carlyle, Colonel Sibthorp, the *Mechanics Magazine* (a Radical periodical), the Chartists (what remained of them) – tended to be those who criticized Free Trade. *The Times* blew hot and cold, first supporting it, then claiming that the exhibition would ruin Hyde Park, finally compelled to acknowledge that in its own terms the exhibition was hugely successful. The sheer scale of it all makes any description, either of the opening ceremonies, or of the visitors, or of the 100,000 exhibits, become a catalogue of hyperboles. Twenty-five thousand season tickets were sold in advance, at 3 guineas each for gentlemen, 2 guineas for ladies. For ten days after the opening, admission cost £1 and was thereafter reduced to five shillings. After 24 May, Mondays to Thursdays cost 1s., Fridays half a crown, Saturdays 5s. There was no opening on Sundays, no smoking, no alcohol and no dogs. On 1 May there were 6,000 extra police on duty and five cavalry regiments on standby in the Tower of London in case of trouble.

By 11 o'clock in the morning, 500,000 people had assembled in the Park to watch Charles Spencer the great aeronaut go up in his balloon at the moment the exhibition was declared open. The jam of cabs and carriages stretched back to the Strand – 1,500 cabs, 800 broughams, 600 post carriages, 300 clarences . . . At noon, the Queen and Prince Albert arrived and were saluted with guns. The great organ struck up 'God Save the Queen'. The archbishop of Canterbury offered a prayer and a choir sang Handel's Hallelujah chorus.

Albert had chosen as the motto 'The Earth is the Lord's and the fullness thereof'. It was not intended as a reference to Lord Palmerston, Pilgerstein as Albert playfully called him, whose foreign policy he so much deplored. *The Times* said it 'was the first morning since the creation of the world that all peoples have assembled from all parts of the world and done a common act'. The Queen was equally ecstatic:

The glimpse of the transept through the iron gates, the waving palms, flowers, statues, myriads of people filling the galleries and seats around, with the flourish of trumpets as we entered, gave us a sensation which I can never forget and I felt much moved . . . The sight as we came to the middle where the steps and a chair (which I did *not* sit on) were placed, with the beautiful crystal fountain just in front of it, was magical – so vast, so glorious, so touching. One felt – as so many did whom I have since spoken to – filled with devotion, more so than by any service I have ever heard. The tremendous cheers, the joy expressed in every face, the immensity of the building, the mixture of palms, flowers, trees, statues, fountains, the organ (with 200 instruments and 500 voices; which sounded like nothing) and my beloved husband, the author of this 'peace Festival' which united the industry of all nations of the earth – all this was moving indeed, and it was and is a day to live for ever.[22]

It would be fascinating to know how we, visitors from the twenty-first century, would have regarded the Great Exhibition had we joined the 20,000 visitors on that opening day, or the 6,039,195 visitors (more accurately one should say visits, since many, like the Queen, returned again and again) before the exhibition closed in October. Would we perhaps regard it as the very emblematic epitome of England in its time? The variety and ingenuity of the exhibits would no doubt astound us. Hibbert, Platt and Son's fifteen cotton-spinning machines demonstrated in anodyne, clean conditions, in a southern exhibition chamber, the kind of machinery which had done the home-weavers out of a living, and to which the northern working classes were now attached like slaves. But here, they seemed like gleaming incarnations of progress and progressivism. The machine section of the exhibition was always the most popular.[23] They were 'the epitome of man's industrial progress – of his untiring efforts to release himself from his material bondage', as James Ward wrote in *The World in its Workshops*. Here could be seen Nasmyth's steam hammer, invented ('after a few moments' thought')[24] to forge the proposed paddle shafts of the *Great Britain*; here were locomotives, talking telegraphs, steam turbines, printing machines, envelope machines; and a wide variety of scientific instruments – air pumps, microscopes, printing telegraphs, cameras and photographic equipment of the most up-to-date kind. J.A. Whipple, a Boston photographer, exhibited a daguerreotype of the Moon, the result of a collaboration with W.C. Bond at the Observatory at Harvard. The Exhibition Jury considered it 'perhaps one of the most satisfactory attempts that has yet been made to realise, by a photographic process, the telescopic appearance of a heavenly body and it must be regarded as indicating the commencement of a new era in astronomical representation'.[25]

In all this, we visitors in a time machine from the twenty-first century would find harbingers of Victorian triumphs – we will see these great inventions used for good and ill in the coming years, cameras capturing for us everything from the Crimean War to Mrs Cameron's Arthurian fantasies; telegraphs playing a crucial role in the establishment of Empire. (The British use of the telegraph was vital in subduing the Indian uprisings in 1857–8.)

But as we have accustomed ourselves to seeing this exhibition as the symbol of nineteenth-century industrial progress and materialism, we turn the corner and – what is this? We are standing in the Medieval Court designed by Augustus Welby Pugin, in which we are confronted with Gothic High Altars, hanging lamps, and statues of the Virgin. So strongly did the Medieval Court offend Protestant sensibility that complaints were made to the Prince Consort and the prime minister and a flood of letters to *The Times* regarded the erection of a Crucifixion on the Rood Screen as an 'insult to the religion of the country'.[26]

While twenty-first-century time visitors, unless from Northern Ireland, would find such complaints bizarre, they might need to remind themselves that 'No Popery' was still a live issue for senior politicians in Britain in 1850–1.

In 1847 the new pope (a liberal called Giovanni Maria Mastai-Ferretti – he had been elected in 1846 and took the name Pius IX) had approved in principle the idea, put to him by Nicholas Wiseman, that English Roman Catholicism – hitherto organized as a mission Church under the care of vicars-apostolic – should be administered differently. England should be divided into Catholic dioceses, taking their names not from the ancient or medieval sees of York, Exeter, Salisbury etc. but chiefly from the modern industrial centres – Birmingham, Liverpool, Nottingham, Northampton, Plymouth and so on. Wiseman, who was rector of the English college in Rome until 1840 and thereafter a vicar-apostolic, who had been consecrated bishop, was a genial fellow on the whole better liked by non-Catholics than by his co-religionists. (He has his 'lobster-salad side',[27] complained one puritanical Catholic.) Browning used him as the model for Bishop Blougram in his fascinating poem on the subject of doubt and faith. Macaulay, visiting Rome in 1839, had found that Wiseman reminded him of Whewell, master of Trinity, Cambridge – 'full of health and vigour . . . He was extremely civil.'[28]

The Year of Revolutions delayed the scheme for the creation of an English Roman Catholic hierarchy. The pope himself fled Rome to Gaeta, the new secretary of propaganda, Monsignor Barnato, who was to set the English schemes in hand, was hidden in an Armenian monastery under Turkish diplomatic protection. When it was safe to emerge, 'Pius IX re-entered Rome in March 1850, a pope who had lost his liberalism.'[29]

It was now part of the pope's need, in the face of widespread anticlericalism and atheism, to rally the Catholic troops, and the act of making 'bishops' of Hexham, Shrewsbury or Birmingham became part of a more general scheme to strengthen Catholic Europe, of which England, for the first time in centuries, was seen to be a part. Wiseman was presiding over a Church which had grown in numbers enormously, but this was to bring its own problems. The English 'Catholic Church' was divided into three quite different groups who did not mix, or sympathize, with one another. By far the largest group was the new influx of Irish immigrants, hugely increased by the Famine. Second, there were the High Church malcontents who had followed John Henry Newman and his other friends from a position of attempting to see the Church of England as a Catholic remnant to a belief that true Catholicism could be found only in the Church of Rome. Some of these converts, most notably F.W. Faber, who built the London Oratory in the flamboyant baroque style of a Roman church – the Via Veneto come to Knightsbridge – gloried in the trappings of contemporary European Catholicism, but most of Newman's converts were swayed by the literature of an earlier age – the early Greek and Latin Fathers, the lives of the medieval saints – and took in effect their Anglo-Catholicism with them to Rome. In terms of ethos they were like travellers who brought with them the English apothecary, travelling library and chaplain on a continental sojourn.

There remained the tiny handful of old Catholic families who had not altered their religious allegiance since penal times and who had lived through times of persecution and prejudice as recently as the Gordon Riots. They feared that the creation of Catholic bishoprics in England would cause an anti-Catholic backlash, and they also took the view that it was unnecessary. The old organization under vicars-apostolic worked perfectly well and cost very little. Wiseman's scheme of new cathedrals which no Catholic could afford was to condemn English Catholics to a century and a half of fund-raising, tombolas and bingo. The older Catholics, the kind romanticized in Thackeray's *Henry Esmond*, who called their priests *Mister*, not *Father*, and who disliked the extremism and bad taste of continental piety purveyed at the Brompton Oratory, felt that something approaching a new religion was being foisted on them in terms which compromised their positions as British citizens.[30]

Though Catholic Emancipation had come in 1829 there were still a few anomalies on the statute books. Wiseman's florid manner of announcing the new hierarchy – he did so as a newly created cardinal, and wrote 'from out of the Flaminian Gate' – was too much for some of his flock. 'Your beloved country has received a place among the fair churches, which normally constituted, form the splendid aggregate of Catholic communion; Catholic England has been restored to its orbit in the ecclesiastical firmament, from which its light had long vanished.'[31] Lord Beaumont, a Catholic peer, said it was impossible to accept the new hierarchy and remain loyal to the Queen. The premier Catholic nobleman, the Duke of Norfolk, agreed with him and publicly became an Anglican by receiving holy communion in his parish church.[32]

As the old Catholics had predicted, the creation of the unpoetic sees of Liverpool and Birmingham provided the No Popery brigade with the excuse for mass hysteria. The papal brief reached the English press in the second week of October 1850. By Guy Fawkes Day the crowds were ready to express their anti-Catholic sentiments in traditional fashion. Some Catholic churches had their windows broken. In many places, Wiseman – or the pope – or both – were burnt in effigy.

These displays were not limited to the uneducated classes. The lord chancellor, at the Mansion House dinner of 9 November, quoted Shakespeare's lines

> Under our feet we'll stamp thy Cardinal's hat
> In spite of Pope or dignities of Church.[33]

He was thunderously applauded. Lord John Russell did not see it as his prime ministerial role to urge moderation. He deplored not only Roman Catholics but also those Anglo-Catholics within the Established Church. In fact he regarded these Puseyites, as they were now called – after the venerable Dr Pusey of Oxford, their High Church champion – as even more dangerous than the real thing. Writing to the Queen he quoted with approval the views of the late Doctor Arnold of Rugby, on the Catholics within the Established Church compared with the RCs – 'The one is the Frenchman in his own uniform and within his own praesidia; the other is the Frenchman disguised in a red coat, and holding a post within our praesidia, for the purpose of betraying it. I should honour the first, and hang the second.'[34]

As so often, the Queen surprises us with her compassion, broadmindedness, common sense. She shared Lord John's horror of unmanly High Church mummery, but as to the outbursts against her Catholic subjects, she wrote, 'I must regret the unchristian and intolerant spirit exhibited by many people at the public meetings. I cannot bear to hear the violent abuse of the Catholic religion, which is so painful and cruel towards the many good and innocent Roman Catholics.'[35]

Lord John, however, the author of the Great Reform Bill of 1832, the pioneer of British Liberalism, had no compunction about abusing the Roman Catholic religion; and he went further. On the tide of prejudice which Wiseman and the pope had provoked, Lord John brought before Parliament legislation to make the new Catholic dioceses illegal. 'I disapprove of such legislation very much,' Earl Grey wrote in his diary, 'and most reluctantly assent to its being attempted, but the country has got into such a state that I believe still greater mischief would result from doing nothing.'[36] A very great deal of parliamentary time in the first half of 1851 was devoted to the promotion of Lord John's bill, with hours of time given to the backwoodsmen to air their anti-Romish prejudices in the chamber of the House. No doubt it gave them great pleasure to vote to fine £100 anyone who claimed to be an archbishop or bishop of any diocese other than an Anglican one. The law they passed – the Ecclesiastical Titles Act – was so absurd that no-one was ever prosecuted by its terms and Gladstone easily, and necessarily, repealed it in 1871.

But all this was going on while Pugin erected his Madonnas and crucifixes, his roods and dossals and reredoses in the Crystal Palace in 1851. For those who had come to share Pugin's – and Newman's – faith there undoubtedly was a 'Second Spring' of English Catholicism in the middle of the nineteenth century. In the year of the Great Exhibition, the former archdeacon of Chichester, Henry Manning, one of the most dynamic churchmen of the age, was ordained as a Roman Catholic priest by Wiseman.

Whatever the religious significance of all this, the visitor to the exhibition – particularly a twenty-first-century visitor coming to the Crystal Palace in Hyde Park in a time machine – might see the outbursts of irrational prejudice against Catholics less in metaphysical than in political terms. The paradox of the exhibition was that while being international in scope, it was fundamentally designed as a demonstration not merely of British superiority to other nations but, in some way, of British independence and isolationism.

We should not fail to notice the internationalism of the displays, and if we read the *Illustrated London News* of 26 April 1851, with its pictures of Bengalis busily carving ivory for the Great Exhibition, we might also see in it signs of colonial exploitation. We might gasp with delight at the stuffed elephant and howdah from India, or at the exoticism of the Tunis Room. As we wandered from the Turkish stalls, the Greek stalls, the French, German and Italian exhibits we might indeed feel that 'the exhibition turned the Crystal Palace into, in the words of so many visitors, a fairyland, a tour round the world'.

Yet it has to be said that the presence of so much exotic foreign material, and so many foreigners, did not diminish the natural xenophobia of the English. Quite the reverse. The Home Office, and the Duke of Wellington, seen as the natural defender of England against foreign foes, were inundated with paranoid letters. '*Woe to England. All the French Socialists* it is understood are coming over to the Exhibition!!!! It will be *well* if *London* is not destroyed by *Fire*!!!! The Pope has successfully thrown the Apple of Discord *amongst us*!!!!' was one letter. A broadsheet printed and published by E. Hodges warned:

> Look out, look out, mind what you're about
> And how you go on, sirs,
> Mark what I say in the month of May,
> Eighteen hundred and fifty-one, sir,
> In London will be all the world,
> Oh, how John Bull will shrill then,
> The Russian, Prussian, Turk and Jew,
> And the King of the Sandwich Islands . . .

It goes without saying that E. Hodges did not thrill to the prospect. Broadly speaking the internationalist minority, including Prince Albert, rejoiced at the number of foreigners, and the xenophobic majority saw the exhibition as exacerbating trade rivalries rather than emphasizing the harmony between trading partners.

To most twenty-first-century eyes, the majority of artefacts in the exhibition would seem lumpen and hideous. For every laugh we might have at a stuffed animal (and Plouquet's famous stuffed rabbits, squirrels, weasels playing cards, holding tea parties and playing the pianoforte were among the great losses when the Crystal Palace was destroyed by fire in the twentieth century) there would be dozens of Birmingham-made epergnes, overmantels, clocks and tables which would not seem beautiful to our contemporaries. The Jewel Cabinet designed for Elkington and Co. by Albert's artistic mentor Louis Gruner, and adorned with panels depicting the Queen and her consort in medieval costume, with silver statuettes at each corner, is a good example: can one ever envisage an age which thought it lovely? It is still treasured in the Royal Collection. As Ruskin bitterly but appositely reminded his readers, 'In the year 1851, when all that glittering roof was built, in order to exhibit the petty arts of our fashionable luxury-carved bedsteads of Vienna, glued toys of Switzerland and gay jewellery from France – in that very year, I say, the greatest pictures of Venetian masters were rotting at Venice in the rain, for want of a roof to cover them, with holes made by cannon-shot through their canvas.'[37]

We should probably conclude if we had seen the original 1851 exhibition through twenty-first-century eyes that none of the exhibits could rival that 'glittering roof' itself.

The original conception of Paxton, so gloriously executed by the firm of Fox, Henderson and Co. of Smethwick, created a building which outsoared the Chatsworth Stove, a magnificent airy structure, entirely of iron and glass, modern, architecturally innovative and without the camp element of pastiche which characterizes almost all other great Victorian buildings. It was the largest greenhouse in the world, incorporating the very trees of Hyde Park. It was the world's first shopping mall, with tier upon tier of shops selling all manner of wares. It was infinitely adaptable to its purpose, containing an Aladdin's cave of variety, but it was also something of great beauty and worth in itself. When the exhibition closed on 11 October 1851, the net profit was more than £186,000 – money which was used to buy the plot of land in Kensington in which the permanent collections would be housed, and in which Prince Albert's memory was immortalized – in the Victoria and Albert Museum, the Imperial College of Science and Technology, and the Royal Albert Hall.

The Palace itself was demolished and re-erected to a slightly different design in Sydenham, South London, where it remained until destroyed by fire in 1936. Incidentally, it was the Sydenham Crystal Palace, and not the one in Hyde Park described as a cucumber frame between two chimneys, which has been seen variously as 'a monstrous Beaux-Arts ferro-vitreous composition' and an important pioneering work of proto-modernism.[38] Certainly if you see the photographs taken by the modernists Dell and Wainwright in the 1930s of the Crystal Palace you understand why Le Corbusier hailed its 'triumphant harmony'. The extension which Paxton added, and the two chimneys, make the Sydenham version much less harmonious than the Hyde Park original.

It would be wrong to think that the Crystal Palace embodied a single monist self-portrait of Victorian England. It was in some ways a glorious fluke, with various types of self-interest and showing-off – by the manufacturers, by Prince Albert, by Paxton – all coming together under Cole's stage-management. For all the vaunted success of the cheap days, the night-trains from Yorkshire bringing iron-workers and miners, the agricultural labourers depicted staring at the machinery in the *Illustrated London News*, and Mary Callinan, the old lady who walked from Penzance – aged one hundred in one account, eighty-four in another – clutching her shilling entrance fee, the exhibition could not be said to be an embodiment of social harmony. The very fact that some people went on 'shilling days' and others had paid £1 emphasized social difference.[39]

Perhaps there were many like Mr and Mrs Sandboys and family, in Henry Mayhew's novel of the name, who came up for the exhibition but, because of their provincial innocence, and the difficulty of finding their bearings in an overcrowded capital, never actually penetrated the Crystal Palace. (Cursty Sandboys inadvertently gives his shilling ticket to Le Comte de Sanschemin, an unscrupulous Frenchman.) Much the best things about this relentlessly facetious novel are the illustrations by George Cruikshank – such as the frontispiece, 'All the world going to see the Great Exhibition of 1851', a globular picture of the nations of the world converging on the Crystal Palace, or the one which shows the boxes at the Royal Opera being used as dormitories (such was the pressure on accommodation), or the double illustration 'London in 1851', in which every spare inch of a street scene is populated and crammed, contrasted with 'Manchester in 1851', totally deserted save for one old man smoking, and reading his newspaper on the empty street corner.

Mayhew's novel captures the Francophobia which was always ready to surface in England during the Victorian period. Franz Winterhalter's *The First of May* is a latter-day Adoration Scene, depicting the old Duke of Wellington kneeling before a Holy Family – Albert, Victoria, and Wellington's infant godson Arthur, future Duke of Connaught. In the background is the Crystal Palace, and some people see this icon as meaning that the old world-view, embodied in the Duke, bows out to the new, embodied in the Prince Consort. The old belligerent attitude to Europe is replaced by international concord based on commerce.

In spite of his misgivings about the exhibition, Wellington did visit the Crystal Palace for the opening, and went so often that he almost became part of the 'Shew'.[40] To the end of his days he took seriously his duties as warden of the Cinque Ports, the guardian of England against continental invasion. Long after the threat of a French invasion had become, to say the least, unlikely, he had strengthened fortifications on the south coast, and it was apt that he was to die in Walmer Castle, the warden's official residence. His funeral in London was an emblem of an old England which had vanished. The poet laureate in his eulogy 'Ode on the Death of the Duke of Wellington' used the funeral as a chance to beg

> O Statesmen, guard us, guard the eye, the soul
> Of Europe, keep our noble England whole,
> And save the one true seed of freedom sown
> Betwixt a people and their ancient throne.[41]

In fact, by then, Britain was involved with a French alliance, and not merely an entente with the nation that Wellington had fought so doughtily forty years since, but with a Bonaparte.

In December 1851, Louis Napoleon Bonaparte, who had been, a little shakily, elected as president of the new republic in 1848, staged a coup d'état and established himself as emperor of France. The foreign secretary, Lord Palmerston, whose antics over the Don Pacifico affair and many another international incident had been so embarrassing to the government of which he was a part, told the French ambassador of his 'entire approbation' of Bonaparte's action.[42] He had not consulted the Queen, or the prime minister, and though he blusteringly claimed that he had only been speaking in a private capacity, such a defence in a foreign secretary was risible. Lord John Russell asked for his resignation. Victoria and Albert were cock-a-hoop. Albert did not believe that British public opinion was pro-Bonapartist and he was probably right – but Palmerston was not long gone from the political scene.[43]

When Lord John's government fell, the Tories came back into office and the Queen asked Lord Derby to form an administration. This was to be the famous 'Who? Who?' government, since when the Duke of Wellington was told the names of the new Cabinet, two months before he died, he had responded with those withering monosyllables.[44] Hindsight is chiefly interested in the *Who Who* administration because it contained Disraeli in his first role as chancellor of the Exchequer. Derby's government did not last the year, however, and by December, Lord Aberdeen had formed his Liberal–Peelite coalition Cabinet – with W.E. Gladstone replacing B. Disraeli as chancellor of the Exchequer, Lord John Russell as foreign secretary and Pam as home secretary. The

Queen was not able to dismiss the 'two dreadful old men' as easily as she might have hoped. Moreover, though Pam lost control of the Foreign Office for the months of 1852, his policy – an alliance with the new French emperor – was still that of the government. Though the reasonable and unbelligerent figure of Aberdeen was the last man to want to break the forty years of European peace, this was the government which was to lead Britain to war.

Marx was never more sparklingly satirical than in his analysis of the French coup d'état in *The Eighteenth Brumaire of Louis Bonaparte* – 'Hegel remarks somewhere that all facts and personages of great importance in world history occur, as it were, twice. He forgot to add: the first time as tragedy, the second as farce.'[45] (The first '18th Brumaire', according to the French Revolutionary calendar, had been the date when Napoleon I seized power). The coup by the farcical Napoleon was, as Marx said, merely the restoration in the eyes of the bourgeois of 'Property, family, religion, order' – you see this obsession in the sweep of Zola's great novels. It was the alliance of royalists (whatever their sentimental horror of Bonapartism) and the Church which enabled Napoleon III's coup to succeed, and it was the danger to property which underlay this revolution – the old propertied classes in France under the Bourbons had been the huge landed classes. But it was capitalism which underwrote the Orleanist monarchy. In a comparable way in England, 'The Tories . . . long imagined that they were enthusiastic about monarchy, the church and the beauties of the old English constitution, until the day of danger wrung from them the confession that they are enthusiastic only about *rent*.'[46]

Prince Albert and Queen Victoria and the Peelites all would have known the truth of that, though they would have hated having it so clearly spelled out for them. The new conservatisms of Disraeli and later of Salisbury, designed to enlist the alliance between the old landed grandees and the emergent petty capitalists of the suburbs, were the most eloquent demonstration of how true Marx's words were. Moreover, on both sides of the Channel the European ruling classes whose rentier interests created such strange alliances depended not only on knowing their friends but on recognizing, and holding in subjection, the enemy. 'Bonaparte would like to appear as the patriarchal benefactor of all classes. But he cannot give to one class without taking from another.'[47]

That is why we cannot understand what is taking place on the international stage in the 1850s without seeing what is happening at home. Industrial manufacturing capital, enriching the shareholders of the rentier class, needed an army of near-slaves to keep the ever-expanding industries going. Economic expansionism cannot exist without territorial expansionism. The condition of the urban poor, the problems of the colonies, the changing face of European realpolitik – what A.J.P. Taylor calls 'the struggle for Mastery in Europe' – are all part of the same selfish Darwinian struggle. This is why in France old political enemies joined forces behind Napoleon III, and in England governments teetered over trivialities, forming and reforming themselves around coalitions of common interest. Once Chartism had been defeated, the main political groupings – Liberals, Peelites, Tories – were all agreed on the fundamentals of economic policy. No real challenge in the mainstream of *parliamentary* politics was offered to the Benthamite laissez-faire ideal.

Given Marx's continental perspective, it is not surprising that he saw Christianity, or perhaps more accurately the Churches, as instruments of oppression. In the English context, however, there were more complex and interesting developments. The capitalist system, like the Darwinian theory which is its mythopoeic expression, depends upon the assertion rather than the denial of the will. Selfishness is its greatest, perhaps its only virtue. It is not surprising, in the decades in which the states of Northern Europe became reordered to absorb the new economic ethos, that religious belief and adherence should find themselves challenged. At the end of *Yeast*, Charles Kingsley's Christian Socialist novel of 1848, the young hero, who has had his eyes opened to the plight of the (rural) poor, comes to London and hears the choir sing the afternoon service in St Paul's Cathedral.

> Shall I tell you what they are singing? He hath put down the mighty from their seat, and hath exalted the humble and meek. He hath filled the hungry with good things, and the rich he hath sent empty away. Is there no life, think you, in these words, spoken here in every afternoon in the name of God?[48]

The words are delivered to the hero by a mysterious stranger who adds, 'No, I dare not despair of you English, as long as I hear your priesthood forced by Providence, even in spite of themselves, thus to speak God's words about an age in which the condition of the poor, and the rights and duties of man, are becoming the rallying-point for all thought and all organization.'[49]

'Let the great world spin forever down the ringing grooves of change,' wrote Tennyson. 'I thought the wheels ran in grooves,' he explained after his first railway journey. (*Above*) This steam locomotive of 1845 appears to be pulling stagecoaches from the Pickwickian era. (*Below*) Tennyson's haunting poetry of doubt and grief made him the ideal Laureate of the age.

The plight of the poor and their political discontent led to many riots and disturbances during the 1840s. This print shows the Chartist riot in Newport, Glamorgan, in 1840.

The desolation of Ireland reached depths of unimaginable horror during the Great Famines of the late 1840s, which killed over 1 million and sent millions more into exile. Out of this suffering the Irish republican movement was born.

Prince Albert's anxious look suggests that one of the Queen's outbursts is imminent. Their marriage was passionate and stormy.

(*Above*) Osborne House, his Italianate villa on the Isle of Wight, was built to Albert's specifications by Thomas Cubitt.

(*Right*) The entrance hall at Osborne reflects Albert's chaste and learned taste. After his early death, his widow filled the place with her beloved 'clutter'.

The Crimean War was the first to be photographed. Seen here is the Cook House of the 8th Hussars, the King's Royal Irish. After the Famine, the army was an obvious career for many young Irishmen.

As many men died of disease as in battle during the Crimean War. Florence Nightingale's organizational skills and compassion created the hospital at Scutari on the Bosporus, and led to the reform both of medicine and of the army.

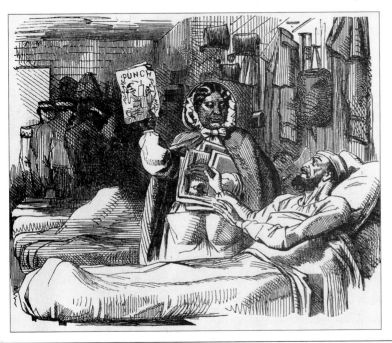

But it was Mary Seacole, whose services Miss Nightingale rejected on racialist grounds, who nursed the sick in the front line of battle in the Crimea itself and whose jolly 'hotel' provided the men with home cooking and, a much-needed commodity, handkerchiefs.

The evolutionary theories of Charles Darwin, caricatured here, emerged concurrently with the popularity of European zoos. (*Below left*) This young chimpanzee in London Zoo, photographed in 1869 on the keeper's lap, and beside a Rhesus macaque, must have prompted new thoughts in the visitors. Darwin's grandfather Josiah Wedgwood made a celebrated medallion depicting an African slave in chains and asking the question, 'Am I not a man and a brother?' (*Below right*) Eighty years later this question becomes for the *Punch* cartoonist a metaphysical conundrum. From now on, humans and apes were kin.

MONKEYANA.

AM I
A
MAN AND
A
BROTHER?

Am I satyr or man?
Pray tell me who can,
And settle my place in the scale.
A man in ape's shape,
An anthropoid ape,
Or monkey deprived of his tail?

Charles Dickens's novels are full of unforgettable children and images of childhood. But in his generation, children did not have 'childhoods', with nurseries, children's books and special food. They were little adults.

Alice Liddell, whose father was Dean of Christ Church, Oxford, befriended a don called the Rev. Charles Dodgson. The results were some photographs in questionable taste and *Alice's Adventures in Wonderland*.

(*Above*) The Great Conservatory at Chatsworth House in Derbyshire (the Chatsworth Stove) was the creation of the gardener there, Joseph Paxton. A brilliant self-taught engineer and designer, he planned the Crystal Palace, which would house the Great Exhibition of 1851, in a doodle on his blotter during a meeting. (*Below*) Paxton's eye for perspective, and his use of metal and glass, made him the object of admiration for such modernist photographers as Dell and Wainwright, who captured the Crystal Palace here during the 1930s just before it was destroyed by fire.

Largely under the influence of F.D. Maurice, professor of theology at King's College, London, Kingsley espoused the Christian Socialist Movement which, though it lasted only six years as an organization, had a lasting effect on the thinking of many English Christians. Maurice has been called 'the greatest of all teachers since Augustine . . . With him it was never an opinion he was offering you; it was the truth of life you were grasping.'[51] Every page of Maurice's theology is informed by the sense that these religious ideas are not esoteric but immediate. The notion that Almighty God took human flesh was difficult enough to believe; but Maurice is one of those rare beings who saw the implications of such a belief outside the purely churchy sphere: 'The State is as much God's creation as the Church.' Newman's glancing and imaginative mind has much to say on the level of personal belief, and he provides ingenious grounds for accepting the 'development' of doctrine. He seldom, if ever, draws any connection between these theological concerns and the real plights and problems of men and women of the nineteenth century. He wrote from the middle of the slums of Birmingham as if he were an Oxford don or – as he fantasized in his boyhood – 'I thought life might be a dream, or I an Angel, and all this world a deception, my fellow-angels by a playful device concealing themselves from me, and deceiving me with the semblance of a material world,'[52] whereas Maurice was always engaged with realities external to himself. To this degree, Maurice – the Anglican professor hounded out of his theological chair for 'heresy' – was in many ways more 'Catholic' than Newman, the Roman convert who was to die a cardinal.

If Marx was unfair to judge England by continental standards and to see Christianity as propping up the status quo – many Victorian Christians from Ashley to Maurice to Kingsley were inspired by their faith to question the very nature of the Benthamite social structure – he would also have been wrong to suppose that the Victorian establishment – to use an unsatisfactory shorthand word – closed ranks against criticism. One of the reasons perhaps that there never was a Marxian revolution in England was the British capacity for adaptation of its system, based on really acute self-criticism. Ashley was not some fringe character – he was at the very heart of the governing class.

'Have you read "Alton Locke" and "Yeast" by Kingsley?' The Queen asked her daughter. 'They are said to be rather strange and show his (supposed) chartist and socialist views.'[53] But this did not stop her from asking Kingsley to be tutor to her children. Yes, Marx was right, a hundred per cent right, that capitalism depended on unbridled selfishness. What is missing from his robust and magnificent prose is the sense of quite complicated agonies, apparent in the Victorians' most widely read philosophers and thinkers – above all Carlyle and Ruskin.

13

Marx – Ruskin – Pre-Raphaelites

True, the only cohesive opposition to the march of capitalism in the 1840s and 1850s came from communism – or its watered-down equivalents – and Christianity. But – this is one of the central questions facing the men and women of the age – were they believable? Their allure explains how such strange alliances could have been formed against the relentlessness of the factory-owners – a Bible Christian such as Ashley, motivated by reading the Gospels, standing alongside radicals and socialists whose views of other matters he might deplore, in his campaign to limit the hours worked by women and children in the cotton mills. It is a curious fact that the leader of the working men's cause in the House of Commons, until the Factory Act of 1850 finally did bring in the desired Ten Hours measure, was a high Tory aristocrat who believed in hierarchy, deference and the literal truth of every word of the Bible. His tireless campaigns to set up ragged schools for slum-dwellers, and to prick the conscience of laissez-faire economists, took over a decade. In the first years of Victoria's reign, the coal flickering cheerfully in your grate would, as like as not, have been dragged through underground tunnels too small for a grown man by child workers as young as six. This was brought to an end in 1844, against the fiercest opposition from the big colliery proprietors, such as Lord Londonderry. It took a further three years to persuade liberals such as Macaulay, Palmerston or Russell so much as to consider limiting the hours worked by women and children to ten hours a day. With their blinkered view of what constituted 'liberty' these liberals felt that legislation interfered with the personal freedoms of workers. Most of the child workers in the mills were employed not by the mill-owners themselves but by adult male spinners who subcontracted work. To make laws about such private arrangements was, in Palmerston's view, 'a vicious and wrong principle'.[1]

We shall fail to understand the Victorians if we do not take note of the word. Their principles were not ours. Some were candid enough to recognize that the greedy logic of their belief in laissez-faire economics was incompatible with a Christian witness. Others, perhaps a majority in the early to mid-Victorian period, tried to live with a double standard, being perfectly prepared to say that they believed the working classes were made in God's image and likeness, while treating them with a severity comparable to that of slave-owners in the West Indian plantations.

Sometimes we can learn more of a past generation by reading the authors who were popular at the time and have now sunk without trace, rather than reperusing the immortals. Harriet Martineau (1802–76) was one of the most highly esteemed journalists of the day, and her weathercock mind gives us the directions in which the mid-Victorian liberal wind was blowing. Born of a long line of (Huguenot) surgeons in Norwich, she was one of the most popular interpreters of the English-speaking nineteenth century to itself. A series of woodenly written short stories illustrative of the political economy of Malthus, James Mill and Ricardo would probably not reach the bestseller lists in the twenty-first century, but in the 1830s they made a very palpable hit, and as she tells us, 'the stern Benthamites' thanked her as a safe and faithful expositor of their doctrines. Her *Half a Century of the British Empire*, begun in 1848, was designed for the educated, self-educated or semi-educated bourgeoisie.

Wordy, authoritative, cliché-ridden, Miss Martineau had the know-all tone which so often wins journalism wide readership and short-term respect. Like many of her modern equivalents, she had all the right views – that is the views espoused by the metropolitan intelligentsia. She was a keen abolitionist – of slavery – but saw no reason why this concern for her oppressed fellow humans in American plantations should lead her to comparable feelings of compassion for English factory-workers. In 1855 she penned *The Factory Controversy – A Warning Against Meddling Legislation*. Factory inspectors in 1853 had drawn the attention of the secretary of state to the 'enormous amount of accidents' in British factories, but clever journalist that she was, Martineau knew how to turn an obvious truth – that, in spite of the best endeavours of Ashley and others, the conditions in factories were still fairly appalling – into something absurd:

The whole number of accidents from machinery, in three years, was reported to be 11,716 of which 3,434 were of a serious character. The serious are all that require any serious notice, as the others are of so slight a nature that they would not be noticed anywhere but in a special registration like that provided by The Factory Act. For instance, 700 are cases of cut fingers. Any worker who rubs off a bit of skin from finger or thumb, or sustains the slightest cut which interferes with the spinning process for a single day, has the injury registered under the Act.[2]

Martineau, a lifetime professional invalid, wrote whole books about her hypochondriacal conditions. Her journalism describes her sick-room languor – 'O what a heavenly solace to the soul is free sympathy in its hour of need!'[3] But she can confidently dismiss the conclusions of factory inspectors, and claim that what they call serious injuries are no more than a bit of skin rubbed off someone's thumb. Likewise, as her belief in religion faded away, she became an enthusiast for mesmerism, believing that her hysterical conditions, rendering her immobile for months on end, had been cured by mesmeric trances. Mobile once more, she could tour America and Ireland, and send back precisely the dispatches the comfortable middle classes wanted to read. Touring Ireland in 1852, she found an island populated by stage Irishmen, tipsy, idle, dirty and inefficient. The chief problems of the place were a want of capital and an excess of religion.[4] No one would make that complaint of the England which Miss Martineau represented, prosperous, intelligent and callous.

Turn to the chapter in *Capital* entitled 'The Working Day' – eighty of the finest pages ever written by Marx or anyone else on the plight of nineteenth-century factory workers – and a very different picture emerges. There we read that although the three Factory Acts of 1833, 1844 and 1847 restricted the working hours of women and children in some circumstances, the liberal capitalists in the House of Commons had, with the passing of each act, clawed back some 'concession' in return. So, for example, when the 'relay system' was regulated in 1844 – making it impossible for factory-owners to work a child from 5 a.m. until noon and then again at 1 p.m. as if this second stint of work constituted a new 'shift' – the Lower House '*reduced* the minimum age at which the exploitation of children could begin from 9 to 8, this being done to ensure that capital could have "the additional supply of children" which capitalists are by human and divine laws entitled to demand'.[5] The various factory acts never changed the basic notion that males over the age of eighteen should work a fifteen-hour day from 5.30 a.m. to 8.30 p.m. Marx, reading through the small print of the 1844 act, was also able to remind his readers that though the law now forbade the employment of children after 1 p.m. who had been employed before noon, a child of eight, beginning now at noon, might be worked from 12 to 1 – one hour; from 2 to 4 – two hours; and from 5 to 8.30 in the evening – in all the legal six and a half hours – in order to make their work simultaneous with the adult workers. So the spirit of the act which desired the protection of children being kept at factories all afternoon and all evening was defied by its letter.[6]

The accumulation of evidence from factory inspectors adduced in Marx's chapter makes the protestations of Martineau and her readers seem as ridiculous as they are offensive. We read the testimony of doctors and factory inspectors who have examined potters, manufacturers of lucifer matches, railwaymen, brick-makers . . . Whatever the category of worker examined, the same story is told: the exploitation of workers to the point where the urban proletariat of Victorian England have become stunted in growth and subject to a whole range of debilitating illnesses, all of which are a direct consequence of their being overworked. The doctor in the North Staffordshire Infirmary, having enumerated the pneumonia, phthisis, bronchitis and asthma, as well as disorders of kidney and stomach, to which his 'ill-shaped and frequently ill-formed' patients were subject, summed up the causes of these complaints in two words – 'long hours'. The match-manufacturers of Manchester, Birmingham, Liverpool, Bristol, Norwich, Newcastle and Glasgow all suffer from 'phossy jaw' – half the workers are under thirteen.[7] Wallpaper manufacturers suffered from comparable chemical poisonings. The hours worked by a London baker must have made the (usually adulterated) bread roll dry in anyone's mouth if he had read *Capital* over his breakfast. Taking his information from the reports delivered to Parliament – the 'Blue Books' – Marx reminds Londoners of what someone else endured to put bread on their table.

The London journeyman baker's work began at 11 p.m., when he made the dough, a laborious task lasting half to three-quarters of an hour. Then he lay down on the kneading board, with a sack for a mattress, and slept for a couple of hours. Then followed five hours of hard, rapid work, kneading, moulding and preparing loaves and rolls. Temperatures in the bakehouse were as high as 90°. When the bread was baked it had to be delivered, and a high proportion of journeymen bakers undertook this work as well, wheeling handcarts or carrying baskets of bread to shops and houses – work which lasted until 1 or 6 p.m. depending on demand. During the London 'season', when bread was required in larger quantities in the evenings, the work of the bakeries was continuous. London bakers, statistics showed, seldom lived beyond the age of forty-two.

Henry Mayhew noted that as the wages of a trade went down, so the labourers extended

their hours of work to the utmost possible limits. 'My employer' I was told by a journeyman tailor working for a large West-end show shop, 'reduces my wages by one-third, and the consequence is, I put in two stitches where I used to give three.' 'I must work from six to eight and later,' said a Pembroke table-maker to me, 'to get 18 s now for my labour where I used to get 54 s a week – that's just a third. I could in old times give my children good schooling and good meals. Now children have to be put to work very young. I have four sons working for me at present.'[8]

And simplest and most life-threatening of all the hazards facing the urban Victorians was the sheer squalor resultant from their failure to understand that cholera, typhoid and typhus fever were water-borne.

The stench of London and its waters was remarked by all writers of the period. When the Queen and Prince Albert attempted a short pleasure cruise on the Thames in 1858 they were forced to turn back to land after a few minutes, the odours were so terrible. (That year of drought, Parliament had to rise early because of the smell becoming unendurable on the terraces outside the Palace of Westminster.)[9]

Mayhew's description of Jacob's Island, Bermondsey in South London, conveys the flavour of the mid-nineteenth-century Thames even more vividly than *Our Mutual Friend*, that murky river-novel:

As we passed along the reeking banks of the sewer [i.e. the tidal ditch] the sun shone upon a narrow slip of water. In the bright light it appeared the colour of strong green tea, and positively looked as solid as black marble in the shadow – indeed, it was more like watery mud than muddy water, and yet we were assured this was the only water which the wretched inhabitants had to drink. As we gazed in horror at it, we saw drains and sewers emptying their filthy contents into it; we saw a whole tier of doorless privies in the open road, open to men and women, built over it; we heard bucket after bucket of filth splash into it . . . we asked if they did drink the water? The answer was, They were obliged to drink the ditch, without it, they could beg a pailful or thieve a pailful of water.[10]

The chief propagandist for proper drainage in Victorian cities was Edwin Chadwick, who drew public attention to the filthy conditions in the large manufacturing towns. But the great scientific demonstration of the fact that disease was water-borne was made (against the fiercest opposition) by Dr John Snow. (He was also the genius who pioneered the use of chloroform during childbirth, and acted as a merciful anaesthetist to the Queen.)

Throughout the nineteenth century, as epidemic followed epidemic, there was heated debate about whether cholera was contagious.[11] Generally speaking, the contagionists were viewed by contemporaries as archaic, even antisocial. The anti-contagionists – modern, bourgeois, mercantile – were reluctant to admit the possibility – as we observed in the last chapter – that trade and traffic could spread pollution, disease, death.

Snow demonstrated his findings in his book *On the Mode of Communication of Cholera*, published in 1849. The crucial example of the contagionist vs. anti-contagionist argument was an outbreak of cholera in Albion Terrace, Wandsworth Road, South London in that year. Cholera extended to all the houses in which the water was tainted. Numbers 1–17 Albion Terrace were supplied with water from a copious spring in the road in front of the terrace, the water of which was conducted by a brick barrel-drain between Nos. 7 and 8 and then flowed right and left to supply tanks in the ground behind each house. Snow followed the stoneware pipes and the leaden pipes to the pump in each back kitchen; then he followed the drains from the privy to the cesspool behind each house. Behind Nos. 1 and 7 the cesspools were quite full and the overflow drain from that at No. 1 was choked up. Behind No. 7 was a pipe for bringing surplus water from the tanks, communicating with a drain from the cesspool. All seventeen houses found the water disagreeable to drink. During the heavy rains of 2 August 1849, a drain burst at No. 8 and overflowed the kitchens.

Two days after the drain burst, there was the first outbreak of cholera, which was fatal in fourteen hours. At No. 8, a lady had choleraic diarrhoea, but recovered. The old lady at No. 6 died on 4 August. The lady at No. 3 by now suffered from diarrhoea – she was dead by 6 August. There were three or four other cases in the terrace, all fatal. More than half the inhabitants of the part of the terrace in which cholera prevailed were attacked by it, and upwards of half the cases were fatal.

The doctor giving evidence to the General Board of Health, Dr

Milroy, was an anti-contagionist. He attributed the mortality in Albion Terrace to three causes – an open sewer in Battersea Fields, 400 feet to the north of the terrace; odour from the sinks at the back of the houses; and an accumulation of rubbish in the cellar at No. 13. Milroy believed that cholera was caused by 'miasma'. He did not explain why hundreds of houses near the stinking sewer of Battersea Fields did not develop cholera; nor did the disease break out in the thousands of households where the kitchens flooded after rainstorms. The crucial fact was the connecting water-pipes between the houses.

The majority of the medical profession refused to accept Snow's findings. It was not until the cholera microbe was isolated and identified by Koch in 1883 that Snow's brilliant hunch – turning to circumstantial deduction – was proved.[12] Snow tried – and Chadwick too – to spread the gospel of cleanliness as a guard against waterborne disease: the creation of good drains; lodging houses for vagrants; public washhouses; quarantine for local visitors. The coal miners were the group who suffered more from cholera than any other – Snow urged that their work conditions be divided into four-hour shifts so that they did not need to use the coal pits as privies. In parts of London where the classes washed their hands – Belgravia – the rate of death by cholera was 28 in 10,000, compared with 186 per 10,000 in poorer districts. But, of course, such measures could not be introduced without control, and – as in the case of the Irish famine – the true laissez-faire liberal would, quite literally, prefer death to state interference. The lampoon in *Punch* in 1852 was only an inch away from reality:

> It is with pride, therefore, I repeat, that whatever may be the case in the country (where I regret to see the hateful Public Health Act seems to be extending its ravages), in London we are enjoying the enormous privilege of self-government, and that if the epidemic cholera should visit us again, we may confidently show him to his old haunts of 1832 and 1849, and so convince him that, in this free country, he, too, is at liberty 'TO DO WHAT HE LIKES WITH HIS OWN'.

Sewage and drainage provided the inspiration for one of Victorian art's most self-conscious efforts to make a social comment in paint: *Work* by Ford Madox Brown, a canvas begun in 1852 to celebrate the Public Health Acts inspired by Chadwick's campaigns, was not completed until 1863 – and not exhibited until 1865.[13] The idea came to the artist when he saw men digging in Heath Street, halfway up the Mount in Hampstead.[14] He painted it under the mistaken impression that they were constructing a fresh water supply, whereas they were in fact constructing new sewage pipes. The picture, a punctiliously executed and still recognizable London view in a blaze of summer sunshine, is heavy with symbolism. Poor ragged children, characters from Mayhew, scrabble in the dirt in the foreground; behind them loll the rich, their superfluity of wealth depicted by the groaning tray of the pastry-cook. To the left, posters on the wall suggest means of improvement for the working classes – 'The Working Men's College', the inspiration of F.D. Maurice, who stands to the extreme right of the picture, his gentle intelligent face curiously reposeful compared with the contemptuous tormented figure at his side, his teeth orange with tobacco smoke, his Diogenes-contempt for Benthamite society apparent in his grin. This is Thomas Carlyle. In the background of the picture are men carrying election posters for Bobus, the imaginary Benthamite parliamentary candidate lampooned in Carlyle's *Past and Present*. Carlyle's pessimism about Parliament and democratic processes had now become absolute. 'What can the incorruptiblest *Bobuses* elect if it be not some *Bobissimus*, should they find such?' – by which he means that the Victorian concept of an 'aristocracy of Talent', if guided solely by 'Midas-eared philosophies' of money-love, will only result in a society which is spiritually rotten and dead.[15]

Past and Present is in part an essay about the medieval chronicles of St Edmundsbury Abbey in Suffolk and in part a rant against the times. Is it possible to recapture the noble spirit of the Middle Ages without their unbelievable superstitions? 'Awake, ye noble workers, warriors in the one true war,' says Carlyle.[16] He looks to a time when 'the Inventive Genius of England, with the whir of its bobbins and billy-rollers shoved somewhat into the background of the brain, will contrive and devise, not cheaper produce exclusively, but fairer distribution of the produce at its present cheapness!'[17] He condemns utterly both the Mammon of the capitalists and the false idols of Christian revivalists – Puseyites, Catholics and others. The 'elect' in Carlyle's heaven are those who see life's earnestness.

Not a May-game is this man's life; but a battle and a march, a warfare with principalities and powers. No idle promenade through fragrant orange-groves and green flowery spaces, waited on by the choral Muses and the rosy Hours; it is a stern pilgrimage through burning sandy solitudes, through regions of thick-ribbed ice. He walks among men; loves men, with inexpressible soft pity, – *as they cannot love him.*[18]

Carlyle's search was for just that dignity and individualism which, we suggested, was Wordsworth's human legacy in *The Prelude*. His belief that the human race – and the British in particular – had gone astray at the time of the Industrial Revolution was widely shared, and his vision of a medieval world in which pure workers look to a hero as their leader – in the case of this book the incorrupt Abbot Samson – has many resonances. 'There is no longer any God for us!' he bleakly exclaims, but the truths embodied in the old Gothic ruins we see at St Edmundsbury would still have the power to revivify society.[19]

Much of this pattern of thought finds its echo in the Pre-Raphaelite Brotherhood – who were young enough to be Carlyle's sons. The 'brotherhood' began in 1848 at 83 Gower Street, when a group of art students vowed 'to produce thoroughly good pictures and statues'. Of the original seven, three members of the PRB – Dante Gabriel Rossetti, aged twenty, John Everett Millais, aged nineteen, and William Holman Hunt, aged twenty-one – went on to be famous artists. Other painters whom we think of as 'Pre-Raphaelite' – such as Ford Madox Brown himself – never in fact joined the Brotherhood, which was never a very tightly knit guild, and which dissolved with the years.

One sees the way in which these young painters set out to criticize the spirit of the age if one considers two of the most celebrated paintings of William Holman Hunt, companion pieces executed within two or three years of one another. *The Light of the World* was the most popular of all Victorian paintings. Engraved by W.H. Simmons and W. Ridgway, copied three times by Hunt himself, and photographically reproduced, it was an icon of faith in a time of doubt, the image of Christ which has hung in a thousand churches and chapels, and on millions of bedroom walls. (In 1905–7 the copy now hanging in Keble College, Oxford, toured the colonies and was viewed by hundreds of thousands who flocked to see it as a sacred object.)

The original models for the figure of Jesus were Christina Rossetti, pious poetess, sister of Dante Gabriel Rossetti, and a whey-faced young woman, herself a painter of some ability, called Elizabeth Siddal.[20] Her family had an ironmongering business in Southwark and, like her sister, she originally worked in dressmaking and millinery. She probably began to work as an artist's model because she herself aspired to be a painter. She both modelled and studied in Newman Street, just north of Oxford Street, where there were drawing schools and where both Ford Madox Brown and Rossetti had studios. To say that there were few opportunities of self-improvement for young female milliners in nineteenth-century London is an understatement. Possibly the first time we see her in a painting of note is in Hunt's *British Family succouring a Christian from the persecution of Druids*. In 1852 she posed in a bath for John Everett Millais as Ophelia, her father taking strong exception, since she might have died of hypothermia. Her face is one of the most haunting of nineteenth-century England. She was a tall woman, in an age which praised the petite. Her lower lip tucked beneath the upper 'as if it strove to kiss itself' – the words are Rossetti's, destined to fall in love with her and, years later when love had faded, to marry her. She had translucent skin, freckles, and abundant red hair.

Meeting her a little later than this – at London Zoo – Georgiana Burne-Jones recalled how 'Lizzie's slender elegant figure – tall for those days, but I never knew her actual height – comes back to me, in a graceful and simple dress, the incarnate opposite of the "tailor-made" young lady.' Georgiana recollected that when she went home with Lizzie:

> I see her in the little upstairs bedroom, with its lattice window, to which she carried me when we arrived, and the mass of her beautiful deep-red hair, as she took off her bonnet; she wore her hair very loosely fastened up, so that it fell in soft, heavy rings. Her complexion looked as if a rose tint lay beneath the dark skin, producing a more soft and delicate pink for the darkest flesh tones, her eyes were of a kind of golden brown – agate colour is the only word I can find to describe them – and wonderfully luminous.[21]

It is not entirely inappropriate that behind the bearded gentle figure of Hunt's *Light of the World*, standing with his lantern, and knocking to be let into our hearts, there should lurk those golden-brown eyes. If suffering could redeem, then poor Elizabeth Siddal would have redeemed us all.

It was widely assumed for years, on no evidence, that Gabriel Rossetti and Elizabeth Siddal were lovers in the modern way between 1851 – the year of their so-called 'engagement' – and their marriage in 1860. Rossetti's most learned biographer, Jan Marsh, has cast doubt on this and plausibly argues that Elizabeth's misery and frustration during these years, and her subsequent decline into drug addiction, were related to Rossetti's coyness, later neglect. Two years before he married, Rossetti probably lost his virginity, aged thirty, with a young woman who was cracking nuts in a bar in the Royal Surrey pleasure gardens, and who flicked a shell in his direction. This was Fanny Cornforth, another of the great icons of nineteenth-century painters, a large girl with abundant golden hair, pouting lips, a strong Cockney accent and a sensual laugh.

As when the last of the paid joys of love

wrote Rossetti, lest one should be in any doubt about how Fanny earned her living

> Has come and gone . . . and with one laugh of satiate bliss
> The wearied man one minute rests above
> The wearied woman, no more urged to move
> In those long throes of longing, till they glide
> Now lightlier clasped, each to the other's side
> In joys past acting, nor past dreaming of . . .[22]

Lizzie was an image to be adored with the heart and the eye. Sick worship can kill its object, as the lives and deaths of modern icons, pop or royalty, demonstrate. Siddal sickened and died of being worshipped as a dead Ophelia, an ethereal Beatrice. Her husband's most loving image of her was of *Beata Beatrix*, the soul of Dante's beloved, painted from memory after her drug-overdose death.

Vulgar, pouting, sensual and strong, Fanny was destined to be housekeeper and muse to Rossetti and his friends for years.[23] She was not, as it happens, the model for what I have called the companion-piece to Hunt's *Light of the World* − *The Awakening Conscience*. This was another 'stunner'; a teenage barmaid at the Cross Keys public house in Chelsea called Annie Miller.[24] Hunt first saw her when she was swabbing beer and spit off the pub floor − she was bare-foot and her red-gold hair fell over her shoulders in flaming ropes. She was soon part of the Pre-Raphaelite circle, affecting to be shocked by Rossetti's claim that 'women are so much nicer when they have lost their virtue', while loving the attention. She was one of the most successful artist's models of her day − much disapproved of by the would-be genteel Lizzie Siddal; she was the mistress of Rossetti and was for a time Hunt's fiancée.[25] In Hunt's view of Annie, communicated in his granddaughter's memoir *My Grandfather His Wives and Loves*, Annie is represented as a spirited girl who could be 'trouble': her attempts to get Hunt to educate her, marry her, find her a position are seen as potential blackmail – but how else was a girl who had grown up in a warren of rooms used as a brothel supposed to make a life for herself?

Carlyle, initially an admirer of Hunt's, had loathed *The Light of the World* – 'You call that thing a picture of Christ! . . . Don't you see that you're helping to make people believe what you know to be false, what you don't believe yourself?'[26] The icon of the Victorian Christ – who was in fact a 'wronged woman' with a beard – represented that side of the Christian religion which was most under threat as the Sea of Faith ebbed away in the nineteenth century: namely a belief in the Divine Saviour, the Man-God. This was the 'falsehood' in which Carlyle and so many Victorian intellectuals refused to believe.

To discard Christian morality, however, was altogether more difficult, and this is one of the reasons for the fascinating double standards which we find in so many individual Victorian lives, particularly where sex and money were in question. Christ had taught that you cannot serve God and Mammon. A state which modelled itself on the socio-economic ideas of Malthus, Ricardo and Bentham had enthroned Money, so it was not surprising they lost their sense of God. Chastity was no easier for Victorians than for anyone else, but their guilt-feelings about sex, combined with their attitudes to economics, could lead to those presumptions of possession, ownership, purchase of women by men against which feminism formed its inevitable Hegelian antithesis. (Hunt was in love with Annie Miller, wanted to marry her; but his very act of 'educating' her, treating her as a Pygmalion creation of his own, was in itself a form of purchase.)

Hunt's nickname among his friends was 'Mad' and his granddaughter tells us that he was a manic depressive – 'when in despair about his future or his work he would shut himself up in a poky bedroom above the studio and shiver with fear. He felt as if icy water were trickling down his spine. Alone in the dark, he raved, holding long noisy conversations with the Devil . . . He frequently lost faith in humanity and in his confused idea of God, but for him the Devil was always real.'[27]

The word 'Pre-Raphaelite' in popular modern parlance does not refer to particular painting techniques or attitudes to the Middle Ages. It means young women with pale faces, pouting lips and abundant hair. The hair was important; so important that hairdressing, for the first time in English history, came out of the private domain of the home.

Women who could afford to now went to hair-stylists – the styles varying much from year to year. No respectable woman wore her hair loose – which is what gives these loose-haired Pre-Raphaelite maidens so much of their erotic charm for the men who painted them and the men who bought the pictures. And in an age where everything was up for sale, the exporters and importers did not stop at hair itself. Great quantities of hair were imported into Britain from the European continent. The 'hair harvest' in Italy was an annual feature in poorer villages and 200,000 lb of hair were sold annually in the Paris markets, at a price of 10s. or 12s. per ounce – 20s. for really long hair. 'We saw several girls,' noted one observer at the Collenée market, 'sheared, one after the other like sheep, and as many more standing ready for the shears, with their caps in their hands, and their long hair combed out, and hanging down to their waists.'[28]

So valuable a commodity had hair become that *The Hairdressers Journal* reflected on 'one most unpleasant feature connected with the business' – the prevalence of hair thieves who would set upon young women whose head showed a valuable crop, shear them, 'and always kept on the safe side of the law, apart from the robbery of the hair'.[29]

In *The Awakening Conscience* Annie Miller's hair tumbles down her shoulders and back, as she rises from the lap of her roué lover. Just as Carlyle saw at once that *The Light of the World* was not so much an expression of faith as – something radically different – a seeking after false consolation, so *The Awakening Conscience* disturbs us with its jingle-jangle of confused imagery and – more – confused sexual feeling on the part of the artist. The picture is meant to depict the 'awakening conscience' of a kept woman who rises from her lover's knee listening to the promptings of morality. It is in fact soaked, like so many Pre-Raphaelite canvases, in *male* feelings about sex – purely mechanical lust clashing noisily with schoolboy masturbation – guilt masquerading as serious moral feeling. This, apart from their sheer technical skill, must explain the enduring popularity of the Pre-Raphaelite painters.

Yet however sheepish a man, and satirical a woman, must feel when standing in front of one of these paintings today, and whatever the final analysis of their aesthetic worth, how pleasing it is that these faces, these images, survive. Lizzie Siddal, Fanny Cornforth and Annie Miller's are among the best-known faces of the nineteenth century – far better known to us than the faces of most of the prime ministers or novelists or civil servants. Next to the Queen herself, theirs are the faces which survive.

The Awakening Conscience, depicting the world of the 'kept woman', awoke some raw nerves among the critics. Carlyle liked it as much as he'd despised *The Light of the World*. *The Morning Chronicle* denounced it as 'an absolutely disgraceful picture'. Although the middle classes liked tut-tutting over the moral dangers of fallen women and lapped up depictions of their decline in novels such as Mrs Gaskell's *Ruth*, they probably felt that Hunt's picture had lifted too many veils. Hunt, while painting it, had lectured Annie on the dangers of going down such a path herself. While she posed for him in an expensive gown, fine linen trimmed with hand-embroidered lace, Annie was supposed to be staring into the pits of hell as her whiskery admirer tries to hold on to her bottom. Many observers of her face must have seen, rather, a young woman with an eye to fun and prosperity ahead if she continues in her 'degrading temptation' – Hunt's words.

The young pre-Raphaelite Brotherhood found themselves to their good fortune with an eminent defender, none other than the greatest art critic of the age (or any age). Ruskin saw at once that the sexual aspect (confused as we may find it) of *The Awakening Conscience* is only part of the story. In his letter to *The Times* of 25 May 1854 expounding the picture's meaning, he sees that the hideous mid-Victorian furnishings speak of the moral destructiveness of new wealth brought in by the 'success' of industrial capitalism:

> There is not a single object in all that room – common, modern, vulgar (in the vulgar sense, as it may be), but it becomes tragical, if rightly read, that furniture so carefully painted, even to the last vein of the rosewood – is there nothing to learn from that terrible lustre of it, from its fatal newness; nothing there that has the old thoughts of home upon it, or that is ever to become a part of home . . .

In the coming decades, William Morris was to wage war on the factory-made ugliness of Victorian domestic interiors, and to expand, even more trenchantly than Ruskin himself, on the intimate connections between morality, as socially and privately understood, and design.

Ruskin in *Modern Painters* had been the great defender of Turner against production-line Academy painting rules. At first sight it might seem surprising that the man who could see Turner's smudgy seascapes as the highest painterly form would be able, at the same time, and so instantaneously, to form a generous judgement of the crystalline Pre-Raphaelite innovation. In both cases, what Ruskin recognized was that the fledgling Brotherhood, like the great old sun-worshipper, were devotees of truth, believers that painting must be true in two senses, both faithfully reproducing nature, and punctilious in its emotional integrity. When Ruskin first impulsively leapt to the defence of the PRB – against those who suspected them of being crypto-Catholics, or worse – he did not do so because they were his friends: 'Let me state, in the first place, that I have no acquaintance with any of these artists, and very imperfect sympathy with them. No one who has met any of my writings will suspect me of desiring to encourage them in their Romanist and Tractarian tendencies.'

As the 1850s unfolded, however, Ruskin's social contact with these much younger men was to have momentous effects in his personal history. In Rossetti's raffish ménage, Ruskin was to find the very opposite of the prim, well-ordered, rich suburban household of his sherry-merchant father – both so stifling and so inescapable. In Holman Hunt, Ruskin was destined to discover a deep and important artistic friendship. But it was Ruskin's acquaintanceship with John Everett Millais which had the first and explosive effect.

Millais, ten years Ruskin's junior and a year younger than Ruskin's wife Effie, had been a child prodigy, admitted to the Royal Academy Schools at the age of eleven. He was twenty-two years old when Ruskin first called on him, and tried to convert him to Turner. 'He believes,' Millais wrote, 'that I shall be converted on further acquaintance with his works, and that he will gradually slacken in his admiration.'[30] Neither thing happened, but the two men had soon become friends, constantly visiting one another, and travelling together. Millais, the painter of Romantic Scottish history, had never been north of the border; Ruskin, ethnically a Scot and devotee of Sir Walter, put right the difference by arranging a Highland tour. In July 1853 they arrived at Glenfinlas, Brig o' Turk, near Stirling. Here, by the falls, Millais set to work to paint a portrait of his hero.

Millais has fixed on his place – a lovely piece of worn rock, with foaming water, and weeds, and moss, and a noble overhanging bank of dark crag – and I am to be standing looking quietly down the stream – just the sort of thing I used to do for hours together – he is very happy at the idea of doing it and I think you [Ruskin's father] – will be proud of the picture – and we shall have the two most wonderful torrents in the world, Turner's St Gothard – and Millais's Glenfinlas.

The picture did get painted, in spite of a very wet summer and a persistent cold suffered by Millais and by Ruskin's wife. Ruskin himself, and his friend Dr Acland, who was for a while of the party, and Millais's brother were all blind to what took place during that wet summer: Millais and Effie Ruskin fell in love. As they did so, Millais discovered that Ruskin, great art historian, was a man who 'appears to delight in selfish solitude. Why he ever had the audacity of marrying with no better intentions is a mystery to me. I must confess that it appears to me that he cares for nothing beyond his Mother and Father, which makes the insolence of his finding fault with his wife (to whom he has acted from the beginning most disgustingly) more apparent . . .'[31]

These words were written to Effie's mother. The Gray family discovered that summer not only that for five years their daughter had suffered neglect and reproach, but that her marriage was unconsummated. On her wedding night, Ruskin (who was completely ignorant of sexual matters) had been unable to consummate – 'he had imagined women were quite different to what he saw I was,'[32] Effie afterwards recalled. Later he was to suggest other reasons – religion, a lack of desire for children – why the marriage should not be consummated, at least until she was twenty-five.

Gladstone said that if one had known all three parties as well as he had done – Ruskin, Millais, Effie – one would be unable to blame any of them. Let this be our line. Ruskin was one of the great men of the nineteenth century, Millais a prodigiously accomplished (if ultimately uninspired) painter, Effie an affectionate, intelligent woman who married Millais – when the Ruskin marriage had been set aside – and bore him eight children. Peace to them all! Vulgarians claim to know precisely what it was about the female anatomy that Ruskin had found so shocking. The truth is actually unclear. Geoffrey Hill is wiser to observe that:

> Ruskin's wedded
> incapacity, for which he has been scourged
> many times with derision, does not
> render his vision blind or his suffering
> impotent.[33]

Far more important than the details of Ruskin's private life were the areas to which his 'vision' and his 'suffering' took him. Having begun as a pioneer student of art history, he had come to see that aesthetic theory cannot be detached from social theory. Increasingly a follower of Carlyle, Ruskin came to see the nineteenth century as a nightmare era, and the core of this horror – the corollary of its materialism – was its loss of faith.

The weathercock mind of Harriet Martineau is a good guide here to the movement of middle-class opinion in the 1850s. Carlyle himself was impressed by her – 'far beyond expectation. She is very intelligent-looking, really of pleasant countenance . . . full of talk though unhappily deaf as a post, so that you have to speak to her through an ear trumpet.'[34]

By the early 1850s the *Punch* wag Douglas Jerrold was quipping, 'There is no God, and Harriet Martineau is his prophet.' Marian Evans could not dispel the impression of Harriet's *vulgarity* when she first met her, but after a few encounters they had become intimate friends.[35]

Miss Evans, known later to the world as George Eliot, was, from 1851 to 1855 (i.e. from the age of thirty-two to thirty-five), living in the household of the radical bookseller John Chapman, 142 The Strand. She had translated in 1844 the revolutionary Hegelian version of Christ's life, *Das Leben Jesu* of David Friedrich Strauss, and in 1854 she was to translate Feuerbach's *Das Wesen des Christenthums* (Essence of Christianity). Both books saw religion as a purely human construct and the Christian religion as an exercise in mythology.

Nowadays, such views are commonplace, even among the clergy. In the nineteenth century they were as revolutionary as George Eliot's unorthodox approach to sexual relations. (Escaping her love affair with Chapman, she lived for many years, even though he had a wife still living, with George Henry Lewes, journalist and German scholar, biographer of Goethe.) Attempts to see Christianity itself as based on a factual mistake – the mistake of supposing Christ to be divine – would inevitably provoke stormy reactions from those who believed that Western civilization itself was founded on the divinity of Jesus and the values he gave to the world. When a very mild, indeed quite possibly orthodox book about Jesus was published – *Ecce Homo* – Ashley decried it as 'the most pestilential book ever vomited, I think, from the jaws of hell'.[36] Great Christian that he was, Ashley's entire motive for establishing Ragged Schools, rescuing women and children from their servitude in mines and factories, was based on the premise that God Himself had chosen to come to Earth as a poor person of no reputation, thereby not merely redeeming the human race from sin, but teaching it that every child born into the world is made in God's image and likeness, every child has dignity and worth, and rights. Remove the truth of Christianity and, for a Christian of Ashley's generation, you have destroyed the very reason for believing in virtue itself. The Benthamite jungle has triumphed.

Unbelief had been taken for granted among the sophisticated Whiggish upper crust which Lord Ashley knew well and which he found so detestable. The Queen herself had been given in marriage to Prince Albert by the most Whiggish of her uncles, the Duke of Sussex, a bibliophile with a huge collection of bibles. In the margin of his *The Book of Common Prayer*, this royal duke had drawn a fatal hand, pointing at the Athanasian Creed, with the comment, 'I don't believe a word of it.'[37]

Ashley's description of the death of Lord Melbourne (his wife's uncle) in 1848 prepares us for how horrible the Darwinian vision of humanity was for a Christian man. 'He died and gave no sign; all without was coldness and indifference; God only can discover what was within. Those who stood around his bed were either ignorant or thoughtless . . . It was not the death of a heathen; *he* would have had an image or a ceremony. It was the death of an animal.'[38]

The cynicism of an educated or upper-class coterie threatened to become endemic among the middle class, thanks partly to the efforts of unbelievers such as Harriet Martineau and Marian Evans in *The Westminster Review*. It would be misleading to suggest that in the 1850s 'atheism was the religion of the suburbs', as G.K. Chesterton claimed was the case for the next generation. But unbelief was widespread. What is perhaps most striking to the eyes of hindsight about the responses to Evans's translations of Strauss and Feuerbach is not the hostile reactions of the few but the silent acquiescence of the many. Yet, enough people shared Marx's view that religion was the opium of the people for conventional believers to be worried. Doubt had been the unspoken secret of sophisticates in the 1820s and 30s, the modish belief of the periodical-reading middle classes in the 1850s. What if it spread to the working classes too? Was not the concept of deference, based on religion, the social glue which held society together? In Catholic France, maybe: in Orthodox Russia, perhaps. The agonized middle-class minds who thought like this (Darwin did – it was one of his chief motives for keeping his evolutionary theories secret so long) had not, as Mayhew had done, gone out and confronted working-class people in England. Had they done so, they would have found religious practice (except among Irish immigrants) all but unknown, and indifference to religious ideas all but total. Dr Pusey was right to say that in 'the alleys of London . . . the Gospel is as unknown as in Tibet'.[39]

Yet, on the surface of things, at least among the middle classes, Victorian England still looked as though it was a Christian culture. Churches were built, Christian books printed, in abundance. But there were signs of edginess. In academic spheres, both in England and America and on the continent, the obsession continued with Hegel, the 'true philosopher of the modern consciousness . . . The crisis that Hegel was striving to describe [was] the crisis of a civilisation that has discovered the God upon whom it depended to be also its own creation.'[40] A self-confident religion, such as Judaism in the great Rabbinic age, or Catholicism at the time of the schoolmen, enjoys vigorous debate with itself. It is not timorous. It might take sides, and argue with trenchancy, but it does not need to bully. The Victorian heresy-hunts should have warned those who conducted them that the ground they defended so loudly was sinking sand. Unable to face the arguments of Strauss or Feuerbach head-on, the hardline Orthodox chose to persecute the faithful innovators and original thinkers within their own midst. Two obvious examples spring to mind – those of George MacDonald and F.D. Maurice. Both, interestingly, came unstuck for the same sort of reasons – a refusal to gratify their more vindictive co-religionists by pretending to believe in Hell – and both at about the same period – in the years just before the outbreak of the Crimean War – a war which itself was entangled from the outset with religious fundamentalisms.

George MacDonald (1824–1905) – the poet and visionary, not the Methodist minister of the same name whose daughters had so remarkable a series of marriages and progeny* – prepared for the Congregational ministry, but his time at the Arundel Congregational Chapel was not a happy one. The congregation offered to lower his salary of £150 (he was by now married) unless he abandoned his declared belief in a future state of 'probation' for heathens: it was

---

* This, the *other* George Macdonald, the Wesleyan minister of Wolverhampton, was the father of Alice, who became Rudyard Kipling's mother; Georgiana, who married Edward Burne-Jones; Agnes, wife of Sir Edward Poynter; and Louisa Baldwin, mother of Stanley Baldwin the prime minister.

altogether too merciful, and too much like the Popish Purgatory for the chapel-goers of Arundel. This is the writer whose visionary novel *Phantastes* (1858) baptized the imagination of C.S. Lewis many decades later. MacDonald went on being a Christian – for twenty-first-century readers he must seem an embarrassingly Christian writer – but for his own flock he was a heretic.[41]

Through the influence of F.D. Maurice, MacDonald became a lay member of the Church of England. But Maurice himself was to suffer at the hands of the heresy-hunters. As a professor at King's College in the Strand, he had pointed out that the Greek word αἰώνιος (aiōnios) when applied to punishment, referred to the quality, not the duration. In *Theological Essays* (1853) he argued that to believe that future punishment would be endless was a superstition. He found himself being fiercely ejected from his professorial chair. Tennyson, who was a friend – Maurice was godfather to the poet's son Hallam – felt indignant on his behalf. With perhaps semi-consciousness of his own absurdity on this occasion, Tennyson wrote:

> Come, when no graver cares employ,
> Godfather, come and see your boy:
> Your presence will be sun in winter,
> Making the little one leap for joy.
>
> For, being of that honest few,
> Who give the Fiend himself his due,
> Should eighty-thousand college-councils
> Thunder 'Anathema', friend, at you;
>
> Should all our churchmen foam in spite
> At you, so careful of the right,
> Yet one lay-heart would give you welcome
> (Take it and come) to the Isle of Wight . . .[42]

Only a very edgy Christianity would try to discard two such obviously deep Christians as MacDonald and Maurice: but we watch this tendency of heresy-hunting going on all over the nineteenth century, in Protestant sects, in the Russian Orthodox Church that persecuted Tolstoy, in the Roman Catholic Church that invented the heresy of modernism and denounced almost every development of modern life from railways and electricity to democracy. Nineteenth-century

Christianity, unlike its equivalents in the twelfth century, could not adapt or absorb the new ideas. Fundamentalism, as it is now called, was a sure sign of uncertainty within the fold of faith, as well as being a reaction against abandonment of religious belief without its confines.

And one rather interesting symptom of this 'fundamentalism' was a revival of interest in the very sites where the Incarnate God had walked the Earth. Holman Hunt shared some of this fascination and set off for the Holy Land to paint *The Scapegoat* on 13 January 1854. All his friends tried to discourage him. 'If you go to the Holy Land now, you will paint things you will be ashamed of in seven years,' warned Ruskin.[43] What began as a sacred pilgrimage swiftly turned, as so much in Hunt's life did, to unintentional farce.

Hunt's passion for authenticity and accuracy demanded that the pure white goat, acquired with some difficulty in Jerusalem, had to be carried with the luggage on the perilous journey southwards to the Dead Sea. Today, tourists whizz through the desert in air-conditioned cars and buses to the shores of the Dead Sea. The former Sodom and Gomorrah, emblems of desolation as those biblical cities of the Plain destroyed by Jehovah in his wrath, are now health spas. For Hunt the journey was perilous. The desert had vultures in the sky, hyenas and bandits in the rocks, poisonous insects flitting through the air. The goat was not made of such strong stuff as Annie Miller (who had taken advantage of Hunt's absence to return to her old profession in London, forming an affectionate liaison with Lord Ranelagh – a viscount who enjoyed drinking champagne from her slippers at Bertolini's, a smart restaurant). It was too weak to walk. Exposed all day to the heat while Hunt captured the background – 'a God-forsaken area of awful and silent solitude, a Dantesque desolation shrouded in mist' – the unfortunate animal died.[44] The next goat had an easier task; Hunt painted it in the garden of his lodgings at Jerusalem, with its hoofs carefully embedded in a tray of Dead Sea salt. The two *Scapegoat* canvases are not among Hunt's best work. Rather than being heavy with religious symbolism, they simply look like goats, against some-what lurid backgrounds reminiscent of the visionary canvases of John Martin. Amusing as it is to contemplate Hunt's visit to Palestine, it is not chiefly about his interest in the place in the mid-1850s that history is concerned. As Ruskin reminds us, as the painter toiled in the desert of the Dead Sea, the cliffs above Balaclava and Sebastopol were white with tents. The Crimean War had begun.

*

Western preoccupation with Jerusalem and the Promised Land showed a mingling of political, religious and colonial interest which in part seems a bizarre reflection of the medieval Crusades, in part a dire harbinger of the still unresolved conflicts of the Middle East. As early as 1841, the Prussian minister Herr Bunsen succeeded in his diplomatic efforts to establish a joint Anglo-German bishopric in Jerusalem. The incumbent was to alternate – a Lutheran followed by an Anglican. If this seemed an attractive idea to the British government – whose head of state after all was the daughter and wife of those who had begun as German Lutherans – it filled the Oxford High Churchmen with theological fury. John Henry Newman gave it as one of his chief reasons for leaving the Church of England and joining that of Rome, this airy assumption by the politicians that a Lutheran 'bishop' could possibly be a bishop in the full Catholic and Apostolic sense of that term.[45]

Others could see that what was primarily in the minds of the statesman was not the theological definition of 'valid orders' so much as staking out territorial possession. If the Ottoman Empire, of which the entire Eastern Mediterranean formed a part, was weak and crumbling, then the Prussians and the English wanted to make it plain that they had a stake in the Holy City, even if nearly all the other bishops in the place – Latin, Greek, Copt, Armenian, Syriac, Maronite – would unquestionably consider the Northern European pretensions to episcopal status as questionable as their political interests. Ever since the 'Holy Land' was invented as a pilgrimage-centre by the Empress Helena in the fourth century, it had been the scene of acrimony and violence among the rival religious groups. Indeed a visitor from another culture, or planet, who did not know what the function of the 'Holy Land' was, could be forgiven for supposing that it had been devised specifically as a battleground, where worshippers of supposedly the same all-loving deity came to denounce, abuse and murder one another.

Throughout four centuries, it had been the task of the Ottoman sultans to preside over these unedifying squabbles, and to impose, for the sake of civil order, a culture of mutual tolerance on the inhabitants of their empire. In cities as various as Constantinople itself, Alexandria and Sarajevo, Christians, Jews and Muslims had been taught by their Turkish rulers that where religious difference was in question there really was only one political option: live and let live. Muslims and Jews were nearly always able to accept this, in relation to one another and to the Christians. The followers of Christ, however, while finding it possible to live at peace with their fellow monotheists of the Islamic or Judaic persuasion, could not always resist outbursts of violence against their co-religionists, and the inter-denominational hatred grew hotter, the closer they came to their most sacred shrines.

An agreement with the Porte (as the Imperial court at Constantinople was known) between the French government and the sultans, signed in 1740, gave the French 'sovereign authority' over the Holy Land. For this reason a silver star, adorned with the royal arms of France, was placed over the very spot where Christ had supposedly been born in Bethlehem. This precedent, of Western Roman Catholics, in the person of Franciscan friars, seeing themselves as the natural guardians of the holiest sites in Christendom, was a throwback to the disputes at the time of the Crusades. It did not alter the fact that apart from the shrine-guardians themselves in their humble brown habits, knotted with rope in imitation of Francis of Assisi, almost no Christians in the actual region were Roman Catholic, or even in communion with Rome. The huge majority were members of one or another of the autocephalous Orthodox churches − mainly Greek Orthodox, some Russian, Bulgarian, Romanian and others − or they belonged to one of the other Eastern churches such as the Armenian or Coptic traditions. To all these, the claim of French friars to look after buildings where nearly all the worshippers came from the Christian East was an outrage which mingled political with religious arrogance.

In 1852, Napoleon III wooed conservative opinion at home by asking for the keys of the church at Bethlehem to be returned to the French clergy. For a quiet life, the Sultan agreed, only to be greeted by protests from the Tsar. It gave Nicholas I the excuse to ask the Porte for certain guarantees, including the assignment to Russia of the general protectorate over Christians in the Turkish Empire.

There certainly seems a strong element of paradox, if not gross humbug, in an increasingly secular Protestant Britain choosing to involve itself in this dispute. Somehow, however, the British managed to persuade themselves that Russian expansionist ambitions were a direct threat to their interests. It was thought that the passage to India and the other trade routes would be in Russian hands if the Tsar continued to bully the Sultan. 'When the Czar makes Russian lakes of the Mediterranean and the Baltic, and holds Egypt and Syria, our merchants will rue their blind folly in declining to stop him while it was yet possible,' opined that newly self-appointed expert on war and foreign affairs, Harriet Martineau, in *The Westminster Review*, January 1854 – this was supposedly the voice of intelligent liberal opinion. The radical petit-bourgeois *Reynolds' News* denounced Prince Albert, whom it believed, rightly, to be urging moderation and negotiation on Lord Aberdeen's government. Aberdeen himself loathed the idea of war, and yet rumours began to circulate that he had imprisoned Prince Albert in the Tower for high treason while the Cabinet put itself on a war footing.[46]

'The state of *tension* is undoubtedly great, and scarcely to be long endured; but I persist in thinking that it cannot end in actual war,' Aberdeen had written, only in November 1853. 'War . . . would not only be an act of insanity, but would be utterly disgraceful to all of us concerned,'[47] *The Times* believed. Yet by Christmas, France and Britain had tied themselves into an alliance with Turkey which made war an inevitability. The Turks had been at war against Russia since October 1853. By the time the Russians sank the Turkish fleet at Sinope – it has been called the Pearl Harbor of the war – British public opinion saw it as a massacre, and the rest – the landing of a huge Anglo-French expeditionary force, headed for the Balkans and the Black Sea – looks like an inevitability.

14

The Crimean War

M. Alexis Soyer, *chef de cuisine* at the Reform Club in Pall Mall, was far from home. To be precise, he was riding by a new-built road and becoming spattered with mud as he descended from the 'Genoese heights', as they were called, to the harbour of the small Crimean port of Balaclava. At the bottom of the ravine, he found his way blocked by French and Sardinian wagons, unloading wine and shipping stores. It was a long while before M. Soyer got through the traffic jam to the Commissariat.

The reports of the Crimean campaign in *The Times* by William Howard Russell had been an historical innovation. Never before had the public heard such candid, or such immediate, descriptions of the reality of war, the bungling as well as the heroism, the horrible deaths by disease, as well as the bloody consequences of battle. Russell's reports of the complete inadequacy of hospital facilities, and the contrast between the woeful British treatment of the sick and wounded and the French military hospitals run by Sisters of Mercy, had prompted Florence Nightingale to pester the Secretary-at-War into allowing young women of good families to go as nurses to Scutari, on the shores of the Bosporus. Russell's legendary dispatches had also alerted Soyer to the knowledge that allied troops could do with some advice about food and provisions. The daily allowance for each English soldier was 1 lb of meat, 1 lb of bread, coffee, salt and sugar. Each man had to prepare this food himself, usually in difficult and – once the Crimean winter had set in – often in impossible conditions.

Soyer, as well as being a cook to the famous, and to the greatest of the new Liberal clubs, was also a man who cared for the unfortunate. He had taken soup kitchens to Ireland, where he had pioneered a practical stove – two steam boilers with a removable container on top. At the outbreak of the Crimean War, he saw that his stove would be invaluable as a way of providing hot food for large numbers of men encamped or entrenched in the field. He adapted many of his recipes from a book he had lately prepared to promote cheap and nutritious eating – *Shilling Cookery* (published 1854). One of his best inventions was a gigantic vegetable cake. Each hundredweight of vegetables was divided as follows – 20 lb carrots, 20 lb turnips, 10 lb parsnips, 15 lb onions, 20 lb cabbage, 10 lb leeks, with a pound of aromatic seasoning, made up of thyme, pepper, bayleaf and cloves, pulverized. This mixture was made into a dried cake of easily divisible portions, each portion steamed into life when needed.

It was to ensure the arrival of these cakes at Balaclava that Soyer now made his way to the Commissariat and approached Lord Raglan. The one-armed veteran of Waterloo and commander-in-chief of the British forces was known to Soyer and had asked the cook to improve the distribution of meat. 'Monsieur Soyer – anything you may propose or point out as an improvement will, so far as it is practicable, be carried out.'

As he galloped off towards headquarters, Soyer noted a group of officers gathered about a sort of gypsy tent by the side of the road. Many of these officers, as London clubmen, recognized the celebrated Frenchman and called out to him. From inside the tent, a stentorian female voice asked, 'Who is my new son?'

'Monsieur Soyer, to be sure,' said one of the officers. 'Don't you know him?'

A plump Jamaican woman, past her first youth, emerged from the tent.

'God bless me; my son, are you Monsieur Soyer of whom I heard so much in Jamaica? Well, to be sure! I have sold many and many a score of your Relish and sauces – God knows how many . . . I had a gross about ten days ago . . .'[1]

The great French cook alighted from his horse and the Jamaican lady invited him to drink a glass of champagne with her friend Sir John Campbell, the senior brigadier-general in the army, who after the battle of Inkerman was temporarily in charge of the 4th Division – destined to be killed in the assault upon the Great Redan, when he displayed 'a courage amounting to rashness'.[2]

The ample Jamaican lady was Mary Seacole, and she too, like M. Soyer, was in the Crimea because she had read Russell's newspaper reports. Sitting in Jamaica, she read of the battle of the Alma and the sufferings of the British soldiers, and realized that many of her army and navy friends, who had been stationed in the West Indies at some point in their careers, were now enduring the winter's cold in the Crimean peninsula. Since she was both a self-trained nurse and a boarding-house keeper, she knew that she could be of use.

Mary Seacole was one of the many extraordinary characters thrown into relief by the Crimean War. Born in 1807, she was the child of a Scottish army officer and a free – not liberated, but born free – black woman who herself ran a boarding house in Kingston, Jamaica. By her late forties, Mary Seacole had travelled all over the Caribbean: Nassau, Haiti, Cuba and Panama. It was a momentous decision, however, to cross the world to Russia as a freelance nurse-hotelier. When Seacole reached London, Florence Nightingale had already left for the Turkish capital. She went to the organization in London which was recruiting nurses for Miss Nightingale's hospital at Scutari (present-day Üsküdar) and was turned down flat, despite her obviously useful qualifications. She then applied to the managers of the Crimean Fund and was also turned down. It was a shattering moment. In Jamaica, where she had always been popular with British visitors and where her own father had been a white soldier, she had allowed herself to associate racial prejudice with the slave-owning citizens of the United States.

'Was it possible that American prejudices against colour had some root here? Did these ladies shrink from accepting my aid because my blood flowed beneath a somewhat duskier skin than theirs? Tears flowed down my foolish cheeks as I stood in the fast-thinning streets.'

This overweight woman of forty-eight years and of boundless energy and spirit did not allow rejection to dash her spirits. She made her own way to Constantinople, and presented herself in person at the famous hospital at Scutari. Many of the wounded soldiers recognized her, and called out cheery greetings to 'Mother Seacole'. Once again, however, she met with rejection. The nursing officer rebuked her with: '"Miss Nightingale has the entire management of our hospital staff, but I do not think that any vacancy . . ." "Excuse me, ma'am," I interrupted her with, "but I am bound for the front in a few days," and my questioner leaves me, more surprised than ever.' Undeterred, she engaged a Greek guide to escort her to the front. She called him Johnny – 'wishing however, to distinguish my Johnny from the legions of other Johnnies, I prefixed the term Jew to his other name and addressed him as Jew Johnnie'.[3]

Florence Nightingale's admirable hospital was several hundred miles from the Crimean peninsula. Mary Seacole did not pretend to Nightingale's formidable gifts of organization, but she was in the very front line. Her 'British hotel' in Balaclava was an important refuge. She served sponge cake and lemonade. 'They all liked the cake, poor fellows, better than anything else: perhaps because it tasted of "home".'[4] The 'ranks' who had a fear of hospitals felt more at ease with 'Mother Seacole' than in the Turkish field hospitals. She treated patients suffering from cholera and dysentery. She was attentive to their practical needs. Officers and men had permanent colds throughout the Crimean winters. There were no pocket handkerchiefs until Mary Seacole established her 'stores'.

> That berry-brown face, with a kind heart's trace
> Impressed on each wrinkle sly
> Was a sight to behold, though the snow-clouds roll'd
> Across that iron sky.
>
> (*Punch*)

Many Crimean veterans had cause to remember Mary Seacole gratefully. (She came back to live in London after the war, and prospered; during the 1870s she was a friend, and masseuse, of the Princess of Wales; she died in 1881.) Miss Nightingale's hospital was where you were taken if you were wounded or fell sick. Mary Seacole was on hand for the troops in the long months when nothing much appeared to be happening and, unlike some of the officers, she showed courage under fire. She saw the fighting on the Redan and witnessed the horrors left behind when they finally lifted the siege of Sebastopol.

Florence Nightingale's was a somewhat different story. Two-thirds of the total casualties in the Crimean War were from disease and hardship, not from battle – the French lost nearly 100,000 by the end, the British some 60,000, the Russians over 300,000.[5] Russell's dispatches had told a truly horrible story. Wellington's first concern for an army on the march – the physical wellbeing of the common soldier – might have been shared by his former comrade-in-arms, now British commander-in-chief, Lord Raglan, but the poor organization of his expedition led from the beginning to unnecessary hardships. Britain declared war on Russia on 28 March 1854. By 8 April expeditionary forces were landing at Gallipoli, that strip of Turkish coast which in a later war was to see so much suffering and slaughter. The British troops watched the French troops being supplied by a flotilla of steamers – bakeries, hospital tents, stores. All their supplies were rushed on shore by a well-organized baggage train. The British, suffering badly from the cold, had no beds to lie on and waited several days for blankets or food to arrive. Disease had already broken out in Malta on the way down. By the time the officer class arrived in their comfortable transport ships and steamers the Sea of Marmara resembled a regatta and disease was rampant. The allied armies were transported through the Bosphorus, many of them decamping on the eastern shore to the makeshift field hospitals at Scutari.[6] The healthy made for the coast at Bulgaria; it was at Varna, on this coast, that the allied command – Marshal St Arnaud, Lord Raglan and Admirals Hamelin (commander of French naval forces), Dundas, Lyons and Bruat considered the orders of the English Cabinet that they should make a descent in the Crimea and besiege Sebastopol. By now cholera had killed 7,000 French. In the villages surrounding Varna, Turks and Greeks perished 'like flies'. The hospitals were full before a single shot had been fired in battle. On 10 August a further calamity was a fire in the stores at Varna, destroying weapons, provisions and 19,000 pairs of shoes.[7]

'The conduct of many of the men, French and English, seemed characterized by a recklessness verging on insanity,' Russell wrote.[8] 'They might be seen lying drunk in the kennels, or in the ditches by the road-sides, under the blazing rays of the sun, covered with swarms of flies.' Those who survived cholera and the fire were severely weakened by 'fever, ague, dysentery and pestilence'. Apart from minor skirmishes (in which a young Russian officer called Lev Nikolayevich Tolstoy took part) in Silistria, there was not much to show for the first six months of the war.

Russell's dispatches had revealed a miserable, unheroic, ramshackle campaign presided over by old men. Lord Raglan, fluent in French as he was, and genial, had a distressing habit – born of his youthful years of serving under Wellington – of referring to the French as 'the enemy'. The inspector-general of fortifications, Sir John Burgoyne, was seventy-one years old. Four of Raglan's aides-de-camp were relations – Major Lord Burghesh, Captain Lord Poullet Somerset, Captain Nigel Kingscole and Lieutenant Somerset Calthorpe. The cavalry was commanded by some truly grotesque specimens of aristocratic eccentricity. The commander of the cavalry division, Lord Lucan, had purchased the command of the 17th Lancers for £25,000, but had left the army in 1837 – since when he had been on half-pay. The closest he had come to seeing military action had been skirmishes with the Irish peasants on his estates in County Mayo. He was fifty-four when the war broke out. His brother-in-law, the 7th Earl of Cardigan, was pushing sixty. The noisy, lecherous life of this upper-class hooligan had been punctuated by scandals. He had been acquitted (by his peers) for fighting a duel in 1841; his command of the 11th Hussars (for which he had paid £40,000) had made him many enemies both among his officers, with whom he quarrelled regularly in the mess, and his men, who suffered merciless floggings.[9]

These were the men who joined the survivors (10,000 Englishmen died of cholera at Varna) for the invasion of the Crimea in September 1854, one of the most extraordinary armadas to set sail in the whole history of warfare. They were pursued by a flotilla of sightseers, well-wishers and busybodies, but none were more important than William Howard Russell, since he revealed to the world the vulnerability and the sheer crass inefficiency of the supposedly great powers. The newspaper reports which prompted the charitable impulses of Alexis Soyer and Mary Seacole to rush to the aid of the British were also capable of revealing, for example, to disgruntled sepoy officers of the native Indian regiments, reading flyblown, yellowed copies of *The Times* in Kanpur and Lucknow, that the British Lion was not necessarily invincible.

But journalism is a curious art. Russell wanted to tell the truth, but he also wanted to tell a story, and a story, if it contains fighting, must have heroes. The public demanded it. Since European literature began, setbacks and defeats were capable of acquiring heroic status just as much as victories. Britain had not been involved in a European war for forty years, and in the pages of *The Times* each morning they found the opportunity for a modern *Iliad* to be played out for them. Unlike the Napoleonic Wars, this one was happening a safe distance away. Everybody was gripped by it. If a plague-ridden army commanded by whiskery, bottle-nosed old roués made unlikely material for heroic literature, the public was perfectly prepared to hear and see what it chose. The invasion of Russian soil was followed avidly week by week. In the Birmingham Oratory, John Henry Newman established a room which, though geographically in the centre of an ugly industrial city, has the remote calm of Oxford in the 1830s. His Oratorian confrères have left the room as it was when he died in 1890. You can still see there the maps cut out from *The Times* with which he followed the Crimean campaign. He gave lectures on the Turks to his parishioners (*Lectures on the History of the Turks*, 1854). Such enthusiasm could be found in all classes in Britain, and all manner of households.

The Silistrian skirmishes of the summer did not have the stuff of which good stories are made. For one thing, it could not be disguised from anyone that, while the English and French troops languished from heatstroke, alcohol and disease, it was largely through the skill of the Turkish army that the Russians had been kept at bay in their Balkan incursions. Russell's narrative pace quickens once the troops had disembarked in the autumn of '54.

The Russian commander, Prince Menshikov, had about 80,000 men deployed in the peninsula. The allied troops numbered 26,000 British (with 66 guns), 30,000 French (with 70 guns) and 5,000 Turks. The first major engagement was when Menshikov established himself with some 40,000 men and 100 guns on the rising ground to the south of the river Alma. The Russians failed to stop the allied advance. After the battle of the Alma, Russell notes, 'there was a sickening, sour foetid smell everywhere, and the grass was slippy with blood'. About 5,000 died, though Raglan listed only 326 casualties, the French 60 and the Russians 1,755. *The Times* had never sold so many copies, and prophesied an early victory and the fall of Sebastopol long before Christmas.

Within the three weeks that followed, the British 'lost as many of cholera as perished on the Alma'.[10] It was on 25 October that they fought the most celebrated battle of the campaign, that of Balaclava. While the Alma had been an allied victory, and Balaclava a Russian one, there was no doubt which made the greater appeal – just as, in a much later war, the British retreat at Dunkirk in 1940 went on being celebrated for decades.

The battle of Balaclava fell into two distinct phases. At first, an unequal artillery duel between Russian and Turkish guns (18-pounders vs. 12-pounders) flew across the valleys above Balaclava. Overlooking the South valley were Lucan's cavalry division and Campbell's 93rd Highlanders. 'Remember there is no escape from here. You must die where you stand.' The Highlanders accordingly opened fire. 'The ground flies beneath their [the Russians'] horses feet: gathering speed at every stride, they dash on towards that thin red streak topped with a line of steel,' as Russell wrote. The Heavy Brigade moved westwards to help the Turkish guns. (Tennyson's own recording of his poem on the charge of the Heavy Brigade is in its way as impressive as his more famous lines on the Light Brigade and

Dahn the hill, dahn the hill, thahsunds uv Rooshians

nicely demonstrates his Lincolnshire vowels.) It was an extraordinary piece of gallantry, 300 mounted men of the 6th Inniskilling Dragoons, the Royal Scots Greys and the 5th Dragoon Guards and the 4th Royal Irish Dragoon Guards, charging with swords at heavy field guns. 'Some of the Russians seemed to be rather astonished at the way our men used their swords. It was rather hot work,' one officer recollected.[11] The charge of the Heavy Brigade was a moderate success, leading to a withdrawal of the Russians into the North valley to regroup behind a battery of eight artillery pieces.

The first phase of the battle was over and had ended in stalemate. The Russians could still threaten Balaclava. Raglan wished the cavalry to advance and reclaim the heights. He sent orders to Lucan to this effect, promising infantry support. Raglan wanted Lucan to move forward at once. Lucan thought he should await the arrival of the infantry before beginning a two-pronged assault. The infantry were slow in coming. Through his telescope Raglan could see the Light Brigade dismounting and idling in the mid-morning sun. He told the nattily dressed Airey (who had caused a sensation in Varna by sporting a red flannel suit) to repeat the orders to advance. Airey scribbled on a piece of paper: 'Lord Raglan wishes the cavalry to advance rapidly to the front – follow the enemy and try to prevent the enemy carrying away the guns. Troop Horse Artillery may accompany. French cavalry is on your left. – Immediate.'

The note was given to the ADC, Captain Nolan, who was a hothead who had been 'talking very loud against the cavalry . . . and especially Lucan'. Nolan rode to Lucan and told him to attack at once. No infantry support had arrived, and it was not clear in which precise direction Raglan wished the cavalry to ride. As Nolan arrived with his ambiguous order – to be greeted with Lucan's 'Attack, sir! Attack, what? What guns, sir?' – Lord Cardigan sent his ADC, Lieutenant Henry Fitzhardinge Maxse, to point out that 'the heights which flanked the valley leading to the Russian battery of heavy guns were covered with artillery men and riflemen'.

Nolan had not completely finished his unintentionally disastrous work. He asked permission to ride in the charge with the 17th Lancers. As the Light Brigade trotted forward, he suddenly galloped ahead, yelling and waving his sword. He was the first of 107 men and 397 horses who would be mown down by Russian guns in the next twenty-five minutes. The Light Brigade rode down into the valley, engaged the waiting Russian cavalry, and – there being no way out of the valley on the other side – they were obliged to turn round and once more run the gauntlet of deadly gunfire. A Russian cavalry officer remarked, 'It is difficult, if not impossible, to do justice to the feat of these mad cavalry, for, having lost a quarter of their number and being apparently impervious to new dangers and further losses, they quickly reformed their squadrons to return over the same ground littered with their dead and dying. With such desperate courage these valiant lunatics set off again, and not one of the living – even the wounded – surrendered.'

When Prince Albert was being 'broken in' by the landed classes, he surprised them all by his preparedness to make daring jumps when hunting with the Pytchley and the Quorn. Cardigan had been his host at Deene Park in Northamptonshire, magnificent hunting country. The celebrated reaction of the French Marshal Bosquet to the Charge – *'C'est magnifique, mais ce n'est pas la guerre'* – was totally accurate. Cardigan was showing himself more a master of foxhounds than a soldier in this magnificent display of bravado.[12] Raglan was furious with him. Lucan has generally been held responsible for the blunder. 'You have lost the Light Brigade,' Raglan curtly told him that evening. He was sacked a few months later. Cardigan had invalided himself out of the war by then – he returned to England to the strains of 'See, the conquering hero comes'. He was painted demonstrating the Charge of the Light Brigade on a plan of the battlefield to the royal family. (When she heard of the extent of Cardigan's depravities – Deene Park little different in atmosphere from a bordello – the Queen had herself painted out of this canvas.) But both men remained in the army – Lucan to become a field marshal and Cardigan the inspector-general of cavalry.

If this had been a serious war – that is, had there been any need for British and French troops to be in the Crimean peninsula (defending, for instance, their own national security) – then the Charge of the Light Brigade would have been a catastrophe. Raglan now could not risk his two infantry divisions in an attempt to move the Russian forces from Causeway Heights; he dared not risk losing possession of the port of Balaclava and being cut off from the sea. The siege of Sebastopol could not get going until the brisk infantry victory at Inkerman had brought about the worst battle casualties of the war, on 5 November. (*'Quel abattoir!* – What a slaughterhouse! – as one French officer observed.[13])

By then the winter had set in, and many seriously wondered whether the allied troops, with totally inadequate summer clothes and provisions, could survive the months of dark, wet and cold on those bleak uplands. But Russell had written one of his great journalistic set-pieces – 'A more fearful spectacle was never witnessed than by those who, without the power to aid, beheld their heroic countrymen rushing to the arms of death . . .'[14] And, reading it over his breakfast porridge at Farringford, Freshwater Bay, Isle of Wight, the poet laureate could be moved to write lines about 'the noble six hundred', one of those rare poems known by those who do not read or know poetry. He had penned it within 'a few minutes' of reading *The Times*.[15] Though Tennyson, in the Epilogue to his poem about the Heavy Brigade, was to assert that

> Who loves war for war's own sake
> Is fool, or crazed or worse;

the public appetite for this war could not be explained by any simple political or religious 'cause'.[16]

An earlier generation of historians was able to read the history of the nineteenth and twentieth centuries as a diplomatic carve-up, organized by the chief ministers and ambassadors of the European powers. One of the most stylish of such accounts was A.J.P. Taylor's *The Struggle for Mastery in Europe 1848–1918*, a work published half a century ago. By this view of events, the Crimean War had nothing to do with the possession or administration of the Holy Places, and not much to do with the administration of the crumbling Ottoman Empire. It was entirely a struggle between the European superpowers, and could be seen as the ominous first stage in a tragedy which would reach a climax on the battlefields of Flanders and Northern France in 1914–18, a fiery denouement thirty years beyond that as the Russians pounded and bombed their way into the smouldering ruins of Berlin. This view of history sees the aims of Russia as opportunistic, wishing to establish its influence in the Christian East, clashing with the revived opportunism of Napoleon III and 'the gang of Bonapartist adventurers who ran France'.[17] Napoleon III had no wish to overwhelm the Russians, merely to check their power, in order to bring them into an alliance with France against the emergent powers of Prussia.

The rivalry between France and Germany, erupting into the Franco-Prussian war and all its cataclysmic consequences, is not something which hindsight can ignore. The defeat of Russia in the Crimean War, if seen in this light, is the crucial event of mid-nineteenth-century European history. Had Russia won, and established a claim on the Ottoman Empire: had she, in effect, taken over the running of the Eastern Empire: had Napoleon III been chucked out, and Palmerston's foreign policy, based on a breezy assumption that Britain allied itself with 'liberal' régimes, been discredited . . . From such unfinished and fruitless speculations, historians can play a parlour-game of what-ifs and might-have-beens. No Napoleon III, no power games in Europe, but a developing recognition of the economic and political strengths of the Prussian Empire . . . Might this have led to the sort of federalism and spirit of European reconciliation which made the closing decades of the twentieth century so much more peaceful than those of the nineteenth? A Europe in which there was no First World War, no Russian Revolution, is tragically unimaginable for us.

Such speculation is painful in special ways for every and each European nationality. Undoubtedly for the Russian patriot, then as now, there must be bafflement not only at the cynical secularism of the French and British governments at the time, but at the secularism of the historians such as Taylor who see the war as something effectively determined and promoted by realpolitik. The more speedily they took leave of the faith and ideas of pre-industrial, pre-Enlightenment life, the more the Victorians loved faking up the externals of the Middle Ages. For each individual medieval 'revivalist', the task of bringing 'back' Gothic architecture, or some other aspect of medieval art, usually involved some protest against contemporary politics, or materialism. This is true of Pugin, Holman Hunt, D.G. Rossetti; it will be even truer, as the century wears on, of William Morris and his associates. Carlyle's great treatise on the medieval ruins and medieval life of St Edmundsbury, *Past and Present*, was their key text because it touched on a matter not simply of concern to aesthetes but which was still a fact of political life. The aesthetic topsy-turvydom of Gothic railway stations, or a neo-medieval Parliament building in which to pass further reform bills, was matched by the cussed and awkward survivals from an actual past clashing miserably with an industrially greedy, culturally blind present.

It was a literal and horrible truth that the Irish had suffered in the nineteenth century a famine of thirteenth-century proportions. By a similar token, neither the secularists of the Russell/Palmerston breed nor their mid-twentieth-century historians could begin to understand the extent to which the Orthodox religion was still a living force for the majority of Russians, and Slavs generally. The Enlightenment Petersburg liberals who had befriended Pushkin or who in a later generation were depicted in the novels of Turgenev were a tiny minority in the Empire. In many respects the Slavophil conservatives in Russia were right to think the influence of liberalism would destroy the whole fabric of Russian life: certainly this was what Dostoevsky came to believe as the century advanced.

But one of the most dismaying things about the Crimean War was the lack of comprehension, ideologically speaking, between the two sides. Kinglake, whose history of the *Invasion of the Crimea* fills many volumes, is best known for his earlier volume *Eothen*, one of the most imaginatively successful travel books, evoking the life and texture of the Near East and the Levant. Few Englishmen possessed Kinglake's ability to understand alien cultures – Russian piety for example. At the beginning of his immense war chronicle he told his readers: 'When the Emperor of Russia sought to gain or to keep for his Church the holy shrines of Palestine, he spoke on behalf of fifty millions of brave, pious, devoted subjects, of whom thousands for the sake of the cause would joyfully risk their lives. From the serf in his hut, even up to the great Tsar himself, the faith professed was the faith really glowing in his heart and violently swaying the will.'[18]

The Times, urging moderation on the government before the Aberdeen coalition found itself at war, could insist that 'a European war over the tomb of our Saviour would be too monstrous in the nineteenth century'.[19] Paradoxically, as things turned out, *The Times* itself, with its newly invented Applegarth presses, rolling out 200 copies per minute of Russell's reports, was able to make this the first war in history which could be treated by a large public as a spectator sport.

And the British loved it. Their love of that war is reflected in almost every town in England to this day, where old men in 'cardigans' or young men in balaclava helmets can still be found in Alma Villas and Inkerman Crescent. The Second World War, whatever the rights and wrongs of how it might have been avoided, was fought – as most British people continue to believe – for high moral motives. It was a war which had to be won, to defend European freedom – or so it is said. Yet surprisingly few Dunkirk Squares or Dresden Terraces have resulted from it. We don't wear Montgomery berets, though some of us still possess Raglan overcoats. No British generals or admirals of the Hitler war were invested with the Homeric status which the Victorians gave to the quarrelsome and incompetent old men who led the Crimean invasion.

Once it was clear that the 'victory' of Inkerman notwithstanding, the Russians and their oldest ally, the winter, would insist on a long struggle, there was an overwhelming case for a negotiated settlement to the war. Such a flat outcome to the story was inevitably going to come, but not until the Peace of Paris in 1856, and many lives were to be lost before then. Tsar Nicholas himself died on 2 March 1855, and perhaps if his successor Alexander II had not been bound to appease patriotic fervour at home, many of the miseries of 1855 could have been avoided – the dreadful sufferings during the siege of Sebastopol, the 'forgotten war' afterwards, the fighting in Armenia (Kars and Erzerum) during that grim year. *The Times* by its repeated exposures of British inefficiency and weakness was the classic example of exercising 'power without responsibility'. Russell's dispatches could work up public rage, most notably during the terrible winter of 1855, about the absence of provisions and supplies. It could find no shortage, moreover, of Guilty Men – sometimes suggesting that The System itself was to blame, sometimes finding a scapegoat – Raglan and his staff officers, Lord John Russell, Aberdeen. At the same time, the newspaper created a public hunger for a satisfactory end to the story, and that end could only be outright military victory. Perhaps this is why the war created such peculiar alliances. Christian socialist F.D. Maurice believed that *The Times* was horribly wicked, that the press was killing the nation's mystic unity. Extremists of left and right, however, could unite in Russophobia.[20]

Marx's obsessions with the dangers of Pan-Slavism filled many of his articles at this time. Read today, they seem indistinguishable from Hitler's comparable fears in *Mein Kampf* – written seventy years later, but reflecting the same dread that the 15 million Slavs subject to the Austrian emperor – or in Hitler's day, living in the scattered remnants of the Austro-Hungarian empire – would unite against the rest of Europe. 'Panslavism is now, from a creed, turned into a political programme, with 800,000 bayonets to support it.'[21] Like Hitler, Marx saw the political structures of Europe as essentially fragile, transitory. The constant of European history was racial difference, the eternal struggle which had been conducted since Attila's warriors first surged over the icy plains of Northern Europe, between Slav and Teuton. Marx influenced Hitler to believe that there was a new player in the power struggle – and that the war would raise again 'a sixth Power of Europe': the Revolution.[22]

One aspect of Marx's thinking on the Eastern Question which has puzzled students of his writings was his paranoid conviction that Lord Palmerston, outwardly the most jingoistic of government ministers, and replacing Lord Aberdeen as prime minister at the darkest hour of the war, was in fact a Russian spy. Marx had been convinced of this theory by reading the voluminous writings of an independent and endearing Tory called David Urquhart. Marxists are coy about this fact – particularly Russian Marxists – since for reasons which do not need to be explained it embarrasses them that the philosopher who inspired the Russian Revolution should have been personally violently anti-Russian.

Urquhart, from 1795, had travelled in the Mediterranean in the lifetime of Lord Byron. Like Byron, he knew Albania well, and in his twenties he spent much time in Constantinople, where he went native, smoked a hookah and became a real expert in Turkish grammar and literature. He was first secretary of the British embassy there in the 1830s but did not get on well with the career diplomats. The Turks loved him, and called him Daoud Bey. From the 1830s he was bombarding the Duke of Wellington with evidence of Russian expansionism and Russian designs on the Ottoman Empire. He was sacked in 1837 at the instigation of Palmerston, which was when his obsession with Palmerston (and his belief that he was a paid agent of the Russians) began. When he came back to England he stood for Parliament as an independent. Like other independent-minded Tories he had sympathies with the Chartists, despite believing them to have been infiltrated by foreign powers. His paranoia did not extend to the Catholic Church however. Though a lifelong Protestant, he believed that the Papacy was 'the only moral force in Europe'. His house in Rickmansworth, decorated with rich Iznik tiles and heavy with the odours of Latakia, was a Turkish haven and he campaigned (semi-successfully) for the introduction of Turkish baths in England. He wore Turkish dress at home, but appears to have been heterosexual – or at least sufficiently heterosexual to marry at the age of fifty-nine. (One of his sons was the legendary Oxford don Sligger Urquhart, outside whose windows an inebriated Evelyn Waugh was to chant, 'The Dean of Balliol wears women's clothes.')[23]

He believed that Palmerston was utterly corrupt and when an MP, Urquhart tried to have Pam impeached: 'England thought herself to be rich because great masses of wealth were accumulated into the hands of the few, whereas she was poor in all real wealth and was, moreover, smitten with the sore distress of corruption and blindness. Material poverty matters little. A nation may be poor in gold and possessions and yet, like Spain and India and the East, in fact all the countries where the old traditions still linger, may be not only healthier, but richer than England.'

Pilgerstein, as Queen Victoria and Prince Albert nicknamed

Palmerston, embodied for Urquhart, as for Marx, all that was most corrupt about Victorian England. Resembling one of the pomaded old lechers in Thackeray's seedier pages, he was in fact an incompetent, not to say near hopeless, war leader when he succeeded to the premiership. Though louder and more vulgar than Lord Aberdeen he was no more decisive. 'I cannot say we have improved in order and regularity under the new chief,' said Sir Charles Wood. Gladstone's description of the first Cabinet meeting with Pam in the chair was equally devastating. 'It was more acephalous than ever; less order, less unity of purpose: Charles Wood had twice cried, "*Will* the Cabinet decide *something* upon *some* point?" P thought he had appeared more éveillé than usual, had taken no lead.'[24]

Though ingenious conspiracy theorists might think this indicated that Palmerston was cleverly contriving that his secret paymasters the Russians should win the war, the likelier explanation for his behaviour in Cabinet is that he was seventy years old – and more than half tight much of the time: as was that other old Harrovian who became a wartime prime minister when full of years, Winston Churchill – though Palmerston was as old at the beginning of the Crimean War as Churchill had been at the end of *his*.[25] There are obvious points of comparison – both aristocratic leaders distrusted by their own kind, both politically indefinable in terms of party, both swept to power in the teeth of objections from the reigning monarch, and from the political classes, because of their populism and their rapport with that indefinable person the ordinary Englishman. There were also very obvious differences. Churchill spent the greater part of his grown-up life in political exile. He was a great war leader but by general consent he allowed the Americans and the Russians to bamboozle him at Yalta. Palmerston was not a great war leader but he was a consummate diplomat and international wheeler-dealer. (One does not use the word diplomat here to suggest tact – but he had trod the stage of international politics for nearly half a century by the time he was prime minister and he knew how to dress up a negotiated settlement to the war – the treaty of Paris of 1856 – as if it were an out-and-out victory.)

Aberdeen's coalition had collapsed at the beginning of 1855 and the Queen had made heroic struggles against the inevitable – a Liberal government with Palmerston as prime minister. She asked Lord Derby to form another administration with a Conservative minority in the Commons; Derby offered Palmerston the post of secretary for war and Pam's reply was that he could only serve if Clarendon – Derby's deadliest political foe – were made foreign secretary. When the idea of a Derby government instantly collapsed, the Queen summoned Lord Lansdowne, but he told her he was too old. (Four years older than Palmerston – the two were rival candidates as MP for the University of Cambridge as long ago as *1806* – when Byron, another Harrovian, in 'Hours of Idleness' had mocked them.)

Then Victoria asked Lord John Russell, who had regarded Palmerston as a political rival for decades, but he found on consulting colleagues that they would not serve under him again – though he was destined to become prime minister one last time when Palmerston died in the office in October 1865. The Queen begged Clarendon to serve under Russell – 'Lord John Russell may resign, and Lord Aberdeen may resign, but I *can't* resign. I sometimes wish I could,' she complained.[26]

There was nothing for it. On 4 February 1855 Palmerston was summoned to Buckingham Palace and invited to form a government. The Queen's objections to him were based partly on deep personal revulsion. Palmerston's wife, when Lady Cowper, had been a much-trusted lady-in-waiting in the dear days of Lord M., but Lord Palmerston had disgraced himself, when staying at Windsor Castle, by a 'brutal attack on one of the ladies' – in effect, a rape. The Queen and Prince Albert had also fallen out with Pilgerstein in 1846–7 when they discovered that he had been sending dispatches to Portugal and taking sides in the civil war without consulting his sovereign.

For others, however, Palmerston's arrival in the premiership was what the middle classes had been longing for, during the previous year of drift and muddle. The man who settled the Don Pacifico matter by blockading Greek ports with gunboats would succeed in 'seeing off' the autocratic Russians. Peter Bayne, a journalist writing thirteen years later, described the feelings of 'the ordinary Englishman' when he heard that Palmerston had become prime minister: 'When we were at war with Russia and when the nation, after trying statesman after statesman, continued in the distressing consciousness that the administration lacked vigour, the man who, for a quarter of a century, had been checkmating the policy of Russia was naturally called for.' The importance here was the perception of the Palmerston 'myth', since as Urquhart and others would wish to say, Pam had been if anything pro-Russian in the years leading up to the war. But – as Bayne told the readers of *St Paul's Magazine* – Palmerston was the man to whom the business of war could be committed, and in whose hands the name of England was safe.[27]

Palmerston was adept at self-promotion. The peace-loving free-trader John Bright could complain that 50,000 men died to make Palmerston prime minister, but with his eye to the populace, the war prime minister could make even this objection seem unpatriotic. Bright, he replied, reduces everything to pounds, shillings and pence. If confronted with the threat of imminent invasion, Bright would 'sit down, take a bit of paper, and would put on one side of the account the contributions which his Government would require from him for the defence of liberty and independence of the country, and he would put on the other the probable contributions which the General of the invading army might levy upon Manchester'.[28]

Sir Henry Layard was a radical MP with a fervent anti-Russian view who had been in the Foreign Office (like Urquhart he had been attached to the British embassy in Constantinople and was regarded by Palmerston as a clever middle-class upstart). His speeches about the inefficiency of the British aristocracy, and their bungles in the Crimea, made a great impression and were cheered on by *The Times*. Palmerston's instinct was to silence Layard by giving him a post in the government, but the Queen was so horrified by his attacks on the aristocracy that she refused. Layard proposed sending MPs to the Crimea who should have the power to overrule and dismiss incompetent commanders. 'I have no doubt that a Cavendish in the Cabinet is a very important thing, but the public think more of 20,000 lives than they do of a Cavendish.' However true this seems in retrospect, the popular mood at the time was against Layard and behind Palmerston.

The Crimean War seems like the archetypal example of Cobden's view that war is an extended form of aristocratic sport. Certainly, the notion of aristocratic superiority would have been hard to sustain in its aftermath. It is probably significant that Samuel Smiles's *Self-help* failed to find a publisher before the war, and became the ultimate self-defining bestseller of the mid-Victorian age when it was published at the end of the decade.[29] But England was and is a very odd place. Those Samuel Smiles businessmen and inventors and manufacturers who appeared to be so much at odds with the aristocrats of Lord John Russell's generation did not invariably establish themselves as democrats and men of the people The tendency was that they aspired to use their money to send their children to the same schools as the aristocrats, to acquire large houses and estates, just like those of the old upper class, and, where possible, to marry into it. 'What is most coveted in this country,' said *The Times* in September 1851, 'more than wealth, more than talent, more than fame, more even than power, is aristocratic position, to obtain or improve which other things are only sought as the means.'

Palmerston, as long ago as 1831, giving a very cautious support to Lord John Russell's Reform Bill, had said that the English people are not fond of political change. 'They formed a striking contrast to their neighbours on the Continent . . . who boasted of the newness of their institutions, while the English were proud of the antiquity of theirs.'[30] A quarter of a century later, Palmerston could turn round Layard's complaints against the atrocious bungling of upper-class army officers in the Crimea and create a picture of aristocratic heroism which made 300 MPs stand up and cheer:

> Talk to me of the aristocracy of England! Why, look to that glorious charge of the cavalry at Balaklava – look to that charge, where the noblest and wealthiest of the land rode foremost, followed by heroic men from the lowest classes of the community, each rivalling the other in bravery, neither the peer who led nor the trooper who followed being distinguished the one from the other. In that glorious band there were the sons of the gentry of England; leading were the noblest in the land, and following were the representatives of the people of this country.

The disastrous cavalry charge has become a political template. The English, to this day, are capable of holding directly contradictory views of the class system. On the one hand they believe in egalitarian notions of no one being better than another just because he is born rich or noble, and they take vindictive delight in the prospect of royal or noble personages whom they dislike being 'brought down a peg'. On the other hand, the *same people* will flood into the Mall to cheer the Queen or pay money to go round some ducal palace – those such as Chatsworth which contain a real live duke being a much greater tourist attraction than those which are mere museums. 'Their neighbours on the continent' might well form into two camps – the haters and the lovers of aristocracy. In England they are one and the same.

Palmerston appealed to this somewhat brutal schizophrenia by himself being an odd mixture of populism and hauteur, insensitivity and genuine good-hearted altruism. The only obvious political belief which you can trace from his long career is the conviction that he had the right to be in the government, whether it called itself Tory, Whig, Peelite or Liberal. Praed had mocked him as a sort of political Vicar of Bray ('I'm not a Tory now!') when he had thrown himself behind the Reform Bill. His ambivalence was unaltered in 1852 when, as a Whig and friend of Radicals, he seriously contemplated taking the post of chancellor of the Exchequer in Derby's first Cabinet – the job which in the event was given to Disraeli.

A comparable double standard applied to his views. After his marriage, Palmerston found himself stepfather-in-law to Lord Ashley – that is, Ashley was married to Lady Palmerston's daughter by a previous union (the former Lady Cowper). It was undoubtedly for this reason that Palmerston supported the Ten Hours Bill. When some trade union leaders called at his house in Carlton Gardens unannounced, he consented to see them. They tried to demonstrate to him the sort of work expected of a child. Surely, he airily suggested, the advent of machinery had hugely improved the conditions even of child labour in a factory. The working men indicated such work was like pushing two large lounging chairs round and round his drawing-room. Calling for the assistance of a footman, Palmerston tried pushing the chairs – to the astonishment of his wife, when she came into the room and remarked, 'I am glad to see your Lordship has betaken yourself to work at last.'[31] Out of puff after a few circumambulations, Palmerston was told that factory children walked as much as thirty miles per day behind their machines. That shocked him and converted him to the Ten Hours Bill. He was equally horrified by slavery. Yet, as we have seen, he treated his Irish tenants abominably, and in spite of the obvious need to reform the army he resolutely refused to do so. He went to his grave believing that flogging was absolutely necessary to maintain military discipline, and the purchase of commissions was not abolished until 1870. Yet this old man, who really belonged to the aristocratic (and high diplomatic) world depicted by Sir Thomas Lawrence, who was ten years old when his father's friend Gibbon died, and who was an MP before the death of Napoleon, became a popular prime minister in the era of photography and modern newspapers. He was voted in by the middle class.

Palmerston was cynical enough to know that the Crimean War could be popular so long as it could be represented as serving the interests of Great Britain. The army consisted entirely of aristocratic officers, most of them buffoons, and working-class men driven to the dire expedient of soldiering by poverty. Many, therefore, were Irish or Scots. The battles took place far away. No English town was reduced to rubble, as was Balaclava. It was an armchair war, fought, as far as the English bourgeoisie was concerned, by classes as remote from their own lives as the Sultan and his entourage in the Topkapi palace. Yet war is a Pandora's box, even when fought at a distance of over a thousand miles. Palmerston's complacent belief in the love affair between the English and the aristocracy was, like most things in England, only half true.

For most Englishmen, hatred of the enemy was not really enough to fuel war fever. It would have been absurd to suppose that the subjects of Queen Victoria in 1854, whether mill operatives or farmers, clergymen or railway engineers, felt so natural a kinship with the Turk that when the Sultan declared war against Russia, they longed, to a man, to fight the Tsar. What happened was more muddled and, from the point of view of the collective consciousness – that mystic unity beloved of Maurice – more complex. A war puts a society on its mettle. While fighting Hitler's war, the British – through the experience of coalition government, rationing and the like – were also working through the dreadful social legacy of the 1930s and determining to refashion a welfare system and their whole attitude to the state. Many on both sides of the political spectrum saw the Crimean War as a comparable test for the British. As fast as the chancellor of the Exchequer throughout the war – through two administrations – William Ewart Gladstone – was trying to pay for it by temporary impositions of income tax, events were challenging even his laissez-faire economic certainties. A modern state, and this was what post-Crimean England was becoming, could not without calamity allow the untrammelled market free rein. Fiscal controls – and a taxation system – arose willy-nilly.

The very lack of political definition at home, and the lack of distinction of the two war Cabinets, in fact points up the questions which Victorian Britain was asking itself *of itself* during this war. 'We working-class and professional men are only listeners in the trial going on between merchants, manufacturers and tradesmen and aristocracy,' F.D. Maurice complained to an audience at the Working Men's College on 31 May 1855. This was to be one of the political conundrums which would preoccupy the British for a hundred years – how to find political representation *both* for intelligent non-commercial middle-class opinion and for the working classes. The result would be that fascinating political hybrid, the Labour Party.

Until that hybrid had grown, however, society was to pass through many transformations, some directly political – to do with parliamentary reforms, extension of the franchise, and so on – others more nebulous, but no less interwoven with the fabric of life.

The war as theatre, as spectator-sport, as tragic absurdity, came to a close. Having reduced Balaclava to rubble, with great loss of life, the British invited the Russian commanders to dinner *en plein air*. M. Soyer describes the scene:

Early the next morning all the people in authority were astir. Generals, colonels, officers, and men in light marching order, might be seen quickly crossing and re-crossing the plateau in every direction. I had, with my brigade of cooks, been busy since daybreak, and a white stream of communication had established itself between the general's palazzo, built of fine white stone, and the villarette of your humble servant, so conspicuously erected in almost the centre of the plateau. This was no other than my cooks in their white culinary attire, running like mad to and fro, fetching and carrying the portions of the collation which I had prepared in my kitchen. At ten, to the minute, the party were to sit down; at five minutes to ten the collation was on the table, and in military order. The bill of fare was as follows:

DÉJEUNER POUR VINGT-QUATRE PERSONNES,
Offert au Général Vassileffsky par le Général Garrett.

Filets de turbot clouté à la Dame Blanche.
Cotelettes de mouton à la vivandière.

Relevées chaudes.
Les hanchettes de mouton à la Bretonne.

Pièces froides.
Le dindonneau farci à l'anglaise.
Les poulets demi-rôtis.
Le gros jambon de Westmoreland glacé.
Le gannet garni d'ortolans à la Victoria.

La Macédoine Lüdersienne à l'Alexandre II.

Petits hors-d'oeuvres.
Les escalopes de mortadelle de Verone.
Le thon italien mariné.
Les olives de Provence farcies.
Les lamproies et sardines marinées.
Les anchois.
Les cornichons à l'estragon.
Indian pickles.

Entremets de douceur.
Gelées d'oranges.
Idem au marasquin.
Plum-pudding à la Exeter.
Un turban Savarin au Madère.

The Crimean cup à la Marmora.

Dessert assorti.
Salades d'oranges.
Compotes de poires.
Figues, raisins, amandes, &c.

My engineer, Tom Shell-proof, as we afterwards called him, undertook to gallop round to the various regimental kitchens, and see that all was in order . . . At ten to the minute, the Russians arrived. After the introduction, the guests sat down, and every jaw was soon doing its best; for in less than twenty minutes there were only the names of the various dishes to be seen, and they were upon the bill of fare – which was not eaten. The Russian general, who has only one arm, ate as much as two men with the use of both. A servant waited upon him, and carved his meat. Better-looking men I have seen, but not more military. He seemed as hard and as round as a cannon-ball. Between three and five was the general's hour of rising in time of peace. When he told me this, I said, 'Then I suppose in war-time you don't lie down at all, general?'

'Very little indeed,' was the reply.

'That I can conceive. But in time of peace you must admit four or five to be rather an early hour to call upon a friend, as you proposed doing to General Garrett.'

The general was a man of very agreeable manners – spoke French rather fluently – had a very quick eye – was no sooner seated than he took a survey of the company. The lunch was much relished – the speeches were short and to the point, and all went on to everybody's satisfaction. The Russian general was particularly pleased, and highly complimented his host upon the dainty repast, which he could not conceive was to be had in the Crimea.

Two things to emerge from the Pandora's box of war, and which could hardly have been predicted when the Powers began their quarrel about the ancient sites of Christian pilgrimage, were the importance of photography, and a change in the Western world's smoking habits.

We do not know why a Scotsman called Robert Peacock Gloag was in the Crimea, but while he was there he saw Turks and Russians smoking cigarettes. 'In them, he found an idea and an ideal. From the war a purposeful man emerged.'

The first Gloag cigarettes on sale in London were cylinders of straw-coloured paper into which a cane tip was inserted and the tobacco filled in through a funnel. These are what Russians call little scorchers, *papirosi*. You can still buy them in Russia. Gloag filled them with strong Latakia tobacco.

By 1860–1, a Greek captain in the Russian army, John Theodoridi, had set up a shop in London – Leicester Square – selling Turkish cigarettes. Four other cigarette-makers followed. Theodoriki Avramanchi, another Greek, opened a shop in Regent Street in 1865, Caranjaki in Great Winchester Buildings, D. Mazzini in Union Court and A. Zicaliotti in Bloomfield Street. Gloag settled in Peckham, a south-eastern suburb of London. He made cigarettes called 'Moscows' for Theodoridi (these had a piece of wool in the end to act as a filter) and 'Tom Thumbs' – 'penny lines to be smoked to the bitter end'. From one room, he expanded to his whole house, then to another. Then he had six houses. He sold his 'Don Alfonso' in bundles of 25 for 1 shilling. This 'Whiff' was introduced in 1871. In 1870 he had founded the church of St Stephen, Peckham, in gratitude for his profits. By now, he had a factory, 40 Boyson Road, Walworth. The text over the door of his 'tobacco church' was – 'But when the blade was sprung up, And brought forth fruit, then appeared the tares also.'

This seemed an intelligent recognition of the fact that, from the first, the habit of cigarette-smoking was seen as both a blessing and a curse. Arthur E.J. Longhurst, assistant surgeon to HM (Prince Albert's) Light Infantry, attributed the decline of the Ottoman Empire itself specifically to the Turkish fondness for cigarettes. Having noted the 'imbecile progeny' of native American tobacco-addicts, Dr Longhurst adds, 'We may also take warning from the history of another nation, who some few centuries ago, while following the banners of Solyman the Magnificent, were the terror of Christendom, but who since then having become more addicted to tobacco-smoking than any of the European nations, are now the lazy and lethargic Turks, held in contempt by all civilized communities.' An American contemporary of Dr Longhurst's, William A. Alcott, noted that 'the slave of tobacco is seldom found reclaimable'. He added that smoking damaged teeth, lungs and stomach, as well as the morals of the addict.

What Gloag had introduced to the West, however, was a narcotic so addictive that social attitudes were forced to change, in order to accommodate the cigarette compulsion. In the pre-cigarette age, smoking was chiefly regarded as a 'low' activity. In 1861 a notice was pinned on the board at the Travellers' Club 'respectfully requesting' members to refrain from smoking, except in one specified area – this was because someone had lit a cigar in the hall.[32] It was not until the 1880s that smoking was generally permitted in the public rooms of London clubs. In respectable households men either had to smoke out of doors or else 'sneak away into the kitchen when the servants had gone to bed and puff up the chimney'.[33] Smoking was first allowed in railway carriages in 1860.

The real smoking revolution happened in the generation after Gloag's, when the Bristol tobacco firm of W.D. and H.O. Wills pioneered the first Bonsack cigarette-making machine, bought from America in 1883.*[34] It enabled them to manufacture approximately 200 cigarettes per minute. Between 1860 and 1900, Britain became a smoking nation, its consumption of tobacco rising 2.4 per cent in 1862, 4.7 per cent in 1863 and an average of around 5 per cent per annum for the rest of the century.

By 1886, the adoption of the Bonsack machinery by Wills had been followed by firms such as Lambert and Butler (London), John Player and Sons (Nottingham) and the Liverpool firms Hignett Bros and Cope Bros. These Liverpool factories competed for the franchise to display and sell cheap cigarettes in the Railway Refreshment Rooms. Spiers and Pond, the company who ran all the refreshment rooms for the

---

*The invention of James A. Bonsack of Salem, Va.

Midland Railways, sold the right to Cope Brothers for £800 p.a.

A price war in the 1880s led to the 'penny cigarettes'. In 1888, Wild Woodbine made its appearance, the most famous cheap smoke in the Western world, forever associated with the men fighting in the trenches a quarter of a century later. It was during this price war that Wills watched their profits rocket – £6.5 million in 1884, £13,961,000 in 1886, shooting to nearly £127 million in 1891. The working classes had become hooked. This was the true opium of the people, and Gloag's legacy of the cigarette habit could be said to be the most lasting and notable consequence of the Crimean War. When the Turkish, Russian and British empires are now as obsolete as the Bonapartist dynasty, the British working class, 146 years after the treaty of Paris, are still addicts of what Gloag brought home – though in other classes the custom, like its adherents, is dying.

One man who was quick to adopt the cigarette habit was Emperor Napoleon III. When Prince Albert and Queen Victoria visited Paris in 1855 they found him chain-smoking.* They brought with them three hundred and sixty photographs of the Crimean campaign taken by Roger Fenton – one of the more successful photographers in that war. Probably the Romanian court painter Carol Popp de Szathmari took more dramatic shots, including scenes of battle, but only one of his photographs has survived.[35] This is a splendid old Turkish irregular soldier, a Bashi-Bazouk, lolling beside a bare-chested female companion. Szathmari's albums belonging to Napoleon III were probably consumed by fire when Communards burnt the Tuileries in 1871. The army photographer Richard Nicklin and two assistants in the Royal Engineers drowned, with sixteen cases of equipment, in Balaclava harbour when their ship, the *Rip Van Winkle*, was sunk on 14 November 1854.[36]

Fenton was a commercial photographer who saw the war as a chance to practise his (comparatively) new hobby. We exclaim at his prints, as at those of James Robertson (an Englishman based at Constantinople):

---

*Prince Albert, who abominated the habit, did not join him. As his verse biographer, the Rev. Paul Johnson, aged 94, recalled,

The Prince a singular example set
And smoked not e'en a fragrant cigarette,
Nor feared to give his royal host offence
As deemed unsocial in this abstinence.

but they are nearly all portraits, and only a very few, if the truth is told, actually convey much of the atmosphere of the war. These are such as *Private Soldiers and Officers of the 3rd Regiment (The Buffs) Piling Arms*,[37] *Carts and Cattle leaving Balaklava harbour*,[38] *Mounted French Infantry Officer*[39] (his képi on one side of his head, the cigarette in his mouth, the pointed bell-tents smudgy behind him on the hillside).

Action photographs were barely a technical possibility. All these photographers used the wet-plate solution which had been developed in 1852 by Scott Archer, an Englishman. A glass plate was immersed in collodion, a solution of ether, guncotton and alcohol, which was blended with silver iodide and iodide of iron. Then the plate was sensitized by means of a coating of silver nitrate solution. The wet plate was then placed inside the camera. Exposure took between three and twenty seconds, which accounts for the air of frozen stillness in most of these frames. The plate then had to be removed at once to a dark room, which is why photographers in the Crimea were encumbered with, in Szathmari's case, a carriage, in Fenton's with a specially covered van. Whereas wet collodion plates in England would probably be usable for up to ten minutes, in the heat of a Crimean summer they dried almost instantaneously.

So, the wonder is that we have any plates at all of the Crimean War. We do, however. Lord Raglan, Sir George de Lacy Evans, Sir James Scarlett, General Sir John Lysaght Pennefather, Sir John Campbell with the Light Company of the 38th (South Staffordshires), Omar Pasha and the French Zouaves all stare into Fenton's lens. Wherever his van (overpoweringly hot in that sweltering summer) turned up, the soldiers clustered round, wanting to be immortalized. They stare at us, or so it seems, just as much as we stare at them. Clearly, Fenton has managed to freeze certain moments in the past, but what strikes us more forcibly is their wistfulness as they look at us, and the future.

15

India 1857–9

On 9 May 1857, in the parade-ground at Meerut, some forty miles north-east of Delhi, a melancholy scene was enacted beneath the rolling stormclouds and the sunless sky. Eighty-five sepoy troops were being stripped of their uniforms – for which they had themselves paid – and handed over to blacksmiths who riveted fetters on their arms and legs. These were no common criminals. Lieutenant (later General) Sir Hugh Gough, who was in Meerut that day, believed they 'were more or less picked men, and quite the *élite* of the corps'.[1] How did it come about that these proud soldiers, who had fought so bravely for the East India Company in the Sikh wars in the Punjab less than a decade before, found themselves humiliated and paraded before their comrades like common criminals? What was their offence?

The new Enfield rifle with which they had been issued could not be loaded unless each and every cartridge had its end bitten off before insertion into the gun. These sepoys had refused, fearing that the grease used on the cartridge came from the fat of an animal forbidden in the dietary laws of their religion. Their commanding officer, Colonel Carmichael Smyth of the 3rd Native Cavalry, was a choleric, unpopular figure. On 23 April he had ordered a parade to demonstrate the use of the new cartridges and a method by which they could be used without biting. It was not in itself an ill-intentioned idea, but as many of the colonel's fellow officers observed, it was crashingly tactless and almost bound to have a disastrous consequence. Ever since the new rifle, with its notoriously greased cartridges, had been introduced to the subcontinent, there had been rumours flying. In January, at Dum-Dum, a low-caste lascar was said to have approached a Brahmin sepoy who worked in the musketry department and told him that the grease used for these cartridges – which had to be put in the soldier's mouth before he loaded his rifle – was made from the fats of forbidden beasts – beef dripping would have most alarmed the Hindus, pork fat the Muslims.

Incredibly – given the sensitivity of dietary matters in religion – it seems as though forbidden fats had, in some instances, been used to grease the cartridges, though as soon as the mistake was noticed the East India Company gave strict orders that the cartridges should be greased with a mixture of tallow (sheep fat) and beeswax.[2] But the rumours were now ablaze. It was widely reported among the sepoy regiments that the British had deliberately engineered a situation in which Hindus would eat beef fat in order to make Christians of them. Although this was not true, it was not so preposterous a suggestion in 1857 as it might have been in the time of Warren Hastings. Lord Dalhousie in his time as governor-general (1848–56) had been a modernizer, an improver, a moral policeman. The Evangelical desire to improve met the Benthamite ambition to organize the lives of others and together they found a perfect object for their busybodydom: Indian religion. William Wilberforce said he really put the conversion of India to Christianity 'before Abolition' (of slavery) as a task for God and His Englishmen. What were the Hindu divinities after all but 'absolute monsters of lust, injustice, wickedness and cruelty. In short, their religious system is one grand abomination.'[3] James Mill lost his faith in God while writing his Indian history, but that classic textbook was to tell generations of Englishmen that 'by a system of priestcraft, built upon the most enormous and tormenting superstition that ever harassed and degraded any portion of mankind, their minds were enchained more intolerably than their bodies; in short that, despotism and priestcraft taken together, the Hindus, in mind and body, were the most enslaved portion of the human race'.[4]

When Viscount Canning took over the governor-generalship of the Company in 1856, he particularly disliked evangelical British army officers, 'terribly given to preach'.[5] Lt-Col. Wheeler of the 34th's 'whole mind' was 'given to religious teaching'. Patronizingly, Canning thought the sepoys 'curious creatures . . . just like children. *Ombrageux* is the word for them I think. Shadows and their own fancies seem to frighten them much more than realities.'[6]

As well as fears, in the late 1850s the sepoys had cause for discontent. As the great Indian scholar S.B. Chaudhuri noted, it was not so much the fear for their religion that provoked the rural classes and their landed chiefs to revolt: 'It was the question of their rights and interests in the soil and hereditary holdings which excited them to a dangerous degree.'[7] The British under Dalhousie had taken over the property of many of the Indian landowners. The rents were now fixed by the East India Company.

The sepoy armies were of use to the Company not merely to police the territories already occupied by the British but also to conquer and subdue more – for example the garrisons of Lower Burma. For Indian troops to be moved efficiently and speedily to Burma it had been deemed necessary by the British to insist on the abolition, or ignoring, of the caste system in such areas as military transport. These 'common-sense' reforms were much resented, especially by Brahmin sepoys who objected for example to having to travel alongside Sikhs. The British need to 'transform the loosely disciplined mercenary army which had survived since the time of Clive into a modern force yielding unhesitating obedience' meant inevitably that Indian sensitivities would be trampled or tormented.[8]

Who were the sepoys? Many were 'distressed gentlefolk' whose families could no longer make a living from the land, or perhaps had been impoverished by British land reform. The Bengal army was largely recruited from a limited number of districts in Southern Oudh, the eastern regions of the North-Western provinces and Western Bihar, where Brahmins and Rajputs (who claimed descent from the ancient Kshatriya soldier caste) belonged to proprietary brotherhoods of small landowners. Military service was a dignified option for these men. Out of their 7 to 9 rupees per month, they had to pay for food, uniform, and transport of baggage. After the wars of conquest and expansion in the Punjab were over, the British cut the allowances to their sepoy troops and hinted that 'foreign' troops, for example the Gurkhas, could be recruited more cheaply if the Brahmins and Rajputs did not want the work. The sepoy was therefore torn, at this period, between a need to make a living and a profound resentment at the high-handed reforms of the British, especially when these reforms were made in the name of Western progress. If 1857 was something more than a disturbance among the troops, if it was a rising against the *angreezi raj*, or English rule, then it was very much a revolt against the Modern. The aggrieved sepoys had more than a little in common with the hand-loom weavers of Lancashire put out of work by machines; with the dispossessed working classes of England who found themselves forced into Benthamite workhouses; with the Irish whose right to their own religion, and even life itself, was questioned in some English quarters; with Canadians and Jamaicans whose livelihood was wrecked by Free Trade; and with those many Radicals and Chartists who demonstrated and petitioned not so much for the creation of a brave new future as for a share of the freedoms they had enjoyed in the past and which the March of the Modern had taken away from them.

So here are the eighty-five sepoys standing in the parade-ground in Meerut in the sweltering, thunderous, sunless heat while the stormclouds gather: eighty-five brave, old-fashioned fighting men manacled like disgraced slaves and marched to the prison house before the shocked gaze of their comrades. Rather fewer than 2,000 sepoys witnessed the spectacle. That evening one of the native officers went to Hugh Gough, who was sitting on the veranda of his bungalow, to warn him that there would be a mutiny of the native troops at Meerut the next day. Gough was an intelligent man who knew that since the discontents at Dum-Dum in January there had been minor mutinies at Barrackpur and Berhampur, and a serious uprising of the 48th Native Cavalry at Lucknow.[9] He went at once to Colonel Carmichael Smyth, who reproved him for listening 'to such idle words'. Later in the evening Gough tried to persuade some of the other senior British officers at Meerut – Brigadier Archdale Wilson and Major-General W.H. Hewitt, commander of the Meerut Division – but they too dismissed the suggestion.

The mutiny began the next day, a swelteringly hot day, so hot that the evening church parade was postponed from half-past six to seven o'clock. Before the padre had time to implore the Deity to deliver the Christians from all the perils and dangers of that night, billows of smoke were rising into the torrid air from the bungalows which had been set alight. The sowars of the 3rd Cavalry rode to the prison to release their eighty-five humiliated comrades. Young Gough – subsequently to win a VC* – and Major Tombs rallied the European troops. Many of the Native troops were on the European side. The colonel of the 11th Native Infantry galloped across to see what 'all the noise was about' and was shot on the parade ground. Mayhem broke out, with Colonel Carmichael Smyth conspicuous by his Duke of Plaza Toro-like skill in taking cover and spending the night in the safety of the cantonment under the protection of the Artillery.[10]

During a night of fires and violence the rabble from the bazaars of Meerut swarmed over the military quarters, looting and killing. Wajir Ali Khan, deputy collector, afterwards gave evidence that though plunder was going on all night the sepoys did not touch a thing.[11] Gough later said that none of the sepoys in the 11th or the 3rd murdered their own officers. By morning, however, some fifty Europeans, men, women and children, had been killed. Gough had

---

*With great prescience the monarch had instituted the Victoria Cross for gallantry on 29 January 1856.

ridden through the baying lines of the 20th Native Infantry as they called out *Maro! Maro!* – Kill! Kill! – but, though he survived, he could see that they were out of control.

Moreover, it was obvious that the mutineering sepoys were now in the reckless position of having nothing to lose. Whether they surrendered or pleaded for clemency, they knew that the gallows or the firing squad inevitably awaited them. They might as well fight on. The Europeans listened to the shouting of slogans, the crackling of flames, the cry of *'Yah! Ali! Ali! e nara Haidari!'*[12] The Indians were crying out that they had 'broken the Electric Telegraph and overturned the British Rule, and boasting they had committed these atrocities in the name of religion'.

By morning, the mutineers had escaped Meerut and had ridden off to Delhi. The Meerut outbreak, however unpleasant in itself, might have been seen as no more than a summer heat-storm had the fire of discontent not spread. 'Oh why did you have a parade?' wailed General Hewitt to the colonel. By then the rebels had proclaimed the last Moghul emperor, eighty-two-year-old Bahadur Shah II, the king of Delhi. The sepoy mutineers also issued the following proclamation:

To all Hindoos and Mussulmans, Citizens and Servants of Hindostan, the officers of the Army now at Delhi and Meerut send greeting:

It is well known that in these days all the English have entertained these evil designs – first, to destroy the religion of the whole Hindostani army, and then to make the people by compulsion Christians. Therefore we, solely on account of our religion, have combined with the people, and have not spared alive one infidel, and have re-established the Delhi dynasty on these terms. Hundreds of guns and a large amount of treasure have fallen into our hands; therefore it is fitting that whoever of the soldiers and people dislike turning Christians should unite with one heart, and, acting courageously, not leave the seed of these infidels remaining . . . It is . . . necessary that all Hindoos and Mussulmans unite in this struggle and, following the instructions of some respectable people, keep themselves secure so that good order may be maintained.

For ninety years after 1857, the British liked to represent the terrible events of that summer as 'the Indian Mutiny'. It was necessary for the British self-image that the outbreaks of incendiarism and violence should have been of a purely military character, an aberration by a few fanatics who (mistakenly, of course) believed that they were being asked to put the fat of forbidden meats in their mouths. These maniacs – so the British historians saw things – were prepared to reverse all the benefits of civilization which had been brought to them by the East India Company for the sake of returning to the most superstitious adherence to a backward-looking religion. They were a few diehards discontented with army life. The huge majority of Indians, it is averred in this notion of events, recognized that the British administered their land and their institutions far more fairly than the corrupt princelings of the decayed Indian dynasties, whether Moghul or Mahratta.

At the other extreme are to be found the Indian nationalist historians who liked to see 1857 as the first serious attempt at a united Independence Movement for the subcontinent. For these historians, the Delhi Declaration is of the utmost significance, giving the lie to the British supposition that Hindu and Muslim could never coexist without a European administration keeping the peace. They would link the Delhi declaration to the momentous Calcutta Congress of 1886 whose spirit was captured by the Nawab Reza Ali-Khan, Bahadur of Lucknow, who said – in Urdu – 'Hindus or Mahomedans, Parsees or Sikhs, we are one people now, whatever our ancestors six or eight hundred years ago may have been, and our public interests are indivisible and identical . . . we Mahomedans (at least such of us as can think at all) think just as all thinking Hindus do on these public questions.'

Most Indian historians today view with some scepticism the notion that 1857 was Act One of the Independence Drama. But its memory undoubtedly fuelled later supporters of the Freedom Movement, just as the memories of the Famine shaped the development of Irish Republicanism. Had the events of 1857 been no more than a mutiny, then there would not have been places, such as Banda and Hamirpur, where civilian mobs rose against the British without military assistance.[13] If, however, one tries to see these uprisings as part of a concerted Independence movement, it is difficult to explain why the greater part of the subcontinent was unaffected. The conflict was a phenomenon of the North-West of India, and central North-West at that. It never spread up as far as Lahore in the Punjab, nor – by a mixture of good luck and clever tactics by the British – did it ever reach the administrative capital, Calcutta. Bombay, Hyderabad, Mysore, the Carnatic, Ceylon remained all but unaffected by the bloody events.

Nor should one forget the chief reason for the successful suppression of the uprisings: namely that the Indian majority fought alongside the British in the various battles and siege-reliefs and – it must be supposed – that the majority of Indian citizens, for whatever reason, did not wish to take part in a violent war either against the Europeans or against their local Indian landlords. In *Narratives of Events at Cawnpore*,[*][14] the Indian author Nanak Chand witnesses the murders, the burnings and the sheer chaos brought about by the uprising. On one terrifying, broiling hot day he found himself cowering in a garden hut for all the hours of daylight without food or water while the mob, who had refreshed themselves by plundering a British wine-cellar, rampaged around the plantations of Madarpoor. These were not aggrieved sepoy officers but peasants on the razzle, completely out of control. At midnight under the cover of dark, Nanak Chand crept to the banks of the Ganges, tiptoeing over untold numbers of corpses. 'These drunken boatmen were armed; some with clubs, others with weapons, and they were running about the woods like wild men. I cannot describe the terror that seized me at that moment. How I sighed for the British rule.'

It is only fair to record this Indian impression of things before recognizing that 'British rule' was not restored without very great cost to the Indian population. The ruthlessness of British reprisals, the preparedness to 'punish' Indians of any age or sex, regardless of whether they had any part in the rebellion, is a perpetual moral stain on 'the Raj', and it is no wonder that in most popular British histories these atrocities are suppressed altogether or glossed over with such a distasteful anodyne phrase as 'dark deeds were done on both sides'.[15] It is not to defend the murders of European women and children that one points out that such remarks suggest an equivalence where none can properly exist. Even if 1857 was not quite an independence war, it was much, much more than a 'mutiny' – a word which not merely, inaccurately, suggests that violence was restricted to the military, but also begs every moral question by assuming the legitimacy of British 'rule'. The sepoy, for reasons of economic necessity, had accepted his 7 or 9 rupees a month from the East India Company for four generations. Did that give a British historian sitting in London, who had never set foot in India, or a Whiggish president of the Board of Control – also in

---

[*]Modern Indians spell this Kanpur, the spelling followed here except when quoting Victorian sources.

London – or a local 'collector' the right to tell the Indian how much rent he should pay, what he should eat, how he should treat his wife or his neighbours? 'The people of this country do not require our aid to furnish them with a rule for their conduct or a standard for their property,' Warren Hastings had wisely remarked in 1773 when Lord North's Regulating Act set up a Supreme Court in Calcutta.[16] The Victorians rode roughshod. There can be no moral equivalence between a people, by whatever means of atrocity, trying to fight for their freedom to live as they choose, without the interference of an invading power, and that power itself using the utmost brutality to enforce not merely a physical but a political dominance over the people.

The terrible story has three phases. It started in the summer of 1857, when the Europeans suffered massacres at Meerut, Delhi and Kanpur – and when the last-named town and Lucknow underwent sieges which, for the heroism and suffering displayed, fast became legendary. Next came the relief of Lucknow and the demonstration that the British were regaining control of the situation. Third came the war of reprisal of 1858–9 in which the brilliant guerrilla leader Ramchandra Pandenanga, known as Tatya Tope, fought a series of heroic rearguard actions and gave the hardened campaigners Sir Colin Campbell and Sir Hugh Rose a 'run for their money'. By then, though, there was no doubt about the inevitable outcome of the war. Nearly all the British accounts dwell, for reasons which do not need to be explained, on the first two of those phases, and turn a blind eye to the third.[17]

When the rebels reached Delhi on the night of 10/11 May 1857, probably no one was more surprised than the eighty-two-year-old king, whose days were largely devoted to composing poetry, illuminating manuscripts and listening to the cooing of his pet doves and nightingales. The city was garrisoned, but largely with sepoy troops – there were no European regiments there – and the cry to massacre the infidels was obeyed in a way that most Indians appear to have deplored. The European women who were lucky enough to escape the cantonments – Mrs Wood, the doctor's wife in the 38th Native Infantry, and her friend Mrs Peile – recorded many acts of kindness from natives who assisted their getaway.[18] Many were not so lucky. James Morley, a merchant from the Kashmir bazaar, was typical in finding his whole family massacred. He escaped disguised as a woman, but that would not have saved him in many quarters where the shootings of women and children were indiscriminate. In the aftermath of the violence, careful inquiries were unable to reveal a single instance of rape or torture being a prelude to the death of European women in any of the atrocities of that summer. One official noted that this information was of some comfort to those who had lost wives, sisters and daughters, but there were many in Britain who simply refused to believe it.[19] So shocking were the Delhi murders of British women that, paradoxically, the British wanted to make them even more shocking, with the automatic assumption that the 'angels of Albion' had been ravished as well as shot. The Reverend John Rotton, British chaplain during the Meerut and Delhi atrocities, reveals the double standards which had crept into British attitudes to the Indian. This clergyman witnessed some terrible things, and buried many of his massacred fellow countrymen, so one does not in any sense wish to patronize him. To say that his partisan attitude is understandable is not, however, to find it especially elevating. He had rushed out his *Chaplain's Narrative of the Siege of Delhi* within a year of the event itself, one of the hundreds of books published in the next thirty years demonstrating comparable habits of mind, steeped in a certainty of racial superiority to the Indians. This is something new since the era of Clive, or even of Wellesley, and it was to shape the pattern of 'British India' for the next century.[20]

The men who perpetrated the murders at Meerut were, in the Reverend John Rotton's view, 'savages'. He titillated his readers by saying 'it is better to throw a veil over the sins which have so indelibly disgraced human nature', but was able to write approvingly of the loyal Gorkha (*sic*): 'The facility with which the Gorkhas wielded the Kukree – a native knife, and a most effective weapon of war in experienced hands – elicited the wonder of every beholder. Once plunged into the abdomen of an enemy, in a second he was ripped up, just as clean and cleverly as a butcher divides an ox or sheep.'[21]

Rotton had no doubt, from the first, that much more was involved in the conflict than a political struggle between conservative-minded, impoverished Indian officers and a thoughtless utilitarian system of reform. The bloodbaths which were unleashed by the original points of contention possessed, for this devout churchman, an unmistakable mystic significance. He likened the Mutiny to the moment in the Book of Kings when:

Ahab and Jehoshaphat went up to Ramoth Gilead, at the instigation of the lying prophets of Baal who said, 'Go up, for the Lord shall deliver it into the hand of the king.' . . . The Christian warrior, taking a retrospective glance, can feelingly say, 'Verily the enemy thrust sore at us that we might fall, but the Lord helped us.' Not only the disciples of Christ, but everyone realized the fact that the divine favour prevented* and followed us.[22]

As for the infidel mutineers:

they little thought that the struggle was a battle of principles – a conflict between truth and error; and that because they had elected in favour of darkness and eschewed the light, therefore they could not possibly succeed. Moreover they had imbrued their hands in the innocent blood of helpless women and children, and of honest and confiding men, who spurned to harbour the thought of suspicion, despite the differences of race and religion. That very blood was appealing to heaven for vengeance. The appeal was unquestionably heard, and its justice fully admitted.

This reading of the events of the summer of 1857 must have been tempered, in the chaplain's mind, by the knowledge that God moves in a mysterious way, His wonders to perform. Vengeance was slow in coming. Besieged in Delhi, the few remaining Europeans had to wait through the hottest months of the year, until August, before Brigadier-General John Nicholson, a tormented homosexual soldier in his mid-thirties who had been in India since 1839, appeared on the ridge above Delhi to relieve the siege. A huge figure, with a long black beard and a deep voice, Nicholson was destined to die in the fighting. Further proof of the mysteriousness of Providence was evinced by the cholera outbreak in the 8th and 61st regiments, which killed hundreds, including General Sir Harry Barnard, in command of the force, and severely weakened his successor General Reed, the provisional commander-in-chief.

Meanwhile, as cholera swept through the camp in Delhi, they heard the news of the disasters at Kanpur. These were perhaps the most shocking losses suffered by the Europeans during the whole summer. The killings were disgusting; the treachery of the local princeling, Nana

---

*i.e. went before.

Sahib, was demonstrable; no one can deny or minimize these facts. From the first, however, Kanpur acquired a mythic significance. The aged poet of Delhi, Bahadur Shah II, or the obese king of Oudh could hardly be represented, even to a furious British newspaper-reading public, as demon-kings. In the local princeling at Kanpur, Nana Sahib, was found an ideal candidate.

Dhondu Pant (Nana Sahib's actual name) was archetypically one of the Indian bigwigs who stood to lose by the modernizing reforms of Lord Dalhousie. Under Dalhousie the East India Company had dethroned the last Peshwa of Bithur, Baji Rao II, and given him a pension worth £80,000 per annum – 8 lakhs of rupees. The Company took his revenues from rents. When he died, however, his adopted son Dhondu Pant/Nana Sahib was not considered by Dalhousie to be entitled to such lavish treatment.[23] No one visiting Nana Sahib in his palatial residence five miles from Kanpur, no one who saw his luxurious carpets, crystal chandeliers, soft Cashmere shawls, his menageries and aviaries, would have believed him to be on the breadline, but the Company had deprived him of vast revenues, which he believed to be his in 1851. In 1857 he would demonstrate the truth of the proverb that revenge was a dish best served cold.[24]

A glance at the map shows the strategic importance of Kanpur. This town – at the time, numbering 60,000 – on the banks of the sacred Ganges was an important post on the Great Road, the trunk road connecting Delhi and Benares. It is fascinating, from the point of view of military history, that Tatya Tope, the 'Napoleon' of the uprising, Nana Sahib's general, never grasped the importance of this road. Had he but managed to block it at one, preferably at two points, he might have inflicted real damage on the British – perhaps, who knows, broken their nerve.

Kanpur was, however, ripe for his picking in summer 1857.[25] The British reorganization of the sepoy regiments had weakened morale. When the 2nd Cavalry mutinied at Kanpur on 2 June, the native regiments were in disarray. All the native officers of the 56th at Kanpur, for example – all – were on furlough, and seconded to mercenary soldiering in districts miles from home, at the time of the rising.[26]

Tatya Tope had the guerrilla leader's knack of seizing a chance, but lacked the weapons or manpower to hold on to Kanpur indefinitely. Useful as it might be to occupy this point of the trunk road for a few weeks (or, if he was lucky, months), he knew that he would not be able to hold out against a fully armed British contingent of trained men when they came marching westwards up the Great Road. Once they had mutinied, the men tended to throw away their uniforms, and the rag, tag and bobtail included unskilled peasants wishing to loot and pillage who 'looked less like a rival Indian army, more like a chaotic collection of civilian insurgents'.[27]

It is in these circumstances that we must envisage the unfortunate Europeans' plight in Kanpur. It would appear that after the outbreak of Mutiny, Nana Sahib offered protection and hospitality to the European women and children, and safe-conduct to those who wished to escape by boat down the Ganges. Conditions within the cantonment quickly became intolerable. Dysentery and heatstroke were rife, and morale was weakened by an apparently accidental fire which destroyed all the medical supplies in the Europeans' possession. The double atrocities with which the name of Kanpur is always associated in British minds concerned the treatment of the British women and children. First – help for Lucknow not appearing – General Wheeler, the British commander, oversaw the European refugees being put on the forty or so boats provided by Nana Sahib. As soon as they were all afloat, their Indian escorts leapt ashore, many of them able to set the thatched roofs of the boats alight before jumping into the water. As the convoy drifted downstream, they were met by an organized firing party of insurgents, who bombarded the boats with musket fire, burning arrows and heavier artillery. They were afloat for two days in these circumstances, the semi-clad survivors being dragged from the river at Satichaura Ghat. Then on 10 July, the women and children were taken to a house known as the Bibighar. It was a large bungalow with a courtyard, formerly the residence of a British officer and his Indian mistress. To the survivors of the boats were added those officers' wives who had escaped the cantonment and been rounded up by Tatya Tope.

He knew that Brigadier-General Henry Havelock was on his way to relieve Kanpur – which he did, successfully, on 16 July. The British troops who went into the courtyard, and peered into the dried-up well at the Bibighar, were too late to save the women. The newly appointed magistrate, J.W. Sherer, wrote to a senior civil servant, Sir Cecil Beadon:

> May God in his mercy, my dear Beadon, preserve me from ever witnessing again such a sight as I have seen this day. The house they were kept in was close to the hotel – opposite the theatre – it was a

native house – with a court in the middle, and an open room with pillars opposite the principal entrance. The whole of the court and this room was literally soaked with blood and strewn with bonnets and those large hats now worn by ladies – and there were long tresses of hair glued with clotted blood to the ground – all the bodies were thrown into a dry well and on looking down – a map of naked arms, legs and gashed trunks was visible. My nerves are so deadened with horror that I write this quite calmly. It is better you should know the worst – I am going this very moment to fill the well up and crown its mouth with a mount. Let us mention the subject no more – silence and prayer alone seem fitting.[28]

It remains uncertain whether Nana Sahib had any prior knowledge that the massacres would take place.[29] They were committed in his name, but he always denied having any part in the murders. This did not stop the British press demonizing him as the very type of oriental duplicity and callousness.[30] Sherer, the magistrate just quoted, recalled that Nana was an '*excessively uninteresting person*'; rather overweight, boring. Nevertheless, *The Spectator* suggested that Nana should be 'caged and exhibited as Macduff intended to do with Macbeth. He should be caged as a matter of study and after exhibition in India should be brought to England and carefully guarded to live out the term of his natural, or unnatural life, a monster without sympathy.'[31] For some years after the Massacres,[32] a well-known 'portrait' of Nana Sahib circulated, comparable to the Wild West 'WANTED' posters of criminals. The same picture was also used to hunt for Rajah Kunwat Singh. It was in fact a picture of a blameless banker from Meerut who had given his portrait to a London barrister named John Lang, who successfully prosecuted a case on his behalf. Lang lent it to the *Illustrated London News*, where it became a serviceable icon 'against which the public could direct their hatred'.

The revenges exacted by the British for the massacres at Delhi and Kanpur were far from being purely emblematic in India itself. From the very first, the British decided to meet cruelty with redoubled cruelty, terror with terror, blood with blood. At Delhi, Nicholson had urged, 'Let us propose a Bill for the flaying alive, impalement, or burning of the murderers of the women and children at Delhi. The idea of simply hanging the perpetrators of such atrocities is maddening.'

Sir Henry Cotton was summoned from his tent by a Sikh orderly. 'I think, sir, you would like to see what we have done to the prisoners.'[33]

Muslims had been stripped, tied to the ground and 'branded over every part of their bodies with red-hot coppers'. With his own hand, Cotton put an end to their agony by blowing out their brains, but no action was taken against the torturers. Russell, the *Times* journalist who had covered the Crimean War, saw Sikhs and Englishmen calmly looking on while a bayoneted prisoner was slowly roasted over a fire.[34] Sewing Muslims into pigskins, or smearing them with pork fat before execution, was another torture favoured by the British. When 'Clemency Canning' – the sobriquet was intended to insult the governor-general – implored army officers not to countenance the burning of villages, his words were met with contempt. Long before the Kanpur massacres, whole villages had been sacked by the British. Rape and pillage were encouraged by the British officers before old women and children were burnt alive in their villages. Officers boasted that they had 'spared no one', or that 'peppering away at niggers' was a pastime which they 'enjoyed amazingly'.[35] The troops who 'relieved' Delhi were drunk, killed hundreds quite indiscriminately, and sent thousands of homeless refugees into the surrounding countryside.

Many Indians had the experience of being lashed, standing, to the mouth of a cannon and blown apart by grapeshot. 'One gun,' recalled a clergyman's wife who had come out to watch the executions, 'was overcharged and the poor wretch was literally blown to atoms, the lookers-on being covered with blood, and fragments of flesh: the head of one poor wretch fell on a bystander and hurt him.'[36]

Colonel James Neill was one of the many British officers who fought in India at this time with a religious sense of duty. (He was to rise to the rank of brigadier-general.) Like Nicholson in Delhi, Neill at Kanpur felt that hanging was too gentle a fate for the murderers. In fact, no sepoy would take part in the massacres in the Bibighar and the disgusting slaughter had been the work of five local butchers. This did not stop Neill embarking on a system of wholesale torture and butchery himself when he and his men retook possession of the station. Prisoners were made to lick the blood from the floor of the Bibighar while a European soldier lashed their backs with a whip. Every means was taken to offend the religious sensibilities of prisoners, whether they had any proven part in the uprising or not. Brahmins, therefore, would be made to lick parts of the floor previously moistened with water by 'untouchables'. 'We broke his caste,' wrote one Major Bingham. 'We stuffed pork, beef and everything which would possibly break his caste down his throat, tied him as tight as we could by the arms and told the guard to be *gentle* with him . . . The guard treated him *gently*. I only wonder he lived to be hung, which I had the pleasure of witnessing.'

Neill killed as many Indians in Allahabad alone as were killed on his own side in the entire two years of fighting. Yet the British continued to feed their self-esteem by representing themselves as the underdogs, heavily outnumbered, never more so than during the legendary siege of Lucknow.

This great feudal court-city, the capital of the nawabs of Oudh, was much the most prosperous precolonial city in India.[37] An Englishwoman who married a Lucknow nobleman (Mrs Meer Hasan Ali) was reminded by the city of the visionary castles of the Arabian Nights. Russell, the war correspondent, saw

A vision of palaces, mirrors, domes azure and golden, cupolas, colonnades, long façades of fair perspective in pillar and column, terraced roofs – all rising up amid a calm still ocean of the brightest verdure. Look for miles and miles away and still the ocean spreads, and the towers of the fairy-city gleam in its midst.

Russell also observed the appalling squalor and poverty of the slums for which the British, like the nawabs before them, had done nothing.[38]

Dalhousie's reforms were especially resented in Lucknow, not least because of Lucknow's religious significance in the Muslim consciousness, site of many holy mosques, and because of the blatant greed with which the governor-general regarded the ancient Muslim kingdom. Dalhousie spoke of Oudh as the luscious 'cherry that will drop into our mouth one day'. The British army annexed Oudh in 1856 and the king lived under a benign house arrest. Dalhousie's much more agreeable successor, 'Clemency' Canning, saw the nawab as a joke figure. The nawab wrote a poem for Canning which translated as 'Thy body is as jessamine. Erect as the Cypress thou art. Minister of the Queen of the World, Protector and Benefactor of all the world, Great thou art.' Sending this effusion home for the amusement of his family and friends, Canning wrote to Harriet, Lady Hodgson:

Pray read the King of Oude's [sic] Ode. It is an old affair – written before he was released; but I had forgotten to send it to you before.

He is very fat; and when he composes, he has all the cushions of his divan laid out in the middle of the floor, and lies down upon them, stomach downwards, dictating his verses, with his arms and legs spread out as far as he can stretch them. Exactly like a turtle.[39]

This was written in 1859, in the peaceful period after the hostilities were over. When the uprising had engulfed the city in the summer, two years before, it was something much more than a mutiny of the sepoy regiments. On the first Sunday of the outbreak, in April 1857, thousands of Muslims marched through the streets under the banners of their faith, while less thoughtful rioters ransacked and burnt houses, looted the shops, and indicated their contempt for the Europeans by staging mock decapitations of life-size dolls dressed in British army uniform.[40]

The British retreated into the Residency of Sir Henry Lawrence, chief commissioner of Oudh, and the financial commissioner, Martin Gubbins, fortified his own substantial house, using seventy-five native servants to build bastions and dig ditches. The siege itself lasted 143 days, and the courage and endurance of the British men, women and children who held out in the entrenchment inspired a mass of literature. Cholera and dysentery carried off as many as did enemy bullets. Food supplies were limited, and morale was undermined by bickerings and resentments. Gubbins and Lawrence were perpetually at odds. The civilian volunteers resented very deeply the lack of gratitude displayed to them by the military. Twenty volunteers, civilians not in the government employ, stood guard at various key positions around the entrenchment.

One half of the soldiers were thus on duty every day, and the other half off duty at the Residency; not so with the volunteers, for *every day and night of the whole five months* [his italics], did they stand sentry and do their duty, yet so unjust were the military authorities, that, while the soldiers got sugar and tea (as long as it lasted) the volunteers got none, while the soldiers drew rum and porter rations *daily*, until Havelock's force came in, the volunteers were refused it – while the soldiers received meat *daily* the volunteers were only allowed it every second day, and while the soldiers got otta, the volunteers were served out with wheat and told to grind it into flour themselves! This will give you an idea of the treatment to which gentlemen of respectability, who never flinched from the post of danger, were subjected during this trying time. The brigadier was always coarse in his speech and harsh in his manners, and fairly led by his staff, his aide-de-camp conceited and impertinent – the adjutant-general the reverse of conciliatory, the Commissariat officer . . . was snappish and insolent in the extreme.[41]

When at last, after several botched attempts, General Havelock relieved the siege, the conquering heroes themselves – Havelock himself and Neill – were exchanging such notes as this – 'I wrote to you confidentially on the state of affairs. You send me back a letter of censure of my measures, reproof and advice for the future. I do not and will not receive any of them from an officer under my command be his experience what it may.'[42]

Havelock contracted dysentery at Lucknow, from which he died[43] – 'Harry,' he said to his son, 'see how a Christian can die.' Henry Lawrence died of wounds during the siege – every one of the soldiers who carried him to his grave kissed him on the forehead. This was not a war when the senior officers escaped. General Barnard died of cholera. At the funeral of General John Nicholson, aged thirty-six, the men of the Multani Horse threw themselves on the ground and wept. 'Probably not one of these men had ever shed a tear before; but for them Nicholson was everything.'[44] It was not only the suffering, and deaths, of women and children which excited passionate British emotion during this tragic period. The Mutiny, as they called it, had caught them all by surprise. The possibility that Indians could, for whatever motives, expose their vulnerability summoned forth in the collective psyche violent and passionate emotions.

The fluttering, torn Union Jack was never removed from the flagpole of the Residency at Lucknow through all the hellish nine months. It was not a moment for national self-questioning about what right they had to be in India in the first place. The uprisings and wars of 1857–8 were seen as the assault of barbarism against Christian civilization. The army officers who suppressed the rebellion were seen as magnificent heroes in the mould of those chronicled by Livy in the schoolbooks. 'Never since the days of old Rome, when "the bridge was kept by the gallant three" have there been heroes more worthy of a nation's honour than that little band of fighting men who held the Temple on the banks of the Ganges and cut their way through a pitiless multitude who were thirsting for their blood'[45] is a typical sentence from *The Great White Hand or The Tiger of Cawnpore* by J.E. Muddock – one of over fifty exciting novels which British men or women wrote about the uprising. 'The "Great White Hand" was triumphant; it had crushed "the House of Timour" into the dust; it had broken and destroyed the power of England's enemies, and had vindicated the outraged honour of the British nation.'[46]

That was how most of the British, however sophisticated, saw the suppression of the 'Mutiny'. *The Illustrated London News*, in a leader-article on 26 September 1857, said:

> The general feeling of India is not only that the mutiny will and shall be suppressed, but that the result of the struggle – bloody and horrible as it may be – will be the re-establishment of British power on a firmer basis than ever. At home the same feeling is prevalent. We have some croakers – as we always must have; but the tone of the public mind is proud, self-reliant, and hopeful; and men the most peaceful – who, prior to these exciting events, had no more notion that they possessed the martial spirit than the good bourgeois in Molière's comedy had that he spoke in prose – burn with an irrepressible desire to punish the murderers of women and children, and to wreak avenging justice upon the traitors and the cowards who have done us this wrong. If anything were needed to show that we were at heart a nation of soldiers this mutiny has effected it.[47]

This was, undoubtedly, the public mood. It is a terrifying example of how short a collective memory can be, how distorted its moral sense. In something like fifty years, the British had radically changed the rules and terms by which the East India Company had operated in India. From being a trading monopoly which worked, where successful, to the mutual advantage of greedy English merchants and greedy, or timorous, Indian princes, it became an administration, claiming the right to the revenues and rents of those princes, and the rents of the peasant-farmers. It had taken upon itself the role of educator, civil servant and improver, making no secret not merely of its disapproval of Indian religions, but, more, of its right to disapprove. The sharp reactions these events in India had produced were seen by the English public at large (apart from the inevitable croakers) as 'treason' – though how you can 'betray' an interloping authority which you do not regard as legitimate, these English imperialists did not trouble to ask themselves. By the next year, when the Act of Parliament abolished the EIC, it was 'provided that the splendid empire raised by the East India Company during the last and present century should be transferred to Queen Victoria'.[48] The nation of shopkeepers had become the nation of imperialists. The late Victorian historian of *Punch*, M.H. Spielmann, saw as the 'masterpieces of Sir John Tenniel his Cawnpore cartoons depicting "The British Lion's Vengeance on the Bengal Tiger." . . . Once this fine drawing is seen, of the royal beast springing on its snarling foe, whose victims lie mangled under its paw, it can never be forgotten.' Spielmann tells us that Tenniel's cartoon served as 'a banner when they raised the cry of vengeance, it alarmed the authorities, who feared that they would thereby be forced on a road which both policy and the gentler dictates of civilisation forbade'.

It is with relief that one turns to the exchanges between the governor-general and his monarch.

> One of the greatest difficulties which lie ahead, and Lord Canning grieves to say so to Your Majesty, will be the violent rancour of a very large proportion of the English Community against every native Indian of every class. There is rabid and indiscriminate vindictiveness abroad, even amongst many who ought to set a better example, which it is impossible to contemplate without something like a feeling of shame of one's fellow-countrymen.[49]

The vehemence of the Queen's response does her great credit. She entirely shared Canning's 'feelings of sorrow and indignation at the unchristian spirit shown – alas! also to a great extent here – by the public towards Indians in general and towards *Sepoys without discrimination!* [her italics]'. She emphasized that the Indians should know 'that there is no hatred to a brown skin'.

These words were totally sincere, and borne out in her unfeigned delight in the company of Indians, an aspect of the Queen's character which would lead to minor troubles later in the reign. Apart from being shaming, the British vindictiveness towards all Indians in general, in the aftermath of what they called the Mutiny, blinded them to the most extraordinary aspect of the period 1857–9 in Indian history: namely that sepoy regiments on the whole remained loyal to the East India Company. Even those which did not conspicuously refused to take part in the worst atrocities upon Europeans.

Historians from Indian and British backgrounds both tend to write as if the defeat of the 'Mutiny' were an inevitability. Certainly, by the end of 1857 the British had largely gained control of the situation: Lucknow and Delhi had been relieved. Tatya Tope, however, and other Indian resistance-fighters, kept up fairly vigorous guerrilla warfare for the whole of the next year. The king of Delhi, who was put on trial in March 1859 for having aided and abetted the 'mutineers', was exiled for life to Rangoon. Addressed by his followers as 'Ruler of the Universe',[50] he was an enfeebled old man, toothless, weak, and powerless as he had always been. Sir Colin Campbell, the veteran Crimean hero, pursued Tatya Tope in some exciting campaigns and the defeat of the Mutiny at Jhansi by Sir William Rose really signalled the end of the war.[51] Tatya Tope was hanged at dawn on 18 April 1859.

Undoubtedly a factor in the Indian defeat was the tendency for rebel groups to disintegrate. At the outbreak, the 17th Native Infantry had marched out of Azamgarh for Faizabad 'with all the pomp of war: elephants, carriages, buggies and horses accompanied Bhundu Singh Rajah their leader'. They fought in the action there – the 200 troops having swollen to 500 non-uniformed rabble. After August 1857 there were no organized sepoy resistance-fighters in the entire Doab district. By contrast the British, who had their share of setbacks, always regrouped, closed ranks. Much has been made of the importance of the telegraph and the railway, which the British had at their disposal and the rebels did not.

Such would be the common-sense or occidental version of events. Perhaps it would be truer to say that India, and the Indians, did not yet have an alternative vision of themselves to put up against the European bullies in their midst. The notion of 'enlightened' politics was itself a Western import which, having taken root, would require nurture before achieving the desired result of British withdrawal. Viewed in this light, it is hard to see who was the victor of 1857–9. The British ground the Indians down, but what followed – ninety years of 'The Raj' – was in fact an odd sort of coalition. The British could not 'govern' India without Indian consent. The subsequent occasions of violence, such as the notorious massacre at Amritsar of 1919, were in fact signs of British weakness, a losing of grip, rather than the reverse. The Raj worked only for so long as the Indians themselves, fearful of the divisions within their own ranks, between castes, religions and cultures, got along as best they could with their European visitors.

Sir Fitzjames Stephen, the political philosopher of the new order in India, took a bleak view of British rule: 'It is essentially an absolute government, founded not on consent, but on conquest. It does not represent the native principles of life or of government, and it can never do so, until it represents heathenism and barbarism . . .' Yet as everyone, English and Indian, knew, India chose in 1857 to conquer itself, and finally to let its rebels cave in. The 36,000 European troops could easily have been defeated had not the majority of 257,000 sepoys chosen to remain on their side.

The knowledge that the Indians had the power, if they chose, to re-enact another Kanpur, another Lucknow, perhaps underwrote the insufferable psychology of bullying conquest which characterized the British military mindset after their supposed victories. Johnny Stanley (1837–78), younger brother of the 3rd Lord Stanley of Alderley, is alas a typical specimen. Having served in the Crimea aged sixteen, and nearly died of fever, he came out to India as Lord Canning's ADC. He wrote home amusedly in December 1868, clearly frustrated to be out of England during the hunting season: 'Yesterday Baring and I had a tremendous race after a ragged black dog, it made for its village, & we crashed through everything scattering cows & niggers & their bamboo fences as if they were nothing.'[52]

While Lord Canning was exchanging kindly letters about the need to establish good relations between Europeans and Indians, his young aide wrote, four days before Christmas:

> The way to keep a Sikh regiment in order is this: of course you will not agree with me, but it is this, an officer commanding one of the irregular regiments of cavalry rides through the Bazaar in plain clothes, he meets one of his troopers whom he orders to salute, the sowar is insolent, the officer rides up to him, takes him by the long hair & throws him off his horse. That is the only way. The man is immediately cowed, if you attempt to parley they get worse. The men have all positive orders to salute any white face, not a private.[53]

The immediate political consequence of the uprising was the abolition of the East India Company, and the placing of India under the direct control of the government in Westminster. Lord Canning became not governor general, but viceroy. This had been planned for years before the sepoy uprisings – Sir Charles Wood's Government of India Bill of 1853 had set in train the process of abolishing the EIC and attempting a programme of modernization, railways, education, land reform[54] – all the blessings of civilization bestowed by whiggish busybodydom on a culture that had not asked for any of them. Inevitably there were Indians who received all or part of these things with the enthusiasm which was deemed appropriate in Whitehall. It is impossible not to smile at the high-mindedness of the British bafflement when their gifts were not appreciated.[55] 'Firing cannon balls at railway engines symbolized a wilful and irrational rejection of technical progress.' One can imagine Carlyle, Ruskin, William Morris, William Holman Hunt, George MacDonald and Cardinal Newman, while not exactly approving of the violence done against 'technical progress', at least seeing the point of it.

Some British men and women, in spite of the bitter legacies of 1857, would always respond sympathetically to the Indian ethos; many married Indians, and it was by no means only in the 'nabob' era that Britons 'went native' in India. Many who did not, like Kipling or Curzon, had a deep love for Indian history, culture and tradition. Yet the cynical judgement of Colonel Chardin Johnson of the 9th Lancers probably felt like truth when he wrote it:

> The Sikhs don't love us one bit but hate sepoys like poison . . . Moreover, they are the lastly conquered of the Indian races and have not forgotten what British Pluck can do. They like the cause now, for the sepoys have mutilated and tortured their men . . . and their blood is up on our side at the present – but, this business over [i.e. the Mutiny] they may play us the same trick as the sepoy ruffians anyday – there is no sympathy between us – we despise niggers, they hate us.[56]

He was wrong about the Sikhs, who became the mainstay of the new Indian army, but his picture of the mutual distrust as the 1850s came to a close has an uncomfortable authenticity.

Ninety years passed before 'midnight's children' reclaimed the subcontinent from the British. It is not a long time *sub specie aeternitatis*, or even when measured by the duration of the Moghul empire or the Mahratta kingdoms. The ambivalence of Indian attitudes to this vivid phase in their country's history can be caught by what happened in two of the legendary shrines of the Raj on Independence Day 1947. In Lucknow, a crowd flocked to the Residency, intent on raising the Indian flag in the very place where the British flag had fluttered bravely throughout the siege, and for the next ninety years without interruption. They were prevented from doing so by 'Dedhu' Pant, the grand old man of United Provinces (now Uttar Pradesh), politics, who spent a lifetime in anti-British struggle. As prime minister of the newly formed state, he told the crowds to disperse and go home, 'and leave in peace a spot sacred to the British dead'.

At Kanpur, however, things were, and are, very different. Until Independence Day all Indians (except Christians) had been barred from entering the shrine garden which contained the dry well where the 'angels of Albion' perished. On Independence Day the crowd surged into the forbidden garden and the nose of the white marble angel was damaged. The European Well Committee agreed to remove the angel to the cemetery of the Memorial Chapel. A bronze effigy of Tatya Tope, the initiator of the massacre, was placed to look down gloatingly on the slaughtered innocents, and one cannot but sympathize with the great colonial historian who saw this as 'a singularly tasteless and vicious reprisal against the hapless dead'.[57]

16

Clinging to Life

In February 1858, lying sick of a fever at Ternate in the Moluccas, Alfred Russel Wallace, an amateur naturalist, began to think of Malthus's *Essay on Population*. Unlike Charles Darwin, who was always rich, thanks to the Wedgwood inheritance, Wallace had had to work his way through the world – as a schoolmaster, self-taught railway architect, and explorer. Like Darwin he had made a trip to South America, and been awestruck by the equatorial forests, the beauty and strangeness of the flora and fauna, and by the native population. Financing his travels by the sale of specimens, he had also spent eight years exploring the Malay Archipelago. Like Darwin, Lyell, Chambers, and indeed most scientists of the day, Wallace was preoccupied by the problem of the origins of life on Earth, what Goethe called 'The mystery of mysteries'. Since the time of Darwin's grandfather, Erasmus Darwin, who wrote *Zoonomia* (1794–6), a work which anticipated the opinions of Lamarck, scientists had believed in the evolution of species. It was Jean-Baptiste Pierre Antoine de Monet, Chevalier de Lamarck (1744–1829), who finally put paid to the notion of the immutability of species, but the question remained – *how* did such changes take place? The caricature of the question is, how did the giraffe acquire a neck long enough to reach the tree? The secondary question is, what happened in the meanwhile to all the generations of short-necked giraffes whose mouths never came near the foliage?

Lamarck's answer to the first question is that species inherited acquired characteristics. The parent acquires some useful survival technique and is enabled thereby to pass this on to the offspring. Lamarckian evolution was popularized in England by Herbert Spencer – a self-taught philosopher, pioneer sociologist and universal wiseacre – and later in the century by Samuel Butler, grandson of Darwin's headmaster at Shrewsbury School. Although it can now be demonstrated that Lamarck was wrong about acquired characteristics being inheritable, it was in fact the metaphor in which most Victorians believed. Darwin, interestingly, adapted his own theories after the publication of his most famous book, adding mistakes to subsequent printings of *The Origin of Species* in order to conform more nearly to the Lamarckian theory he actually set out to disprove. This alerts us to the truth that two things are always going on during scientific research, even in the case of scrupulous scientists such as Wallace and Darwin: on the one hand there is a painstaking search for objective reality, on the other there is the medium in which this search is conducted – language, a metaphor-encrusted tool which dates as easily as clothes. Thus, while we can see the Victorian evolutionary biologists as making truly world-changing 'discoveries' of verifiable (in Popper's terms) phenomena, likewise we can see their ideas as shaped by their times: the 'origin of species' question being to this extent as much a phenomenon of the 1850s as stovepipe hats, steam railways and Pre-Raphaelite art. It is in this sense and context that we see how Lamarckian evolution is the perfect metaphor for the self-made rentier class, such as the Wedgwoods and Darwins. Owd Wooden Leg Wedgwood lived and slept in his 'works' in Stoke-on-Trent, cheek by jowl with his workers. He made a fortune and was enabled thereby to acquire the houses and lands of a country gentleman. It was Josiah II at Maer Hall who had inherited so many of Jos the First's acquired gentilities that he left 'the works' entirely in the hands of managers. It was at his uncle's house at Maer that Charles Darwin learnt to shoot – and 'my zeal was so great that I used to place my shooting-boots open by my bedside when I went to bed, so as not to lose half-a-minute in putting them on in the morning'.

But – back to Wallace in 1858, sweating through his fever and thinking of Malthus. Within two hours, he suddenly thought out the whole theory of natural selection. Three days later he had finished his essay.

It is very typical of the difference between the two men that Wallace worked out in a couple of hours what it took Darwin twenty years to decide to publish. Like Wallace, Darwin had been inspired by Malthus – only in 1838. He had sat on his theory, mulled it over, concealed it from himself and his wife, agonized about it. Then, when Wallace sent him his own essay on natural selection, he decided to act. The Wallace–Darwin theory was duly read out at the Linnaean Society in London on 1 July 1858, and the first person to apply it, and to publish it, was Canon H.B. Tristram a clergyman–ornithologist who, in an article in *Ibis*, October 1859, used it to explain the colours of desert birds. Charles Darwin, who had written and rewritten several drafts of his essay, expanded it to *On the Origin of Species by Means of Natural Selection, or the Preservation of Favoured Races in the Struggle for*

Life. It was published by John Murray, himself an amateur geologist. Murray was in fact unconvinced by the theory, but when the whole edition of 1,250 copies sold out in one day he saw its commercial potential. It was to be one of the bestsellers of the age. The number of pamphlets, debates, books, speeches, sermons, quarrels it generated is numberless. It was a book which grew out of pure observation of Nature, but which on another level seemed to define the age to itself. Its primary discovery, that an impersonal process of selection is at work in nature, comparable to the process by which pedigree dogs or hybrid roses are 'improved' by breeders, was seen by the Victorians themselves as a picture of a competitive world. Perhaps it was only in the late twentieth century that some of its other implications – the need to be a Friend of the Earth, since we are all descended from the same roots and sources – were worked out.

Wallace and Darwin had been working on the same material for twenty years quite independently. It was twenty years since a rough version of the theory had been penned by Wallace. Graciously, however, he allowed Darwin to publish and resigned himself, for a lifetime, to being 'the moon to Darwin's sun'.[1] Since he was still in Malaya when Darwin's *Origin of Species* appeared, Wallace did not read the book until 1860. He read it five or six times, 'each time with increasing admiration'. He later said he was glad that it had been Darwin, fourteen years his senior, and not himself who had been called upon to set forward the theory in detail. Later he did publish his own *Contributions to the Theory of Natural Selection* (1870), which confirmed that his mind and Darwin's had been working towards the same conclusions by completely independent means.[2]

Darwin and his beloved cousin-wife Emma moved quite early in their married life to the village of Downe,* near Sevenoaks, Kent. Here he battled with his lifelong mystery illness, which left him breathless and exhausted for half of every day. Here he basked in the love of his wife and children and cousins, here he fulfilled his duties as a local citizen, sitting on the parish council, befriending the vicar, even sitting as a magistrate. Darwin, in his diffidence and self-doubt, is one of the most attractive of all men of genius. Wholly typical is the story told of some quite unimportant discussion at the parish council. Much later that night, the vicar of Downe, the Rev. John Innes, was surprised by a

---

*In those days, Down.

knock at his front door. The tall, bald, troubled figure of Charles Darwin stood there. 'He came to say that, thinking over the debate, though what he had said was quite accurate, he thought, I might have drawn an erroneous conclusion, and he would not sleep till he had explained it.'[3]

Given that this was the nature of the man, it is not surprising that he was so unwilling to test the waters by publishing *The Origin of Species*. Darwin was acutely aware of the intellectual objections to his theory, and this was his primary reason for anxiety; *was it true?* In 1844, when Chambers had anonymously published *Vestiges of the Natural History of Creation*, there had been an outcry. 'Mr Vestiges' or 'The Vestigarian' was seen as a 'practical Atheist'.[4] The Church had seen, even in Chambers's generalized transmutationist tract, that such a view disposed of the need for any kind of interventionist God. Scientists had trod very warily since the furore. Figures such as Sir Richard Owen (1804–92), the finest anatomist of his day, first Hunterian professor of anatomy at the Royal College of Surgeons, Gold Medallist in the Geological Society, and in his latter days in charge of the natural history departments at the British Museum, provided a good example of the difficulty faced by any Victorian scientist who wished to get on in the world. In private he freely discussed evolutionary theory. In public he offered simple-minded defences of the literal truth of the Old Testament.[5] He denounced *Vestiges* and in time he would denounce Darwin.

Today we live in an age of scientific triumphalism. It is difficult to recapture the spirit of Victorian England before Darwin published his famous theory. The Church and the clergy still had tremendous power. Not only did they control nearly all university posts, but the convention remained (whatever was said in private) that Parliament and the Press all supported Orthodoxy. For so retiring and shy a man as Darwin to stand up against them all was a formidable challenge. Added to these was the religious distress caused to his wife Emma. Darwin knew that there would be those, including himself, who felt that his theory of natural selection did away with the necessity of believing in a Creator. The Captain of the *Beagle*, by now a rear admiral married to a pious evangelical lady, had already made furious objections to Darwin's highly acclaimed journal of the *Voyage*. Darwin's observations that there were discernible differences between species from island to island in the Galapagos Archipelago did not, in *The Voyage of the Beagle*, lead to any particular conclusion, but Captain Fitzroy was not slow to grasp the implications which Darwin later spelt out in *Origins*. Consider the absence of Batrachians – i.e. frogs, newts and toads – on small oceanic islands. 'As these animals and their spawn are known to be immediately killed by sea-water, on my view we can see that there would be great difficulty in their transportal across the sea, and therefore why they do not exist on any oceanic island. But why, on the theory of creation, they should not have been created there, it would be very difficult to explain.'[6]

It is the gentle way in which the very concept of creation is thrown away in parenthesis which perhaps made *The Origin of Species* seem so injurious to the faith of certain Christians. For Captain, later Rear Admiral, Robert Fitzroy if you did not believe that each individual frog, newt, finch, butterfly, dandelion had been made, in its present form, *immutable*, then you were denying the principle of Creation. In the summer of 1860, the rear admiral went along to the meeting of the British Association at Oxford to take part in that celebrated debate on Evolution in which Bishop 'Soapy Sam' Wilberforce begged to know whether 'it was through his grandfather or his grandmother that [T.H. Huxley] claimed his descent from a monkey': and in which Huxley – Darwin's St Paul as he has been called, his representative on Earth – replied that 'If . . . the question is put to me, would I rather have a miserable ape for a grandfather or a man highly endowed by nature and possessed of great means of influence and yet who employs these faculties and that influence for the mere purpose of introducing ridicule into a grave scientific discussion, I unhesitatingly affirm my preference for the ape.'[7]

How grateful Darwin was, not to be present during these embarrassing displays of fisticuffs, but poor Fitzroy was there, and he spoke in support of the bishop. His own publication, *A Very Few Remarks with Reference to the Deluge*, had attempted to demonstrate that the geology of South American can best be understood in terms of the volcanic catastrophes which took place at the time of Noah's Flood in the book of Genesis. ('Lyell says it beats all the other nonsense he has ever read on the subject,' said Darwin.) Fitzroy was professionally involved with the weather, being in charge of the meteorology department at the Board of Trade. His disastrously inaccurate weather forecasts were pilloried in the press in the spring of 1865 and he sank into depression. He took the same remedy as his uncle Castlereagh and cut his own throat.

Darwin could hardly have been blamed, but the suicide was to grieve him. Beneath the rear admiral's expressions of religious certitudes lay terror. We can never forget this when observing the phenomenon now generally termed 'fundamentalism', which is why it so often turns to violence. The real voice of sanity in the Oxford debate was neither Huxley nor Soapy Sam but Darwin's friend, Sir William Jackson Hooker, director of the Botanic Gardens at Kew. It was, Lyell believed, Hooker who turned the debate against the bishop. The botanist struck to the purely scientific arguments. When Francis Huxley was collecting his father's letters for a book which was to have included an extensive quotation from T.H. Huxley's reply to Bishop Wilberforce, it was Hooker who dissuaded him from publishing what he called 'far too much of a braggart epistle'.[8] Yet if, from the beginning, the Theory of Natural Selection was seen as incompatible with religious belief, much of the blame for this must rest with the churchmen who were too timorous to study the scientific, too lazy to work out the theological implications in sufficient depth. No wonder the perception took root that a choice must be made, *aut Darwin, aut Christus*, Darwin or Christ.

In his highly readable book *Darwin for Beginners* (1982), for example, Dr Jonathan Miller stated that 'for pious Christians, it was an article of faith that the living world was an unaltered replica of the one which God had created at the outset. No species had been lost and none had been altered.' It would seem as though some Christians, such as Rear Admiral Fitzroy, made this curious notion into an article of their faith, but if so it was not an idea of very ancient or creditable vintage. St Augustine of Hippo (354–430), who was the first great philosopher-theologian of the Latin West, had taught that the original germ of living things came in two forms, one placed by God in animals and plants, the other scattered through the environment, only destined to become active in the right conditions. It wasn't necessary for God to create each living species. The Creator provided the seeds of life and allowed them to develop in their own time.[9]

The Renaissance was the period during which the doctrine of Special Creation emerged. This was an idea of nature which saw all species as the direct, unchanging creation of God. Milton depicts the Creation in this manner in *Paradise Lost*. A pioneer of the viewpoint was the Spanish Jesuit Francisco de Suárez (1548–1617), who specifically denied the evolutionary ideas of Augustine and – more importantly, since he was seen as a definitive theologian – of Thomas Aquinas. With the Renaissance obsession with Mutability, and the changeableness of all sublunary things, would go the yearning for God to have created living forms all at one shot:

> The grassie Clods now Calv'd, now half appeer'd
> The Tawnie Lion, pawing to get free
> His hinder parts, then springs as broke from Bonds,
> And Rampant shakes his Brindled main; the Ounce,
> The Libbard, and the Tyger, as The Moale
> Rising, the crumbl'd Earth above them threw
> In Hillocks . . .
>
> *Paradise Lost* VII: 463–9

Against this is the Wallace–Darwin view that species all emerge, ultimately, from a single life-form. The theory does not suggest, as Bishop Wilberforce mischievously inferred, that we are descended from monkeys, but that the higher primates, human beings among them, share a common ancestry. The monkeys are cousins, not grandmothers. Pooh-Bah in *The Mikado* is closer to the Wallace–Darwin notion when he boasts, 'I am, in point of fact, a particularly haughty and exclusive person, of pre-Adamite ancestral descent. You will understand this when I tell you that I can trace my ancestry back to a protoplasmal primordial atomic globule.'[10] *The Mikado* appeared sixteen years after *The Origin of Species* and five after *The Descent of Man*. In *The Origin* Darwin does not directly discuss the question of human origins at all.

If one had to isolate a single all-consuming idea which has taken hold of the human race in the post-political era in which we now live, it is the interrelatedness of natural forms – the fact that we are all on this planet together – human beings, mammals, fish, insects, trees – all dependent upon one another, all very unlikely to have a second chance of life either beyond the grave or through reincarnation, and therefore aware of the responsibilities incumbent upon custodians of the Earth. 'Let it be borne in mind,' Darwin writes in *The Origin*, 'how infinitely complex and close-fitting are the mutual relations of all organic beings to each other and to their physical conditions of life.'[11] This surely explains why, in our generation, Darwin has grown in importance and stature, whereas almost all his contemporary thinkers and sages are half-forgotten. Herbert Spencer is all but unread. With the demise of European communism, it seems to many – especially to the majority who have not read much Marx – as if *The Communist Manifesto* and

Das Kapital are dead. Freud, in many schools of psychology, is discredited; Hegel is of more interest to historians of philosophy than as a living inspiration to many of our contemporary philosophers. Carlyle and Ruskin are unknown to general readers; Mill is read selectively by students, but is no household name. But neo-Darwinians – Richard Dawkins, Daniel C. Dennett and the rest – can still write bestsellers.

'Let me lay my cards on the table,' writes Professor Dennett. 'If I were to give an award for the single best idea anyone has ever had, I'd give it to Darwin, ahead of Newton and Einstein and everyone else. In a single stroke, the idea of evolution by natural selection unifies the realm of life, meaning and purpose with the realm of space and time, cause and effect, mechanism and physical law.'[12]

The success of *The Origin of Species*, however, as opposed to the more general question of the philosophical influence of Darwin on the way *we* think, resides precisely in its quietness, its unhectoring tone. Though Darwin caused Emma such distress by his unbelief, and wept at the distress he caused – on one of her letters on the subject he scribbled, 'when I am dead, know that many times I have kissed and cryed over this' – he was not an adamant unbeliever, as some of his followers were, and are. His unbelief was quiet and sad. Downe House used to be a parsonage, and in many respects his life resembled that of the naturalist parson, such as Gilbert White, who he could so easily have become after Cambridge. His attention to detail, his patience, his homeliness as well as his punctilious quality of observation are all things we find in Gilbert White. The examples he chose – spaniels, racehorses, pigeons – ensured that hardly an English reader from working-class pigeon-fancier to tweedy female Cocker-breeder to aristocratic racehorse-owner would not recognize Darwin's world as his or her own. Though earlier readers of Lyell and Chambers were horrified by the pitilessness of nature red in tooth and claw, Darwin manages to make nature appear almost as gentle as himself. In what is almost a quotation from Malthus, he depicts the struggle for existence thus: 'All we can do, is to keep steadily in mind that each organic being is striving to increase at a *geometrical ratio* [my italics – note the Malthusianism]; that each at some period of its life during some season of the year, during each generation, or at intervals, has to struggle for life, and to suffer great destruction.'[13] But there is consolation offered by gentle Darwin – 'When we reflect on this struggle, we may console ourselves with the full belief that the war of nature is not incessant, that no fear is felt, that death is generally prompt, and that the vigorous, the healthy and the happy survive and multiply.'

The literature on Darwin and his impact is almost limitless. The truth remains that the majority of Victorian scientists went on being Christian, or at least holding on to some form of religious belief.[14] Initially at least, the assaults on the authenticity of the Bible were much more damaging to faith than was Darwin. The religious reactions against Darwinism, from Sam Wilberforce, and later from the Catholic Church, can perhaps now be seen as horror at the notion of a natural world which is always changing, never still, never the same, rather than a fully considered philosophical consideration of God's creative power (or its lack). Marx and Engels saw Darwinism as making an entire *Weltanschauung* out of laissez-faire capitalism – progress through struggle. It is perhaps for later generations of philosophers and scientists to ask questions about 'Darwin's metaphor'. In simple terms, where there is talk of 'struggle' and 'progress' in Darwin, or in Spencer of 'the survival of the fittest', how much of the theory survives examination?

We shall return to Darwin and Darwinism at the point when he publishes *The Descent of Man*, but it is worthwhile to ask whether any of the four major scientific objections to *The Origin of Species* still stand up. In no particular order the objections are as follows. One, that Darwin's view depended on a miscalculation of the age of the Earth. This was the view of the physicist William Thomson – Lord Kelvin. He was right to think Darwin got the age of the Earth wrong: but as a matter of fact the Earth is older – not, as Kelvin thought, younger – than Darwin's calculation, so there is plenty of time for evolution to have occurred by Natural Selection.

Another objection, posed by a Scotch engineer, Fleeming Jenkins, was based on ignorance (shared by Darwin) of genetics. Jenkins could not see, if natural selection produced a favourable variation, how it could be preserved for the next generation rather than being diluted. While he made the objection, Father Mendel in his Czech monastery was proving that genetic factors don't dilute over time by somehow averaging out, but behave as if they were indivisible (although some are dominant, others recessive). By the 1880s Weisman was advancing his theory that the perishable generations are linked by imperishable genetic material, identified in 1931 as deoxyribonucleic acid – DNA – whose structure was not demonstrated until the 1950s. Here at last was hard and fast evidence that Darwin's critic, Jenkins, was definitely wrong, and in the imperishability of DNA we see the way in which natural selection *could* pass on favourable variations without breeding out.

The Catholic biologist H. St George Mivart objected to Darwin's theory on an almost metaphysical point. While we might understand the manner in which the process of natural selection might work once it was under way, how does it explain the initial development? How did a 'useful' organ like the eye get started in the first place? Some of St George Mivart's objections seem to be based on a confused metaphor of purpose. The Darwinian does not believe in purpose, so that Darwin's own metaphor of 'struggle' is probably unfortunate. One is not to imagine the giraffe in one generation striving to some imagined state of long-neckedness: merely that the longer the neck, the more leaves the animal can eat, hence an inexorable development of giraffes to browse at tree height.

These three objections, all brought on scientific, or quasi-scientific grounds, have been answered in time. There is one puzzle, however, which worried Darwin the most and to which he could not supply an answer. As Dr Jonathan Miller has said, 'the process of evolution is more episodic than Darwin supposed'. The concept of the 'hopeful monster', the species which appears to have arrived from nowhere, or to have fast-forwarded through the infinitesimal and slow processes of evolutionary change, cannot be dismissed. How do you leap from having a couple of stumps to having workable wings? Can you or can't you breathe in air, having been previously aquatic? *Most* such objections can be answered half-plausibly by Darwinians. Some, however, can't. Darwin hoped that fossil evidence or something comparable would eventually demonstrate the 'missing links' in the chain. But in the case of some structures in the natural world – such as that of the eye for example – modern biochemistry has revealed a complexity which makes Darwin's explanations seem clumsy. In the view of Michael Behe, 'Each of the anatomical steps and structures that Darwin thought were so simple actually involves staggeringly complicated biochemical processes that cannot be papered over with rhetoric. Darwin's metaphorical hops from butte to butte are now revealed in many cases to be huge leaps between carefully tailored machines – distances that would require a helicopter to cross in one trip.'[15] The use of the word 'tailored' here begs huge questions. Many would think that the 'argument by design' or the 'creationist' viewpoint, however satisfying to those who entertain it, still fails on a scientific or analytic level to explain how, in the evolutionary story, you get from a to c without passing an invisible b. This is the objection to Darwin which, for some people, has never been answered.

The success of *The Origin of Species*, however, does not depend in the first instance on any polemical stance, so much as on its picture of the natural world as a teeming, changing and infinitely various abundance of interacting species – plant, insect, fish, bird, mammal only the most visible. This explains its initial impact. In common with the novels of Dickens, the canvases of Frith (his famous overcrowded *Derby Day* was exhibited in 1858), or the socio-economics of Marx with his vast variety of allusions and examples, Darwin's most famous book is superabundant. Plenitude is its first, and most overwhelming, quality.

Natural selection, it need hardly be explained, means not selection by the conscious will of men or of gods, but by successful procreation. The 1858 Matrimonial Causes (or Divorce) Bill became law in England, but not in Ireland, enabling men and women to obtain divorces through a special court, at a cost of around £100. Prime Minister Palmerston, the old roué, told Parliament, 'we shall return here and sit day by day, and night by night, until this Bill be concluded'.[16] His chancellor of the Exchequer – Gladstone – was horrified by the measure, intervening in the debate seventy-three times, and devoting long speeches to the horror of bringing divorce to the doors of all classes. (Hitherto, divorce had only been possible in England by introducing a special Act of Parliament for each marital breakdown. By 1872, with the new law, some 200 decrees were granted annually.)

The existence of the new divorce law formalized the recognition that Victorian men and women committed adultery – thus, it defined them not merely as property-owning, but as sexual beings. Predictably the law remained biased against women; whereas husbands could sue for divorce on the simple ground of adultery, a wife could do so only if she could prove that her husband was guilty of bestiality, bigamy, incest, rape or cruelty in addition. Though Darwin very consciously and conspicuously omitted a discussion of human behaviour from *The Origin of Species*, its first readers brought to it, and extracted from it, a new sense of the human place in nature, and this sense in part was inevitably something which found its expression in the many novels and poems which touched on relations between the sexes.

The art-form, however, which was most blatantly concerned with adultery and sexual feeling was the music drama of Richard Wagner. The year which saw the publication of *The Origin of Species* in November had also been that in which Wagner completed *Tristan und Isolde*[17] – though the music drama was not performed until June 1865. The extent to which the inspiration for the work was Wagner's guilty passion for Mathilde, the wife of his benefactor Otto Wesendonk – or indeed how far it anticipates the feelings he would have for Cosima, the wife of his first conductor Hans von Bülow before she married Wagner – this is the stuff of gossip-biographies. Already in the midst of his great *Ring* dramas, Wagner paused to return to the medieval romance of Gottfried von Strassburg's *Tristan*. In so doing, he wrote an erotically charged manifesto; the hero's preparedness to betray his liege-lord King Mark is an act of magnificent anarchy.

Capitalism, and its creation of a large *haute bourgeoisie* and a large rentier class with endless leisure, both hugely increased the opportunities for adultery and heightened its dangers. The divorce lawyers whose very existence Gladstone so deplored had come into existence to determine how the iron structures of capitalist society, held together as modern conservative politicians still delight to remind us by the 'building-blocks' of family life, could coexist beside the sexual appetites of men and women. The needs for control and hypocrisy and the weapons of financial ruin or public humiliation were obvious when you consider what damage the Tristans and Isoldes of the suburbs could do if they chose. This must be part of what gives the opera its stupendous, almost narcotic power.

Wagner is a supreme innovator, not merely musically, but imaginatively. Like Marx and Darwin, he draws heavily on the works of predecessors and contemporaries, especially Berlioz. Darwin would be unthinkable without the other evolutionary thinkers – just as Marx owes more than he would ever allow to Proudhon, and to Hegel – but it still makes sense to hail them as world-changing intellects. Wagner's dreams of the uses to which human beings put their powers – now the slaves and now the masters of greed and passion – are, like Darwin's, with us still. *Tristan und Isolde* is perennially 'modern'. Its Second Act is a sustained musical evocation not merely of erotic feeling but of the sexual act itself. Had such a thing ever been attempted in European art – and has it ever been bettered? And yet it speaks not merely of the ecstatic joys of coition, but also of the impossibility of two human beings ever fully getting beyond sex to union of mind or soul. Its reason is the tragic and realistic one that Western humanity could no longer energetically believe in an afterlife. This great theme of *Tristan*, its *Liebestod*, therefore transcends sex just as Dante had done when he wrote the *Paradiso*. But whereas the great medieval poet could synthesize the personal and the erotic into a grand political and religious vision, culminating in Paradise, Wagner – a genius of comparable power – sees all human aspirations, their hope of political progress, of philosophical enlightenment, of religious comfort or of sexual ecstasy, interwoven with their consciousness of mortality. As he would expound in his extended mythical *Ring* dramas, the gods themselves cannot escape the extinction which awaits each one of the species being swept down the evolutionary river; whereas the dream of Marx is one of ultimate triumph for the poor, and the fascination of Darwin's theory for Darwinian optimists was in the concept of progress through struggle, Wagner, with a realism which perhaps only comes to artists, saw the progress of his century – and ultimately of the human race – as one towards destruction.

In England, the *Liebestod* is transposed into a minor key when we turn to the home life of Queen Victoria, doomed for most of her reign to be a grief-stricken widow, her emotional life a blend of yearning and morbidity, which if not Wagnerian in tone at least matched Wagner's dramas in intensity. So aware are we of her last forty years as a half-life, an epilogue to the *Morte d'Albert*, that we must sometimes suppose there was an inevitability about the Prince's death, aged forty-two, or that he had already begun to decline into melancholy and inactivity before he was struck down by typhoid fever. This fiction began with Lytton Strachey's life of *Queen Victoria* which asserted that Prince Albert 'believed that he was a failure and he began to despair'. But he wasn't a failure, he had not begun to despair, and despite a premature baldness and paunchiness (he wore a wig indoors during his latter days because the Queen kept their rooms so cold)[18] and despite his very bad teeth, there was no reason to think that, had he escaped the typhoid fever, he would not have continued to lift himself from gloom and lead a full, happy life. In the very closing months of his life he thanked God 'that he has vouchsafed so much happiness to us', and this was heartfelt, even if life with his temperamental wife had its tribulations, and life among the unserious and ungrateful English its trials. (When the Queen was finally allowed to dub him Prince Consort in 1857 *The Times* cattily imagined that this would lead to increased respect for Albert, 'on the banks of the Spree and the Danube'.)[19] In fact, this is one of those feeble jokes which rebound on the teller, for hindsight makes us see what a valuable European dimension Albert brought to the political scene in England, and forces upon us the wistful game of wondering what might have been, had, for example, Albert (whose international, and in particular whose pan-German, stature grew by the year) lived into the era of Bismarck and beyond . . . No man single-handedly could have prevented the disastrous growth of rival nationalisms which came to catastrophe in 1914, but one can say that, had Albert's policies, rather than those of Lord Palmerston and those of subsequent prime ministers, been pursued, world war would have been less likely.

We see what he was like from the letters of Edward White Benson who, in his late twenties, was appointed as the headmaster of the newly founded Wellington College. This school, established in memory of the Great Duke, was always of interest to Prince Albert. He helped choose the site, in Berkshire, he gave advice about the architecture, where to plant trees, what the uniform should be like. Benson, whose appointment was owing to Albert, was typical of the sort of man the Prince encouraged – young, by no means well-born, energetic, serious. In one of his letters, he describes going to the Palace of Westminster, before the school was opened, for a meeting of the School Council:

> At the foot of a great staircase which I reached I turned round and saw a moustachioed gentleman drive up in a carriage, but I turned round and ran upstairs and on reaching the top found that the gentleman had run upstairs after me and that it was the Prince himself. He smiled very graciously and sweetly and shook hands with me, and he went on into the room where the Council had met already . . . The Prince is a prince of princes – thoroughly interested and hearty.[20]

This good-heartedness, and energy, came to be applied to all aspects of Albert's life, to his patronage of the arts, to his chancellorship of Cambridge University, to his punctilious management of Balmoral, Osborne, Windsor, their households and estates, to his large family, to his charitable work, and to his involvement with politics both at home and abroad.

After the suspension of the East India Company, Asia itself fell, in effect, under Albert's benign supervisory fiefdom. 'All despatches, when received and perused by the Secretary of State to be sent to the

Queen,' the new civil servants were told in 1858.[21] 'We are over-run with visiting royalties, present and prospective,' Greville complained to his diary in 1857. 'It is a new feature of the present day, the flitting about of royal personages.'[22]

In the marriage of his firstborn – Vicky – to Prince Frederick William (Fritz) of Prussia, there occurred the first of those dynastic alliances by which Albert, had he been spared, might have exercised an influence on a European scale. The marriage took place in the Chapel Royal at St James's Palace on 25 January 1858. The bride was just seventeen, the bridegroom twenty-six.[23] Disraeli, attending the bridal ball at Buckingham Palace, thought there were as many European princes as at the Congress of Vienna – here were the King of the Belgians, the Duke of Brabant, the Count of Flanders, the Prince and Princess Frederick William of Prussia, the Prince and Princess of Prussia, Prince Albert of Prussia, Prince Frederick Charles of Prussia, Prince Frederick Albert of Prussia, Prince Adalbert of Prussia, the Prince of Hohenzollern Sigmaringen, the Duke of Saxe-Coburg-Gotha, the Duchess of Orleans, the Comte de Paris, the Duc de Chartres, the Princess of Salerno, the Duke and Duchess d'Aumale, Prince Edward of Saxe-Weimar, the Prince of Leiningen, Prince Victor of Hohenlohe Langenburg and Prince Julius of Holstein Glücksburg.[24]

This was Britain 'at the heart of Europe' at a period of crucial European change. Prince Albert wanted this dynastic marriage because he saw that the future of Europe was to be shaped by the future of Germany. From his earliest years, under the tutelage of Baron Stockmar, and later as a student of Bonn University, Albert had come to want the unification of Germany.[25] Ever since his arrival in England, partly through his friendship with the German ambassador the Chevalier Bunsen, Albert had formed the view that a strong Anglo-German alliance could influence the direction this unification took. For as long as the German duchies and states were divided, the forces of reaction – in the states themselves, in Russia and in Austria – could go unchecked, save by the dangerous forces of revolution. Albert's view was that a Germany united by Prussia – but a Prussia which had adopted constitutional government – could be the safest bulwark Europe could have against tyranny on the one hand, anarchy on the other. Many within his own family disagreed with his view – old uncle Leopold, king of the Belgians, was afraid of a 'Prussian super-nation' if German unity took place.[26] 'An efficient Germany can come of it, only it would in a kind of way be a Germany subordinated to Prussia.'[27]

Albert, persuaded partly by Stockmar, partly by his own observation, thought that the little duchies, such as Coburg, were going to be swept aside anyway. The only question was not *whether* there would be a united Germany, but what kind of nation it would be – a Peelite (as it were) well-balanced Germany, with parliaments and representative government, living at peace with itself and its neighbours and allowing learned men like Chevalier Bunsen to continue educating the world (Germany's destiny), or a more tragic, belligerent Germany, economically and politically unstable, falling back on militarism as a poor substitute 'quick fix' to achieve national unity.[28]

It is possible to disagree with the drift of Albert's hopes for Europe; it is not possible to be blind to the fact, however, that he was a very well-informed, intelligent and moderate-minded German who knew whereof he spoke. Palmerston, who liked crossing swords with the Prince over European policy, was an old man, a very old man, who never saw that the rise of modern Germany was going to change Europe forever. One sees this in his well-known joke about the Schleswig-Holstein question. Palmerston made the remark when prime minister in 1863 – namely that there were only three people who had ever understood the Schleswig-Holstein question. One was a German professor, and he had gone mad. One was the Prince Consort, and he was dead. The third was himself, and he had forgotten all about it.[29] This 'forgetfulness' was a handy cloak for diplomatic ineptitude and political-cum-military impotence.

But if the intricacies of the question were of proverbial complexity, its broad historical implications – in terms of what it meant for the political balance of Europe – were very simple. Throughout the late 1840s and particularly after the revolutions of 1848, Albert was urging Pilgerstein to accept the claims of the overwhelmingly German duchy of Holstein to belong to the German Federation. The position of the predominantly Danish Schleswig was rather different.[30] Palmerston's diplomacy held the pass in 1852, when the London Protocol put both duchies under Danish suzerainty. But ten years later the problems had not gone away. The German-speakers of Holstein wanted to be part of Germany. Bismarck could win popularity at home by invading the duchies – in 1864. 'God forgive you for it,' the Queen wrote to Vicky, by then Crown Princess of Prussia. Then – seeing that events would be no different whether God forgave them or not – Victoria urged, 'only make peace – give the Duchies to good Fritz H[olstein] and have done with it'.[31] By the time she wrote this letter Albert was dead, and the

Schleswig-Holstein question had become a family row – the Prince of Wales (Bertie) being married to Princess Alexandra of Denmark, and the Princess Royal to the Crown Prince of Prussia. Pilgerstein was prime minister, and he was in the humiliating position of realizing, after the Crimean War, that Britain was militarily powerless against Prussia.

After the war over the Danish duchies it was left to the Austrians and Prussians to pick over the pieces. Britain had lost any real European influence. For the next thirty years the British could conceal this fact from themselves by greater and greater imperial expansion and concerns with Empire. But it is true, as a modern historian has put it, that by 1864, 'Britain had ceased, in any real sense, to be a great *European* power at all.'[32] This is the true legacy, not merely of the Crimean War, but of the aristocratic principle, which enabled an old man of Palmerston's very limited qualities to remain in positions of power for the best part of half a century.

Would any of it have been different had Prince Albert lived? It is hard to believe his influence would have been absolutely negligible. The Queen's grief-stricken language about him after he died is so hyperbolic that we are apt to dismiss Albert as a figure of some absurdity, overlooking how enormously he was respected by scientists, diplomats, academics, politicians – and by his own children. The traditional patterns of a 'Victorian' family were largely reversed at Osborne and Windsor. It was very much the Queen who was the stern one. Prince Albert once confided in Lord Clarendon that the disagreeable task of punishing the children had always fallen on him, and he regretted not resisting the harshness of the Queen towards her children for fear of exciting her if she were thwarted.[33] Lady Lyttelton became superintendent of the Royal Nursery. She was amazed by how severely the children were punished. At four, Princess Alice received 'a real punishment by whipping' for telling a lie. The young children were often admonished with their hands tied together, and the Prince of Wales and his brother received even harsher treatment.[34] The children did not however seem to respond to Albert either with fear or resentment. At a Royal Academy banquet some years after Albert's death the Prince of Wales tried to speak of his father and broke down sobbing. After her marriage to Fritz, Vicky wrote – on board HMY *Victoria and Albert* on the Scheldt – 'The pain of parting from you yesterday was greater than I can describe; I thought my heart was going to break when you shut the cabin door and were gone – that cruel moment which I had been dreading even to think of for 2 years and a half was past – it was more painful than I had ever pictured it to myself' – and so on for pages. 'All your love, etc. I shall most earnestly endeavour to deserve. To you, dear Papa, I owe most in this world.'

The Princess Royal had comparably intense feelings about her mother. Their frequent correspondence she was to describe as 'so natural and like thinking aloud'. Certainly these remarkable letters, spanning forty years, give an insight into the Queen's character and psyche which is like no other. The candour of Queen Victoria's dislike of her eldest son, the Prince of Wales, is shocking. 'Poor Bertie! He vexes us much. There is not a particle of reflection, or even attention to anything but dress! Not the slightest desire to learn, on the contrary, il se bouche les oreilles, the moment anything of interest is being talked of! I only hope he will meet with some severe lesson to shame him out of his ignorance and dullness' (17 November 1858).[35] Bertie 'is not at all in good looks; his nose and mouth are too enormous and as he pastes his hair down to his head, and wears his clothes frightfully – he really is anything but good looking. That coiffure is really too hideous with his small head and enormous features' (7 April 1860).[36]

Her imperiousness and her attention to detail were, on occasion, provoking. Poor Vicky was given advice by her mother about every conceivable area of life – the temperature to keep her rooms, the desirability of installing water closets not only in her palaces but 'throughout Germany',[37] as well as every aspect of political life. Sometimes the stream of opinions – the Queen's dislike of the Anglican Communion Service, her love of the novels of George Eliot, her distaste for babies – might have been entertaining. Sometimes the mother's need to interfere caused distress, and even fears – expressed by Baron Stockmar when the Queen was in manic or hysterical mode – that she had inherited the malady of her supposed grandfather George III.[38] When it came to a stream of bullying letters to the Crown Princess about whether she stood or sat during her son's christening – 'Let German ladies do what they like but the English Princess must not' – Lord Clarendon approached Albert and asked him if he could tell the Queen not to be so interfering. The suggestion put Victoria in 'a towering passion'.[39]

The Queen's temperament, ever volatile, became actually unhinged on the death of her own mother, the Duchess of Kent, on 16 March 1861. Like many egomaniacs – and was not the whole success of Dr Freud to be based on the universality of the condition? – Queen

Victoria had sustained her leap from adolescence to young womanhood by the inner belief that her parent was her enemy. When she
became Queen, her rejection of her mother had been total, though with
the passing years there had been some rapprochement, not least
because her twenty-year marriage to Albert had strengthened her sense
of belonging to Coburg. After her mother died, however, the Queen
went through the Duchess's belongings and found the incontrovertible
evidence that her mother had always loved her, saving and treasuring
every scrap of childhood memorabilia. For a month, Victoria became a
morbid solitary, refusing to see her own children, eating her meals
alone, and leaving Albert 'well nigh undone' with managing the
Queen's business as well as his own. Clarendon said to the Duchess of
Manchester, 'I hope this state of things won't last, or she may fall into
the morbid melancholy to which her mind has always tended and
which is a constant cause of anxiety to P[rince] A[lbert].' So alarming
were the reports of the Queen's melancholy-madness that old Uncle
Leopold – the brother of the Duchess of Kent – crossed the Channel to
find the court still in full mourning in August.[40]

There is no doubt that Albert was weakened by living with the full
blast of his wife's hysteria. As the summer of 1861 wore on he drove
himself to work harder and harder, partly, one suspects, because her
behaviour had become insufferable. He took her to Ireland to inspect
the troops – the Prince of Wales was serving ten weeks in the army there.
She complained constantly – of feeling 'very weak and nervous'. The
chief reason for his, and the court's, insistence that she went was to
show her in public, since rumours were now flying all over Europe that
she had been incarcerated in a padded cell. They saw Bertie – not
deemed real officer material by his seniors in the Grenadiers. His coevals
had played him the trick – no doubt very welcome to that young
sensualist – of insinuating Nellie Clifden, a young 'actress', into his bed.

By the autumn, rumours of this silly escapade had reached the
London clubs and the royal family was looking more than usually
absurd. On 24 November, in drenching rain – *entsetzlicher Regen* –
and with a heavy head cold, Albert inspected the troops at Sandhurst.
The next day he went to Cambridge, where Bertie was supposedly a
student, to upbraid him, and there followed a painful reconciliation
between father and son. The general feeling of overwork and of being
'run down' had turned into something more serious. For some time
Albert had been depressed, and suffered from stomach pains,
toothache and exhaustion.

Something had died in him. *Ich hange gar nicht am Leben; du hängst sehr daran* . . . he had said to the Queen when he was at a low ebb – 'I do not cling to life; you do; but I set no store by it. I am sure that if I had a severe illness I should give up at once; I should not struggle for life. I have no tenacity for life.'[41]

A very strange moment had occurred about a year before when Albert and Victoria visited Coburg. Riding alone in a carriage drawn by four horses, which suddenly took fright, Albert found himself being taken rapidly towards a railway crossing. He tried to take control of the horses, which crashed towards a wagon on the road. Albert leapt free, and he rushed at once to the aid of the coachman whose wagon was wrecked. One of his horses was killed. During this accident – and he was only forty when it happened – he sensed that 'my last hour had come' – *mein letztes Stündlein gekommen wäre*.[42]

By the beginning of December 1861, it was clear that the Prince Consort was gravely ill: the likeliest explanation for this is that he had succumbed to typhoid fever. (Back in November 1858, the Queen had been complaining to Vicky that 'that horrid fever' was sweeping through Windsor; he who had done so much to encourage Edwin Chadwick's campaign for proper sanitation might well have died because of the drains at Windsor Castle; or, some say, it was cancer.) When Princess Alice told him on 7 December that she'd written to Vicky to say he was ill he replied, 'You did wrong. You should have told her I am dying.'[43]

The doctors, as so often, were worse than useless, but perhaps it was a hopeless case. On 14 December, the Queen knelt by his bed and said *Es ist kleines Fraüchen* (It is your little wife). He signalled his consent when she offered him *ein Kuss*, but he was slipping away into the only condition which guaranteed a respite from her moods, tantrums and noise.

As the Princess Royal knew from her mother's letters on the subject, Queen Victoria was insistent on the installation of 'very necessary conveniences' near the bedrooms in royal residences . . . 'A real blessing'.[44] Such was her need to avail herself of this modern provision that it was left to the ladies in waiting, the equerries and the Prince Consort's children to witness his actual demise.

By the time she returned, she exclaimed, 'Oh, this is death, I know it. I have seen this before' . . . 'I took his dear left hand which was already cold and knelt down by him. All, *all* was over.'

When she withdrew to the Red Room the equerries and her children, all 'deeply affected but quiet', gathered round her. She clutched the hand of Prince Arthur's governor, Sir Howard Elphinstone, and pleaded, 'You will not desert me? You will all help me.'[45]

In an instant, everything had changed, not merely in the Queen's life, and in that of the court and the royal family, but in England and Europe generally. Put bluntly, there was no longer an intelligent member of the royal family. British constitutional monarchy had been a very limited power, but now there was no serious check on the oligarchy of politicians who could flatter, cajole or sidestep the royal ego entirely. Whereas, in Albert's day, an intelligent influence was brought to bear, as it were, downwards from the throne, on social questions in particular but to a smaller degree on foreign policy, the relationship between politicians and the Crown now became merely a camp joke. Over the next half-century, the progeny of Victoria and Albert would marry and be given in marriage to all the important royal houses of Europe except the Austrian. Within seventy years of Albert's death nearly all these dynasties would be swept away – in Russia, Prussia, Austria, Spain and the Balkans. The fact that the monarchy survived in England was not a token of its strength but of its triviality. Had Albert lived, Britain, too, might have paid its monarchy the compliment of wishing to check, or even to abolish, its influence. As it was, the Widow of Windsor, living as a virtual recluse for years and performing almost no constitutional function, helped to lead the monarchy into a position where it was not worth abolishing. The claim that Britain was a monarchy in any but the most titular sense was now a fantasy.

PART III

The Eighteen-Sixties

17

The Beloved – Uncle Tom – and Governor Eyre

The little boy holding up a small golden bucket of roses in Rossetti's canvas *The Beloved* wears a doleful expression, not altogether suitable for this supposed celebration of connubial bliss. The melancholy of the child, whose name is not remembered, is understandable when we know that he was suffering from a cold. Rossetti had spotted him on the steps of a London hotel and realized that he would make an exotic adjunct to this work, which had been commissioned as a Christmas present for the wife of a wealthy Birkenhead banker called Rae. The child, a black boy, was a slave, travelling with his American master. Finding himself whisked off to Rossetti's studio in Chelsea, the boy had wept copiously, an object of fascination to the painter, who noticed that the moisture on his cheeks made his dark skin even darker. While Dante Gabriel Rossetti patiently sketched and painted, the destiny of the boy's fellow African-Americans was being forged in the bloodiest war of the century. While the child wept, and Rossetti begged him to keep still, Sherman's army was advancing through Georgia to Atlanta, burning and pillaging, while in an opposite direction on ox-drawn carts and makeshift wagons black refugees fled from slavery, some to a new life which was an improvement on the old, many or most to poverty and ill-treatment every bit as horrible as their lives under the old dispensation.

As in the late medieval canvas celebrated by Auden, 'everything looks away quite leisurely from the disaster' in Rossetti's picture. Few, if any, who looked at *The Beloved* today in a gallery would be able to find a glimmering of political significance in the child's presence. He has, surely, been added for purely aesthetic reasons to this crowded and not entirely successful composition for which Mr Rae paid £300 – about a third as much money as he would have had to pay for the boy himself.

It is this, the concept of actual ownership by one person of another, which makes slavery not merely an abhorrent concept but to almost all modern sensibilities an unimaginable one. W.H. Russell, following his success as a war correspondent in the Crimea and in India, attended a slave auction in Montgomery, Alabama, and filed this dispatch in *The Times*, 30 May 1861:

I am neither a sentimentalist nor Black Republican, nor negro worshipper, but I confess the sight caused a strange thrill through my heart. I tried in vain to make myself familiar with the fact that I could, for the sum of £975, become as absolutely the owner of that mass of blood, bones, sinew, flesh and brains as of the horse which stood by my side. There was no sophistry which could persuade me the man was not a man – he was, indeed, by no means my brother, but assuredly he was a fellow creature.

Such feelings were hardly new in England. 'No man is by nature the property of another,' Samuel Johnson had averred. And visiting Oxford in his sixty-ninth year he gave as a toast, 'Here's to the next insurrection of negro slaves in the West Indies.' (Of the Americans in 1777, he had asked, 'How is it that we hear the loudest *yelps* for liberty among the drivers of negroes?')

The same paradox which Tory Johnson had observed in the 1770s was on glaring display in the 1860s. Those states which insisted on their liberty to secede from the Union (though Jefferson Davis would never have done anything so undignified as to *yelp*) were those which also insisted on their right to perpetuate slavery, at a period in history when even the Russians were liberating their serfs.[1] (The emancipation of the serfs happened on 19 February 1861, two months before the bombardment of Fort Sumter; nearly two years before Lincoln proclaimed the emancipation of slaves in those states in arms against the Union, on 1 January 1863.)

Yet even from the remote perspective of Dante Gabriel Rossetti's studio, the question of American slavery was not one which could be seen in morally simple terms. The Englishman, particularly the English liberal, might deplore the notion of purchasing 'blood, bones, sinew, flesh and brains', but what else was the nineteenth-century factory-owner doing to his workforce? What – come to that – was the status of English women, of whatever class, in relation to their father or husband? (Not until 1882 did the Married Women's Property Act grant to married women the full right of separate ownership of property.)

Then again, there was the intimate economic connection between the English capacity to mass-produce cotton goods, and hence increase their national wealth immeasurably, and the American capacity to grow and harvest cotton in ever greater, ever cheaper quantities. If James Hargreaves, the poor weaver of Blackburn, had never pioneered the spinning-jenny in 1764, and if Richard Arkwright had never invented the water-frame spinning machine a little later, or Cartwright invented the power-loom, the quiet home-weavers of Lancashire, rustic characters who belonged in the pages of Wordsworth, might still have been pursuing their calm, untroubled lives deep into the third decade of Queen Victoria's reign. But they weren't.[2] The population-explosion had occurred; the Malthusian struggle was conjoined; the masses had thronged into the mills and factories of Northern England – Lancashire by now contained 12 per cent of the population. Between 1821 and 1831 17,000 persons per annum had flocked to Lancashire. By 1860 there were some 2,650 cotton factories, worked by a population of 440,000, their wages amounting to £11,500,000 per annum. In order to employ this population at this rate it was necessary to import 1,051,623,380 lb of cotton: nearly all of this raw material came from America.[3]

If the population-explosion in England fed upon and needed the industrial genius set in motion by Arkwright, Cartwright, Hargreaves and others, cotton itself could not have supplied their need had it not been for comparable advance in American agriculture. In 1793 Eli Whitney had invented the cotton gin, which enabled the cotton seed to be easily separated from the lint. The declining agrarian economy of the South was immediately revitalized. Cotton was an easy crop to grow in the rich virgin lands of the Mississippi basin, and a cheap labour force was to hand – in the slaves. Article 1, Section 9 of the American Constitution had envisaged the ending of the *trade* in slaves, though not the institution of slavery, by 1808. A number of enlightened planters had followed Jefferson's example and liberated their slaves in their wills. Had the agrarian economy of the South continued to decline, had Eli Whitney never made his ingenious cotton gin, had there been no industrial revolution in Lancashire, then the quiet old Southern ways might have gradually evolved into a poor, but slave-free culture, a sort of eighteenth-century England, underpopulated but genteel.[4] As it was, to meet the demands of nineteenth-century trade, slavery in America actually increased, from 1 million slaves in 1800 to approximately 4½ million in 1860.

There are few more tragic examples in history of the truth of Ezra Pound's observation, 'Nature overproduces. Overproduction does no harm until you over-market.'[5]

Those who profited from the overproduction of Southern cotton were not just planters. They were the Northern middlemen, the New York merchants who bled the Southerners dry by selling them manufactured goods at ever-increasing prices; and they were the English merchant class, liberals almost to a man, loud in their advocacy of the abolitionist cause, but only after they had made millions out of a system which had depended, for its initial profitability, on American slave labour to harvest, English child labour to manufacture, cheap cotton goods for the export market.

These uncomfortable truths were not lost on observant Englishmen and women in the 1860s, which is precisely why we find many English people turning a blind eye to America at this time, or almost wilfully missing the point of what was going on there; and also perhaps why we find some of the keenest abolitionists in the ranks of those who had defended capitalist industrialism. (Harriet Martineau was typical.)

We should expect that most paradoxical of political figures, Gladstone, to typify the many-stranded complexity of this matter. Prince of humbug, yet deeply the man of principle; guilt-ridden profiteer from his father's Demerara slave-plantations, yet defender of the old man's good intentions; stern, in youth an unbending Tory, yet in old age visionary radical; populist with an eye to the main chance, yet prepared throughout his long political life – from resignation over the Maynooth Grant to his destruction of the Liberal Party over Irish Home Rule – to stand on firmly rooted moral conviction; visionary prophet, but crashing bore: at the time of the outbreak of the American Civil War, Gladstone was, aged fifty-two, the chancellor of the Exchequer in Lord Palmerston's 'Liberal' government. Lord John Russell was foreign secretary. England was still being governed by the 'two dreadful old men' who had been around at the time of the 1832 Reform Bill, the Irish Famine and the Indian Mutiny. Victorian England was a gerontocracy, which made the life of the politically ambitious keenly frustrating. While his opposite number in the Commons, Disraeli, made a comparably agonizing ascent of 'the greasy pole', patiently awaiting the retirement or demise of Lord Derby, the Conservative leader, Gladstone was the Liberal leader in waiting, ever anxious to establish himself as the only possible successor to Palmerston.

At this date, the North-Eastern region of England was as prosperous – from exports to Europe, from shipbuilding, from coal – as the North-Western cotton-producing towns of Lancashire were distressed. As

Liberal chancellor of the Exchequer Gladstone was widely credited with this prosperity, and he was invited to address a dinner at the town hall in Newcastle on 7 October 1862. He was given 'the reception of a king', in the words of his biographer and admirer Morley. A great procession of steamers followed him to the mouth of the Tyne, and workers from the forges, furnaces, coal staiths, chemical works, glass factories and shipyards lined the river bank to cheer: 'and all this not because he had tripled the exports to France, but because a sure instinct had revealed an accent in his eloquence that spoke of feeling for the common people'.[6] This is not, of course, a reference to the Liverpudlian timbre which is (just) detectable in the recorded voice of Etonian and Oxford-educated Gladstone but to his streak of populism, his feeling, amounting to genius, for public mood. At the grand dinner, no doubt carried away by the warmth of his reception in Newcastle, Gladstone moved into one of those oratorical flights for which he was long remembered. On this occasion, his words occasioned a diplomatic incident between Britain — in the person of the foreign secretary — and the American minister in London, Charles Francis Adams. Was it a gaffe as is generally supposed? Or did Gladstone, who was a most unusual combination of passionate impulsiveness and deviousness, *intend* his words to cause the discomfiture which they unquestionably did?

'We know quite well,' he said, 'that the people of the Northern States have not yet drunk of the cup — they are still trying to hold it far from their lips — which all the rest of the world see nevertheless they must drink of. We may have our own opinions about slavery; we may be for or against the South; but there is no doubt that Jefferson Davis and other leaders of the South have made an army; they are making, it appears, a navy; and they have made what is more than either, they have made a nation.' The words were greeted with loud cheers.

Adams — of the great dynasty — did not have an easy task. From the beginning of the Civil War, over the question of British neutrality, he had been forced to emphasize that Britain could not recognize the Confederacy without putting itself on terms of hostility with the Union. Russell smoothed things down, and forced Gladstone to withdraw his implication that the British government believed in the inevitability of a Confederate victory. Much later in life, Gladstone expressed dismay at his words. He had never, he said, desired a division of the American Union and indeed feared that such a thing would put a 'dangerous pressure on Canada'. The 'tokens of goodwill' which, over the last twenty-five years of his career, he received from the American people made him all the more anxious to dissociate himself from his earlier position. This was because it suited Gladstone the octogenarian democrat to believe that he had always been a fervent believer in government of the people, for the people and by the people. The new orthodoxy of a shared political vision, linking Britain and America, enabled early twentieth-century historians to see the 1860s as the great turning point for both countries, the era when both put the old world, and with it old hostilities, behind them. 'The Reform Bill of 1867 brought a new British nation into existence, the nation decrying American institutions was dead, and a "sister democracy" holding out hands to the United States had replaced it' was one genial American view, published six years after Woodrow Wilson had imposed his disastrous conclusions on the Versailles Peace Agreement.[7] This is still very much the way some people, on both sides of the Atlantic, see the 1860s.

At the time, things looked very different. Many would have shared Disraeli's view that the 'immense revolution' taking place in the United States would 'tell immensely in favour of aristocracy'.[8] The greatest Tory intellectual of the age, Lord Robert Cecil, perhaps influenced this view. (Although Cecil at the time abominated Disraeli, the feeling of antipathy was not reciprocated. And Cecil, as Lord Salisbury, was destined to be Disraeli's foreign secretary, and his successor as Conservative prime minister – *vide infra*.) Writing in the *Quarterly Review* Cecil insisted – in October 1862 – that the democratic idea

is not merely a folly. It is a chimera. It is idle to discuss whether it ought to exist; for, as a matter of fact, it never does. Whatever may be the written text of a Constitution, the multitude always will have leaders among them, and those leaders not selected by themselves. They may set up the pretence of political equality, if they will, and delude themselves with a belief in its existence. But the only consequence will be that they will have bad leaders instead of good. Every community has natural leaders, to whom, if they are not misled by the insane passion for equality, they will instinctively defer. Always wealth, in some countries birth, in all intellectual power and culture, mark out the men to whom, in a healthy state of feeling, a community looks to undertake its government.[9]

These are sentiments with which the bulk of the political class, Conservative and Liberal, agreed in England until the First World War, which is why the idea of England becoming more democratic, or more like America, in the 1860s or 1870s must be taken with a pinch of salt. Naturally there were pockets of such opinion.[10] Cobden and Bright's use of American flags at election rallies to represent freedom excited rancour and ridicule. Most British opinion – *The Times*, Bagehot, Disraeli and the Conservatives, as well as Gladstone – assumed the likelihood of a Confederate victory; and many, perhaps a majority, hoped for it. Matthew Arnold was one of the first commentators to express the view that secession was final. This prophet of liberalism thought it was a good thing for the North, allowing the Yankees to develop a modern enlightened society, and free from blacks, who he imagined would be sent back to Africa. As a schools inspector, Arnold noted in early January 1865 that of students in training colleges who had been set a composition which touched upon the American crisis, almost every one had taken 'the strongest possible side' with the Confederacy.[11]

The neutrality of the British government was certainly not based on any form of natural common feeling with Lincoln or the Federal government. Adams noted that when it became clear that the North would fight on to victory the attitude of Palmerston and Russell became favourable to the Union, but this was 'no special sympathy, but merely a cool calculation of benefits to Great Britain in maintaining that policy of friendship determined upon in the fifties'.[12] (In the early stage of the war, they had taken no chances, though, and dispatched 11,000 troops to Canada to protect the border.)[13] Lincoln's secretary of state, Seward, the man who had himself hoped for the Republican nomination for the presidency, described Britain, perhaps understandably, as 'the greatest, most grasping, and most rapacious power in the world'.

That power depended on trade, on manufacturing, on exports; and a crucial part of that trade was concentrated upon the cotton-mills and factories of Lancashire. Jefferson Davis's decision to impose a cotton embargo, rather than attempting to defy Federal blockades of the ports, was a major political blunder. In the first year of the war it was ineffectual. Canny British merchants had seen the danger of raw materials running out and had bulk-bought cotton in a year when its price was in any event low. By the following year, however, in May 1862, the situation in formerly prosperous Lancashire was desperate. In a cotton town such as Blackburn 'of 84 mills, 23 were silent and smokeless';[14] 9,414 persons had applied for poor relief; the pawnshops were crammed with furniture and clothing; starvation beckoned.

The British press, on the whole, took the view that the commercial and human calamity which had now befallen Lancashire mattered far more than the issue of slavery. *The Times* reminded its readers that abolitionists had been persecuted in the North, as well as in the South, before the war; and that even at the outset of the conflict, Lincoln and his allies had not come out unambiguously against slavery. The more populist *Reynolds' Newspaper* urged, if necessary, force to break the blockades.[15] 'England must break the Blockade or her millions will starve.' 'Better to fight the Yankees than starve our operatives.'[16] The American consul in Manchester reported that public opinion among the working classes was 'almost unanimously adverse to the Northern cause'. This was hardly surprising. 'A few soldiers may indeed be pierced by shot and bayonet or shattered by cannon, but what are their sufferings compared with the miseries of thousands of capitalists who view with alarming eyes the gradual disappearance of their stock? What are bullets flying about you compared with the heavy fall of securities which have utterly lost their buoyancy?'[17] At a meeting in the Temperance Hall, Little Bolton, on 14 February 1863 to consider such questions as 'Is not the recent policy of President Lincoln worthy of sympathy and support of all lovers of freedom and constitutional government?' there were raucous interruptions, laughter, booing and catcalls when the worthy Liberal speaker, Mr John Edward Kirkman, tried to defend Lincoln.[18]

Urged on by the English abolitionists and the economic radicals, Lincoln himself wrote to the people of Lancashire recognizing their plight, and trying to imply that the English working classes would prefer to starve rather than tolerate the existence of slavery on the other side of the Atlantic. 'I cannot,' he wrote, 'but regard your decisive utterances upon the question as an instance of sublime Christian heroism which has not been surpassed in any age or any country.'[19] The truth is that in years of prosperity the working classes, as well as the factory-owners themselves, had been content to make profits out of cheap imported cotton which, without slaves to harvest it, would have been twice the price. Equally true was that most workers would have preferred an early end to the war in exchange for regular paid work in the mills and factories. The factory operatives of Lancashire did not have any influence, one way or another, either on the conduct of the war in America, or on the decisions by Palmerston and Russell about their policy of neutrality.

But while this is undoubtedly the case, and while from month to month of the crisis the import of the American Civil War, its monumental significance as a turning point in the tide of world history, was very largely lost on English politicians and the English public, on another level the issue of slavery was perfectly clear.* Gladstone's biographer, Lord Morley, explains the superficial English myopia over the matter by saying, 'we applied ordinary political maxims to what was not merely a political contest, but a social revolution. Without scrutiny of the cardinal realities beneath, we discussed it like some superficial conflict in our old world about boundaries, successions, territorial partitions, dynastic preponderance. The significance of the American war was its relation to slavery.'[20]

Another way of putting it if one were not, as Morley was, a paid-up Liberal, was that the English at this date took an ambivalent view of the disturbance of 'the aristocratic settlement', to use Disraeli's phrase.[21] The English preserved in large measure their 'aristocratic settlement' while advancing towards modern democracy. They were not confronted, as the Americans were, with a stark choice, because they did not have slaves, or indeed large numbers of black people, living in their towns and villages. Rossetti's little black model was an exotic who stood out in a London street, which is how the artist came to spot him.

At Balmoral in September 1863 there was another instance of how strange a black face could seem to the untravelled:

> Princess Alice has got a black boy here who was given to her, and he produces a great sensation on the Deeside where the people never saw anything of the kind and cannot conceive it. A woman, and an intelligent one, cried out in amazement on seeing him, and said she would certainly have fallen down, but for the Queen's presence. She said nothing would induce her to wash his clothes *as the black would come off*! This story the Queen told me in good spirits.[22]

---

*Compare Carlyle's squib 'Ilias (Americana in Nuce) [America in a Nutshell]'.
PETER *of the North* (to PAUL *of the South*) 'Paul, you unaccountable scoundrel, I find you hire your servants for life, not by the month or year as I do! You are going to Hell you _____!'
PAUL 'Good words, Peter! The risk is my own ... Hire you your servants by the month or the day, and get straight to Heaven; leave me to my own method.'
PETER 'No, I won't. I will beat your brains out first!' (*And is trying dreadfully ever since but cannot yet manage it.*)

Macmillan's Magazine, August 1863, p.301

The author is Gladstone himself. Black people were people, on the whole, who were abroad. Many Victorians would have shared the kindly minded and in all respects Liberal Thackeray's view – 'Sambo is not my man & my brother; the very aspect of his face is grotesque and inferior' Many, too, if they had visited Virginia as Thackeray did in 1852–3, would have concluded, 'they are not suffering as you are impassioning yourself for their wrongs as you read Mrs Stowe: they are grinning & joking in the sun'. He wondered how they would survive after abolition, believing that the need to compete with whites in the labour market would lead to 'the most awful curse and ruin . . . which fate ever yet sent' the black man.

By the cruellest of ironies, these views, which seem so unenlightened to us, were borne out by events in America. The Northern victory which landed Jefferson Davis in jail and in irons led to the destruction of those rich estates and plantations where benign slave-ownership was at least possible. The existence of the Ku Klux Klan would have been unimaginable in the old South. It sprang up, like National Socialism in Germany, in reaction against the sheer lack of magnanimity of the supposedly liberal victor: and as a result of economic hardship. The plight of the poor, white and black, in the Southern states over the next hundred years was unimaginably horrible. As the left-wing black historian W.E.B. Du Bois was to put it in *Black Reconstruction*, written in 1935, 'God wept; but that mattered little to an unbelieving age; what mattered most was that the world wept and is still weeping and blind with tears and blood. For there began to rise in America . . . a new capitalism and a new enslavement of labour.'[23]

There were indeed changes in the 1860s. The 'social revolution' seen by Morley in America drove the labour force in the same direction in which the British and European labour force had been driven in the earlier decades of industrialization, but with fewer protections and much less willingness on the part of the big capitalists or the governing class to appease its proletariat. The 'aristocratic settlement', though as Ashley had seen, totally opposed to the selfish cut and thrust of capitalism, nevertheless provided checks, in England, to an unbridled market economy. If it is true that Christianity and communism provided the only real opposition in dialectical terms to the Market, the existence of an aristocracy provided a background against which pure Darwinian competition was tempered by a notion of *noblesse* or *nouvelle richesse oblige*. Not only did many aristocrats remain in positions of real power and influence in the nineteenth century but, with their new-found wealth, many of the new rich chose to live their own versions of an aristocratic life. Of course this involved a system of hierarchy which to modern eyes appears arcane; also, we moderns might bridle at the concept of patronage. But it is no accident that when the British chose formally to dismantle their aristocratic system after the Second World War, they modelled the state, with its system of welfare and patronage, less on the Soviet monolith than on the old-fashioned Christian aristocrat who looked after the poor on his estate from cradle to grave, built them schools and cottages, and provided them with specially created work projects when economic crisis dried up the demand for work in mills, factories or mines. Attlee and Sir Stafford Cripps were more the heirs of the 7th Earl of Shaftesbury than they were of Karl Marx.

A major crisis in capitalism occurred during the Cotton Famine when many Northern landlords, Gladstone included, devised schemes of work. At a rally in Manchester on 2 December 1862 Derby praised the 'noble manner, a manner beyond all praise in which this destitution has been borne by the population of this great country'. He gave £5,000 at one time to the relief fund, the largest single subscription, it was said, made by a single Englishman to a public fund for a single purpose or a single time.[24] It inspired others to give – altogether Derby was to raise £130,000, and donate £12,000.[25] The numbers of those seeking relief rose from half a million in January 1813 to 1,260,000 in 1865. There was, no doubt, practical self-preservation instinct at work here. Derby feared the mob. As the greatest landowner in Lancashire he was always careful to keep quiet about his personal sympathies for the Confederacy, knowing that some of the working classes had sympathies with the 'democratic' Northern states.

Thus – to return for a moment to the little black boy in Rossetti's *The Beloved* – we can legitimately find, in the work of this least political of painters, echoes of the socio-political world in which the artist took so little interest. There is, for a start, the object itself, the gilded, framed icon: an erotic or semi-pagan altarpiece intended not for a church but for the house of a financier, a banker, Mr Rae of Merseyside. The picture supposedly illustrates a biblical text – 'My beloved is mine and I am his: let him kiss me with the kisses of his mouth': but it is designed as a Christmas present for a Victorian capitalist's wife: it is not merely an exploration through symbol of erotic and spiritual desire, it is also a social status symbol and an expensive object of domestic furniture. Rossetti's very detachment from the contemporary political debate lends the little black boy, by paradox, a greater eloquence for us than he would have if he had been made to carry a burden of symbolism – such as Wedgwood's famous ceramic medallion 'man and a brother' in chains. Rossetti's sister Christina and his brother William as well as Burne-Jones, Holman Hunt, Browning – to name a few in his circle – were keen abolitionists. Whistler on the other hand had a brother in the Confederate army, and Ruskin would have followed Carlyle's line – of which more later. Rossetti chose to remain aloof, laughing when his friends quarrelled about the issue.[26]

In a sense, however, the aloofness was its own form of political comment. The British response to the American Civil War struck a liberal like Morley, in retrospect, as astonishing. He might well have echoed *The Morning Herald*, when the war had been won – 'We have been false to our principles and neglected an opportunity . . . we have been guilty of a crime as well as a blunder, and assuredly we or our children will pay for both.'[27]

History ridiculed this liberal angst. When it suited the United States to become the close allies of Great Britain, they did so, without too many memories of the ambivalent attitude of Palmerston and Russell to the Civil War.

What the distance of a century and a half suggests is that the British could afford to shed tears over *Uncle Tom's Cabin* as a nursery-book, but perhaps not to inquire too deeply into their own highly ambivalent attitude to the peoples and races of the world whom, by commerce or empire, they had subdued without the means of overt slavery. We have observed how British self-congratulation at having escaped an 1848 revolution needs to be tempered by a recognition of the many areas of conflict in different parts of the globe – Canada, the Caribbean, South Africa, and throughout the Indian subcontinent – where there were disturbances and minor wars every bit as 'revolutionary' as what happened in Berlin, Vienna or Paris in 1848. Moreover, post 1857–8 in India, we noted that a change had come over the British attitude. Those who saw the Indians, with their ancient dynasties and princi-palities, their culture, languages and religions, as independent beings, to be won over in commercial arrangements by the East India Company, were now heavily outnumbered by those who believed that the Indians were savages who must be subdued – either on Benthamite principles of social economy or for reasons of Christian evangelicalism or through an amalgam of the two. The culture of British imperialism had evolved, and with it, the need for the British to persuade themselves that the white man was superior to the black man.

Anthony Trollope, for example, visited the West Indies in 1858 and concluded that the 'liberated' black workers were unable to reason and that they were innately lazy. 'To recede from civilization and became again savage – as savage as the laws of the community can permit – has been to his taste. I believe that he would altogether retrograde if left to himself.'[28]

A writer who probably had more influence than Trollope, perhaps more than any other, in shaping the way that the British thought about the other people in the world was George Alfred Henty (1832–1902), who began his writing career in the 1860s. Henty – educated at Westminster and Caius, Cambridge, the son of a wealthy stockbroker – had been commissioned in the Purveyor's Department of the army, and gone to the Crimea during the war. There he had drifted into journalism, sending back reports for the *Morning Advertiser* and the *Morning Post* before catching fever and being invalided home. He continued to work in the Purveyor's Department until the mid-Sixties, when the life of the war correspondent and the writer of boys' adventure stories seemed overwhelmingly more interesting and better paid. Four generations of British children grew up with Henty's irresistible stories, beautifully produced, bound and edited, on their shelves.

The Henty phenomenon – over seventy titles celebrating imperialistic derring-do – really belongs to the 1880s, but deserves a mention here not only because of his radical and political views, but because of the direction taken by his career as a writer. The Henty story, by the time he had got into his stride, followed the formula that a young English lad in his early teens, freed from the shackles of public school or home upbringing by the convenient accident of orphanhood, finds himself caught up in some thrilling historical episode. The temporal sweep is impressive, ranging from *Beric at Agincourt* to *The Briton: a story of the Roman Invasion*; but the huge majority are exercises in British imperialist myth-building: *By Conduct and Courage, A Story of the Days of Nelson, By Pike and Dyke, By Sheer Pluck, A Tale of the Ashanti War, Condemned as a Nihilist, The Dash for Khartoum, For Name and Fame: or through the Afghan Passes, Jack Archer, A Tale of the Crimea, Through the Sikh War. A Tale of the Punjaub (sic); The Tiger of Mysore, With Buller in Natal, With Kitchener in the Soudan*, and so on.

The stereotypes are not necessarily what a twenty-first-century reader would expect: Henty is keenly Turcophile, for example, and holds in contempt those English in India – whether mercantile or military – who do not trouble to acquaint themselves with Indian languages and culture. This, for many modern readers, will make all the more distressing Henty's view that 'the negro is an inferior animal and a lower grade in creation than the white man'.[29] It seems strange to think of his books standing on the same nursery-shelves as *Uncle Tom's Cabin*, but both were staple fare for English children.

By the standards of a later generation, European childhood, up to the 1860s, was like human life itself, nasty, brutish and short. Not only was infant mortality high. Childhood itself, if we define childhood in modern terms as a time of play, of learning, of innocent idleness and amusement, was virtually non-existent for the majority. Two of the most celebrated early nineteenth-century childhoods are those of Charles Dickens and John Stuart Mill. We tend to think of them as freakish, but really the only thing which was unusual about them was their genius. Millions of children in the nineteenth century had the experience of working in a grown-up world when aged ten. Thousands of middle-class boys like Mill would have been expected to conform in manner and even in dress to the *mores* of middle-aged parents.

Childhood as Americans or Europeans of the twenty-first century understand the term is really quite a new phenomenon in human history and began – roughly speaking – in the 1860s. It was the privilege of the ever-expanding middle classes and of the upper classes. The working classes continued to go to labour in factories from an early age – though they might receive some rudimentary study in the afternoons. As soon as may be, they left the parental roof and began themselves to breed. 'No one who has ever attended the morning service at Manchester Cathedral will forget the ceremony of asking the banns of marriage,' wrote R. Arthur Arnold in 1864. 'When the happy couples make their appearance after the third publication it is hoped that they are not so confused as are most of those listeners to this long-drawn string of some hundred names . . . Boy husband and girl-wife, themselves oftentimes not fully-grown, became the parents of weakly children, specially requiring what they rarely get, a mother's care.'[30]

By contrast, between the dates 1840 and 1870 the average age of gentlemen, aspirant gentlemen and aristocrats for getting married was twenty-nine.[31] Arthur Hughes's painting *The Long Engagement* depicts an emotional predicament stemming directly from an economic situation. The prosperity which had created the vast bourgeoisie with its gradations from lower to upper middle class had also created a code. You could not marry, and maintain the position in society to which you aspired, until you had a certain amount of money in the bank. This was the age of savings, of investment incomes, of unearned income. Marx was wrong to consider the proletariat to be the equivalent of a slave class. Everyone who could do so aspired to rise from a condition of dependency. In 1861 there were 645 banks and the value of the ordinary deposits was £41,546,475.[32] Many of these deposits were extremely modest. The Savings Bank movement initiated in Ruthwell, Dumfries, by the Rev. Henry Duncan in 1810 had blossomed, via Penny Banks, Friendly Societies and such, to the larger Trustee Savings banks; these had been regulated by Act of Parliament in 1863, and in 1861 the Post Office Savings bank had protected the small saver after a number of swindles. The whole system of society began to revolve not simply on how much you earned but on how much you could squirrel away.[33] Lord John Russell spent nearly fifteen years campaigning (unsuccessfully as it turned out) for the extension of the franchise on the basis of your possessing £50 on deposit. Those whose good fortune had put them in possession of an appropriate accumulation could afford to marry and to set up an establishment.

There were innumerable tracts, books, pamphlets and even poems on the theme of 'prudent marriages and their effects on posterity' (to quote the title of one such, of 1858).[34] In S.W. Partridge's *Upward and Onward, a Thought for the Threshold of Active Life* (1851), potential householders were cautioned

> A good house
> Is no unconvertible thing, large rooms,
> Servants, gay drapery, new furniture,
> Nor undesired, nor undesirable.
> But first take counsel of thy income; wait
> Till prudence speak in the affirmative.

Mrs Warren reckoned in *A House and its Furnishings* that a six-roomed house could be run if you had an income of £200 p.a. *A New System of Practical Domestic Economy* estimated that you should set aside 10 per cent of your income on horses or carriages, which would mean you needed £1,000 for a four-wheeler with horses. (The coachman would be paid for out of the 8 per cent you would spend on the wages of male servants.) If you had £600 a year you could keep two horses if your groom doubled as a footman. A gig cost £700: that is, a one-horse carriage – a tilbury or a chaise.

Running costs broke down as follows:

Food for 1 horse	£24 10s.
Duty on 1 horse	£1 8s. 9d.
Shoeing, stable rent	£8 3s. 3d.
Duty on a gig	£3 5s.
Repairs, wear and tear	£8 15s.
Occasional groom	£7 18s.
Total	£54[35]

This was the great era of 'carriage folk'. At the beginning of the century, elliptic springs had made this soon-to-be-obsolete mode of transport enjoy a magnificent flowering.[36] The berlin, barouche, calèche, coupé, clarence, daumont, landau and phaeton all crowded the streets of London in that supposedly prosaic railway age. In 1814, there were 23,000 four-wheeled vehicles in the capital; by 1834, 49,000; by 1864, 102,000, with a further 170,000 two-wheelers.[37] This represents a huge social class, as well as huge congestion in the streets; and it is this class, this immensely privileged class, probably more comfortable than any human class who had ever existed on the planet, whose offspring were the first with the leisure and time to have a childhood.

Everyone who could do so in the 1860s was settling down into domestic life. The Marxes abandoned their cramped flat in Soho and moved to a variety of new-built family-houses in Kentish Town on the edges of Hampstead Heath where, on Sundays, the great economic philosopher would walk with his few surviving children and tell them stories. At the same point in time, Philip Webb was designing the Red House, Abbey Wood, for William Morris, that young idealist-aesthete, destined to become a revolutionary socialist, but not before he had founded his firm, Morris and Co., on the back of the domestic bourgeoisie, hungry for his wallpapers, carpets, curtains and cushion-covers. How wise Disraeli was. 'It is a privilege,' he wrote in 1862, 'to live in this age of brilliant and rapid events. What an error to consider it a utilitarian age! It is one of infinite romance! Thrones tumble down, and crowns are offered, like a fairy tale, and the most powerful people in the world male and female, a few years past, were adventurers, exiles, demireps.* *Vive la bagatelle!*[38]

*Women of doubtful reputation.

Disraeli, as so often, appears to be dabbling in paradox or wit for its own sake, but had actually described what was the case. Capitalism was not just the relentless machine, crushing the wage-slaves at the bottom: it had also created a fantasy-world of rapid social change, leisure, fairy-tale. It is not accidental that the decade of the consolidation of the rentier class, the decade of carriage-folk, of the expansion of the suburbs, the growth of the savings banks, the era of the nouveau-riche business man and the stockbroker, should also have been the golden age of children's literature. In the Victorian day nursery a picture of the world could emerge, simply from reading the books on offer to a child of that time, which would not differ materially from turning the less interesting pages of Hansard or *The Times*. Prompted by Disraeli's insight that 1862 was 'an age of infinite romance . . . like a fairy tale', I want to examine the 1860s through the prism of children's literature: Thackeray's *The Rose and the Ring* (1855), Christina Rossetti's *Goblin Market* (1862), Kingsley's *The Water Babies* (1863). This era of expanding schools for the middle classes also saw the publication of *Tom Brown's Schooldays* (1857) and *Eric, or, Little by Little* (1858). It also witnessed the prodigious popularity of Hans Christian Andersen, the prolific Louisa May Alcott began to write for children (*Little Women*), and Alice entered Wonderland in 1865.

We shall not abandon the grown-up world but look at it, as it were, from the nursery window, recognizing always, of course, that the concerns of the middle and upper classes – war and peace in America; the extension of the franchise; the final emergence of Gladstone and Disraeli as the two titanic opposites of the political world; the continuing controversies between science and religion; the dread of revolution and the pricking of conscience in the face of poverty; the Woman question, and the beginnings of modern feminism; the story of literature, of Trollope, the later Browning; the growth of Morris and Co., the origins of the aesthetic movement; the expansion of the British Empire; and the ever-widening circle of the Queen's European dynastic connections through her children's marriages – these and many other matters about which articles and books have been written and which concerned the periodical-readers of the day in clubs and rectories and suburbs were of little or no concern to those urchins who never had a nursery, never learnt to read, never in many respects had that middle-class privilege, a childhood.

*

The poor, and the children of the poor, continued throughout this decade to lead their scarcely endurable existences. On 13 April 1861 the Statistical Society of London visited a single room, occupied by five families. A separate family ate, drank, and slept in each of the four corners of the room, a fifth occupying the centre. 'But how can you exist?' asked the visitor of a poor woman whom he had found in the room (the other inmates being absent on their several avocations).[39] 'How could you possibly exist?' 'Oh, indeed, your honour,' she replied, 'we did very well until the gentleman in the middle took a lodger.'

Victorian children had to be seen as expendable, life had to be seen as cheap, when so it was, since there was no remedy in that unreformed and in many regards unformed society. In August 1861 a lunatic was brought before Thames Police court, 'charged with revolting assaults upon female children'. He had been the terror of his neighbourhood for some time, but – having nowhere else to dispose of him – the magistrate sent him back to the workhouse.[40]

In that same year, in April, Lord Palmerston rose to his feet in the Mansion House and praised the beneficial effects of Free Trade. He spoke of the healthy 'internal condition of the country'. By many standards what he said was perfectly reasonable. Yet while he spoke in the Mansion House, a horrifying murder took place in the picturesque village of Danbury in Essex when a married woman called Martha Weaver strangled an illegitimate little boy aged three, named John Gipson. The murderess was the wife of a respectable mechanic. No motive was ever found for her crime.[41]

A few days earlier, a much more disturbing case occurred in Stockport, in the North-West of England. It is doubly extraordinary for the modern reader, since it is a case with obvious parallels with the murder of James Bulger in 1993. When the defendants, Peter Henry Barratt and James Bradley, were brought to trial at Chester Assizes before Mr Justice Crompton in August 1861, their heads hardly appeared over the dock, since they were only eight years old, 'quite incapable of giving a plea or knowing what was going on'. The prisoners, utterly neglected and uneducated, had murdered a little boy called George Burgess aged two years and nine months.

The infant's parents both worked as cotton operatives at a mill and farmed out young George Burgess to Sarah Anne Warren, described as a nurse, who allowed her charges to play on waste land near the Star Inn. A little before three o'clock in the afternoon a woman called Whitehead saw Barratt and Bradley, with the two-year-old, walking towards Hempshaw Lane, where the body was eventually found. Barratt was pulling the younger child by the hand. It was crying and Whitehead had asked whether it was a boy or a girl. She was told it was a little boy. By four, two other witnesses, Emma Williams and Frank Williams, saw Barratt dragging the child, now naked, into a field, and Bradley got a stick from the fence with which he hit the child. Emma Williams called out, 'What are you doing with that child undressed?' but the boys made no reply and walked on in the direction of a brook where the body was at length discovered.

The corpse was found the next day, face down in the water, naked save for a pair of clogs on its feet. It was badly bruised and since the bruises were ecchymosed they must have been administered before death.

It was on Saturday 13 April that a police officer called Morley questioned first Barratt, and then took Barratt to Bradley's house. Morley asked Barratt, 'Who did you play with on Thursday afternoon?' He said, 'With Jimmy Bradley.' Morley said, 'Where did you go?' He said, 'We went beside the Star Inn, down Hempshaw Lane and up Love Lane.' Morley then said to Bradley, 'Did you see anyone in Love Lane?' He said, 'Yes, we saw a woman.' And he also said, in answer to a question from Morley, 'We had a little boy with us as we met beside the Star Inn.' Slowly the story emerged, with Bradley confessing, 'Peter said I must undress it' and Barratt interposing, 'Thou undressed it as well as me.' Morley said, 'Then you both undressed it?' Bradley said, 'Yes.' Morley said, 'What did you do then?' Bradley said, 'Peter pushed it into the water, and I took my clogs off and went in and took it out again. Peter then said, "It must have another."' Morley said, 'Another what?' Bradley said, 'Another dip in the water.' And there followed a dispute between the two boys about who exactly hit the child where and when.

The killing of this child, George Burgess, who actually went unnamed in *The Times* account, is fascinatingly similar to the killing of Jamie Bulger in the late twentieth century by two comparably cruel little tykes. The contrast between the treatment of the killers in the two cases throws an interesting light on the difference between ourselves and the Victorians. Though this case, 'unparalleled in the annals of crime', clearly horrified both police and court, as well as *The Times*, there seems to be none of the sentimentality, none of the vindictiveness or spite, none of the hysteria which accompanied the twentieth-century case. Bulger's killers were sent down for murder, and when they approached their eighteenth birthdays there were howls for vengeance not only from the working-class 'communities' from which they sprang, but also from the press.

Barratt and Bradley's counsel at Chester pleaded that they were themselves mere babies, with no notion of the injury they were committing. He called upon the jury to acquit altogether and 'not to let the brand of felons fall upon such infants as they saw before them'.

The learned judge then summed up and told the jury that if they were not completely satisfied that the children had considered the full effect of what they were doing, then the crime should be reduced to manslaughter. Judge Crompton did in effect direct the jury to reach this merciful and sensible conclusion – unlike the judge in the Bulger case. Whereas in the case of the Bulger killings, the populist home secretary intervened – unlawfully as it subsequently transpired – to try to extend the prison sentences of the children responsible, the judge in this case of 1861 imprisoned the boys for one month, followed by five years in a reformatory. There were some 3,712 children in reformatories in 1866, and some 8,029 juveniles in British prisons.[42]

It would be interesting to know what befell Bradley and Barratt in later life. Almost certainly, like so many juvenile criminals in Victorian England, they will have joined the army, perhaps going to some such heroic fate as befell 'the Private of the Buffs' in Sir Francis Hastings Doyle's poem – 'poor, reckless, rude, low-born, untaught'. The Victorians had many vices but they did not have the bad taste to make the dead infant into a saccharine icon, nor to victimize the almost equally wretched killers. Nor could they pretend that such abominable cruelty in two young boys was altogether unique. At Birkenhead at about this time one boy knifed another in the jugular, killing him instantly, while at a farmhouse near Barnard Castle, a twelve-year-old shot dead his housekeeper with no obvious provocation.[43]

A case which was much more disturbing to them, since it happened in a middle-class household – not in the unimaginable slums, but actually within the shrubbery where good bourgeois children played – was that of Constance Kent. On the night of 19 June 1860 the almost decapitated body of a nearly four-year-old boy, Savill Kent, was found in the garden privy, hidden by shrubs, of Roadhill House in Wiltshire. He was the son of Samuel Kent, a factories inspector, and his second wife, the former governess to the children of the first Mrs Kent. (She gave birth to ten, five of whom survived infancy.)

'Shall not God search this out? For he knoweth the secrets of the heart?' were the words which his grief-stricken parents put on the child's gravestone. The police arrested the child's nurse, Elizabeth Gough, and released her for lack of evidence. No 'leads' appeared, and the case seemed insoluble until Constance Kent, the murdered child's half-sister, now aged nearly twenty-one, was unable to keep her secret any longer. She had become religious – specifically, Anglo-Catholic – and had turned to the Reverend Arthur Wagner, perpetual curate of St Paul's Church, Brighton. Wagner was a colourful figure, who spent a considerable fortune building Anglo-Catholic churches in that jolly seaside town. His father, the vicar of Brighton, watching the family money evaporate as yet another incense-drowned brick fane was erected, once preached a sermon on the text 'Lord have mercy on my son, for he is a lunatick.' He it was who prepared Constance Kent for baptism and confirmation. When she was twenty-one she inherited £1,000 from her mother's estate and offered it to Wagner. He refused, and it was then that she made her confession to him, adding that it was her intention to give herself up to the police and to make a clean breast of it. She made the written statement, 'I, Constance Emilie Kent, alone and unaided on the night of the 19 June, 1860, murdered at Road Hill House, Wiltshire, one Francis Savill Kent. Before the deed, none knew of my intention nor after of my guilt: no one assisted me in the crime, nor after in my evasion of discovery.'

It seems as though Wagner made it a condition of pronouncing absolution over her in the confessional that she should answer before the law. Her motive seems truly like something in the darkest Greek tragedy. Her governess had persuaded her to hate her own mother. As she grew into her teens Constance came to see that her mind had been corrupted against her mother, that the governess, now the stepmother, had poisoned the love which was most important to her. She took revenge by killing her stepmother's child.

When the truth emerged there was enormous public interest, not least because it enabled the newspapers to deplore the Puseyite excesses of Father Wagner. He was a steadfast friend to her, interceding on her behalf at the highest level. After the trial, he wrote to his fellow Puseyite Gladstone, then chancellor of the Exchequer:

I cannot of course but feel very thankful, for her friends sake that Her Majesty has been pleased to commute Constance Kent's sentence to penal servitude for life, yet that Commuted Sentence is in her case who was, I trust, well prepared for death, and possessed of great courage, almost a worse punishment than the original one, not so much because it involves a life-long penance, as because it cut her off from some of the means of grace to which she has become accustomed, and from the use of many spiritual books, which may be of great benefit to her soul, exposed as she is likely to be as life advances, and with such sad antecedents, to great internal temptations.[44]

Wagner begged the home secretary to permit her to be incarcerated in some Anglican sisterhood, or similar institution, but the request was refused. She served twenty years. There, it was assumed, the story fizzled out, until a brilliant piece of detective work by Bernard Taylor – *Cruelly Murdered* – *Constance Kent and the Killing at Road Hill House* (1979, revised 1989) – presents convincing evidence that she emigrated to Australia, worked as a nurse, and did not die until she was over a hundred, in 1944. She appears to have been a saint-like figure who devoted herself to the welfare of others.

There is an apocryphal story that when tiny Harriet Beecher Stowe, less than five feet in height, was presented to the tall lanky president at the White House in 1862, Abraham Lincoln said, 'So, you're the little woman who wrote the book that started this great war.' Even if this exchange did not take place, Lincoln certainly did entertain the author of *Uncle Tom's Cabin*. Moreover it is from this book, now classifiable as children's literature but not especially meant as such, that many people in the Western world formed their impressions of the United States, and of the convulsions which would engulf them during the momentous 1860s. More than a million copies of the book sold in England on its first publication there in 1852, ten times as many as had previously been sold of any work except the Bible.

Yet, as we have seen, the American Civil War and its aftermath by no means inspired the English to support or even much to sympathize with the Union. It is possible to generalize and say that many English people, particularly those who had admired *Uncle Tom's Cabin*, took a pride in the part their country had played in the abolition of slavery, but would defend the right of the Southern states to determine their own affairs. But this generalization might provide too sweet an interpretation of public mood. One wonders whether *Uncle Tom's Cabin*, so popular in the England of 1852, would have gone down so well in the England of, say, 1868. The Sixties were a decade, after all, in which the English were compelled to confront their own attitudes to the issues raised by the liberation of slaves. But the theatre in which the drama was played out was not Alabama or Mississippi but the colony of Jamaica.

In 1865, when the war between the Confederacy and the Northern states was concluded in the supposed liberation of African Americans, Jamaica had a population of something over 440,000. Thirteen thousand were white, the remainder were the descendants of the former slave population (320,000 Jamaican slaves had been liberated in 1807). The island was ruled by a governor, flanked by a council, and an elective assembly of forty-seven members. Two thousand Jamaicans, by virtue of being property-owners, were entitled to vote. As a 'settled' colony, Jamaica was under the law of England – a crucially important fact in the story, since technically exactly the same laws should have applied there as in Britain. There were very strong feelings of discontent among the blacks, especially those who, through the medium of the Baptist Church, had acquired a modicum of political education. They resented their political destiny being determined by an assembly overwhelmingly supported by the planters, the former slave-owners, and the triumphs of the anti-slavery armies, marching through Georgia, had fired them with dreams of liberty: government of, for and by the people.

Edward John Eyre became the governor of Jamaica, aged forty-nine, in 1864. Of English birth, the son and grandson of clergymen, his colonial career in Australia and New Zealand had been conspicuous for its fairness. He defended the aborigines against white Australians. In 1845 he took two abo boys with him to visit the Queen and Prince Albert at Buckingham Palace.[45] It was his enlightened experience with aborigines and the Maoris which led to his appointment first as captain-general, then governor, of the Caribbean sugar-island.

Eyre tried to broker peace between the planters and the political malcontents, and in so doing excited the scorn of George William Gordon, the illegitimate son of a wealthy white planter and a slave woman. Gordon was elected to the assembly in 1863 and made the new governor's life as difficult as possible. 'When a Governor becomes a dictator, when he becomes despotic, it is necessary to dethrone him . . . I have never seen an animal more voracious for cruelty and power than the present Governor of Jamaica . . .' Gordon predicted 'anarchy and bloodshed' if the franchise were not extended.

In October 1865 there was an uprising of black peasants in the planting district of Morant Bay. The courthouse was burned to the ground and at least twenty whites were killed. A riot spread. There was talk of the slaughter of Frenchmen when the natives of Haiti proclaimed a republic. The governor received reports that 'the most fearful atrocities were perpetrated . . . The Island curate of Bath, the Rev. V. Herschell, is said to have had his tongue cut out whilst still alive, and an attempt is said to have been made to skin him. One person (Mr Charles Price, a black gentleman, formerly a Member of the Assembly) was ripped open and his entrails taken out.'

Eyre had to act and the possibility of total anarchy, of the British being driven from the island altogether, made him act with great severity. First he declared a state of martial law in Morant Bay. Then he had Gordon arrested in Kingston, but rather than allowing him a civil trial there, Eyre had him moved to Morant Bay, where he was tried by court martial and summarily hanged. Over the next month, 608 people were killed or executed, 34 were wounded, 600, including some women, were flogged and about 1,000 leaf-hut dwellings were destroyed. Eyre was regarded by the whites on the island as their saviour. The Council was abolished and Jamaica became a Crown colony. The magistrates and clergy, and many other groups, showered Governor Eyre with loyal addresses. 'We the undersigned, Ladies residing in the County of Cornwall, Jamaica, and on its borders, beg to tender our heartfelt thanks to you for the prompt and wise measures which we believe, under God, to have been the means of saving us and our children from a fate too terrible to contemplate.'

But on his return to England in 1866, Eyre found a country divided around the issue. At Southampton where he docked, a huge dinner was given in his honour – with speeches in his praise by the Earl of Cardigan, 'hero' of the Light Brigade, the Earl of Shrewsbury and Talbot, and rather surprisingly, the Rev. Charles Kingsley, since 1860 regius professor of history at Cambridge. Others dubbed the dinner 'the Banquet of Death', and a mob collected in Southampton High Street. In London, there was more mob violence, denouncing 'the Monster, ex-Governor Eyre' – for the poor fellow, entirely dependent on his salary, had been deprived of his governorship. The Jamaica Committee was formed, with such worthies as Thomas Hughes, lately elected MP for Lambeth, and John Stuart Mill, believing that Eyre had no more right to declare martial law in Jamaica than he would in England. The fact that he deliberately moved Gordon from a civil legislature to a place where he could be condemned without a proper

trial was seen by Eyre's critics as murder. When he had retreated to
Market Drayton in Shropshire, Eyre was indeed forced to stand before
local magistrates and face charges of murder. They were rejected by the
justice and the bells of Market Drayton rang out in consequence.

The liberals then tried to assign on murder charges Colonel
Alexander Abercromby Nelson – he it was who had confirmed the
capital sentence which hanged Gordon – and Colonel Brand, who had
presided at that court martial. Once more, magistrates rejected the
lengthy legal arguments in favour of prosecution. For Mill and the
Liberals, the question was, 'Who are to be our masters: the Queen's
Judges and a jury of our countrymen, administering the laws of
England, or three military or naval officers, two of them boys,
administering as the Chancellor of the Exchequer tells us, no law at
all?'

For Eyre's supporters – Tennyson, Ruskin and, most eloquent of
them all, Carlyle – it was clear that the governor had been justified in
restoring order, even if his justice had been rough:

> The English nation never loved anarchy, nor was wont to spend its
> sympathy on miserable mad seditions, especially of this inhuman and
> half-British type; but have always loved order and the prompt
> suppression of seditions, and reserved its tears for something
> worthier than promoters of such delirious and fatal enterprises who
> had got their wages from their sad industry. Has the English nation
> changed then altogether?

It was largely through the influence of Carlyle that Parliament voted the
ex-governor a pension. But the answer to the question was, yes,
England had changed, and the Eyre controversy was but a symptom of
it. The mobs who called Eyre a murderer were concerned less with the
fate of a few seditious Jamaicans than they were with what Eyre
represented – the suppression of fair government. Old Palmerston had
died days after the Jamaican rebellion. The successive governments of
Russell, who took over as prime minister, and Derby, who became
Tory prime minister in 1866, had to face the question of how to extend
the franchise without losing the aristocratic balance. (That they very
largely did so was one of the triumphs of the Conservatives, and of
Derby himself.)

Meanwhile, the attitude displayed at this time by the British towards
blacks, and towards the subject peoples of the Empire in general,

showed that there had been a perceptible change. The 'burden' of Empire coarsened public sympathy. The nation which at the beginning of the century had prided itself on the moral beauty of the anti-slavery cause had the greatest sympathy with a man who had flogged, tortured, burned and hanged the descendants of slaves whose rebellion Dr Johnson himself would have applauded. Was this because they wanted such rough justice applied in England? Or was it that, in imperial times, they had come to believe that there was one law for the white man, and another for the black? Eyre himself, who had defended the Australian aborigine, had come to the view that Caribbean aspirations to freedom were illegitimate, based on 'the indolence, apathy, improvidence, profligacy and crime which characterize the mass of the people'.[46] This view of black people, so widespread among the white Europeans of the coming decades, was believed to justify, even to necessitate, the subjugation and conquest of Africa itself.

'We are too tender to our savages,' Tennyson protested to Gladstone when they quarrelled over Governor Eyre. 'We are more tender to blacks than to ourselves . . . niggers are tigers, niggers are tigers.'[47]

Is it entirely accidental that the European 'Scramble for Africa' began only after such views had become entrenched, in the decades which followed the supposed 'emancipation' of the friends and family of Uncle Tom?

18

The World of School

When the Prince Consort died, his son Albert Edward, the Prince of Wales – Bertie – was not yet twenty-one; and by German standards his education was far from complete. In boyhood, he had developed a mastery of German and French, but to his parents' dismay he had no taste for history, or book learning, or mathematics, or science. He spent part of 1860 as an undergraduate at Christ Church, Oxford, where Dean Liddell – joint compiler of the Greek Lexicon and father of Alice – was the head of house, and where his tutor was the professor of ecclesiastical history, Arthur Penrhyn Stanley. Then in the fateful year of his father's demise Bertie had a spell at Cambridge, where his tutor was the regius professor of history, Charles Kingsley. Earnestly as Prince Albert had chosen Stanley and Kingsley for their progressive religious views, Bertie, with his incorrigible amiability, had developed no spiritual or intellectual interests, preferring hunting, drinking and, when occasion presented itself, wenching. It must have taxed the ingenuity of Oxford's chancellor, Lord Derby, to find reasons why Bertie should be made a doctor of civil law in 1863 – a ceremony which took place after Bertie had married Princess Alexandra of Denmark. In a speech of his own composing (how many twentieth- or twenty-first-century prime ministers could pen Latin prose which was praised for its ease and excellence by professional scholars?)[1] the three-times prime minister chancellor of Oxford wisely chose to dwell on Princess Alexandra's enchanting beauty rather than the Prince's academic attainments.*

One can be perfectly certain that amiable Bertie did not understand a word of it. After his father's death, his mother made no attempt to

---

*'Ipsa adest; et in egregia formae pulchritudine in benigna dulcium oculorum luce, in fronte illa nobili et pudica, nobis omnibus qui hic adsumus innatus virtutes animae velut in speculo licet . . .' (She is here present; and to all of us who are gathered here it seems as though, as in a looking-glass, these innate virtues are reflected, in the surpassing beauty of her appearance, in the kindly lights of her sweet eyes, in her noble, modest face.) *Oratio ad illustrissimum principem Albertum Edwardum Principem Walliae ab Edwardo Galfrido Comite de Derby.* 16 June 1863.

restrain her feelings of bitterness against the young man; she irrationally blamed him for Albert's death, since the Prince Consort had made the trek to Cambridge when he was going down with his last illness, to admonish Bertie for his part in the Nellie Clifden affair. Now the Queen was 'Alone!' She said of Bertie, 'If he turns obstinate I will withdraw myself altogether and wash my hands of him, for I cannot educate him.'[2]

It was proposed that a tour of the Levant, scheduled before the Prince Consort's death, should go ahead as a way of rounding off Bertie's formal education. The entourage was to be led by the Prince's governor, Colonel Robert Bruce – who had already accompanied the young man to Canada, the United States and Prussia. The unfortunate Bruce – son of the 7th Earl of Elgin, and aged a mere forty-nine at the beginning of the tour – was destined to contract a fever in the marshes of the Upper Jordan from which he died on 27 June 1862.[3]

Given the heterogeneity of temperament, and varieties of intellectual attainment of the royal entourage, everyone in the party acquitted themselves creditably. They included a medic, Dr Minter, various equerries, and the Prince's Oxford tutor, Arthur Penrhyn Stanley. As they drifted down the Nile in their boat, Bertie persuaded the eminent ecclesiastical historian to read Mrs Henry Wood's trashy novel, *East Lynne*, 'which I did in three sittings. Yesterday I stood a tolerable examination in it. A brisk cross-examination took place between HRH, APS, Meade and Keppell [two equerries]. I came off with flying colours, and put a question which no one could answer: "With whom did Lady Isobel dine on the fatal night?" It is impossible not to like him [the Prince] and to be constantly with him brings out his astonishing memory of names and persons.'[4]

This delightful holiday snapshot reveals the true Bertie. We can imagine what his father would have thought of their all reading *East Lynne*: Albert forbade Bertie to read *any* novels – even Sir Walter Scott had been deemed too 'demoralising'.[5]

As they approached the fateful marshes on those reaches of the Jordan which were to prove Colonel Bruce's undoing, there occurred one of those mildly ridiculous incidents which remind one how tightly knit was the Victorian 'upper ten thousand', that is, the aristocracy, the literary and political classes, and those educated at the universities, and one sees that much of the point of 'education' for the Victorians was not merely to impart knowledge but to create a class who, regardless of social, ethnic or religious origin, were all part of the same club.

The royal party were eating a picnic near the ford of Jabbock when a number of mounted Arabs came galloping down to the ford, headed by their sheikh. A messenger came to the royal tent, crossing the water with a man in a flat boat. His request was a surprising one – could the sheikh please meet with Dr Stanley. Everyone had been alarmed by the arrival of the warlike Arabs; Colonel Bruce had fingered his pistol; but the courageous Arthur Stanley, a small man with a delicate quiet charm, walked over unarmed to his interview with the 'sheikh'. The sheikh had dismounted from his great charger and laying both hands on his shoulders, said, 'Arthur Penrhyn Stanley.' The professor, after a moment of confusion caused by the Arab costume and the deep sunburn of the sheikh's face, recognized his old Oxford friend William Gifford Palgrave – who had been up at Trinity when Stanley was collecting all the prizes at Balliol.

Palgrave's own journeys, spiritual and geographical, could fill a book. His grandfather, Meyer Cohen, had been a successful member of the London Stock Exchange. His father, Sir Francis, had, on his marriage to a Gentile, changed his name to Palgrave. A distinguished antiquarian, he had been one of the founding fathers of the Public Record Office, and as such surely deserves a statue in London. Sir Francis's most celebrated son, also called Francis, edited *The Golden Treasury of best songs and Lyrical poems in the English language*, and was the friend of Gladstone, Tennyson and literary London. Gifford had stranger lands to travel in. Always drawn to the East, he had served a commission in the 8th Bombay Native Infantry. On his way home he learnt Arabic, and developed the desire to convert the Arabs to Roman Catholicism, a religion he had recently embraced himself. At the time that Stanley met him dressed as a sheikh, Gifford Palgrave, or the Abbé Sohail as he liked to be known, was a Jesuit priest. He lived much in the desert, and in 1858 had gone to the Palace of the Tuileries dressed as an Arab to tell Emperor Napoleon III about the plight of the Syrian Christians. He changed his name several times, sometimes in his letters home signing himself Michael Cohen. Not long after meeting Stanley and the Prince of Wales, he put himself at the service of the Prussian court as a diplomat, and left both the Jesuits and the Catholic Church. Shortly thereafter he joined the British diplomatic service and, having been consul in the Virgin Islands, he was destined to die as Our Man in Montevideo. Having returned to the Judaism of his forefathers, and dabbled in Islam and Shintoism, he was reconverted to Roman Catholicism at the end. He crammed a wealth of experience into sixty-two years.

Arthur Penrhyn Stanley, in his lifetime (1815–81) so infinitely more celebrated than Gifford Palgrave, has sunk to a comparable obscurity in the minds of many twenty-first-century readers. Indeed, if he is remembered at all he is, for many people, best known as a character in fiction – the delicate young Arthur in *Tom Brown's Schooldays* who dares to risk the sneering laughter and hurled bedroom-slippers of the bullies by kneeling down in a dormitory and saying his prayers – 'a snivelling young shaver' – before getting into bed. 'It was no light act of courage, in those days, my dear boys, for a little fellow to say his prayers publicly, even at Rugby. A few years later, when Arnold's manly piety had begun to leaven the school, the tables turned; before he died, in the school-house at least, and I believe in the other houses, the rule was the other way.'[6]

In this, the most celebrated of many Victorian school stories (published in 1857), Arthur expounds the scriptures to Tom Brown and his madcap friend East. 'The first night they happened to fall on the chapters about the famine in Egypt, and Arthur began talking about Joseph as if he were a living statesman; just as he might have talked about Lord Grey and the Reform Bill; only that they were much more living realities to him.'[7] There were clearly only the smallest of differences between young Arthur the schoolboy and Arthur Penrhyn Stanley who, in 1864 became dean of Westminster, appointed by Queen Victoria herself. Like the Queen, and like his hero, Dr Thomas Arnold of Rugby, Stanley was Broad Church, a variety of Christian which has all but died out, which is a puzzle, since in many respects it seems the most obvious sort of Christian to be. He sat light to doctrines. Many of his contemporaries doubted whether he was worthy to be counted a Christian at all. 'In Westminster Abbey,' wrote his biographer, 'he found the material embodiment of his ideal of a comprehensive national church, an outward symbol of harmonious unity in diversity, a temple of silence and reconciliation which gathered under one consecrated roof every variety of creed and every form of national activity, whether lay or ecclesiastical . . . He insisted that the essence of Christianity lay not in doctrine, but in a Christian character.'[8] This was the essence of Dr Arnold's teaching at Rugby when 'little Arthur' was a boy there.

In the novel, Thomas Hughes makes Arthur into the son of a 'clergyman of a parish in the Midland counties, which had risen into a large town during the [Napoleonic] war, and upon which the hard years which followed had fallen with a fearful weight'. This gives

Hughes, a socialist, the chance to explain Arthur's virtues by allusion to the 'manliness' of his father's parish experiences. (The clergyman has died of typhus fever among his poor parishioners.) Stanley's father was actually the bishop of Norwich, a scion of the Stanleys of Alderley, a cadet branch of the family of the earls of Derby.[9] When Derby became chancellor at Oxford the professor of poetry had apostrophized him as the

True Heir of England's old Nobility!

The Stanleys of Alderley could claim descent or collateral relationship with the Stanley who fought at Flodden ('"Charge, Chester, charge! On, Stanley, on!" were the last words of Marmion'); he had been a pall-bearer of Edward IV: his father at Bosworth Field had taken the crown of England from Richard III's corpse and placed it on the head of Henry Tudor (King Henry VII), who was his stepson. In Victoria's reign, three hundred and fifty years after Bosworth, the Stanleys were still powers in the land. Derby was the first Victorian prime minister to hold office three times. The Stanleys of Alderley, though not like the earls of Derby 'kings of Lancashire', were considerable magnates in neighbouring Cheshire, chairmen of the Quarter Sessions, and related to many of the powerful aristocracy. (The second Lord Russell, for example, who succeeded to the prime minister's earldom, was via his mother the grandson of the 2nd Baron Stanley of Alderley.)[10] When Arthur Stanley was installed as dean of Westminster, having married Lady Augusta Bruce (sister of the unfortunate colonel who had accompanied him to the Holy Land), the postmaster general was his brother-in-law, the 8th Lord Elgin; the foreign secretary Lord Russell was a cousin, as was the next prime minister, Lord Derby, and the next foreign secretary, Lord Stanley.

It was, presumably, the high reputation of Thomas Arnold (1795–1842), who became headmaster of Rugby in 1828, which persuaded Bishop Stanley to educate his delicate little son at the famously rough Midland boarding school.[11] 'Unfortunately,' Arthur wrote home to his sister in his first term there, 'the writing master here is called Stanley, and so I think I shall get the nickname of Bob Stanley's son.' It showed a charming optimism. When they saw the tiny lad, in his blue many-buttoned jacket and grey trousers adorned by a pink watch-ribbon, the boys devised a somewhat better nickname. They called him Nancy.

One of the mysteries of English life, from the 1820s to the present day, is why otherwise kind parents were prepared to entrust much-loved children to the rigours of boarding-school education. Stanley's mother remarked, 'Arthur says he doesn't know why, but he never gets plagued in any way like the others; his study is left untouched, his things unbroken, his books undisturbed.'[12] Stanley himself considered it all the more remarkable 'considering what I am'. His fastidious loathing of ragging, fisticuffs and the rough fights which form a part of daily existence at boys' boarding schools is perhaps reflected in his description of the martyrdom of Thomas Becket. In his *Historical Memorials of Canterbury Cathedral* Stanley bemoans Becket's use of strong language to his assassins[13] – 'I will not fly, you detestable fellow!' exclaims the resolute archbishop, like a plucky junior resisting the bullies of the Fifth at Rugby. Stanley sadly admits that 'the violence, the obstinacy, the furious words and acts, deformed even the dignity of his last hour, and well nigh turned the solemnity of his "martyrdom" into an unseemly brawl'.[14]

A school moment. By contrast, the death of Dr Arnold of Rugby is full of dignity, offering instruction and edification to the last. Even as his wife read to him from the 'Visitation of the Sick', the great headmaster said emphatically 'Yes' at the end of many of the sentences, as though the *Book of Common Prayer* were school work submitted for his approval.[15]

Thomas Arnold was generally credited not merely with the revival of Rugby School from a state of moral and intellectual torpor, but also with the invention, in some sense, of the public school ethos, as understood for the next century. Stanley's two-volume biography of his hero (published 1844) sees Dr Arnold's achievement as an essentially religious one. It ends, indeed, with a near-apotheosis, in which an old boy of the school, writing to Arnold's widow, imagines the headmaster actually set down at the right hand of God:

As our Saviour's wounds were healed on the morning of the Resurrection, so shall his mortal disease be healed, and all that we most loved in him shall become immortal. The tone of earnestness shall be there, deepened perhaps into a more perfect beauty by a closer intercourse with the Son of man . . . and how will the most aspiring visions of reformation that ever filled his mind on earth be more than accomplished in that day of the restitution of all things![16]

Even in heaven, it would seem, the headmaster was to be earnestly looking for something to reform.

Arnold's achievement, perhaps, historically, was to see the public school as the ideal social expedient by which the liberal–conservative ideals of the early nineteenth-century reformers could be put into practice. Rather than the bourgeoisie, as on the continent, displacing the aristocracy as the governing class, they could themselves acquire some of the attitudes, and speech inflexions, of the upper class by having the education of 'gentlemen'. From a comparatively small pool of privately educated boys, the colonial governors, senior ecclesiastics, politicians, statesmen, lawyers and other professionals could be drawn. An easily expandable governing class could quietly be created in which aristocrats did not lose their place, but in which there was room for those clever enough to push for, or rich enough to buy themselves, a position. Of course, this cynical Benthamite explanation of Arnold's campaign to make the boys of Rugby into 'Christian gentlemen' misses out the personal and religious sincerity of Arnold's ideals: but it is a fair description if not of Arnold's aims, then of the effects of his reforming zeal at Rugby. (The numbers of which we are speaking remain proportionately tiny – only 7,500 boys were at boarding school in England during the 1860s.)[17]

Tom Brown's Schooldays, unconsciously perhaps, mirrors the feelings of the Victorian middle classes towards the public schools. Although a sunny book, devoted to celebrating the manly joys of pure comradeship, games, Bible-reading and hero-worship of Dr Arnold, the bits we all remember are about bullies tossing the little boys in blankets and roasting them before the fire. (It was inspired of George Macdonald Fraser, in his late twentieth-century series of novels about the Rugby bully, to see that Flashman was an archetypical Englishman.) Flashman, in fact, takes over the story in spite of all Hughes's desire to the contrary, rather as Satan defies Milton's pious intentions at the beginning of the epic and becomes the hero of *Paradise Lost*.

Those 'first-generation' families who sent their sons off to public school were not necessarily appreciative of what they found. Arnold had high academic standards. The cleverer boy, taught by his principles, would certainly have been very good at Greek; and the more receptive might have imbibed muscular Christianity. But after Arnold's premature death, aged forty-seven, the major public schools remained insanitary nests of bullying, sexual depravity and – as far as a general knowledge of the natural or social world was in question – ignorance.

Gladstone was just such a middle-class product of a public-school education bought by parents who had learned to see these places as the training-grounds of a new aristocracy. Eton made him, and he remained obsessed by the place to his dying day. But the Liberal in him was forced to recognize that public schools, like everything else in the world, would benefit from Reform. For this reason Gladstone, when chancellor of the Exchequer in Palmerston's second Cabinet, was largely instrumental in the setting up of a parliamentary commission under Lord Clarendon to investigate the condition of the public schools.[18]

The commission worked for almost three years, from 1861, and interviewed 130 witnesses. It investigated such matters as school administration, the syllabus, the necessity or otherwise of teaching children science, the desirability of 'fagging' (that is, younger boys working as servants for older boys), the place in life of games and athletics, the need or otherwise for examinations ... Yet throughout its deliberations, and the discussions in both Houses of Parliament of its final report – leading eventually to the Public Schools Act of 1868 – it is hard to avoid the feeling that the main thing under discussion was class. Even when it came to the anodyne question of whether science was a suitable subject to which to draw a young gentleman's (or would-be gentleman's) attention, you have the sense that they are not really discussing whether boys ought to know chemistry. An impressive array of scientists appeared before Clarendon to urge the adoption of a scientific education, and interestingly Dean Farrar (author of such school classics as *Eric, or, Little by Little*) was thoroughly in favour of this. But the headmaster of Shrewsbury, B.H. Kennedy, carried the day. The natural sciences, he told Clarendon, 'do not furnish a basis for education'.[19] As the author of *The Public School Latin Primer* he had a nice little earner on his hands: speaker after speaker in Parliament, including Gladstone, emphasized the undesirability of science as a school subject. Lords Derby, Stanhope and Carnarvon all argued that it would lead to 'cramming' and overwork, and cut into time needed for games, and the Earl of Ellenborough was able to spell out exactly where this could lead: examinations in which tradesmen's sons could succeed against, for example, the sons of army widows 'who had learned truth and honour at home'.[20]

All the public schools had, as a matter of historical fact, been founded to teach poor scholars. It was centuries since a poor person had been to Eton; and those public schools which retained places for poorer pupils found them in a distinct minority, though a witness to Clarendon said that at Charterhouse 'gown boys were not looked down upon'.[21] Other schools found it less embarrassing actually to found new establishments for the worthy townsfolk, lest the 'young gentlemen' boarders in Eton collars from richer homes should have to mix with the children of local tradesfolk or even of artisans. The Lower School of John Lyon came into being in the town of Harrow in 1875. Dulwich in 1857 had created Alleyn's School for the more plebeian pupils; Oundle's amputation was called Laxton Grammar School; Repton had the Sir John Port School and Rugby the Lawrence Sheriff – in both cases named after the founders of the original charitable enterprise.

So popular was the idea of public-school education that even as the Clarendon Commission sat, new 'public schools' were founded – Beaumont in 1861, Clifton and Malvern in 1862, Cranleigh and St Edward's, Oxford, in 1863. For the clearer it became in everybody's mind that the schools were to be the reinforcement of the new class system – indeed its seedbed – the more necessary it was to have a hierarchy of schools. An extension and elaboration of this hierarchy was indeed the life's work to which the Reverend Nathaniel Woodard (1811–91) was devoted. Woodard was a keen Tractarian, and wanted to educate children in the High Church principles which he had himself imbibed at the feet of Newman, Pusey and Keble at Oxford, where he only got a pass degree, having married and had children as an undergraduate.[22] The religious motive notwithstanding, Woodard was always perfectly open about the need to see boarding schools as vehicles of social engineering. His manifesto, *A Plea for the Middle Classes*, was published in 1848, and his *Letter to Lord Salisbury*, published twenty years later, was a progress report on his remarkable success in raising the money by public subscription for the establishment of no fewer than sixteen schools – 'providing a good and complete education for the middle classes at such a charge as will make it available for most of them'. Salisbury himself when still Lord Robert Cecil, Longley, archbishop of York (former headmaster of Harrow), Gladstone, Bishop Wilberforce, Temple when headmaster of Rugby and Charles Kingsley all gave Woodard money and encouragement, so in spite of his Anglo-Catholic credentials he appealed to a wide spectrum.

From the first he recognized that 'middle class' was now a term which applied both to 'gentlemen with small incomes, solicitors and surgeons with limited practice, unbeneficed clergymen, naval and military officers' and to a second class of 'respectable trades folk'. There was also a third category who could afford his fees but who were not, strictly, respectable – the keepers of 'second-rate retail shops, publicans, gin-palace keepers', etc.[23]

Woodard established three sorts of school: the first were mini-Etons, which would educate boys until they were eighteen and then send them to university or into the army; the second class would keep them until sixteen; the third until fourteen. All would have the architecture of an 'old school' – a chapel, a quadrangle, masters and headmasters in academical caps and gowns, all the bogus appurtenances of 'public school'. Such is the eagerness of the socially mobile that the publicans were only too happy to send their sons to the third-class Woodard schools, such as St Saviours, Ardingly, knowing that these boys might so better themselves in later life that they could aspire to send their own sons to grander Woodard establishments, such as Lancing. Who knows? Within three generations they could even have escaped the Woodard group altogether, and be rubbing shoulders with the upper middle classes at Charterhouse or Shrewsbury.[24] Woodard was clever enough to see that such arcane transformations would be hindered by too much of the stabilizing influence of home, which is why from the first he insisted on the need for boarding schools.

The non-hierarchical or anti-hierarchical spirit of our age is so much at variance with Canon Woodard's ideals that we are in danger of ignoring the obvious fact that they were ideals. The children of gin-palace keepers deserved educational opportunities just as much as the children of the ducal palace, the vicarage, the suburb or the slum. The Victorians invented the concept of education as we now understand it; even if we believe ourselves to be more egalitarian than they, it is from them that we derive our axiomatic assumption that learning should be formalized learning, education institutionalized, the imparting of knowledge the duty of society and the state to every citizen. The 1860s, which began with the Clarendon Report on Public Schools and ended with the parliamentary Act guaranteeing elementary education for all, was the decade in which this culmination of Benthamite control was accomplished. Bishop Stanley, choosing to send the delicate Arthur Penrhyn Stanley, his son, to Rugby School, was emblematic of the change which had come upon England with the coming of the age of Reform. The bishop had not been to school himself. John Ruskin did not go to school. Nor did Queen Victoria, nor John Stuart Mill, George

Eliot or Harriet Martineau. It would be absurd to suggest that Disraeli, Dickens, Newman or Darwin, to name four very different figures, who attended various schools for short spells in their boyhood, owed very much to their schooling. Had they been born in a later generation, school would have loomed much larger in their psychological stories, if only because they would have spent so much longer there, and found themselves preparing for public examinations. It is hard not to feel that a strong 'syllabus', or a school ethos, might have cramped the style of all four and that in their different ways – Disraeli, comparatively rich, anarchically foppish, indiscriminately bookish; Darwin, considered a dunce, but clearly – as he excitedly learned to shoot, to fish and to bird-watch – beginning his revolutionary relationship with the natural world; Newman, imagining himself an angel; Dickens, escaping the ignominy of his circumstances through theatrical and comedic internalized role-play – they were lucky to have been born before the Age of Control. For the well-meaning educational reforms of the 1860s were the ultimate extension of those Benthamite exercises in control which had begun in the 1820s and 1830s. Having exercised their sway over the poor, the criminals, the agricultural and industrial classes, the civil service and – this was next – the military, the controllers had turned to the last free spirits left, the last potential anarchists: the children.

As Woodard had realized from the first, in creating his hierarchy of boarding-schools with their bogus traditions, faked-up slang, and imitations of the older public schools, education was a necessary part of the new class system which capitalism had brought into being. To be truly effective, it was necessary not merely to set up new middle-class schools, but to deprive the poor of the education which had been provided them for generations. The original founders of the public schools had all meant them to educate the poor. In 1442, Henry VI had instructed that 'no one having a yearly income of more than five marks' was eligible to attend his foundation at Eton. In the early nineteenth century, however, the public schools had begun the process of social segregation on which Victorian England very largely depended. Thomas Arnold, for example, closed the free lower school at Rugby so that, without hiring a tutor to teach their children, the poor could not reach the standard necessary to pass into the upper school. Winchester in 1818 claimed that its pupils were the 'poor and needy' specified by the founder William of Wykeham: it was only their parents who were rich. The Public Schools Act of 1868 took over any remaining endowments dedicated to poor pupils and gave them to the rich schools. In Sutton Coldfield, for example, whose poor were educated free by virtue of an endowment, £15,000 was plundered from the old charitable foundation in order to provide a 'high school for well to do children'.

The independence which education provided was thus removed from the poor, as was the element of choice. After 1870, and W.E. Forster's Education Act, it was to become compulsory for everyone to attend schools, but to do so in places strictly assigned to them according to income and social status.[25]

For the first time in Protestant history, even females were not exempt. Here is in fact the central, the classic example of the rule that, in order to find liberty in the Benthamite controlled world, you had to submit to its slavery. Education, first at schools, a little later in the century at university colleges, was the key means by which women were to enter upon a professional world on terms with men. Florence Nightingale founded a school of nursing in 1857 and provided others with a template of how women might, independently of men, establish a professional identity – hence, eventually, a political one. But in order to compete with boys, girls had, from the very first, to fight for such dubious privileges as the right to sit for public examinations.

F.D. Maurice had been the chief inspiration behind the setting-up of Queen's College, Harley Street, as an adjunct to the University of London, and from that institution emerged two of the most important educationalists of the nineteenth century:[26]

> Miss Buss and Miss Beale
> Cupid's darts do not feel.
> How different from us,
> Miss Beale and Miss Buss.

The lines, invented by a Clifton schoolmaster when Miss Buss insisted on attending a Headmasters' Conference to discuss public examinations, rebound upon their own masculine limitations. The glory of Miss Beale and Miss Buss is that they established, for educational purposes, that women are *not* 'different from us'.

Frances Mary Buss opened the North London Collegiate School for Ladies on 4 April 1850 at No. 46 Camden Street. Her great triumph, apart from the establishment of the school – and with it an inspiration to other 'Girls' Public Day Schools' – was to battle for the right to sit public examinations. The Cambridge Syndicate in 1863 was at first fiercely opposed to girls sitting exams. Through the influences of her friends Elizabeth Garrett and Emily Davies she was able to win this vital concession. (In 1869 Miss Davies opened, at Hitchin, the college eventually known as Girton – it moved to Cambridge in 1873.) Miss Buss was a tiny woman with an extraordinary flair for teaching and an intelligent fervour for the rights of women. In a long career, and a violent century, she never raised her hand against a child, though pupils, like the men who attempted to check her reforms, quailed in her presence.[27]

Her friend Dorothea Beale had witnessed, as a teacher, the rough end of school life. While Buss left Queen's College, Harley Street, to establish the North London Collegiate, Beale was appointed, at the age of twenty-six, head teacher of the Clergy Daughters' School, Casterton, Westmorland. This establishment, which had been founded in 1823 by the Reverend Cairns Wilson at Cowan Bridge, was destined, by the hand of its most famous pupil, to become the most notorious girls' school in European history: for it is none other than the Lowood of *Jane Eyre* (1847).

Patrick Brontë, himself born in a hovel in Northern Ireland and educated entirely by the local parson, is one of the many brilliant men and women who, not having been to school themselves, inflicted school on their offspring. In the case of the Brontë sisters, poverty decreed that they should be trained as governesses, and a training meant to endure Mr Wilson – Mr Brocklehurst in the novel.

'If ye suffer hunger or thirst,' he exclaims, to the housekeeper, 'happy are ye. Oh madam, when you put bread and cheese, instead of burnt porridge into these children's mouths, you may indeed feed their vile bodies, but you little think how you starve their immortal souls!'[28]

Lowood was, Jane Eyre tells us, 'the cradle of fog and fog-bred pestilence . . . Semi-starvation and neglected colds had predisposed most of the pupils to receive infection; forty-five out of the eighty girls lay ill at one time.'

There was, for the Brontë sisters themselves, a bitter and truthful reality in Mr Brocklehurst's catechism:

'No sight so sad as that of a naughty child,' he began, 'especially a naughty little girl. Do you know where the wicked go after death?'

'They go to hell,' was my ready and orthodox answer.

'And what is hell? Can you tell me that?'

'A pit full of fire.'

'And should you like to fall into that pit and to be burning there for ever?'

'No sir.'

'What must you do to avoid it?'

I deliberated a moment; my answer when it did come, was objectionable: 'I must keep in good health and not die.'[29]

Maria and Elizabeth Brontë both died – aged less than twelve – because of fever contracted at the school. Emily Brontë's health was immeasurably weakened by the place – she died aged less than thirty, as did her sister Anne. 'Lowood' was no less severe, indeed sadistic, in atmosphere when Dorothea Beale went there as principal, and she left after a disagreement with the governors in her first year.[30] In 1858, against a list of fifty rival candidates, she was chosen as the principal of a newly established school – Cheltenham Ladies' College. It was one of the first schools in England for children of either sex to offer what in modern terms would be seen as a rounded education, teaching mathematics and science, art and history, as well as languages. It remained, until the twentieth century, a school for Ladies. Whereas Miss Buss's schools in London were open to the daughters of respectable merchants, businessmen or traders, Cheltenham waited until the 1920s before opening its door to such, and throughout Miss Beale's lifetime (she died in 1906) only offered its considerable intellectual resources to the daughters of gentlefolk or the professional classes.

The Victorians invented school as a social instrument which moved forward the potentiality of the bourgeois revolution while it retained old hierarchies, and invented new ones. The freshly founded public schools – Bradfield, 1850; Cheltenham, 1841; Clifton, 1862; Dover, 1871, Glenalmond, 1841; Lancing, 1848; Malvern, 1865; Marlborough, 1843; Rossall, 1844; *et al.*[31] – all sprang ready formed with the bogus school slang, arcane brand-new traditions and firm hierarchies. Their ethos both enshrined and evangelized the combination of individualism with the crushing of self by institutionalism which is so distinctive and paradoxical a feature of the Victorian experience.

Tom Brown arrives at Rugby a free spirit, a child of the pre-industrialized English countryside. He could, for all the difference it makes, be an Elizabethan or an eighteenth-century child. He is confronted by the rough world of school – both the admirable 'hearty' Brooke and the bullies, Flashman and Speedicut. It is often supposed that the morality of the novel derives from the pure athleticism of these earlier chapters, and that Hughes was advocating a philistine pursuit of games and hero-worship. The book is deeper than that.

In 1858 *The Times* confessed that it was an 'unsolved problem' how a public school education tamed uncivilized boys and 'how the licence of unbridled speech is softened into courtesy, how lawlessness becomes discipline, how false morality gives place to a sound and manly sense of right, and all this within two or three years, with little external assistance, and without any strong religious impressions'. It concluded that 'Parents may well abstain from looking too closely into the process and content themselves with the result.'[32]

Dr Arnold had encapsulated his ideal 'to form Christian men, for Christian boys I can scarcely hope to make; I mean that, from the natural imperfect state of boyhood, they are not susceptible of Christian principles in their full development upon their practice, and I suspect that a low standard of morals in many respects must be tolerated amongst them, as it was on a larger scale in what I consider the boyhood of the human race'.[33]

Hughes depicts in *Tom Brown's Schooldays* how this transformation took place. It has been skilfully pointed out that many of the jolly boyish reminiscences in the first part of the story – the football game, the bullying, the birds-nesting and so on – were in fact derived by Hughes from the written recollections of other old Rugbeians; the apparently unrealistic second half in which Tom experiences a spiritual renewal through his friendship with little Arthur (and Arthur's near-death experience) is all purely autobiographical. The crucial thing is that Tom has become institutionalized. He has become a team player. This is of vital significance to Hughes the socialist. At the last cricket match, a master remarks that it is 'a noble game'.

'Isn't it? But it's more than a game. It's an institution,' said Tom.

'Yes,' said Arthur, 'the birthright of British boys old and young, as *habeas corpus* and trial by jury are of British men.'

'The discipline and reliance on one another which it teaches is so valuable I think,' went on the master, 'it ought to be such an unselfish game. It merges the individual in the eleven, he doesn't play that he may win, but that his side may.'[34]

The thought is further advanced that 'Perhaps ours' – i.e. the world of the public school – 'is the only little corner of the British Empire which is thoroughly wisely and strongly governed just now.'[34]

'The world of school' in other words – to use the subtitle of another famous story (*St Winifred's, or, the World of School*, by Dean Farrar) – was seen as a microcosm of the political world and as a preparation for it. That is why failure to conform to the conventions of school is seen as so anarchic; and why expressions of individualism are seen as so potentially damaging. This socio-political attitude colours what might be considered a prudish Victorian attitude to masturbation. *Eric, or, Little by Little* has been described as 'the kind of book Dr Arnold might have written had he taken to drink'.[35]

The 'little by little' is the gradual slither of Farrar's eponymous hero from small sins to great. He begins by laughing when a grasshopper gets into a lady's hat in church – for which he receives a flogging from the headmaster, Dr Rowlands. Before long, he is indulging in far worse sins than laughing in church. At first, the filthy talk in dormitory No. 7 shocked Eric 'beyond bound or measure'. Dark though it was, he felt himself blushing scarlet to the roots of his hair, and then growing pale again, while a hot dew was left upon his forehead. Ball was the speaker . . . Farrar himself apostrophizes: 'Now, Eric, now or never! Life and death, ruin and salvation, corruption and purity, are perhaps in the balance together, and the scale of your destiny may hang on a single word of yours. Speak out, boy!'

But Eric is silent, and after half an hour 'in an agony of struggle with himself' he falls. Farrar never spells out the precise nature of Eric's sin but a sermon by Dr Rowlands on Kibroth-Hathaavah (in the book of Numbers) makes it abundantly clear what is meant. Kibroth-Hathaavah is the burial ground of those who have lusted.

Kibroth-Hathaavah! Many and many a young Englishman had perished there! Many and many a happy English boy, the jewel of his mother's heart – brave and beautiful and strong – lies buried there. Very pale their shadows rise before us – the shadows of our young brothers who have sinned and suffered. From the sea and the sod, from foreign graves and English churchyards, they start up and throng around us in the paleness of their fall. May every schoolboy who reads this page be warned by the warning of their wasted hands from that burning marle of passion where they found nothing but shame and ruin, polluted affections and an early grave.

Masturbation, in Farrar's story, leads inexorably to death. One of the most painful aspects of the Ruskin–Effie Gray divorce is the possibility that she revealed that he masturbated while sharing the non-consummated marital bed with her. He wrote to his friend Mrs Cowper, 'Her words are fearful – I can only imagine one meaning to them – which I will meet at once – come of it what may. Have I not often told you that I was another Rousseau?' – i.e. a masturbator – 'except in this – that the end of my life will be the best – has been – already – not best only – but redeemed from the evil that was its death.'[36]

The school story was one of the most distinctive of Victorian contributions to literature. There are no Elizabethan or Jacobean tragedies about school. Novels about school did not come from the pens of Richardson or Fielding. Yet Jane Eyre's experiences at Lowood, Nicholas Nickleby's at Dotheboys Hall, remain some of the most vivid experiences in our reading of nineteenth-century fiction. School, as well as being for Dr Arnold and his followers an archetype of society, becomes too a paradigm of the inner life, the waking nightmare that we will be snatched from the emotional comforts of home and thrust into the hardship, the psychological and physical torture, of a single-sex institutionalized existence. No wonder, for pupils and teachers alike, this should prove so endlessly addictive a theme. *Tom Brown's Schooldays* was published in April 1857, and by November of that year it had gone through five editions, selling 11,000 copies.[37] Twenty-eight thousand copies had sold by the end of 1862. Altogether fifty-two editions were printed by Macmillan before 1892. *Eric* sold comparably well. It, and Farrar's other stories, *St Winifred's, or, the World of School* and *Julian Home*, the continuation of the hero's education at Cambridge, seem so unrealistic to us as an attempted portrait of the speech or thought-processes of actual schoolboys that we blink in amazement in recalling that Farrar was in fact a teacher – first as a master at the newly founded Marlborough College, then at Harrow – where he was appointed in 1855. (After teaching at Harrow he became, first master of Marlborough, then dean of Canterbury.) *Eric, St Winifred's* and *Julian Home* were all composed while Farrar was a Harrow master and all, as it happens, date from one of the most extraordinary periods in that school's history.

While Farrar was penning his distinctive fables about the perils of onanism, the school in which he was actually teaching was a hotbed of homosexual bullying, where every pretty boy was given a girl's name and faced the possibility either of being labelled public property – in which case he was frequently compelled into (often public) acts of incredible obscenity – or of being taken over and becoming the exclusive 'bitch' of an older boy. If Farrar turned a blind eye to this – and he eventually became a housemaster at Harrow – was he also unaware of the personal tragedy engulfing the headmaster himself?

Charles John Vaughan was a pupil of Arnold's at Rugby, a contemporary of Arthur Stanley's, whose sister Catherine he married in 1850. He had a brilliant career at Cambridge, was elected to a fellowship of Trinity, was ordained, and became headmaster of Harrow aged twenty-eight. From 1844 to 1859 he was one of the most revered teachers in England. He had arrived to find Harrow demoralized and depopulated. He increased the numbers of boys from 60 in 1844 to over 200 within two years. 'No headmaster, Arnold excepted, gathered round him a more gifted band of scholars or colleagues.'[38] Yet, at the age of forty-three, he suddenly resigned his headmastership. Those were the days in which a headmaster of a great public school – who would invariably be in holy orders – could expect rich preferment in the Church. (Two of Queen Victoria's archbishops of Canterbury, Temple and Tait, had been headmasters of Rugby.) Accordingly, Palmerston, the Old Harrovian prime minister, offered Vaughan the bishopric of Rochester. Vaughan accepted but then, as the mysterious entry puts it in the *Dictionary of National Biography*, 'a day or two later, probably after a severe struggle with his ambition, the acceptance was withdrawn'. No one who had seen the mere surface brilliance of Vaughan's career could understand why he did not want to be a bishop. He worked for years as the vicar of the poor Northern parish of Doncaster, and ended his days in the comparative obscurity of the deanery of Llandaff. 'He left,' concludes the *DNB*, 'a strict injunction that no life of him should be published.'

It was only in the twentieth century that Vaughan's pathetic secret was revealed. In 1851 one of the boys at Harrow was John Addington Symonds, destined to be one of the century's most articulate (if secret) homosexuals, but in boyhood terrified of his sexuality and loathing the atmosphere of school. In 1851 another boy, a lively, good-looking youth called Alfred Pretor, informed him in a letter that he was having an affair with the saintly Dr Vaughan. He was horrified, and remembered the manner in which Vaughan used to stroke his thigh when he, Symonds, read his essays to the headmaster.

Symonds kept his secret for eight years. Then, when he had escaped

'Dr Vaughan's malign influence' as he saw it, and he was an Oxford undergraduate, he blurted out the whole story while on a reading party. His confidant was the professor of Latin, who, when he had read Pretor's letter, told Symonds he must inform his father. Dr Symonds wrote to Vaughan assuring him that there would be no exposure on condition that he resigned at once. Vaughan went down to Clifton to plead with Dr Symonds, followed a few days later by his wife, who flung herself on her knees, weeping and begging for pity. Dr Symonds was adamant: Vaughan must go. It was further a condition laid down by the Symondses that if Vaughan ever attempted to accept senior office in the Church, he would be exposed and ruined. The secret was kept from public knowledge until Phyllis Grosschurch published her biography of John Addington Symonds in 1964: a good example of the brilliance with which the Victorian public-school classes, if we may call them that, could close ranks and look after their own.

Farrar's novels exude unwholesome sexual feeling like tightly lidded pressure-cookers giving off steam. The secret life of Vaughan hints at the extraordinary emotional atmosphere of these enclosed and (save for the presence of the occasional matron or housemaster's wife) single-sex establishments.

Combined with the differing degrees of homo-eroticism, which was in almost all cases covert, or actually in those pre-Freudian times unrecognized or only half-recognized, was found the wholehearted acceptance of canings and floggings, notionally as punishment, but manifestly a form of tormented emotional release. The 1860s which saw such a flowering of popularity of school stories were also the decade when Swinburne's *Poems and Ballads* first shocked and delighted the world. The published work – so shocking in its overt atheism, so luxuriantly decadent, and for English readers who had not read Baudelaire so completely novel – hinted, with its invocations to 'Our Lady of Pain', at a sadistic interest which is rampant in the poet's secret and pornographic outpourings, in such works as *The Pearl* and *The Whippingham Papers*. Swinburne's overwhelming obsession with flagellation appears to be a compulsive repetition, in the very core of his erotic being and imagination, of the especially violent corporal punishment at the Eton of his day.[39] Eton made a speciality of public floggings – or 'executions' as they were called – and it is impossible not to suppose that these occasions made a profound impression on Swinburne's febrile imagination. Flogging and caning were much discussed at the time of the Clarendon Commission. The most learned monograph on the subject of nineteenth-century flagellation opines that the following anonymous letter, printed in *The Morning Post*, was probably the poet:

> I can vouch that, from the earliest days to the days of the immortal Keate [a notorious flogging headmaster of Eton, 1809–34], and thence to those of the present headmaster, they have one and all, appealed to *the very seat of honour*. 'Experientia docet'. And, mark me, flogging, used with sound judgement, is the only *fundamental* principle upon which our large schools can be properly conducted. I am all the better for it and am, therefore, ONE WHO HAS BEEN WELL SWISHED.

The popularity – overt – of school stories and – covert – of flagellant pornography, sado-masochistic prostitution and its twilight psychological hinterlands are all tokens of how potent the boarding-school experience was, for generations of English boys. You see how firmly it was embedded in the consciousness of the next generation in Henry Newbolt's (1862–1938) anthology piece 'Vitaï Lampada', in which memories of the breathless hush in the Close at Clifton are carried into the Imperial Wars.

> The sand of the desert is sodden red –
> Red with the wreck of a square that broke; –
> The Gatling's jammed and the Colonel dead,
> And the regiment blind with dust and smoke.
> The river of death has brimmed his banks,
> And England's far, and Honour a name,
> But the voice of a schoolboy rallies the ranks:
> 'Play up! play up! and play the game!'

Newbolt, like Hughes, was a man of the left, who saw in the team-spirit of public schoolboys on the cricket pitch a useful paradigm of the cooperative unselfishness of an ideal society.

The games ethos affected not merely the men, but their wives. Arthur Stanley showed no aptitude for cricket when he was a boy; indeed, when at Rugby, he rather disliked the game. Yet when he was installed as the dean of Westminster, all this was forgotten. The boys of the Abbey choir-school were entertained to a cricket-tea by Dean Stanley and Lady Augusta and politely wrote to thank for it. Clearly neither

Stanley nor his wife had stayed to watch the close of play, but this did not prevent Lady Augusta from seeing the games afternoon as an admirable excuse for a sermon. 'My dear Boys,' she wrote:

I am much pleased to have the 'score' and to see how the game went & that though you had had so little practise [sic], you had not forgotten your cricket – It made the Dean & me very happy to see you enjoying yourselves and to learn by the nice letters I have received, that you continued to do so.

We love dearly to see you happy and joyous & making the most of the opportunities given you, both for work and relaxation – I am sure you all feel the delight of exercising the bodily strength & skill & activity which Cricket calls into play – but I am no less sure that you will learn day by day, if you apply yourselves, the truth of the lesson that this teaches us, namely that our happiness in life consists in the right exercise of all the faculties Our Heavenly Father has in His goodness given us . . .

On she bores, concluding after several pages,

I am sure that you will all strive, down to the youngest among you, to make the Dean happy by shewing that not only in the Cricket field but in Church – in yr Houses – in School & at play – the 'score' may be such as to gladden the hearts of those who desire your good.[40]

It is so easy to mock this, so hard to recapture a world where grown-ups took children and childhood so passionately seriously that they could see in an afternoon of cricket, interrupted by lemonade and buns, an occasion for recalling the essentially moral texture of existence itself.

The illogic of the 'Broad Church' position would infuriate, on the one hand theological bigots, on the other those heirs of Enlightenment thought who believed the human race had left behind the need for a religious framework to life. But viewed differently, the intellectual 'inheritance' of Dean Stanley and friends was precisely a source of strength. They accepted the rigours of the scientific principle when it applied to science; they went on reading Plato, convinced that a religious attitude to the universe was allowable even when the mind had recognized the implausibility of many, perhaps most, perhaps all, Christian dogmas. In rather comparable ways, the alliances and rivalries of the changing political scene allowed an aristocracy to survive in England while a bourgeois democracy was forged: the two were not, as on the continent, deemed incompatibles. This ability to live with contrarieties which are not necessarily contradictions was one of the foremost strengths of Victorian England, seen in many aspects of life, not least – a theme for later in the century – in the writings of those British Hegelian philosophers who in large degree grew out of, though many would come to despise, the Broad Church theology of which Arthur Penrhyn Stanley was so charming and delicate an exponent.

19

Charles Kingsley and *The Water-Babies*

Most of us first read Charles Kingsley's *The Water-Babies* in some lavishly illustrated edition – though whether the illustrator was Heath Robinson, Mabel Lucie Attwell or Margaret Tarrant, they tended to overlook the fact that water-babies, having returned to a state of innocence and redemption, were naked. Kingsley explicitly states that the drowned chimney-sweep's boy Tom 'felt how comfortable it was to have nothing on but himself'.

This story, however, 'a Fairy Tale for a Land-Baby', first appeared not as a beautiful 'children's book' but serialized in two grey, unillustrated columns of *Macmillan's Magazine* from August 1862 to March 1863. Those who first wanted to follow the adventures of Tom, who works for the cruel Grimes the chimney-sweep, who is shoved up a chimney flue at Harthover Place, comes down into the bedroom of little Ellie and is accused of being a thief, had to do so by turning over prolix articles by Leslie Stephen on the economic-liberal case for supporting the Confederacy, lengthy reviews by Matthew Arnold on Stanley's *Jewish Church*, scientific disquisitions on oysters, on geology, or the antiquity of man; or a worthy consideration by Thomas Hare on the ideal form of local government in the Metropolis.

There is something apt about the fact that we must search for *The Water-Babies* among the periodical literature of the day, jostling with Kingsley's eminent contemporaries. Kingsley's energetic engagement with his times, his taste for controversy, his extraordinary range, can all be found reflected in *The Water-Babies*. His wife said it was 'perhaps the last book he wrote with any real ease'; he dashed it off, completing the first chapter exactly as published, and without alteration (5,000 words at least?), in an hour.[1]

He was forty-two when he wrote it: destined to die aged fifty-six, exhausted by an American lecture tour, by chain-smoking, and hyperactivity. Staring at Kingsley's dead face in late January 1875, Dean Stanley thought him 'like the stone effigy of an ancient warrior, ... resting as if after the toils of a hundred battles, this was himself idealised. From those mute lips there seemed to issue once more the living words with which he spoke ten years ago before one' – i.e. the

Prince of Wales – 'who honoured him with an unswerving faithfulness even to the end. Some say' – thus he spoke in the chapel of Windsor Castle – 'some say that the age of chivalry is past, that the spirit of romance is dead. The age of chivalry is never past, so long as there is a wrong left unredressed on earth, or a man or woman left to say "I will redress that wrong, or spend my life in the attempt."'[2]

A grave in the Abbey was offered, but the family preferred to bury Charles Kingsley in the graveyard of the parish church at Eversley, south of Reading, where he had been rector since the 1840s. The concourse was huge. The Bramshill Hunt, complete with their horses and hounds, stood respectfully as eight villagers bore to his grave this keen sportsman, naturalist, countryman. Dean Stanley read the service. The bishop of Winchester – Harold Browne, an Etonian Gladstone appointee who succeeded Soapy Sam two years before – gave the blessing. The Hon. A. Fitzmaurice represented the Prince of Wales, who had been taught by Kingsley at Cambridge. Macmillan the publisher was there at the graveside of his bestselling author. But separated by the churchyard wall from the academics and the clergy and the London literati were the local gypsies, and the villagers. No figure comparable to Kingsley could be imagined in the twenty-first century.

Apart from his personal distinction, Kingsley's was a splendid illustration of the flexible use which could be made of a country parsonage in the nineteenth century before motor cars and a bureaucratic Church of England waged their war on the amateurism of the clergy. Himself a parson's son, Charles Kingsley was – in spite of occasional forays to local grammar schools – educated largely at home. At four, he enjoyed composing poetry and sermons, and from early life he was a keen and well-informed natural historian, starting by collecting shells by the Devonian shore of Clovelly. At Cambridge, while gaining a classical first and 'senior optime' in the mathematical tripos, he devoured Coleridge, Carlyle, and above all F.D. Maurice, the guiding light of his life. He hated team games, but learnt boxing from a negro prize fighter.[3]

He was ordained aged twenty-three to a curacy at Eversley, becoming rector of the parish a couple of years later, a position he retained for the rest of his life. At the same time he was deeply engaged with the Christian Socialist movement (Thomas Hughes was to become his best friend); a popular author of novels – *Alton Locke* (1850) and *Yeast* (1851) popularized the Chartist position; a queen's chaplain;

and, from 1860 to 1869, regius professor of history at Cambridge. (He tried living in Cambridge but found it too expensive, and took to merely staying overnight to deliver his lectures before returning to Eversley.) In spite of all this activity, he was a far from negligent parish priest – witness the grief of the villagers, the hunt servants, the farm labourers and cottagers when he died.

Edward White Benson – future archbishop – discovered when he became its headmaster that Wellington College was 'within a fairly easy walk of Eversley'. The two men saw a lot of one another, though rather different both in character and ecclesiastical politics. Kingsley sent his eldest son Maurice to Wellington, despite Benson's reputation for severity. Kingsley, it was noted by the sacerdotalist Benson, wore a suit of rough grey cloth, knickerbockers and a black tie. He seldom dressed as a clergyman. He was such an addict of tobacco that he hid clay pipes in bushes and tree roots around Eversley in case the need to smoke came upon him while visiting the houses of his parishioners. The services in the parish church startled Benson by their lack of formality. For example, when the curate preached, Kingsley sat in the rectory pew in lay clothes but rose at the end to bless the congregation. He sat behind the Jacobean screen during Matins, taking no part whatever. But then the congregation would hear the rector's sonorous voice reciting the Lord's Prayer and knew that the Communion Service had begun. They were always surprised that the stammer which caused him such nervous agitation during conversation appeared to leave him when he recited the liturgy. He was a proper Church of England man, despising what he deemed the unmanliness of the Puseyites, but insistent on, for example, the eastward position when celebrating the Communion – that is, standing facing east, symbolically facing Jerusalem, or the new Jerusalem – and recognizing that the holy table was a symbol of the altar of God; and bowing low (as Dean Swift had done in the reign of Queen Anne) at the Gloria and the name of Jesus. The devotion of this Anglican priest and his country congregation was compared to the parish of George Herbert in the seventeenth century.

The Victorian parson did not ask for great riches – Archdeacon Grantly (the worldling of *Barchester Towers*) was a rare bird. Kingsley was never a rich man, but the living of Eversley gave him independence, and this is surely reflected in the robust unpredictability of Canon Kingsley's views. He abominated slavery, for example, but he tried to persuade Thomas Hughes that 'the Northerns had exaggerated the case against the South infamously'. All the same he thought the Civil War 'a blessing for the whole world breaking up the insolent and aggressive republic of rogues, & a blessing to the poor niggers, because the South once seceded, will be amenable to the public opinion of England; & also will, from very fear, be forced to treat its niggers better'.[4] He was also a supporter of Governor Eyre against the Jamaica Committee. Perhaps the most that a twenty-first-century reader can make of this is to suggest that, regrettable as we may find it, the huge majority of our forebears had attitudes to race which would horrify us. Kingsley can be absolved of racialism. A year before the Governor Eyre episode he had entertained Queen Emma of the Sandwich Islands at Eversley. Fanny Kingsley, his wife, had wondered at 'the feeling of having a Queen civilised, and yet of savage, even cannibal ancestry sleeping under one's roof in Charlie's and my room – eating at one's table – talking of Tennyson and *Tom Brown's Schooldays*!'[5] They had also accommodated the Queen's entourage of servants, black and white, and found her black chaplain, who stayed in the Rectory, 'a delightful man'. It was in fact the socialist in Kingsley that approved of Governor Eyre's severity; the point for Kingsley was not that those massacred and hanged had been black but that they had been creating mayhem: the severe justice was to protect the security of the majority.

But in his attitudes to race, as in his attitudes to other aspects of life, Kingsley was intuitive more than drily ratiocinative. To read *The Water-Babies*, with its teasing denunciations in Chapter Two of scientific materialism, and its attacks on Professor Owen and Professor Huxley, you might think Kingsley was anti-scientific, but:

> The great fairy Science, who is likely to be queen of all the fairies for many a year to come, can only do you good, and never do you harm; and instead of fancying, with some people, that your body makes your soul, as if a steam engine could make its own coke . . . you will believe the one time . . . doctrine of this wonderful fairy-tale, which is that your soul makes your body, just as a snail makes his shell.[6]

Or again:

> Ah, . . . when will people understand that one of the deepest and wisest speeches which can come out of a human mouth is that – 'It is so beautiful that it must be true?' Not till they give up believing that Mr John Locke (good and honest though he was) was the wisest man

that ever lived on earth: and recollect that a wiser man than he lived long before him; and that his name was Plato the son of Ariston.[7]

In fact Kingsley enjoyed a friendly correspondence with Darwin. The dean of Chester once asked Kingsley how he reconciled science and Christianity. 'By believing that God is love' was the reply. And to one who objected that the explanation of the development of the Mollusca given by Darwin could not be orthodox, Kingsley answered, 'My friend, God's orthodoxy is truth; if Darwin speaks the truth, he is orthodox.'[8]

This did not prevent Kingsley, in *The Water-Babies*, developing one of his most successful satires on his selfish, hedonist, capitalistic contemporaries: the lazy Doasyoulikes who evolve backwards, moving from houses to caves, through savagery and ugliness ('when people live on poor vegetables instead of roast beef and plum-pudding, their jaws grow large, and their lips grow coarse, like the poor Paddies who eat potatoes'). Pass five hundred years and they have grown hairy and stupid and are forgetting the use of language; in subsequent generations they go back to being apes. The point of this parable, however, is not to mock Darwin, but to suggest that human individuals, and societies, can choose between 'a downhill and an uphill road'.[9] It is an almost unbelievable fact to us that children were still being sent up chimneys until the publication of *The Water-Babies* and that a year after its publication, Parliament abolished the abuse.

As with science, so with politics, Kingsley derived his view from the belief that God is love. His socialism derived from a simple sense of decency, and from his reading of Maurice's *Kingdom of Christ*, a book which Fanny Grenfell gave to Kingsley before she married him and which, by his own confession, changed his life. It was a book which deplored the narrowness of the High Church and Low Church squabbles and looked for a true Catholicism which was both truly inclusive, and which saw that an obsession with the minutiae of doctrine was meaningless: the glaring and obvious call for nineteenth-century Christians was to recognize the incarnate Christ in the suffering poor, and to make society more just, more equal and more fair.

Since the gift came from Fanny, one cannot help recognizing how closely interwoven Kingsley's religion was with his sexuality. As a young undergraduate at Cambridge, he had been a variety of pantheist, highly sexed and incapable of celibacy. His first physical encounter with a woman was probably with a prostitute at Barnwell or Castle End, and he was so bugged by guilt about it that he felt the need to confess it to Fanny. 'You, my unspotted, bring a virgin body to my arms. I alas do not to yours. Before our lips met I had sinned and fallen. Oh, how low! If it is your wish, you shall be a wife only in name. No communion but that of mind shall pass between us.'[10]

Clearly at this stage of the courtship, Kingsley was worrying about venereal disease. To punish himself for impure thoughts he fasted and prayed. On 1 November 1843, when temperatures must have been sinking towards zero, 'I went into the woods at night and lay naked upon thorns and when I came home my body was torn from head to foot. I never suffered so much. I began to understand Popish raptures and visions that night, and their connexion with self-torture. I saw such glorious things.'[11] During a long engagement when he was separated from Fanny he wrote a life of St Elizabeth of Hungary and drew lavish illustrations of this story of naked young women being tortured by monks. A Cambridge tutor who saw the drawings said that no pure man could have made them, and Kingsley admitted that 'St Elizabeth is my Fanny, not as she is but as she will be.'

Before their wedding Fanny wrote in anticipation:

After dinner I shall perhaps feel worn out, so I shall just lie on your bosom and say nothing but feel a great deal, and you will be very loving and call me your poor child. And then you will perhaps show me your *Life of St Elizabeth*, your wedding gift. And then after tea we will go up to rest! We will undress and bathe and then you will come to my room, and we will kiss and love very much and read psalms aloud together, and then we will kneel down and pray in our night dresses. Oh! what solemn bliss! How hallowing! And then you will take me up into your arms, will you not? And lay me down in bed. And then you will extinguish our light and *come to me*! How I will open my arms to you and then sink into yours . . .[12]

Twelve years after they were married, Kingsley wrote to Fanny, 'I am sitting in my mother's old dressing room where we spent four days of heaven twelve years ago. I have turned it into a study though the room is so full of the gleam of your eyes and the scent of your hair. I cannot help thinking of you and love all the while.'

Not only did it remain, for its entire duration, a marriage which was soaked in shared sexual appreciation and pleasure, but much of the language of their commonly held eroticism drew like some Gothic novel on the imagery of Catholicism. Not only was the marriage bed 'our altar . . . there you should be the victim I the priest, in the bliss of full communion!'[13] but some of the more kitsch accoutrements of 'Monk' Lewis or Horace Walpole – whips, penances – were fed into their mild consensual sadomasochistic games. 'St Elizabeth' in Kingsley's reworked *The Saint's Tragedy* is found in Act II naked in her bedroom, and wincing as her husband touches her body and finds it covered with self-inflicted welts and lash-wounds.

> Alas! What's this! These shoulders' cushioned ice,
> And thin soft flanks, with purple lashes all,
> And weeping furrows traced![14]

Kingsley was more than ordinarily aware of the connections between kinky sexuality and religious symbolism, and like many Protestants of the period the fact that he found titillation in the thought of naked nuns, copulating monks, pious doses of flagellation made him view with all the more suspicion those who wanted to put the clock back and, instead of Maurice's progressive Catholic Christianity, to revive the mummeries, perversions and superstitions (as he saw them) of medieval religion. Kingsley's erotic drawings, accompanying his poems and fantasies, only saw publication in the late twentieth century. They depict such subjects as 'the hallowed lovemaking of Charles and Fanny'. They are naked and roped to a large cross: or they show Fanny, her long hair loose, her feet bare in Magdalene-pose, kneeling before Kingsley as he says, 'I absolve thee from all thy sin in the name of the Father, the Son and the Holy Ghost!'

Far from it being a post-Freudian perception that religious emotions were in reality a substitute for sexual feeling, Victorian Protestantism took it for granted that Catholicism, whether in Roman or Puseyite manifestations, went naturally and hand in hand with sexual perversion. Protestant propaganda abounded in quasi-pornographic descriptions of what the Puseyites and Roman Catholics enjoyed doing behind their sinister grilles, or Gothic convent-gates.

'"Take that thing off," said the Mother Superior. I replied, "I cannot, Reverend Mother, it's too tight." The Nun who was present was told to help me to get it off. A deep feeling of shame came over me at being half-nude. The Mother then ordered the Nun to say the *Miserere* and while it was recited *she lashed me several times with all her strength*.'[15] Or:

'Archdeacon Allen . . . told me *he had known three clergymen* who had practised this teaching of habitual Confession as a duty, *who had fallen into habits of immorality with women who had come to them for guidance.*'[16] In addition to the belief that Catholicism, real or ersatz, Anglo or Roman, was a form of erotic inversion, there was also the widely held view that as well as wanting your daughter for immoral purposes, they also were after your money. 'In the Sisterhood of All Saints, Margaret Street, it is provided by the Statutes, that no Sister leaving the Sisterhood, even if "dismissed", shall have any right to any portion of the money or property which she has given to it whether as a dowry or otherwise.'[17] If anything could be calculated to outrage decent bourgeois opinion more than Reverend Mothers wielding the cat-o'-nine-tails, it was the thought of these 'cults' who lured young women into their clutches laying claim to their capital.

All this should be remembered as a background to Kingsley's celebrated spat with John Henry Newman. There was a temperamental gulf between them. 'In him and all that school, there is an element of foppery – even in dress and manner; a fastidious, maundering, die-away effeminacy, which is mistaken for purity and refinement; and I confess myself unable to cope with it.'[18] In the course of a review in *Macmillan's Magazine* Kingsley threw away the line – he was writing about Froude's ultra-Protestant *History of England* – 'Truth for its own sake, had never been a virtue with the Roman clergy. Father Newman informs us that it need not, and on the whole ought not to be; that cunning is the weapon which Heaven has given to the saints wherewith to withstand the brute male force of the wicked world which marries and is given in marriage. Whether his notion be doctrinally correct or not, it is at least historically so.'

If you go through the works of Newman and watch that serpentine mind wrapping itself around such questions as the credibility of medieval miracles – the flight of the Holy House from Nazareth to Loreto for example – or the legitimacy of persecuting Galileo, you see the force of Kingsley's straightforwardness. Newman, one suspects, did not really believe in the possibility of Mary and Joseph's house flying through the air; did not believe it was right to torture Galileo, nor that Galileo's arguments were wrong. Yet for some perverse reason of party-loyalty he appears to suggest that he does so believe. Unfortunately Kingsley concentrated his fire on one rather harmless sermon of Newman's – which had been preached when he was an Anglican. Ah ha! said Kingsley – so you were a crypto-papist all along, even when you pretended to be Church of England.

Newman responded with an intensely personal, not to say egomaniac, account of how his mind had moved from a boyhood evangelical conversion, through High Church Anglicanism, to embracing the Roman Catholic faith.

> It is not pleasant to reveal to high and low, young and old, what has gone on within me from my early years. It is not pleasant to be giving to every shallow or flippant disputant the advantage over me of knowing my most private thoughts, I might even say the intercourse between myself and my Maker.[19]

But this of course is what Newman does reveal and give in the *Apologia Pro Vita Sua* – The Defence of His Own Life – which was dashed off; sometimes he was writing for twenty-two hours at a stretch, often in tears.[20] Nearly all Newman's contemporaries felt he had won the argument. 'A more opportune Protestant ram for Father Newman's sacrificial knife could scarcely have been found,' said the editor of *The Spectator*. This view has been largely endorsed by the subsequent generations. Newman became, first, a cardinal, then in the eyes of history a great sage of the Church. He was beatified and is due to be canonized as a Catholic saint. As well as a mellifluous spiritual autobiography, his *Apologia* of 1864 is seen as being a turning-point in the history of English attitudes to Catholicism. It checked anti-Catholic prejudice when literary and political London were forced to admit the sincerity and attempted truthfulness of the celebrated convert.

How would a reading of the two books, *The Water-Babies* and the *Apologia*, strike the dispassionate reader of the twenty-first century? Newman's book chronicles in obsessive detail the squabbles between High Church and Low Church divines during the 1830s – the occasions when Dr Pusey published a tract on Fasting, and when Newman himself began to read the early Fathers of the Church, and why a cunning comparison between the Donatists – North African heretics of the fourth century – and the Anglicans made by Dr Wiseman in the *Dublin Review* made Newman begin to doubt the validity of his own Church. Never once in the whole book do we get a sense of the world outside Newman's college walls – or come to that, outside his own head. It is something of a shock at the end to be told 'I have never seen Oxford since, excepting its spires as they are seen by the railway.' The reader is jolted into a recognition that all these intense theological debates happened not in the time of St Augustine, but in the Railway Age. Never once does Newman's quest for a perfect orthodoxy, a pure belief in the Incarnate God, appear to prompt him to consider that if God took flesh, then this has social implications, that the Church should be engaged with the lives and plight of the poor.

The *Apologia* made many readers think more kindly of the Oxford converts to Rome. Within a year of the publication of *The Water-Babies*, Parliament had banned pushing little boys up chimneys. But Kingsley's is more than a social gospel. Newman came to believe that there were but two alternatives, the way to Rome and the way to Atheism. Not only does Kingsley's religion seem altogether more humane: he would seem to be thinking about larger issues. The journey of little Tom the sweep to his watery paradise engages mind as well as heart rather more than the crotchety Oxford don's – Newman's – journey from the Oriel Common Room to the Birmingham Oratory. Speaking of Huxley, Darwin and the others, Kingsley wrote to Maurice, 'They find that now they have got rid of an interfering God – a master-magician, as I call it – they have to choose between the absolute empire of accident, and a living, immanent, ever-working God.'[21] To another correspondent, an atheist, he wrote, 'Whatever doubt or doctrinal Atheism you and your friends may have, don't fall into moral atheism. Don't forget the Eternal Goodness, whatever you call it. *I call it God.*'[22]

20

Goblin Market and the Cause

'One of the strange things about the Victorians,' wrote Anthony Powell in his *Notebook*, 'was seeing refinement in women, whereas one of the attractions of women is their extreme coarseness.'[1] From the scrappy unannotated nature of the great novelist's *cahier* it is impossible to know whether this contention was intended to be placed in the mouth of one of the more outrageous characters in *A Dance to the Music of Time* or whether it was an opinion he held himself. In either event, one senses it might on one level have been an opinion shared by the Hon. Caroline Norton who, in the September 1863 issue of *Macmillan's Magazine*, reviewed jointly Coventry Patmore's verse novel – and hymn to married love – *The Angel in the House* and Christina Rossetti's brilliantly hectic verse fairy story *Goblin Market*. The Angel, it is perhaps unnecessary to remind intelligent readers, is not an idealized picture of woman: it is the Domestic Love which exists between men and women. 'We rejoice,' says Mrs Norton, 'that "the Angel in the House" has come to dwell in the Royal Palace' – a reference to the recent marriage of the Prince of Wales. 'Yet that part of a royal destiny, which seems to us so superlatively bright, is within the reach of any man who chooses so to school his passions and affections as to make a sane choice in life.'[2]

The words come from painful experience. The granddaughter of Richard Brinsley Sheridan, Caroline and her two sisters had taken London Society by storm in 1826. She was married at nineteen to the Hon. Richard Norton and it was an unhappy match – they were extravagant, there were many quarrels, and he beat her. After one particularly bitter row, when Caroline was taking refuge with one of her sisters, Norton took their three children and put them in the charge of one of his cousins, refusing the mother access. It was then that Caroline discovered the status of Englishwomen under the law. Not only, at that date, did any property of a married woman, whether earned or inherited, legally belong to her husband, but so did the children. Richard Norton had the power, without the decree of a court, to forbid his wife ever to see their children again. In 1836 he brought an action against Lord Melbourne – then prime minister. The jury dismissed the case without even retiring, so obvious was it that Norton was acting from pure spite – no serious evidence was produced of an adultery. But it had demonstrated that married women in England in the last year of the reign of William IV had *no rights whatever*. They were non-people, being the same legal status as American slaves, regardless of social class.

Because she was educated, and a published author, Caroline Norton was in a position to raise agitation, but not to do much on her own behalf. The bitterest thing about her experience was the separation from her children:

> What I suffered respecting those children God knows, and He only. What I endured and yet lived past – of pain, exasperation, helplessness, and despair . . . I shall not even try to explain. I believe men have no more notion of what that anguish is than the blind have of colours . . . I REALLY lost my young children – craved for them, struggled for them, was barred from them, and came too late to see one that died . . . except in his coffin.

She found a sympathetic lawyer, Mr Talford, who as MP for Reading was prepared to bring in an Infants' Custody Bill which would prevent other married women suffering comparable horrors. (And he knew *many* comparable cases.) The *British and Foreign Review* when it got wind of this called Mrs Norton a 'she devil' and a 'she beast', and openly libelled her, claiming she was having an affair with Talford. In effect it was impossible to libel a married woman, since married women could not sue. In 1839, after much difficulty, the Infants' Custody Act passed into law; by modern standards it was extraordinarily modest, allowing that a judge in equity might make an order allowing mothers against whom adultery was not proved to have the custody of their children under seven, and access to older children at stated times. Full and equal guardianship of their children was not granted to English women until the Infants' Custody Act of 1925.[3]

In 1855 Caroline Norton was forty-eight years old, and she again entered the lists when Parliament was debating the Divorce Bill. She campaigned, successfully, to get written into the Bill that if a woman was obliged to leave her husband she might resume possession of her own property, or at least of her future inheritance and earnings. She also secured – with Lord St Leonards taking up her points for her in Parliament – the crucial right for a married woman to sue and be sued, and to enter contracts in her own right. In her pamphlet, she apostrophized the reader, 'Why write? Why struggle? It is the Law! You will do no good! But if everyone lacked courage with that doubt, nothing would ever be achieved in this world. This much I will do, woman though I be. I will put on record what the law for women was in England in the years of civilisation and Christianity, 1855, and the eighteenth year of the reign of a female sovereign!'[4]

Yet the modern reader would be surprised to learn that Mrs Norton did not support 'ill-advised public attempts on the part of a few women to assert their "equality" with "men"' and she ridiculed the 'strange and laughable political meetings (sanctioned by a chairwoman) which have taken place in one or two instances'. The original of Meredith's *Diana of the Crossways*, Mrs Norton was an independent-minded girl of the Regency who had grown to maturity in very different times. By the time she reviewed *The Angel in the House* and *Goblin Market* she was fifty-six and feminism as we might understand the term had begun its history.

Returning to the nineteenth century in a time-machine, the twenty-first-century traveller would notice immediately dozens of differences between our world and theirs: the smells of horse-dung and straw in the streets, and, even in the grander houses, the sweaty smell of the servants who had no baths – just the kitchen tap, very often; the darkness at night without electricity; the gas-flares against sooty skies; the fatty food and 'smell of steaks in passageways'; the beautifully made hats, worn by all social classes, and the properly tailored clothes, even on window-cleaners or factory-hands; the continued acceptance of social hierarchy and, with the obvious perky exception, the underlying deference; the racial coherence – Dante Gabriel Rossetti, we recall, found the sight of a slave boy in London exotic – no one in today's London would find anything odd about seeing a little black boy in the street; the superiority to ours of the postal service – four or five swift deliveries per day – and the splendour – red coats and gold or blue piping – of the postman's uniform; the excellence of the rail services; the truly terrifying inadequacy of dentistry and medicine – and with these, the toothache, the halitosis; the generalized acceptance of infant mortality, the familiarity of children's coffins being trundled in glass-sided hearses down cobbled streets; the poverty of the children who survived, the ragamuffins who swept crossings and still, in spite of Lord Shaftesbury's reforms, continued to work, and run about at large, in the alarming, overcrowded cities – all these things and more would assail the eye, heart and nostril and make us know that the Victorian world was utterly different from our own. But the greatest, and the most extraordinary difference is the difference between women, then and now.

We can seek all manner of reasons for the existence in the past of 'patriarchal attitudes', for the fact that the world was male-dominated and phallocentric. The 1860s were the decade in which these things seriously began to change. One of the things which paradoxically occasioned the change was a step backwards, a further diminution of women's rights in English law. It is an episode in history which occupies about twenty years, from the 1860s to the 1880s, when there came into effect, and then were abolished, the Contagious Diseases Acts.*

Among the surgical outpatients at Bartholomew's Hospital in London, one half had venereal disease, mostly the deadly syphilis – at Guy's it was 43 per cent. At Moorfields Eye Hospital and at the Throat Hospital in Golden Square, one fifth of patients admitted were suffering from venereal or contagious diseases, VD or CD, as they were called.[5] That there was a crisis of the greatest magnitude no one could doubt. How the repeal of the CD Acts became enmeshed with the growth of feminism will belong to a later chapter. What is so revealing – and to our eye so extraordinary – is the manner in which these parliamentary acts came into being in the first instance. The Acts were an attempt to apply the continental system of regulated prostitution to British garrison towns, in order to control the spread of disease. It was taken for granted that British soldiers and sailors needed prostitutes. It now became enshrined in British law that women were a source of contamination. No attempt was made to regulate the spread of disease by, for example, penalizing the men who tried to pay for sex. The working-class women whom economic circumstances moved in this direction were, by the standards of their contemporaries, 'fallen' women. Their sin was much greater than the man's.

The CD Acts meant that any woman found by the police within a certain radius of the garrison areas could be arrested. Quite inevitably, from the first, there were dreadful mistakes made – 'innocent' mothers and daughters were rounded up together with prostitutes themselves. Any woman so arrested was deemed by the law *ipso facto* a common

*The first was passed in 1864, amendments in 1866, 1868 and 1869. The Acts were repealed in 1886.

(*Above*) The State Opening of Parliament, 1851. Charles Barry's new Houses of Parliament replaced those which burnt down in 1834. They provided a mock Gothic theatre for the beginning of modern politics. (*Right*) The brand-new throne designed by Augustus Welby Pugin for the chamber of the House of Lords provided the Age of Railways and Reform with a piece of instant history, rather in the manner that the *nouveaux-riches* elevated by capitalism could buy themselves pedigrees and titles.

Landseer's *Windsor Castle in Modern Times* presents two young lovers, Prince Albert and Queen Victoria, looking forward to the new era. The Prince was destined not to survive middle age.

The catastrophe of the British retreat from Kabul, in which all 16,000 British and Indian troops (save one) were slaughtered, gets regularly forgotten. Lady Butler's painting of the sole survivor, an army doctor, arriving in Jalalabad serves as an iconic reminder of the likely consequences of foreign intervention in Afghanistan.

Two of the most celebrated paintings by William Holman Hunt bristle with ironies, conscious and unconscious.

(*Left*) In *The Awakening Conscience* the model, Hunt's sometime mistress, looks rather less conscience-stricken than the subject-matter demands.

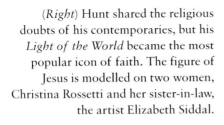

(*Right*) Hunt shared the religious doubts of his contemporaries, but his *Light of the World* became the most popular icon of faith. The figure of Jesus is modelled on two women, Christina Rossetti and her sister-in-law, the artist Elizabeth Siddal.

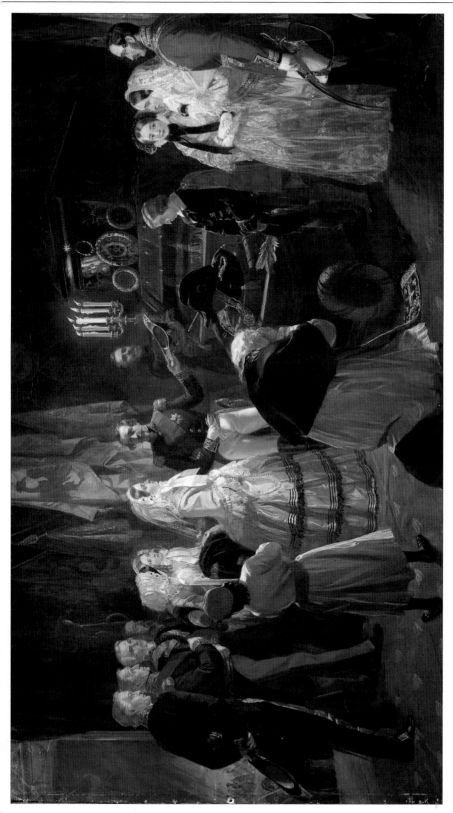

Relations between France and England were always ambivalent. Napoleon III, as he was to become, took Queen Victoria to visit the tomb of the great Emperor at Les Invalides on her visit to Paris in 1855. When, in 1870, he was exiled to England, and Paris suffered bombardment and starvation at the hands of the Prussians, the Queen was delighted. 'Surely that Sodom and Gomorrah as Papa called it deserves to be crushed,' she crowed to her daughter, the Crown Princess of Prussia.

When Ford Madox Brown saw navvies digging in Hampstead, he thought they were bringing a new water supply. In fact they were digging drains, an even more vital necessity in disease-ridden, stinking London. The result was *Work*, a symbolic painting in which Christian Socialist F.D. Maurice stands beside Thomas Carlyle (in a hat) in the foreground, prophets looking at the toilers.

Cardinal Manning's intervention in the Great Dock Strike of 1889 continued the tradition of enlightened alliance between workers and middle-class sympathizers. The splendid banner in his honour was made by the Amalgamated Society of Watermen and Lightermen, Greenwich.

The little boy in Rossetti's *The Beloved* was a slave, spotted by the artist with his American owner in the doorway of a London hotel. Rossetti felt largely untouched by the American Civil War which waged while he laboured on this carefully allegorical work.

General Gordon, evangelical Christian and military hero, came to be an emblem of the virtuous Briton, bringing enlightenment to Africa and Asia, whether they wanted it or not. His death was seen as a martyrdom, as this famous picture would suggest.

prostitute. The law of habeas corpus had been suspended. If she refused to comply, and to undergo an medical examination, she could be imprisoned indefinitely. The medical examinations were horrific and, literally, intrusive. Josephine Butler, the great opponent of the CD Acts, and the woman who would eventually succeed in her campaign to have them repealed, wrote, 'By this law, a crime has been *created* in order that it may be severely punished, but observe, that has been ruled to be a crime in women, which is not to be a crime in men.'[6]

In the context of the 1860s the CD Acts were not, by most, seen as an issue of sexual politics so much as of public health. The war on cholera in the earlier decades of the century, and Edwin Chadwick's attempts to sanitize the towns and clean up the water supplies, were all part of a great Benthamite programme of state-fuelled improvement and control of the expanding populace. As well as the CD Acts the British Parliament brought in the Sanitary Act of 1866, tightening up the 1848 Act on sanitation; and in 1867 the Vaccination Act greatly enlarged the penalties for failure to vaccinate infants and children against smallpox.[7] It is easy to see why the British Medical Association was overwhelmingly in favour of the CD Acts. The increase in social status of the doctor, from village sawbones – often the very same person as the barber – to lofty professional, exactly follows the growth of Benthamism from private fad of the Philosophic Radicals in the Regency period to the underlying ideology of the whole Victorian state machine. Doctors were essential officers of control.

At the same time, the spread of sexually transmitted diseases in an age which knew no effective cure for syphilis, with all its debilitating and deadly consequences to the second and third generation, was a cause for desperate concern. If we criticize the government of Lord John Russell in the 1840s for failing to do enough to fight hunger in Ireland, we should try, perhaps, to understand why the government of Lord Derby twenty years later felt it had a duty to control the spread of a disease which affected – obviously – not merely soldiers, sailors and the women they sought out in garrison towns, but their children; and nor was anyone blind to the fact that middle- and upper-class families were also likely to be infected.*

So monstrous was the phallocentric ideology which so unthinkingly framed the CD Acts in their particular form that the abuses caused by

---

*Though statistically less likely than the working classes. *Vide infra.*

the Acts, and the debates which led to their repeal, worked as a powerful stimulus to the Women's Movement. The fact remained, however, that a huge population, no more or less chaste than any other generation in human history, was capable, every time nature prompted one of them to sexual intimacy with another, of passing on a condition which would lead first to painful lesions, rashes and enlargement of the lymph nodes; later, in the one third of cases who were unlucky enough, to major disorders of the cardiovascular and central nervous systems – paralysis and insanity.[8]

That is why, when the feminists turned to the only woman in England practising as a doctor, Elizabeth Garrett (1836–1917), and asked her to attack the Contagious Diseases Acts, she refused. 'Degradation cannot be taken by storm and the animal side of nature will outlive crusades,' she believed. Some members of the women's movement never forgave her support for the CD Acts. She saw them as 'very limited in scope' and an 'attempt to diminish the injury to public health which arises from prostitution'. As an experienced hospital doctor, Elizabeth Garrett saw it largely as a class matter – 'Every member of the medical profession knows only too well how terrible are the sufferings of this class, and how difficult it is for them to get out of their life of vice, or even to discontinue in it for a time when in a state of urgent bodily suffering . . . Hospitals do not as a rule admit them, dispensaries cannot cure them; even soup kitchens for the sick will not help to feed them.'[9] Garrett saw no alternative for these women than that they be compelled to undergo treatment in accordance with the Acts.

Incidentally, all modern research confirms Garrett's contention that this was a problem overwhelmingly affecting the lives of the poor. Analysis of court and poor law records, hospital and penitentiary reports following the CD Acts in York shows that 73 per cent of men associating with prostitutes were working class.[10] In many working-class districts women were prepared to take the risk of catching venereal diseases since, unlike their 'respectable' sisters, they were able to afford rooms of their own, new clothes, heat, cooked food, and above all alcohol; unlike the dressmakers and laundresses working fourteen hours a day, the prostitutes tended to avoid consumption.[11] The very concept of prostitution was a vague one in such classes. When one Harriet Hicks was on trial for soliciting in 1870 the magistrate asked if she was still a prostitute. 'No, only to one man' was the reply. 'You mean that you are not a prostitute, other than as living with one man without marriage?' Hicks: 'Yes, that's what I mean.' In the poorer parts of Plymouth and Southampton where the sailors poured off the ships looking for women, the notion of middle-class respectability did not exist. A female parish visitor at St Peter's, Plymouth, found one woman with three children; they had three different fathers. She was now living with a sailor and passed for a married woman. 'She says she is not ashamed of her baby – she never professed to be a Christian, and is not so bad as many.' Another was 'married at the registry office to a man whose wife is living and argues that it is all right as the first wife is remarried, and wrote a letter to give him leave to follow her example'.

One should remember these women if one tries to form too neat a picture of middle-class men corrupting or seducing working-class women. When we read of Elizabeth Garrett, pioneer medic and keen supporter of women's suffrage, it is almost as if there are two issues at stake in the 1860s – the Subjection of Women and the Improvement of the Working Classes. It is clear from her support of the CD Acts that she did not wish them muddled.

In her introduction to the Virago paperback edition of Harriet Taylor Mill's essay on the *Enfranchisement of Women* and her husband John Stuart Mill's *The Subjection of Women* Kate Soper wrote in 1983:

> What is likely to jar most on today's readers, however, is the central argument of the essays, that sees the issue of female rights primarily in terms of the opportunity equality will allow for individually talented women to emerge to prominence and realize fulfilment. This is a theme in conflict with that strand of the contemporary women's movement, which stresses not the individual's right to compete, but the iniquity of the competition itself, and which appeals to a collective identity for women in their common struggle against patriarchy.[12]

In this context it is perhaps worth noting how our perceptions of gender politics, as with our notions of race and class, are still in a state of flux. A feminist of 2003 might write differently from Soper in 1983 about the women of the 1860s, and perhaps be less sceptical about the value of individual talent. In the case of Garrett's career as a doctor what one sees is not so much 'competition' as a struggle of titanic heroism against seemingly insuperable odds. (You could as well describe a lone round-the-world yachtswoman as 'competing' with the sea.)

The resistance put up to a woman studying medicine by the entirely male medical establishment was huge. *The Lancet*, champion of liberty for the poor, for the teaching hospitals, for scientific research against obscurantists and for the independence of coroners' courts against whitewashing politicians, had a disgraceful record in opposing Elizabeth Garrett's very presence at lectures and demonstrations. Its objections were based on the supposed 'refinement' of women which we began by noting, or quoting. There are few clearer examples of how the idea of female delicacy was invented as a way of keeping women down. *The Lancet* dismissed Elizabeth Garrett, the sensible daughter of a merchant from Aldeburgh, as an hysteric. It congratulated the students of the Middlesex Hospital for trying to get rid of her. The editorial marvelled 'that this lady is able calmly to go through the manipulations of sounding for stone in the male bladder . . . insensible to the unpleasant feelings which her presence must arouse'.[13] The article omitted to mention that the male bladder in question belonged to a child about two years old.[14] Against all the odds, and with the help of Elizabeth Blackwell, who obtained an MD in the United States and was then admitted to the British Medical Register, Elizabeth Garrett became a doctor. (She studied in London but only got a *degree* in Paris, partly through the support of the British ambassador, Lord Lyons, partly through that of Napoleon III himself.) Thereafter came the foundation of the London School of Medicine for Women by Dr Sophia Jex-Blake (in 1874), and though for many years Dr Garrett Anderson (she married George Skelton Anderson in 1871) was the only female member of the BMA, the barricades had been broken.

In some inevitable senses, though, Kate Soper was right. The nineteenth-century women's movement was largely, if not essentially, a bourgeois movement. It certainly grew out of the prosperity of the early capitalist decades. The women who changed the lives of their sisters and daughters by campaigning for equal educational rights, equal, or at any rate just, parental rights, or for political suffrage were overwhelmingly either from the rich merchant class like Dr Garrett Anderson or daughters of the parsonage, the rentier class or the minor aristocracy. Dr Garrett's friend Emily Davies was typical in being the daughter of a clergyman. Bessie Parkes was the daughter of a rich Birmingham businessman. Barbara Leigh-Smith – in marriage Mme Bodichon – was a cousin of Florence Nightingale, the daughter of the

Radical MP for Norwich. Mme Bodichon helped Emily Davies found Girton College, Cambridge, in 1873, though it was not until after the Second World War that that university permitted women to take degrees.

Just as the Broad Church appeared to demolish Christianity but actually helped it to survive;* just as the Reform Bill appeared to undermine aristocracy but actually enabled it to remain politically powerful; so the incipient women's movement grew out of rentier and bourgeois money, seemed at odds with (some) new bourgeois values, but actually preserved and underpinned the strength of the class system. These women were all asking for preferments – professional qualifications and university degrees – which were denied to all but a handful of the *male* populace. Except for the heady days of Chartism, and for certain unusual moments since – in the days of Lloyd George, for instance, or during the election immediately following the Second World War – the English working classes have not been politically engaged, any more than they aspired to be barristers or surgeons. The Women's Suffrage Movement could be seen as the final confirmation of the triumph of the *haute bourgeoisie*, not the first blast on the trumpet of revolution.

The Kensington Ladies Discussion Society met four times a year; under the chairmanship of Dr Garrett it rounded up the usual suspects – Mme Bodichon, Miss Beale, Miss Buss and Miss Helen Taylor, stepdaughter of the newly elected MP for Westminster, John Stuart Mill. In 1866 they presented to him a petition signed by 1,498 women asking for – demanding – women's suffrage. Mill believed that bringing about the first parliamentary debate on the subject was 'by far the most important public service' which he was able to perform in the Commons.[15] When one considers the size of the opposition both in Parliament and in the country at large, it is remarkable that eighty MPs voted with Mill. It was a battle which took half a century to win, but Mill's rallying-cry is still impressive:

> I know there is an obscure feeling, a feeling which is ashamed to express itself openly – as if women had no right to care about anything, except how they may be the most useful servants of some

---

*Elizabeth Garrett was typical of those who nearly abandoned religion but recovered a version of it under the influence of F.D. Maurice – see Manton, p.97.

men . . . This claim to confiscate the whole existence of one half of the species for the supposed convenience of the other appears to me, independently of its injustice, particularly silly.[16]

He ended on a dark note:

I should like to have a return laid before this House of the number of women who are actually beaten to death, kicked to death, or trampled to death by their male protectors; and in an opposite column, the amount of the sentences passed, in those cases where the dastardly criminals did not get off altogether.

As the Norton case had made clear thirty years earlier, these cases were not limited to the poorer classes.

The Position of Women question, then, would have been much in the mind of the editor of *Macmillan's Magazine* when he asked Caroline Norton to review together Patmore's *The Angel in the House* and Christina Rossetti's *Goblin Market*.

Coventry Patmore (1823–96) immortalized the joys of life's ordinariness in a manner which must have inspired both Hardy and Betjeman:

> I, while the shop-girl fitted on
> The sand-shoes, look'd where, down the bay
> The sea glow'd with a shrouded sun.
> 'I'm ready Felix; will you pay?'
> That was my first expense for this
> Sweet stranger whom I called my wife.

Not long after the poem was published, with all its warm evocations of life and love in a cathedral town, Patmore was widowed. He became Roman Catholic, which so often marginalizes and narrows an English imagination, and the immense popularity of *The Angel in the House* was not enjoyed by the in many ways much finer Odes and the erotic/mystic work *The Unknown Eros*. Poets, and critics of perception, have seen him as something like a great poet, though his impossible character lost him friends in life, and in death he was satirized by Joseph Conrad in *Chance*. The 'incandescent austerity'[17] of his later verse will only ever appeal to cognoscenti. It was not only the cosy Anglicanism of *Angel* which appealed to his contemporary readers

– it was what a hostile friend found repellent: 'the mingling of piety and concupiscence'. Yet *no* modern woman could identify with the young wife in Patmore's poem. Whether they *could* identify with either of the sisters in *Goblin Market*, it has been part of feminist criticism's task to determine. Since *Goblin Market* was published at the beginning of a time of stupendous change in the lives of women in Britain, it is not surprising that modern literary criticism should have tried to tease out gender-politics and references to overt sexuality in the poem which its author insisted was 'just a fairy story' but others perceive as 'a Victorian nursery classic, like many works, somehow considered appropriate for children . . . actually full of sinister, subterranean echoes fortunately too sophisticated for their understanding'.[18] Many critics in the late 1960–2000 period went further than this and imagined that this poem, one of the undoubted masterpieces of the mid-nineteenth century, was too sophisticated for its author to understand either.

Having refused various marriage proposals, Christina Rossetti lived much under the shadow of a pious mother and of Maria, her elder sister who was a member of the Anglican sisterhood of All Saints. Much has been made of the harsh pieties of the Anglo-Catholics of the period and of Christina's morbid feelings of guilt and depression which this religion supposedly fed. To discourage her from moping, Christina worked in the Highgate penitentiary, a House of Mercy for 'fallen women'. The volunteers – Christina was known as Sister Christina in the House – undertook the work of reclaiming the fallen. They would 'by sympathy, by cautious discipline, by affectionate watchfulness . . . teach them to hate what has been pleasant to them, and to love what they have despised, that so after a while they may go forth again into the world and be able to serve amid the ordinary temptations of life, the merciful Saviour whom they have learnt to serve and love in retirement'.[19]

Christina conceived *Goblin Market* as a moral tale to be read aloud in the penitentiary.[20] Just as Milton's *Masque at Ludlow Castle* (i.e. *Comus*) was first performed for a noble family rocked by the grossest sexual scandal – an audience which would have responded with particular eagerness to the moral: 'Love Virtue, she alone is free' – so the girls and young women in the Highgate penitentiary had probably learnt early that excess could bring wretchedness as well as ecstasy. This is the simple theme of *Goblin Market*, a theme as old as the story of the Garden of Eden.

The poem tells of two sisters, Laura and Lizzie, who are tempted by the tiny goblin merchants who haunt the woods and glens offering ripe fruit for a penny. Laura succumbs, and when she has run out of money, like a true addict she pays with anything to hand – in her case a lock of her golden hair. Then she really lets rip – 'She sucked and sucked and sucked the more/Fruits which that unknown orchard bore./She sucked until her lips were sore.' Lizzie goes to the wood to obtain an antidote for her sister's sickness. The goblins try to force her to eat their fruit but she 'laughed in heart to feel the drip/of juice that syrupped all her face'. She remains virginal, runs back to her sister, knowing she has it in her power to save – 'Did you miss me?/Come and kiss me./ Never mind my bruises,/Hug me, kiss me, suck my juices/Squeezed from goblin fruits for you.'

One does not need to bring a blush to the reader's cheek by spelling out some of the 'explanations' which critics have brought to these vivid lines. They are faced with a ludicrous dilemma. Either they have to imagine that Christina was so emotionally stupid that she did not know what she was writing. Or they have to suppose that the nun-like Christina was a pornographer. Neither is true. Christina's relationship with her nun sister Maria is reflected in this poem – as, no doubt, is her observation of the excesses which led her brother Dante Gabriel into alcoholism, and the 'fallen women' with whom she worked in Highgate into ruin. The poem is about the dangers of excess – of an unbridled appetite. To say it is 'really' about rape, incest, lesbianism is to miss the point. It is about the human tendency, which could no doubt be shown by incestuous lesbians but is actually more general, to self-destruction by means of self-indulgence. A child who had been sick after eating too much chocolate would understand *Goblin Market* better than many of the academic commentators.

The inability of some modern critics to grasp the surface meaning of *Goblin Market*, their insistence that its author could not have known the *kind of things* going on beneath that surface, is suggestive of the gulf between the women of the twentieth and of the nineteenth century respectively. (The greater proportion of the critics are women.) Christina Rossetti's most sensitive late twentieth-century biographer, Jan Marsh, wrote earlier studies of 'the Pre-Raphaelite sisterhood' and on 'the Legend of Elizabeth Siddal', which cunningly showed how much an interpretation of these Victorian women, of their lives and deaths, reveals about the historians and biographers who have tried to present them to contemporary readers.

Elizabeth and Gabriel Rossetti's marriage, never perhaps very happy, entered a dark phase with the birth of a stillborn child on 2 May 1861. When Ned and Georgie Burne-Jones called on them they found Lizzie, dosed to the eyeballs with laudanum, rocking an empty cradle.[21] From now on, other visitors noticed Gabriel wincing and shrinking when his wife spoke sharply to him. Her behaviour has been described as disruptive, ill-tempered, jealous.[22] 'She was almost certainly suffering from post-natal depression.' Some visitors, she enjoyed – Swinburne, for example, who came and read to her from Jacobean plays – Fletcher's *The Spanish Curate* was a favourite. But it was the friendship with Swinburne which precipitated the crisis. The poet met the Rossettis at the Sablonniere restaurant in Leicester Square for dinner: Lizzie was tired and Gabriel took her home at about eight, himself setting out, once she was in bed, for an evening, first at the Working Men's College where he taught – in Great Ormond Street – then for some hours unaccounted for. When he came home Rossetti found that his wife had taken a huge overdose of laudanum: she died at 7.20 in the morning on Thursday 11 February 1862. Impulsively he buried with her, in the family plot in Highgate Cemetery, the manuscript of his poems which, as the years of his widowhood passed, he came to miss.

From 1864 to 1870 Rossetti was at work on his masterpiece, one of the great morbid statements of all nineteenth-century art, the *Beata Beatrix* in which he depicted Elizabeth as the Beatrice of Dante's *Vita Nuova*. Though he began painting it in her lifetime it seems unmistakably the face of a dead woman who has outsoared the shadows of earthly existence – a quite sublime combination of the spiritual and the merely morbid. We sense in it both the sickbed smell of an unhappy woman who died of an overdose, and the ultimate hope that we are more than flesh and blood. Growing out of a deep domestic pathos, and a sordid failure to make emotional connections and sympathies, and created in the first decade when Doubt had become not merely a coterie-secret but the norm for millions of people, it gently speaks both of religion's glory and its tragic impossibility. It is in a way the ultimate icon of what was going on inside men and women during the 1860s.

Elizabeth Rossetti, destined thus to be immortalized in this painterly likeness of a resurrection body, was also destined to have her sleep disturbed in Highgate Cemetery. By the end of the decade Rossetti wanted his poems back, and in one of the most macabre scenes in the history of literature, on 5 October 1869 the coffin was opened. Lizzie was holding her Bible and Rossetti's poems. Some believe – the lawyers entrusted with the gruesome task found all 'quite perfect' in the casket – that the opium had preserved her as if in formaldehyde, and that her hair was still red-gold, but this is mere speculation, a good example of the iconic status which Elizabeth achieved in death.[23] For later generations, Elizabeth Siddal could become the ultimate female victim of male neglect or emotional violence: or else, viewed differently, she could be seen as a Sixties raver, the sort of young woman who in the Sixties of the twentieth century would have married pop stars, not painters. Later writers could take more interest in her own achievements and aspirations as a painter, which Ruskin always championed.

Modelling and drawing were, for a woman of her socio-economic background, a means of escape. If, for the less economically advantaged feminists of the Beale, Buss, Bodichon school of thought, the Cause – college, education, professional life – was an escape from the fate of being a governess, then for the Elizabeth Siddals art was the means of not being a domestic servant or a seamstress. The higher feminists wanted to save their sisters from becoming Jane Eyre: practically speaking, far more had to choose between becoming Dickens's Marchioness or the Doll's Dressmaker.

A concentration on the exotic life and death of Elizabeth Siddal should not make us forget those who did not end up either as painters or paintings. The largest occupational group among nineteenth-century women in England was, overwhelmingly, the servant class. In 1851 there were 751,540 domestic servants in the census; forty years later the number had swollen to 1,386,167.[24] In London one person in every fifteen was in service. It was a simple matter of supply and demand. As the rentier class grew more prosperous, more and more servants were required, and figures lower and lower in the social scale not merely employed servants but considered any menial activity – such as putting coal on their own fires – as demeaning. If this seems to a modern mind like exploitation, one has to remember from the other point of view the comparative restfulness of the servant life. The master was expected to provide food, housing and a modest cash wage; and for those working in larger households, there was the camaraderie of the servants' hall. Many found such a life in every way preferable to the long hours and daily grind of factory work. Only in the 1930s in England did the number of domestic servants sink below one million.[25]

For a record of the lives of working-class women in the middle of the nineteenth century, we go to the diaries of one of Rossetti's confrères at the Working Men's College, a minor poet and civil servant, who came along one or two evenings per week to conduct a Latin class. Arthur J. Munby's (1828–1910) not very good poems occasionally appeared in *Macmillan's Magazine* alongside those of Christina Rossetti and Matthew Arnold. A graduate of Trinity, Cambridge, the son of a York solicitor, Munby had a dullish job as an ecclesiastical civil servant, having failed to make a career at the Bar. It is, however, not for his verses, but for his remarkable diaries that Munby will be remembered. He was obsessed by working-class women. 'Blessed is the land whose peasant women measure four feet round the waist, and have arms as thick as a bed post! Those who prate of women's rights, if they knew their own meaning, would honour such mighty daughters of the plough as much at least or more than the "strong-minded females" who have neither the shrinking graces of their own sex nor the bold beauty of ours.'[26]

These are typical Munbyisms, but while this might have been true in his physical predilections for the female crane-driver type, it does not really reflect his socio-political stance. He was in love with a servant girl called Hannah Culluick, a native of Shropshire, who first met Munby when the family with whom she was in service brought her to London for the season. She was twenty-one, he was twenty-six. He accosted her in the street as he did dozens, hundreds, of young women and learnt her story. He saw 'a robust hardworking peasant lass, with the marks of labour and servitude upon her everywhere'. She saw 'such a nice manly face with a moustache'.[27] Eighteen years later, they were secretly married. Their courtship had been chaste, as were his encounters with the colliers, milkmaids, waitresses, prostitutes, fisherwomen etc. etc. whose lives he recorded and whom he so obsessively photographed or had photographed. Clearly, there was a strong sexual attraction which led Munby on, but one suspects that had he only been interested in a string of Simenonesque *conquests* his diaries would make less compelling reading.

The immediate and continuing impression they leave upon the reader of the twenty-first century is the prodigious gulf created by the class structure. At times it is literally a gulf, as when Munby:

met my Juno [i.e. Hannah] at the Haymarket Theatre, to see Tom Taylor's ingenious & spirited piece, the 'overland Route'. We went to the gallery of course; Hannah has never been to any other part of a theatre, except once, when 'William the groom' took her with an order to the boxes – actually the *boxes*! at Astley's. Poor child! She did not presume to recognize me in the street, but waited alone in the crowd.

When Munby looked over the rail of the gallery

down upon my equals in the stalls and boxes, I am sensible of a feeling of placid half-contemptuous indifference: but how if they were to look up and see me thus? Should I feel ashamed, worthy of *their* contempt? I think not: yet, if not, would it not be only because I know that she is worthy to be one of them? And so we get back to class distinctions: I love her, then, because she is *not* like her own class after all, but like mine!

It is a fascinating entry because it shows that for all his empathy for the large, red-handed women whose lives he chronicled in his diary, he does not really question the Victorian class system. He meets the Prince of Wales at dinner in Trinity: the archbishop of Canterbury comes into his office – 'a mild patriarchal old man' – it was Sumner. He dines with the Rossettis, Ruskin, Swinburne. He frequents gentlemen's clubs and Inns of Court. All the while he is recording conversations with female acrobats, parlour-maids or – during a holiday in Scarborough – the 'bait girls' who lowered themselves down the cliff face on a strong rope to gather winkles and mussels in baskets. 'Noo then, coom on, we're gahin!' He liked sketching, as well as making verbal descriptions – Mary Harrison, 20, a waggon-filler at Pewfall pits near Wigan; or Jane Matthews, also 20, 'mending her stocking, seated on a heap of ironstone' at the Dowlais Works, Merthyr Tydfil. A typical Munby diary entry was for 26 October 1865, the funeral of Lord Palmerston – 'a most *poor* & mean business':

I saw no one of either sex who was at all noteworthy, except one, & that was a servant maid belonging to the Guards' club. A kitchen wench she was; the word "kitchen" or "kitchenmaid" was stamped on a corner of her coarse apron. With two common-place fellow-servants, she had come up from the cellars, & stood within the railings, holding on thereby, in her humble dress of lilac cotton frock and coarse clean apron, while some of her moustachio'd masters lounged on the steps above. A robust country looking lass of good height, pleasant to behold in such a spot . . . Thus she stood, gravely gazing, while sumptuous ladies, silked & furred, looked down from balconies all around.

Some modern readers will find Munby's attitude to the 'specimens' collected vaguely disconcerting or downright offensive. There is something more than condescending, and bordering on the sexually deviant, about his preoccupations. His wife called him 'Massa' in imitation of a black slave. Yet without his obsession, posterity would be the poorer. Thanks to Munby, dozens of human lives that would otherwise have passed unrecorded into oblivion have been preserved to us. We can see their beauty and their struggle. They remind us, even more than the early feminist heroines such as Miss Davies, Miss Bodichon or Dr Garrett Anderson, of the huge spiritual and imaginative divergence between our own times and the Victorians.

21

Wonderland

The changes which had come upon the world – and upon industrialized Britain in particular – during the first quarter-century of Queen Victoria's reign were without historical parallel. The population explosion; the revolutions, industrial, social and political; the changes of world-view; the collapses and revivals of belief-systems were all prodigious. Historians can still play the game of cause and effect and ask which of these disruptive events was the origin, which the consequence of the other. 'The more we consider these mid-Victorians,' wrote Munby's biographer Derek Hudson, 'the more we realise how many, including some of the most sensitively intelligent, were forced by the pressures of a materialist age to live out a world of fantasy in their daily lives.'[1]

The age which had begun to fear that materialism was the only truth built railway stations in the manner of Gothic cathedrals. The Pre-Raphaelites were not alone in choosing for theme, not the changing industrial townscapes and ever-varying modern fashions in clothes and houses, but historical tableaux. David Wilkie Winfield, who changed his name to Wynfield, was a characteristic creature of his age.[2] Having trained at 'Dagger' Leigh's (the model for Barker in Thackeray's *The Newcomes*) studio in Newman Street, he painted such subjects as Oliver Cromwell in the night before his death and – his most acclaimed work – *The Death of Buckingham*, which depicted the murdered body of Charles I's favourite. Wynfield and his friends constituted the 'St John's Wood Clique', self-consciously Bohemian young men whom he photographed in a variety of fancy dress – Elizabethan ruffs, skullcaps redolent of Colet and Erasmus, breastplates and turbans. Wynfield's photographic portrait of Frederic Leighton, whose own early canvases included *Dante in Exile*, shows a figure who is every inch a young man of the 1860s with his slightly wispy moustache and bushy beard, but whose costume – medieval? ancient Roman? – suggests the child's dressing-up box. The 'Clique' were of course going out of their way to stand apart from their bourgeois origins; but as is so often the case, rebels seem as much characteristic of their age as conformists – in some ways more so, the retreat into fantasy being an urgent, even a central compulsion of the mid-Victorians, their literature, architecture, religion or lack of it. (F.D. Maurice had objected to the Tractarians: 'Their error . . . consists in opposing . . . the spirit of a former age, instead of the ever-living and acting Spirit of God.'[3] It makes a reasonable commentary on many of his contemporaries, not just those High Church or Roman clergymen who wished themselves back in the age of Saint Augustine of Hippo.)

It was typical of them to use the modern invention of photography for the furtherance of fantasy. Just as Newman did not want to be a clergyman of the nineteenth, as much as of the fourth century, so Wynfield could use the means of collodion (a gummy solution of gun-cotton) spread over glass plates to immortalize his friends as if they were figures in Ainsworth's *Tower of London* or Bulwer-Lytton's *The Caxtons*. Meanwhile, Julia Margaret Cameron had persuaded her much older husband to go and live at Freshwater on the Isle of Wight to be near the poet laureate. Her villa, Dimbola, became a centre of photographic activity, social voraciousness, affection, noise. William Allingham – poet of 'Up the airy mountain, Down the rushy glen . . .', diarist and friend of the Tennyson circle – recorded:

> Down train comes in with Mrs Cameron, queenly in carriage by herself, surrounded by photographs. We go to Lymington together, she talking all the time. 'I want to do a large photograph of Tennyson and *he objects*! Says I make bags under his eyes – and Carlyle refuses to give me a sitting, he says it is a kind of *inferno*. The *greatest* men of the age (with strong emphasis) Sir John Herschel, Henry Taylor, Watts say I have immortalized them, and these other men object!! What is one to do, h'm.'[4]

Mrs Cameron's lens, eye, imagination, transformed the great men of the age, and anyone else she could persuade to sit for her – parlour-maids, children, friends and relations – into creatures of fantasy. Her Benthamite old husband with his long white beard became King Lear. The American artist/model Marie Spartali, who sat for Burne-Jones and Rossetti, becomes Mnemosyne the Goddess of Memory and mother of the Nine Muses.[5] Lady Elcho posed beside a tree as a spectre in Dante . . . Tennyson was perhaps never better depicted than in the Cameron portrait known as The Dirty Monk. And who is this – looking half away from the camera in 1872, a full-bosomed twenty-year-old woman, her hair loose against the shrubbery? Cameron entitled the picture *Alethea*, truth, and the model was Alice Liddell.

Very different she seems in one of the most celebrated of all nineteenth-century child-images, 'Beggar Child', as photographed by the Rev. Charles Dodgson, leaning against a rough stone wall in the Deanery Wall at Christ Church, Oxford, and lifting her ragged slip to reveal a slender knee and a hint of thigh. Dodgson must have taken dozens of pictures of Alice and her sisters Lorina and Edith. The dons' wives seemed content to allow this stammering clergyman to photograph their daughters completely nude, though only when they were very young. More than one friendship came to a sudden end when he asked to photograph a girl of eleven or older.[6]

No one knows why Dodgson so abruptly ceased to be friends with Alice's parents. When Liddell arrived at Christ Church as dean, in 1856, Dodgson (1832–98) was already installed as the young mathematics lecturer and sub-librarian. (He was ordained deacon, aged twenty-nine, in 1861, but never became a priest.) Alice was his most devoted little 'child friend' during her ninth and tenth years, and it was during a picnic in July 1862, when she was ten, that the first version of *Alice's Adventures Underground* were told to her as an oral narrative. The written version was finished the following year, with Dodgson's own illustrations. The next year – 1863 – Tenniel agreed to illustrate the much-expanded *Alice's Adventures in Wonderland*. By the time *Through the Looking-Glass* was published (1872) Alice had grown into the wistful young figure photographed by Mrs Cameron.

It was no less a figure than Lord Salisbury, no fanciful observer, who wrote to a friend six years later, 'They say that Dodgson has half gone out of his mind in consequence of having been refused by the real Alice. It looks like it.'[7] If true, then the rift with the Liddells, occurring in 1863, would have been caused by the thirty-one-year-old Dodgson proposing to Alice when she was eleven. This probably seems more shocking to a twenty-first-century sensibility than it might have done to the Victorians. Edward White Benson, future archbishop, proposed to Mary Sidgwick when she was twelve and he twenty-four – though they waited six years before marrying. The 1861 census shows that in Bolton 175 women married at fifteen or under, 179 in Burnley.[8]

Alice Liddell, however, was evidently capable of exciting affection from older admirers. Dodgson's photographs, which might produce queasiness in the eyes of some, conform to that most horrible cliché of paedophile fantasy – the little child who 'wants it' is leading on the voyeur. (Voyeurism, we may be sure, is all that was at work with

Dodgson, and he was probably so much in denial about the erotic nature of his photographic pursuits that he believed the asexual nature of the naked poses he set up for his child models made them 'innocent'.)

After 1870, she befriended the Slade professor of art, John Ruskin, who in *Praeterita* recalls sneaking an evening with her and her sisters when Dean and Mrs Liddell were supposed to be dining at Blenheim Palace with the Duke of Marlborough.[9]

> Well, I think Edith had got the tea made, and Alice was just bringing the muffins to perfection . . . when there was a sudden sense of some stars having been blown out by the wind, round the corner; and then a crushing of the snow outside the house, and a drifting of it inside; and the children all scampered out to see what was wrong, and I followed slowly; and there were the Dean and Mrs Liddell standing just in the middle of the hall, and the footmen in consternation, and a silence, – and –
>
> 'How sorry you must be to see us, Mr Ruskin!' began at last Mrs Liddell.
>
> 'I was never more so,' I replied.

Snow had made the expedition to Blenheim impossible – 'and I went back to Corpus, disconsolate'.

Alice would have been seventeen or eighteen when described here as a scampering child; but Ruskin could most cheerfully relate to females when he regarded them as presexual infants. His own hopeless and painful love affair – one has to use this word, though it was of course entirely Platonic, and indeed largely something taking place inside his head – was with Rose la Touche. They met when she was 'nine years old . . . rising towards ten; neither tall nor short for her age; a little stiff in her way of standing. The eyes rather deep blue at that time, and fuller and softer than afterwards. Lips perfectly lovely in profile; a little too wide, and hard in edge, seen in front; the rest of the features what a fair, well-bred Irish girl's usually are; the hair perhaps, more graceful in short curl round the forehead, and softer than one sees often, in the close-bound tresses above the neck . . .'[10] Ruskin was nearly forty when he fell under Rose's spell, forty-seven when he proposed. The mother and father were appalled – not least when Ruskin's former wife wrote to Mrs la Touche revealing the secrets of her own marriage to the sage. Poor Rose, anorexic religious maniac, half wanted to marry Ruskin. 'Do you think,' she wrote in 1872, when in her early twenties and about to die, 'that the Professor would really, really care to have me and be happy with me – just as I am?'[11] We can all guess the truthful answer to what would have happened had Rose recovered, and had Ruskin and she attempted a 'normal' married relationship. In later life when he had gone mad, Ruskin was something of a 'liability' with the little girls at the local school, near his Coniston home. Long before this, however, in letters to his cousin Joan Agnew (whose destiny, with her husband Arthur Severn, it was to nurse Ruskin in his insane old age) he had employed extraordinary baby-talk – e.g. of Scotland, he wrote to her (he aged forty-eight, she newly married to Arthur), 'There was once a bonnie wee country marnie dear – ey called it Totland – I pose because it was so nice for wee tots to play at pushing in wee bookies . . . When I was the weest of tots – it oosed to be so pitty, mamie.'[12] And so on.

Ruskin did not limit himself to baby-language in private correspondence. The 1860s, which saw him emerge as a self-appointed social prophet with *Unto this Last* – a tract on the meaning of labour which enjoyed quasi-scriptural status in the old British Labour Party, pre 1980s – also saw him developing his talents as an educator of females. He taught at a girls' school in Winnington, Cheshire, and the lectures he gave there were chiefly on crystals and geology.

No one could call *The Ethics of the Dust* a dry textbook. Its subtitle is *Ten Lectures to Little Housewives on the Elements of Crystallization*. There is much brilliance in these lectures, particularly when he expounds the fact that diamonds and coal are chemically all but identical, and moralizes about the capitalist greed for both. But the whimsy is absolutely overwhelming.

Lecturer: (*perceiving various arrangements being made of footstool, cushion, screen, and the like*). Yes, yes, it's all very fine! and I am to sit here to be asked questions till supper-time, am I?

DORA: I don't think you can have any supper tonight: we've got so much to ask.

LILY: Oh Miss Dora! We can fetch it him here, you know, so nicely!

Lecturer: Yes, Lily that will be pleasant . . . Really, now that I know what teasing things girls are, I don't so much wonder that people used to put up patiently with the dragons who took *them* for supper . . .

Ruskin and Dodgson came to know one another, through the Christ Church connection. Dodgson took a fine photograph of Ruskin but, we are told, 'Ruskin never appreciated the odd, puckish personality of Dodgson.'[13] Perhaps there was not much personality to appreciate? The author of the *Alice* books has been the subject of innumerable biographical studies, quack psychiatric examinations, and bogus in-depth analyses. He has been shewn to be crypto-homosexual, crypto-atheist, crypto-more or less anything. The evidence for these speculations is usually sought – and being sought, conveniently discovered – not in his letters or diaries but in the pages of a whimsical story about Alice. Since the first publication of *Alice's Adventures in Wonderland* Lewis Carroll (as Dodgson styled himself) has been much the most celebrated 'children's author' in the English language. The stories have never been out of print, and they have been translated into almost as many languages as the Bible.

The secondary literature on Carroll and the *Alice* books – vast, and mostly more nonsensical than the stories themselves – tells us much about the commentators from generation to generation. Some try to enter into the Carroll whimsy. Others offer joke 'explanations' of the tales – such as Sir Shane Leslie's brilliant spoof, purporting to have made the discovery that Carroll was writing about the religious controversies of the day: the Cheshire Cat is Cardinal Wiseman, the Blue Caterpillar Benjamin Jowett, the battle between the Red and White Knights the controversy between Thomas Huxley and Samuel Wilberforce. Others have taken such jokes seriously and attempted different interpretations – political, philosophical, psychoanalytical and so on. Or there have been the attempts to link the events in the book to actual events in the course of its composition. The royal visit to Christ Church – Queen Victoria coming to visit the Prince of Wales when he was an undergraduate – has as much absurdity as anything in the pages of Carroll's fantasy: 'I had never seen her so near before,' noted Dodgson, 'nor on her feet, and was shocked to find how short, not to say dumpy and (with all loyalty be it spoken) how *plain* she is.'[14]

Likewise, commentators have found real-life, or rather real dead, hatters, who died as Victorian hatters tended to, of mercury poisoning – symptoms of which included rushing manically about stuffing bits of bread and butter in their mouths. Others, not all medics, have joined sides and tried to prove that Alice's Hatter does not demonstrate the symptoms of mercury poisoning.

When Carroll first showed the story to George MacDonald,

however, we can safely assume that none of these qualities were what arrested the greater writer's attention. MacDonald will have seen that Carroll was in some ways borrowing the techniques of his own *Phantastes* of 1858. MacDonald was a master myth-maker, intuitively aware of the way that fantasy works precisely by not having specific allegorical or symbolical equivalence. Just as the 'originals' of the story were all 'recognized', so one can see, particularly in their published form with the Tenniel illustrations, that the tales bristle with contemporary allusion. The Reverend Robinson Duckworth, who was present at the picnic in July 1862, afterwards 'saw' himself as the Duck, the Lory as Lorina, the Eaglet as Edith Liddell and the Dodo as poor stammering Do-do-dodgson. But it would be mad to read the *Alice* books as autobiography, any more than the clear resemblance between Disraeli and the gentleman sitting opposite Alice in the train in Chapter 3 of *Looking-Glass* has any satirical significance. The liberating thing about reading *Alice* – both *Wonderland* and *Looking-Glass* – is that they are *games*: they are what Wittgenstein called language-games, playfully and brilliantly exposing the fact that signifiers such as words and numbers will not bear the weight or fixity which systems of language, theology, metaphysics or logic often wish to place on them. To this extent, they represent an intellectual holiday for the author, a teacher of mathematical logic who as a devout churchman did think that theology was important, and voted against giving a proper salary to Professor Jowett because of his supposed heresy.

What many of the serious commentators miss about the Alice stories is their surface-obviousness. They do not work – if they do work for us, rather than embarrassing us by their archness – on a secret level but on a superficial level. The failure of language-games to do their work, the very simple failure of human beings of the same language-group to understand what one is saying to another, this is the essence of the Carroll comedy, found in the relentless puns, double-takes and double entendres of the dialogues. There is also the additional 'comedy' of children being kept out of the grown-up world by language-games. This is perhaps the least attractive feature of the books as far as real children are concerned.

Carroll's painstaking New York biographer, Professor Morton Cohen, quotes with approval a seventeen-year-old student of his, who wrote:

Lewis Carroll gives equal time to the child's point of view. He makes fun of the adult world and understands all the hurt feelings that most children suffer while they are caught in the condition of growing up but are still small.[15]

To which the reader must respond – Well, yes and no. Carroll *understands* children being baffled and upset by grown-ups, but we can seek in vain in either of the *Alice* books for the kind of soppy empathy with children discovered there by this college student of 1995. Carroll's is a merciless eye, as cold as the collodion spread on the glass plates of his camera. Innocent of full paedophilia in the physical sense, he has the paedophile's habit of viewing children as objects: the suffering and bewilderment of Alice is preserved in the stories as funny – just as funny as the antics of the grown-up creatures, and just as unreasonable. The Reverend Charles Dodgson jokes about the little girls' failures in comprehension in the same callous way in which Mr Murdstone and his friends joke about 'Brookes of Sheffield', laughing all the more merrily when David Copperfield, unaware that he himself is being guyed, tries to join in the joke. To compare Carroll with Dickens is to recognize the essentially callous quality of the mathematics don's humour. Far from empathizing with little children everywhere, as his various saccharine postscripts* to the books suggest (as the tales went into their endless bestselling reprintings), the evidence of his letters, diaries and photographs suggests that he did not really have sympathy for children at all – still less the obsession with his own boyhood without which it would be difficult for the biographers to enflesh the essentially dull life of this shy, dry old stick of a man.

*e.g. 'To all my little friends, known and unknown, I wish with all my heart, "A Merry Christmas": . . . May God bless you, dear children, and make each Christmas-tide, as it comes round to you, more bright and beautiful than the last – bright with the presence of that unseen Friend, who once on earth blessed little children,' etc. etc.

22

Some Deaths

Our decision to use children's literature as a prism through which to view the Sixties of the nineteenth century has helped, perhaps, to focus the decade as one which was indeed an 'age of equipoise'. That the mid-Victorian era knew a special flowering of literature for children is itself, as we have seen, a fact of sociological reverberations and significances.[1] So, too, is the fact that books such as *Uncle Tom's Cabin* (1852), which were not meant for children in the first instance, could so easily and so soon have found a place on the shelf beside *The Children of the New Forest* (1847), *Tom Brown's Schooldays* (1857), *Eric, or, Little by Little* (1858), *Goblin Market* (1862) or *Alice's Adventures in Wonderland* (1865). This was also the period when Hans Christian Andersen's tales were first translated into English (1846 onwards) and began their prodigious world popularity. All these books differently reflect the ways in which the world was changing, and some reflect how it was not.

While the gerontocracy lasted, England resembled one of those arrested families where, the ancient parents still living, the grown-ups, even in middle age, continued to see themselves as 'the children'. Hence, perhaps, in large measure, the truth of Disraeli's view that the era was like a fairy-tale, and hence too the fittingness of so many of its great writers being the authors of books for children.

But in the 1860s the older generation at last began to die off. Palmerston died on 18 October 1865. 'Gladstone will soon have it all his own way,' he had said to Shaftesbury, 'whenever he gets my place, and then we shall have strange doings.' But he was succeeded as the Liberal prime minister, not by Gladstone, aged fifty-six, but by Russell, aged seventy-three. Russell (Earl Russell since 1861) was determined to deal with the matter of electoral reform. The author of the first Reform Act in 1832 was prime minister in 1865: no more potent symbol could be found of the gerontocratic nature of early to mid-Victorian England. The first Reform Act had done little enough to enfranchise the middle classes. Now, the bourgeoisie, both *haute* and *petite*, was huge. And five out of six adult males in the population were voteless.[2] How far this mattered, and how far the population as a whole really minded about the vote per se, may be an open question. At the time, the extension of the franchise was the great object of political debate. 'It was the flag and shibboleth of the new nation against the old.'[3]

At this historical distance, it seems extraordinary, if an electoral process was accepted at all, that the franchise should not be extended to all, regardless of income or gender; but this is not how it appeared to those in the thick of the debate, either inside or outside Parliament. The order of events was dramatic and exciting. In 1866, Russell's Liberal government brought in a very moderate Bill to extend the franchise to householders of a certain level of wealth. There was a right-wing revolt within the Liberal ranks at the notion of such a concession to Radicalism, and the Bill was defeated. Russell resigned, to be defeated in the general election by Lord Derby. The (minority) Conservative government then surprised everyone by bringing in a more far-reaching Reform Bill. The diehards in Derby's Cabinet – General Peel, the Earl of Carnarvon and Viscount Cranbourne (the future prime minister, as the 3rd Marquess of Salisbury) – resigned in protest. This in itself helped the purposes of Derby and his political genius of a leader in the Commons – Disraeli. What Disraeli and Derby were able to do, by an *apparently* more radical extension of the franchise, was to have a much greater say over the distribution of constituencies and, without open gerrymandering, to make it likely in the future that they would have a good chance of forming majorities in the House of Commons. This is what was going to happen – Conservatism, of a sort, was the dominant political creed of the second half of Victoria's reign. 'Disraeli was educating his party, and preparing it for the inevitable future.'[4]

Derby, his leader and prime minister, had seen that the Liberal Bill of 1866 – the one they defeated – was 'the extinction of the Conservative Party and of the real Whigs'. As a man who had actually been a member of the Whig government which brought in the 1832 Act, Derby knew whereof he spoke. What we are able to see more clearly was how remarkably successful the Conservatives were in preserving some element of aristocratic government down to, and even after the First World War. There was at least an alliance between the landed classes and the new bourgeoisie, and that large portion of the population, the working-class Tories. How much Disraeli foresaw all this, how much he was even its architect, there will always be room to debate. Though, in the short term, the Second Reform Act did not do the Tories any good – the Liberals won the election of 1868, bringing in Gladstone as prime minister for the first time – there is no question that without it the Conservative Party would have been annihilated. Gladstone would eventually have come in, come what may, and 'strange doings' would have been the ineluctable consequence.

Yet to diehards, the extension of the franchise by some 938,000 voters was all a disaster. Carlyle put it more trenchantly and gloomily than anyone in his pamphlet *Shooting Niagara: and After*, in which he imagined civilization plummeting over the rapids. 'That England would have to take the Niagara leap of completed Democracy one day' was now regarded as an inevitability. 'Swarmery', he called it, the swarming together, not even of mobs, but of Constitutionally Reformed Majorities. The notion that things could be changed or reformed by the holding of elections, by making speeches on the hustings, by the return to Parliament of Honourable Members for this borough and that, was palpably absurd to the author of *Heroes and Hero-Worship*:

> Inexpressibly delirious seems to me, at present in my solitude, the puddle of Parliament and Public upon what it calls 'the Reform Measure'; that is to say, the calling in of new supplies of blockheadism, gullibility, bribeability, amenability to beer and balderdash, by way of amending the woes we have had from our previous supplies of that bad article. The intellect of man who believes in the possibility of 'improvement' by such a method is to me a finished-off and shut-up intellect, with which I would not argue.

Carlyle wrote, as he said, in solitude. His wife was dead. She had died in April 1866, when Carlyle was making one of his periodical visits to his 'ain folk' in Scotland. Mrs Carlyle, who had received numbers of visitors at Cheyne Row in his absence, had continued her London life which, as so often, featured the exercise of a little dog. Nero, the dog who had shared some of the more intensely depressing of the Carlyles' years together in Chelsea, was long since dead and buried in the garden. She took his successor to exercise in Hyde Park, holding it in her arms in the back of a brougham until they reached Victoria Gate. There she had released the dog, and it had had its paw run over accidentally by another carriage. She leapt out of her own carriage to rescue it, and took the dog back into the brougham, sinking on to the seat. The coachman trotted on round the park, twice round the drive, down to Stanhope Gate, along the Serpentine and up again.

Receiving no directions from his passenger in the back, he had turned round. Something was amiss. He stopped the carriage and asked a gentleman to look into the back. The gentleman told the cabby to take the lady at once to St George's Hospital – now an hotel – opposite the Duke of Wellington's Apsley House, at the south-east corner of the park. They opened the door of the brougham when they reached the hospital, and found Jane Welsh Carlyle sitting upright on the back seat with the dog on her lap: she was dead.[5]

Carlyle's anguish for the death of his wife, his guilt for the things done and undone during their long shared pilgrimage together, deepened the misery of that already miserable man. He often walked to the spot where she must have died, and reverently removed his hat – 'in rain or sunshine' – the gesture implying a form of penance, comparable to Samuel Johnson standing hatless and wigless in the rain at Uttoxeter market where he had been unfilial towards his father (who had a stall there).[6] Froude was criticized for making public so many of the details of the Carlyles' marriage; and twentieth-century authors have been further able to piece together the non-evidence and evidence of such friends as Jane's lifelong confidante Geraldine Jewsbury, who was with her on the day she died, and who allegedly had been told that the marriage was unconsummated. Sometimes it is not the secrets of a marriage but its obvious surface life which tell the truest story. The Carlyles had a miserable time quite visibly, often at odds, often snarling and snapping at one another in the presence of friends. Equally, in the presence of friends, they were intellectual soulmates and enjoyed a similar acerbic sense of humour; and many friendships there were.

They had been the centre of 'literary London' in the 1840s. Small wonder that Carlyle in his seventies found the new age little to his taste; the 'Niagara' rapids of 'Swarmism' nothing short of ridiculous. 'The Aristocracy, as a class, has as yet no thought of giving up the game,' he wrote, 'or ceasing to be what in the Language of flattery is called the "Governing Class"; nor should it until it has seen farther.' That was his view. Some readers in the twenty-first century would find it bizarre, as a positive suggestion for the way the future might shape itself. What is easier to agree with in Carlyle's pamphlet is his negative assessment of the English. 'We are a people drowned in Hypocrisy; saturated with it to the bone – alas, it is even so, in spite of far other intentions at one time, and of a languid, dumb, ineradicable inward protest against it still . . . Certain it is, there is nothing but vulgarity in our People's expectations, resolutions or desires in this Epoch. It is all a peaceable mouldering or tumbling down from mere rottenness and decay . . .'[7]

Carlyle's is a voice which we can hardly understand now. The great novelists of the early to mid-nineteenth century, Dickens and Thackeray, remain freshly alive. They were destined to die before the old Chelsea curmudgeon, much younger as they were.

Thackeray's death at the very end of 1863 – he was aged fifty-two – brought an end to a career which in many respects never began. His finest achievements – *Vanity Fair*, *Henry Esmond*, the first half of *Pendennis* – are better than anything in Dickens, but it would be paradoxical to consider him, on the whole, the greater writer. He was worn out by journalism, by syphilis, by the need to maintain himself as a gentleman, his beloved daughters as ladies, in difficult domestic circumstances – his wife having for many years been humanely confined as a lunatic. His imagination was not at home in the Age of Equipoise – his best work all depicts the time of the Regency, or even the eighteenth century. Curiously enough, he seems closest to his own age in the pantomime-burlesque written for children, *The Rose and the Ring* (1855): his old trick of puncturing snobberies and class-obsessions was never more deftly employed than in chronicling the fortunes of Rosalba, first seen as an urchin in the Park, to be condescended to by the odiously bourgeois Princess Angelica, but soon revealed as a princess. The physical unimpressiveness and general dinginess of the British royal family is never actually alluded to, but you feel it constantly hinted at in Thackeray's satire. Children still find it funny, but it remains one of those many mid-Victorian children's books which are ultimately written for the amusement of the adults who had to read them aloud.

Dickens, by contrast, wrote as a child, he understood as a child, he thought as a child: and when he became a man he never put away childish things. It is often suggested that Dickens was restrained by the conventions of his age from writing openly about sex, but this is to beg many questions. You could equally point out that he did not write as Balzac or Zola would have done about money: and there was no Victorian taboo about the open discussion of shillings and pence. He writes about the world as a highly intelligent, profoundly imaginative child would write about it. Balzac would be able to take us through every stage of Mr Dorrit's ruin, and when the rescue takes place, we should feel that we had had an interview with the Dorrit auditor, the Dorrit family solicitor and the Dorrit banker. But as Dickens tells the story it is a fairy-tale, a romance. Dorrit is in the Marshalsea, unable to clear his debts, and it is the world of the Marshalsea which matters to us more than the exact financial troubles which took him there. We see him through the eyes of Little Dorrit, who was born in the debtor's prison. Then – hey presto! – Pancks the rent collector exposes the wickedness of Mr Casby, and the lost inheritance of Mr Dorrit is found with the arbitrariness of a story in the Brothers Grimm.

The events and concerns which a grown-up might consider important – sexual feeling and finance, and politics – do not interest Dickens. Or they interest him only as they have an effect on the lives of children. That is why *Great Expectations* and *David Copperfield*, which tell the story of childhood with raw and unforgettable realism, are the finest things he ever wrote. Not to see the merits of Dickens is more than a literary myopia: such an absence of sensibility would suggest a failure to see something about life itself. That is why Dickens occupies a place of all but unique importance in the minds of the English. One of his acutest readers, G.K. Chesterton, was also able to see that in his cast of characters there was something archetypical, if not actually symbolic. 'The first and last word upon the English democracy is said in Joe Gargery and Trabb's boy. The actual English populace, as distinct from the French populace or the Scotch or the Irish populace, may be said to lie between those two types. The first is the poor man who does not assert himself at all, and the second is the poor man who asserts himself entirely with the weapon of sarcasm.'[8]

There is deep truth here. Marx did not see the truth it contained, which is why he waited in vain for an English revolution. The English rich have never understood the sarcasm of Trabb's boy and they have taken the silence of Joe Gargery for deference. The middle-class liberals, with their sanitation acts, education acts, board schools and churches, throughout the nineteenth century and beyond, wanted not merely to improve conditions for the poor but to improve the poor. From the beginning of his early *Sketches by Boz*, through his tales of workhouses, vagrants and petty criminals, Dickens always knew that this was a misguided, not to say odious, ambition. If all Dickens characters possess some of the qualities of pantomime, he allows to all an equal dignity. There was something apt in his dying – that he who had excoriated the early Benthamites and mocked the improving workhouses, and the parish-pump bossiness of early nineteenth-century liberalism, should have died as its second phase – of sanitation and an extended franchise – began.

He was fifty-eight when he died, at Gad's Hill in June 1870, worn out by overwork, and by the insanely energetic public readings from the novels with which he had entranced theatre audiences on both sides of the Atlantic.

The funeral was in Westminster Abbey, the national Valhalla. It could have been nowhere else. Dean Stanley read the funeral service from the book of Common Prayer. There was no singing, though the organist played the Dead March from *Saul*. When reporters arrived at half-past nine to inquire when the ceremonies were to begin, they were informed that they were over: but the dean left the grave open all day – on the edge of Poets' Corner. All day – Waterloo Day, 1870 – a crowd flowed past and looked down at the coffin. 'No other Englishman,' said Walter Bagehot, 'had attained such a hold on the vast populace.' They still trudged into the Abbey as the hour of midnight approached. The truth of Bagehot's words – the importance of Dickens – tells us as much about the English as it does about the novelist himself.

If you had to seize on one way in which Britain had changed during the 1860s, you could do worse than focus on the theme of public executions. 1868 saw the last of these ghoulish spectacles in England. Was this liberal progress? Or was it part of the mid-Victorian bourgeoisification of life, an indication of prudery, not compassion? What is so interesting is that liberals, who had been in favour of the abolition of capital punishment altogether in the 1840s, had, by and large, changed their minds in the Age of Equipoise. They had decided that for a heinous crime such as murder, execution was permissible so long as it did not happen in public. 'In the end it was squeamishness, not humanity, that won the day.'[9]

Dickens and Thackeray had both been keen abolitionists in the early years of Victoria's reign. They had both, by chance, been present at a celebrated hanging back in 1840. Courvoisier was a French valet who murdered his aristocratic master Lord William Russell, uncle of Lord John, who as home secretary had presided over the abolition of the old penal code (which had allowed hangings of petty criminals). Thackeray had attended in a light-hearted spirit: he was a twenty-nine-year-old journalist hoping to make a good piece of copy out of the experience. He had been horrified. He watched unblinking until the body dropped. 'His arms were tied in front of him. He opened his hands in a helpless kind of way, and clasped them once or twice together. He turned his head here and there, and looked about him for an instant with a wild, imploring look. His mouth was contracted into a sort of pitiful smile.'[10]

Thackeray 'came down Snow Hill that morning with a disgust for murder and it was for the murder I saw done . . . I feel myself ashamed and degraded at the brutal curiosity which took me to that brutal sight; . . . I pray to Almighty God to cause this disgraceful sin to pass from among us, and to cleanse our land of blood . . .'*

Charles Dickens shared his brother-novelist's distaste for public hangings and campaigned against them, writing impassioned articles in the *Daily News* and letters to *The Times*.[11] At the Courvoisier execution he noted the 'odious' levity of the crowds. There was 'no emotion suitable to the occasion. No sorrow, no salutary terror, no abhorrence, no seriousness; nothing but ribaldry, debauchery, levity, drunkenness and flaunting vice in fifty other shapes.' When he attended the execution outside Horsemonger Lane Gaol of the Mannings, a husband and wife jointly hanged for murder, Dickens wrote that 'the mirth was not hysterical; the shoutings and fightings were not the efforts of a strained excitement seeking to vent itself in any relief. The whole was unmistakably callous and bad.'[12] Yet while deploring the behaviour of the mob – and the crowds were huge: over 20,000 came to see the Mannings hang – Dickens found it hard to keep away from these murderous pieces of street theatre, these festivals of violence. The night before the Mannings were hanged he arranged a supper party at the Piazza Coffee House, Covent Garden, at 11 p.m. and he spent the night wandering the streets among the drunks, the rowdies and the whores. He had hired an apartment overlooking the gallows: 'We have taken the whole of the roof (and the back kitchen) for the extremely moderate sum of ten guineas or two guineas each.'[13] When Mrs Manning finally dropped, he noted her 'fine shape, so elaborately corseted and artfully dressed, that it was quite unchanged in its trim appearance, as it slowly swung from side to side'.

Yet in the twenty years which intervened between the death of Mrs Manning and the last public hanging, Dickens had, like John Stuart Mill, abandoned his wish 'to advocate the total abolition of the Punishment of Death as a general principle, for the advantage of Society, for the prevention of crime'.[14]

In 1868, Mill in the Commons opined that 'when it was shown by clear evidence that a person was guilty of murder with atrocity, it

---

*The death mask of Courvoisier was an 'attraction' at Madame Tussaud's waxworks until the twentieth century.

appeared to him that to deprive that criminal of the life which he had forfeited was the most merciful and most proper course to adopt'.[15] Of the commission set up to pronounce on the question, only four were in favour of total abolition. The rest wanted the abolition of public executions.

When Mill spoke of the merciful nature of hanging, he presumably meant that he would rather be hanged than do penal servitude in a Victorian jail. Part of what he meant, though, must have been that to kill murderers, to get them *out of the way*, was neater, tidier, more efficient. It was the old Benthamite in him speaking. He would have shared the later Dickens's contempt for the mob enjoying themselves, and supported the removal of the obscene contraption of the gallows behind the prison walls. It was, as the best modern historian of the gallows, V.A.C. Gatrell, has said, an act of 'social sanitization'. It was more 'civilized', hardly more humane, to hang men and women in secret. The middle- and upper-class legislators had not made the law kinder. They had merely demonstrated their contempt for the mob who loved the drama, the obscenity and the sheer cruelty of public hangings. In 1868 the rough world of *The Beggar's Opera*, of eighteenth-century gallows humour, of folk festival entwined in law-enforcement, came certainly to an end.

It is an eloquent fact that the last man to be hanged publicly in England was an Irishman. Gladstone's mission, when he finally took over leadership of the Liberal Party, and became prime minister in December 1868, was to 'pacify Ireland'. The Fenian movement – the notion that Ireland could become independent of British rule by violent means – was focused after the close of the American Civil War when many Irish soldiers in the Federal army, supplied with American money, decided to imitate the Polish, or Italian nationalists and stage outrages – first in Canada, then in Britain. As many as 1,200 Fenians assembled at Chester in February 1867.

Gladstone, anxious to demonstrate that he had outgrown his wrong-headedness at the time of the Maynooth Grant (1845), brought in a Bill to disestablish the Irish Church. Meanwhile, Fenians had been arrested on a number of charges. A policeman in Manchester had been killed. An attempt was made to rescue two Fenian prisoners in Clerkenwell jail, less than a mile from St Paul's Cathedral, the Bank of England and the Guildhall. A barrel of gunpowder was placed against the outer wall of the prison and blown up. Twelve persons were killed, 120 others injured. Gladstone pressed on urgently with the Irish Land Act (1870), demonstrating a lesson which was eagerly learnt by the Fenian movement: that the English move slowly over Irish affairs when the Irish are at peace, but develop an astonishing capacity to expedite pro-Irish legislation when a few bombs have been exploded, particularly if they have been let off in London.

The English, for their part, could use the opportunity of the Clerkenwell bombing to demonstrate another sorry pattern of behaviour which, in the course of Anglo-Irish relations, would be repeated for a hundred years: namely the belief that draconian punishment of the bombers and gunmen would cow or silence Ireland rather than dignifying the murderous activities of buccaneers and turning them into political martyrs. Michael Barrett, who had been arrested shortly after the Clerkenwell bombing, demonstrated another fact by the manner of his death: that the Irish 'issue' has always been one between the Irish people and, not the English people, but the English governing class who, with their large houses and estates in Ireland, had an interest in the matter which was largely absent in the middle and lower classes in England. Whereas an old-fashioned murderer could attract 30,000 Londoners to stay up all night drinking, the Irish bomber did not draw more than 2,000. Compared with the huge numbers who came to see the executions of the more entertaining murderers, there were few women in the crowd – and almost no middle-aged or old women. The boozy old boilers, the Mrs Gamps and Betsy Prigs whom Dickens love-hated, stayed away, the young and bonnetless girls being clearly Irish, as were a good portion of the crowd.[16]

The street preacher who had started to rant at 6 a.m. would, in the case of a regular murderer, have been heckled with blasphemous cat-calls. This man was heard in reverent silence – another indication that here was a largely religious, Irish crowd. At half-past seven a bell began to toll for the passing soul and the convict was pinioned in his cell. When he was led out to face the crowd, they were quite unlike the mob described by Dickens and Thackeray. Everything was still, silent. Barrett was calm while Calcraft, the hangman, strapped his legs together. He held the hand of the prison chaplain, the Rev. Dr Hussey, and quietly joined in the prayers being said for his soul. 'The wretched man did not struggle much. His body slowly swung round once or twice, and then all was over.' After the silence, the crowd dispersed into the traffic on Ludgate Hill. London resumed its life.

On the same page, the *Annual Register* recalls a successful Derby

Day for 1868, good weather, and some excitement for the punters. The favourite, Lady Elizabeth (7 to 4 against), came nowhere – she was flagging by the mile post, and the race was won by a horse called Blue Gown.[17]

PART IV

The Eighteen-Seventies

23

Gladstone's First Premiership

In 1870–1, Europe was involved in wars and ideological conflicts of a cataclysmic dimension. Two pairs of immense irreconcilables clashed together: on the one hand, France and Germany; on the other, Catholicism and the new secularism – in particular, atheistic communism. As things played out, these two archetypical, monstrous struggles for power – ideological and territorial – were interwoven with the last vainglorious political posturings of Napoleon III. For he had guaranteed the safety of the pope and the temporal power of the Papacy with French troops which had to be withdrawn when he declared war on Prussia in the summer of 1870. In the space of one year, the ideological map of Europe was changed, and it was to be locked in a geopolitical rivalry, and a war of ideas, unresolved – if ever – until the late twentieth century.

1870–1 was in the truest sense a European catastrophe. The sheer slaughter was something without parallel – first in the war in which the well-disciplined Prussians inflicted such total defeat on the French at Metz, then in the Paris Commune. (During the Bloody Week of 21–28 May 1871, 25,000 French died at the hands of their own compatriots.) The ominous drama of it all makes almost intolerable reading, since we know what will happen forty, fifty, seventy years later. The victory of Prussia led directly to the creation of a united Germany. The treaty of Versailles of 1871 absorbed the kingdoms of Bavaria and Württemberg, and the grand-duchy of Baden, the grand-duchy of Hesse and many of the other German states were now incorporated in the Reich, centred on Berlin and recognizing the king of Prussia as their emperor. The king of Prussia – Wilhelm – was proclaimed the Kaiser. Bismarck his chancellor was triumphant. In the Hall of Mirrors, at the Palace of Versailles, the proclamation was made before the devastated government of France – a humiliation which would be revenged in 1919, repeated in 1940 . . .

Britain was at best tangentially involved with these conflicts which were to leave everything so changed: Germany united at last under Prussia; the Italians at last a nation, in occupation of the pope's temporal domains; the pope gamely fighting back with weapons of the

Spirit by the declaration of his own infallibility; the Commune in Paris attempting the complete obliteration of the cathedral of Notre Dame – together with the Hôtel de Ville, the Palais de Justice, the Tuileries and a large part of the rue de Rivoli – only themselves to be massacred by the thousand in May; those who survived death being, in prodigious numbers, exiled or condemned to penal servitude.

By what some would call an irony, Georges Seurat's huge canvas *Bathers at Asnières* – 201 × 300 cm – now hangs in the National Gallery in London, far from the Seine-side scene it depicts. Parisian workers loll beside the river enjoying their recreation. In the background a calm factory adds a few puffs of smoke to the grey-blue smudge of sky. Such a scene of peace – painted in 1884 – could be taken for granted if these were Londoners on the banks of the Thames. Few of the English who look at this picture hung in their national collection will realize that the workers are sitting on the site of a battlefield where French blood has been spilt – first by invading German troops, and then in turn by the soldiers of the Versailles government which had abandoned the capital to the hands of the Communards. The peacefulness of Seurat's scene is worked for – the tranquil semi-naked Parisians are cast in one equal light. There is something both dogged and precarious about this peace.[1]

A lens which is focused on Britain at this watershed of European history, the opening of the 1870s, depicts then a scene which is out of kilter with the rest of Europe, almost comically so. After his release from imprisonment in the palace of Wilhelmshöhe above Cassel, Napoleon III went into exile in England, living with Empress Eugénie at Chislehurst, Kent, for the last two painful years of his life. (She survived until 1920.) He merely crossed the English Channel, but in some ways he could have been crossing to a different universe.[2] He had left behind the bloodshed, passion and wretchedness depicted in Emile Zola's 1892 novel *La Débâcle* (which must be the best war novel ever written, set in 1870–1) and entered *Middlemarch* (published in 1872 the year *after* Marx's *The Civil War in France* but holding up a mirror to a world whose continental equivalent had been pounded, mortared, out of existence, but which would survive in England for another forty years). So it was that, while the Fathers of the First Vatican Council were declaring the pope to be infallible, the fellows of Balliol were at last electing Benjamin Jowett as master; while in Paris they formed a Commune, in London they played the first Football Association Cup; and while the Communards were being butchered at the 'Federates'

Wall' – as it came to be known – in the Père Lachaise cemetery, the English Parliament was setting up the Local Government Board.

'What a base, pot-bellied blockhead this our heroic nation has become; sunk in its own dirty fat and offal, and of a stupidity defying the very gods' was how Carlyle saw matters.[3]

As he had laboured through long years on the life of the great German Enlightenment monarch – years poor Mrs Carlyle had dubbed 'the valley of the shadow of Frederick' – Carlyle had prophesied the eventual dominance of Europe by Germany. Froude describes the outcome of the Franco-Prussian war as 'an exhibition of Divine judgement which was after Carlyle's own heart'. Carlyle shared with the majority of the British an anti-French prejudice – not dissipated in his case by the fact that Napoleon III (as Prince Louis Napoleon) had once visited the sage of Cheyne Row. (A mean, perjured adventurer, Carlyle had thought him; Napoleon had got into his carriage asking if 'that man was mad'.)[4] Most English followers of events on the continent felt pity for France in its desolation, and above all for Paris, the hunger and despair of the siege, the internecine destructiveness of what followed. London alone sent £80,000 worth of provisions to the starving,[5] but here her kindly-minded subjects were not at one with the Queen, who was cock-a-hoop at the Prussian victory. 'How dreadful the state of Paris is! Surely that Sodom and Gomorrah as Papa called it deserves to be crushed,'[6] she wrote to her daughter the Crown Princess of Prussia. 'The joy of our army,' Vicky gushed back to her mother, 'around Paris is not to be described.'[7] (But Queen Victoria changed her mind after the Prussian annexation of Alsace-Lorraine.)

Salisbury, who was far from being philoteutonic, was fluent in French and kept a house in France, did not rejoice in the Prussian victory, but spoke for Conservatives everywhere when he wrote (to G.W. Sandford, 24 September 1870), 'whatever else Bismarck does I do hope he will burn down the Faubourg St Antoine and crush out the Paris mob. Their freaks and madnesses have been a curse to Europe for the last eighty years.'[8]

Carlyle, in a long and measured letter to *The Times*, bemoaned 'this cheap pity and newspaper lamentation over fallen and afflicted France'.[9] He reminded readers that 'a hundred years ago there was in England the liveliest desire, and at one time an actual effort and hope, to recover Alsace and Lorraine from the French'.[10] He concluded, 'That noble, patient, deep, pious and solid Germany should be at length welded into a Nation, and become Queen of the Continent, instead of vapouring, vainglorious, gesticulating, quarrelsome, restless and over-sensitive France, seems to me the hopefulest public fact that has occurred in my time.'[11]

The British government retained a neutral stance. Vicky was displeased by her mother's speech from the throne on 9 February 1871 which referred to the belligerents, in a war as yet unresolved, as 'two great and brave nations'. She must have known that the Queen's Speech at the State Opening of Parliament was simply an expression of the politics of her government; that, though the sovereign read out the words, they had been scripted by the prime minister – in this case Gladstone.

As had happened before in Gladstone's career, there was a tortuous moral and intellectual complexity in his attitude to the Franco-Prussian war, to the annexation of Alsace-Lorraine in particular, to Europe generally. He told the Queen 'in a very excited manner' that there would 'never be a cordial understanding with Germany if she took that million and a quarter people against their will'. But his sovereign, and his Cabinet, were against Gladstone, favouring the neutral stance adopted in the Queen's Speech. That wasn't the end of the matter, however. Although in public Gladstone was a neutral, he let off steam by writing, anonymously, in *The Edinburgh Review* an article entitled 'Germany, France and England' in which he deplored Bismarck's action, and denounced 'Bismarckism, militarism, and retrograde political morality'. The *Daily News* seized on the obvious identity of the author and 'leaked' it. It was a moment comparable to the Newcastle speech at the beginning of the American Civil War when Gladstone, as it were, accidentally blabbed out his sympathy with the Confederacy. Consummate politician that he was, he knew how to use such supposed gaffes to play to the gallery, to signal to his supporters that he would like to take particular views, populist or otherwise, were he not restrained by party, or Cabinet, colleagues. He was 'the People's William'.

Setbacks – such as Disraeli trouncing him and introducing a more radical, and fairer, second Reform Bill than his own – could be represented by Gladstone to his huge and adoring audiences as triumphs of his own. 'God knows I have not courted them,' he recorded in his diary after a deliberately rabble-rousing tour of Lancashire.[12] His consummate political skills and his long run of political luck could, in his own mind, be very easily explained – 'The Almighty Seems to Sustain me.'[13] A.J.P. Taylor, in *The Struggle for Mastery in Europe*, maintained that Bismarck encouraged the idea of himself as a Machiavel, and revelled in the idea that he had tricked Napoleon III into declaring war on Prussia over the trivial question of the candidature for the Spanish throne. The more people read the confusion of events as a subtle spider's web of Bismarck's invention, the stronger Bismarck's hand. Gladstone, in his prime, had some of these qualities, not of overt humbug, but of quite instinctual political genius, knowing when to surf with, when to swim against, each rolling wave.

Little as he liked what Bismarck had achieved, a part of Gladstone envied it. He must in fact have been quite pleased when his Cabinet colleagues reminded him of how humiliated Palmerston had been when attempting to guarantee the independence of Danish Schleswig-Holstein when Britain had neither the diplomatic backing nor the military expertise to resist a well-organized Prussian army. Even over so complex and for Gladstone emotionally charged an issue as religious freedom, he had to confess an admiration for the intolerant *Kulturkampf*. Gladstone's own attitude to Catholicism, as a High Churchman many of whose closest friends had converted to Rome, was to say the least ambivalent. Yet when he watched Bismarck enact legislation against *political* Catholicism – prohibiting the Jesuit order in Prussia, banning church weddings and absorbing Church schools into state control, Gladstone could not but be impressed: 'Bismarck's ideas & methods are not ours,' he wrote to Odo Russell at Berlin; it was one of those ominous phrases awaiting a 'but', and it comes syntactically late in the sentence, as if the People's William and champion of liberty, the (new) friend of the Irish, and the demagogue from largely Catholic Liverpool cannot quite believe what he is thinking, let alone not daring to say. 'Bismarck's ideas & methods are not our own . . . I cannot but say that the present doctrines of the Roman Church *destroy the title of her obedient members to the enjoyment of civil rights*' (my italics). Gladstone 'would have to say this publicly, for I want no more storms; but it may become necessary'.[14]

As the 1870s unfolded, Gladstone's preoccupation with Christian Europe as a morally cohesive union was to develop alongside, paradoxically, the distrust of that Roman Catholicism which historically had been the guardian of all the things he held dear: Latin language and culture, theology, the spiritual ideals of the author. Next to Homer, he most idolized Dante. Like the trecento visionary, Gladstone looked for a Catholicism in which the temporal vanities and political ambitions of the Papacy had been crushed; he longed instead for a true Catholicism – i.e. universal Christianity – which would unite the people of Europe against the Muslim culture of the Ottoman Empire and the atheist encroachments of scientific materialism. These thoughts lay behind all Gladstone's realpolitik, and nothing could be more different from his general view of the world than Disraeli's definitive speech after the Prussian seizure of Schleswig-Holstein and its victory at Königgrätz:

> It is not that England has taken refuge in a state of apathy, that she now almost systematically declines to interfere in the affairs of the Continent of Europe. England is as ready and willing to interfere as in the old days, when the necessity of her position requires it. There is no Power, indeed, that interferes more than England. She interferes in Asia, because she is really more an Asiatic Power than a European. She interferes in Australia, in Africa, and New Zealand.[15]

England, and the world, are still living with these polarities: on the one hand England, a European nation, culturally at one with Europe, is politically detached from it; on the other, while a portion of Britain will always by commerce or politics feel involvement with Europe as a primary interest, others will draw on the historic trading traditions of a seafaring race and look to a greater world. The great contrast between modern Britons and those of the 1870s – speaking now of the intellectual and social elite – is in their sense of German cousinhood.

Gladstone was perhaps not in the normally understood sense of the term an intellectual, though no one who has surveyed his enormous library at Hawarden, or struggled to read his prolix and eccentric book on Homer, could question that he was a bookish man, one to whom the life of the mind was supremely important. Yet he had the Tractarian narrowness; not ignorance – he was widely read in German, Italian, French – but adopted, deliberate narrowness.

How different the fortunes of the Church of England might have been if Newman had known German. Mark Pattison in his *Memoirs* recalls his own struggle with the language, which he did not reckon to have mastered until 1858.[16] In the 1820s, there were said to be only two men who knew German. As a High Church bigot who followed the banner of Dr Pusey, Gladstone would have seen the German biblical critics as undermining the Christian faith itself. (For one of those two with perfect German was, of course, Pusey himself, who had been to

Germany in his youth, studied at Göttingen and Berlin, heard Johann Gottfried Eichhorn lecture on Balaam's ass and decided, having been half seduced by the German critics, that their alarming discoveries must be suppressed, ignored, persecuted, silenced.)[17] George Eliot satirizes, with a sad gentle satire, this Oxford generation when she makes the dry-as-dust scholar Mr Casaubon, destined to marry Dorothea Brooke, the heroine of *Middlemarch*, write a worthless and unfinishable compendium *A Key to all the Mythologies* – worthless because he had not read . . . the Germans.

George Eliot, as the young Marian Evans, had translated into English those very works of German scholarship of which Dr Pusey was (rightly) so afraid: David Friedrich Strauss's *Leben Jesu* and Ludwig Andreas Feuerbach's *Wesen des Christenthums* (her version was called *The Essence of Christianity*, 1854). Both were attempts to interpret Christianity in the light of Hegel's philosophy. Hegel, toweringly the most important philosopher of the nineteenth century – one states this as an objective fact in the History of Ideas, quite regardless of whether one agrees with or accepts any part of Hegel's thought – was all but unread in England during his lifetime (1770–1831). Those who had read the German metaphysicians – Kant, Hegel, Fichte – included Samuel Taylor Coleridge, Carlyle, and in Edinburgh Sir William Hamilton. They disseminated some of their ideas, but it was really in the mid-century onwards that their true importance became known to literate English men and women. George Eliot was of central importance in this development. Her life-companion George Lewes was also influential, as the author of the first biography of Goethe, published in 1855. Many devout Germans disliked Lewes's book, because of its candour about Goethe's promiscuity, but there could be no doubt about its impact in England, particularly in a world which was only semi-capable of reading German. For here was a figure – a scientific prodigy, a great poet, a dramatist, and a herald of modern views of religion and politics – who in his range and depth and size and confidence was quite unimaginable on the English scene. Here was a true Universal Genius, and no one reading Lewes's book could suppose that it was an accident that he was a German, any more than it was an accident that Beethoven, Mendelssohn (much more highly regarded by the Victorians than by us), Fichte, Schiller, Kant or Hegel were Germans. No English reader of Lewes's *Goethe* when it first appeared could fail to meditate, too, on the contrast between Prince Albert – accomplished musician and linguist, good art historian, amateur architect, politically aware, liberal in religion and politics, intelligently abreast of contemporary scientific discovery – and his wife and her frankly ludicrous uncles.

A discovery of German philosophy, literature and culture was, for the mid-Victorian generation, the eye-opener into a larger world. It was in 1844 that Benjamin Jowett and Arthur Stanley set out for a walking holiday in Germany and met Erdmann, Hegel's chief disciple. Thereafter, not only was German philosophy to be the chief source of inspiration for British logicians, metaphysicians and political thinkers for half a century and more; but the whole German educational method – from universal state primary schools to the treatment of science as an essential academic discipline – was to be the envy and inspiration of British schools and universities. One of the chief things to impress George Lewes about Germany – and not merely about Prussia – was the advanced state of scientific education. At Munich in 1854, he had worked in the laboratories where 'extensive apparatus and no end of frogs' were put at his disposal. Those very few professional scientists in England would envy the salaries paid to German scientists. (The Hunterian professor of anatomy at the Royal College of Surgeons, Richard Owen, used to say he could not live on his salary.) 'When the government establishes a physiological Institute professors (and amateurs) can work in clover,' Lewes predicted.[18]

As the nineteenth century drew to its close, the British love of all things German would widen from the intellectual to the middle classes. But it would go hand in hand with a growing awareness that there was now a power in Europe which was actually preparing to outstrip Britain not only in military power but also in economic prosperity. The aged Carlyle with his last gasp could point to the fact that England had fought a war against Napoleon with Prussia as its ally, and consistently feared and hated France: he could also point out – which a railway journey across the European land-mass could make clear to anyone – that the German states, and the German-speaking peoples of the Austrian Empire with whom they were in a perpetually uneasy relation, made up the huge proportion of the European peoples. Not since the Thirty Years War in the seventeenth century had the peoples of Europe learned to live at peace with one another. If they were ever able to do so it would probably be on the basis of some German federalism, of the kind favoured by Prince Albert, and which appears to be the basis of the modern European Union.

What can't be denied in terms of population and land-mass is the inevitability of some kind of German 'domination' of Europe. The only thing which held this in check was that very French nationalism and expansionism which the British most dreaded. Once, under Bismarck and the new Kaiser, 'noble, patient, deep, pious and solid Germany should at length be welded into a nation' the foundations of the Reich had been laid. The figures for the next forty years or so show the dramatic increase in German power vis-à-vis Britain. In 1871, Britain had a population of 32,000,000, Germany 41,000,000. These lived respectively in territories of 120,000 and 208,000 square miles. Their respective armies numbered 197,000 and 407,000. By 1914 the British army numbered 247,000, and the German a staggering 790,000. The British navy had 60,000 men in 1872, 146,000 in 1914: the German navy had expanded from a mere 6,500 men to 73,000. Prussian military expansion was being paid for by vast investment in the infrastructure, and by prodigious industrial growth, comparable to Britain's expansion in the first half of the century. In 1850 there were 10,000 miles of British railway and 6,000 miles of German. By 1910 there would be 38,000 miles of British railway and 61,000 miles of German. In 1880 Britain produced 980,000 tons of steel, to Germany's 1,550,000 tons. By 1913 this had increased to 6,900,000 tons in Britain and 18,600,000 tons in Germany. As European 'players' Britain, for decades easily the most modern, the most technologically efficient and the most industrially productive, now had a major rival against whom competition, in purely European terms, was impossible.

The area where Britain bore up, and continued to dominate, was in exports and world trade: though Britain's *share* of world trade fell from 38 to 27 per cent between 1870 and 1913, Germany's rose only by 5 per cent.

		Britain	Germany
Exports	1870	235,000,000	114,000,000
	1913	525,000,000	496,000,000[19]

Britain's colossal wealth, and her world influence, would increase in the last half of Victoria's reign, but this increase would be dependent on her empire. Hence, for the purposes of a full picture, one must always remember that 'the Victorians' were not merely the British, but the Indians, the Egyptians, the Sudanese, the Zulus, and many other peoples of the globe caught up for commercial and political reasons into the drama, their destinies and futures irrevocably changed. To this extent, Disraeli's semi-serious definition of Britain as an Asiatic, not a European power is true. But the spectre of a mighty Conservative empire in Europe, ruthless enough not merely to annex Danish provinces but if necessary to starve the people of Paris and reduce their monuments to rubble, had a wonderful power to concentrate Liberal English minds.

Alan and Rex Hargreaves, the sons of Alice Hargreaves, née Liddell, both died in the First World War. Alan crossed the Channel in the Expeditionary Force as a captain in September 1914, was twice wounded and died a year later. Rex, a captain in the Irish Guards, was killed in the attack on Lesboeufs on 25 September 1916. Alice herself lived until 1934.[20]

The world of the 1870s is in touch with our world, in a way that earlier decades of Victoria's reign is not. We can reach it. Many of my generation (born 1950) have met very old people born in the 1870s. The reforms, the changes, the plans, the modernizations all seem with hindsight to be preparations for the tragedy of 1914–18, which would obliterate the Victorian universe. The Free Traders of Cobden and Bright's generation had believed that the abolition of the Corn Laws, the replacement of hierarchy by commerce, aristocracy by bureaucracy, would herald a universal peace. War, they believed, was a noblemen's sport, and those who watched the bungling of the aristocratic officers in the Crimea might have been inclined to agree with them.

In the event, however, increased population and increased international commerce went hand in hand with increased armaments in all the prosperous countries. Inevitably, the expertise which had been devoted to ingenious machinery in factories was turned to the development of weapons. If the human race could mass-produce it could also mass-destroy. The Russian shells at Sinope had annihilated the Turkish fleet, and the British warships, little changed since the days of Nelson – wooden ships with masts and sails – had suffered badly from the bombardment by Russian guns at Sebastopol. Inevitably, new technology would be required in the event of another war. The French pioneered *La Gloire* in 1859, a wooden ship protected above the water-line with a corselet of iron behind which the guns were mounted. The British, not to be outdone, produced *The Warrior* in 1860, the first all-metal battleship with an iron hull, and a belt of iron armour thick enough to resist shells.

During the next thirty years, iron replaced wood as the material for ships' hulls.[21] Armour was incorporated; breech-loading, rifled ordnance firing explosive or armour-piercing shells replaced smooth-bore, muzzle-loading cannon. Gun turrets replaced broadside guns, and locomotive torpedoes, hydraulic machinery and electricity all eventually made their appearance on warships. These developments were the inevitable consequence of industrial expansion at home and colonial-cum-commercial expansion abroad. To be the world's biggest trading nation, Britain needed to have the most powerful navy. Nothing could have been more false than Bright and Cobden's belief that more trade meant more peace.

The fact that Britain did not fight a European war between the time of the Crimea and August 1914 should not abet the assumption that this era of plenty was achieved peacefully. The Empire and its spoils were preserved, and won, at the end of guns. There was scarcely a year, from the 1860s onward, when some British troops, somewhere in the world, were not fighting. This book is not exclusively, or even primarily, a history of warfare. It is worth recalling, though, that even when the narrative does not mention a war – minor or not so minor – acts of belligerence are taking place. From 1863 to 1872 there was the Third Maori War. In 1870 Canada saw the Red River expedition; in 1871–2 there was the Looshai expedition in Bengal; in 1873–4 the Second Ashanti War in West Africa; in 1874 the Duffla expedition. In 1875–6 there was the Perak campaign in Malaya, and race riots in Barbados. In 1877–8 there was the Jowakhi campaign and the Ninth Kaffir War. Indian troops were sent to Malta in 1878 in readiness for a showdown with Russia over the apparently insoluble Eastern Question. In 1879 came the Zulu War, coinciding with the Second Afghan War. In 1880, Britain fought its first war with the Boers. That is just one decade – and one could make a similar list for the 1880s and 1890s which would include major conflicts in the Sudan, Burma, Matabeleland and China, culminating in the Boer War and the Boxer Rebellions as the century drew to its close. But just as the British – who saw numberless troubles in their colonies or would-be colonies in 1848 – could claim they survived the Year of Revolutions without incident, so the free-trading Manchester Liberals could imagine that their imperial revenues came to them unstained with blood; or at least, to put it a little less melodramatically, without a strong navy and an adequate army on land to defend, where necessary, British interests.

Throughout the latter part of the nineteenth century, Britain was basically a sea-power, and the navy took priority over manpower. In terms, though, of political trouble for Gladstone's government, the army was more to the forefront of attention. While it came unstuck over the question of expenditure on the army and the navy – 'the critical factor in the decision to dissolve Parliament' in 1874 – much parliamentary time in the earlier sessions – which Gladstone and his Liberal backbenchers would like to have devoted to Ireland, to educational matters, to reform of the tax system – was taken up with army organisation.[22]

Gladstone's administration of 1868–74 is seen by us as his first. It is abundantly evident from his diaries, however, that he thought of it as his one and only chance of leading a government. He had come in with a landslide victory, with a majority of over 100, many of them Northern Nonconformist Liberals. It is only hindsight which enables us to see this as the first Liberal government – to be followed in 1874 by a Conservative government. The two-party system as understood by modern political historians was being born. Contemporaries would have seen Gladstone's Cabinet as a coalition of old Peelites such as himself and Cardwell, seven Whigs – Clarendon, Granville, Fortescue, Hartington, Kimberley, Hatherley and Argyll; two Radicals – Lowe and Bright; and three Liberals – Childers, Goschen and Bruce. There was much to do, and military reform was never meant to dominate their agenda in the way that it did.[23]

But against the background of the Franco-Prussian War, the British government could not but examine its own military resources. Under the treaty of London (1839) Britain was committed to defend the independence and neutrality of Belgium. In answer to a question in the Commons, the secretary of state for war, Edward Cardwell, was obliged to confess that he was not sure that the army was in a position to send the 20,000 men who would be necessary in the event of Prussian aggression in Belgium. Cardwell was deliberately exposing the army's flank here. He wanted the response he got – namely a clamour for army reform. 'The great events on the Continent seem to have given rise to a great feeling in this country which may make the question of army organisation a less hopeless one than it has been hitherto.'[24]

Mid-nineteenth-century government in Britain has been described as 'minimalist'. The editor of Gladstone's diaries, for example, Colin Matthew, stated that 'no industrial economy can have existed in which the State played a smaller role than that of the United Kingdom in the 1860s'. This is certainly true if Victorian governments are compared with today's British governments, or with the regimes in France, Italy,

Germany and Russia in the nineteenth century. Gladstone's aim had been fiscal minimalism – the reduction of tax had been his ideal. But as a Peelite he recognized that there was a need for elements of state control, and the trauma of the Corn Laws, from which the Tories only began fully to recover in the 1860s or early 1870s, had been a demonstration of the fact that social engineering was possible when governments chose to withhold money, grants and tariffs, as much as when they intervened. As Gladstone in his middle age developed into his own version of political radicalism, he was very far from being a minimalist. He and his parliamentary friends wanted to change things – in Ireland, in schools, in a multiplicity of areas which a Tory would not necessarily consider to be the state's business.

Army reform showed the true colours of Gladstone's government: and they are somewhat paradoxical colours. On the one hand, Cardwell wanted to reduce expenditure on the army: he proposed to do this by withdrawing 25,709 men from colonial service, cutting £641,370 from the stores vote, and by reducing the size of infantry battalion cadres to 560 other ranks (later reduced to 520).[25] On the other hand, the populist and egalitarian side to the Gladstone government wished to reform the army on political grounds, to drag it into modern times, to abolish the system of purchasing commissions, and to do away with some of the more violent disciplinary procedures, such as flogging and branding, which were deemed inconsistent with the sunny spirit of the times.

The impetus for many of these reforms came not in the first instance from the back benches of the House of Commons, but from the Press. It saw in the victorious Prussian army overrunning France a well-trained machine where officers were chosen on merit, rather than because they could afford to buy their positions. And how did the Prussian officer material achieve the necessary range of skills? Why, through an effectively organized system of education in which the government took an active interest. If any one thing in 1870 emphasized the moribund character of the aristocratic system in Britain, was it not the system of purchase? Abolish it, and Britain might become as efficiently meritocratic as the Germans!

There is a paradox in the fact that these attacks came from the Press, since in Prussia the newspapers were strictly forbidden to criticize the government in any way. If those newspapers such as *The Daily News* and *The Times* were consistent in their desire to imitate Prussia they would have invited Mr Gladstone to close them down. In any event, what the newspapers really wanted was not to build up an escalation of arms, leading eventually to a European Armageddon in the trenches – though we can see this was the eventual consequence of making the army more 'efficient'. What the newspapers, and the Radical backbenchers, wanted was to strike a blow against the aristocracy, who ran the army.

Gladstone on this as in many other areas of life was double-minded. This isn't the same as hypocrisy, but the two can be confused. When Ruskin accused Gladstone of being a 'leveller', he elicited the reply, 'Oh, dear no! I am nothing of the sort. I am a firm believer in the aristocratic principle – the rule of the best. I am an out-and-out *inequalitarian*' – a confession, we read, 'which Ruskin treated with intense delight, clapping his hands triumphantly'.[26]

As the son of a Liverpool merchant who had been to Eton and married into the landed gentry – the Glynne family – Gladstone lived at Hawarden the life of an aristocrat: a huge house, and many acres, and the income from farm rents and coal mines. His brother likewise lived like a Highland laird at their great house, Fasque, in Aberdeenshire. His entire life, except when in the House of Commons, or wandering the streets of London to rescue prostitutes whom he engaged in interminable conversations about the state of their soul, was spent in a country-house world. He was an habitual guest at Chislehurst, Walmer Castle and Hatfield, finding Lord Salisbury's High Anglicanism much to his taste. ('In few chapels is all so well and heartily done.')[27]

Yet on the hustings he could tell the citizens of Liverpool, 'I know not why commerce should not have its old families rejoicing to be connected with commerce from generation to generation . . . I think it is a subject of sorrow, and almost a scandal, when those families which have either acquired or received station and opulence from commerce turn their backs upon it and seem to be ashamed of it. (Great applause.) It is not so with my brother or with me. (Applause.)' One wonders how often he came out with such sentiments at the dinner table at Chatsworth or Hatfield.

The man whom he placed in charge of reforming the army was Edward Cardwell, like himself a Peelite, like himself the son of a Liverpool merchant. There were a number of reasons why his reforms, embodied in the Army Enlistment Act (1870) and the Army Regulation Act (1871), were of very limited efficacy.[28] First he wanted to redress the balance of troops by reducing the colonial garrisons and basing the army in Britain. This measure, overwhelmingly popular with Northern grocers because of the money it saved, did not work out in practice. By February 1879 there were eighty-two battalions abroad and only fifty-nine at home, for the simple reason that, the Fenian threat in Ireland apart, there were few reasons for troops being in Britain and many – during an Ashanti or a Zulu war – for them being abroad.

Nor did events bear out Cardwell's belief that he would improve recruitment by the Localisation Act (1872), whereby one of two linked battalions was based at home while the other served abroad. Localization, the establishment of barracks in the provinces, enabled recruitment to reach hitherto unvisited areas, and led to the further depopulation of rural Britain.* The establishment of these local depots was very slow, and many line regiments rarely visited their nominal locality, so Cardwell was not really attracting a much wider range of recruits. No doubt those who did enlist preferred life after he abolished branding and flogging, and enjoyed the possibility of shorter service, but the pay was still poor and it was noticeable that most soldiers belonged to the British army because of poverty. The great majority of recruits hailed from worlds where they would have been labourers, artisans and mechanics;[29] rural Ireland was one of the areas from which most came.[30] There were also very many Scots in the army. The military authorities reckoned that a serving soldier would be marginally better off than the lowest-paid agricultural worker in England, Scotland and Ireland – their wages calculated at £30, £33 14s. and £18 9s. per annum respectively. In fact, military wages lagged very slightly behind those of English agricultural labourers, but were considerably greater than the Irish: a fact which easily accounts for the high proportion of Irishmen who enlisted.[31] But of course it was not in the livelihood of the rank and file that the Liberal Parliament of 1868–74 was chiefly interested.

Of all the aspects of military reform to capture Press attention, public interest and parliamentary time, it was the system of purchase which was the most contentious. And like so many reforms imposed by politicians on a non-political class, it actually had only partial effect, since officers went on selecting members of the 'officer class', regardless of whether their pips and coronets had been bought or awarded gratis. Cardwell was adamant that he was not attempting a class war. 'It is a

* Vide infra.

libel upon the old aristocracy to say that they are ever behindhand in any race which is run in an open arena, and in which ability and industry are the only qualities which can insure success,' he told Parliament in March 1871. But after three months in which his diehard opponents had questioned every clause of his Bill, and after they had filibustered in committee, he complained to Gladstone, 'there sits below the gangway on our side a plutocracy – who have no real objection to Purchase – and are in truth more interested in its maintenance than the Gentlemen opposite'. He referred to the Whig aristocrats. 'They say in private that they want something *more* for the money involved; that something being the removal of the Duke of Cambridge: – while in truth they wish to purchase an aristocratic position for personal connections, who would never obtain it otherwise.'[32]

It is a strange fact, but the purchase of commissions had already been made illegal in 1809, except where regulated by royal warrant. When, after months of parliamentary time had been wasted, Cardwell's Bill had been rejected by the Lords, Gladstone cancelled the warrant. 'It was a brilliant manoeuvre,' says Lord Jenkins: but it wasn't very brilliant. The government had to pay out £8 million in compensation to officers who suffered from the measure.[33] And if this was the neatest way of dealing with an obvious abuse, why didn't Gladstone think of it in the first place?[34]

The Duke of Cambridge, whose florid mustachioed face is familiar to the English today from innumerable inn signs, and who so incongruously lived into the twentieth century – his dates are 1819–1904 – could not be expected to take kindly to Cardwell's reforms. He had been field marshal and commander-in-chief since the Crimean War, and he shared passionately with his cousin the Queen* a sense of the importance of maintaining a link between the Crown and the army. One of Cardwell's rationalizations was to abolish the dual government of the army, whereby it looked both to the commander-in-chief and his staff *and* to the secretary of state for war. In September 1871 the commander-in-chief was definitely subordinated to the War Office – Cardwell became in a manner the Duke's boss, his office and staff in Horse Guards Parade were removed, and he was required to move to the War Office in Pall Mall. The Queen herself protested, to

---

*He was a grandson of George III, being the only son of the 1st Duke of Cambridge and Augusta Wilhelmina Louisa, daughter of Frederick, landgrave of Hesse-Cassel.

no avail.

The Duke, who had become a colonel in the Jäger battalion of the Hanoverian guards when aged nine,[35] disliked intensely the abolition of purchase. He had been a brave soldier since joining the British army (he lived in Hanover until he was eleven), serving in Corfu, Ireland and the Crimea. He saw action – after Alma 'I could not help crying like a child' – he was mentioned in dispatches for his gallantry at Inkerman, and he was far from being a figurehead commander-in-chief. As a professional soldier he was understandably aggrieved by what he took to be Cardwell's interference. Until his appointment as secretary of state, Cardwell had been a mere paper-pusher in the Treasury. The Duke's career lasted long into the 1880s; he was a dutiful member of the royal family, standing in after the death of the Prince Consort and performing such functions as entertaining foreign dignitaries and supporting hospitals. Cardwell, worn out by the whole business of army reform, retired, exhausted, in 1874. This enemy of the aristocratic principle asked for, and was granted, a peerage by the same Gladstone who won applause from the Liverpool burghers for thinking it 'a subject of sorrow and almost a scandal' when persons such as himself and Cardwell sought ennoblement.

Gladstone's poor relations with the Queen coincided, not perhaps altogether accidentally, with a period when the monarchy was markedly unpopular. Although Gladstone was a devout monarchist, and a believer in the Church of England, he could not compete with Disraeli as a royal flatterer. The period of Gladstone's greatest triumph coincided with the Queen's decline in public esteem, and she would not have been unaware of this. In 1874, when Gladstone was so unexpectedly defeated, she was able to express relief that 'It shows that the country is not *Radical* . . . what a good sign this large Conservative majority is of the state of the country.'[36] 'How far the monarchy really was in danger in 1868–72 no one can say for certain,' said Lord Blake in his Romanes lecture, 'Gladstone, Disraeli and Queen Victoria'. 'But if it was, much of the credit for removing the danger goes to Disraeli.' Some of the credit, too, must go to the republicans. Although some of the working classes were Radicals or republicans, most were not. Those who attempted to stir up republican sympathy seemed a little too slick, a little too like metropolitan sophisticates or pushy, rising plutocrats.

The rich young Radical Sir Charles Dilke (1843–1911), now Liberal

MP for Chelsea, was openly republican, as was his fellow Radical Joseph Chamberlain (1836–1914), not yet an MP, both destined to be bright stars in the late Victorian political sky. The Queen had been a virtual recluse since being widowed, and refused to perform even simple public duties such as the State Opening of Parliament. She did so in 1871 solely because they were about to debate royal allowances, and then only on four more occasions in the next thirty years. *What Does She Do With It?* was a popular pamphlet, anonymously published but written by G.O. Trevelyan, another young Radical. (It rightly opined that the Queen was squirrelling away money given to her from the Civil List, amassing a private fortune from public funds, the basis of the colossal personal wealth of the present British royal family.)

The young Radicals were representative of a widely held and modern view of life. They wanted to be rid of the Queen. They had no time for the Church. (Trevelyan, travelling with Gladstone in 1867, had been disgusted that the Grand Old Man 'was reading nothing but a silly little *Church* goody book'.)[37] They were unlikely to be impressed either by the Queen or by her heir.

Bertie had been obliged to appear as a witness in the scandalous Mordaunt divorce case in 1870 – narrowly avoiding being cited as a co-respondent. The Queen asked Gladstone to 'speak to him'. 'I cannot help continually revolving the question of the Queen's invisibility,' Gladstone told his colonial secretary Lord Granville. Speaking 'in rude and general terms, the Queen is invisible and the Prince of Wales is not respected'.[38] Then in December 1871 Bertie went down with enteric fever. It was approaching the tenth anniversary of his father's death when he nearly died himself. The illness did something, temporarily, to restore the fortunes of the monarchy in the eyes of Press and public. The Duke of Cambridge approached Gladstone and they arranged for a Thanksgiving Service in St Paul's Cathedral on 27 February 1872 which made one of those royal spectacles which the British public enjoy. They forgot to invite Bertie's doctors, causing the more agnostic of them to feel that some of the thanks accorded to the Almighty might more politely have been offered to the medical profession. There was even talk of Professor Tyndall, of University College Hospital, being asked to lecture on 'The Pointlessness of Prayer', but nothing came of this suggestion.[39]

God and the Queen remained allies, as John Ruskin increasingly came to feel. Ruskin's visit to Hawarden was organized by Gladstone's daughter Mary Drew (married to the Rev. Harry Drew). It is instructive, not just because it elicited quotable exchanges between the two great men, which make us smile (they both undoubtedly enjoyed teasing one another), but because each discerned in the other an ambivalence of attitude to their contemporary social and political problems, an ambivalence which was the consequence less of their own divided natures than because the times actually called for ambivalent, not to say contradictory responses.

Hindsight helps here. Who, reading of the plight of the nineteenth-century poor, could be other than some species of socialist or 'equalitarian'? Who, witnessing the consequences of the communist experiment in Russia, could not view with dismay the socialist aspirations of the late nineteenth century? For this reason we can empathize with a whole contrariety of Victorian political viewpoints, easily able to understand how, for example, Marx or William Morris on the one hand, Lord Salisbury on the other, could think as they did. But perhaps the most interesting of those who reflected on the nature of society in the 1870s were those like Ruskin and Gladstone who tried to hold these contradistinctions together. Ruskin was *both* the inspiration of English socialism, the keen supporter of working men's colleges, the denouncer of the destructive effects of industrialization on the lives of the poor; *and*, as he described himself in his *Praeterita*, 'a violent Tory of the old school – Walter Scott's school, that is to say, and Homer's'. The People's William, particularly when he was daily on his knees in Church, retained an element of an 1830s John Keble Tory in his nature.

Gladstone genuinely believed that the times were out of joint, and that he had been given a golden chance, with his triumphant election victory of 1868, to bring real changes to pass, changes which would be based on justice and which would make life fairer for more people. He had swallowed his Anglican pride and realized that Ireland would never be pacified so long as the law appeared not to recognize that the majority of the Irish were Catholics. The Irish Church Bill of 1869 disestablished the Anglican Church in Ireland, making it one Christian denomination among others. The Irish Land Act of the following year was a step towards giving Irish peasant farmers freedom and independence. The introduction of the Secret Ballot in 1872 was a protection of the independence and liberty of voters. The civil service was made more open, with the possibility of posts being advertised and competed for by likely candidates.

Yet all this begged the question of whether the passing of parliamentary Bills was what society needed; whether Liberalism always brought sweetness and light. When he stood as a candidate for the position of rector of Glasgow University against the Radical John Bright, Ruskin asked the students:

> What in the devil's name have *you* to do with either Mr D'Israeli or Mr Gladstone? You are students at the University, and have no more business with politics than you have with rat-catching. Had you ever read ten words of mine with understanding you would have known that I care no more either for Mr D'Israeli or Mr Gladstone than for two old bagpipes with the drone going by steam, but that I hate all Liberalism as I do Beelzebub, and that, with Carlyle, I stand, we two alone now in England, for God and the Queen.[40]

This was the side which Ruskin acted up when he stayed as Gladstone's guest – 'We had a conversation once about Quakers,' Gladstone recalled, 'and I remarked how feeble was their theology and how great their social influence. As theologians, they have merely insisted on one or two points of Christian doctrine, but what good work they have achieved socially! – Why, they have reformed prisons, they have abolished slavery, and denounced war.' To which Ruskin answered, 'I am really sorry, but I am afraid I don't think that prisons ought to be reformed, I don't think slavery ought to have been abolished, and I don't think war ought to be denounced.'[41]

It would be a mistake to treat this remark too seriously, or too unseriously. In fact, Ruskin came away from the visit to Hawarden, 'almost persuaded to be a Gladstonian'.[42] Gladstone for his part discerned in Ruskin's political views 'a mixture of virtuous absolutism and Christian socialism. All in his charming and modest manner.'[43] Gladstone, addict of parliamentary politics that he was, was by no means a citizen of the secular city. He knew that for many or most people there was a life outside politics, and that politics were meaningless if they did not take account of this fact.

Nowhere was this more obvious than in the Liberals' education reform. 'Amid dire controversies that in all countries surround all questions of the school,' Morley wrote, 'some believe the first government of Mr Gladstone in its dealing with education to have achieved its greatest constructive work. Others think that, on the contrary, it threw away a noble chance.'[44] The 'others' in Morley's phrase were those secularists like himself who believed that there should have been introduced a system of universal and uniform secular education. Gladstone, partly because he was so preoccupied with Irish questions, partly perhaps because he did not wish to expose the contrast between his private feelings and his public persona as a radical figurehead, remained aloof from much of the parliamentary debate and left the framing of the Education Act to W.E. Forster (1818–86), a Quaker wool merchant who was vice-president of the committee of the privy council for education. Forster was torn between two warring factions. Joseph Chamberlain of Birmingham, R.W. Dale, a Congregational minister, and others formed the National Education League, in favour of freeing schools altogether from denominational association. But there were others, such as H.E. Manning, the Roman Catholic archbishop of Westminster, who could point to the burning churches and lawcourts of Paris, torched by Communards at the very moment Forster's Education Bill was being discussed, and ask whether secularism always brought enlightenment and peace. Some would see the Forster Education Act as an extension of Benthamite control over the populace, particularly over the masses. Advocates of 'state education' like to see 1870 as the beginning of educational opportunities for poor people in Britain, but this is by no means the case. To believe that Forster brought literacy to the working class, for example, is to underestimate people's capacity to take education into their own hands. Surveys of adult literacy in the early part of Victoria's reign suggest that, for example, 79 per cent of the Northumberland and Durham miners could read, and about half of them could write. Eighty-seven per cent of children in the Norfolk and Suffolk workhouse in 1838 could read and write. Thanks to the growth in freelance schooling, all privately financed, literacy levels had risen to about 92 per cent in the nation at large by the time of Forster. There was no pressing need for the state to involve itself in education at all. By 1948, 5 per cent of state-educated school leavers were still classified as illiterate.[45]

In the end there was a compromise which pleased no one – some schools were Church-run, others not. Complete religious liberty was given to all schools. Specifically denominational teaching was forbidden. Disraeli's quip was that this created a new 'sacerdotal class' of schoolteachers with the duty of interpreting the Bible in any way they pleased, so long as their interpretation was not that of any Church formulary. The Act provided for education to be available for everyone under thirteen – but of course it was years before enough schools were built, or teachers recruited, and secondary education was still limited to the middle and upper classes. The Act did not provide free education: everyone had to pay for a place at one of the 'board schools' which it created, unless they could establish their poverty.

To all the reforms and changes brought in by the Liberals, their changes to the educational system – both at the level of elementary schools and of universities – Gladstone was ambivalent. The Universities Terms Act, 1871, which made it possible to attend Oxford or Cambridge without subscribing to the Thirty-Nine Articles of the Church of England, had tested Gladstone. The Liberal in him won – and he forced it through Parliament as an act of justice. But the Anglican in him had taken some persuading.

Jowett, now master of Balliol, maliciously captured something of Gladstone when he wrote to Florence Nightingale, 'Mr Gladstone . . . makes no secret of his conversion to disestablishment. Neither did he when I met him about six years ago. But then it became a secret again which no friend of the Ministry was allowed to question.'[46]

By 1874 the radical programme of Gladstone's government had run out of energy, as had Gladstone himself. After a number of setbacks – a defeat in a Commons vote over the Irish universities, a government defeat in a by-election (Stroud) – he declared that he wanted a dissolution of Parliament. As one last fling at popularity, he went to the hustings with the promise to abolish income tax, but the Conservatives won the election with a majority of 83 seats, and Gladstone's first administration was over. Since he was sixty-five years old, it would have been reasonable to suppose that as well as being his first, it would also be his last. He was able to devote the first year of his retirement as prime minister to the subject which interested him most: religion.

24

The Side of the Angels

On Low Sunday, 1873, a new curate arrived in Wapping, to serve at
the mission church, St Peter's, London Docks. He was Lincoln
Stanhope Wainwright, the son of an old military family (his father was
ADC to Lt General Sir Willoughby Cotton), educated at Marlborough
and Wadham College, Oxford, and now aged twenty-six. He was to
spend the remaining fifty-six years of his life in this slum parish. He
never took a holiday. He hardly ever thereafter slept a night out of
Wapping. He led a life which, compared with the comfortable world
into which he had been born, was one of extraordinary austerity. He
slept on a straw mattress in an uncarpeted room. 'One cannot understand poverty unless one knows what it is to be poor,' he used to say.[1]

His vicar, Charles Lowder, emphasized how very poor the
parishioners were:

> There were a large number of small tradespeople, costermongers,
> persons engaged about the docks, lightermen, watermen,
> coalwhippers, dock labourers, shipwrights, coopers &c., the poorer
> of whom in the winter, or when the easterly winds prevented the
> shipping from getting up Channel, were for weeks, sometimes
> months, without work, and unable to support their families; their
> clothes, their furniture, their bedding, all pawned, they lay on bare
> beds, or on the floor, only kept warm by being huddled together in
> one closed, unventilated room.[2]

Drink was an obvious narcotic to numb the hell of Wapping life.
Children grew up with drunken parents, 'with brothers and sisters
already deep in sin, and abroad thieves and prostitutes a little older
than themselves'.[3] The pubs of the parish doubled as brothels for the
sailors – Greeks, Malays, Lascars, Dutch, Portuguese, Spanish, French,
Austrians – who crowded the cobbled streets, and 'there were frequent
fights between foreign and English sailors about the girls with whom
they were keeping company'.

No one who came to this exotic part of London could fail to be
impressed by the fact that this squalid, wicked and poverty-stricken

square mile yet 'contains one of the main supplies of London's wealth and commerce, as well as one of its most curious sights, the London Docks. The extensive basins, in which may be seen the largest ships in the world; the immense warehouses which contain the treasures of every quarter of the globe – wool, cotton, tea, coffee, tobacco, skins, ivory; the miles of vaults filled with wines and spirits; the thousands of persons employed – clerks, customs officers, artisans, labourers, lightermen, and sailors – make the Docks a world of itself, as well as a cosmopolitan rendezvous and emporium.'[4]

When Wainwright arrived as Lowder's curate, he was shown into St Peter's church and 'it was far beyond what, ritualist as I was, I had been accustomed to'.[5] The first generation of the Oxford Movement or High Church revival – Newman, Pusey, Keble – had been concerned primarily with doctrine: much of that doctrine, such as the impossibility of reducing the number of Anglican bishoprics in Ireland since Anglicanism was the one true Church, now seems esoteric to us. These founding fathers of the Movement would have seemed, to all outward appearances, indistinguishable from Low Churchmen or Broad Churchmen when conducting the liturgy. In the next generation, however, High Churchmen were, very gradually, to adopt customs which came to be known as Ritualist. Instead of standing at the north end of the Communion table, they stood facing east, as a symbol of the fact that the Eucharist was Christ's banquet to be celebrated in the (New) Jerusalem. They lit candles on the Holy Table. Some wore coloured stoles over their surplices. Others wore full Eucharistic vestments. Whether these customs were permissible to the clergy of the Church of England was a matter of dispute, depending on how you interpreted the rubric in the Book of Common Prayer.

Some would maintain, accurately, that vestments, incense, altar-lights and other elaborations of ritual *were* practised in the reign of Edward VI. What could not be denied is that in the middle years of Queen Victoria these observances became popular. Samuel Wilberforce visited Manchester and was told in the city that laymen were showing a love of ritual. 'There is, I believe, in the English mind a great move towards a higher ritual.' The churches where these rituals were practised tended to be the poorer parishes. The clergy who laid on the incense-drowned, candle-lit ceremonials brought colour, mystery, a sense of the numinous, into the lives of people who had nothing. But moreover, they were visibly men, like Lowder, like Wainwright, like Alexander Heriot Mackonochie at St Alban's, Holborn, who were themselves prepared to embrace poverty and to fight the poor's battles for them. They had absorbed the Catholicism of F.D. Maurice, which saw that in order to worship Christ, who became man – and a poor man at that – it was necessary for the Church not merely to preach orthodoxy from its pulpits but to engage with the lives of those most victimized and oppressed by the capitalist experiment: the urban poor.

No doubt it was this fact which, combined with gut anti-Catholic prejudice, made the 'Ritualists' so disturbing a presence for the Victorians. As early as the 1850s at St Barnabas, Pimlico, mobs had burst into the church to protest at the allegedly Romish goings-on, hissing in the aisles and rattling at the chancel gates.[6] When Bryan King had introduced Ritualism to the parish of London Docks – St George in the East – there had been similar riots, and again when St Peter's was established as a mission church in Wapping. Services were regularly interrupted with 'execrations, hisses, and laughter, the same bursts of groans and howlings, the same stamping of feet and slamming of doors, the same hustling of the clergy and maltreating of helpless little choir-boys, the same blasphemies, the same profanity, the same coward-liness, the same brutality as ever'.[7]

Thomas Hughes and Dean Stanley, no Ritualists they, had intervened to persuade the bishop of London, however 'illegal' the rituals might seem to him, not to side with the mob, but to support his clergy. (In any case, many of those who rioted in London Docks were not motivated by Protestant frenzy: some were Irish Roman Catholics angered at what they took to be the aping of true Catholic ways; others were pimps, publicans and prostitutes who feared that Christianity, if authentic, would have a disastrous effect on trade.)

You would have thought that an attempt by Anglican clergy to engage with the lives of the poor in an imaginative and unselfish way might have received support, even from those who found the 'smells and bells' bizarre. Archibald Campbell Tait (1811–82), a Rugbeian Liberal, was certainly inclined to reach accommodation with the Ritualists when he was bishop of London. He yearned to bring Christianity to the poor – he it was who insisted on services at Westminster Abbey being free and open to the public. He built churches. He preached in omnibus yards, in Covent Garden Market and in ragged schools. Had the Ritualists been prepared to tone down some of their departures from the liturgical norm, Tait's inclination was to sympathize with their pastoral devotion.[8] Nine hundred people came to hear Tait preach when he and his wife visited the survivors of the cholera epidemic of 1866 and to speak at the newly consecrated St Peter's, London Docks.[9] But during Disraeli's brief tenure of the prime ministership (1868) Tait had succeeded Longley as archbishop of Canterbury, and on Disraeli's return in 1874 Tait found himself as primate while a Parliament now composed of a handful of Jews and atheists as well as many Nonconformists brought on to the statute-book the Public Worship Regulation Act, forbidding certain ritual acts – the mixing of wine and water in the chalice, the wearing of Eucharistic vestments – which emphasized the Catholic nature of the Church of England and seemed to some Protestants to be letting in Popery by the back door.

Unlike Gladstone, Disraeli was not an ecclesiastical obsessive: indeed he felt somewhat out of his depth when Church was being discussed. 'Ecclesiastical affairs rage here. Send me Crockford's Directory. I must be armed,' he had written in some panic to his private secretary from Balmoral.[10] Quite why Disraeli should have chosen to spend much of his first session introducing this Bill remains something of a mystery, but perhaps he saw it as a comparatively easy way of bringing cheer to his monarch. Queen Victoria was obsessed by the Ritualists. When staying at Balmoral she made her Communion with the Presbyterians at Crathie parish church, a fact which scandalized loyal Anglicans. Ten days after doing so, she wrote to Dean Stanley, 'She thinks a *complete Reformation* is what we want. But if *that* is *impossible*, the archbishop should have the *power* given him, by *Parliament*, to *stop* all these ritualistic practices, dressings, bowings, etc. and everything of that kind, and *above all, all* attempts at *confession*.'[11]

Needless to say it was Church ritual to which she objected. She still expected 'bowings etc.' to herself by her subjects, and on her rare appearances in Parliament would have been shocked had the Lord Chancellor not walked backwards down the steps of the throne. She had an instinctual fear that the Church of England was becoming too high for her – 'I am very nearly a Dissenter – or rather more a Presbyterian – in my feelings, so very Catholic do I feel we are.'[12] And though she believed Bismarck had gone too far in his persecution of the Catholics, 'they are dreadfully aggressive people who must be put down – just as our Ritualists'.[13]

The sovereign was not alone in her detestation of the Ritualists. Pamphlets and sermons by the score rolled from the presses denouncing them for their crypto-Romanism, their 'mass in masquerade', their advocacy of auricular confession ('the enemy of domestic peace'), their links with 'the bondage of Judaism' (this from the dean of Carlisle, who believed their sacerdotalism to derive from the Jews); there were even those who saw Father Lowder and Father Wainwright and their friends as 'the enemy of national independence'. The Rev. W.F. Taylor Lt.D. of Liverpool, lecturing to the Church Association in St James's Hall, London, could say, 'I am old-fashioned enough to agree with old Bishop Hall, who said, "No peace with Rome till Rome makes peace with God" . . . . The object of the Church of Rome is the subjugation of this land . . . If we go back to Rome we go back to our national slavery, and national subjugation to Rome . . .' And so on.[14]

Some Ritualists, a minority, were aspirant Roman Catholics or in two minds about the question. For most of them, it was not an issue. For such as Mackonochie or Lowder, the point was, first, to bring Christ to the poor, next – in reaction to the intrusive parliamentary interference – to preserve the 'doctrines, rights, and liberties of the Church'.[15] The 1874 Act provided the Ritualist movement with its 'martyrs'. Five clergymen were imprisoned for refusing to comply with the requirements of the Act, Arthur Tooth of Hatcham (22 January 1877 to 17 February 1877), Thomas Pelham Dale of St Vedast's, Foster Lane, in the city of London, 30 October 1880 to 24 December 1880; R.W. Enraght of Bordesley, Birmingham, 27 November 1880 to 17 January 1881; S.F. Green of St John's, Miles Platting, Manchester, who had much the longest imprisonment – 19 March 1881 to 4 November 1882; and Bell Cox of St Margaret's, Liverpool, 5 to 21 May 1887. The Gladstone scholar Dr Matthew says, rightly, that 'no industrial economy can have existed in which the State played a smaller role than that of the United Kingdom in the 1860s', but the British, in their persecution of Ritualists, had found their own version of the Prussian *Kulturkampf*. Nor can one forget that these laws were brought into effect when the Contagious Diseases Act defined any woman detained by the police in garrison towns as a common prostitute; when many forms of sexual 'deviancy' were outlawed; when the 'rights' of married women were on a par with those of children and horses; when most adults still had no vote.

For those, perhaps, who actually knew the Ritualist heroes, these political points counted for less than the witness of their lives and deaths. Charles Lowder was the first secular priest known by his people as 'Father' – a custom subsequently imitated by Roman Catholics. The people of Docklands called him 'the Father', 'Father' or just 'Dad': he had quite simply made the island parish feel like a family. The funerals of these priests tell us so much. When Lowder died, exhausted, in September 1880, Wainwright preached at his Requiem from the text 'Weep not!' No one, the preacher included, could keep the injunction.

> The wonderful stillness as the procession left the densely packed church for the bridge in Old Gravel Lane was one that could be felt. There were hundreds of people lining the lane. Round the bier were grouped priests representing all shades of opinion, but all at one in their respect and veneration for him who never spoke unkindly of others or showed want of respect for those whose religious convictions kept them apart from us. And when one remembers that twenty-four years before the crowd had tried to throw him over that bridge, one sees that it was the ultimate triumph of the right.[16]

The Ritualist movement was, as Canon Scott Holland was later to remark, 'the recovery in the slums by the Oxford movement of what it had lost in the university . . . It wore poverty as a cloak, and lived the life of the suffering and the destitute. It was irresistible in its élan, in its pluck, in its thoroughness, in its buoyancy, in its self-abandonment, in its laughter, in its devotion. Nothing could hold it. It won, in spite of all that could be done by authorities in high places, or by rabid Protestant mobs to drive it under.'[17]

A pleasing evidence of human counter-suggestibility is revealed by the statistics. In 1874, the year of the Public Worship Regulation Act, 14 Anglican churches in England used incense, and 30 Eucharistic vestments. In 74 the clergyman stood to the east, rather than at the north end of the Holy Table when celebrating Holy Communion. By 1879 one had dropped the use of incense, but 33 were using vestments, and the number of priests using the eastward position had risen to 214.

Taking the country at large, in 1882, outside London, 9 churches used incense, and 336 vestments; 1,662 used the eastward position. By 1901, 2,158 churches used vestments – about a quarter of all the parish churches in England; 393 used incense; 7,397 used the eastward position. Customs which before the 1874 Act had been the esoteric preserve of a handful of exotic slum-shrines had become, within a generation, the normal practice of Anglicans.[18]

Of course, if this had simply been a matter of the aesthetic and liturgical preferences of a few churchgoers a century ago, it would not have been worth the space we have devoted to it. But it was more than that. Disraeli's government introduced these anti-Ritualistic measures in part, surely, as a consequence of something which had nothing to do with a few High Churchmen in the slums. It was a self-defining gesture, in response to what had been happening in Europe over the previous five years. No one was more conscious of this than Gladstone himself.

As a High Churchman who went to church every day of his life, Gladstone was dismayed by the Public Worship Regulation Act, partly because he sympathized with the religion of the Ritualists – though it was not quite his type of Anglicanism – chiefly because he distrusted the Erastian thinking behind the legislation. All his adult life he had been considering the relationship between Church and state. His change of heart over Ireland, his wish to liberate the Irish Catholics from the implication that they *ought* to be Anglicans, had lost him many friends among the Irish Protestant Ascendancy, but he had done what he deemed to be right. There were those Anglicans (whatever they thought about the comparatively trivial question of whether incense was desirable) who saw the 1874 Act as an interference by the Secular Power in what should be a sacred sphere. They began to talk of not merely the Irish but also the whole English Church cutting its ties with the state – disestablishing itself.

Gladstone did not want this, but, keen student of Dante that he was, he knew that this conflict between Church and state, pope and emperor, ran through European history like a fault-line. Dante, who believed all power came from God, consigned to hell those popes and ecclesiastics who seized for themselves powers which should be exercised by the emperors. St Peter, in Dante's heaven, goes crimson with rage at the sight of Boniface VIII's corrupt practices and gives utterance to the belief that his throne, the Papacy, is now in effect vacant while the corruption of popes and anti-popes poisons the Church Militant. Gladstone really did believe, with the majority of thinking Anglicans, that his Church, for all its faults, was closer to the ideal Catholicism of Dante than was the Church of Pope Pius IX. That is, he thought you could be a Catholic without owing obedience to a pope who, in the theological sphere, peddled the blasphemous notion of his own infallibility, and in the political sphere had so far left behind him the liberalism of his youth as to support such dreadful tyrannies as the kingdom of Naples, whose prisons and police-cruelty had so shocked Gladstone when he saw them.

Pius IX had lined up his Church behind the forces of extreme reaction. The case of Edgar Mortara had shocked Europe. The

Mortaras were a rich Jewish family from Bologna whose maid – a Christian – baptized their son without, needless to say, the consent of the parents. The papal police arrived at the house when the child was seven and abducted him. When, at the customary papal audience with the Jews of Rome on New Year's Day 1859, the boy's parents pleaded for his return, Pius IX replied, 'In the past year you've given a fine example of submissiveness! To turn all Europe topsy-turvy on account of the Mortara case . . . But let the newspapers, for their part go on talking all they want . . . I don't care a rap for the whole world!' Two years later, Pius IX displayed Edgar Mortara, now dressed as a Catholic seminarian, to the Jews of Rome. Ten years later, Pius ordered two Italian revolutionaries, Monti and Tognetti, to be beheaded in the Piazza del Popolo for attempting to blow up the papal barracks; and just two weeks before Rome was taken by storm, one Paolo Muzi was hanged in Frosinone, the last citizen of the Papal States to be executed.[19]

It is against this background that one is to consider the debate over the First Vatican Council and the doctrine of Papal Infallibility. (Or, indeed, the contemporary debate about whether Pius IX – now the Blessed Pius, should be promoted to full Catholic sainthood.) The twentieth century saw a Roman Catholic Church, stripped of all temporal lands though not devoid of political influence, spiritually revitalized though shaken by doubts and dissensions within its own ranks, still playing political roles in the world. In the 1930s, this role was conspicuous, in Spain most markedly, for its identification with fascism. In the 1960s and 1970s by contrast, in Central and South America, Catholics influenced by Liberation Theology lined up with the Left. In the closing decades of the twentieth century a Polish pope used his mighty influence to contribute to the collapse of materialist–atheist Soviet governments throughout the Eastern bloc.

It would be a mistake to identify Catholicism, or the Papacy, solely with any one of these political developments – and this perhaps was Gladstone's mistake: to identify the extreme political, as well as theological, authoritarianism of Pius IX with the Roman Catholic religion *per se*. After all, his once-close friend Archbishop Manning, one of Pius's keenest supporters in a theological way, was a man of the Left politically.

Nevertheless, the Council itself had caused grave concern to many Catholics, not least to the Fathers assembled in Conclave. There was no real opportunity given to the bishops and theologians to debate the matter of the pope's supposed Infallibility. The official minutes of the Council state that all the bishops present rose and gave their assent, but this is not what happened. Seeing the sort of doctrines they would be required to ratify, many of the nearly 700 bishops left Rome before the vote was cast. The Infallibility definition received just 451 placets, 88 non-placets and 62 placets *juxta modum* (Church Latin for 'Don't know') and the constitution *Pastor Aeternus* was passed by 533 placets.[20] 'Quite a few men in the minority were caught napping,' wrote Bishop Joseph Hefele, on 10 August 1870, 'and gave way before the roaring fanaticism. It really took a little strength to fight off the importunate people from the majority, to remain seated and not to sign.'[21]

The bishop was writing to the most distinguished historian of Catholicism in Germany, arguably in Europe, Ignaz von Döllinger, who had been such an influence on English Catholics and Anglicans, including on Newman, whose *Essay on the Development of Christian Doctrine* owes much to him. It was to visit Döllinger, now resident in Munich, that Gladstone set out in September 1874. Döllinger had written, as recently as 1861, in *Papstthum und Kirchenstaat* that Churches which separate themselves from the Papacy risk dissolving themselves into chaos. But he did not like the extreme ultramontane theology of the First Vatican Council and following the Declaration of Infallibility he let it be known that he was opposed. He was excommunicated in 1871. In the year that Gladstone visited him (they'd met before back in the Forties) Dr Döllinger was seventy-five years old. He had refused to join the so-called Old Catholics who formed what was in effect a non-papal Catholic Church – a little like a Church of England only for Dutch, Germans and others; but he had taken part in conferences at Bonn with the Old Catholics, Anglicans, Orthodox and others to see if there was a way forward.[22] Very many theologians and historians flocked to talk to Dr Döllinger. Gladstone and he appear to have got on well. Gladstone called on him 'at six o'clock in the evening', Döllinger recollected; 'we began talking on political and theological subjects and became, both of us, so engrossed with the conversation that it was two o'clock at night when I left the room to fetch a book from my library bearing on the matter in hand. I returned with it in a few minutes and found him deep in a volume he had drawn out of his pocket – true to his principle of never losing time – during my momentary absence.'

Gladstone had subsequently enjoyed a brief walking tour in the

Bavarian Alps with a son and daughter and then came home to write his pamphlet *The Vatican Decrees in their Bearing on Civil Allegiance*. Writing it, Gladstone would have found himself thinking of the wreckage of broken friendships with which his circle was littered as a result of the many English conversions to Rome. He no doubt thought of his sister Helen, whom he had failed to see in Germany – a Catholic convert living in Cologne. When he had finished the pamphlet he had an emotional collapse – 'Broke down from over work and hurry in afternoon from diarrhoea. In the night I rose & took castor oil.'[23] It is a curious work for a man who regarded it as his prime political mission to pacify Ireland. For if disestablishing the Irish Church was calculated to alienate the Protestants of that island, the *Vatican Decrees* pamphlet was calculated to offend the Catholics. It questions whether, after the First Vatican Council, the Catholic could be a completely loyal citizen of a non-Catholic state. It ends with a peroration whose meaning in intellectual terms is opaque, but whose patriotic music is unmistakable. It is frankly rabble-rousing, and Gladstone can only have been pleased that his pamphlet sold 145,000 copies, with a large number also buying its sequel, *Vaticanism*, in the following year of 1875:

> It is not then for the dignity of the Crown and people of the United Kingdom to be diverted from a path which they have deliberately chosen, and which it does not rest with all the myrmidons of the Apostolic Chamber either openly to obstruct, or secretly to undermine. It is rightfully to be expected, it is greatly to be desired, that the Roman Catholics of this country should do in the Nineteenth century what their forefathers of England, except a handful of emissaries, did in the Sixteenth, when they were marshalled in resistance to the Armada, and in the Seventeenth when, in despite of the Papal Chair, they sat in the House of Lords under the Oath of Allegiance. That which we are entitled to desire, we are entitled also to expect: indeed, to say we did not expect it, would, in my judgment, be the true way of conveying an 'insult' to those concerned.

Gladstone appears either to be stating the obvious – that Roman Catholics should be loyal citizens and, in the case of members of both Houses of Parliament, prepared to take an Oath to the Crown; or he is making the surely monstrous suggestion (for a Liberal) that Roman Catholics should give up their religion and join the Church of England. His wild pamphlets finally brought his friendship with Manning to a close, and drew from Newman the graceful rebuke in his *A Letter Addressed to his Grace the Duke of Norfolk on Occasion of Mr Gladstone's Recent Expostulation*: 'If I am obliged to bring religion into after-dinner toasts . . . I shall drink – to the Pope, if you please – still, to Conscience first, and to the Pope afterwards.'[24]

Yet the gracefulness does not really get round the difficulty. If Gladstone was impugning the political loyalty of Catholics, then his pamphlets were unpardonable. But very many Catholics knew what Pius IX and his more extreme supporters would make of Newman's after-dinner toast; and many, including Döllinger, knew that though they chose to remain in the Church for reasons of spiritual solidarity, Catholics of Newman's colouring were, to put it mildly, dismayed by the infallible pretensions and political posturings of the Papacy. After all, this bizarre debate stirred up by Gladstone, with its appeals to the memory of the Spanish Armada, was taking place at a period of history when many Europeans, far from worrying about the rival claims of infallible popes versus scholarly Döllingers, of Presbyterian monarchs or ritualist saints, were asking the more searching question, whether religion itself was true.

In the year that the pope declared his own infallibility Darwin published *The Descent of Man, and Selection in Relation to Sex*, with its humbling conclusion: 'Man still bears in his bodily frame the indelible stamp of his lowly origin.'[25] There are certain passages in this book which make disturbing reading for us in the twenty-first century. One of the core beliefs of the Western world, post-National Socialism and its *Götterdämmerung*, is in the equality of all the races of humankind. The easy way in which Darwin assumes the superiority of Northern and Western and white human beings to those of other climates and hemispheres will bring a blush, or an embarrassed smile, to many readers today. There is something, for us, chilling in Darwin's meditations on the contrast between those 'Eastern barbarians' who overran the Roman Empire, and the 'savages' who wasted away at the prospect of British colonization. He cheerfully speaks of the 'inferior vitality of mulattoes'.[26] Savages have 'low morality', insufficient powers of reasoning to recognize many virtues, and 'weak power of self command'.[27] Darwin accepts Malthus's view that barbarous races reproduced at a lower rate than civilized ones and he appears (he who so abominated the cruelty of Brazilian slave-owners in *The Voyage of a Naturalist*) to believe that acts of genocide, if perpetrated by the British, were somehow part of the Natural Process:

When Tasmania was first colonised the natives were roughly estimated by some at 7,000 and by others at 20,000. Their number was soon greatly reduced, chiefly by fighting with the English and with each other. After the famous hunt by all the colonists, when the remaining natives delivered themselves up to the government, they consisted of 120 individuals who were in 1832 transported to Flinders Island . . . The grade of civilisation seems to be a most important element in the success of competing nations.[28]

This is the element which the twenty-first-century reader would find most shocking in Darwin. Most Victorian readers would be untroubled by the notion that European races were superior to those in other parts of the world. Had not Tennyson spoken for all of them by stating, 'Even the black Australian, dying, dreams he will return a white'?[29]

What upset Darwin's contemporaries was the possibility that evolutionary theory eliminated the need for God as an hypothesis. 'The declining sense of the miraculous,' as Lecky called it in 1863, 'was pushed further into decline by Darwin and the public acceptance of evolution. By removing special creation of species, Darwin removed the need for very numerous interferences with physical laws.'[30] Those words are by a Church historian. We should now see, as the late Victorians in general began to see, that even to talk about 'laws' of nature – if by that is implied any external agency or mind behind matter or grand Designer of the universe – is to talk in metaphor. Things happen in certain ways. Darwin's patience in assembling evidence for why he believed evolution worked by a process of sexual selection is untainted by rhetoric or noise. His is a quietly reasonable tone of voice. The metaphysical implications of what he so slowly and so gently worked out caused him grief. His disciple Huxley and others could shout these implications through a megaphone, but not Darwin. It makes him all the more deadly as a voice to undermine traditional theism.

Whatever he did or did not do for God, Darwin certainly cut the human race down to size. In a year when one man persuaded the greater part of Christendom that he was infallible, there was surely a corrective, in the reminder (Darwin's part I, chapter VII) of 'the wonderfully close similarity between the chimpanzee, orang and man, in even the details of the arrangement of the gyri and sulci of the cerebral hemispheres'.[31]

Already, a decade and more after T.H. Huxley and Samuel

Wilberforce had their spat at the Oxford conference of the British Association for the Advancement of Science, the debate had moved on. Wilberforce, to whom posterity has been unjust, left Oxford in 1869 and became bishop of Winchester. He was not there long. In July 1873 – when he was sixty-seven – he was thrown from his horse while riding with Lord Granville on the Surrey downs at Abinger, and was killed instantly.[32]

Huxley, a materialist Don Quixote tilting at religious windmills, was to continue waging a campaign to promote evolutionary thought for the next two decades. If the Church of England was run by men like Wilberforce, he opined, 'that great and powerful instrument for good or evil, the Church of England will be shivered into fragments by the advancing tide of science'. As for the Church of Rome, it was 'the great antagonist' of science. Huxley, as late as 1889, believed that only secular governments prevented the Inquisition from persecuting scientists – 'the wolf would play the same havoc now, if it could only get its blood-stained jaws free from the muzzle imposed by the secular arm'. There were, he asserted, only two intellectually honest beliefs: strict orthodoxy and agnosticism. Since 'a declaration of war to the knife against secular science' was the only position 'logically reconcilable with the axioms of orthodoxy', there could be no neutral ground.[33]

Human nature, however, is more complicated than Huxley wanted it to be. Many Christians absorbed Darwinism, or other versions of evolutionary theory. Perhaps theologians were, in the decades after Darwin, more inclined to stress God's indwelling in the creation than his part in its origin, but men and women continued to go to church. Nonconformism, with its heavy reliance upon a literal interpretation of Scripture, might have been more vulnerable to the assaults of scepticism if it had numbered among its adherents more Herbert Spencers, George Eliots or Edmund Gosses. It is unlikely, however, that the American evangelists Dwight L. Moody or Ira D. Sankey, who visited Britain in 1874–5, found many in their large audiences whose evening lamp shed its rays on the pages of Feuerbach or Darwin. Their meetings took the form familiar in our own day to those who have watched such American revivalists as Dr Billy Graham. 'It was an impressive sight to see masses of human beings hanging or sitting on the shelves, and to all appearance on the clefts of the rocks behind the preacher,' wrote a reporter when Moody and Sankey held an open-air meeting in Edinburgh, 'for it reminded us of the time when men and women will be crying to the rocks to fall on them, and cover them from the face of him who sitteth on the throne, and from the wrath of the Lamb.'[34] In Belfast there was another 'soul-stirring sight', when three thousand stood up to sing. 'It was like the sound of many waters to hear this multitude sing the new song as all stood and sung in one burst of praise,

> O happy day, that fixed my choice
> On thee, my Saviour and my God![35]

Of course there will always be mockers. 'A London Physician' wrote a pamphlet claiming that 'The People Go Mad Through Religious Revivals.' 'Alas! judged by the low standard of an American ranter, Mr Moody is a third-rate star,' wrote this acerbic, anonymous medical gentleman. 'As for Mr Sankey, the friend who can sing, his voice is decidedly bad, and, like all worn-out singers, he endeavours to conceal this by startling alternations of high and low notes.'

Similar sneering was no doubt directed to the activities of William Booth (1829–1912), who started as an Anglican layman, became a Methodist lay preacher, and then adopted the uniform and style of a musical army – 'The Salvation Army'. 'Its impact upon slums can easily be exaggerated,' says a modern historian of this well-meaning movement, established in 1878.[36] We need not be so dismissive, even though William Booth's most famous rhetorical question – 'Why should the Devil have all the best tunes?' – must puzzle anyone with an ear. To compare the hurdy-gurdy noises made by the Sally Army with Haydn's masses, or even with the conventional Anglican psalm-settings, would suggest that the Devil was in fact comparatively lacking in musical advantage. The Salvation Army particularized a general tendency among the many movements to improve the lot of the Victorian poor, whether these worthy efforts were sacred or secular. In general, there was no evidence of the populace at large taking kindly to schemes of human improvement. Improve their houses, their conditions of work, their drains and, if you must, their doctors – this seemed to be the mood: but hold back from the rather less attractive wish to improve *them*. This surely is what distinguishes the liberal from the conservative temperament throughout the ages and helps to explain, in a time when there was such continuing inequality and such evident hardship in some quarters, why electors chose to return Conservative governments.

There was also the fact that in Disraeli the Conservatives had a leader of consummate charm, wit and lightness of touch. This by no means suggests, because his surface shone, that he was a man of no depths. Over the religious questions of the day, for example, Disraeli was in his way as keen to preserve the orthodoxies as Gladstone, though less anxious to be seen like the Pharisees praying in the marketplace. Though he quipped, 'I am the blank page between the Old and the New Testament'[37] he was in fact a simple Church of England man, as far as observance was in question. As to belief – when he addressed the dons and undergraduates of Oxford in 1863, who were agonizing about whether humanity was of the apes or the angels – 'My Lord, I am on the side of the Angels.'[38] Disraeli's wit, in such marked contrast with the prolixity and the intense seriousness with which Gladstone wished to be seen to take not only the world, but himself, opened up a fascinating gulf in the politics of the 1870s. If Gladstone's first administration was the first really Liberal government, Disraeli's second – of 1874 – was the first clear Conservative government in the modern understanding of the term. The electorate were choosing not simply between two great coalitions, new-formed into political machines; nor yet alone between two of the giants of British political history; but, as it were, between two visions of life itself.

To savour the spiritual distance between the two men, you have only to turn from Gladstone's speeches on Ireland, quoted in Hansard, or his pamphlets on Ritualism and the Vatican decrees, to Disraeli's novel *Lothair* (1870). Gladstone wrote and spoke like a mad clergyman – earnest, excitable, unstoppably prolix. Disraeli's novel covers much the same ground. Its themes are the predatory character of modern Catholicism, with a sub-plot involving Italian radical nationalists and Fenian terrorists. Its settings are just those grand London dinner-tables and country houses with which Gladstone and Disraeli were both familiar. But *Lothair* has fizz, and like the best satire it delights in what it mocks. During his brief period of premiership in 1868, Dizzy had tried to set up a Catholic university in Ireland. Archbishop Manning had at first been supportive of the scheme. Then he withdrew from it and threw his support behind his old friend Gladstone. Disraeli's Irish policy was in ruins – a key factor in losing him that year's election. The retiring prime minister – then aged sixty-five – sat down and wrote his sprightliest and best-constructed novel, his first (by the time it was published) for a quarter of a century. The chief target of its satire is the figure of Cardinal Grandison. Etiolated (he never eats, and turns up at grand houses after dinner), interfering, worldly and fanatical, Cardinal Grandison is a genuinely seductive character. And he is quite unmistakably a portrait of Manning. Ecclesiastical obsessives might mock Disraeli's hazy grasp of the raiment and ritual of the Catholic clergy, but as a work of High Camp fantasy *Lothair* is richly enjoyable in its own right, as well as being, clearly, the inspiration for much of Ronald Firbank and for Waugh's *Brideshead Revisited*. As the cardinal discourses of the Japanese government at the soirée of Mrs Putney Giles, Bayswater hostess, 'the Mikado himself was not more remarkable than this Prince of the Church in a Tyburnian drawing-room, habited in his pink cassock and cape, and waving, as he spoke, with careless grace his pink barrette'.[39]

The novel as it happens makes the same point, and shares the same view, as Gladstone's pamphlets on Vaticanism. At first Lothair, the young aristocratic hero, is nearly seduced by the atmosphere of the old Catholic families, and by the delicious mystery of Tenebrae chanted in a chapel not unlike Knowle ('Vauxe' in the book). Then, after a series of improbable adventures fighting for Garibaldi in Italy, he escapes the wiles of the cardinal and of the religious maniac Miss Arundel, and marries the lovely Protestant Lady Corisande. The cardinal is left to 'my banquet of dry toast'.[40]

Disraeli's novel irritated his more pompous parliamentary colleagues who thought that ex- and aspirant prime ministers ought to be boring. But it sold very well. By the time he became prime minister again in 1874 *Lothair* had earned Disraeli £10,600.[41]

One reason for the book's appeal is that it is an obvious *roman à clef*. Lord and Lady St Jerome are based on Lord and Lady Howard of Glossop; Monsignor Catesby is a portrait of Monsignor Capel, the 'society' priest; the Bishop is Soapy Sam Wilberforce and the Duke is clearly the Duke of Abercorn. Lothair himself is a clear portrait of the 3rd Marquess of Bute (1847–1900), who was indeed seduced by the Church of Rome and who devoted a comparatively short life to the pleasures of ecclesiastical aestheticism. He translated the Roman Breviary into English, and commissioned William Burges to rebuild Cardiff Castle and to build Castell Coch. He beautified and transformed many churches. He was prodigiously rich.

J.A. Froude was surely right to say that:

the students of English history in time to come, who would know what the nobles of England were like in the days of Queen Victoria, will read "Lothair" with the same interest with which they read "Horace" and "Juvenal". When Disraeli wrote, they were in the zenith of their magnificence. The industrial energy of the age had doubled their already princely revenues without effort of their own. They were the objects of universal homage – partly a vulgar adulation of rank, partly the traditional reverence for their order, which had not yet begun to wane. Though idleness and flattery had done their work to spoil them, they retained much of the characteristics of a high-born race. Even Carlyle thought they were the best surviving specimens of the ancient English. But their self-indulgence had expanded with their incomes.[42]

Money enabled eccentricity to flourish on a prodigious scale in the Victorian upper class. They ranged from a low-life peer such as the 4th Marquess of Ailsbury, whose heavy box coat had real half-crowns for buttons and who spoke in rhyming slang, mixed with bookies and actresses and gambled away £175,000,[43] to rarer creatures such as Robert, 2nd Baron Carrington (1796–1868). He owned Wycombe Abbey in Buckinghamshire and Tickford Park near Moulsoe. Lord lieutenant of Buckinghamshire, a Fellow of the Royal Society and an enterprising landowner who left £70,000, he was known in clubland as 'glass-bottom Carrington' because of his unshakeable belief that 'an honourable part of his person was made of glass, so that he was afraid to sit thereon and used to discharge his legislative and judicial functions standing'. Grenville Murray, illegitimate son of the 2nd Duke of Buckingham, revealed this fact to the world the year after the unfortunate peer's demise, and was horsewhipped by Carrington's son on the steps of the Conservative Club for doing so.

During the whole of his uneventful life, he persistently refused to sit whenever it was possible by any exercise of ingenuity to stand up or lie down . . . He even adopted a recumbent posture with many precautions; and when he retired for the night was accustomed to go gingerly on his stomach in order that the lower part of his body might be uppermost. He then trusted that, if lightly covered, it might escape crack or damage. When he walked abroad, he could never hear the sound of approaching footsteps from behind without emotion.

Loathing both his county houses, Carrington took a twenty-year lease on the neighbouring Gayhurst, where he commissioned William Burges to build kitchens, brewhouse, dog kennels and of course lavatories in the most ornate Gothic manner.[44]

The 1st Earl of Dudley, 'the Lorenzo of the Black Country', died insane in 1833 after a lifetime of conversing with himself in two voices, one squeaky, one bass. In 1847 his town house, 100 Park Lane, was taken over by Lord Ward, who installed a stupendous Louis XVI-style ballroom, heavily gilded, and a number of magnificent drawing-rooms.

The grand houses of London at this date were palatial on a scale difficult for the imagination to recapture, even with the aid of photographs. The saloon at Bridgewater House, completed in 1854, the picture galleries and the state drawing-rooms, were inspired by the Palazzo Braschi in Rome. Popes or emperors might have found the rooms ostentatious: they were occupied by an obscure Gloucestershire squire called R.S. Holford,[45] who had made a fortune from shares in the New River Company. The grandeur of the residences of the Rothschilds, the Beits (by the end of the century) or the dukes of Devonshire beggared belief. Dickens's Mr Merdle in *Little Dorrit* was not an exaggerated figure. The high Victorians worshipped money, and the grander you were, the more you were expected to flaunt it. What Lady Eastlake experienced at Devonshire House in 1850 could have been replicated in many London palaces any year of Queen Victoria's reign:

There was an immense concourse of carriages in Piccadilly – a party at Miss Coutts' and Lord Lansdowne's besides . . . We drew up under a large portico, where, as it was raining, hundreds of servants were clustered. Then we entered a very large hall, with pillars in couples, looking like the crypt of the whole building. This hall led to the grand staircase, which encompasses a space big enough for billiard table, statues, etc. Nothing could be more grand and princely than the *coup d'oeil* – groups sitting and lounging about the billiard table, where the Duke of Argyll and others were playing – crowds leaning over the stairs and looking down from the landing above: the stairs themselves splendid, shallow broad steps of the purest white marble, with their weight of gorgeous crystal balustrade from the wall; and such a blaze of intense yet soft light, diffused round everything and everybody by a number of gas jets on the walls. The apartments were perfect fairyland, marble, gilding-mirrors, pictures and flowers;

couches ranged round beds of geraniums and roses, every rare and sweet oddity lying about in saucers, bouquets without end, tiers of red and white camellias in gorgeous pyramids, two refreshment rooms spread with every delicacy in and out of season, music swelling from some masterly instrumental performers, and the buzz of voices from the gay crowd, which were moving to and fro without any crush upon the smooth parquet. The [6th] Duke [of Devonshire] looks just fit for the lord of such a mansion; he is tall and princely-looking with a face like a Velasquez Spanish monarch.[46]

It is perhaps difficult for a sensibility of the twenty-first century to understand how such showy displays could take place in a capital city so riddled with poverty and disease, without some insurrection of an envious populace. There are a number of possible reasons why there was no London Commune, no socialist mob charging up Piccadilly, or into the new-built Belgrave Square, to maul the rich as they stepped from their carriages on to the well-lit marble stairs.

One reason is the fact that rich and poor were kept apart in Victorian England to an unimaginable extent. The poor simply were not allowed into Piccadilly. Even quite bourgeois streets and squares were gated and barred against proletarian ingress. The moneyed classes were well-policed and well-armed. The parishioners of Father Lowder and Father Wainwright were not.

Another reason is the numbers. In an ever-expanding industrialized population, there were more aspirant than there were despondent members of the working or lower-middle classes, more who hoped for that lucky break, more who by saving or by luck or by enterprise had made a little bit more money than their neighbour. As in twentieth-century America, in nineteenth-century Britain the money-making process was seen by a majority of the populace to be a matter not for apology but for enthusiasm. The palaces of London which groaned with mountains of camellias and sweetmeats were not merely the playgrounds of the old landed families: had they been, some latter-day Chartists or British sans-culottes might have stormed their ornate balustrades. The nouveaux riches, so disgusting to the old upper-class snobs, were incarnate symbols to the rising bourgeoisie of what a little bit of luck or hard work could turn into. The British class-system was always fluid, and anyone with luck, money or panache could always penetrate it. Not only was the nineteenth century a great era for the refurbishment of old country houses such as Chatsworth, it was also a time of astounding new building – much of it paid for with new money.

Sir William Armstrong (1810–1900) was the son of a prosperous Newcastle merchant, who became mayor in 1850. After the Crimean War so humiliatingly exposed the inadequacy of British artillery, there was room for some clever Englishman to rival the Prussians in the manufacture of an efficient gun. That Englishman was Armstrong, whose gun, breech- instead of muzzle-loaded, fired a shell instead of a ball, with a rifled barrel instead of a smooth one; it was made of coiled and welded steel instead of cast iron. By the time of his death in 1900, when he had been ennobled as Lord Armstrong, his Elswick works competed with Krupps for being the biggest armaments factory in the world.

Between 1869 and 1884 Armstrong employed Norman Shaw to build him Cragside, an enormous neo-Tudor country house, the first private house to be lit by electricity. The Chinese and Japanese warlords, the King of Siam, the Shah of Persia and the Crown Prince of Afghanistan all came to Cragside to admire the 1,729 richly planted acres, the abundant rhododendrons, and 7 million other trees, and the extraordinary house where hydraulic electricity not only lit the innumerable rooms but turned the spit in the kitchen, operated the central heating, and rang the gongs for meals. The rooms were connected with telephones. The foreign potentates did not come principally to admire Norman Shaw's half-timbered gables, medieval inglenooks and panelled billiard-room, but they provided a congenial setting in which to negotiate the purchase of automated weapons of death from the mild-mannered millionaire-owner. Of all the nineteenth-century palaces, Cragside perhaps most embodies the paradoxes of Victorian capitalism: the aesthetic of Shaw deriving from his inspiration by Ruskin and Morris, and in turn holding up a lantern to the Arts and Crafts movement, bought with world-conquering money and the ingenious automated capacity to kill.[47]

The old-rich and the new-rich helped to keep Britain as a whole rich. That was the idea. That certainly was the idea which underpinned late Victorian politics, making it a contest not between plutocrats and 'equalitarians' (to use Gladstone's mocking word) but between two parties who, much as they might differ over some aspects of foreign policy, of Irish policy and even of domestic administration, were united in a willingness to keep the power and accumulated wealth of the plutocracy and the aristocracy largely undisturbed.

25

The End of Lord Beaconsfield

Britain became so used to being governed by what could be called an aristocratic consensus or settlement that it was years before the existence of a so-called democracy took hold of the collective political imagination. Indeed, it is open to question whether an enthusiasm for democracy has ever counted for much in Britain, if by that is meant such things as a Bill of Rights, a democratically chosen judiciary or an elected head of state. Prime ministers, Cabinets, civil servants continue to govern Britain with only nominal reference to the results of ballot box or poll. The exclusion of adults from the voting process on grounds of income or gender would now be abhorred by all but a few maniac diehards. But the electorate, being given the right to choose its government, has seldom shown any enthusiasm for changing the Constitution, the method of dividing power between the two Houses of Parliament, or the composition of the Cabinet, the actual decision-making political body.

Until very recently, the hereditary peers of England sat in the upper chamber as of right: a proportion, at the time of writing, still do so. Their rights and privileges were removed, not as a result of some populist movement, but by modern-minded politicians who felt for whatever reason that enough of that particular system was enough. All the same, whatever happens to the House of Lords in our own day or in the future, we can say that the way Britain was governed remained substantially unaltered from the time of Disraeli to the premiership of John Major and Tony Blair. The electorate has been extended, but elections still take place in roughly the same manner. Thereafter, parliamentary members claim to represent, not a political faction but a place – the members are not announced as 'The Labour Member' or 'The Conservative who has just spoken', but as 'The Honourable Member for Scunthorpe' – just as might have been the case at any time since the reign of Edward III. The Cabinet and the government are still referred to as *administrations*, their task being primarily to administer the business of the government on behalf of the Crown.

In this sense, Britain retains a largely aristocratic (or perhaps oligarchic would be more accurate) form of government, even though the prime minister and his or her team do not come from the landed section of society. The parties do not, as in other parts of the world (or as in one specific part of the United Kingdom to this day, Northern Ireland), represent single sections of society or single interests. Only very seldom in British history – the most obvious example is the General Strike of 1926 – does the populace appear to divide along purely class lines.

How far any of this is the achievement of the politicians of the 1870s, historians and political analysts must decide. Many paradoxes resulted from the 1867 Reform Act. Not only were some of the working class enfranchised by the Act natural Tories; but also, paradoxically, many of the natural Liberals who had voted Gladstone to power in 1868 became alarmed by the rise of the working classes and thought the Conservative Party was a safer bastion against communism. So the Tory Party could appeal to the working classes, to the petits bourgeois of the suburbs *and* to the old aristocracy who, from the repeal of the Corn Laws until 1874, had inclined to remain aloof from political engagement. The left, if you can call it that – the Radical wing of the Liberal Party – found itself in comparably broad coalition with the old Whigs, the Peelites, and those who were attracted to the milder side of Gladstone's 'energy'.

Gladstone himself, though, believed himself to be beaten in 1874.[1] He retired as Liberal leader in favour of Lord Hartington. Disraeli was at last, and unambiguously, on top of the 'greasy pole'. Having spent a lifetime clambering up, he found himself the commander of the first majority Conservative government since 1841, and it was a substantial majority: taking account of the new Irish Home Rule Party in the Commons, 48 in actual parliamentary terms.[2]

In a lampoon for *Weldon's Christmas Annual*, 1878, entitled *Dizzi-Ben-Dizzi*, Disraeli is seen as an Oriental Potentate. After the election

Then Ben was left sole ruler of the land[3]

able with his Vizier, 'Salis' – i.e. the 3rd Marquess of Salisbury – to do more or less as he chose. Another spoof, by one 'Politicus', envisages the former Tory prime minister, the 14th Earl of Derby, coming to Disraeli from beyond the grave to visit him in his library at Hughenden. This, like the *Weldon's Annual* squib, comes from the end of Dizzy's premiership.[4] Derby is merciless. He accuses Disraeli of disregard for the old Tory aristocratic values – by virtue of his 1867 Reform Act –

and because of his belligerent foreign policy in the 1874–80 government he also lambastes him for the bloody consequences of international cynicism.

On the first point, the ghostly Derby loftily says, 'I thought that *Conservatives* had a peculiar regard for the Glorious Constitution in Church and State.'[5] Over foreign policy (Derby's son was foreign secretary for the first four years of Disraeli's second Cabinet, being succeeded by Salisbury) the ghost is much more scathing:

> You, sitting in your cosy room, with the ambition cherished through a life-time all but gratified, do not know what is taking place in thousands of homes in the land. I can pass from home to home unseen. With the speed of lightning I can pass from town to town and from land to land. I have visited the battlefields where Russian and Turk meet in deadly struggle, and where thousands of sons and husbands and fathers are now mouldering to dust. Your vacillating policy caused all that . . .

The ghost of Derby accuses Disraeli of cynically siding with the cruel, and tottering, Ottoman Empire against the legitimate aspirations of young nations 'struggling for liberty in the East of Europe':

> You are ready enough, with your dreams of 'a scientific frontier' to strike weak and semi-civilized people like the Afghans or Zulus; but you, with all your talk . . . take care not to strike at a nation which is powerful enough to meet you in the field. With your petty wars in every part of the world, with your ceaseless 'surprises' and your bombastic talk about 'a spirited foreign policy', you destroy confidence and cripple trade. While the resources of the people lessen, the taxation increases. Where are the millions that Gladstone left in the Exchequer? Where are the millions that you have received from the increased taxes upon a growingly impoverished people?[6]

The spirit, now beginning to sound a little more like Marley's ghost than Derby's, blames 'Benjamin' for the phenomenon of poverty in English cities:

> I have seen the tears yet wet on the faces of children who, in their hunger, have cried themselves to sleep. I have seen mothers, sitting over fireless grates, shivering and looking round their desolate homes

to see what articles they could pawn on the morrow to get a meal for their children . . . Conservative as I was, and *am*, I always thought, and still think, that the best things for a Government to *conserve* are the liberties, the prosperity, and the happiness of the people.[7]

How far does any of this mud stick? Evidently it is mud prepared for the election which threw Disraeli out of office so decisively in 1880: the Liberals came back with a majority of 137 over the Conservatives.

Disraeli's greatest biographer and interpreter, Lord Blake, sums up his predicament in 1874 with typical aplomb: 'He had given very little thought to what his Government would actually do if he won a general election.'[8] Dizzy himself, four years after his victory, was heard to murmur, 'Power! It has come to me too late . . . There were days when, on waking, I felt I could move dynasties and governments; but that has passed away.'[9]

He was sixty-nine years old when he formed his second Cabinet, and he was destined to die a year after leaving office. He was never in the best of health as prime minister, especially in the winter months when he was subject to severe bronchitis. His premiership, then, was inevitably a series of inspired energetic bursts rather than a sustained marathon or a carefully considered programme. In so far as this government of 1874–80 did have a long-lasting consequence, it was to confirm Britain as 'an Asiatic power' rather than a European one. The phrase is typical of Disraeli's playfulness but it was meant. He would no doubt have liked to make Britain more influential in Europe, but after the triumph of Prussia in 1870, and the establishment of the *Dreikaiserbund* – the alliance of the three emperors of Austria-Hungary, Russia and Germany – Britain was condemned to a marginal role in Europe. It is difficult to know whether Lord Derby's ghost, in the spoof by 'Politicus', was being fair in his implication that Britain would have had any influence over the Balkans even if she had pursued a different policy in the mid-Seventies when the crisis blew up there.

In the first major foreign policy decision of his administration, however, Disraeli showed a decisiveness, and a flair, which were all his own – and which it is difficult to imagine any other statesman of the time achieving with such expedition and style.

The Suez Canal had been opened in 1869. It cut the journey from Britain to India by several weeks and thousands of miles, and by 1875 four-fifths of its traffic was British. In the event of an invasion of India by Russia through Afghanistan (an ever-present possibility in British paranoia if not always in Russian foreign policy), or if there were another Mutiny, the Suez Canal could carry troops from England far more quickly than the old route round the Cape.

In 1870, when Lord Granville was foreign secretary, there was a chance of the British government buying either the Egyptian khedive's interest in the Canal Company, or the whole concern. The French engineer, Ferdinand de Lesseps, who had constructed the canal and founded the Suez Canal Company, was happy to negotiate either arrangement but, incredibly, the British could not see what advantage would be gained. In 1875 Khedive Ismail was again very short of money and was looking to dispose of the 176,602 ordinary shares (out of a total of 400,000 in the Suez Canal Company as a whole). Frederick Greenwood, editor of the *Pall Mall Gazette*, was told by the financier Henry Oppenheimer that the khedive was negotiating with two French groups. Greenwood told the foreign secretary, the young 15th Earl of Derby, who did not at all like the idea of the purchase.[10]

Disraeli himself now intervened. The Cabinet opposed him, but he overruled them. Undoubtedly his friendship with the Rothschilds helped. Disraeli's secretary, Monty Corry, went to see Lord (Lionel) Rothschild in his office at New Court, Lincoln's Inn, and the banker advanced the British government £4 million. He charged a commission of 2½ per cent and made £100,000 for his firm out of the deal. Those were the days before 'insider trading' was made a sin. Henry Oppenheimer with his syndicate 'was the speculator who made most out of the deal', buying shares before the government purchase was public knowledge. The Rothschilds themselves however did not speculate on the Stock Exchange with their secret knowledge.[11] Nor, as was suggested, did Natty Rothschild – a member of Parliament – directly profit from the deal negotiated by his family's bank.[12] (A Mr Bigger alleged that Nathaniel Rothschild was in breach of the Act on Privilege, 22 Geo. III, c. 45, but he was neither a partner in the firm, nor privy to the deal.)

It was paid for by the chancellor of the Exchequer, Sir Stafford Northcote, passing an Exchequer Bonds Bill, raising £4,080,000 from the Post Office Savings Bank at 3½ per cent; and by raising income tax to 4*d*. in the £ – a 'penal' level, as has been said by a later member of the Rothschild family.[13] It was, however, one of the best investments ever made by a British government. In purely financial terms, the profits were huge. The shares were bought for £22 10*s*. 4*d*. per share and had risen, by January 1876, to £34 12s. 6d. By 31 March 1935 they were worth approximately £528 per share.

Even more important than the paper valuation of the shares, however, was the symbolic importance of Disraeli having secured British control of the Canal Company. As Cairns, lord chancellor, put it to Disraeli, 'It is now the *Canal and India*; there is no such thing now to us as India alone. India is any number of cyphers; but the Canal is the unit that makes these cyphers valuable.'[14] The Canal was a symbol of British imperial dominance of the world. It is apt that the end of that dominion should have been signalled by Colonel Nasser, in 1956, nationalizing the Canal. British impotence to reclaim it made unambiguous her reduced power and status among the nations. It had become in any case meaningless since the loss of India in 1948 and the gradual dismantling of the Empire. But Disraeli's purchase was the beginning of that period – which extended perhaps until the Second World War – when British political power could be defined in terms of overseas dominion.

Discarding (as she coquettishly allowed him to do) the convention by which the prime minister and his Sovereign conversed in the third person, Disraeli wrote to the Fairy (his special nickname for her), 'It is just settled; you have it, Madam!' To his friend Lady Bradford:

> We have had all the gamblers, capitalists, financiers of the world organized and platooned in bands of plunderers, arrayed against us, and secret emissaries in every corner, and have baffled them all, and have never been suspected. The day before yesterday, Lesseps, whose company has the remaining shares, backed by the French whose agent he was, made a great offer. Had it succeeded, the whole of the Suez Canal would have belonged to France, and they might have shut it up . . . The Fairy is in ecstasies.[15]

Sir William Harcourt wrote in *The Times*, 'there was something Asiatic in this mysterious melodrama. It was like "The Thousand and One Nights", when, in the midst of the fumes of incense, a shadowy Genie astonished the bewildered spectators . . .'[16]

The next spectacle, which did not even require the painful expedient of putting up the income tax, was to make the diminutive, pudgy little Fairy into an empress. If Bismarck could become a prince, and the king of Prussia an emperor, why could not Victoria? Hers would be an Imperium to cock a snook at, if not to rival, the European

Dreikaiserbund. She could scarcely be the empress of Britain, and although her government now had a toe-hold in most discovered corners of the planet, it would have been vainglorious to style herself empress of the world. Without so much as consulting the Liberals, let alone debating the matter in Parliament, Disraeli slipped into the Queen's Speech in 1876 that the Prince and Princess of Wales would be visiting India – and by the way, from now on the Queen would be known as the Empress of India: Victoria R.I.[17] At a time when the monarch had never exercised smaller actual power, she invested herself with a title which would have embarrassed her despotic predecessors. If, to some, the phrase 'Empress of India' was more suggestive of a pig or a railway engine than a constitutional monarch, it made her happy, and it helped to define her country's self-image during that un-characteristic period – again, lasting until the Second World War – when it thought of itself in terms of Imperial pomp. It was a very short period under the eye of eternity, and we may wonder in retrospect whether the Imperial mantle ever really suited the British.

How does one define an empire, or imperialism? Empires of the past – Persian, Roman, Byzantine – tended to be continuous land-masses, taking in differing lands, language and racial groups, all administered with some ultimate reference to a centralized autocracy. Clearly the 'British Empire' could not conform to this pattern, scattered as it was all over the globe. What astonishes posterity, considering the com-paratively primitive state of communications in the nineteenth century, was how cohesive this 'empire' managed to be. Germany, France and Belgium continued in rivalry with the British to lay claim to various parts of Africa and Asia as part of their colonial dominion.

This is all rather different from the old empires which, like dozing dragons nested too close together, alarmingly gave off signals of dis-content with one another throughout the period – namely the Austro-Hungarian, the Russian and the Ottoman empires.

This is not the place to attempt a full analysis of the history or extent of the Ottoman Empire, but its decline – the decline of the power of Turkey – is the dominant political fact in the last quarter of the nineteenth century. We live today with its consequences. For Gladstone and the Liberals, it was axiomatic that rebellion against the Ottoman Empire was a legitimate 'nationalist' aspiration. They thought that any group that wanted to declare its 'independence' of the sultan was like the Irish Home Rulers, and should be supported. Disraeli and the Conservatives took a more cautious approach, but they – together with the senior statesmen and diplomats of Russia, Germany and Austria-Hungary – saw it as their business to decide the future of the Ottoman Empire. They all accepted the Russian emperor's contemptuous definition of Turkey as 'the sick man of Europe'. They took it as axiomatic that the Ottoman Empire should be broken up, and if they did not have the Liberal belief in nationalism (for Bulgarians, Albanians, Bosnians, Egyptians *et al.*) they nonetheless believed that they could use the weakness of the Turks to seize these territories, or influence them.

Such instinctive territorial interference was not carefully considered. Opinions might differ about the quality of administrative efficiency, or its degree of justice, in those places administered by the Turks and their dependency. It is a different question, whether any plausible alternative, agreeable to all peoples in any given region, would provide the utilitarian ideal of the greater happiness to the greater number. Go to twenty-first-century Bosnia, Romania, Bulgaria, Macedonia, Kosovo, Albania, Syria, Lebanon, Israel/Palestine. What you will find is warring peoples, often of wholly irreconcilable aspirations, being encouraged by the Western powers to believe in Gladstonian dreams of independence, national identity. The same powers, in the United Nations, are then obliged to behave as if they were sultans attempting to impose ideals of mutual tolerance on the warring parties.

Life in all these places was more poverty-stricken under the sultans; differing religions and racial traditions tended to live together more peaceably – *faute de mieux* – when Turkey was a Sick Man than when the Russians, the British and the Germans decided to effect a cure for the sickness. The 'cure' was administered from a position of complete ignorance of the actual conditions of life in the sultan's dominions, and, it need hardly be said, without consulting either the Turkish authorities or their subjects. The individual outbursts of fighting and discontent were seen entirely against a background of rivalry and fear between Russia and Austria-Hungary, with Count Andrássy, the Hungarian prime minister and Austro-Hungarian foreign minister (from December 1871 onwards), looking to Britain as his ally to shore up the Ottoman Empire and prevent the Russians fulfilling their dream – the occupation of Constantinople, the annexation of the empire. Russia was not merely looking for advantage of this kind. It was gripped by a quasi-religious Pan-Slavic fervour, so that the plight of the Serbs harassed by their Muslim neighbours became a matter of anxiety for the Great Russian Soul.

Perhaps if the Powers had not persisted in believing that there was an 'Eastern Question', a phrase which suggests that there might have been an Eastern answer, the consequences of collective failure would not have been so catastrophic. Count Andrássy, prime minister of Hungary, was right to foresee that 'if Bosnia-Hercegovina should go to Serbia or Montenegro, or if a new state should be formed that we [i.e. Austria-Hungary] cannot prevent, then we should be ruined and should ourselves assume the role of the "Sick Man"'. The Magyar determination for separate nation states for Hungary would follow, and the collapse of the Habsburg Empire. No one can forget that the participants in these international discussions would all be plunged into world war by the assassination of Archduke Francis Ferdinand in Sarajevo by a Serbian terrorist in 1914, a conflagration which would destroy in turn the aspirations of Bismarck, the House of Hohenzollern, the Romanov dynasty in Russia and with it all that the Russian emperors believed by civilization and religion. Hindsight can sometimes provide historians with a parlour-game: in this case it is difficult to see what could have turned the tides, given the ambitions and composition of the countries and statesmen concerned. We can see clearly enough what went wrong: but what might have prevented the disaster?

Money might be one answer. Probably there would have been no 'Eastern Question' had Turkey in the 1870s not been financially ruined, actually bankrupt. Foreign trade had suffered badly since the Crimean War. Turkey was largely non-industrialized. Eighteen and a half million people in the Ottoman Empire were employed during the 1870s in manufacturing cotton textiles, and their incomes gradually declined in competition with the industrialized nations.[18] Agriculture, though, fared better. Between 1840 and 1913, despite substantial declines in population and losses of land, exports increased fivefold.[19]

Britain increased her trade with the Ottoman Empire by 400 per cent in the decades after the Crimean War.[20] The Turks imported almost all their machinery, iron, coal and kerosene, and the sale of cotton, cereals, dyestuffs, silk, opium, dried fruit and nuts did not balance the books. The extravagance and fiscal incompetence of the sultans at this period is staggering.[21] Abd-ul-Aziz had 5,500 courtiers and servants, 600 horses, 200 carriages and a harem of 1,000 to 1,500 women. He built two palaces on the Bosphorus, Ciragan and Beylerbey. 'General discontent reigns in the Ministries,' said Abraham Bey, in 1871. 'There is no money. It is the Palace that rules.' In 1874 over half of government expenditure was devoted to servicing external debt, and in

1875 the Ottoman government issued a declaration of bankruptcy.[22]

When the Balkan crisis – which we are about to describe – arose, Abd-ul-Aziz faced a profound discontent at home, demonstrations in the mosques and squares of Istanbul, and eventually deposition by a military coup. The army appointed Murat V as sultan. Abd-ul-Aziz, under house arrest in the Feriye Palace, was found dead on Sunday 4 June 1876 with his veins cut and one artery slashed, having committed suicide with a pair of nail-scissors.

The reign of Sultan Murat V lasted only a few months. His early manhood had been marked by intelligence and political acumen. He was seen as a potentially enlightened reformer, but the situation was such that he suffered an emotional collapse. It was given out that he was dead, though he actually lived until 29 August 1904, making several attempts to regain his throne.

The Cabinet next appointed Abd-ul-Hamit II, a thirty-four-year-old destined to be sultan for the next thirty-three years, until 1909.[23] He it was who had to face, in the first few years of his reign, the formidable task of coping with a war with Russia, a collapsed economy, unrest all over the Balkans, and international outrage in consequence of the Turkish treatment of these uprisings.

In the summer of 1875 a revolt by a few peasants in several small villages in Hercegovina began one of those waves of violence which have periodically disrupted the Balkans for the last thousand years. The cause of the riots was economic. The peasants had set upon collectors who demanded full payment of a sheep tax in spite of a failed harvest the previous year. The military were brought in. The deaths of Muslim peasants were ignored; those of the Christians were trumpeted as religious martyrdoms.[24]

Refugees started to flood into Serbia, Montenegro and Austria, many with exaggerated stories to tell, and the Porte was issued with an ultimatum from Count Andrássy – broadly supported by Britain: namely that tax-farming would be suppressed, and religious liberty guaranteed by the setting-up of a special commission composed of equal numbers of Christians and Muslims. This was followed by the Berlin Memorandum of the Dreikaiserbund, insisting on the inflammatory condition that Christian subjects of the sultan should be allowed to bear arms.

In July 1876 Montenegro – under the leadership of the swashbuckling adventurer Prince Nicholas – joined Serbia in declaring war on the Turks. (Sultan Murat with his incipient nervous breakdown had just been installed.) The Ottoman government, and the world, knew what this meant. Serbia was seen by the Russians, and by many Slavs in the Austro-Hungarian Empire, as the plucky little Christian country standing up against the infidel tyrant. As General Fadeyev, a leading pan-Slavic Russian propagandist, encapsulated the matter in his *Opinion on the Eastern Question* of 1876:

> The liberated East of Europe, if it be liberated at all, will require: a durable bond of union, a common head with a common council, the transaction of international affairs and the military command in the hands of that head, the Tsar of Russia, the natural chief of all the Slavs and Orthodox . . . Every Russian, as well as every Slav and every Orthodox Christian, should desire to see chiefly the Russian reigning House cover the liberated soil of Eastern Europe with its branches, under the supremacy and lead of the Tsar of Russia, long recognized, in the expectation of the people, as the direct heir of Constantine the Great.[25]

Disraeli's position, as British premier, differed from that of his foreign secretary Lord Derby and, to a lesser extent, that of his secretary for India, the increasingly influential Lord Salisbury. 'If the Russians had Constantinople' – this is Disraeli's view – 'they could at any time march their Army through Syria to the mouth of the Nile, and then what would be the use of our holding Egypt. Not even the command of the sea could help us under such circumstances . . . Our strength is on the sea. Constantinople is the Key of India, and not Egypt and the Suez Canal.'

Salisbury as the younger man felt Disraeli was fighting old battles and imagining, twenty years after the event, a re-enactment of the Crimean War. Derby – described by A.J.P. Taylor as 'the most isolationist Foreign Secretary that Great Britain has known',[26] wanted non-involvement at any cost. Events were to spiral, however, in such a way that British isolationism was no longer really possible.

The nationalist mood in the Balkans had spread across the Maritsa to Mount Rhodope, where the Christians fought against the Pomaks or Muslim Bulgars, fanatical devotees of Turkish rule. The village of Batak on the northern spurs of Rhodope was preparing to join forces against the Muslims when a force of Bashi-Bazouks (tribal irregulars) arrived there under the command of Achmet Aga of Dospat and his colleague

Mohammed Aga of Dorkoro. In the course of the summer of 1876, the Christians had probably killed some 4,000 Muslims. Achmet Aga's forces of volunteers undoubtedly visited a merciless reprisal on the Christian villagers of Batak, though whether it was 'the most heinous crime that has stained the history of the present century' (the words of the British commissioner) will probably depend on what you think of the massacres of tens of thousands in Napoleonic battles such as Austerlitz or Borodino; the deaths of 1 million Irish in the famine; the reprisals against 'innocent' Indians after the troubles of 1857–8 or the murder of thousands of Muslims in the previous years of Balkan conflict. A thousand Christians perished in the village church at Batak, the Bashi-Bazouks first firing through the windows, then tearing off the roof tiles and setting fire to the building with burning rags dipped in petroleum. Possibly 4,000 Bulgarian Christians died that summer, though the figure was soon multiplied to 15,000, 30,000 or even 100,000.[27]

This was one of those instances where British political life was fanned into a state of frenzy by a newspaper article: in this case in the *Daily News*, which first told an excited but morally disgusted British public of the 'Bulgarian atrocities'. In British political terms, there were two immediate consequences, one of tangential import to the surviving Bulgarian hill-villagers, the other a more purely British and local drama. First, then, it became all but impossible for Disraeli to maintain an openly Turcophile foreign policy without appearing to side with the rapists and pillagers in Achmet Aga's brutal army. Second, the arrival of the *Daily News* in the Temple of Peace at Hawarden convinced Gladstone that he must lay aside his theological researches into 'Future Retribution' – the uplifting task he had set himself in his retirement – and re-enter the political fray. Dizzy, after two years as a giant facing comparative pygmies in the Opposition, was once more to confront his old sparring partner: but a new Gladstone, a Gladstone even by the milder standards of later years transformed into something between an old-fashioned revivalist preacher and an entirely modern campaigning politician, taking the issue of the Bulgarian Atrocities to the people, and reaping mighty political advantage.

Disraeli dismissed the stories of 'The Bulgarian Atrocities' as 'to a large extent inventions', a 'coffee house bubble'. It is an interesting reflection of the comparatively relaxed political atmosphere of the times that in early September 1876, after a summer in which newspapers and journalistic circles had been buzzing with the Eastern crisis, the prime minister found time to attend a farce at the Haymarket

Theatre – *The Heir-at-Law*. He noticed that three seats were empty in front of him in the stalls. 'Into one of the stalls came Ld. Granville; then, in a little time, Gladstone; then, at last Harty-Tarty!' That is, Lord Hartington, the leader of the Opposition. We owe the ridiculous vignette to a friend of Disraeli's who added, 'Gladstone laughed very much at the performance; H-T never even smiled.'[28] There is something truly absurd about the scene: the solemn, boring, forty-year-old Harty-Tarty must until that evening have imagined that as (somewhat reluctant) leader of the Liberal Party he would eventually become the prime minister. Of Gladstone's two companions, however, it was Harty-Tarty's cousin Lord Granville who was the angrier. The Grand Old Man had, they imagined, retired to Hawarden, leaving the Liberal Party in the hands of the old Whigs. But the Bulgarian news had come to him as a call from God to return to public life. He had been seized with one of his periodic fits of manic energy combined with psychosomatic illness. During his frenzy over the Vatican Decrees in 1874 he had suffered from diarrhoea. Now it was lumbago which afflicted him; but like other 'driven' persons, William Ewart Gladstone used periods of physical illness as a time of preparation for immense outpourings of energy. As soon as back-pain allowed, the old man – sixty-six – made his way to the Reading Room of the British Museum (did his eyes meet those of Karl Marx, engaged on the second volume of *Das Kapital*?) to check references and quotations. His spell of lumbago the previous week, which he had spent in bed at Hawarden, had been passed scribbling his pamphlet *The Bulgarian Horrors and the Question of the East*. On his completion of this inflammatory text he had shown it to Granville and Hartington. Though Granville persuaded him to delete some of the wilder passages, both he and Hartington must have realized that Gladstone was back in the political fray, intent – though out of Parliament and with no seat in the Commons – on seizing back the leadership and taking the party in the direction of radicalism, demagoguery and something akin to, if not actually related to, religious revivalism.

John Murray ordered a print-run of 2,000 copies of the pamphlet, and increased that to 24,000 by 7 September. By the end of September 200,000 copies of Murray's printing had been sold, with innumerable pirated and cut versions in the newspapers. Anthony Trollope read it aloud to his family.[29] The pamphlet caught that mood of public indignation to which Disraeli in his cynicism had been deaf. Lord Lytton, viceroy of India, could dismiss such feelings as 'an outbreak of pseudo-Christian John Bullism, about the Bulgarians and other people utterly unknown to us, who have been or are being murdered and ravished by the Turks; not by any means without having murdered and ravished more or less on their own account'.[30] But the incident had all the ingredients of a story calculated to thrill and excite the British. 'If you want to drive John Bull mad,' said Fitzjames Stephen, replying to Lytton, 'the plan is to tickle (rather delicately – yet not too delicately) his prurience with good circumstantial accounts of "insults worse than death" inflicted on women, then throw in a good dose of Cross and Crescent, *plus* Civilization v Barbarism, plus a little "Civil and Religious liberty all over the world", & then you have him, as the Yankees say, "raging around like a bob-tailed bull in fly-time".'[31]

On the Saturday after his pamphlet appeared Gladstone spoke for an hour at Blackheath to a crowd of 10,000 people. 'When have I seen so strongly the relation between my public duties and the primary purposes for which God made and Christ redeemed the world?' he asked his diary. It was undoubtedly the religious inspiration of Gladstone's feelings which urged him on and which gave such electrifying power to his moral message. He spoke, and not just to the Nonconformists who formed a natural constituency of radical Liberalism, where the established Church was silent. Canon Liddon, rigid High Churchman par excellence (still smarting, admittedly, from Disraeli's attempt to 'put down Ritualism' by the clumsy Public Worship Regulation Act), made the point trenchantly:

> I may do him an injustice; but I have a shrewd suspicion that Archbishop Tait sees in the Ottoman Porte the Judicial Committee – in the Bulgarians and Serbians, the refractory Ritualists – and in the Circassians and Bashi-Bazouks the wholesome and regenerative influences of Lord Penzance [i.e. the judge appointed by the 1874 Act to deal with the ritualists].[32]

The historian E.A. Freeman saw Gladstone as the voice of truth and righteousness, worthy of Isaiah castigating the corrupt ministers of Hezekiah, or Demosthenes denouncing the hirelings of Philip.

Even Gladstone himself, however, could not have known quite how successful he was going to become as an orator and a populist. As he went round the country, speaking to huge crowds, the Queen could dismiss 'that half madman' as 'most reprehensible and mischievous . . . shameful . . .' Meanwhile, events in the Balkans moved on.

The Sick Man of Europe was not so sick after all. The Bulgarian agitation was put down. The Montenegrin 'war' against the Turks resulted in defeat. The new young sultan might be short of cash, but he still administered a potentially powerful government and he had well-trained armies at his disposal. The British had been happy to believe this during the Crimean War. The Russians reawakened memories of that era by declaring war on Turkey on 24 April 1877. Cossack troops were soon visiting on Muslim villagers reprisals no less horrible than the massacre of Christians by Turkish irregulars the previous year. No English newspaper bothered to mention these new 'Bulgarian atrocities',[33] and the 'barbarity' of these Orthodox Christian soldiers did not prevent Gladstone escorting Madame Novikov from the platform at an anti-Turkish rally.

Disraeli's attitude to the Russian war was that, by showing military strength at once, Britain could force Russia into peace and hold her back from occupation of Constantinople. He sent Lord Salisbury – increasingly, his closest ally in the Cabinet – on a tour of European capitals to ensure support for the armed resistance to Russia if she could not be brought to the conference table. In November he addressed the Lord Mayor's banquet and said that Britain's resources for a righteous war were 'inexhaustible' – 'She is not a country that when she enters into a campaign has to ask herself whether she can support a second or third campaign. She enters into a campaign which she will not terminate till right is done.'

Undoubtedly this bullish stance was popular with a large proportion of the British populace. If one section enjoyed working themselves into a frenzy about the Bulgarian horrors, another derived equal pleasure from the prospect of a war. Many, of course, would have enjoyed both prospects. Mass hysteria does not always follow logic. The term 'jingoism' was coined, based on 'The Great Macdermott's song':

> We don't want to fight, but, by Jingo if we do
> We've got the ships, we've got the men, we've got the
>   money too.
> We've fought the Bear before, and while Britons shall be
>   true,
> The Russians shall not have Constantinople.[34]*

---

*The song was written by G.W. Hunt (1829–1904) but performed and popularized by Gilbert Hastings Macdermott (1845–1901).

Both Disraeli and Macdermott were wrong, as it happened. Britain didn't have 'the men' to mount an all-out war against Russia. Immediately after the speech at the Lord Mayor's Banquet, Disraeli tried to extract from the War Office the numbers needed to hold Gallipoli and the lines north of Constantinople. Having said 46,000 they upped their estimate to 75,000 men. 'The Intelligence Dept. must change its name,' wrote Disraeli to Monty Corry. 'It is the Department of Ignorance.'[35] It was just as well that the Russians were not as belligerent as Disraeli supposed. After the treaty of San Stefano, signed with the Turks in a small village near Constantinople on 3 March 1878, ratified and emended at the Congress of Berlin in the summer, peace was secured: for a while.

Disraeli, however, had identified himself and his party with the policy of jingoism. Lord Derby, for thirty years his friend and colleague, resigned as foreign secretary when Disraeli insisted on the British fleet sailing through the Dardanelles. Indian troops were dispatched to occupy Cyprus, since it was deemed necessary for Britain to have a Mediterranean base to strengthen her negotiating position with Russia. By the time the sepoys had warmed up their first billycan of curry on Cypriot soil, the Russo-Turkish crisis was over. Rather than withdraw from the island Britain held on to Cyprus – a real rod for its own back in the twentieth century. This was Salisbury's acquisition, but Gladstone did nothing to hand it back to Turkey when the obvious chance presented itself in his later premiership, at the time of his withdrawing the military consuls from Asia Minor. The partition of the island between Greek- and Turkish-speakers and the farcical humiliations of the British at the hands of a buccaneer archbishop in the 1950s were all the consequence of Salisbury's nifty (as it must have seemed at the time) annexation of territory which was, for all its difficulties, much better off under the loose suzerainty of Constantinople than under the Union Jack.

If the prospect of Indian troops occupying Turkish Cyprus to show what Britain thought of Russia seems bizarre to our perspective, the agitation of the Second Afghan War seems little more than a footnote to the proceedings in Turkey. Lord Lytton, the erratic viceroy of India, decided that the Russian approaches to Afghanistan represented a threat to British interests. This would probably have been true if, by the time he decided on this show of strength, Salisbury and Disraeli had not been cosying up to the Russians in Berlin.[36] The invasion of Afghanistan was temporarily successful. Thanks to the diplomatic interventions of Sir Louis Cavagnari, a good old English name, an Afghan band was playing its own extraordinary rendition of 'God Save the Queen' in Kabul on 24 July 1879. The line, for the time being, had been held.

But jingoistic imperialism was not without cost, either in human life or in the self-disgust which from its beginning it was likely to engender. While the Russo-Turkish War was being fought, ended and negotiated, and while the Afghans under Ayub Khan were engaging disastrously with the forces of Roberts – an immensely skilful general – a very different story was being played out in Southern Africa. Sir Bartle Frere, a convinced imperialist who had lately been appointed high commissioner at the Cape, decided that the power of the Zulu people must be broken. He had not reckoned on the courage and military skill of Chief Cetewayo, one of the most charismatic and ruthless of nineteenth-century Africans. Not only did he enjoy keeping Europeans on their toes by periodic massacre of missionaries, but he also had a way with prime ministers which would on occasion have been the envy of Queen Victoria: having murdered Masipula, his father's prime minister, he exclaimed to Sir Theophilus Shepstone (secretary for Native Affairs in Natal), 'Did I ever tell Mr Shepstone I would not kill? I do kill!'[37]

On 20 January 1879, four invading columns of African troops, led by British officers, entered Zululand. One, under Lt Col. Durnford, encamped at Rorke's Drift ready to act in concert with General Lord Chelmsford. They marched ten miles and camped under the southern face of a steep hill called Isandhlwana, 'The Little Hand'.

Four days later two men, speechless with panic, exhaustion and hunger, staggered to Sir Bartle Frere's bedside at Pietermaritzburg with the news that 800 white and 500 native soldiers had been killed, their camp routed. Meanwhile 3,000 to 4,000 Zulus led by Cetewayo's brother had marched on Rorke's Drift and been beaten off by a much smaller force of British. The defence of Rorke's Drift by the British inflicted heavy casualties on the Zulus and they lost over 3,000 of their bravest warriors.

Chiefly for reasons of honour, Cetewayo now held back from further killing. Partly persuaded by Bishop Colenso of Natal (who had been tried in London for heresy by his fellow ecclesiastics for doubting the literal truth of the Pentateuch), Cetewayo believed the British were his friends. His was the morality of Achilles or Beowulf; Lord Chelmsford seized the advantage. After his defeat at Ulundi (4 July 1879) Cetewayo was captured and the Zulus defeated. They had given the British a run for their money, and in the course of the fighting Prince Louis Napoleon, only child of Emperor Napoleon III and Empress Eugénie, educated at Woolwich, was killed. 'A very remarkable people the Zulus,' observed Disraeli, 'they defeat our generals; they convert our bishops; they have settled the fate of a great European dynasty.'[38]

In fact, the Zulu War was a calamitous mistake. Disraeli did not really approve of Frere's disastrous policy, and by alienating the great Zulu people he had merely lost valuable potential allies against the Boers.

Disraeli had always been brilliant at seizing political advantage from a situation – improvising opinions and positions, and then, in the aftermath of triumph, consolidating his position and making something of it which was truly statesmanlike. He had used the Corn Laws – about which he did not care very passionately – as an occasion to ridicule Peel and destroy him. He had subsequently rebuilt the Conservative Party over long painstaking years and become the effectual architect of modern Conservatism. In the international crises of the late 1870s he had taken a bold Russophobic view and beaten the patriotic drum. It brought him momentary popularity in the country – though not enough to win him another election – and it crowned his career with a place of apparent importance at the Congress of Berlin, summoned in the summer of 1878.

At home, the opposition which Gladstone was preparing against Disraeli was fuelled by an unedifying arsenal of anti-semitism, a flaw which has historically been *more* a feature of the Left and Centre-Left in England than it has of the Right. When Gladstone was roundly beaten in the 1868 election, his wife took it not only as an almost personal affront, but as a defeat for the Church by unbelieving Jewry – even though Disraeli was as much a baptized member of the Established Church as herself. 'Is it not disgusting after all Papa's labour and patriotism and years of work to think of handing over his nest-egg to that Jew?'[39] Gladstone himself, after the success of the prime minister's Guildhall speech – the Jingo one – threatened to obscure his own rabble-rousing, blood-curdling evocations of massacres in Bulgaria, mused, 'the provocation offered by Disraeli is almost incredible. Some new lights about his Judaic feeling in which he is both consistent and conscientious have come in upon me.'[40] The historian E.A. Freeman referred in print[41] to 'the Jew in his drunken insolence' as his measured view of Disraeli's Guildhall speech; and when the Queen lunched at Hughenden he described her as 'going ostentatiously to eat with Disraeli in his ghetto'.

Such anti-semitism would become more general in the coming decades after the huge influx to London of poor Russian Jews during the 1880s.[42] Of course they all lived in the innocent pre-Nazi years when the human imagination could not conceive of what the anti-semitic mania might ultimately be capable. They therefore spoke more freely and allowed themselves jokes and levels of mild verbal anti-semitism which would seem distasteful in the post-1945 era. But Freeman's views would have seemed ridiculous in many of his English contemporaries of whatever class, and Gladstone, who felt real hatred of Disraeli, knew his decent-hearted if erratic public well enough not to air his rather creepy views of Disraeli's 'Judaic feeling'. Not, of course, that Disraeli would appear to have felt remotely prickly about anti-semitic attitudes. He was gifted with a superiority complex in relation to the rest of the world and would seem genuinely to have believed the fantasies of his earlier fictions – that the Jews are natural aristocrats. Perhaps if your mind is the mind of Disraeli, and the Jews you meet inhabit the Rothschild palaces at Waddesdon and Mentmore, this is an easy enough belief to maintain.

Bismarck, who disliked Gladstone as cordially as did Queen Victoria and Disraeli,[43] got the measure of the man at the Congress of Berlin, at which the Great Powers, France, Austria-Hungary, Britain and Russia, gathered in the Prussian capital to discuss the future of the Ottoman Empire, and to unpick the somewhat draconian Russian conditions of the treaty of San Stefano. It is characteristic of the way diplomacy was conducted in those days that no representative of the Porte, no ambassador from the sultan, not a single Turk, was invited to Berlin.

Disraeli, in poor health, attended in the company of Salisbury. He was the 'lion of the Congress'[44] and his incisiveness, intransigence and charm all deeply impressed Prince Bismarck. Britain deprived Russia of almost all the Turkish territories seized in the war and returned them to the Ottomans. The sultan retained military rights in southern Bulgaria. Disraeli had indeed won 'peace with honour'.

Der alte Jude, das ist der Mann! (The old Jew, he's the man!) Bismarck's judgement is that of posterity. When Disraeli came back to London, the Queen offered him a dukedom. He turned down all the honours she wished to shower upon him, except the Garter, which he accepted only on the condition that it was also given to Salisbury. 'High and low are delighted,' crowed the Fairy, 'excepting Mr Gladstone, who is frantic.'[45]

She had created Disraeli Earl of Beaconsfield in the very summer of the Bulgarian atrocities. When he made his final speech in the House of Commons in August 1876 he let on to no one that it was his last appearance on that stage where he had been such a scintillating presence for forty years. Someone noticed – that was all – that there were tears in his eyes that night.[46]

As the time approached for a general election, Disraeli badly miscalculated the Conservative Party's chances. He hoped that the diplomatic triumphs of the Congress of Berlin would give him another victory. Two by-elections, one in Liverpool, another in Southwark, were won by Conservatives where the Liberals might have been expected to win. So he asked the Queen for an early election, and Parliament was dissolved on 24 March 1880. Disraeli retreated to Hatfield as the guest of Lord Salisbury to imbibe copious quantities of Grand Château Margaux 1870 and wait for voting to start on 31 March. He had ignored all manner of factors which would have been apparent to a more humdrum politician. Harvests had been bad for two years running and the rural economy had collapsed. The Conservatives lost 27 county seats. A slump in trade and the continuation of the hated income tax led to catastrophic results for them in the boroughs. In fact they did badly everywhere. The seats in the Commons when counted were as follows, with the figures at the dissolution in brackets: Liberals 353 (250), Conservatives 238 (351), Home Rulers 61 (51). 'The downfall of Beaconsfieldism,' wrote Gladstone gleefully, 'is like the vanishing of some vast magnificent castle in an Italian Romance.'[47]

Gladstone himself had spent the previous two years campaigning, not for an English seat – though he was offered, and won, the seat for Leeds* – but for Midlothian, or Edinburghshire as it was sometimes called in Scotland. It was a comparatively unpopulous seat to win – only 3,260 registered electors, as against the 49,000 in Leeds – but since he won *both* it would not be fair to say he feared failure in either. Perhaps he liked the notion of returning to his Scottish roots for this remarkable transformation of himself in his late sixties into a modern-style campaigning politician.

The campaign-manager, Lord Rosebery, had attended Democratic rallies in the United States and modelled the meetings partly on

---

*He passed it to his son Herbert. In those days you could contest as many seats as you liked.

The death of Prince Albert removed an incomparably intelligent and astute figure from royal and public life. In the household of the Queen, his cult became something akin to an alternative religion.

The condition of society, for all its prosperity and progressivism, filled many intelligent observers with disquiet. (*Above left*) Karl Marx, long exiled in London, foresaw the self-destruction of capitalism, which may yet come to pass. His daughter Eleanor (alongside him) championed his ideas. She befriended Annie Besant (*above right*), who was at first a liberal radical, then a socialist, then a Theosophist. Annie Besant's defection from radicalism distressed the secular campaigner Charles Bradlaugh (*below left*), who was repeatedly excluded from the parliament to which he had been elected for refusing to swear an oath to a God in whom he did not believe. (*Below right*) John Ruskin, perhaps a greater prophet than them all, tried to rescue England's soul from the assaults of industrialization, and fell prey to 'the storm clouds of the 19th century'.

W.E. Gladstone (*below*) and Benjamin Disraeli (*right*), the two giants of mid-Victorian political life, embodied two different views of civilization. Disraeli, a brilliant novelist, offered popular Conservatism to a wider electorate. Gladstone's earnest desire to improve the human race made him popular with Nonconformist Northern grocers.

'A very remarkable people, the Zulus,'
quipped Disraeli. (He regarded the Zulu
War of 1879 as a catastrophic mistake.)
'They defeat our generals; they convert
our bishops; they have settled the fate
of a great European dynasty.' This last
was a reference to the death of the
Prince Imperial of France in the Zulu
campaign. (*Top*) At Rorke's Drift, 103
white men resisted a huge Zulu army.
The survivors are photographed here.
(*Right*) After the slaughter of thousands
of Africans, magazine readers at home
could comfort themselves with images
such as that of Lord William Beresford
running a sword into a Zulu.

The engineering achievements of the age are among its lasting monuments – the great Forth Bridge (seen here during construction) being a notable example.

Gilbert and Sullivan were an unlikely alliance, the coarse satires and cruel jokes of the former at first sight an unsuitable vehicle for the lyrical musicality of one who wanted to write great oratorios. The Savoy Operas, however, held up an hilarious mirror to the age and remain one of its glories. In *Patience* they guyed Oscar Wilde and the Aesthetes, a decade before the legal system sent Oscar to prison.

The diaries of Arthur J. Munby, minor poet and ecclesiastical civil servant, reveal an obsession with working women. Munby secretly married a domestic servant. (*Above left and right*) His studies of collier girls remind us of a world far removed from the drawing-rooms of the middle classes. (*Below left*) Thanks to the Pre-Raphaelite painters some of the Victorian faces most familiar to us are not those of male politicians but of modestly born women. Fanny Cornforth, the model for many of them, was really called Sarah Cox. (*Below right*) Elizabeth Siddal, known to us as Millais's *Ophelia* and Rossetti's *Beata Beatrix*, was a good painter in her own right, admired by Ruskin.

Journalism was changing. (*Top*) Information was on sale, like everything else. (*Left*) W.H. Russell, war correspondent for *The Times*, reported the Crimean War, the Indian Mutiny and the American Civil War. In so doing, he transformed the modern perceptions of warfare. (*Above*) One of the great pioneers of sensationalist modern journalism was W.T. Stead, whose exposé of child prostitution in London landed him briefly in prison. You can't put a bad journalist down, however, and even after he perished in the *Titanic* disaster, Stead made emanations and appearances at spiritualist seances.

American political conventions, partly on the evangelical rallies of Moody and Sankey. Of the thousands who attended, very few were eligible to vote in an election and over half were women. Proceedings began with a selection of Liberal songs, set to familiar hymn-tunes, to 'warm up' the audience. Then the Grand Old Man would arrive, often in a carriage pulled by cheering Liberals. Then the speechifying would start – often with a theatrical admission that he had mislaid his eyeglass. The old Pro was capable of speaking for hours and hours and hours on any of his pet subjects, and he and his team could build up a formidable list of the crimes and blunders of the Conservative government. The purchase of the shares in the Suez Canal could be seen as a profligate waste of taxpayers' money; the acquisition of Cyprus as a major blunder. (Once in office the Liberals would not reverse either.) The bloodshed of the Zulu and Afghan wars could be represented *both* as a shaming loss of British dignity and as an immoral exploitation of a people weaker than the Europeans. He insisted that we should ever 'remember the rights of the savage, as we call him'. There would follow the set pieces which were soon to be famous – 'Remember that the sanctity of life in the hill villages of Afghanistan, among the winter snows, is as inviolable in the eye of Almighty God as can be your own. Remember that He who has united you as human beings in the same flesh and blood, has bound you by the law of mutual love . . .'[48]

F.D. Maurice had emphasized the obligation on Christians to believe that the law of Christ is 'applicable to all persons and all cases . . . he must believe that it lies at the root of all politics'. The cynicism which kept Christianity for Sundays or believed that politics was a necessarily dirty business was one of Maurice's most persistent targets. Though Gladstone's Midlothian campaign speeches seem hammy to modern tastes, it would be unfair not to understand how deeply he meant what he said, and how wide was his appeal to some sections of the electorate. Disraeli's management of the economy was as easy to lambaste as his moral record, particularly since the election coincided with an economic slump. So Gladstone came back from his retirement – not just to restart his political career at the age of seventy-one, but to put to his wider public – who read his speeches in the newspapers – a fundamental choice. The election was a chance to throw out the cynical Utilitarianism of the early nineteenth century, in favour of the applied social Christianity – if not quite Christian socialism – of Maurice. Did we say not *quite* socialism? Not *at all* socialist. Gladstone offered the Northern Nonconformists and Scottish Presbyterian businessmen who were his natural constituents the chance to vote for a specifically moralistic, indeed religious, political programme without having to do anything so disturbing as to dig into their pockets. They could huff and puff about the sanctity of life in the hill villages of Afghanistan without feeling an immediate need for state-funded (i.e. tax-funded) aid to the poverty-stricken families of the big British cities.

Disraeli captured the essence and nature of Gladstone's character and appeal in his last, unfinished novel, *Falconet*. Joseph Toplady Falconet is a young prig who is adopted as a parliamentary candidate for a pocket borough belonging to Lord Bertram – a composite portrait of Palmerston and, possibly, of Disraeli himself. It seems an unlikely combination, it is true, but there is a hint of it in one of the quips for which the fragment is famous. The young Gladstone–Falconet devotes his election address to a fervent speech on the revival of the slave trade in the Red Sea. 'True it was,' remarks the narrator, 'that it subsequently appeared that there had been no revival of the slave trade in the Red Sea, but that the misapprehension had occurred from a mistake in the telegraph, manipulated by a functionary suffering from *coup de soleil* or *delirium tremens*.' But then the Earl advises his young protégé, 'I think I would leave the Red Sea alone. It was a miracle that saved us being drowned in it before.'[49]

When the fragment was first published in *The Times* in 1905, that newspaper asked:

> Who is the noble Earl . . . to whose interest the young Falconet owed his first seat in Parliament, and who advised him to 'leave the Red Sea alone?' . . . Might he have proved to be one of the chosen people; of whom alone this statement is historically true? Is it conceivable that the author intended to treat the world not only to a portrait of his great rival, but also to an idealized picture of his own career and personality as well?[50]

We shall never know. He died – in a house he had acquired since leaving office – in Curzon Street on 19 April 1881, aged seventy-five. The grief-stricken Queen ('The loss is so *overwhelming*')[50] was in favour of a public funeral and burial in the Abbey: but Disraeli's will was specific:

> I DESIRE and DIRECT that I may be buried in the same vault in the Churchyard of Hughenden in which the remains of my late dear Wife

Mary Anne Disraeli created in her own right Viscountess
Beaconsfield were placed and that my Funeral may be conducted
with the same simplicity as hers was.

There is an obvious sincerity and quiet dignity in this which seems to
suggest that with all his love of show, and all his overweening political
ambition, Disraeli was with a large part of himself a detached observer
of the public scene. Archbishop Tait had been appalled by Disraeli's
last completed novel *Endymion*. He read it 'with a painful feeling that
the writer considers all political life as mere play and gambling'. Those
who admire, indeed love, Disraeli find the hint of this spilling into his
political performance highly sympathetic. (The hint only – most of the
time he was in deadly earnest about his political aims just as,
effortlessly witty and eloquent as he always was, there was nothing
frivolous about his manner of public speaking – no *smiles*, let alone
giggles.) When the time came for election defeat, though, he took the
news with immense dignity. He did not go off in a huff, as Gladstone
had done in 1874, ostentatiously retiring from politics. He remained
Lord Beaconsfield, leader of the Conservative Party, and made regular
visits to the Lords. But the novels, and the instructions for a private
funeral, bespeak an admirable detachment. This was incomprehensible
to Gladstone. 'As he lived, so he died – all display and no genuineness,'
wrote Gladstone in his diary when he heard of Disraeli's wish to be
buried quietly with his wife. He assumed that there could be no other
explanation for the behaviour of a politician other than to draw
attention to himself. The malice of Gladstone's comment tells us more
about himself than about Disraeli who, as Lord Blake says, 'had a rare
detachment, an extraordinary ability to survey the scene from outside
and to wonder what it was all about'.[52]

He was a unique being – one of the very few English prime ministers
who could be described as a lovable human being, and one of the few
with any claim to be thought of as a writer. Disraeli has a greater claim
than that. He is a singular novelistic wit, only now perhaps, after an
interval, being appreciated again. It is hard to think of many other
Victorian novelists being a safe pair of hands as prime minister for so
much as a week, let alone stage-managing the Congress of Berlin. An
England with Dickens at the Dispatch Box might have been funny;
Charlotte Brontë might have managed Irish Famine Relief more
mercifully than Lord John Russell. Thackeray and Trollope of course
both stood unsuccessfully as (Liberal) parliamentary candidates. It is

hard to imagine any of them staying the course. George Eliot (assuming a change in the law to allow women MPs) is the only Victorian novelist one can imagine having the gravitas or staying power, but only on condition that she were merely placed in office, like one of the Platonic Guardians. One can't see her loving, as Dizzy did, all the intrigue and calculation of the political life.

George Eliot, as it happens, was one of those who saw the great merits of Disraeli. During the public debates about Bulgaria in 1879 she was vehemently pro-Disraeli and anti-Gladstone. Dizzy was ambitious, she argued, and no fool, 'so he must care for a place in history, and how could he expect to win that by doing harm?' She was 'disgusted with the venom of the Liberal speeches from Gladstone downwards'.[53]

She would also, as one who in *Daniel Deronda* (1876) had written so intelligently and sympathetically about the Jews, have seen the importance for England of having so brilliant a prime minister of Jewish birth and parentage. (She was an accomplished amateur Hebraist as well as philosemite.)[54] When the question first arose in 1848 of whether to admit Jews to Parliament, Lord George Bentinck wrote to Lord John Manners, 'This Jewish question is a terrible annoyance. I never saw anything like the prejudice which exists against them.' Disraeli was brave enough to vote against his party over the question, consistently siding with the Liberals and bravely scandalizing the House by suggesting, in effect, that Judaism was a religion with at least as good a pedigree as Christianity. The Jews were admitted in 1858. It was in no small measure owing to Disraeli. His own career (baptized Anglican though he was) exemplified the willingness of the English political class to make a sensible compromise. Seeing his qualities, the Tory grandees were quite happy to convert Disraeli into a Conservative country gentleman and to treat him accordingly. But though his father had left the synagogue – on the grounds of insufficient belief and a wish to assimilate his children into Anglican culture – Disraeli was always loyal to his roots. His career, ambivalent and exotic, utterly sui generis, was among other things a signal that although anti-semitism existed in England, it was something from a *political* viewpoint above which the British determinedly and deliberately rose.

26

The Devils – Wagner – Dostoyevsky – Gilbert and Sullivan

With money came time; with time, leisure, even for those classes who in former ages toiled and struggled all week long. The professional and commercial classes were the first to obtain a Saturday half holiday. By the 1850s, the textile mills in the North tended to close at 2 p.m. on Saturday. (Wordsells, the Birmingham engineering works, seems to have been the first factory to give its workers Saturday afternoon off – in 1853.) The combination of time, leisure and money led to the increase of leisured activity, and the invention of popular pastimes to fill the newfound vacant hours. There was an enormous growth in the popularity of the turf – with 62 new racing events added to the calendar in the 1850s, 99 in the 1860s, 54 in the 1870s. The growth of railways, combined with the growth of free time, made this possible.[1]

Football, whose rules became formalized by 1859, became the British national game, linking undergraduates and public schoolboys to the chapels and trade unions and working men's associations who formed many of the early clubs. The Football Association began in 1863. Thirty clubs had joined by 1868, this largely southern phenomenon echoed by a northern equivalent in Sheffield.[2] A Birmingham FA was formed in 1875, and a Lancashire one in 1878. Aston Villa Wesleyan Chapel was typical as an example of the religious origin of many of these clubs, as was Christ Church, Bolton, which became Bolton Wanderers in 1877.[3] There was big money to be made by those with the wit to build stadia, charge at the turnstiles and to link home and away matches by arrangement with the railway companies. Bramhall Lane, Sheffield, was drawing crowds of 10,000 by the late 1870s.[4] (It was also used for cricket matches.) Very many clubs could draw crowds of seven or eight hundred, and more than thirty clubs in this decade could draw two to five thousand on a Saturday.[5]

For those with a taste for crowds of a different kind, shopping had become an activity in itself, not just a means of acquiring goods and groceries. William Whiteley started as a draper's assistant in Wakefield, and first came to London to see the Great Exhibition in 1851. He started his own haberdashery; by 1867 he was selling silks, linens, drapery, costume jewellery, furs, umbrellas, artificial flowers. The 1870s were the great era of his expansion, with his huge emporium in Westbourne Grove catering for that expanding part of London. His assistant John Barker asked to be taken into a partnership. Whiteley instead offered Barker £1,000 per annum – an enormous sum for a drapery employee. Barker refused, setting up on his own in Kensington High Street with prodigious success. These big stores, still in existence though differently owned and managed, owed much of their success to being on the doorstep of newish suburbs. Many other big shops cashed in on this principle, some such as James Marshall (of Marshall and Snelgrove) and William Edgar (founder of Swan and Edgar) moving in to the centre of London having made fortunes in the suburbs. The vast Marshall and Snelgrove building on the corner of Oxford Street and Vere Street replaced an attractive row of miscellaneous Georgian houses and shops in 1879. It is built in a pseudo-Parisian manner, trying to suggest that the middle-class clientele who went there to sample the newfangled ready-made costumes were as sophisticated as their richer sisters who patronized the great houses of the French capital.[6]

If shopping and games and race-meetings flourished with the arrival of ready-made leisure, so too did the arts. The 1870s witnessed a remarkable musical revival in Britain, with a flowering of concerts and operas. This in turn led to the founding of the Guildhall School of Music in 1880 and the Royal College of Music in 1883, with Hubert Parry and Charles Villiers Stanford as professors.

Parry (1848–1918) and Stanford (1852–1924) are the best British composers to appear before Elgar (1857–1934). It seems unfair to them to draw attention to the fact that while they were writing their apprentice-work, Verdi (1813–1901) was writing *Don Carlos* (1867), or Brahms (1833–97) his *German Requiem* (1868) and his four symphonies in 1876, 1877, 1883 and 1885 – works which were contemporary with Tchaikovsky's *Evgeny Onegin* (1879) and the Hungarian Rhapsodies (1846–85) of the Abbé Liszt. One cannot blame the few heroic souls who kept orchestral and choral music alive in Britain for the general philistinism of churches, colleges and schools which led to the near-death of music in Britain in the generations after the Industrial Revolution. *Daniel Deronda*, that wonderful novel, captures among many other nuances of life in the 1870s the essentially philistine attitude of the Victorian upper class to music. They thought of it as a diversion, no more. When Gwendolen thinks she can earn her living as a singer, the composer/conductor Klesner is forced to confront her with the unwelcome truth. 'You have exercised your talents – you recite – you sing – from the drawing-room *standpunkt*. My dear Fräulein, you must unlearn all that. You have not yet conceived what excellence is.'[7]

Parry and George Eliot both played their part in the visit of the most distinguished musical visitor to London in the 1870s. Of all the unlikely customers in Whiteley's new department store in Bayswater, few could have been more incongruous among the genteel suburban folk than Richard Wagner, who went there in May 1877 with Chariclea Dannreuther. She helped him choose frocks for his daughters and he bought a rocking-horse for his sons which he called Grane, after Brünnhilde's horse in *The Ring*. Edward Danreuther was an American-born German living in London; he was a virtuoso pianist who introduced English audiences to Grieg, Liszt and Tchaikovsky and hosted the London Wagner Festival.

Wagner's visits to London were made when he was strapped for cash. In 1855, concert versions of his early and more accessible operas had good receptions, though he can't always have been pleased by the manner in which this praise was expressed. The author of the 1850 polemic *Das Judentum in der Musik* (Judaism in Music) was depressed by the English fondness for Meyerbeer and Mendelssohn. So when the leading music critic of the day, George Hogarth, still going strong at seventy-three – he lived until eighty-seven – thought to pay Wagner a compliment, he said that a concert rendition of 'highlights' from *Lohengrin*, 'with scenic action and adjuncts of the opera house . . . would be as effective as the music of Meyerbeer himself'.

Wagner left twenty-two years before visiting London again. By then his tempestuous artistic and personal career had stamped itself on the European imagination. His revolutionary status, and his uncompromising consciousness of his own genius, received the predictable philistine mockery from *Punch* – 'Having been a considerable time accustomed to play the trilogy [*sic*: i.e. the Ring cycle] with one finger on the accordion, I was naturally anxious to hear the same work of art performed by a band of two hundred, at the Albert Hall' etc. etc. *The Daily Telegraph*, being edited by a Jew, could hardly take kindly to Wagner the man. 'In the midst of whatever honours are paid to Herr Wagner – and the deserts of his genius are great – there should be no false sentiment about the master's personality.' Dannreuther, whose wife took Wagner to Whiteley's to buy the rocking-horse, accompanied the great man to the grill room at the South Kensington museum.

> There, over a chop and a pint of Bass's ale, he began to pour out story after story . . . about German Jews, told in their peculiar jargon. A young foreigner, a painter apparently, had taken his seat at a table opposite, and was quietly watching and listening. Soon, his face began to twitch – I could see that he was making efforts to look serene. But the twitches increased – and when one of the stories came to the final point he snatched up his hat and vanished.[8]

Francis Hueffer, the music critic, overheard George Eliot remarking to Cosima Wagner, with that straightforwardness which was so conspicuous and so lovable in her character, 'Your husband does not like Jews; my husband is a Jew.' (It was said as a tease – Lewes was not in fact Jewish.) Neither Lewes nor George Eliot herself appear to have been remotely put out by Wagner's anti-semitism. They saw the Wagners at least a dozen times during the course of that month-long visit, more than once for suppers à six with the Dannreuthers, and evidently got on very well with both Cosima and Richard Wagner.[9] The Prince of Wales, famously philosemitic, attended the concerts, and the Wagners were received at court – at Windsor – by Queen Victoria. The concerts conducted by Wagner himself were conspicuously less successful than those under the baton of his great interpreter Hans Richter. Wagner's beat was completely lost during an extract from *Tannhäuser*, and when Richter resumed the podium the audience greeted him 'almost uproariously'.

Richter's English was no better than Wagner's, however, and this led to some confusing social exchanges. He and his wife were invited to dine with the Beales, but Richter turned up alone. On being asked why Madame had not come too, he answered, 'She is lying; when she does not lie, she schwindles' – his hosts, unaware that '*schwindlen*' in German means to faint, were duly baffled.[10]

Wagner's music, said Lewes, 'remains a language we do not understand'.[11] Cosima Wagner was as baffled by the harmonious, quiet, civilized relationship between Lewes and the great novelist with whom he shared his life. '*Ils nagent dans une mer de calme perpetuel*,' she told someone, '*mais nous savons très bien qu'il y a tout autant de requins et de choses pernicieuses dans une mer calme que dans une mer orageuse.*' (They swim in a sea of perpetual calm, but we know very well that there are as many sharks and harmful things in a calm sea as in a stormy sea.)

This is certainly a misreading of Lewes's 'marriage' with his Polly – i.e. George Eliot. But how does it work as a survey of the contemporary scene? Going down the Thames by steamer, and passing the docklands where Father Wainwright toiled among the Wapping poor, the Wagners found that 'the industrial landscape made a tremendous impression'. Wagner said, 'This is Alberich's dream come true – Nibelheim, world dominion, activity, work, everywhere the oppressive feeling of steam and fog.' In the very same year, Henry James made the same journey and noted:

> like so many aspects of English civilisation that are untouched by elegance or grace, it has the merit of expressing something very serious. Viewed in this intellectual light, the polluted river, the sprawling barges, the dead-faced warehouses, the frowsy people, the atmospheric impurities become richly suggestive. It sounds rather absurd, but all this smudgy detail may remind you of nothing less than the wealth and power of the British Empire at large; so that a kind of metaphysical magnificence hovers over the scene.[12]

One of the most disturbing novels of the 1870s was Trollope's *The Way We Live Now* – disturbing because genial, comic Anthony Trollope, who had so consistently amused his public with tales of country-house gossip and cathedral-feuds, chose to depict an England entirely vulgarized, sold to Mammon, dominated by money-worship. His swindling financier Augustus Melmotte, whose high reputation is based completely on corruption and fraud, is a perennial figure in English life. There is always, at any one time, an Augustus Melmotte in London, idolized by politicians, fawned upon by society, until his exposure, when all those who have been happy to enjoy his largesse howl at his dishonesty. Melmotte (like Dickens's Mr Merdle, a comparable figure) commits suicide. Professor Polhemus, an American scholar quoted by Trollope's biographer James Pope-Hennessy, makes the point that Trollope saw the same truth as Marx and Engels – 'a world where there is no other bond between man and man but crude self-interest and callous cash-payment', a world that 'has degraded personal dignity to the level of exchange-value', creating 'exploitation that is open, unashamed, direct and brutal'. Professor Polhemus points out that, while Karl Marx was an optimist, Trollope's later years were suffused with pessimism and gloom.[13]

The Way We Live Now was published the year before the opening of the Bayreuth Festival Playhouse and the first complete performance of Wagner's *Ring*.[14] As Bernard Shaw reminded 'The Perfect Wagnerite' in 1898, 'the Ring, with all its gods and giants and dwarfs, its water-maidens and Valkyries, its wishing-cap, magic ring, enchanted sword, and miraculous treasure is a drama of today, and not of a remote and fabulous antiquity. It could not have been written before the second half of the nineteenth century, because it deals with events which were only then consummating themselves.'[15]

Shaw rightly saw Alberich the dwarf, amassing power through his possession of the ring, and forcing the Nibelungs to mine his gold, as the type of capitalism. 'You can see the process for yourself in every civilized country today, where millions of people toil in want and disease to heap up more wealth for our Alberichs, laying up nothing for themselves, except sometimes agonizing disease and the certainty of premature death.'[16]

Shaw saw *The Ring* as an allegory which ultimately failed. Wagner had first sketched 'the Night Falls on the Gods' when he was thirty-five. 'When he finished the score for the first Bayreuth festival in 1876 he had turned 60. No wonder he had lost his old grip and left it behind him.' Others have suggested, however – to my mind more plausibly – that what the conclusion of *Götterdämmerung* implies is a transcendence of politics. 'The message of *Götterdämmerung* was that if heroes fall short . . . they fail and with them all their achievements; their whole world passes, while nature prepares another renewal of the life-force.' It is indeed surprising that Shaw with his quite preternaturally acute musical ear was so deaf to the beautiful resolution of the Cycle – 'Nature, the Rhine rises to take again the ring from the finger of the dead hero, whence no lesser power could wrest it. Peace comes through nature . . .'[17]

It is strange that William Morris, who had published a verse adaptation of the Nordic myths, *Sigurd the Volsung* (1876), should have so mistaken the nature of Wagner's purpose. He met the composer, holding out a hand to him which was bright blue – he was experimenting with dyes at this period. But he thought the *Ring* was a 'pantomime' version of the *Niberlungenlied*. 'It is nothing short of desecration to bring such a tremendous and world-wide subject under the gaslights of an opera: the most rococo and degraded of all forms of art – the idea of a sandy-haired German tenor tweedledeeing over the unspeakable woes of Sigurd, which even the simplest words are not typical enough to express!'

Fiona MacCarthy, Morris's best biographer, says that 'in his notorious belittlings of Wagner, Morris appears at his most pig-headed and parochial',[18] which is true; but she could have added 'most ignorant'. It is obvious that a man who imagined that Wagner's operas involved 'tweedledeeing' had not heard a single chord of the composer's work. It would have been interesting to take Morris to Bayreuth and hear his reaction if he had actually sat through *The Ring*: he might have been converted.

No allegory of any work is exhausted by drawing too punctilious a match between symbol and signified. The audience to Wagner's musical drama is caught up in an experience which is profound in itself, and to say Alberich = the Big Capitalist or that the befriending of Alberich by Loki and Wotan = the Church and the Law embracing the power of capital is too narrow and too specific an account of what stands as a universal work of art. Shaw was right, however, to say that Wagner's masterpiece was rooted in its time.[19] What is suggested in the final opera in the cycle is a universal collapse – the Gods themselves hurtling towards self-destruction. As the 'storm-clouds of the nineteenth century' – John Ruskin's phrase – gather, we sense impending disaster in many of the great artworks of the period.

Fyodor Mikhailovich Dostoyevsky died a couple of months before Disraeli. His vision of the human condition was as disturbed, as dark, as demonic as Wagner's. Those who read *Besy* (*The Devils*), his novel of 1871–2, might, when it first appeared, have thought it was merely a farce about a group of liberals in a provincial town being taken over by a manipulative lunatic, a nihilist. To us, reading it 130 years after it was published, *The Devils* is still as funny as the day it was written, but it is also uncannily prophetic. This is, in very truth, what is about to happen to Russia. Just thirty-six years after the death of Dostoyevsky the mighty Russian Empire will fall into the hands of a psychopath and his group of destructive followers.

Dostoyevsky was haunted, as are the musical dramas of Wagner, by the Death of God, the ultimate moral and imaginative calamity for the human race. He believed it was possible to undo the knowledge of this horrible fact by falling at the feet of Jesus and by accepting Russian Orthodoxy. The Russian People, the God-bearing people, might yet save the world by their loyalty to this mystic Christ.

It is strange to think of this great genius pacing the streets of London on his one visit there, in 1862. Like many visitors to Victorian England

– both contemporary visitors from abroad and time-travellers who write about the period – Dostoyevsky was forcibly impressed by the sheer numbers of prostitutes swarming in the Haymarket. 'Here there are old women, here there are beauties at the sight of which you stop in amazement. In the whole world, there is no more beautiful female type than the Englishwoman . . .'[20]

So one could believe if looking at the canvases of Dante Gabriel Rossetti. In a casino he sees a girl and 'I stopped, simply thunderstruck; I have never seen anywhere anything like that ideal beauty. She also seemed very sad.' What Dostoyevsky saw in the faces of Londoners were those 'marks of woe' which William Blake had seen as their hallmark. The 'white negroes' as he called the British working classes, the toilers in the East End of London who 'seek salvation in gin and debauchery', fill him with gloom.

> What you see here is no longer even a people, but a systematic, resigned loss of consciousness that is actually encouraged. And looking at all these pariahs of society, you feel that it will be a long time before the prophecy is fulfilled for them, before they are given palms and clothed with white robes, and that they will long continue their appeal to the throne of the Almighty: How long, O Lord?

Dostoyevsky's solutions, in so far as they were thought through, to the malaise of modern European life could hardly have been more different from that of the communists, but many have noted the similarity between his observations on the English poor in 1862 and those of Engels in 1844.

By the time of Dostoyevsky's death in 1881, nearly forty years had passed since Engels reported on the condition of the working class in England. And England, and the world, had changed quite enormously. America had torn itself apart in a great civil war, with huge loss of life, and the president most associated with the release of the slaves had been assassinated. An assassin, too, murdered the tsar of Russia who liberated the serfs.

There had been several unsuccessful attempts to kill Alexander. On 1 March 1881 a bomb was thrown at his carriage on his return from a military parade, and this seemed like another failed assassination. The emperor got out of his carriage and was standing in the street making inquiries when a second bomb was thrown, which mortally wounded him. This liberal and gentle man was sixty-three years old.[21]

The murder sent reverberations far beyond the Russian borders. The anarchy predicted by Dostoyevsky seemed all too likely to be about to be loosed upon the world. 'Man cannot possibly exist without his former God' – this is the view thrown out by the anarchist Kirillov in *The Devils*, during one of the most dramatic scenes in the whole of fiction.

The malaise of the late nineteenth century was not primarily a political or an economic one, though subsequent historians might choose to interpret it thus. Men and women looked at the world which Western capitalism had brought to pass since Queen Victoria had been on the throne – over forty years now! – and they sensed that something had gone hideously awry. Dostoyevsky is – like so many geniuses – capable of holding contrarieties of view in his head, which is why his vision is so interesting. With a part of himself he was a completely modern, progressive thinker, who for example gave a favourable review to G.H. Lewes's *The Physiology of Common Life*, who had read Darwin, or reviews of Darwin, and dipped into J.S. Mill, both the political thought and the system of logic.[22] On the other hand, as he did so, he felt things falling apart, the centre not holding. Ruskin and Carlyle were writing about a similar phenomenon. So too was the wholly secular Trollope in *The Way We Live Now* who 'says nothing about the gross disparity between rich and poor',[23] concentrating merely on the vanity, the sheer pointlessness of the lives of the rich.

Gladstone bellowing on the windswept moorlands of Midlothian; Wagner in the new-built Bayreuth Festival Theatre watching the citadel of the Gods go down in flames; world-weary Trollope scribbling himself to death in the London clubs; Dostoyevsky coughing blood, and thrusting, as he did, his New Testament into the hands of his son[24] – these could hardly be more different individuals. Yet they all at roughly the same moment in history were seized with comparable misgiving. It is like one of these disconcerting moments in a crowd of chattering strangers when a silence suddenly falls; or when a sudden chill, spiritual more than atmospheric, causes an individual to shiver and to exclaim 'I feel as if a man has just walked over my grave.'

His London concerts complete, Wagner had returned to Germany long before November 1877, when the curtain went up at the Opera Comique Theatre, just off the Strand, which had been leased by the theatrical impresario, Richard D'Oyly Carte. The German musical dramatist was therefore not in a position to see the Gilbert and Sullivan opera, *The Sorcerer*.[25]

The first hit,* *Trial by Jury*, had played at the Royalty Theatre from 25 March to 18 December 1875 with prodigious success. 'It seems, as in the great Wagnerian operas, as though poem and music had proceeded simultaneously from one and the same brain' – as *The Times* critic put it. The music was sublime. The play absurd. Yet in a bizarre way, it was a recognizable picture of the audience's actual world. Those who saw the operas as they first appeared went out into the street with words and music in their heads which – love them or loathe them – are ineradicable. But more than that, for the fans, of whom there are millions to this day, the world itself is transformed by the Gilbert and Sullivan experience.

There is a pathos, not to say tragi-comedy, about the fact that the operas did, and do, indeed seem as if they had proceeded simultaneously from one and the same brain. Arthur Sullivan (1842–1900), the son of a sergeant bandmaster from the Royal Military College, Sandhurst (formerly a clarinettist and music teacher), rose through the route of choirboy at the Chapel Royal and star pupil at the Royal Academy of Music to being a serious aspirant musician and composer. He had studied at Leipzig, and if it had not been for his frivolous association with Richard D'Oyly Carte and William Schwenck Gilbert (1836–1911) he might have had an illustrious career as a minor nineteenth-century musician, known only to the devotees of kitsch as the composer of 'The Lost Chord' – one of the most popular of all English songs – and to churchgoers as the composer of the most rousing tune to 'Onward Christian Soldiers' ('St Gertrude', 1871).[27] As it was, this dignified biography was denied him. He was fated to be prodigiously rich and famous – and to be 'and Sullivan' for as long as the English language endures.

Gilbert, a failed barrister with a grotesque penchant for rather cruel burlesque, was a most unlikely collaborator for Sullivan. For parallels you have to imagine what it might have been like had Mendelssohn gone into partnership with Dickens.

The defendant in *Trial by Jury* is accused of that hoary old Victorian joke, Breach of Promise. It enables Gilbert to indulge in two of his great stand-bys, mockery of the outward forms of English law – judges in their wigs, juries vacillating in their opinions: these are naturally comic – and the ageing process in women. There is hardly an opera in which

*There had been a flop in 1871 with an imitation of Offenbach entitled *Thespis, or The Gods Grown Old*.[26]

the joke does not resurface. In *Trial by Jury* the Judge himself recalls his days of impecunosity as a young barrister:

> But I soon got tired of third-class journeys,
> And dinners of bread and water;
> So I fell in love with a rich attorney's
> Elderly ugly daughter.

The attorney, delighted to get the daughter off his hands, is able to assure the judge:

> 'You'll soon get used to her looks,' said he
> 'And a very nice girl you will find her!
> 'She may very well pass for forty-three
> 'In the dusk with the light behind her!'[28]

Versions of this joke, which to modern taste seems merely cruel, run through the entire Gilbertian oeuvre, from Ko-Ko's

> I've got to take under my wing,
> Tra la,
> A most unattractive old thing,
> Tra la,
> With a caricature of a face[29]

in *The Mikado* (1885) to Jane's song in *Patience* (1881):

> Fading is the taper waist,
> Shapeless grows the shapely limb,
> And although severely laced,
> Spreading is the figure trim!
> Stouter than I used to be,
> Still more corpulent grow I –
> There will be too much of me
> In the coming by and by!

Sullivan's harmonious and beautiful settings of these words make them seem all the more outrageous.

But however much a modern prude might abhor Gilbert, or a musical snob be foolish enough to despise Sullivan, they are essential objects of study if we want to catch the flavour of the late Victorian world. 'Mere entertainment' is all they are; but they share with great art the capacity to make us see their world in a particular way.

Now, as the example of Gilbert's ungallantry about women makes clear, this is not a way of viewing the world of which we would necessarily approve. I could imagine a Marxist critique of *The Savoy Operas* – as the works came to be known when D'Oyly Carte built the Savoy Theatre in 1881 on the south side of the Strand (the first theatre in Britain to be lit by electric light). Perhaps the Marxist might argue that the audiences who streamed into that brightly lit world, who were beguiled by Sullivan's tunes and who laughed at Gilbert's burlesques and puns, were being numbed with a real opiate, something much more potent than religion. The institutions of the Law, Parliament, the Armed Forces, the Class System are all held up to ridicule in *The Savoy Operas*: but it is an essentially undisturbing ridicule, on the whole inspiring affection not loathing for its objects. No one coming out of *Trial by Jury* – which represents the judiciary as ludicrous and corrupt – stands on the pavement wanting the destruction, or even the overhaul, of the legal system. In fact the opposite.

> JUDGE   Though homeward as you trudge,
> You declare my law a fudge,
> Yet of beauty I'm a judge
>
> ALL   And a good Judge too![30]

No one comes out of *The Sorcerer* wanting to overthrow the Church.

> Now for the tea of our host –
> Now for the rollicking bun –
> Now for the muffin and toast –
> And now for the gay Sally Lunn![31]

as Dr Daly – the only clergyman in the canon – sings in happy chorus. There is no danger here, no real satire – only suburban reassurances. Anyone – my fictitious Marxist would argue – who has been 'brought up' on Gilbert and Sullivan expects England to be absurd, corrupt and badly organized – but instead of this making us wish to reform the system, purge it from top to bottom, it induces affection for the most moribund and unjustifiable abuses.

> And while the House of Peers withholds
> Its legislative hand,
> And noble statesmen do not itch
> To interfere with matters which
> They do not understand,
> As bright will shine Great Britain's rays
> As in King George's glorious days![32]

This obvious burlesque was in fact the political creed of the huge majority of the Liberal and Tory first audiences for *Iolanthe* in 1882.

This was one of the great eras of education for women, with the foundation of colleges of higher education for them. The prospectus for 'Vassar Female College' – Poughkeepsie, NY – was published in 1865, 'to accomplish for young women what our colleges are accomplishing for young men'.[33] British equivalents included the opening of the London Medical School for Women in 1875, against tremendous opposition; the foundation of the Royal Holloway College in Egham, Surrey, in 1879; and the admission of women to Oxford and Cambridge. Newnham College became part of Cambridge University in 1871, though women had to take separate exams, and were not considered capable of studying Latin and Greek. In 1880 the British-American Charlotte Scott (1858–1931) studied at Girton College, Cambridge, and was allowed to take the same mathematics examination as the men. She came eighth, which, had she been of a different gender, would have allowed her the title 'eighth wrangler'. Since women were not allowed degrees, she was not allowed. When the name of the eighth *male* wrangler was read out in the Senate House, a party of doughty feminists chanted, 'Scott of Girton! Scott of Girton!'[34]

It is hard to recall these things without being moved. For Gilbert and Sullivan fans of course the very notion of females in higher education is inherently ludicrous, as their version of Tennyson's *The Princess* – *Princess Ida* (1884) – confirms.

> In Mathematics, Woman leads the way:
> The narrow-minded pedant still believes
> That two and two make four! Why, we can prove,
> We women, household drudges as we are –
> That two and two make five – or three or seven;
> Or five-and-twenty, if the case demands![35]

The downside of Gilbert and Sullivan mania – as an expression of the English character and attitude to life generally – is that it can make large sections of the populace who ought to think a bit harder snigger instead. There is no doubt that the progress of feminism – both the education of women and the extension of the franchise – was held back by decades simply because so many people, women as well as men, could dismiss it as a joke.

And, in England, events did so attempt to force themselves into Gilbertian, farcical mode. What could be more satisfying to the philistine public than the legal spat between James McNeill Whistler, American aesthete, painter and author of *The Gentle Art of Making Enemies* (1890), and John Ruskin, who by 1877 was beginning to exhibit symptoms of the insanity which would at length enclose forever that lovable and wonderful prophet? Ruskin went to the Grosvenor Gallery to see the Whistlers on show there, and in the next instalment of his highly distinctive *Fors Clavigera*, a sort of open letter to the labouring classes and others – a stream of consciousness which contains some of his finest writing – he was to observe fatefully, 'I have seen, and heard, much of Cockney impudence before now; but never expected to hear a coxcomb ask two hundred guineas for flinging a pot of paint in the public's face.' Whistler sued. The trial was heard by Sir John Huddleston, famous for 'the tiniest feet, the best kept hands and the most popular wife in London'[36] (i.e. Lady Diana Beauclerk, daughter of the Duke of St Albans). The trial was a farce. Poor Burne-Jones was asked as a witness on Ruskin's behalf and lost Whistler's friendship. The jury found Ruskin guilty of libel and awarded Whistler a farthing's damages. W.S. Gilbert on a particularly whimsical day could not have dreamed up anything more absurd. But the opera about the aesthetes, *Patience* – which in an earlier draft was to have been a spoof of the Ritualist clergy – has about it that whiff of cruel satire which in England has the occasional tendency to turn into mere bullyism. In 1881 they were laughing at an aesthete who walks down Piccadilly with a poppy or a lily in his medieval hand, and has 'an attachment à la Plato for a bashful young potato, or a not-too-French French bean'. Fourteen years later, the spectator-sports were the Wilde trials.

Likewise, in the most popular of the Savoy Operas, *H.M.S. Pinafore* (1878), it would be a po-faced member of the audience who had not laughed at the 'ruler of the Queen's Navee', Sir Joseph Porter KCB, First Lord of the Admiralty.

SIR JOSEPH Now landsmen all, whoever you may be,
      If you want to rise to the top of the tree,
      If your soul isn't fettered to an office stool,
      Be careful to be guided by this golden rule –
      Stick close to your desks and never go to sea,
      And you all may be Rulers of the Queen's Navee![37]

Any observer of the English scene over the last two hundred years knows that this is archetypical – that the political history of Britain is one of chancellors of the Exchequer who know nothing about money, education ministers who can't spell, bishops with little or no religious faith. The original audiences for *Pinafore* would have roared their recognition at the first lord of the Admiralty played by George Grossmith, who had made so many of the 'patter songs' his own. For here *was* Disraeli's first lord of the Admiralty in person, that landlubber son of the Methodist chain of newsagents, W.H. Smith. In fact, this Wesleyan grammar-school boy of philanthropic mien who had probably never stepped aboard a paddle-steamer, let alone a battleship, was destined, first as first lord of the Admiralty, then – in Lord Salisbury's second administration – as secretary of state for war, to oversee an extraordinary transformation in British naval policy.

HMS *Devastation*, 285 feet long by 62 feet, was built in 1873, four years before Smith became first lord. It has been described as 'a floating armoured castle, invulnerable to any foreign guns'.[38] The name alone sends a chill into the spine. Throughout the late Seventies and early Eighties – the time of Disraeli's last, Gladstone's second, governments – there was agitation by the jingoists for an ever-bigger and more devastating navy. Both Smith as a Tory, Gladstone as an old Peelite, were more anxious by instinct to save money than to increase military or naval expenditure. But events, and the large political fact that Britain had an economy which was bound up with an ever-expanding empire, made so judicious a hold on the purse-strings only a partial possibility. During the war scare of 1878–9 Smith was obliged to think of a greatly expanded navy. And in 1884, when Gladstone was in power, a series of scaremongering articles by W.T. Stead – 'The Truth About the Navy by One Who Knows the Facts' – jumped the government into programmes of rearmament. A supplementary vote of £5,525,000 was given by the Exchequer in 1885 – '£3,100,000 of it to be devoted to building one ironclad, five protected cruisers, ten protected scout vehicles and thirty torpedo boats'.[39]

Since no weapon or ship in the history of warfare has been invented without being used, these belligerent developments could only lead to the inevitable *Götterdämmerung* of war – not in the lifetime of W.H. Smith, but in the lifetime of many who attended the first night of *Pinafore*. Only a lunatic would blame Gilbert and Sullivan for the build-up of armaments and the sparring of the Great Powers. But it is fair to observe that a culture which threw up, and feasted upon, *H.M.S. Pinafore* (and the operas of Gilbert and Sullivan are effectively the *only* memorable music produced by the English in the 1870s and 1880s) was also the culture that failed to ask itself any serious questions about the desirability of a country which was still *au fond* a small trading island – albeit a prodigiously rich and energetic one – playing the role of world-dominator, superpower and 'Empire'. Its lifetime of so doing was short and on the whole disastrous; which is why, though Gilbert and Sullivan can still delight us with their zany jokes and whistleable tunes, the operas themselves in the context of their times seem like Neronic fiddling against a fiery sky.

27

Country Parishes – Kilvert – Barnes – Hardy

It is difficult for me to conceive of any more agreeable way of life than that of the Victorian country parson. If I had to choose my ideal span of life, I should choose to have been born in the 1830s, the son of a parson with the genetic inheritance of strong teeth. (Improvements in dentistry are surely among the few unambiguous benefits brought to the human race by the twentieth century.) I should avoid a public-school education through being 'delicate', and arrive at Balliol with a good knowledge of Greek to be taught by Benjamin Jowett. (The Tractarians would pass me by, but after my ordination, upon being elected to a fellowship, I should take a bemused and tolerant interest in the Ritualist churches while having no wish to imitate their liturgical customs.) After a short spell – say, five years – teaching undergraduates at the Varsity, one of them would introduce me to his pretty, bookish sister, and we should be married. I should resign my fellowship and be presented with a college living, preferably a medieval church, a large draughty Georgian rectory and glebe enough to provide the family with 'subsistence'. By now it would be, let us say, the 1860s, and I should remain here for the next forty years, a faithful friend to generations of villagers to whom I would act as teacher, amateur doctor and social worker, as well as priest. My wife, cleverer than I, would read French, German and Italian with our innumerable children and be pleased when the daughters entered St Hugh's or Somerville. Whether any of the sons – keen cyclists, antiquarians, butterfly-collectors and botanists all, like their father, all good at Latin and all admirers of William Morris and George Bernard Shaw – would follow me into a clergyman's career is unlikely, for we should all have Doubts, and the children, as they grew up, would be more honest than their father about expressing them. Perhaps as the country parson, approaching fifty by the time of Disraeli's death, I would instinctively feel that I had entered upon a drama which was coming to an end; that the Age of Faith, embodied in the old medieval building where, every day, I read aloud from the Book of Common Prayer, had irrevocably been destroyed – whether by Capitalism, or Darwin, or Railways or Imperialism, or a nebulous Zeitgeist, who could say?

My fantasy-life as a Victorian parson can be lived out when I take down from the shelves the diaries kept by the Reverend Francis Kilvert, curate of Clyro in Radnorshire from 1865 to 1872, from 1872 to 1876 at his father's parish of Langley Burrell in Wiltshire, and vicar of Bredwardine in the Wye Valley of Herefordshire from 1877. He married in 1879, which is probably why the diaries (candid in their aching, unfulfilled heterosexuality) came to an end. (We shall never know. He died five weeks after marrying.) The best entries in the diary are the snapshots, rather than the set pieces – such as this, for May Day, 1871:

> Up early, breakfast at 7 and the dog cart took me to the station for the 8 train. It was a lovely May morning, and the beauty of the river and green meadows, the woods, hills and blossoming orchards were indescribable. At Hereford two women were carrying a Jack in the Green about the High Town. In the next carriage a man was playing a harp and a girl a violin as the train travelled.[1]

Or

> May 29 1876
> Oak-apple day and the children all came to school with breast-knots of oak leaves.[2]

Kilvert has painted England and Wales before they were 'wrecked' by cars, macadamed roads, supermarkets, factory farms, holidays for all – with their attendant holiday-cottages – retirement bungalows, theme parks, science parks, carparks and railway stations called parkway. No wonder the readers of the twenty-first century escape into his pages as into the most delightful fantasy. And yet, the world Kilvert depicts is in fact one of desperate poverty.

> Tuesday, 9 January 1872
> Went to see old Caroline Farmer and read to her the latter part of Luke vii. On my way thither I fell in with a boy in the lane named George Wells. He was going to beg a bit of bread from a woman who lived at the corner of the Common under the Three Firs. He said he did not know the name of the woman but she knew his mother and often gave him a bit of bread when he was hungry. His mother was a cripple and had no parish relief, sold cabbage nets and had nothing

to give him for dinner. Then a very different figure and face came tripping down the lane. Carrie Britton in her bright curls and rosy face with a blue cloak, coming from the town with a loaf of bread from the baker's for her grandmother.[3]

The abolition of the Corn Laws in the 1840s had been for the radical economic liberals the means of bringing about a glorious era of meritocracy and plenty. Cobden, the chief agitator for Corn Law repeal, has his statue in many an English town. Working men's clubs are called the Cobden Club. Meaner terraces of houses in industrial conurbations are named Cobden Crescent and Cobden Terrace. 'The people of this country look to their aristocracy with a deep-rooted prejudice – an hereditary prejudice, I may call it – in their favour; but your power was never got, and you will not keep it by obstructing that progressive spirit which is calculated to knit nations more closely together by commercial intercourse . . .'[4]

Twenty years later, the agricultural poor of Britain were, on the whole, more wretched than ever, though the big landlords continued to own most of the agricultural land. Though land values and rents fell in the course of the century, half the entire country was owned by 4,217 persons in 1873.[5]

In the 1860s Cobden exclaimed, 'If I were five and twenty . . . I would have a League for free trade in Land just as we had a League for free trade in Corn.' He and his economic liberal allies could not see what effects were visited upon the land by treating farming as just another 'industry'.

In 1860 the United States had some 30,800 miles of railway; by 1870 this had reached 53,200 miles and by 1880 some 94,200. It was now possible for the grain-producers in the great prairies to send their grain to market fast and cheaply. Transatlantic steamer-transport also reduced transportation costs. In 1873 the cost of sending a ton of grain from Chicago to Liverpool was £3 7s.; by 1884 it had fallen to £1 4s. – a cheapening equal to 9s. 9d. on every quarter of corn *for water-freight alone.*[6]

Almost every country in Europe responded to this threat by introducing tariffs on imported corn – i.e. by introducing Corn Laws very similar to the ones so enthusiastically abolished by Sir Robert Peel and his Liberal friends in 1846. Russia – itself a big corn exporter now, much of its cheap grain coming into Britain along with the American – slapped on import tariffs, as did France and Germany. Only

427

industrialized Britain and Belgium chose to believe Cobden's discredited dogma that commercial intercourse between nations inevitably spells progress. Wheat – the largest arable product of English farms – fell in price from 56s. 9d. per quarter in 1877 to 46s. 5d. in 1878. By 1885, the British area under wheat had shrunk by a million acres. By the 1880s the British were importing an absurd 65 per cent of their wheat, and nearly a million workers had left the land, most of them by emigration, though others had swarmed into the industrial towns.[7]

In addition to the devastating ravages of capitalism, rural England in late Victorian times suffered a series of terrible natural calamities. In 1865–6 and 1877 outbreaks of cattle plague (rinderpest) and pleuro-pneumonia were so severe that the government had to restrict the movement of cattle and pay compensation to the owners of slaughtered beasts to check the spread of infection.[8] A run of wet seasons from 1878 to 1882 produced an epidemic of liver-rot in sheep in Somerset, north Dorset and the Lincolnshire marshes – 4 million sheep were lost in the period.[9] The floods caused wipe-out for many arable farmers. Foot-and-mouth disease raged, out of control, through British livestock from 1881 to 1883.

Wheat and wool – the two staples of English and Welsh prosperity since the Middle Ages – fell into the hands of overseas markets.[10] One must not exaggerate the agricultural depression of the closing decades of the nineteenth century, nor simplify its causes. Farmers who did stay in business during these bad years managed not merely to survive, but to increase their profits.[11] There was an increase in meat-production, dairy produce and vegetables, and the introduction of machinery improved economic efficiency, so the period saw the grubbing up of many hedges. Wiltshire at this period acquired the bleak leafless look which it retains today.[12]

But – overall – the cost to the rural poor, to the agricultural labourer, was terrible. Life had always been tough for them, but in the glossily wealthy new world of the 1870s onwards, rural poverty must have seemed even bleaker. When the Earl of Yarborough died in 1875, his stock of cigars was sold for £850, and this has been calculated as more than eighteen years' income for the agricultural labourers on his estate.[13] Child labour is an inevitable part of agricultural life for the poor. Lord Shaftesbury's reforms, which began to better the lives of factory children, did little to help those in the country. The Gangs Act of 1869 aimed to remedy the abuses brought on the children by gangmasters, who dragooned their gangs − sometimes as young as six years old, numbering anything from ten to a hundred persons − as itinerant cheap labour, offering stone-picking, weeding, turnip-singling, potato-setting, hoeing. Life in these gangs was brutal. The children were knocked about a lot, the women forced to drug their babies with opium and leave them in the hedgerows while they worked.[14] The new Act laid down that no child could work in such a gang under the age of eight, but this did not stop small farmers who needed cheap or free labour from setting children to work as young as six. One such, named George Edwards − who rose to become a Member of Parliament − recalled that he started work aged six, and was paid 1s. per week.[15] Poor families in the Celtic fringes could live at incredibly low levels of subsistence: crofters in the Highlands of Scotland were living on as little as £8 a year.[16] In the south, where there simply was no work, and where the farms were not broken up into peasant smallholdings, there was no option. The labourers had to leave the land or starve.

Canon Girdlestone, victor of Halberton in north Devon, organized single-handedly the migration of between 400 and 500 men with families over six years from areas where they were trying to survive on as little as 7s. or 8s. a week for a 10½-hour working day to towns, factories or parts of the country which were more prosperous and could afford to pay a living wage. In a letter to *The Times* to publicize their plight this good country parson described how 'almost everything had to be done for them, their luggage addressed, their railway tickets taken, and full plain directions given to the simple travellers written on a piece of paper in a large and legible hand'. Though their destination was Kent or the north of England, they often timorously inquired if they were going 'over water'.[17] By 1881, 92,250 fewer labourers were at work than in 1871.[18]

By 1901, males employed in agriculture in England and Wales had diminished by one third, and British farming which had led the world had been reduced by doctrinaire Free Trade to a state of ruin. Only in the two world wars of the twentieth century, when isolationism and protectionism came about perforce and when governments were forced once again to consider the primary importance of a nation husbanding its own land and feeding its own population, did British agriculture revive. Even so − as recent unhappy decades have shown − this revival was but an 'episode in a general drama of pain'. Short of another world war, or a British political party with the imagination to repeal the repeal of the Corn Laws, the decline will continue. Much as we have praised Disraeli in these pages, one cannot leave this painful subject without pointing out that he rose to prominence, and splintered the Tory Party, by his eloquent defence of the Corn Laws and his attacks upon Sir Robert Peel. When he was prime minister and the men and women whose livelihood depended on wheat were being destroyed by the grain-giants of the American prairies, Disraeli did nothing to help them.

So – my dream of being a country parson during the middle to closing years of the nineteenth century is not a pure idyll. It is shot through with suffering and pain. And yet. How one longs to be *in* that photograph, taken on an autumn day in October 1882 in the garden of the Rectory at Winterborne Carne. The rector, with a shovel hat, black coat and long white beard, is seated in the foreground. He is the Dorset poet William Barnes, surrounded by his women folk and by his son – William Miles Barnes, also a clergyman in a shovel hat with a long beard. One knows this is a world where extreme hardship and poverty are the norm, but in the verses of this old man, written in the dialect of his native Dorset, there is an elegiac note, a regret for a way of life which will never come again:

> An' oft do come a saddened hour
> When there must goo away
> One well-beloved to our heart's core,
> Vor long, perhaps vor aye:
> An' oh! it is a touchèn thing
> The lovèn heart must rue,
> To hear behind his last farewell
> The geäte a-vallen to.[19]

Another Wessex poet, and one who owed much to Barnes, visited the old man, accompanied by Edmund Gosse, in his last illness. They found him lying in bed with a scarlet bed-gown and a 'soft biretta of dark red wool on his head', his beard abundantly covering his breast, 'lying in cardinal scarlet in his white bed'. Thomas Hardy wrote a memorable poem, 'The Last Signal', about his friend's funeral. He set out from his house, Max Gate, a little late just as the elm coffin was being pushed out into the road. Through the gloom of cloud there flashed a sudden ray of yellow sun as it was setting.

Looking hard and harder I knew what it meant –
The sudden shine sent from the livid east scene;
It meant the west mirrored by the coffin of my friend there,
    Turning to the road from his green,

To take his last journey forth – he who in his prime
Trudged so many a time from that gate athwart the land!
Thus a farewell to me he signalled on his grave-way,
    As with a wave of his hand.[20]

Thomas Hardy (1840–1928) is one of those great writers – Carlyle was one, in the late twentieth century Solzhenitsyn was another – who do not merely produce great artworks, but who seem to embody in their life-pilgrimage deep truths about the nature of their own times. None were 'typical' – whatever that may mean – as Scot, Russian or Englishman. All were in fact outsiders. But in their lives and writings they were instinctively attuned to *what was going on* in their society. Dostoyevsky, half-crazy as he was, had this quality where Tolstoy for example, though obsessed by the state of Russia and the world, did not. I'm talking here less of the writers' *views* per se – though these are clearly affected by the phenomenon – and more of the sense of inevitability about what they wrote and what they were. Whereas lesser writers imitate, pose, strike attitudes, these unfailingly truthful men have something in them of Luther's *Hier stehe ich, ich kann nicht anders*. Carlyle and Dostoyevsky with their despondent fury saw through the lie of nineteenth-century Liberalism: Solzhenitsyn saw through the much bigger and much uglier lie of Soviet communism. Hardy in his oblique, gentle, provincial English way had a bigger target in his ever-bright blue countryman's eyes. 'I have been looking for God for 50 years, and I think that if he had existed I should have discovered him.'[21]

It does not matter that many of Hardy's novels have creaking plots, any more than it matters that he can write on occasion with immense clumsiness – tears are 'an access of eye-moisture'; early morning or suspense do not chill a man, they 'cause a sensation of chilliness to pervade his frame'.[22] There is a greatness of scheme, a truthfulness about Hardy which makes his faults seem trivial.

A master mason's son born in an obscure Dorset parish, he knew poverty from birth, both in his own family and that of his neighbour. As a little boy he dipped his toy wooden sword into the blood of a freshly killed pig and danced about the garden crying, 'Free trade or blood!'[23] Like the majority, the Hardys believed that the repeal of the Corn Laws (it happened when Hardy was six) would bring down the mighty from their seats and exalt the humble and meek; but from an early age he had a sense that life was not to be explained politically. This was the little boy who dressed up as the vicar and preached sermons to his cousin and grandmother. By the time the depression in British agriculture had begun to show itself, Hardy was grown up, a trainee architect in London – his Church interest transferred to the stones and glass in which the Almighty was worshipped rather than to the Holy Orders he supposedly instituted. It was while 'restoring' – wrecking, we should say – the church of St Juliot in North Cornwall that Hardy met his first wife, Emma Gifford – the niece of an archdeacon, as he proudly informed readers of *Who's Who*.

His most successful early novel, *Under the Greenwood Tree*, is a Shakespearean comedy about his parents, who met when members of the same church choir: it lovingly evokes the pre-Tractarian Church of England, the world of box pews, wheezing parish clerks, and the music played not by an organ but by string instruments. The many twists of irony in the plot, however, and the whole *tone* of the thing, can leave the reader in no doubt where Hardy stood, even at this early stage of his writing life (the book was published in June 1872).[24] In his notebook for 30 October 1870 Hardy had written, 'Mother's notion, & also mine: that a figure stands in our van with arm uplifted, to knock us back from any permanent prospect we indulge in as profitable.'

In the great novels – *Far From the Madding Crowd, The Return of the Native, The Mayor of Casterbridge, Tess of the d'Urbervilles, Jude the Obscure* – we encounter human beings against whom all the odds are stacked. One reviewer said that *Tess*, the most popular of all Hardy's works, 'except during a few hours spent with cows, has not a gleam of sunshine anywhere'.[25] *Jude the Obscure* (1895) was burnt by a bishop, which provided Hardy with an excuse to give up writing novels and concentrate on the poetry. Not that the novel did not cost him dear, both in domestic peace (his pious wife gave him hell for the supposed 'immorality' of Jude and Sue) and in reputation. He valued his membership of the Athenaeum Club, where gaitered bishops were found behind their newspapers in the library. (He was elected in 1878.)[26]

Hardy is certainly the most religious of all great English novelists, the most spiritually engaged of all great Victorian writers. He went on regarding himself, after a fashion, as a churchman. 'The struggle between an intellect subdued to determinism and an imagination nourished upon the Christian assertion of spiritual and moral order wrought Hardy to poetry'[27] – that is well said by J.I.M. Stewart, and perhaps is most apparent in the obliquer shots in the poetry than in the doctrinal statements, powerful as 'God's Funeral' and 'God's Education' are. I am thinking of such matchless poems as 'The Impercipient', 'I Look into my Glass', 'A Wet Night', 'Drawing Details in an Old Church', 'A Church Romance', 'Where the Picnic Was', 'A Wife in London', 'We Sat at the Window (Bournemouth, 1875)', 'Afternoon Service at Mellstock' and dozens more. 'Much confusion has arisen and much nonsense has been talked latterly in connection with the word "atheist". I believe I have been called one by a journalist who has never read a word of my writings,' he stated during the First World War. (The journalist was G.K. Chesterton.) 'Fifty meanings attach to the word "God" nowadays, the only reasonable meaning being *the cause of Things*, whatever that cause may be . . .'

Hardy's was a dignified witness, not merely for a cultural nostalgia for churchy things, much as he loved all that – and as *Jude* shows, he had a taste for the new urban ritualist churches as well as for the old country ways – but for the shared spiritual life which a national Church could uniquely supply. He went on hoping all his days for intellectual candour from the Church, and was bitterly disappointed by its failure to speak seriously to modern thinking minds.[28] It is entirely apt that Hardy's most famous piece of writing is not the Schopenhauerian wretchedness of the great fiction, nor yet the almost whimsicality of 'God's Funeral', but the honest yearning of 'The Oxen':

> Yet, I feel,
> If someone said on Christmas Eve,
> 'Come, see the oxen kneel
>
> 'In the lonely barton by yonder coomb
> Our childhood used to know,'
> I should go with him in the gloom,
> Hoping it might be so.

PART V

The Eighteen-Eighties

28

A Crazy Decade

Photography made rapid advances in the 1880s, chiefly in consequence of the invention of the dry plate. It was pioneered by various British researchers. By the end of the 1870s, Sir Joseph Swan's company was selling them, and the famous 'Ilford' plate was introduced in 1879. With smaller, more portable cameras increasingly available, and exposure time reduced to a matter of seconds, it began to be possible to capture moments which earlier photographers could never immortalize. Eadweard Muybridge (his name was originally Muggeridge), working in Paris, invented his photographic gun – *fusil photographique* – in which he mounted tiny glass plates in a disc to facilitate quick changing. Muybridge was able to establish the pattern of birds' wings in flight, and to show that a galloping horse lifts all four feet off the ground simultaneously. His zoopraxiscope was to be the pioneer motion-camera – a mere step away from moving pictures. Meanwhile his, and others', pioneering work could be applied and commercially marketed by Eastman in the form of a portable box-camera, Eastman Number One – slogan 'You press the button – we do the rest!'[1]

The 1880s therefore come to life to us in a way that earlier decades do not: for here have been captured unposed moments. Queen Victoria's smile during her Golden Jubilee in 1887, caught by Charles Knight, would have evaporated by the time Julia Margaret Cameron or Étienne Carjat or David Octavius Hill had anointed their glass plates with collodion and set up their laborious contraptions of an earlier vintage. The 1880s therefore are the first decade we can see unfrozen, and turning the pages of its photographic achievements is *both* like watching the modern world beginning to rouse and like intruding into a world which is about to evaporate: as cadavers preserved for centuries in their lead coffins are said to turn to dust when exposed to sunlight.

So: we can see men laying cobbles outside the photography shop of the Oxford photographer Henry Taunt; look into the eyes of old Lord Shaftesbury with his ragged boys of 1883 (by the time they are thirty, the guns will be thundering in the trenches); watch the dons process with Jowett from Balliol Hall to the Sheldonian for the annual

Encaenia in 1884; see the old woman selling magazines at Piccadilly, and the children playing in the slums of Pounder's Court, Leeds; witness – thanks to Henry Taunt – the last Baptist baptism-ceremony in the River Thames at Hatchetts near Cricklade; see the horse-drawn omnibuses rattle down Regent Street and the steam trains pull into Tunbridge Wells Central; glimpse the recruiting sergeants smoking outside the Mitre and Dove pub in Westminster; see working women packing matches in the Bryant and May match factory in Bow (it was where Freddie Demuth, Marx's natural son, worked). The rich women descend the staircase at a fancy-dress ball at Iveagh House in Dublin; men trudge the treadmill at Wormwood Scrubs; merrymakers lower their bathing machines on to the shingle at Brighton.[2] And some of these faces seem – like Amazonian tribesmen who believe, rightly, that the camera is an instrument of aggression – to look at us, the future, with the distrust of those who have destroyed all that was tranquil in their lives, all that made for good, while others seem not merely to meet, but to anticipate our outlook, our preoccupations.

The very fact that we look at these photographic images at all and take them as emblems of reality, or imagine their reality to possess a new authenticity denied for example to the author of an Icelandic saga or to the canvas and brush of Sir Joshua Reynolds, is a symptom of how deeply we collude in the Victorian love-affair with science, the confused empiricism which supposes that the distinctions between Appearance and Reality can be made by some organ independent of a human mind. The camera is then elevated into an arbiter. The belief that it can never lie becomes itself not merely an invitation to hoaxers but the source of a tremendous confusion about the very nature of truth.

Between 30 August and 15 September, in the rhubarb patch at Llanthony Abbey in the Black Mountains between Hay-on-Wye and Abergavenny, a number of people, first some little boys, then the Reverend Father Abbot himself (Father Ignatius O.S.B.) and other adults, all witnessed 'a most Majestic Heavenly Form, robed in flowing drapery'. It was gigantic, but reduced in size to human dimensions as it approached, a static image facing sideways toward the rhubarb – now designated the 'Holy Bush'. Not only did all of those who saw the apparition attest that it was Our Ladye (sic), but the leaves of the rhubarb over which the apparition manifested itself became possessed of healing properties, for example healing the abscesses on the leg of an Anglican nun. For these were not Roman Catholics who saw Our

Ladye of Llanthony, but – tangentially – still members of the Church of England. There had to be sceptics. Sister Mary Agnes believed that a local railway-clerk with a penchant both for photography and for practical joking had somehow managed to project a magic-lantern image of the Miraculous Apparition of Lourdes on to this rain-sodden rhubarb patch in Wales. For some, this will be a more satisfactory 'explanation' than the suggestion that the monk and his companions 'saw' what their faith wanted them to see.[3]

In January 1882 a group of intelligent and scientifically-minded scholars, public figures, clergymen and university graduates founded the Society for Psychical Research. The founders were Sir William Barrett, professor of physics at the Royal College of Science in Dublin, Henry Sidgwick, the Cambridge philosopher, Frederic W.H. Myers, Edmund Gurney and Frank Podmore – representing the scientific, or at least sceptical, spirit: the spiritualist founder-members were the Reverend W. Staintin Moses, Morell Theobald, Dr George Wild and Dawson Rogers. In time, the Society would include two prime ministers – Gladstone and Arthur Balfour – Alfred Lord Tennyson, Lewis Carroll, John Addington Symonds, and eight Fellows of the Royal Society including Alfred Russel Wallace.[4]

They all apparently believed that science could establish whether there was truth in the spiritualist claims. None seemed troubled by the fact that spiritualism itself came to birth in the age of science and offered apparently scientific 'proofs' for its validity – such as spirit photography. W.H. Mumler, principal engraver at the Boston jewellery firm of Bigelow Bros. & Kennard, was the first amateur photographer to receive the impression of departed spirits on his collodion plate, and though he was subsequently prosecuted for witchcraft in New York, and for obtaining money under false pretences, he was acquitted at his trial.[5] In the great majority of spirit photographs – usually ghosts hovering in smudgy form behind or beside the sitter – we have been assured by those who took and developed the plates that no tampering or dishonesty has occurred, allowing sceptics to scorn and believers to believe exactly as if no such scientific evidence had been produced in the first place.

What seems so characteristic of the age is the attempt to confirm one type of belief by means of an essentially alien mental process: enlisting science to verify the resurrection of the body and the life everlasting seeming as inappropriate as appointing mystics to a chair of physics. But the 1880s are an era of kaleidoscopic muddle when the future of

Ireland or the Liberal Party is determined not by political discussion but by sex scandals. Aesthetes turn from wallpaper design to redesigning society. One of the most famous atheists of the age became a convert to Theosophy. And journalism, that ultimate fantasy magic-lantern, laid its first serious claims to be not simply a purveyor of news, but a moral mirror to society as a whole.

We cannot hope in the space available to provide more than a series of snapshots of this extraordinary ten-year period. What is so striking, as we consider the history of socialism; the relations between America and Europe; the Press and sex; the story of Ireland; the expansion of the Empire into Africa; the life of India; the Ripper murders; the Jubilee itself, is how often, as in some huge novel, the same characters recur in different incarnations. During this decade human visions and revisions took bizarre and violent forms: it is the decade when Marx died, Nietzsche published *Also Sprach Zarathustra* and socialism began to lead to riots and conspiracies worthy of Dostoyevsky's *The Devils*; when the Irish scene was peppered with assassinations and explosions and the British dreams of Empire shed much African blood; when modern America begins the relationship with Europe that will shape the twentieth century. Life became, for millions, more comfortable yet more constrained, and for yet more millions no less wretched than it had been for their grandparents. Not so much 'a low dishonest decade' like Auden's 1930s, as a decade that is high as one might be high on narcotics, and so painfully honest that parties and parliaments would rather tear themselves apart than compromise their idea of truth. It was a crazy, uncontrolled decade, over which Dostoyevsky, dying at the beginning of it, seems to hover like a godfather. Who, at the beginning of Queen Victoria's reign, could have predicted that the decade culminating in her Golden Jubilee would begin with intense parliamentary rumpus and debate about *atheism* and end with the most disgusting series of unsolved murders in the East End of London?

'The only way to start a revolution is to start with atheism,' maintains one of the characters in *The Devils*.[6] Charles Bradlaugh the social reformer and Jack the Ripper are both in their different ways like Dostoyevskian *emanations* – difficult to separate from fiction. The perennial task set for themselves by patient minds, of distinguishing Appearance and Reality, grew no easier as the nineteenth century hurtled on, a mad ghost-train out of control.

29

The Plight of the Poor

The gulf between rich and poor and the numbers of the poor, the grinding degradation of their state and the ever-greater prosperity of the rich: these things escaped the notice of no one with eyes to see in the 1880s. Lev Nikolayevich Tolstoy, novelist turned prophet, beheld in the streets of Moscow a reproach to himself and his class which could not be evaded. On a visit to Paris he had witnessed a man being guillotined and felt that, merely by attending such an atrocious act, he was colluding in murder.

> In the same way now, at the sight of the hunger, cold and degradation of thousands of people, I understood not with my mind or my heart but with my whole being, that the existence of tens of thousands of such people in Moscow – while I and thousands of others over-eat ourselves with beef-steaks and sturgeon and cover our horses and floors with cloth or carpet – no matter what all the learned men in the world may say about its necessity – is a crime, not committed once but constantly; and that I with my luxury not merely tolerate it but share in it.[1]

The diatribe, perhaps rightly called the most powerful of all Tolstoy's works,[2] calls for everyone to follow the law of Christ and give up surplus wealth; for those with two coats to give to those with none; for landowners to give their property to their peasants, for householders to do their own chores instead of expecting others to do them for them; for the richer classes to be less greedy, more imaginative about the plight of the poor.

A failure for them to do something would be met, Tolstoy predicted in 1886, by a terrible retribution. 'The hatred and contempt of the oppressed masses are growing and the physical and moral forces of the wealthy classes are weakening; the deception, on which everything depends, is wearing out, and the wealthy classes have nothing to console themselves with in this deadly peril.'

Thirty-one years later, Lenin would arrive at the Finland Station in St Petersburg. No two thinkers could have been more at odds – Lenin believed that Tolstoyan pacificism and simple-lifing would seriously impede the revolution; Tolstoy abominated violence, hated the industrialism which is really the material background taken for granted by Marxist-Leninism, and had an essentially agrarian solution to the problems of Europe. His account of the money–labour relationship which must be the starting-point of economic theory only really works in an imagined world of small crafts and agriculture.[3]

But the book had enormous impact, and the title *What Then Must we Do?* expressed the truly urgent question for the Europeans of the 1880s. The *problem* was observable all over Europe: its danger and, if unaddressed, its sheer moral ugliness. It is a great decade of political novels – Zola's *Germinal* (1885) has an unmatched picture of the sufferings of working-class people, coal-miners, and the overwhelming forces which drive them to strike action against their managers, and to violence. Even Henry James, pacing the streets of London, found material for his novel of socialist insurrectionaries *The Princess Casamassima* (1886). The hero of that book feels utterly excluded. 'In such hours the great, roaring, indifferent world of London seemed to him a huge organisation for mocking at his poverty, at his inanition.'[4] Staying in grand country houses in Yorkshire, James acknowledged that all the wealth and privilege of such places was based upon 'a sooty and besmirched landscape'. He predicted that 'in England, the Huns and Vandals will have come *up* – from the black depths of the (in the people) enormous misery . . . Much of England is grossly materialistic and wants blood-letting' (6 December 1886).[5]

If you did not dare to climb on an omnibus and ride through the poorer parts of a late Victorian city, you could read the articles by George Sims, reprinted in book form as *How the Poor Live* and *Horrible London*; or you could read the Congregationalist Andrew Mearn's pamphlet *The Bitter Cry of Outcast London*, or the punctilious sociological surveys of Charles Booth, whose multi-volume *Life and Labour of the People in London* showed that London could present a human being with sights every bit as troubling as those which caused Tolstoy moral exasperation in Moscow. The dirty, cramped living conditions, the disgustingly high rents, the foetid water supplies, the near impossibility of scraping together enough to eat in such places, let alone to pay for your child to go to school – all these daily humiliations were widely publicized.

Asked what was the most signal fact in contemporary history, shortly before his death in 1884, Mark Pattison replied without hesitation, 'The fact that 5,000,000 of our population possess nothing but their weekly wages.'[6] Florence Nightingale scribbled a pencil note: 'It is always cheaper to pay labour its full value . . . Labour should be made to pay better than thieving. At present, it pays worse.'[7] In a private letter of 1865 Gladstone had remarked on how much the privileged classes needed to remember 'that we have got to govern millions of hard hands; that it must be done by force, fraud or goodwill; that the latter has been tried, and is answering.'[8]

As the 1880s unfolded, however, the goodwill broke down, prompting in many areas, not just in Ireland, the question, Were merely extending the franchise, or offering elementary education, solutions radical enough to cope with an unsteady labour market, and a growing population? Jerry-built suburbs sprawled out of London, put up in a hurry by speculative builders in such places as West Ham, whose population rose from 19,000 in 1851 to 267,000 in 1880. Office-building, new streets and railways within the confines of the City of London led to a decline in the population here, which fell from 113,387 in 1861 to 51,439 in 1881. The construction of Farringdon Street alone displaced 40,000 people. But a survey by the Metropolitan Board found that many of the new suburbs were empty – in Tottenham, Stamford Hill, Peckham, Battersea and Wandsworth the jerry-built streets were unpopulated. There was no underground railway as yet. The unemployed could not afford to live there. Those employed upon precarious terms, either in manual or clerical work, needed to be able to walk to work, which led to gross overcrowding of areas within hailing distance of the City, such as Bethnal Green. The rebuilding programmes and the haphazard migrations of workers (and this was not a problem unique to London) took place without any central planning at all. No government or political party in England saw it as any part of its business to house the workers. 'They must put up with dirt, and filth, and putrefaction; with dripping walls and broken windows; with all the nameless abomination of an unsanitary hovel, because if they complain the landlord can turn them out at once, and find dozens of people eager to take their places who will be less fastidious.' That was George Sims, who said, 'Is it too much to ask that in the intervals of civilizing the Zulu and improving the condition of the Egyptian fellah the Government should turn its attention to the poor of London, and see if in its wisdom it cannot devise a scheme to remedy this terrible state of things?'[9]

The governing classes did not consider socialism to be an option. The debates within the upper echelons of the Liberal Party boil down to the alternatives spelt out by Gladstone in 1865, whether the rich govern the poor by force, fraud or goodwill. Even those, such as the younger radicals Joseph Chamberlain and Sir Charles Dilke, who advocated a more radical social programme than the old Whigs or Gladstonians are deemed by at least some historians to be deliberately counter-revolutionary – killing working-class agitation with kindness.[10] In this they were entirely at one with Lord Salisbury, who began at this time to concern himself with the problems of housing, recognizing that the conditions described by George Sims, Charles Booth and others could not long endure without great social disruption.

And disruptions there were. Trade union militancy was common throughout the middle and late years of the century – there were frequent strikes, even before the official inauguration of the Trades Union Congress (1868)[11] and the change in legislation, under Disraeli's second term, by which peaceful pickets were not automatically deemed in law to be criminal conspiracies.

By the early Eighties, the socialist ideas of Marx had begun to reach an influential audience. Bernard Shaw read Marx in French translation at this date. So too did an Old Etonian called Henry Hyndman, who read the French Das Kapital on the way home from Salt Lake City in the 1870s.[12] In 1881 he founded the Democratic Federation, and asked radicals such as Helen Taylor (Mill's stepdaughter) and Professor Beesly to the preliminary meetings. Hyndman was an unintentionally absurd figure. Marx found his unsolicited visits to his house in Kentish Town a great bore, and many must have raised an eyebrow at the sight of Hyndman, who never abandoned his silk hat, frock-coat and silver-topped cane, addressing the toilers as his comrades.

William Morris joined the Democratic Federation in January 1883 because it was 'the only active Socialist organisation in England', not because he was attracted to Hyndman. He had 'never so much as opened Adam Smith, or heard of Ricardo, or of Karl Marx'[13] when he was converted from radical liberalism to being a socialist revolutionary.[14] The simple unfairness of life under capitalism, the poor becoming no better off in many quarters as the rich became richer, inspired Morris. It was not a carefully thought out but a deeply felt decision, more akin to religious conversion than reasoned argument. He had not even heard Henry George, the American who was such an influence on Tolstoy, who preached the nationalization of land and who had been to London for a lecture tour in 1881. Rather, an inner hankering drew Morris on. He confided in his friend Georgie Burne-Jones, wife of the painter, 'You see, my dear, I can't help it. The ideas which have taken hold of me will not let me rest: nor can I see anything else worth thinking of . . . One must turn to hope, and only in one direction do I see it – on the road to Revolution: everything else is gone now. And now at least when the corruption of society seems complete, there is arising a definite conception of a new order . . .'[15]

Morris was to demonstrate in his own personal pilgrimage one of the key reasons why the Left took so long to become an effective political force in England in the years up to the First World War: namely a fatal tendency to sectarianism. The psychology of the rebel against the system is unlikely to be that of the team-player. However much he or she believes themselves converted to a system of universal comradeship, they are always likely to rebel against the actual comrades' way of going about things. The Democratic Federation was destined to splinter in the mid-Eighties, with Morris and others forming the Socialist League on 30 December 1884 (it included an old Chartist veteran), only to leave it three years later when it had drifted into the hands of anarchists.

Here was a second reason why socialism was slow to appeal to the British public – and especially to the British working class. Those who have lived in England since 1945 and the Labour government of Clement Attlee think of socialism as the imposition of order. Those who dislike it accuse it of bureaucracy, or incompetence; those who wish it worked better in Britain yearn for its more efficient administration at the levels of government, civil service, or in the local and immediate nationalized hospital, school, dole office. For many in the nineteenth century, as the novels about socialism demonstrate – *The Devils, Germinal, The Princess Casamassima, The Secret Agent* – socialism was indistinguishable from anarchism.

Morris himself wasn't above a few fisticuffs in Hyde Park. At a meeting of the unemployed in Trafalgar Square in 1886 – organized by the Tory Fair Trade Association – Morris wanted his Socialist League to hold back, but the Socialist Leaguers were intent on stirring up the crowd. There were between 8,000 and 10,000 people marching down Pall Mall towards Hyde Park, past the most grandiose club buildings in London. As they passed the Liberal Reform Club, the servants pelted the unemployed with shoes and nail-brushes. The marchers returned the hoots and jeers of the clubmen and their servants, and by the time they had turned the corner into St James's Street, tempers were high.

The Tories of the Carlton Club jeered at them and soon found metal bars and paving stones hurtling through the broken glass of the club windows. The rampage then became total, with rioters running amok in Piccadilly and smashing shop windows. At another meeting in Hyde Park, at which inflammatory speeches were made, the demonstrators crossed Park Lane into North Audley Street and Oxford Street, smashing shop windows – narrowly avoiding No. 449 Oxford Street, the showrooms of Morris & Co.

The middle classes who so eagerly bought William Morris curtains, wallpaper and carpets were not so keen on William Morris's socialist ideals if they led to such scenes as this. For several days afterwards London behaved as if it were under siege.

But this is to race ahead chronologically. There were three other cogent reasons why socialist ideas such as those of Marx and Morris had no hope of wide adoption in the early 1880s. The first is that while the condition of the poor was as truly awful, throughout Europe, as Tolstoy, Zola or Morris observed, the evidence about overall growth in wealth and prosperity is very mixed. One recent account observes: 'Even if there were substantial gains in real income or in real wages for the working class in the second quarter of the nineteenth century, these were more than outweighed by other features of the environment – urbanisation, disease, diet and possibly work intensity.'[16] Yes: and this is not an opinion. It is based on the demonstrable fact that in some industrial English towns, the average height of human beings – a sure indicator of nutritional and general well-being – went down between 1830 and 1880. But against this melancholy statistic must be placed the unquestioned fact that many felt more prosperous – not the unemployed, not the agricultural workers, not the day-labourers in the building or docking industry when trade slumped: but for many, even in the working class, and particularly in the upper working and lower middle classes, the opportunity of self-betterment, self-promotion, even against a cruel atmosphere of risk, was preferable to nihilism and ideas culled from foreigners with funny names. E.P. Thompson has suggested that when Morris became a socialist in 1883 probably no more than 200 people made the same journey.[17] It is only because we know, with hindsight, how important socialism was to become that we note its burgeoning in such detail. In British political life *at the time* it was a minor issue. There were far more pressing things on the agenda – a crisis in Egypt, a very unsettled Ireland, and the preparedness of Gladstone's second government to work towards extending the franchise to all males. The 1884 Franchise Act increased the electorate from about 3 to 5 millions. (It was not until 1918 that everyone – all males, that is – got the vote.)[18]

This leads to the second reason why socialism was not a political option for the late Victorians. If the first was that the majority of voters were too prosperous to need or want it, the second is a double and contradictory fact: the strength of Liberal Radicalism during Gladstone's second term of office. Over such questions as education, or extending the franchise, the Radical wing of the Liberal Party was strong, and represented by figures as diverse as Charles Bradlaugh and Joseph Chamberlain. But, as mention of the last name indicates, radicalism meant different things to different people. Chamberlain, the dynamic embodiment of commercial and municipal power in a great industrial city, a thrusting atheist who had made his fortune manufacturing screws and was then going to advance – from mayor of Birmingham, to Cabinet minister, to prime minister-in-waiting – was by no normal definition a man of the Left. Gladstone's parliamentary majority depended on the old Whigs, on urban radicals like Bradlaugh, on Northern Methodists, on Chamberlain and the brass tacks contingent: none were sympathetic to the Irish Home Rulers towards whom Gladstone was inexorably moving. Dostoyevsky voiced the fear of many Europeans in *The Devils* when he imagined the Liberals being the 'front' who were too weak to prevent the incursion of nihilist–socialist–anarchists into society, wrecking and tearing apart. The story of English Liberalism is stranger, for Gladstone's parliamentary dependency on so many contradictory groups did indeed 'let in' to the forefront of political life a force which many would deem diabolical: it was not Russian nihilism but Birmingham Unionist–Imperialism.

But first, let us consider the figure of Bradlaugh. He had neither the gloss of the patrician Liberal Charles Dilke nor the flashiness of Chamberlain, the businessman who had transformed Birmingham. Charles Bradlaugh's background was that of a minor character in Dickens – his father a lawyer's clerk, his mother a nursemaid from Hoxton, now a London district combining working class and designer chic, sandwiched between the City Road and Shoreditch, but in 1833, when he was born, a village. Bradlaugh belongs to the good old English political tradition of cussedness, and could as well have ended up a Tory of the Colonel Sibthorp school as a Radical in the manner of Cobbet. He stood for the little man being allowed to speak his mind, and for the poor man having as much say in the scheme of things as the rich. He was a quintessential English protestant, small p, allowing his questioning of any established authority to lead him to virulent atheism. He was also a republican. From the 1850s onwards, he had identified with the Polish nationalists against the Russians, the Italian nationalists against the Austrians and the pope, and the Irish nationalists.

He was also a keen Malthusian, but unlike the Reverend Thomas Malthus, Bradlaugh saw that the logic of attributing all social ills to overpopulation was to advocate birth control. In 1877 the British government decided to prosecute the English publisher of an American book – *The Fruits of Philosophy* – written by a physician named Knowlton and advocating birth control. Together with his friend Annie Besant, the runaway wife of an Anglican vicar and at that stage an unbeliever, Bradlaugh produced a new version of the book and after an absurd trial the jury decided, 'We are unanimously of opinion that the book in question is calculated to deprave public morals, but at the same time we entirely exonerate the defendants' – Bradlaugh and Besant – 'from any corrupt motives in publishing it.' They were sentenced to six months' imprisonment and fined £200 each, but the Court of Appeal quashed these sentences on a legal technicality.[19]

So this was the man who in the election of 1880 stood as a Radical candidate for Parliament for the seat of Northampton. He was elected – and Henry Labouchere, moderate Liberal, was elected for the other Northampton seat. Labouchere is perhaps a notorious figure nowadays, since in 1885 when Parliament was debating homosexuality he proposed a clause in the Criminal Law Amendment Act which made all forms of male homosexual activity, and not just buggery, illegal. It seems likely that Labouchere did this to demonstrate the absurdity of the law, but the effect of his amendment was, among other things, to send Oscar Wilde to prison ten years later.[20] His other claim to fame, perhaps more cheerful, is the quip, 'I do not mind Mr Gladstone having an ace up his sleeve, but I do object to his always saying that Providence put it there.' To Bradlaugh, a man utterly different in background and outlook, he was a loyal parliamentary friend.

Bradlaugh arrived at Westminster in 1880 and refused to take the oath required of all sitting MPs. The idiotic Speaker of the House, Sir Henry Brand, could have easily allowed Bradlaugh to affirm, rather than take an oath, with a warning that he might be liable to prosecution. As it was, he referred the matter to the House – then to a private committee. At one crazy moment Bradlaugh was imprisoned in the Clock Tower by some arcane piece of medieval law. Meanwhile the Tories could make capital from the episode and waste hours and hours of parliamentary time, worrying the Irish members and many of Gladstone's Northern Methodist grocers with the imputation that the Liberal government was a Radical atheist sham.

It was an occasion which brought out the best in Gladstone, from the point of view of parliamentary theatre. He made one of the greatest speeches of his career rebutting the young Tory firebrands such as Lord Randolph Churchill and A.J. Balfour. Gladstone saw Bradlaugh as a 'parliamentary impediment'. Each time the House rejected him, the good people of Northampton re-elected him. Eventually, in spite of the vociferous extra-parliamentary intrigues of Cardinal Manning, the opposition of most of the Anglican bishops and the blustering fury of the Tories (Churchill said Bradlaugh – 'a seditious blasphemer' – was supported by 'mob scum and dregs'),[21] Bradlaugh was allowed to affirm rather than take an oath involving the mention of a God in whom he did not believe. He had won his case, and made a point, but it is questionable how far Bradlaugh had helped those who were, in political terms, his primary concern – the poor.

Bradlaugh deeply resented the notion that their cause was best advanced by the socialists, or by any form of agitation which involved violence. He believed that just as the spread of collectivist ideas in Ireland had engendered violence, forcing the British government to reintroduce coercion, so the result of socialism would also be violent: 'You are driving poor people into danger,' he told the followers of Marx, 'you are giving excuses for coercion, you are trying to lead my people wrong, and therefore I bar your way.'[22] He was bitterly hurt when Annie Besant joined the socialists in 1885.

The Irish situation, from the very beginning of Gladstone's second Parliament, dominated domestic politics. To write separate chapters about Ireland and England, as historians of the period tend to do, makes for clarity and convenience; but it begs a number of questions – chief of which is the notion that 'Irish nationalism' is detachable from the matters we have been so far discussing in this chapter. If peasant-farmers in County Cavan had grown as rich over the previous forty years as certain Birmingham businessmen they might have been as passionate for the United Kingdom as Joseph Chamberlain. But because of the history of Ireland since the famine – the religious differences, the poverty, the articulate anti-British witness of Australian and American Irish – the cause had become both nationalistic and every bit as violent as the nihilists in Dostoyevsky's nightmares. It was also just as vague, in terms of its actual, concrete, political definitions. R.F. Foster provides the verdict: 'Dazzling as the political structure of Parnellism had been, it had never really defined what Home Rule meant.'[23]

30

The Rise of Parnell

In January 1880 a correspondent from the *Daily Telegraph* – in those days a Liberal newspaper – visited Connemara and was shown round by the parish priest of a place called Ernlaghmore. Father Flannery pointed to a mound of rubbish by the roadside – heaps of soil, trash, a few domestic items. From this mound a little column of smoke emanated. The rubbish was inhabited by a man who had been evicted by his landlord. The journalist was amazed when, from this hole in the ground, a fine-looking woman emerged, holding a baby. A little way down the shore, Father Flannery found for the Englishman a small cave whose mouth had been stopped by a lobster pot from whose aperture, once more, a trail of smoke proceeded.[1]

Stories such as this could be replicated all over rural Ireland at the time – in Galway, in Connemara, in the Ballina district of Co. Mayo, where small tenant-farmers had been driven off their land by high rents. An average of 200 per week were leaving the port of Larne alone for the United States, and hundreds were crossing the Irish Channel for Liverpool or Glasgow.

It is to such poor people as these on 21 August 1879 that Our Lady, St Joseph and St John the Evangelist appeared over the south gable of the church at Knock,*[2] in South Mayo. Perhaps the vision 'inspired' the Apparitions at Llanthony the next summer, mentioned at the beginning of Part V.[3] Some, including the *Daily Telegraph*, opined that the figures had been projected through magic lantern by a hoaxer on the gable of the church – just such a theory has been advanced to explain the Llanthony apparitions. Meanwhile, one of the children who saw the vision at Knock was able to describe in punctilious detail the book being held by St John the Evangelist, the rose on Our Lady's brow and the featheriness of the angels' wings. The Welsh Appearances – though there is a small annual pilgrimage to commemorate them to this day – were, so to say, *sui generis*. The monk in whose rhubarb patch they occurred was rejected by the Church of his baptism and eventually

---

Cnoc is Gaelic for a hill.

sought ordination from a 'wandering bishop' of no Church. The event did not resonate with the almost entirely chapel-going Welsh – even though Father Ignatius, also known as Dewi Honddu, was a keen Welshman by adoption, and a nationalist. Wales in the 1870s and 1880s knew great hardships, and the farmers, especially when non-churchmen, strongly objected to paying tithes – i.e. a tenth of their income – to the local Anglican parson. (The Church in Wales was still the Established Church.)

Wales had escaped famine – unlike Ireland and Scotland. On the other hand, unlike these lands, it had a living language spoken by a significant proportion of the population, it had suffered from bullying landlords and agricultural depression and – in the winter of 1887–8 – the Hussars were used to quell Welsh riots.[4] But though resentment against the English would continue to be felt to this day by the Welsh, for a number of legitimate grievances, the separatist movement would never be so strong as to lead to the creation of a Welsh Free State or a Welsh Republic. Rather, within the United Kingdom, the Welsh would establish their distinct identity by cultural and linguistic means, and by identifying, when the Labour Movement took shape, with the left wing of socialist political programmes.

In Ireland things were otherwise, where 'Mary the Mother of God comes from heaven, to console and strengthen her children. They are in dire need of a helping hand.'[5] 'Whatever public spirit exists in Ireland just now,' the MP and historian W.J. O'Neill Daunt had written in his Journal in 1859, 'is rather religious than political.'[6] But, as in Poland, it is difficult to distinguish between piety and patriotism: the two go together, and the multitudes who made their pilgrimages to Knock, wishing for cures and blessings, were caught up in an atmosphere in which something more than the purely rational was in the air. There was poverty, and hunger, and rage: there were the memories, folk memories and actual, of the Famine: there were the Fenians – a Gaelic brotherhood naming themselves after the Fianna army in the medieval saga of Fionn MacCumhail: there were also the murderers, the professional malcontents, the anarchists.

Michael Davitt's (1846–1906) Land League, heavily subsidized from America, was a pivotal agent in the story. Born during the Great Famine, Davitt had been evicted, with his father and mother, from a smallholding in Co. Mayo when still a boy. They emigrated to Lancashire, where he was put to work in a factory and lost an arm aged eleven. Unsurprisingly, when he grew up, he had taken part in the unsuccessful raid on Chester Castle and became involved in gun-running, for which he was sentenced to grim treatment in Dartmoor jail. Because he could not as a one-armed man break stones on the moor he had been harnessed to a cart like an animal.[7]

Captain Moonlight was a truly Dostoyevskian 'horror'. It was the codename of the Land League, and it meant what happened to tenants who did not conform to the Land League's patriotically rebellious attitude to landlords. Ricks were burned, cattle maimed, houses and barns torched – all at night by Captain Moonlight. Anyone taking a farm from which a tenant had been evicted was to be 'isolated from his kind as if he were a leper of old'.

The first man to do so was, in his rashness, to add a word to the English vocabulary. When Captain Boycott took over a farm in Co. Mayo not far from Knock, he was besieged by angry expelled tenants who henceforth refused to work or trade with him. An expedition of Ulster Protestants marched to rescue him. The first Boycott in history had taken place. Captain Moonlight dug graves beside traitors' back doors but at first there were no actual murders – at first.[8]

In 1882 the viceroy, Lord Cowper, and William Forster, the chief secretary, resigned and were replaced by Lord Spencer and the Duke of Devonshire's brother, Lord Frederick Cavendish. On 6 May Cavendish and an undersecretary, T.H. Burke, were walking in Phoenix Park in Dublin when a murder gang – the 'Invincibles'[9] – sprang out and hacked them to death with twelve-inch surgical knives. Even the Fenians were shocked by the brutality and brazenness of the outrages. The leader of the Invincibles was an Irish American, Edward McCaffrey. To murder anyone is undesirable: the murder of an amiable young man like Lord Frederick who had only just arrived in Ireland sent a good indication to the politicians that they had to deal here with something rather more formidable than the Welsh nationalists. In January 1881 a Fenian bomb had injured three people in Salford (Manchester); an unexploded bomb was found in the Mansion House in March; and again in the May of the following year. In 1883 bombs exploded in Glasgow and London, and the next year four London railway stations were closed because of terrorists, Irish conspirators attempted to blow up London Bridge, and the newly opened Underground Railway was closed by bombers.

It was against this background of anarchic violence that we are to understand Mr Gladstone's conversion to Home Rule for Ireland – just after the election of 1885 – as well as the extraordinary political career of Charles Stewart Parnell (1846–91), whose name, incidentally, was pronounced not Parn-*elle* but *Parn*-ull, with emphasis on the first syllable.

Parnell, a young Protestant landlord from Avondale, Co. Wicklow, was destined to die in his wife's arms in Brighton, in 1891, aged forty-five. It is hard for any British or Irish person to contemplate his early end, and his failure, without intense emotion; for we have lived through thirty and more disgraceful years at the end of the twentieth century in which the government of Ireland, in accordance with the wishes of its inhabitants, has been perceived, or made into, an intractable problem by generations of politicians and pundits. The nature of 'the Irish problem' in our time has been what to do about Ulster, prompting the question, had Parnell any idea of the strength of resistance to his Home Rule scheme which would have come from the hard-core Scottish Protestants of four Ulster counties?

We shall never know the answer to that. It was never put to the test. The story of Ireland, and of Parnell, dominates the 1880s, and this political genius, this inspired visionary, seems all the more impressive with the perspective of the years. His very great achievement was double-handed. First – and this was the real tribute to his finely attuned political intelligence and quite extraordinary charismatic gifts, still felt at this distance as one reads about him – he persuaded the Irish nationalists, old and new-style, to rally behind his very conservative and in some respects ambiguous programme of Home Rule. That is, Ireland would have its own parliament, but remain part of the British Empire.

The finer details – who would appoint the police, or the judges? would Irish MPs – any of them – sit in Westminster? could Britain declare war on another country and Ireland remain neutral? – were never fully worked out. Great disputes with the British Liberal Party went on regarding these issues, even when Home Rule was a going concern. The point was that even 'Land Leaguers' such as Davitt joined up behind Parnell, and in the course of the 1880s not only the 'Irish party' at Westminster but in effect the whole Irish nation united behind him. This was never to happen again, with any other figure on the Irish scene, however skilled or attractive to his followers.

It would be out of place to tell the whole story at once, but it is necessary to realize that within a remarkably short space of time Parnell and his parliamentary party had moved from being imprisoned outlaws to coming within a whisker of 'pacifying Ireland' – Gladstone's long-cherished dream. It was indeed said that for the twelvemonth of 1884–5, 'for over a year, in a manner almost unbelievable today – Salisbury and Churchill being Parnell's dependants first, Gladstone and Morley afterwards – the uncrowned king of Ireland had been a dictator in British politics'.[10]

Parnell held on to his own revolutionary wing, his Captain Moonlight practitioners, his American desperado friends and potential bomb-makers, not by theatricality but by a genuinely radical attitude to the Land Act, brought in by Gladstone in 1881. He did not believe it went nearly far enough, and he was arrested and imprisoned at Kilmainham for urging Irish tenants to disregard it and withhold rents. It is perhaps necessary to labour the obvious and remind readers who presumably would not be holding this book in their hands if they were not comfortable and well-fed of the troglodyte existence forced upon Irish people by obdurate landlordism – described on page 452. The harvests of the late Seventies, so ruinous to many English agrarian workers, threatened in Ireland a repetition of the Great Famine. Parnell was not putting on an act to win over the Fenians when he resisted the Land Bill and landlordism. He defied it with every ounce of his political blood – which is largely why landlordism was defeated, even though he himself died a failure. After the Liberal government did him the favour of locking him up in prison, the Irish felt they could trust Parnell, Protestant and landlord though he be.

Partly through his own skill, partly as a matter of electoral good fortune, Parnell held a balance of power, both during Gladstone's second administration of 1880–5 and, after the 1885 election, during Salisbury's brief minority government (June 1885 to the beginning of 1886). After the election of 1880 the Liberals held 354 seats, the Conservatives 238 and the Home Rulers 65 seats; after the election of 1885, the Home Rulers had 86 seats; the Liberals 335 and the Tories 249.

But it was at the end of 1885 and during that election that Parnell's most outstanding political achievement was, as we should say, 'leaked' to the public. That is, he had converted Gladstone himself to an out-and-out commitment to Home Rule. The 'leak' occurred in a characteristically eccentric fashion. Just before Christmas Gladstone's son Herbert (also his secretary) told several newspaper editors, and the National Press Agency, of his father's conversion.[11]

The timing of the 'Hawarden Kite', as this leak was dubbed – some say the coinage was Salisbury's – was perhaps designed to cheer up the

Irish voters, and to flush out the Tories as proponents of coercion: that is forcing tenant farmers to either pay their rents or take to the hedgerows. But it was a bold move, the beginning of the boldest and noblest phase and aspect of Gladstone's career. Though we may think harshly of Gladstone the Christian hermit of Hawarden, the penny-pinching economic liberal who allowed the English poor to fester in their slums through four administrations; though his theatrical piety and hammy rhetoric may impress us as little as his impertinent belief that he could 'improve' prostitutes by talking to them for hours on end, then whipping himself with thongs given to him by Dr Pusey; though some of his foreign policy seems dictated by a need to strike moral poses while the rest was forced upon him by events; though in short we might share the personal aversion from Gladstone felt by many of his contemporaries, in his Irish policy he was more enlightened than any British leader before or since. In 1930 King George V said to his prime minister, Ramsay MacDonald, 'What fools we were not to have accepted Gladstone's Home Rule Bill. The Empire now would not have had the Irish Free State giving us so much trouble and pulling us to pieces.'[12]

True, the Ulster question – still 'pulling us to pieces' – was never put to the test by the Parnell–Gladstone idea; but had things turned out differently in Parnell's personal fortunes, he might well have overcome even this perennially impossible problem.

Gladstone's conversion was to throw his own party, the English Liberals, into considerable disarray. His worst enemy within his own ranks, and whom he woefully underestimated, was the Flash Harry from Birmingham, Joseph Chamberlain, soon to begin the distinctive Odyssey which would take him from the Radical wing of the Liberal Party into Lord Salisbury's third Cabinet as a rabidly jingoistic colonial secretary. Other senior Liberals, most notably Hartington, by now 8th Duke of Devonshire, would leave the Liberals and as Liberal Unionists ally themselves with the Tories over the Irish issue.

This is a story which we must resume towards the end of our consideration of the 1880s, when we have had time to think of some of the other events of the decade. Whether or not Home Rule ever had a chance of succeeding is one of the most agonizing historical 'ifs' which can occur to an Irish or British mind. How many lives would have been saved, and how much misery avoided, is incalculable.

Parnell in 1885–6 was in the ascendant. He was only forty, he had

Ireland, and the most eminent of all British statesmen, on his side. He also, known to a handful of insiders, was having an affair with the estranged wife of Captain O'Shea, one of his own MPs. Triumphant as he was at this time, it is impossible to imagine that he did not view with foreboding the tragic case of Sir Charles Dilke, another extraordinarily talented parliamentarian – a Radical who was seriously spoken of in many quarters as a potential successor to Gladstone himself.

Dilke (1843–1911) was the youngest member of Gladstone's outgoing Cabinet. He was rich, being the heir to the second generation of a fortune based on journalism: not on the sensational stuff which would be the means by which his ruin could be told to a salacious public but on then-popular periodicals such as the long-defunct *Athenaeum* and the – heroically, still with us – *Notes and Queries*. As a rich young man in Chelsea, Dilke was well-read, well-travelled and knew 'everyone'. At the end of his life he wrote that he had 'known everyone worth knowing from 1850 until my death' and those who share or are impressed by this approach to life can count off a roll-call with which few could compete – from the Prince of Wales to Cardinal Manning, from Bismarck to George Eliot. One senses a great chilliness, not to say hollowness, about Dilke – it would be hard in fact to find any man more different from Parnell.

When Gladstone took office for the second time, Dilke and his great political ally Chamberlain had issued the old man with the joint ultimatum that neither would serve under him unless he appointed both to Cabinet office. After some humming and hawing they had accepted a compromise – Chamberlain was made president of the Board of Trade, and after a reshuffle in 1882 Dilke got the presidency of the Local Government Board. Moreover his friend of some years, Emilia Pattison, the much younger wife of the crabby old rector of Lincoln, was now a widow and had agreed to marry Dilke on her return from India.

But on Sunday 19 July 1885, Dilke heard the fateful news that Mrs Donald Crawford – sister of his brother's widow – had told her husband that after her marriage, Dilke had been her lover. Crawford was to sue for divorce, citing Dilke as co-respondent.

The case of *Crawford* v. *Crawford and Dilke* was heard before Mr Justice Butt on Friday 12 February 1886. The decree nisi was given by the learned judge, though he did not accept Mrs Crawford's fairly hair-raising testimony against Dilke. Indeed he appeared to accept the truth of Dilke's denial that he had slept with Mrs Crawford and as Roy

Jenkins says in his biography of Dilke, 'the verdict appeared to be that Mrs Crawford had committed adultery with Dilke, but that he had not done so with her'.[13]

Mrs Crawford lied in court – of that there's no doubt. She lied in the divorce hearing, and she lied when, in the following July, Dilke tried to clear his name through a process whereby the evidence was presented to the Queen's Proctor. (In this he failed – and Mrs Crawford's decree was made absolute in the summer of 1886.)

The lurid nature of Virginia Crawford's evidence – allegations that Dilke had a long-standing affair with a maid called Fanny Gray, whom he persuaded to have three-in-a-bed sessions with Mrs Crawford – is only one of the puzzling features of the whole sordid affair. We are not here dealing with Doll Tearsheet. When Virginia was seventeen she married the law don at Lincoln College, Oxford, Donald Crawford. He was a colleague of Pattison's, so Emilia – Mrs Pattison, the future Lady Dilke – knew her independently of her family connection with Dilke. She was having an affair with a Captain Forster at the time she told her husband that Dilke was her lover. Why did she choose to blacken her own name in public with these allegations – whether they were true or false?

Cardinal Manning is a figure in the story. As a political ally and social friend of Dilke's, he was taken into the confidence of the beleaguered politician. He maintained Dilke's innocence, and continued to associate with him, which one suspects he would not have done had he believed Dilke had lied about the matter in court. (Manning was to play a decisive role in the downfall of Parnell, as soon as *his* adultery became public, ruling it out of the question that a man cited as a co-respondent in a divorce could lead a political party.)

At the same time, Manning was the confidant, and eventually the confessor of Mrs Crawford, whom he received into the Roman Catholic Church. She went on to lead a blameless life of social work and membership of the Labour Party, dying deep into the twentieth century. She never recanted her evidence against Dilke, as perhaps conscience would have prompted her to do – if only in a posthumous written note – had her story been substantially false. Perhaps the key ingredient in the story was her discovery that Dilke had also been having an affair with her mother.

Roy Jenkins's biography, sunnily at home with the complexities of political intrigue in the higher echelons of the Liberal Party and the social upper reaches of late Victorian London, whirls into eddies of incoherence when trying to come to grips with the psychology of this young woman. As his story stands – and it remains easily the best account of the case, and one of the best vignettes ever written of political life in Victorian England – the baffling figure of Virginia remains incomprehensible.

Some things are clear. She wanted to carry on her love affair with Captain Forster, so she didn't confess it to her husband. Instead she named Dilke. In spite of all his protestations it looks as if he did have *something* going on with her, even if some of the incidents (such as three-in-a-bed with a maid) were either inventions or as Jenkins says *transferred*: i.e. happened in actuality with Forster. Presumably she blurted out her story to her husband because their marriage had become intolerable, but could not have dreamed of the terrifying cross-questioning from lawyers that lay ahead.

So, some of the mystery of the case, which will always cling to it, emanates from the confused motives of an evidently unhappy young woman. But there is another element to all this, which makes the case something more than a sexually titillating scandal. The extraordinarily innocent childish-all-knowing Henry James was so scandalized by the 'revelations' of the two legal cases – not so much what they alleged against Dilke as what they suggested about the sexual mores of those whose drawing-rooms he had frequented as an eager diner-out – that he could fashion two exquisitely mysterious disquisitions of innocence in the face of sexual depravity – *The Awkward Age* and *What Maisie Knew*. Most people were not so naive as the virginal novelist. They knew how, in the present reign, Lord Melbourne and Lord Palmerston had conducted their lives; hence whether or not this or that bit of filth, aired in a divorce court and greedily reprinted in the *Pall Mall Gazette*, was strictly true was less interesting than the bigger question, *Why was this coming out at all?* It would be a fair assumption that in the summer of 1885 very many distinguished figures in London were involved with affairs which would cause scandal if made public. Why was Dilke singled out?

The answer is, we don't know that he was, and the notion of any sort of conspiracy against him got up for political purposes has never been proved. But nor has the evidence of ex-Inspector Butcher ever been explained either. Two days before she made her confession to her husband, Virginia Crawford was spied upon by a detective, Inspector Butcher, calling at Joseph Chamberlain's house in London. Chamberlain had no previous acquaintance with Virginia Crawford.

He did not tell Dilke, supposedly his dear Radical ally, about the visit, and when challenged about it, he never supplied an adequate answer.[14]

What we know in the political sphere at this time is that Dilke was Chamberlain's only serious rival as a leader of the Radicals and as a potential successor to Gladstone. We also know that Dilke had moved into a position of broad general sympathy with Home Rule, an idea which would drive Chamberlain out of the Liberal Party eventually but which that summer he might have hoped (five months before the 'Hawarden Kite') to scotch. Who will ever know? Whether or not Chamberlain, or another, deliberately set up the Dilke scandal for political ends (and there are those who favour the theory that Rosebery was the instigator),[15] we shall probably never know. What is certain is that the Dilke case demonstrated how utterly the scandal of a divorce case could ruin a political career. To have affairs is one thing; to have them published in the newspapers is quite another. The incident would give powerful ammunition to those who knew of Parnell's love-affair with Katharine O'Shea and gave an ugly boost to what could be called the power of the Press. The Press, and the anti-Parnellite politicians, would use any weapon which came to hand to destroy the workability of Home Rule. When it is examined, what is the 'Irish question' but another version of the poverty question? It was a question of whether grotesquely few landlords should be allowed to go on squeezing the very life out of millions of Irish men, women and children; and whether an English Parliament should continue to criminalize those who did not have the money to pay their rent. Under the gaudy embrace of a Union Flag, politicians and public could disguise the raw nature of the question, make it one of patriotism and decency versus dynamiters and superstitious papists. But the glaring, brutal injustice – the sheer weakness and poverty of the Irish, the wealth and strength of their overlords – though it could be dressed up *then* as the nature of things, or even as a political virtue, returns to haunt us with its moral ugliness.

The Fourth Estate – Gordon of Khartoum –
The Maiden Tribute of Babylon

One of the strangest legacies left to the world by the Victorians is the popular Press – and by extension, the radio and television journalism which has largely modelled itself on 'the New Journalism'. The ways in which human beings have observed, noted, told stories about the world have varied much since they first began to paint versions of their doings and preoccupations on the walls of caves, or to devise mythologies to make sense of their puzzlements or calm their fears. Since classical times, historians and chroniclers had attempted to draw a distinction between narratives which were fictitious and those which bore some resemblance to what had taken place, though in many cultures this distinction did not seem markedly important.

The need for 'news', an instantaneous impression of the world on a weekly or daily basis, evolved within a century or so of the invention of printing, but the great age of journalism in Britain was undoubtedly the nineteenth century. By then there was a plethora of locally produced daily newspapers, and in addition to the provincial press there were many London newspapers printed with a national audience in mind. Of these, *The Times* at 3*d.* was pre-eminent under the editorship of J.T. Delane. There were many other dailies selling for a penny, including *The Daily Telegraph, The Daily News, The Daily Chronicle, The Morning Post* and *The Standard*. One of the stories of the 1880s, and the direct result of Gladstone's Irish policy, was how many of these originally Liberal papers, such as *The Telegraph* and *The Morning Post*, became Conservative.[1]

Then, as now, politicians shamelessly used the newspapers to 'leak' their views, and to carry weight against their Cabinet or parliamentary opponents. When Sir Charles Dilke realized that his Cabinet colleague was moving in the direction of using a policy of coercion in Ireland, he leaked the fact to his tame editor, Hill of the *Daily News*. 'The result of it was that the *Daily News* had an article the next morning which smashed Forster's plan,' said Dilke.[2] Chamberlain frequently leaked government secrets to the Press – using Escott, editor of the *Standard*. W.E. Forster himself (now chief secretary for Ireland) whispered in the ear of the editor of *The Times*. We have seen how Gladstone used his son to brief the Press about his change of heart about Home Rule. John Morley, destined to become chief secretary for Ireland in Gladstone's third government – and Gladstone's biographer – was editor of the *Pall Mall Gazette* during the second Gladstone administration. 'It would be worth silver and jewels,' he told Dilke when still in journalistic mode, 'if I could have ten minutes with you about three times a week.'[3]

Morley (1838–1923) was one of the great exponents of Victorian Liberalism, and even those of us who involuntarily smile at that creed cannot deny the sheer intellectual impressiveness of his career. A doctor's son from Blackburn in the North of England, he went up to Lincoln College, Oxford, and in spite or because of the example of the rector, Mark Pattison (who maintained a cynical public silence about his disillusionment with religion), the young Morley came clean about his own unbelief. These were the days when Oxford undergraduates were still obliged to subscribe to the Thirty-Nine Articles of the Church of England. Morley got a second in Mods – the exams taken after five terms in Latin and Greek – but opted to go down with only a pass degree rather than stay and take Honours in the name of a Holy Trinity he disbelieved. Intellectual honesty and a dogged agnosticism guaranteed him a life of poverty for the next few years but were to be the most marked features of his character for the rest of his life.

Morley was a 'journalist' in the glory days of nineteenth-century periodical literature: its exponents were such as George Eliot, Mill, Huxley, Matthew Arnold, Leslie Stephen, Walter Bagehot, George Meredith, Robert Cecil (before and after becoming 3rd Marquess of Salisbury) and many other great names. As editor of the *Fortnightly Review* for fifteen years, Morley published many of these names, always giving space to such important articles as Huxley's 'The Physical Basis of Life'. Morley made a special study of the French thinkers of the Enlightenment and wrote books on Rousseau and. Voltaire, as well as two short books on Burke.[4]

In periodicals such as the *Fortnightly Review* or the Liberal *Spectator* under Hutton's editorship, or the *Westminster Review*, the Victorian upper and middle classes could mull over what they thought of the news, of science, of religion, literature and their place in the world. This higher journalism is one of the great evidences of their sophistication and moral literacy. But something which Matthew Arnold called 'the New Journalism' was on its way, and its most energetic exponent was

Morley's deputy at the *Pall Mall Gazette*, William Thomas Stead (1849–1912). When Gladstone offered Morley the post of Irish secretary, Morley is reported to have said, 'As I kept Stead in order for three years, I don't see why I shouldn't govern Ireland': just the sort of remark that the liberal Governor von Lembke might make in Dostoyevsky's great prophecy in *The Devils*: for of course neither Morley nor any other Englishman was henceforth able to 'govern' Ireland. Nor could his sensible Enlightenment viewpoint restrain the hydra of the new journalism, a monster machine whose twin-turbo was fuelled by sensationalism and moralism.

No visitant from another age who landed in the midst of our twenty-first-century culture would begin to make sense of our popular journalism – prurient, self-righteous, spiteful and pompous – unless they were able to trace its origins to the chiefly North Country traditions of the nineteenth-century Nonconformists. Dickens had ridiculed the Puritan conscience in such grotesques as Mr Chadband (*Bleak House*). What happened in the following generation was that a fervour, a craving for the emotional excitement of the prayer-meeting and the conversion experience, was awkwardly translated into secular spheres. As has been well said, 'in an epoch of varied achievements, scientific, literary and commercial, the elect of God related themselves to mundane reality almost exclusively through their aptitude for money-making; balancing this imperfect contact with a complex epoch by self-complacency'.[5]

Stead was the son of a Congregationalist minister from Yorkshire. 'I was born and brought up,' he wrote:

in a home where life was regarded ever as the vestibule of Eternity, and where everything that tended to waste time, which is life in instalments, was regarded as an evil thing . . . Hence in our North Country manse a severe interdict was laid upon all time-wasting amusements . . . Among them in my youth three stood conspicuous from the subtlety of their allurement, and the deadly results which followed yielding to their seductions. The first was the Theatre, which was the Devil's Chapel; the second was Cards, which were the Devil's Prayer Book; and the third was the Novel, which was regarded as a kind of Devil's Bible, whose meretricious attractions waged an unholy competition against the reading of God's Word. Where novel-reading comes in, Bible-reading goes out, was a belief which, after all, has much to justify it in the experience of mankind.[6]

Stead, and the sort of journalism which he pioneered, was to provide for the rising tide of lower-middle-class chapelgoers a marvellous substitute for the dramas of the Devil's Theatre, the frivolous triumphs and disasters of the Devil's Prayer Book. He was to redefine the world as a lurid back-drop for a new literary form, every bit as diverting as the three-decker novel from the Satanic circulating libraries.

Gladstone, who made such a powerful appeal to this class, was to learn by vertiginous experience its fondness for whipping itself up into frenzies of moral indignation: useful for the Grand Old Man in the case of the Bulgarian Atrocities, embarrassing in the case of Dilke's adultery – and in the case of Parnell, politically calamitous.

Stead was twenty-two when he became editor of the *Northern Echo*, a daily paper published in Darlington, and he remained there until 1880. It was the articles he wrote on the Bulgarian Atrocities in 1876 which first brought him to notice, and which were crucial in demonstrating to Gladstone that there existed a 'constituency' who could be swayed on supra-political moral grounds. Stead had cheered when Gladstone promised to boot the Turks out of Bulgaria – 'their Zaptieks and their Mudirs, and their Bimbashis and their Yuzbashis, their Kaimakams and their Pashas, one and all, bag and baggage, shall, I hope, clear out from the province they have desecrated and profaned'. But Gladstone when swept to power in 1880 did nothing about renegotiating the terms of the Congress of Berlin which trisected Bulgaria and left two of the three sections under Turkish rule.[7] Few of the subscribers to the *Northern Echo* would much care, because by then they had moved on to some other excitement.

In 1880 Stead became Morley's deputy in London on the *Pall Mall Gazette*, becoming editor in August 1883.[8] The type of journalism which he espoused and developed was to become an essential prism by which the modern world observed itself. It was based on a threefold alliance, between an eagerly opinionated public, a political class anxious to test and ride these opinions like surfers waiting for the next roller to bear them crashing to shore, and the conduit that brought these two together, the solicitors or procurers known as journalists. Of Stead it was observed, 'Nothing has happened to Britain since 1880 which has not been influenced by the personality of this extraordinary fanatic, visionary and philanthropist.'[9] The opinion was that of Reggie Brett (later Lord Esher), the private secretary of Lord Hartington. Brett had introduced Jackie Fisher to Stead – a meeting which led to the 'Truth about the Navy' articles.

In 1882–3 Brett's mind had turned to Egypt and the Sudan. The Cabinet was, as on most issues, divided about Imperial affairs generally, Egypt in particular, with the secretary for India (Hartington), the president of the Board of Trade (Chamberlain) and the first lord of the Admiralty (Northbrook) taking a hawkish and interventionist view; John Bright (chancellor of the Duchy of Lancaster) was the most extreme in the opposite direction, being a Quaker and a pacifist. Gladstone was chiefly worried by the possibility of spending public money, and still believed that the purchase of Suez Canal shares had been a risk not worth taking. But, as Frederic Harrison declared, 'a hollow and ghostlike laugh of derision' was to be heard from Disraeli's burial-vault as the Gladstone government of 1880–5 responded to events in Egypt.

Having spent the Midlothian campaign denouncing 'Beacons-fieldism' and opposing British involvement in Egypt, Gladstone had to recognize that the United Kingdom's commercial interests were intimately bound up with Egypt and the Suez Canal. Forty-four per cent of Egyptian imports came from the UK, and 80 per cent of Egyptian exports came to Britain. The canal was a vital route to India, for both commercial and military reasons. The political situation was, to put it mildly, unstable and the system of Dual Control – by which the khedive governed with the cooperation of Franco-British advisers – did not work well. For reasons which had more to do with French domestic politics than with Egypt itself, the French did not have the concerted will to persist with a policy of European intervention when the situation became complicated. The mutiny of the Egyptian army in 1879 had been followed by the uprising of Colonel Arabi Pasha in 1881 – which many French liberals saw as a legitimate nationalist aspiration. The French fleet which together with the British had been patrolling the waters of Alexandria harbour was withdrawn, leaving the British fleet alone. Alexandria saw riots during the summer of 1882, with 50 Europeans killed and 60 wounded on 11 June. Gladstone with great reluctance sent in the army, under Sir Garnet Wolseley. It was a highly popular campaign with the public, the more so since Wolseley gave Arthur, Duke of Connaught (1850–1942), command of the 1st Guards Brigade. 'When I read that my darling precious Arthur was really to go, I quite broke down,' the Queen told her journal. 'It seemed like a dreadful dream.'[10]

But it turned out to be a triumph, one of the most successful small campaigns of the Queen's reign. The general took with him a group of brilliant soldiers known as 'the Wolseley gang' who had proved themselves in the Ashanti War of 1873–4 – Redvers Buller, who interrupted his honeymoon to take part, William Butler, Hugh McCalmont and others. The Cardwell reforms of the army bore fruit: 17,401 British troops with 61 guns and supplies were successfully shipped to Alexandria – which the navy bombarded. Bright resigned from the Cabinet – no one much minded. Wolseley marched westward across the desert and engaged Arabi's forces about 16 miles east of Zagazig at a village on the Sweetwater Canal, and beside the railway line, called Tel-el-Kebir. The Egyptian fortifications would, Wolseley saw, be a 'tough nut to crack', but it was a perfectly managed operation. The 'butcher's bill' for the battle was 57 British killed, 382 wounded and 30 missing, half the casualties being Highland Scots.[11] On 18 September Wolseley reached Cairo and found a letter from the Queen – 'as cold-blooded effusion as you have ever read'.

Gladstone's Cabinet intended to withdraw the troops as soon as possible. This, however, was one of the classic examples in history of how easy it is for a Western power to intervene in apparently anarchic situations abroad, and how difficult it is to withdraw. Over the next forty years sixty-six promises were made by British governments or their consuls announcing their firm intention of leaving Egypt. Somehow the moment was never quite right, and there was in fact a permanent presence of British troops on Egyptian soil until President Nasser drove them out in 1956.[12]

In September 1883 Major Evelyn Baring, who had been in India as a finance member of the viceroy's council for three years, was recalled to London, knighted, and sent to Egypt as British agent and consul-general. He would hold the post for the next twenty-three years.[13] Gladstone, of all unlikely people, had annexed Egypt, but he was not happy as a colonialist, still less as an imperialist. He quite failed to understand or to capture the mood described by Dilke at this time – 'our side in the Commons is very jingo about Egypt. They badly want to kill somebody. They don't know who.'[14]

Baring had set out for Egypt with the doubtless admirable intention of 'leading the Egyptian people from bankruptcy to solvency, and then onward to affluence, from Khedival monstrosities to British justice, and from Oriental methods veneered with a spurious European civilization towards the true civilization of the West based on the principles of the Christian moral code'.[15] Alas, this good Liberal banker was immediately faced with a danger which was not obviously soluble by reasonable means. An Egyptian government official, a former slave-trader called Mohammed Ahmed, declared himself to be the Mahdi ('one who offers divine guidance in the right way'). He raised a rebellion in the Sudanese province of Kordofan. The khedive dispatched 10,000 troops under the command of General William Hicks: a good soldier, but one who was in an impossible position. The 10,000 Egyptians under him had not been paid, their morale was poor, their willingness to fight low. The Mahdi was established in the capital of Kordofan, El Obeid, a fortified city of 100,000 inhabitants, and though many of them were armed with nothing but sticks[16] they fought as those who had God on their side. By a series of clever ambushes, and the use of treacherous guides who lured Hicks Pasha's men into wooded ravines, the Dervishes were able to massacre all 10,000 of the Hicks army.

This was the situation facing Baring when he arrived as consul in Cairo.

General Charles George Gordon (1833–85) – from the British point of view, destined to be the tragic hero of the unfolding drama in the Sudan – was in Jerusalem when El Obeid surrendered to the Mahdi. When the news came of the Hicks disaster, he had been in Palestine ten months, basing himself in a house at Ain Karim, a village three miles west of the city. By the simple method of walking about Jerusalem with a bible in his hand, this devout Christian soldier managed to persuade himself that he had identified the actual Place of the Skull at which the crucifixion of Christ occurred, and the very 'Garden Tomb' which was the scene of the Resurrection. Since it looks so much more like the watercolour illustration of the Garden in a Victorian children's bible than does the Church of the Holy Sepulchre, encrusted with centuries of ecclesiastical piety, it is not hard to see why Gordon's 'Garden Tomb' appeals to Protestant pilgrims to this day.

Mysterious are the ways of Providence – in which Gordon, Gladstone and the Mahdi all fervently believed. While in Jerusalem, Gordon read of the unfolding events in the Sudan and favoured granting it independence under native rulers. 'He rules there and is working out His Will and I like to think, as I verily believe, the end of it will be the end of slavery.'[17] What neither Gordon nor Gladstone knew was that the Mahdi was to die of natural causes by the middle of 1885 and that the entire crisis occasioned by his uprising would thereby have been averted.

Gordon appeared to be destined for quite another sphere of glory, since while he was in Jerusalem the king of the Belgians offered him the governorship of the Congo. He was admirably qualified, having been in his time governor of the Sudan – he administered the place in happier pre-Mahdian times with almost no European troops – and the successful victor over the 'Celestial King' who had tried to raise the Taiping rebellion in China (hence his nickname – 'Chinese Gordon'). The very man to exercise a kindly Christian influence over the Congolese.

But pressure was mounting on the Gladstone government to do something about the situation in the Sudan. The British generals in Cairo advising Baring – General Stephenson, Sir Evelyn Wood and General Baker – were all of the view that the Egyptian government could not hold on to the Sudan, and it was essential to withdraw the garrisons.[18] It was a formidable, if not impossible operation. The combined number of Egyptians and British, civilian and military, at risk from the Mahdi in Khartoum was 6,000. How were they to be transported to safety? The prospect of thousands of men, women and children making their way across waterless deserts, at the mercy of fanatical Dervishes, was too horrible to contemplate. The government which was swept to power on a wave of horror at the Bulgarian atrocities could not overlook this.

When the news of the Hicks disaster reached England, a colonel in the Royal Engineers living at Folkestone remembered twenty years before seeing another fanatical horde in China collapse before the genius and skill of a young British officer. Colonel Edwards wrote to the inspector general of fortifications, General Sir Andrew Clarke RE, 'There is one man who is competent to deal with the question – Charlie Gordon.'[19] Clarke told his friend the chancellor of the Exchequer, who in turn told the foreign secretary, Lord Granville. On Sunday 1 December, Gladstone wired to Baring in Cairo, 'If General Charles Gordon were willing to go to Egypt, would he be of any use to you or to the Egyptian Government, and if so, in what capacity?'

The idea that 'Chinese Gordon' would save the day gathered force. It was once believed[20] that the Hartington 'party' within the Cabinet deliberately set up a meeting between Gordon and W.T. Stead, engineered by Reggie Brett, who had such belief in Stead's powers. The truth is, there was more chance, or Providence, at work than conspiracy. Gordon had accepted governorship of the Congo. Hartington and Granville were in correspondence about whether a commissioned British officer could legally accept such a post without resigning his commission and his pension.[21] Hartington would scarcely have been writing in confidence to a Cabinet colleague about Gordon's departure for the Congo if he seriously entertained hopes of nobbling him for the Sudan. Later, when Gordon was sent to the Sudan, Hartington was a supporter – but that was after two changes of mind.

Gordon went to Brussels, accepted governorship of the Congo from King Leopold and wrote resigning his commission in the British army. The next day, 8 January 1884, Gordon was staying with his sister in Southampton. An old friend, Captain Brocklehurst of the Horse Guards, was with him when a short bearded man presented himself at the door.

'Can I see General Gordon?' – 'I am General Gordon' – was the exchange which took place on the doorstep – itself a token of Gordon's eccentricity. How many other generals of this date would open the front door rather than wait for a servant to do it for them? For both men, it was a religious moment. Stead 'knew he was in the presence of one of God's doughiest champions'. Gordon at first declined to speak of the Sudan, but once he started on the subject, it was difficult to stop him. The government policy of evacuation could not work, and he explained to Stead why. 'You must either surrender absolutely to the Mahdi or defend Khartoum at all hazards.'[22]

Before Stead left, Gordon presented him with a copy of *The Imitation of Christ*. The next day the *Pall Mall Gazette* had the headline *Chinese Gordon for the Sudan*:

We cannot send a regiment to Khartoum, but we can send a man who on more than one occasion has proved himself more valuable in similar circumstances than an entire army. Why not send Chinese Gordon with full powers to Khartoum, to assume absolute control of the territory, to treat with the Mahdi, to relieve the garrisons, and to do what he can to save what can be saved from the wreck in the Sudan?

Gladstone's government worked on this advice. It was the most disastrous political mistake of Gladstone's career, and it was based on two fundamental errors. First, he could not decide – as Gordon earnestly desired him to do – whether Gordon in Khartoum was being sent as an adviser, or as an alternative executive. And secondly, he would not commit the government, until it was too late, to sending troops as a reinforcement for Gordon's mission. These two mistakes were compounded by dithering. After Gordon had set out for Khartoum, the government changed its policy. In January, Gladstone's son Herbert had made a categorical assurance that the British would *not* hand over responsibility for the crisis to anyone else. On 19 February Hartington shamelessly changed gear with: 'I contend that we are not responsible for the rescue or relief of the garrisons either in the Western or the Southern or the Eastern Sudan.'[23]

The Cabinet dithered about whether to send a relieving force to Gordon in Khartoum. When General Sir Garnet Wolseley was at length dispatched with the Wolseley gang, they had on their hands a much more difficult campaign than their victory over Arabi at Tel-el-Kebir. In January 1885 10,000 Dervishes struck a column led by Sir Herbert Stewart at Abu Klea, 45 miles from Korti – 'the most savage and bloody action,' according to Winston Churchill, 'ever fought in the Soudan by British troops'. Colonel Burnaby was killed, with 8 other officers and 65 other ranks. Stewart was mortally wounded. Khartoum was by now besieged, when Sir Charles Wilson, an experienced staff officer but no commander, received the fateful message by Nile steamer from Gordon that men and women were dying in the streets and relief was desperately needed. Wilson delayed for three days – the most fateful three days of Gordon's life.

Two days before his fifty-second birthday, at 3.30 a.m., General Gordon lit a cigarette and sent that message to Wilson. By 5 a.m. he was dressed in his white uniform and his sword and holding his revolver. The noise of the Dervishes in the streets had been echoing all night. He walked to the top of the stairs which led to the palace council chamber. A throng of Dervishes stood at the foot of the stairs brandishing spears. Their leader, a warrior called Shahin, advanced with his spear. Gordon shrugged before Shahin's spear hit him. As he spun round, another spear hit his back. He fell on his face and the other Dervishes attacked him. It was 5.30 on the morning of 26 January 1885.*

The scene has been painted by G.W. Joy and now hangs in the City Art Gallery, Leeds. Reproductions of it are legion. I must belong to the last generation of Englishmen whose first history lessons took place in a schoolroom where *Gordon's Last Stand* hung on the walls. It is an

---

*The man who actually killed Gordon did not so much as know who he was. The Mahdi had decreed that he wanted Gordon taken alive. This did not stop the death of Gordon achieving instantaneous iconic status at home.[24]

icon of Christian civilization, stoical in the face of anarchic savagery. It is also, paradoxically, an image of white supremacy and power, even though it is a picture of one quite small white man about to be speared by a gang of black men. Partly, the message of supremacy is reinforced by the fact that Gordon stands at the top of the steps while his assailants come up from below. But more than that, he stands as the emblem of what is necessary in the face of such murderous anarchy: calm discipline, goodness such as only the English can bring to the world. This is the message of this powerful picture: it justifies a British presence, not only in the Sudan, but anywhere else in the world where the indigenous population lack the self-discipline or restraint to conduct themselves according to the mores of North-West Europe.

Nor, when contemplating this icon which still possesses a power to move, should one overlook the very considerable charisma of Gordon himself. He was not the sort of general whom every officer would like. (Some good men were killed in the march to relieve Khartoum, including the popular General Earle, and it was understandable that Redvers Buller was dismissive of Gordon – 'the man was not worth the camels'.)[25] But one has to remember that when he arrived in Khartoum Gordon was greeted by thousands of inhabitants as 'Father' and 'Sultan'. 'I come,' he told them, 'without soldiers but with God on my side, to redress the evils of the Sudan. I will not fight with any weapons but justice.' Cynicism does not tell the whole truth. Nevertheless, Lytton Strachey looked ahead to the 'glorious slaughter of twenty thousand Arabs, a vast addition to the British Empire, and a step in the Peerage for Sir Evelyn Baring'[26] when General Kitchener conquered the Dervishes at Omdurman. These horrors are not to be denied, and we can see they were a combined consequence of the new generation's imperial ruthlessness, and the old generation's vagueness about intervening.

Gordon's death at the time and afterwards was seen as a martyrdom. If it could be used to justify later atrocities that is not Gordon's fault. If Joy's canvas suggests not so much a martyrdom as a Passion, it was not alone. He who gave Stead his *Imitation of Christ* was seen as something very close to Christ by his contemporaries. The day of his death was commemorated annually with special sermons. In 1898, preaching in Sandringham parish church, the bishop of Ripon, William Boyd Carpenter, said of Gordon, 'his name is a summons to all to live more courageously towards ill, more unselfishly towards men, and more simply towards God'.[27] The previous year at Sandringham the bishop of Thetford had exclaimed, 'Oh brethren, we have known others like him, with that beautiful combination of courage and tenderness, the reflection of Him who was and is the Lion of the tribe of Judah and the Lamb of God.'[28]

Warrior of God,

Tennyson called him,

> man's friend, not here below,
> But somewhere dead far in the waste Soudan,
> Thou livest in all hearts, for all men know
> This earth hath borne no simpler, nobler man.[29]

It was this quality which Stead noted during his pioneering 'interview' with Gordon. Gladstone completely failed to grasp the public mood, while all along Queen Victoria had understood it. 'If not only for humanity's sake, for the honour of the Government and the nation he must not be abandoned,' she had instructed Gladstone when she urged him not to delay sending relief to Khartoum.[30] When Gordon was killed, she wired Granville, Hartington and Gladstone in an uncoded telegram – so that all the Press knew her hectically expressed indignation – 'These news from Khartoum are frightful, and to think that all this might have been prevented and many precious lives saved by earlier action is too fearful.'

There is no doubt that Gladstone's perceived callousness to Gordon, and his inability to see why the death in Khartoum caught the imagination of so many people, was a symptom of his having lost political grip. Five days after the news of Gordon's death reached London, Gladstone went to the theatre, a gesture of indifference which caused public fury. 'No single event in Gladstone's career made him more unpopular.'[31] Quite apart from anything happening in Ireland, it was the beginning of his coming adrift and a major cause of his electoral failure in 1885. Of course, within six months of Gordon's death, the *Pall Mall Gazette* had forgotten the hero of Khartoum and moved on to something even more exciting.

There can be no doubt that in the eyes of Stead himself, his greatest journalistic coup was his exposé of child prostitution, 'The Maiden Tribute of Modern Babylon'.

Josephine Butler, the wife of a Cheltenham schoolmaster, George Butler, had been stung into public good works by bereavement, her agony following the death of her little daughter Eva in 1864. (She fell downstairs.) Mrs Butler never recovered her own health fully, but decided to reach out of her own suffering to help others. ('I had no clear idea beyond that, no plan for helping others; my sole wish was to plunge into the heart of some human misery, and to say to afflicted people, "I understand. I too, have suffered."')

She began by visiting the workhouse in Liverpool. (To escape the associations of their home in Cheltenham the Butlers had moved to Liverpool, where George had become principal of Liverpool College.) Sitting among the women of the workhouse, and picking oakum with them, Josephine Butler began to understand the conditions of working-class women – and above all to feel anger at the Contagious Diseases Acts. The Report of the Royal Commission of 1870 to inquire into the workings of the Acts (of 1864, 1868 and 1869) saw the behaviour of those who visited prostitutes as 'the irregular indulgence of a natural impulse'. The law institutionalized the notion that to use a prostitute's services was 'natural' even though the woman who provided the service was wicked. In order for this institutionalized rationale of prostitution to be effective, it required, in the Contagious Diseases Acts, giving to the law the right to apprehend, and to examine, women at will.

> Men have, from time to time, attempted to deal with this disorder and disease by regulation or suppression. Both methods have been aimed solely at the women who were alleged to be prostitutes, and no attempt was made to deal with the vastly greater body of men who consorted with them, and who were, if only by reason of their greater numbers, a far greater source of danger to the general community.[32]

It is hard to overstate the courage of Josephine Butler in bringing this abuse to the attention of the public. Decent women did not talk about sex in public – still less about sexual diseases, or the double standards employed by men when legislating about them. At the Colchester by-election of 1870, when Mrs Butler spoke in support of the Abolitionist who challenged Sir Henry Storks, Tory, a keen supporter of the Acts, her hotel was mobbed and its windows smashed. But Storks lost by 500 votes – 'bird shot dead' as Josephine Butler was told by a telegram. A Royal Commission was set up to review the Contagious Diseases Acts, to which Mill gave vital evidence, emphasizing that this was a matter of basic civil liberty. After years of campaigning by Mrs Butler and friends, the Acts were eventually repealed in 1886.

Fascinatingly, although Gladstone did preside over the ultimate repeal of the Contagious Diseases Acts, he was not much of an ally to Mrs Butler over the years. He used to regret her *intensity*. Before he died, he admitted in a pamphlet, 'It has been my misfortune all my life, not to see a question of principle until it is *at the door* – and then sometimes it is too late!'[33] In the case of the Contagious Diseases Acts, it was late, but not 'too late', after all. They were repealed, but it is odd that a man whose divine calling was to reclaim prostitutes should have been so blind as to the moral principles at stake in legislating for state-registered brothels. For this is what the Contagious Diseases Acts provided in garrison towns. In order to check the spread of disease, the state had brothels which were regularly checked by doctors. Any woman found in the street could be picked up by the police and forced to submit herself to intrusive medical inspection, whether a prostitute or not.

In the course of her campaigns to repeal the Acts, Josephine Butler came across many abuses in England and abroad. In her investigations into the abuses of the French system, in 1874 she had confronted the notorious M. Lecours, Prefect of the *Police des Moeurs*, the vice squad, who attributed the huge increase in the numbers of Parisian prostitutes since state regulation was brought in to the influence of the Commune and to 'female coquetry'.[34] She went to Brussels, and exposed the kidnap of British children and young women for use in Belgian brothels. And what she found out so scandalized her that she decided to approach Stead and expose the fact that you could purchase a child on the streets of London for the purposes of sexual abuse. In Liège, she had been told, 'waggon-loads of girls had been brought into Belgium'.[35]

It was, from the point of view of those English puritans with a taste for such things, sublime 'copy'. But in order, as they say in the trade, to make the story stand up, it was necessary for an actual man to purchase an actual child-prostitute and be prepared to admit that he had done so. Who better than our Northern crusader himself, W.T. Stead?

Readers of the *Pall Mall Gazette* during the first week of July 1885 were warned not to buy the issue of 6 July, since it would contain matters to upset the squeamish. Even without these inducements, 'The Maiden Tribute of Modern Babylon' would have been a sell-out – a full account of the sale or violation of children, the procuration of virgins, the international trade in little girls and the unnatural vices to which they were subjected. Headlines such as 'THE FORCING OF UNWILLING MAIDS' and 'DELIVERED FOR SEDUCTION' had all the hallmarks which this type of journalism has had ever since. That is, while professing to deplore what it describes, it offers the readers the pornographic thrill of reading all about it. Stead described a clergyman calling regularly at a brothel to distribute Christian literature, but with equal regularity succumbing to the erotic allure of the little girls. Whether or not this reverend gentleman existed in fact, he was an emblem of Stead and his readership, hovering self-righteously about unsavoury places to which they were irresistibly drawn.[36]

On Derby Day, 1885, Stead claimed he had witnessed a girl being purchased from her mother for £5. In fact, this sale was a masquerade. The girl was called Eliza Armstrong. She was taken to a brothel in Lisson Grove, Marylebone, and rested on the four-poster bed while Rebecca Jarrett, a retired prostitute now under the protection of the Salvation Army, administered chloroform. Around the curtains of the bed there now appeared our puritanical editor, Stead, holding a glass of champagne and a cigar as tokens of his status as a roué. He paid his money, and Liza was bundled off to a Salvation Army hostel in Paris, then on to Drôme in the South of France, before being returned to Stead's house in Wimbledon. But Stead in his zeal had overstepped the law, and Liza's father, who did not have a part in the proceedings, brought a prosecution for abduction. During the trial it emerged that Rebecca Jarrett worked as a housemaid for Josephine Butler and that the whole story was a fabrication. George Bernard Shaw wrote of Stead:

I was a contributor to the *Pall Mall* under his editorship; but as my department was literature and art, and he was an utter Philistine, no contacts between us were possible. Outside political journalism such as can be picked up in a newspaper office he was a complete ignoramus. I wrote him a few letters about politics which he acknowledged very sensibly as 'intended for his instruction', but he was unteachable except by himself.

We backed him over the Maiden Tribute only to discover that the Eliza Armstrong case was a put-up job of his. After that, it was clear that he was a man who would not work with anybody; and nobody would work with him.[37]

Rebecca Jarrett was sent to prison, the others involved in the fraud being let off – except Stead, who went to jail for three months. For every year afterwards he wore his prison clothes on the anniversary of his imprisonment, attracting some notice as he paced over Waterloo Bridge to his office in a jacket and trousers covered with arrows, and a badge with his number. The gesture, like the offence for which he was originally sentenced, was an expedition in the cause of some higher truth into the realms of fantasy. Although Stead had worn prison uniform on his first day in prison, as a 'first class misdemeanant' he was in fact allowed to wear his own clothes for the remainder of his sentence.[38]

The childhood custom of regarding novels as the Devil's Bible had probably resulted in the habit of mind, very common among newspaper editors, where the distinction between truth and falsehood had grown so blurred as to become indiscernible. Other things remained from the chapel – the glow of righteous indignation, and the essential vindictiveness of the elect when contemplating the more enviable sins of their fellow-mortals. Stead became obsessed, for example, by Sir Charles Dilke's supposed adulteries, and even gave Mrs Crawford a job on the *Pall Mall*, presumably hoping that some salacious confession would fall from her lips as she sat at her desk: but she saved that for Cardinal Manning.

Stead was not a bad man. He was that much more dangerous thing, a morally stupid man doing bad things which he believed to be brave because they made a stir. He and his like predetermined the essentially unserious nature of modern journalism: determined, that is to say, that particular kind of moral silliness whose unseriousness is disguised from the practitioners themselves. Spreading misery and embarrassment, mostly they leave actual abuses unaltered. The repeal of the Contagious Diseases Acts in 1886 really owed far more to James Stansfeld than to Stead. Stansfeld, who had been a Cabinet minister in Gladstone's first government, gave it all up to become a 'one-issue' campaigner from the back benches, he was so impressed by Mrs Butler. She – and he – had far more influence on the raising of the age of consent than did Stead.

As Shaw implied, after Stead's fraud over Eliza Armstrong was exposed, he was not so highly regarded, and took to editing something called the *Review of Reviews*. There were a few attempts to revive the old sensationalist magic, some of which sold very well – especially *If Christ Came to Chicago* of 1892, in which Stead 'named and shamed' the brothel-owners. In latter years he became more and more obsessed by spiritualism and – as befitted a man with an eye for the headline – he did not die in his bed at home: he went down with the *Titanic* in 1912. He was last seen helping women and children on to the lifeboats.

Yet, having said that one must add that like so many sentences about Stead, it is not completely true. It remains to be tested when he will be *last* seen. After his body sank with the transatlantic liner in the icy waters of the Atlantic, Stead made a number of manifestations of himself to those with faith enough to see him. Speaking through the medium of Mrs Coates of Rothesay, he announced on 3 May 1912 that he was glad to have given help to so many on board the *Titanic* and to pray with them. He was, he promised, surrounded by friends in Spirit-land.[39] In London, he was actually seen by Mrs Harper and Mr Robert King. He dictated messages *via* automatic writing, suggesting that since he passed over he had not lost that journalistic fizz which made *Maiden Tribute* and *If Christ Came to Chicago* into bestsellers. 'Thank you for understanding – the human Marconigram – strange, strange, strange.'[40] Not limiting his manifestations to Blighty, Stead appeared in Melbourne and Toledo.[41] Most remarkable of all, perhaps, are Mr William Walker's Spirit Photographs of Stead, when he manifested himself in Kingston-upon-Thames about a year after he was drowned.[42] Another, even more striking manifestation shows Stead peering over the shoulder of one Archdeacon Colley. The archdeacon, in an academic square cap or mortar-board, stares firmly at the camera, apparently unaware of Stead hovering in the background. Stead's earnest expression is a moving testimony to the essential irrepressibility of the Fourth Estate.

32

Politics of the Late 1880s

The densely knotted drama of British political life from June 1885 to August 1886 will perhaps interest only the addict of the parliamentary roulette wheel. The general effect of what emerged from those crisis-ridden months, however, reverberates through British political life until the Second World War – arguably beyond it.

In outline what happened was this. Gladstone's second administration, which had been dogged by so many problems from the start – the Bradlaugh affair taking hours of parliamentary time, the unignorable Irish crisis, the problems of Egypt and the Sudan, the question of extending the franchise at home – ran into terminal trouble in the summer of 1885. The Cabinet was split over Ireland. But the ostensible reason for the collapse of the government was the budget which proposed a tax on beer and liquor. Behind the shield of this comparatively minor issue the shattered Liberal Party tried to disguise from itself the irreconcilable nature of its differences over the larger matter of Ireland. When Sir Michael Hicks Beach – what we would call the shadow chancellor of the Exchequer – moved an amendment on the budget, 76 Liberals abstained. The Irish members voted with Gladstone, giving him the tiny majority of 264 to 252 in the Commons. But the warnings were clear and Gladstone – who, remember, had not yet had his conversion to Home Rule and was still trying to hold the party together – resigned.

He went to Osborne to do so, and the Queen did not even offer him luncheon. Still less, during what both must have assumed to be his last audience in fifty-five years of political life, did she express one word of regret at his departure. On his way home across the Solent by the early-evening ferry, Gladstone was too absorbed in Robert Louis Stevenson's *Kidnapped*, just published, to feel much grievance.[1]

The Conservatives formed a minority government on 24 June 1885, but they knew that it could not last long. Parliament had voted the previous year to increase the franchise by 2 million individuals, and this could not fail to favour the Liberals. The procedures – establishing the names and addresses of the new voters, and the boundaries of the new constituencies – would take until November. In December 1885 the election led to a Liberal victory, as anyone could have predicted. A deep paradox was now going to unfold. Chamberlain, leader of the Liberal Radical wing, could boast that 'government of the people by the people . . . has at last been effectively secured'.[2] He could believe that a great programme of democratic reform would unfold – including abolition of the House of Lords and the monarchy. But as the election came to its slow conclusion, his leader, Gladstone, flew the Hawarden Kite and announced his conversion to Home Rule – anathema to Chamberlain, and to a significant proportion of Liberals, both old Whig and new Radical. When the results were counted in December 1885, the Liberals had 334 members, the Conservatives 250 and the Irish 86. It was clear that with the profound fissure in Liberal ranks caused by the Irish issue, Gladstone was never going to collect enough votes to secure Home Rule in the session of 1886. His Home Rule Bill came before the Cabinet in March 1886 – Chamberlain and Trevelyan resigned. In the Commons the Home Rule Bill was defeated by 30 votes – 341 noes against 311 ayes. Chamberlain had voted against his chief and changed sides – with extraordinary results both in his own career and in the history of politics. The short-lived third Gladstone government resigned, and Salisbury took office as prime minister in August 1886, and would serve a full term until the summer of 1892.

The question which forces itself upon our minds at the distance of one and a quarter centuries is how much of a true political shift took place as a result of the electoral reforms of 1884. Did the granting of a vote to 4,376,916 male adults (as opposed to 2,618,453) before the passage of the Representation of the People Act[3] appreciably change the way in which Great Britain was governed over the next few decades? Believers in Parliament might see British history as an unfolding progression of freedoms by which, as general election followed general election, more and more people – first the urban males, then the entire working class (males), then all adults, male and female – were empowered. But empowered to do what? To elect representatives who for the most part perpetuated the system which had placed them there. The great majority of British members of Parliament since W.H. Smith became 'ruler of the Queen's Nav-ee' in *H.M.S. Pinafore* have followed his example –

I always voted at my Party's call
And I never thought of thinking for myself at all.

If the majority of the population was working class, how did it come about that until the twentieth century there were next to no working-class parliamentarians thrown up by this supposedly democratic system? Was the Reform Act of 1884 a step in the direction of democracy, or was it a piece of legislation which allowed 4,376,916 male individuals to go into a ballot box and choose between two party candidates who in many fundamental areas had identical political aims? Is the reason that Irish Home Rule split the Liberal Party quite simply that it was the only issue about which the political classes were seriously divided, and the only issue, thanks to the solidarity of the Irish MPs, in which a vote cast in a ballot box might make an appreciable difference to the way politicians conducted public life?

We have already seen that Gladstone, who moved thousands to tears with his evocation of Bulgarians shivering on their icy mountains, did nothing to change the terms of the Congress of Berlin; nor did he, who so deplored 'Beaconsfieldism' and its jingoistic creeds, hesitate to make Sir Evelyn Baring the effective king of Egypt. Tory brewers could fight with teetotalling Nonconformists over duties on beer and spirits, but this was a comparatively minor issue confronting the parties compared with the political issues which, with hindsight, we might consider primary. In 1886, with a slump in trade, London saw the riots which we have described on pages 445–6. The socialist ideas of Hyndman or Marx or Morris were simply not considered by the political classes. We can see that the position of women in society is a question which emerges from the localized debates over the Contagious Diseases Acts and their reform, so bravely raised by Josephine Butler and James Stansfeld. We can see how closely the feminist issue raised by that drama relates to the growth in women's education – the extraordinary struggles of women to receive a university education on a par with men. In Britain, London University was alone in allowing women to sit examinations and receive degrees. The numbers of women at Girton College or Newnham in Cambridge, Lady Margaret Hall (founded 1878), Somerville (1879), St Hugh's (1886) and St Hilda's (1893) at Oxford, were tiny, but significant. The actual texture of life for women of all classes was eventually to change as a result of these places. It is something far less quaint than the old photographs of the Girton girls' rowing eight would suggest: it is the empowering – professionally and intellectually – of their sex.

Those who believe that Parliament is an institution with a serious political function might be surprised that the first woman member to take her seat did not do so until 1919 and that the proportion of men to women in Parliament is still in the twenty-first century overwhelming. But this is one of the many issues where the real agents of change were extra-parliamentary. Women's colleges, trade unions, the churches, the cells of non-parliamentary political groups and – in time of war – the meeting-together of people in ships, squadrons and regiments were all far more effective agents of change in Britain than any political party pre-1945 – arguably beyond. The function of Parliament was to preserve the power of the political classes; and this in effect meant the Rich.

Twenty-seven years after the Reform Act, a disillusioned Radical MP named Hilaire Belloc wrote a brilliant analysis of the Party System.

We are not surprised at Romeo loving Juliet, though he is a Montague and she is a Capulet. But if we found in addition that Lady Capulet was by birth a Montague, that Lady Montague was the first cousin of old Capulet, that Mercutio was at once the nephew of a Capulet and the brother-in-law of a Montague, that Count Paris was related on his father's side to one house and on his mother's side to the other, that Tybalt was Romeo's uncle's stepson and that the Friar who had married Romeo and Juliet was Juliet's uncle and Romeo's first cousin once removed, we should probably conclude that the feud between the two houses was being kept up for dramatic entertainment of the people of Verona.[4]

The deadly accuracy of this analysis, published in 1911, can be shown by analysing the guest-lists at country house parties from any time between 1880 and the outbreak of the Great War.

'*Pace* Bagehot,' wrote David Cannadine in his magisterial *The Decline and Fall of the British Aristocracy*, 'the spirit and substance of the mid-Victorian Commons was aristocratic, not plutocratic.' One sees what Cannadine means when he goes on to remind us that in 1880, of 652 MPs, 394 were nobles, baronets, landed gentry or their near relations, and that after 1884 this balance was somewhat reduced.[5] (In the 1910 elections the youngest candidates on both sides were the sons of peers.) There is, though, something misleadingly romantic about the distinction between a plutocracy and an aristocracy. The Victorian aristocracy might have enjoyed the fiction that it was a race apart. Its strength actually derived from its adaptability, its ability to absorb new blood and new money into its ranks. While romantic snobs such as Proust's Baron de Charlus might think that an aristocrat was a person with many quarterings, tracing a pedigree back to the Carolingian nobility, the Victorian nobleman as like as not was making sensible injections of cash into the family kitty. The decline in agriculture and the collapse of money from rents and farms both made this a necessity and allowed the new money to buy up landed estates. It took very few years to make an aristocrat. So, the *Peerage* might tell us that the 5th Earl of Harrowby, for example, had been born in 1844 and in 1887 married the Hon. Dame Ethel Smith. Her mother, Emily, became Viscountess Hambleden in 1891. This deeply aristocratic lineage was created to add a touch of nobility to her second marriage. The viscountcy passed through her to the first male born of this marriage. This was our old friend W.H. Smith, whose fortune was made from station bookstalls but who was by then, like the truly Gilbertian figure he inspired, some time first lord of the Admiralty, first lord of the Treasury and lord warden of the Cinque Ports.

Not only did the banking families of the Barings, the Glynns, the Marjoribanks and the Rothschilds all enter the peerage, but by the 1880s trade of all sorts could do so. Arkwright's partner, Jedediah Strutt, was a poor weaver who developed the revolutionary spinning jenny. His grandson Edward Strutt became 1st Baron Belper in 1856. His son married a daughter of the 2nd Earl of Leicester. His great-granddaughter married the 16th Duke of Norfolk. By the 1890s 'the proportion of business and commercial families achieving peerage was 25 per cent and rising'; under Gladstone or Salisbury, the families of Hardy (iron), Guest (steel), Eaton (silk), Armstrong (engineering), Brassey (railways), Guinness, Allsop and Bass – all beer – ascended to coroneted grandeur. Between 1886 and 1914 200 new peerages were created.[6]

'Relying on God, not on Fortune' is the family motto of the W.H. Smiths – aka Viscounts Hambleden. *Deo non fortuna fretus*: but a fortune helped; and stationery and magazines made more money than arable or sheep.

Chamberlain in 1883, campaigning for the extension of the franchise, had denounced the 3rd Marquess of Salisbury:

Lord Salisbury constitutes himself the spokesman of a class – of the class to which he himself belongs, who toil not neither do they spin; whose fortunes – as in his case – have originated by grants made in times gone by for the services which courtiers rendered kings, and have since grown and increased, while they have slept, by levying an increased share on all that other men have done by toil and labour to add to the general wealth and prosperity of the country.

The election was to be a 'Mend Them or End Them' contest for the aristocrats, declared Chamberlain,[7] but he was soon brokering deals, on the one hand with the Whigs such as Lord Hartington, on the other with the Conservatives such as Lord Salisbury, in whose third Cabinet he would serve as colonial secretary. Chamberlain's mercurial political career makes best sense when one realizes that he made an absolute identification between Power and Money. Beatrice Potter, who was in love with Chamberlain, and excited by his Radical ideas, was herself the child of a first-generation millionaire who had made his money out of railways. She longed for a creed, and believed in the early to mid-Eighties that Chamberlain's radicalism might be what she sought. Yet she was shrewd enough to see that the big Birmingham business families, 'the Kenricks and Chamberlains form the aristocracy and plutocracy of Birmingham. They stand far above the town society in social position, wealth and culture, and yet spend their lives as great citizens, taking an active and leading part in the municipal, political and educational life of their town.'[8]

She was devastated when four years later, in November 1888, Chamberlain, twice a widower, remarried. The day before the ceremony she prayed for them in Westminster Abbey – 'I prayed that the love of a good woman might soften and comfort him' – and the next day observed:

> This marriage will, I think, decide his fate as a politician. He must become a Tory. The tendencies of his life are already set in that direction: hatred of former colleagues, sympathy with the pleasure-loving attractive class of 'English gentleman' with which he now associates . . . by her attraction to the 'good society' she will draw him closer to the aristocratic party. She is, besides, an American aristocrat and like the aristocrats of a new country is probably more aristocratic in her tastes and prejudices than the aristocrats of the old country.[9]

This was shrewdly judged, and it is probably a truth which needs to be set beside the artistic truths of the novels of Henry James which, for the last two decades of the nineteenth century, chronicled the meeting of the old and new worlds: usually in the form of American innocents, often heiresses of great wealth, failing until a crucial and late moment to perceive the moral duplicity of the Europeans. For all their elaborate manner, many of James's great novels have the simplicity of *The Tale of Jemima Puddleduck*, a female who does not understand why a foxy-whiskered gentleman should bid her return, bringing sage and onions, to his feather-bespattered lair. Isabel Archer's fox in *The Portrait of a Lady* (1881) is Gilbert Osmond, aided and abetted by the wicked Madame Merle. But there is a shift between *The Portrait of a Lady* and *The Golden Bowl* (1904) which perhaps reflects a political reality. Whereas Isabel Archer is the victim of Merle and Osmond's plot, Maggie Verver is comparatively robust. In the end, it is the immense wealth of the old man, Adam Verver, which shows itself stronger than the title of an Italian prince. He can force the treacherous Charlotte, his second wife, to return with him to the United States while his daughter Maggie keeps her prince in Europe – a premonition of the strength of American money in relation to the old world order, a strength which President Woodrow Wilson would demonstrate within fifteen years of *The Golden Bowl*'s publication.

It is interesting that as well as Chamberlain, Lord Randolph Churchill, another rising political star of the 1880s, should have married an American. Chamberlain married Mary Endicott, aged twenty-four, the daughter of the American secretary of state for war.[10] Randolph Churchill married Jennie Jerome, a figure more reminiscent of Edith Wharton's novels than those of Henry James. She had grown up in a superb mansion in Madison Square. They met during the Cowes regatta in 1873 and were engaged within a week. Though her son saw Jennie as 'a fairy princess: a radiant being possessed of limitless riches and power',[11] it was not a happy marriage. By the time that mother-loving little boy, Winston Spencer Churchill, was a schoolboy at Harrow, London buzzed with rumours of Jennie's and Randolph's affairs, and rocky relationship.[12]

Politically, at this distance, it is hard to see why Lord Randolph Churchill so impressed his contemporaries. Pop-eyed, small of stature and caddish in manner, he seems like the archetypal career politician. He led the Tory attacks on Bradlaugh in the Commons, for example, with expressions of fervent Christian shock that an atheist should be admitted to that assembly, while privately admitting to his wife that he thought 'all religious differences senseless'. At home he ridiculed 'the monotonous exhortations of a clergyman in a white surplice', while in public he spoke as if the Heavens would fall if Bradlaugh took his seat.

'God forbid that any great English party should be led by a Churchill!' Gladstone exclaimed when someone spoke of the young Randolph as a potential leader of the Conservative Party. 'There never was a Churchill from John of Marlborough down that had either morals or principles.'[13] It is hard to make much sense of his 'Fourth Party', a group which consisted of Churchill, John Eldon Gorst, Sir Henry Drummond Wolff and – some of the time – Arthur Balfour: Gorst saw it as 'the rise of the Democratic Tory party which was always Dizzy's dream'. Some saw Lord Randolph as a Liberal trapped, as it were by accident, in the wrong party – this was the theme of W.S. Churchill's hagiographical treatment of his father. Some of his more erratic judgements are perhaps attributable to the illness which eventually killed him, aged forty-five, in January 1895. Bouts of euphoria followed manic states, and his speech – a cruel fate for one who so eloquently entertained the Commons – became incoherent. Paralysis set in. Gossips diagnosed syphilis – probably correctly. Certainly this was not helped by the family disease of alcoholism. But Churchill also had something else wrong with him – a brain tumour, or maybe multiple sclerosis.[14] Perhaps he sensed that all was not well when he so impulsively resigned as the very young chancellor of the Exchequer in Salisbury's government in December 1886, because W.H. Smith (secretary for war) questioned his limitation of expenditure on defence. Since the details of the budget were as yet undisclosed to the public, the reasons for his resignation were mysterious to them, and the career which began as the meteoric rise of the Democratic Tory fizzled into obscurity.

33

Into Africa

During the month of October 1885 – which saw the funeral of Lord Shaftesbury in Westminster Abbey, a general election in France, and the removal of 14 tons of rock by dynamite to form the tunnel in New York harbour known as the Hell gate, while a cyclone swept southern Italy, and a horse called Plaisanterie won both the Cesarewitch Stakes and the Cambridgeshire Stakes[1] – a thirty-eight-year-old Englishman was lying in a small hut in the East African region north of Lake Victoria Nyanza – Masai country. In his Lett's monthly pocket diary, measuring 4½ inches by 2¾, he wrote, in a tiny handwriting, 'Eighth day's prison. I can hear no news, but was held up by Psalm XXX, which came with great power. A hyena howled near me last night smelling a sick man, but I hope it is not to have me yet.'[2]

Though he was not to be eaten by hyenas, James Hannington's (1847–85) confidence was misplaced. His arrival as the newly consecrated bishop of the newly created diocese of Eastern Equatorial Africa had been full of hope and prayer. Docking at Mombasa, he had established his diocesan headquarters at Frere Town and then began a progress westwards through land which he had persuaded himself was 'his' diocese. The Masai were disturbed by the party – 226 strong – which the bishop took in his entourage, and the Christians suffered frequent attacks as well as bad weather and illness. At Kwa Sundu, in October, Hannington reduced the party to 50 – and pressed on towards Lake Victoria Nyanza, covering 170 miles in five days. All in all it had been an heroic trek – starting with a walk of well over 400 miles to plant the Cross of Christ on Kilimanjaro, and marching onwards down routes which had been trodden by traders – from Mombasa, through Taita by the lakes of Naivasha and Baringo to Uganda.[3] But the new young king of Ganda, Mwanga, found the advance of a white man along such a route undoubtedly threatening. The bishop and his party were surrounded, overpowered and arrested. The pocket diary reveals that Hannington applied to himself the words of the Psalmist – 'I had fainted, unless I had believed to see the goodness of the Lord in the land of the living. Wait on the Lord. Be of good courage. Wait, I say, on the Lord.' On 28 October, inquiring the reason why his custodians were drumming and shouting louder than usual, the bishop was told that he and his companions were to be taken to Uganda. As they set off, Hannington's party was surrounded by Masai. The bearded young man looked his murderers in the eye and bade them tell King Mwanga that he had purchased the road to Buganda with his life. Then he pointed to his own gun which was being brandished by a Masai warrior. The gun went off and, as his friend the Rev. E.C. Dawson put it, 'the great and noble spirit leapt forth from its broken house of clay, and entered with exceeding joy into the presence of the King'. The Masai then massacred, with spears, all but four of the fifty men accompanying the bishop.

Ugandan Christians revere Hannington as a martyr. He was not the last Anglican martyr to meet a violent end there – in our own lifetimes President Idi Amin saw to that. Archbishop Janani Luwum was among the untold numbers massacred in the years 1971–9 in Uganda.[4]

Hannington, who earned the timeless crown of martyrdom, was also a man of his time – an archetypical new man, young, energetic, certain – very recognizably a man of Chamberlain's world rather than, say, that of Lord Melbourne. Like Benson, the archbishop of Canterbury, like many of the new electorate, he came from the lower middle class – his father ran a warehouse in Brighton. Hannington himself worked in the warehouse from the age of fifteen to twenty-one. The family, originally dissenters, joined the Church of England in 1867, when Hannington was twenty. He was thereafter entitled to go to Oxford, though he attended a private hall – St Mary's – rather than a college, and barely scraped a degree, being twenty-six before he did so. He was priested when he was twenty-nine, so had a mere nine years of ministry, nearly all of it exercised abroad for the Church Missionary Society.

It has been said by one of its liveliest historians that 'the scramble for Africa bewildered everyone, from the humblest African peasant to the master statesmen of the age, Lord Salisbury and Prince Bismarck'.[5] In a speech in May 1886, Salisbury stated that when he left the Foreign Office in 1880 'nobody thought about Africa', but when he returned to it five years later 'the nations of Europe were almost quarrelling with each other as to the various portions of Africa which they could obtain. I do not exactly know the cause of this sudden revolution.'[6]

Hannington, making his great missionary journey, clearly imagined himself to be bringing to the Africans salvation and the Word of God, with their inestimable concomitants, commerce and what he would have imagined to be civilization. King Mwanga and his Masai warriors would have seen in the young bishop's caravan an embodiment of the Modern World on the March. Like the peasant farmers of Ireland who wanted to be allowed a life of independence in which to practise an ancient faith and pre-eighteenth-century methods of agriculture; like the Ottoman sultans, ruling a dusty old empire in which clocks were forbidden; like the popes who, as the custodians of the oldest and most durable monarchy in Europe, had wanted to hold on to their temporal rights and lands; and like the young sepoy officers who dreaded much more than what had passed into their mouths when they bit the new-fangled cartridges; like the Polish gentry holding out against Russian intrusion and the Boer farmers of the Transvaal who now found themselves annexed by British soldiers, King Mwanga was confronting the nineteenth century in all its unstoppable energy. It was an energy which took the physical form of territorial conquest. But it was something more than this. The 'Scramble for Africa'[7] (a journalese phrase coined by *The Times* in September 1884) was the Victorian equivalent of the penetration of outer space for the superpowers of the twentieth century. It was of a piece with the Benthamite desire to control human groups and societies, and with the scientific desire to systematize, to classify, to museumize. To stick a label on something and to give it a Latin name is to comprehend it, to understand, to master.

Africa sat defiantly in the middle of the world throughout the Industrial Revolution, refusing to be classified, penetrated or understood. The extraordinary significance, for the Victorians, of David Livingstone, patron saint of missionary explorers, and of his St Paul, the American journalist Henry Morton Stanley, is that they had been where no white man had trod, and done it in a *scientific* spirit. Livingstone had died in May 1873 at a village in the county of Ilala, the very heart of the continent. They had sun-dried his body and brought it back for burial in the national Valhalla, Westminster Abbey. Stanley – the illegitimate son of Welsh-speakers who had been brought up in the local workhouse, St Asaph's near Denbigh, before going to America aged seventeen – saw Africa, as many explorers and missionaries did, as the metaphor for the uncharted territory of their own personal 'struggle'.[8] At Livingstone's grave in the Abbey, he voted to be, 'if God willed it, the next martyr to geographical science, or if my life is spared, to clear up not only the secrets of the Great River throughout its course, but also all that remained problematical and incomplete of the discoveries of Burton and Speke and Speke and Grant'.[9]

The Scramble for Africa was not a plot. It was something which happened because of the nature of the times in which it happened. The restlessness and scientific curiosity and by their lights the wish to be helpful of some travellers and explorers went hand in hand with the commercial greed and appetite for power in others. Then again, these explorations took place at the time of growth in European nationalisms. Livingstone penetrated the Congo, but in so doing he found a world in which cannibalism, slavery and rampant sexual promiscuity were waiting to be abolished, tidied away and disapproved of. The king of Belgium, Leopold II, was the first to give voice to the idea that '*Il faut à la Belgique une colonie*', Belgium must have a colony,[10] but it was not long before the other European countries were wanting what he called 'a slice of this magnificent cake'.[11] *The Times* saw Central Africa as a land of 'unspeakable richness' only waiting for an 'enterprising capitalist'. Once on African soil, however, even some of the greediest Europeans felt the itch not merely to plunder but to improve the African.

No one can say that the post-colonial problems faced by Africans in the twenty-first century do not grow out of the preoccupations of the nineteenth-century conquerors. The artificial boundaries imposed on mapless tribal lands by analogy with European borders, the deliberate shattering of traditional sociopolitical structures among African peoples, and their exploitation by Western commerce continue to cause and to highlight the difficulty. But which Western observer confronted by child slavery in an East African cocoa plantation, or female circumcision, or rampant AIDS, does not feel the impulses of benevolent Victorian missionaries to 'improve' and to 'civilize' the continent? The United Nations and the Commonwealth of Nations continue to assert the moral imperative of democracy for the new African states. Their fervour on the subject recalls the energy with which early missionaries attempted, with only limited success, to recommend monogamy.

None of us can entirely detach ourselves from the Imperial experiment and its consequences. At the same time, we cannot fail to wonder at the speed with which the European nations discovered Africa, mapped it, carved it up among themselves. France took the largest share geographically: the French Congo was a larger area than all Germany's African colonies put together.[12] By 1890 Salisbury and Bismarck had brokered deals with the other European powers and the 'map of Africa' was drawn – with Italian Somaliland looking out over the Indian Ocean, neighboured by British East Africa (Kenya), German

East Africa (Tanganyika) and Portuguese Mozambique. The real and unresolved area was in Southern Africa, where the Boers had been annexed against their will by the British – and this would escalate into a major war at the end of the century. France had meanwhile taken over a large area of the Congo and established Tunis and Algeria as French territories, as well as establishing the vast territories of French West Africa beside which the German Cameroons or Portuguese Angola look small.

One of the most vigorous historians of the British Empire, Lawrence James, has rightly pointed out that there were two scrambles for Africa during the 1880s and 1890s: on the one hand there was the diplomatic game in which de Brazza, Salisbury or Bismarck pored over maps. The other was the 'more robust business in which individuals ventured into largely unknown hostile regions and cajoled or coerced their inhabitants into accepting new masters and new laws'.[13]

Of these individuals, Frederick Lugard DSO (1858–1945) – later 1st Baron Lugard – was one of the most extraordinary. The whole colonial experiment – from the discoveries of the first missionary-explorers to the two world wars and to the beginnings of change in Africa – was contained within the period of Lugard's lifetime. Within twenty years of his death, the countries he helped to colonize and administer – Nigeria, Kenya, Uganda – had become independent.

Lugard was a Sandhurst-educated professional soldier, both of whose parents were missionaries. His father had been senior chaplain on the Madras establishment, and Lugard's early service was in India, where he developed a taste for big game-hunting. He was a slight, trim figure with enormous moustaches – 'exceptionally extravagant at a time when no self-respecting fighting man went bare-lipped in the tropics'.[14] Having fallen in love with a beautiful divorcee called 'Clytie', while campaigning in Burma he heard news that she was close to death after overturning her carriage at Lucknow. By the time he came back to India she had sailed for London, and when he pursued her there, Lugard had the shocking experience of finding her in bed with another man. It was a turning-point in his life. He lost his religious faith. He was prostrate with exhaustion.[15] He abandoned the Indian army and put himself at the service of the missionary African Lakes Company, waging war against slavers around the shores of Lake Nyasa. The Arabs and the Swahilis were the slave-traders making regular swoops in Nyasaland. Lugard had only limited success in fighting them and was severely wounded in 1888.

After a brief return to England in 1889, Lugard was commissioned by the Imperial British East Africa Company to establish their interest in Uganda, and to open up a new route from Mombasa to the interior by the Sabaki river. Since murdering Bishop Hannington in 1885, partly to gratify the Muslim slave-traders who had occupied his capital of Mengo, King Mwanga had fallen under the influence of the French White Fathers missionaries. Uganda was in a state of near civil war, with Muslims, Catholics and Protestants all at odds, and the pagans, devotees of witchcraft, hashish or bhang and polygamy, representing the forces of conservatism. Lugard made his first appeal to the pro-English Protestants (the Wa-Ingleza) and seemed to find the French missionaries themselves more inimical than the Wa-Bangi or pagans. The French bishop out there, Monsignor Hirth, 'would not look you in the face when speaking'.[16] Back in England Lugard tried to enlist the help of the Roman Catholic bishop of Emmaus, who was staying in Cadogan Street and with whom he was on 'cordial terms', but the bishop would not be drawn. It was beyond Lugard's comprehension that the Duke of Norfolk could support the French missionaries, who openly favoured handing Uganda over to the Germans.

With great expedition, Lugard got Mwanga to sign a treaty giving the British East Africa Company the right to intervene in the affairs of Uganda. He then went on an adventurous journey up-country through the Ruwenzori mountains as far as the Albert Nyanza, where he enlisted 600 Sudanese soldiers and marched back to the capital Mengo. He found (it is now 1892) fighting between Catholics and Protestants, and the Catholics attacked his headquarters in Kampala. Lugard possessed two Maxim guns in a somewhat battered state, and with these he defended his position at Kampala. About a week after the so-called battle of Mengo, the king took refuge on an island sanctuary – the island of Bulingugwe. Lugard pursued him and started firing the Maxim guns across the water at the considerable crowds of men, women and children. 'A crowd of women and children fled with us. How many fell! We had soon gained the other shore of the island; the bullets could no longer reach us. But what a sight! Just a few canoes, and a crowd of 3,000 or 4,000 throwing themselves into the water to cling to them; it was heart-breaking. What shrieks! What a fusillade! What deaths by drowning.' The account comes from the Church Missionary Society's *Intelligences*.[17]

There is no record of this atrocity in Lugard's copious Diaries, and in his book *The Rise of Our East African Empire* he dismisses the notion that 'hundreds, if not thousands' had been killed. His estimate is about twenty-five dead on the island, and no more than sixty in the water.[18] A fortnight before the massacre was alleged to take place, he noted:

> It is not for us to say that all Islam, or all Rome, will be damned. Let us hear all sides, and select what our reason and conviction teach us to be the best form of worship . . . If missionaries would preach *Charity*, Charity, Charity, 'which thinketh no evil, suffereth long and is kind' – I am convinced that they would do more to reclaim Africa, than most subtle distinctions between Catholic and Protestant and Islam. Teach them civilization too – raise them in their own self-respect.[19]

Elsewhere he says, 'the curse of Africa and of Uganda in especial is guns', and 'the curse of this poor country is that every man in it is a liar, and one can never get at the truth of things'.[20]

Lugard was almost certainly not a partaker in the atrocities,[21] at the end of which 50,000 Catholics had, it was claimed, been sold into slavery, their cathedral and several schools destroyed.[22] Throughout his long career as a colonial administrator – as high commissioner in Nigeria (1900–7), as governor of Hong Kong (1907–11) and once again in Nigeria – he believed in a system of 'dual control' by which the traditional institutions of native peoples provided the best foundation on which to progress. By his old age, he had come to see that African self-government was not only inevitable but desirable.[23] He considered the prime reason for military intervention to be the liberation of slaves. He abhorred the moral cowardice of having an 'active and pushing' anti-slavery policy 'so long as the whole difficulties of the matter fell on the shoulders of a native ruler', but a lukewarm or even retrogressive policy 'from the day it devolved upon us to carry out these measures ourselves'.[24] His ideal was a politics of 'self-development' for the African colonies with the minimum of interference from Europeans except to correct abuse.[25] To this extent Lugard was very different, in his conception of the Imperial role, from Cecil Rhodes, who made himself a fortune out of diamonds and whose first military–political coup was the annexation of Bechuanaland in 1884–5. He really did dream of an unbroken chain of British territory from the Cape to Cairo: but these dreams and their consequences belong a little later in the story.

34

Kipling's India

The confidence with which white Europeans assumed racial superiority over the African or the Indian is one of the most shocking aspects of the Victorian sensibility. Bogus notions of racial stereotype, and fervour for the salvation of souls, sometimes combined in the same individual to produce an alarming cocktail of imperialistic motivation. The story of Gordon all but alone in Khartoum with his bible and his self-belief, or Livingstone penetrating the unknown territories of the Congo, or Bishop Hannington, with fifty bearers, confronting the angry warriors of King Mwanga, are all stories which suggest a primeval and physically equal struggle in which the white man's superiority to the black is demonstrated in moral terms. The truth is that the expansion of the Empire took place at a time of rapid technological advance. The new inventions changed everything, both in Europe and in the Imperial world: changed the pattern of trade, disrupted the normal pattern of political relationships both within and between nations, created a global economy, a global technological world with which politicians could only partially come to terms.

Technology is the vital factor in the Imperial story. We have already alluded to the fact that the British possession of the telegraph played a vital role in defeating the sepoy uprisings of 1857–8 in India. At the same time, Speke and Burton were setting out to discover the sources of the Nile, Livingstone to explore the Zambezi. Shallow-draft steamers were an essential part of the enterprise. Having begun his unlocking of the African mystery, Livingstone could also produce the bestselling book which would publicize it. Steam printing enabled him to roll off 70,000 copies of *Missionary Travels and Researches in South Africa*. Before its invention, 10,000 books sold would have been a prodigy.

Travel speeds, thanks to railroads and steamships, had now been reduced. Jules Verne sent the fictional Phileas Fogg around the world in eighty days; in 1889–90 the American journalist, Elizabeth Cochrane – 'Nellie Bly' – accomplished the round trip in a little over seventy-two. This was the era when the world was divided into twenty-four time zones one hour apart, because it was now technologically possible 'to put a girdle around the earth', like Shakespeare's Ariel. Steel had replaced iron as the preferred material for boiler and hull construction, with purpose-built ships bringing frozen meat or petroleum across the ocean.[1]

Petroleum fuelled the newly developed twin-cylindered engine developed by Gottlieb Daimler (1834–1900) of Württemberg.[2] In 1885 he devised his surface carburettor; and while he was designing his high-speed vertical engine, Karl Benz (1844–1929) of Mannheim was developing his first motor-vehicle[3] (his first four-wheeled car was constructed in 1893), though Daimler can take the credit or blame for inventing the internal combustion engine itself.

Joseph Swan, familiar since the late 1840s with primitive filament lamps and arc-lamps, demonstrated his electric glow-lamp, the first carbon-filament incandescent light bulb, on 18 December 1878. We have already alluded to his lighting the house of Sir William Armstrong. The House of Commons was lit with incandescent electric light by 1881; Peterhouse, Cambridge, was the first institution to follow suit in 1884.[4]

At the same time, wireless telegraphy was being developed by Heinrich Hertz (1857–94). Sir Oliver Lodge (1851–1940) pioneered the use of an induction coil as a means of tuning an electric resonator – a system he perfected in 1897, and whose commercial possibilities were almost instantly exploited by Guglielmo Marconi (1874–1937). Before that, Alexander Graham Bell (1847–1922), basing his experiments on the work of the German physicist Hermann Helmholtz (1821–94), had pioneered the telephone. The first telephone exchange was established in London in 1879.

The Home Insurance Company in Chicago in 1883 commissioned William Le Baron Jenney (1832–1907) to build them a 10-storey office block – since demolished – which would be fireproof and would let in as much light as possible.[5] The lower stories were constructed with wrought-iron beams and girders. Wrought-iron was also used by Gustave Eiffel (1832–1923) when he designed a 985 ft tower for the Paris Exhibition of 1889, its masonry piers bedded in huge pits of concrete 50 feet deep, its swooping heights attainable by means of mechanical elevators.[6] (Jenney's Home Insurance Building used Bessemer steel for its upper storeys.)

The world of King Mwanga, of the Turkish sultans, or of the Reverend William Barnes in Dorset, with his long beard and his knowledge of a vanishing dialect of rural Dorset, was now to be replaced by another world altogether – petroleum-fuelled, steel-girdered, telephonically-connected, electric-lit.

'It is useless to rail against capitalism. Capitalism did not create our world; the machine did.'[7] Just as it could be said that the arms race got out of control merely because technology was unbridled, not because politicians willed it to do so, it could also be said that the Imperial expansion was part of the technological revolution. Given the possibility of steamships and railways covering vast distances in previously unimaginable journey-times, or the advance of cable telegrams, or the development of the machine gun, it was inevitable that those who possessed this technology would feel bound to use it. Those cultures with no such technology could not resist the incursions of those with Maxim guns, telegrams, railways and steel-framed steamships. One way of looking at this would be to say that the technologically advanced culture was dominant or even (as nearly all Victorians would have believed) superior. Another way of viewing matters, however, would be to suggest that the notion of 'control' was itself a patriarchal illusion. If it was right to begin Part IV by quoting from Dostoyevsky's *The Devils* and seeing it as a prophetic work, then much of the technological advance of the 1880s could be seen as a blind march to murder, arson, mayhem. In 1879 Alfred Nobel (1833–96) invented blasting gelatine – 92 per cent nitroglycerine gelatinized with 8 per cent of collodion cotton.[8] The initial difficulties of manufacture were great, but by 1884, with the use of soluble nitro-cotton (rather than collodion), large-scale production could begin. The human race now possessed the capacity to blast quarries, mines and dams on an unprecedented scale, but it had also taken an irrevocable stride towards the capacity to obliterate itself altogether.

The bard of the technological revolution, the artist who felt most instinctively, and understood with the most immediate intelligence, the connection between technology and imperial strength, was Rudyard Kipling (1865–1936). His Browningesque dramatic monologue 'McAndrew's Hymn' – a glorious poem almost better than anything, even, that Browning wrote – puts into the mouth of an old Scottish ship's engineer the bizarre thought:

> From coupler-flange to spindle-guide I see Thy hand, O God –
> Predestination in the stride o' yon connectin'-rod.[9]

And in 'The King' the poet sees Romance itself, the Boy-god who most poets teach us to suppose is vanished from the Earth, bringing up the nine-fifteen train.

> His hand was on the lever laid,
> His oil-can soothed the worrying cranks,
> His whistle waked the snowbound grade,
> His fog-horn cut the reeking Banks;
> By dock and deep and mine and mill
> The Boy-god reckless laboured still![10]

Kipling was also the first writer to admit the sexual appeal of imperial expansion. Whatever the political or economic motives of empire, its existence and its growth expanded the world for a great many people who could not conceivably have come into contact otherwise with races and cultures utterly different from their own. The 'Burma girl' who sits by the 'old Moulmein Pagoda' in 'Mandalay' offers delights which are not in the repertoire of the 'fifty 'ousemaids' dated by the common soldier-narrator since his return to London:

> When the mist was on the rice-fields an' the sun was
>   droppin' slow
> She'd git 'er little banjo an' she'd sing *Kulla-lolo!*
> With 'er arm upon my shoulder an' 'er cheek agin my
>   cheek
> We useter watch the steamers an' the *hathis* pilin' teak.[11]

Kipling's reputation is one of the most complicated in the history of literature. It would be an obtuse reader who did not recognize his brilliance as a short-story writer – 'our greatest' according to the poet Craig Raine . . . 'our greatest practitioner of dialect and idiolect'.[12] It would also be hard to think of anything but priggishness or intellectual snobbery which refused to see merit in Kipling's enormous output of verse. Yet it is impossible to imagine the revisionist reader, however much under Kipling's spell, who could endorse the views in 'The White Man's Burden', with its picture of

> Your new-caught, sullen peoples,
> Half-devil and half-child.[13]

(A reference to the American conquest of the Philippines.) When Kipling's talent first shone upon the world, he was seen less as an imperialist than as an exotic. Those marvellous early stories in *Plain Tales from the Hills* opened up a world which many stuffier defenders of the Raj would probably have wanted concealed. He depicts in dozens of incomparable vignettes the silliness and triviality of English society in the hill stations, the casual adulteries and flirtations, and the continual allure, imaginative and sexual, of India itself. 'It is the strength of this new story-teller,' wrote Edmond Gosse, 'that he reawakens in us the primitive emotions of curiosity, mystery, and romance in action. He is the master of a new kind of terrible and enchanting peep-show, and we crowd around him begging for "just one more look".'[14]

Perhaps the most terror, from the early collection, is to be found in the story called 'Beyond the Pale', in which an Englishman called Trejago wanders down a dark narrow gully in the city – Lahore, presumably – and peers through the grating to see who owns 'a pretty little laugh' coming from the darkened room behind. It is little Bisesa, a fifteen-year-old widow, and he woos her with singing the Love Song of Har Dyal in her own language.

> In the day-time Trejago drove through his routine of office work, or put on his calling-clothes and called on the ladies of the Station, wondering how long they would know him if they knew of poor little Bisesa. At night, when all the City was still, came the walk under the evil-smelling *boorka*, the patrol through Jitha Megji's *bustee*, the quick turn into Amir Nath's Gully between the sleeping cattle and the dead walls, and then, last of all, Bisesa, and the deep, even breathing of the old woman who slept outside the door of the bare little room that Durga Charan allotted to his sister's daughter.[15]

Trejago falls in love with Bisesa, and she believes that he will marry her; but when the rumour of their liaison gets out, Trejago returns to the window-grating through which he has previously crawled to his young lover to find her holding out 'her arms to the moonlight. Both hands had been cut off at the wrists . . .'[16] The next thing Trejago knows, a knife is being thrust out from the grating and cuts into his groin. The strong implication is that he is rendered impotent by the wound.

If this is one of the darkest stories Kipling ever wrote, there is, throughout his work, a very strong ambivalence about the supposed superiority of whites over Indians. The unnamed subaltern who commits suicide because he feels he has disgraced himself with women and debt[17] ('Thrown Away') hasn't learnt the lesson that 'India is a place beyond all others where one must not take things too seriously – the midday sun always excepted. Too much work and too much energy kill a man just as effectively as too much assorted vice or too much drink.' There is multi-layered irony here, of course, and like so many of Kipling's stories, it is cruel. The narrator and the major who help bury the Boy give out that he has died of cholera. They think of sending home a lock of his hair but 'there were reasons why we could not find a lock fit to send'. (He has blown his head off.) They send a lock of the major's instead and, hysterical on whisky, write back to the Boy's mother 'setting forth how the Boy was the pattern of all virtues, beloved by his regiment . . . it was no time for little lies, you will understand – and how he had died without pain'.[18]

In what is Kipling's most successful sustained evocation of Indian life, *Kim*, written when he had long since left India (1901), Kimball O'Hara, the son of an Irish colour-sergeant and (one infers) a Eurasian nursemaid, befriends a Tibetan lama and follows him on the religious pilgrimage to Benares and the river which will wash away sin. Contrasted with the lama and his essentially serious perception of things are the British intelligence agents who want to train Kim as a spy in 'The Great Game'. The most memorable and moving characters whom Kim and his Tibetan friend encounter, and the most realistic, are all Indians – Hindu and Muslim and Sikh.

The spies seem to have wandered into the 'felt life' of a masterpiece from adventure stories on a railway bookstall. One feels that Kipling's imagination has seen something to which his developed political brain is blind: namely the absolute inevitability that the Raj will one day end. In this story, everyone of course takes the Raj for granted. There are no Indian nationalists. Yet India itself in all its cultural abundance, in all its geographical varieties, its colours, lights and smells, comes alive in this book quite incomparably: larger and stronger than any temporary political system.

Sixty years is not long under eternity's eye. There must have been plenty of children alive in Kim's Lahore who lived to see the end of the Raj. Lahore, no longer a city of Kipling's India, is, like most of the Punjab, part of Pakistan. The Sikhs – about 4 million of them – found their homeland crudely divided down the middle in the territorial carve-up hastily contrived by Sir Cyril Radcliffe and Lord Mountbatten in 1947. (Sikhs had been largely eliminated from Lahore, as had Muslims, on the 'Indian' side of the border, from Amritsar.)[19] Exile, migration and massacre were what awaited these people – at least half a million dead.

Knowing this as we do might make us, if we are European, have some sympathy with the views of those Victorians who believed that the Imperial system was the only one beneath which multiculturalism could flourish.[20] Modern Indian historians who see the Raj, probably correctly, as founded on notions of white racial superiority can quote letters such as Secretary of State Lord George Gordon writing to Lord Elgin (viceroy and son of a previous viceroy in the 1890s), 'I am sorry to hear of the increasing friction between Hindus and Mohammedans in the North West and the Punjab. One hardly knows what to wish for; unity of ideas and action would be very dangerous politically, divergence of ideas and collision are administratively troublesome. Of the two the latter is the least risky, though it throws anxiety and responsibility upon those on the spot where the friction exists.'[21] In other words, the British could be seen as operating a policy of divide and rule. No doubt the administrators *did* think like Lord George Gordon, but whether they deliberately fomented division between Sikhs, Muslims and Hindus is rather more questionable. In *Kim* everyone takes multiculturalism, and the Raj, for granted. India and Pakistan over the last fifty years have not offered the world a very perfect model of mutual tolerance.

The tensions in British thinking about the Raj concerned themselves less with rival interest-groups in India, and more with the contrast between Liberal and Conservative administration. After Gladstone replaced Lord Lytton as viceroy with Lord Ripon in 1880, there were no more Conservative viceroys until the end of the century. The Liberal viceroys attempted to satisfy the 'legitimate aspirations' of Indians. The phrase is that of Sir Courtenay Ilbert, whose reform of judicial procedure – enabling Indian judges and magistrates to try Europeans in country districts – caused a storm of protest. Ripon backed down: in concession to the racists he allowed a provision whereby, in such cases, the white defendant could insist on a jury half of whom would be European.

The Liberal viceroys encouraged the growth of an Indian professional class. Between 1857 and 1887, some 60,000 Indians entered universities.[22] One third of the 1,712 Calcutta graduates in 1882 entered government service, slightly more became lawyers. Most of those who joined the Indian National Congress – 'collaborators' in the term of a modern historian – were Hindus.[23]

The inevitability that self-government would come is obvious to the eyes of hindsight. Lord Curzon, in some ways the greatest of all the viceroys, who took up his post in 1899, was the most out-and-out Imperialist, believing that 'through the Empire of Hindustan . . . the mastery of the world was in the possession of the British people'. Yet he sensed almost as soon as he got to India, in his fortieth year, that 'The English are getting lethargic and they think only of home. Their hearts are not in this country.'[24]

Curzon was one of the only viceroys with a deeply learned love of Indian language, lore, architecture and archaeology. In a speech to the Asiatic Society in 1900 he defined one of his roles as a guardian of India's past. 'A race like our own, who are themselves foreigners, are in a sense better fitted to guard, with a dispassionate and impartial zeal, the relics of different ages, than might be the descendants of warring races or the votaries of rival creeds.'[25] One perfectly understands Indian distaste for the patronizing tone here, but any Indian antiquary has reason to be grateful to Curzon for preserving and conserving so much – including such bold innovations as attempting to take over Bodh Gaya, site of the Buddha's enlightenment, which had been in the possession of a Hindu merchant since 1727, and hand it back to the Buddhists. (Political pressure made Curzon unwillingly back down here.) In his antiquarianism and taste for old Indian artefacts, buildings, philosophy and literature, Curzon seems, like the muse of Kipling, both imperialistically arrogant and culturally humble. A large part of him bowed before a great Asiatic past, and seemed to know by instinct that British imperial ambitions would never have the power, or importantly the will, to dominate it.

'Right-wing' critics of liberalism in the Raj looked with satisfaction to the journalism of Sir James Fitzjames Stephen, who in 1883 famously said that the Raj was 'founded not on consent but on conquest'. Obviously, after the quite horrifying trauma of 1857–8, this was in part true. The reform of the Indian army after the Mutiny raised the ratio of Europeans to Indians in the armed services to about half by the mid-1860s.[26] But it must have been obvious to all that on another level, both the army and the ICS only functioned on a principle of consent. In the 1860s the army numbered 120,000 Indians and 60,000 Europeans, and it was the constant aim of penny-pinching laissez-faire British governments to cut these numbers. Once Indian nationalism became an even half-serious proposition, the Raj could not long endure. Racist, by any standards, it undoubtedly was; economically exploitative too, as nearly all modern historians wish to point out; but the British will to govern by force had its limits when consent was absent. The massacre of protesters at Amritsar by General Dyer – 379 killed and 1,200 wounded – on 13 April 1919, followed by a proclamation of martial law, was a disgrace from which the British Raj never recovered its semi-legitimate self-estimation for decency and justice. Thirty years before independence it sealed the Raj's fate, but one can now sniff the obsolescence of the imperial ambition in the wind much earlier – in the closing decades of Queen Victoria's reign.

35

Jubilee – and the Munshi

To the crowds who assembled in London for the Queen's Golden Jubilee in June 1887, however, the British Empire was manifested as a visible pageant. As the Queen's carriage was drawn to Westminster Abbey for the Service of Thanksgiving on 21 June, it was preceded by an Indian cavalry escort, each member of which was presented with a special medal at Windsor Castle before going home.[1] The crowds gave rousing cheers to the brilliantly dressed Indian princes who attended the ceremonies in honour of their Queen-Empress. The Maharao of Cutch, his diamond-and-ruby-encrusted turban sparkling in the sunshine, received especially warm applause. The Maharaja Holkar of Indore was clad with equal magnificence. And there must have been gasps of wonder at the superb gold and silver trappings and saddle on the proud Arab stallion of His Highness the Thakor of Morvi. In fact the colonial princes and monarchs such as the Thakor Sahib of Limbdi or the Maharaja and Maharani of Cooch Bihar, or the majestic figures of Queen Kapiolani and her daughter Princess Liliuokalani of Hawaii, rather outshone the visiting European royalties – the men whiskery and uniformed, the women for the most part plain and long-suffering – who must have been more or less indistinguishable as they trotted by in their open landaus.

One figure stood out from the grandees in their gilded epaulettes, sashes, uniforms, helmets, turbans. The Queen herself wore a black satin dress, and a bonnet trimmed with white lace. Many will have noted her corpulence, to which the previous day's luncheon (the actual anniversary of her accession) amply contributed. With its Potage à la Royale, its Filet de Boeuf au Macaroni, its Poulets, its Venison steaks, its lobsters, ducklings, jellies and *Reis Kuchen mit Aprikosen*, it was of a positively Hanoverian heaviness.[2]

One witness to the Abbey service remarked how apt it was that the Queen dressed so simply – 'she was mother and mother-in-law and grandmother of all that regal company, and there she was, a little old lady coming to church to thank God for the long years in which she had ruled over her people'.[3] A comparable observation was made once when she was being driven through Dublin, and a woman in the crowd remarked, 'Sure, and she's only an old body like ourselves.'

She was no such thing. Those admitted to her presence attested to her personal charm and strength of character, which was 'both shy and humble . . . But as Queen she was neither shy nor humble, and asserted her position unhesitatingly.' This could form no part of public perception of her character, however, since for most of the previous quarter-century she had been a recluse, squirrelling away the £400,000 per annum awarded to her as Head of State, and seldom seen. Journalists and those whose hobby was to 'follow' the royal family singled out particular members as 'popular', 'scandalous' and so on, but very little was publicly known about any of them, least of all about the Queen.[4] Even those who might be expected to have come across Her Majesty – such as the 3rd Marquess of Salisbury – found her character a total surprise when actually encountered.

The parade of the Queen's children, grandchildren and in-laws was distinguished neither by its beauty or health, nor by its morals. It was widely agreed in the Abbey that the most impressive figure was the German Crown Prince (Fritz) – married to the Princess Royal. He had arrived at the ceremonies, with Vicky, arrayed in cuirass and silver helmet, from a hotel in Norwood where they were staying to conserve their strength for a summer at Balmoral.[5] They had also consulted Dr Morell MacKenzie of Harley Street, who had confirmed that Fritz had cancer of the larynx. (He died in 1888.) Their son Willy (the future Kaiser Wilhelm II) had been damaged at birth – one arm was crushed and he was deaf. He had also inherited the strain of madness in the family. His relations with his parents were of the most painful. In some moods he was so Anglophobic that once when he cut himself he hoped he would lose every drop of his English blood. When he heard of Lord Frederick Cavendish's assassination he said it was 'the best news I have received today',[6] and he regarded Queen Victoria – at least when the fits of the most extreme Anglophobia seized him – as 'an old hag'. Those who cheered the arrival at the Abbey of the governor general of Canada, the Marquess of Lorne, might have wondered why his wife, Princess Louise, had produced no heir. Did it have anything to do with the fact that she had been in love with the sculptor Edgar Boehm (a substantial figure – it was said a winch was necessary to lift him from his royal mistress when he died in flagrante) and that Lord Lorne was a promiscuous homosexual, much given to meeting guardsmen in Hyde Park until his exile to the land of the lumberjack? The Prince of Wales was a by-word for scandalous adulteries, and poor Prince Leopold was haemophiliac, a condition for which Princesses Alice (already ten years dead at the time of the Jubilee) and Beatrice were carriers – as was the Princess Royal. (They spread the disease through most of the royal houses of Europe.) This was no 'old lady like ourselves': it was an extraordinary matriarchy of medical and psychological oddities.

One of the more markedly eccentric – and to me attractive – features of the Queen's character was shown in her passionate partiality for individual servants. John Brown, the Highland ghillie, certainly enjoyed an intimacy with his royal employer which gave rise to gossip.[7] There was even a scurrilous pamphlet published – *Mrs John Brown*. Courtiers who saw them together were irritated by Brown's throwing his weight about. He 'could do practically what he liked with the other servants' and was impertinent to equerries, royal doctors and the like. But Frederick Ponsonby – son of the Queen's private secretary and himself a royal servant of long standing, was surely right to conclude that 'whether there was any quite unconscious sexual feeling in the Queen's regard for her faithful servant I am unable to say, but judging by what I heard afterwards . . . I am quite convinced that if such a feeling did exist, it was quite unconscious on both sides, and that their relations up to the last were simply those of employer and devoted retainer.'[8] The court grew used to the Queen's adopting Brown's locutions. When the Duchess of Roxburgh and Miss Stopford (a woman of the Bedchamber) were not on speaking terms, Sir James Reid, the Queen's doctor, suggested that the Duchess might visit her. 'Oh no,' exclaimed the Queen. 'There would only be what Brown calls Hell and hot water.'

Perhaps only those, in our own day, who have befriended old ladies who still employ servants can recognize how deep and close the bond between them can grow. The Queen had been in effect an only child – though she had a half-sister she was brought up as a solitary, uncertain of her mother's love and yet monarch of all she surveyed. She also inherited the classic Hanoverian distaste for her heir, and she had the terrible misfortune to be widowed young. Neither from parent nor from first-born son could the consolations of affection be found, nor the even more deeply consoling qualities of dependability, obedience, affection for her whims. It is no surprise that she numbered her servants among her best friends.

When Brown died in 1883 she was devastated, and was still thinking loving thoughts of him on her deathbed nearly eighteen years later. No servant ever replaced him in her affections, but there was one 'about whom' – to quote from her doctor – 'the Queen seems off her head'.[9]

At the end of June 1887 she engaged her first two Indian servants – Mahomet Buksh, a plump smiling young man, and Abdul Karim, aged twenty-four, both of them *khidmutgars* (waiters). They were engaged to serve at table, but it was not long before the Queen had given her secretary a Hindi vocabulary to study. 'I am learning a few words of Hindustani to speak to my servants. It is a great interest to me for both the language and the people,' she said.[10]

After a couple of months at Osborne the Queen, exhausted by the rare experience of fulfilling a few public engagements for her Jubilee, moved the court, as usual, to Balmoral, giving to Major-General Sir Thomas Denneby, her groom-in-waiting, important instructions:

Mahomet Buksh and Abdul Karim should wear in the *morning out of doors* at breakfast when they wait, their *new* dark blue dress and always at lunch with any 'Pageri' [pagri] (Turban) and sash *they like* only not the *Gold ones*. The Red dress and gold and white turban (or Pageri) and sash to be *always worn at dinner in the evening*. If it is wet or cold the breakfast is *in doors* when they should always attend. As I often, *before* the days get too short take the tea out with me in the carriage, they might do some extra waiting instead, either *before* I go out, or when I come in. Better before I go out, stopping half an hour longer and should wait *upstairs* to answer a handbell. They should come in and out and bring boxes, letters, etc. *instead* of the *maids* . . .

And so on for pages.

Purists will note with interest that the Queen refers to 'lunch' not 'luncheon' and that in the frenzied excitement of contemplating her beautifully dressed new servants, she has abandoned the protocol of referring to herself in the third person.

Abdul Karim soon became the favourite. Evidently he was very charming, and he was the master of 'laying it on with a trowel', the prerequisite, as Disraeli had noted, when flattering royalty. Abdul was – to the amazement of the other courtiers – given John Brown's room to occupy, almost a sacred shrine in the Queen's eyes. He was – he assured Her Majesty – the son of a Surgeon General in the Indian army and it was most inappropriate for him to be waiting at table. Before long he was given the title of Munshi Hafiz Abdul Kasim – the Queen's official Indian secretary. Young Frederick Ponsonby, son of Sir Henry and now a member of the royal household, was dispatched to India to establish the credentials of the 'Surgeon General'. He found the Munshi's father was the apothecary in the jail at Agra. The Queen was furious with Ponsonby and told him he had met the wrong man. She did not invite Ponsonby to dine with her for a year.[11]

During the summer of 1889 the Queen noted that a brooch had gone missing – it had been given her by the Grand Duke of Hesse and had been pinned to a shawl. The courtiers made investigations and discovered that Hourmet Ali, the Munshi's brother-in-law, had stolen it. Mrs Tuck the Queen's dresser retrieved the brooch from Wagland the jeweller in Windsor, who confirmed that he had paid Hourmet 6/– for it. When confronted with this hard-and-fast evidence, the Queen erupted with rage against Mrs Tuck. It was one of those wild tantrums which had so terrified the Prince Consort. 'That is what you English call justice!' she shouted, instructing the dresser that no one – not the housekeeper at Balmoral, not Rankin the footman, *no one* – must be told of this disgraceful episode.

Historians and biographers have, alas, tended to share the snobbish and racialistic attitudes of the court to the Munshi; even, it has to be said, Lady Longford adopts a tone which implies that there is something inherently ridiculous about an Indian being a royal servitor. The Queen, who could be so maddening and so foolish on many levels, was also able to see that a capable and pleasant fellow such as the Munshi would have got nowhere if he had told the truth about his supposedly low origins. Resuming the haughty and formal third person, the Queen begged to inform Sir Henry Ponsonby that 'to make out that the poor good Munshi is so *low* is really *outrageous* & in a country like England quite out of place . . . she has known 2 Archbishops who were sons respectively of a Butcher & a Grocer'.

True, she was insensitive to the dangers of accepting advice on Indian affairs from a Muslim at a time when there were tensions – when were there not? – between Hindus and Muslims. Perhaps she saw some kinship between the moral and scriptural simplicities of the Mosque and the austere Presbyterian worship at Crathie, which she in every way preferred to the Anglican service. Not all her notions were crazy. Salisbury pooh-poohed the notion that he should send Mr Rafuddin Ahmed, a young friend of the Munshi's, to Constantinople as an attaché at the embassy.[12] Surely a Muslim voice representing Britain in the Ottoman capital was perfectly sensible. Victoria's idea to have not merely decorative servants in turbans but Indian members of the

Household contrasts impressively with the record of Elizabeth II, who during a period when her country became supposedly multiracial and multicultural employed not one secretary, equerry or household servant of an Asian or Afro-Caribbean background.

So, the Golden Jubilee passed away – with a children's party for 30,000 in Hyde Park, a review of the fleet at Spithead, and well-wishers from all over the three kingdoms, and all over the Empire, saluting their sovereign with bunting and telegraph messages and songs. To read the Queen's own, and understandably self-satisfied, account of the matter in her Journals you could be forgiven for believing that 1887 had closed in a glow of happiness, with the Empire calmly and prosperously in love with its sovereign and – to borrow a phrase from a modern politician – 'at ease with itself'. Nothing could have been further from the truth.

36

The Dock Strike

In May 1887, the Queen had been to the East End of London and heard what she described to her prime minister as a 'horrid noise (*quite* new to the Queen's ears) "booing", she believes it is called'. Salisbury was 'much grieved to hear it', but explained to his Sovereign that 'London contains a much larger number of the worst kind of rough than any other great town in the island; for all that is worthless, worn out, or penniless naturally drifts to London.' He opined that the 'booing' almost certainly emanated from socialists or the Irish – 'very resentful men who would stick at nothing to show their fury'.[1]

The only plausible political group within the parliamentary system who might have represented the interests of the poor against the views of Lord Salisbury were the Liberal Radicals. Yet their leader Joseph Chamberlain had brought down Gladstone over the question of Ireland and would himself one day serve in a Salisbury Cabinet. The split in the Liberal Party put the Conservatives in power for most of the rest of the reign.

As will always happen eventually when strong interests are not represented within the political system, people took to the streets. Under Gladstone's government, a new word had been coined to describe the dreadful effects of the slump – 'unemployment';[2] it was matched by the conditions already described in rural areas – devastation in Ireland, and to a small extent in England, too. The people described as 'worthless, worn out and penniless' did indeed come to the cities in a desperate attempt to find work, and in the Jubilee Year they were not always very successful. In the winter of 1886–7 there had been almost daily demonstrations organized by the Marxists, in which lines of ragged men marched out of the East End.[3]

During the autumn they had tended to congregate in Trafalgar Square – 'the most convenient place in all London for an open air meeting' according to William Morris, but dangerously near the Westminster Parliament at the end of Whitehall, or Buckingham Palace at the end of the Mall. The newly appointed chief of the Metropolitan Police was instructed by Salisbury to crack down on demonstrations. It was Salisbury himself who conceived the idea of railing in the Square –

'with gates of course',[4] so that in the event of trouble the agitators could be penned in.

On Sunday 13 November – it was to earn the sombre nickname of 'Bloody Sunday' – the Radical Federation announced that it would hold a demonstration to protest against coercion in Ireland, and to demand the release of William O'Brien MP. Both sides, the socialists and the police, had a strategy in place. The demonstrators tried to baffle the police by approaching in many different groups from all sides of the Square. Morris and Annie Besant marched from Clerkenwell Green. Another group marched from Holborn and were met at Charing Cross station by the Radical MP and author R. Cunninghame Graham and John Burns the trade unionist. Others, trying to march from Bermondsey and Deptford, met with mounted police on Westminster Bridge – where twenty-six people were so badly injured that they were carried back across the river to St Thomas's hospital. What the demonstrators did not realize was that the police, tipped off by spies, had surrounded Trafalgar Square at points in a radius of about quarter of a mile and that behind them were two squadrons of Life Guards with fixed bayonets. Once the marchers had passed through the strategic points marked out by the police they were surrounded and at their mercy. *The Times* reported that 'the police, mounted and on foot, charged in among the people, striking indiscriminately in all directions and causing complete disorder in the ranks of the processionists. I witnessed several cases of injury to men who had been struck on the head or the face by the police. The blood, in most instances, was flowing freely from the wound and the spectacle was indeed a sickening one.'[5]

Part of the trouble was that the demonstrators, in so far as they were organized at all, imagined that they could fight well-coordinated troops and police against whom they stood no chance. They would have been much better advised to conduct the sort of non-violent resistance to the police pioneered by Gandhi in South Africa – inspired in part by the pacifist writings of Tolstoy.[6]

The police numbers were so great – probably 2,000, backed up by 400 armed soldiers – that the 10,000 marchers, many of them beaten up, dispersed without a shot being fired. Cunninghame Graham and Burns, having been badly clubbed, were arrested – and subsequently imprisoned for six weeks. The following Sunday, a smaller number tried to hold another demonstration in Hyde Park. At the same time police in Northumberland Avenue, just south of Trafalgar Square, knocked down a young law-writer named Alfred Linnell, who subsequently died. After some weeks of legal wrangling about whether he had died as a result of injuries caused by a horse kicking him, Linnell's body was released for burial. It was decided to make the funeral held on 18 December a demonstration.

It was choreographed by Annie Besant.[7] To the solemn music of the Dead March from *Saul*, fifty wand-bearers, veterans of the Chartist agitation, preceded the coffin, which was emblazoned with the legend, 'Killed in Trafalgar Square'. They set off from Soho with an open hearse, four horses and six pall-bearers – William Morris, Cunninghame Graham, W.T. Stead, Herbert Burrows, Frank Smith and Annie Besant herself.[8] Huge crowds (Mrs Besant reckoned 100,000 people) lined the wayside to the Mile End Road, and the cortège did not reach the cemetery until half-past four. It was nearly dark and rain fell as the burial service was read by Christian Socialist leader the Rev. Stewart Headlam. Orations and laments were spoken, by the light of lanterns, to a vast crowd. Eleanor Marx might have reflected on the strange fact that when her father had been buried in Highgate cemetery in March 1883 only a huddle had collected in Highgate to hear Engels' panegyric. The obsequies of an unheard-of clerk, however, symbolized for hundreds of people present why the struggle was so important. As Morris put it,

> there lay a man of no particular party – a man who until a week or two ago was perfectly obscure, and probably was only known to a few . . . Their brother lay there – let them remember for all time this man as their brother and their friend . . . Their friend who lay there had had a hard life and met with a hard death; and if society had been differently constituted from what it was, that man's life might have been a delightful, a beautiful one, and a happy one to him . . .

Morris's hymn 'A Death Song', set by Malcolm Lawson to music, was not his most accomplished effort but its refrain sent out a message to 'the rich':

> *Not one, not one, nor thousands must they slay*
> *But one and all if they would dusk the day.*[9]

Quite how the revolution might be accomplished or prevented would occupy the politically minded for the next half-century. In England, on the Left, the debate at first was between those who sought purely political remedies, and by revolutionary means – Morris, Eleanor Marx, Hyndman in their differing ways – and those such as Bernard Shaw and ultimately Beatrice (née Potter) and Sidney Webb who advocated gradualism – Fabianism. But it is hard, when reading the writings of the Fabians, to avoid the conclusion that they shared with the bossy Benthamites at the beginning of the century an essential distrust of the working classes; their ambition was not merely to improve the conditions of society but to improve the members of the lower orders themselves. Shaw mocked the Social Democratic Federation as Chartism 'risen from the dead'; they could have replied that he was Jeremy Bentham with a long red beard. Beatrice Potter, not yet either Mrs Webb nor a fully-fledged socialist, but a close chronicler and observer of the lives of the poor in dockland and among the sweatshops of the new Jewish immigrants in the East End, did not believe that the working classes were capable of organizing themselves.

The events of the next few years would prove her wrong. 'The strike,' she told her diary, of the Dock Strike in 1889, 'is intensely interesting to me personally, as proving or disproving, in any case modifying my generalizations on "Dock Life". Certainly the "solidarity of labour" at the East End is a new thought to me.'[10]

One of the first triumphs for organized labour happened at the Bryant & May match factory in the East End. The development of the lucifer match in the 1860s had been so successful that Bryant & May had added an extra storey to their factory, thereby destroying the ventilation. Phosphorus fumes filled the premises, and many employees – they were nearly all female – developed 'phossy jaw', a form of bone cancer, or skin cancer. The hours were long – in summer, 6.30 a.m. until 6 p.m., in winter starting at 8 a.m. Latecomers were fined half a day's pay. There were also fines for dropping matches, talking, or going to the lavatory outside of two short mealtimes. Eating happened on the premises, so that phosphorus was ingested, and those with rotten teeth had them pulled, often against their wishes, by the foremen. Piecework could make a girl 5s. or 9s. per week – many started as young as six. A really hard-working adult could make between 11s. and 13s. It was Annie Besant who drew attention to conditions in this factory (where it will be remembered Karl Marx's illegitimate son Freddy Demuth worked as a foreman) and her three informants were promptly identified and sacked. In late July 1888, Annie Besant announced that a Matchmakers Union had been formed. They went on strike, and within three weeks the employers had conceded most of their demands – shorter hours, better pay and some improvement in working conditions.[11]

In March 1889 there was formed the National Union of Gasworkers and General Labourers of Great Britain and Ireland. After their strike of 1889, initially over the disgusting working conditions at the Beckton Gas Works, they made history, being the first to win the concession of working only an eight-hour day.

Gasworkers were busy in the dark cold months of winter, but in the summer months, when people needed less heat and light, the workers were laid off. Similar problems faced the London dockers, and after their strike in the late summer of 1889, relations between labour and capital were never again the same. The power of peaceful organized labour had been demonstrated, and it was not a forgettable lesson. Much of its drama stemmed from the fact that, as has already been observed, London's docklands exhibited with hyperbolic forcefulness the contrasts and injustices of the capitalist system. Thanks in part to the surveys of Charles Booth – *The Life and Labour of the People in London*, for which some of the research was done by Beatrice Potter – and thanks also to photographic evidence, and to the anecdotal recollections of those who worked with the priests mentioned earlier, in chapter 24, we know in profound detail about the lives of the poorest of the poor in the capital of the richest city in the world. The great ships which came into London Docks from all over the world, bringing to their owners, and to the investors and merchants who profited from them, colossal wealth, were unloaded by men who worked piece-rates. When trade was slack, the men were paid nothing. The pay was variable. In August, the strike began for 6*d.* an hour.

You can't separate the three big things going on at once in the political life of Britain at the end of the 1880s – Ireland, the growth of organized labour in trade unions, and Imperialism. They are all intertwined. The Imperialists saw the Empire as the ultimate dumping-ground for troublemakers, and the best solution for hunger and discontent caused by overpopulation at home. (Without it, Cecil Rhodes believed there would be a civil war in England.) Yet the desire of the Irish for independence cut at the vitals of English power and unity. If a Westminster government could not even hold together a tiny United Kingdom, how could it sustain an empire stretching across the world? Of course it could not, and the ill-starred 'scramble for Africa' which took place within a few decades produced an Imperial experiment which could be neither administered nor paid for. The wonder is that it lasted the sixty or seventy years it did before coming apart. (Just about as long as that equally ill-starred venture, the Union of Soviet Socialist Republics.) It could only work economically by a system of exploiting markets and labour at home and abroad. In India, for example, the shoddily produced cotton fabrics of Lancashire factories or the gimcrack metalwork of Birmingham were bought by an artificially created 'market' while indigenous textile or metalworkers were sweated for cheap export.

The place where all this came home, in every sense of the phrase, was the dock; nor was it entirely accidental that those poor enough to be driven to accept the lousy wages for loading and unloading – the stevedores – were overwhelmingly of Irish extraction.[12] The strike was led by Ben Tillett (1860–1943), himself an itinerant labourer, an English-born Irishman, a slight man with the gift of impassioned oratory. Beatrice Webb said he had the face of a 'religious enthusiast'.

It was easy enough for Tillett to call the strike; altogether more difficult to persuade perhaps 30,000 strikers, with no previous tradition of solidarity or union discipline, to stay on strike for no pay for as long as the dispute with the directors lasted. (And it lasted five long weeks during which some men were close to starvation, in spite of the soup kitchens set up by well-wishers and the funds collected from as far afield as Australia.)

Tillett could not have led such a mighty movement on his own. He owed much to the help of Will Thorne (1857–1946), Tom Mann (1856–1941) and John Burns (1858–1943), all members at one time of the SDF. Thorne was the leader of the Gasworkers Union, and could offer the benefit of his experience of a successful strike. Mann had helped – and he alone of the group remained to the end of his days a Marxist, being a founder member of the Communist Party of Great Britain in 1920.

In some ways, though, the most powerful figure among the strike-leaders was John Burns – he who had been arrested on Bloody Sunday. His Scottish father died when he was young. One of eight children, he grew up in poverty in South Lambeth. On his re-election as a Member of Parliament he said, in a speech in 1901 in the Commons, 'I am not ashamed to say that I am the son of a washerwoman. Two of my sisters used to be the ironers in the laundry which now does the laundry work for the House of Commons.' He trained as an engineer, but all his life he was not merely bookish but a voracious collector and reader of books. One of his boyhood memories dated from when his mother had moved to Battersea. Crossing the Thames, Burns found himself walking in Cheyne Walk, Chelsea, where he saw an old man in plaid trousers, a long Inverness cape and a wideawake hat. A gust of wind blew the hat away and Burns retrieved it for its owner. 'Thank you verra much, my little monnie,' said the old man. A policeman who witnessed the incident told Burns, 'Go home and tell your mother and father you have picked up the hat of a great man, Thomas Carlyle.'[13]

As a foreman engineer, the teenaged Burns, like some character in Conrad, sailed the West African coast. He once dived into the sea to rescue the cook, who had fallen overboard, and it was while recuperating that he read John Stuart Mill's *Political Economy*. The chapter on communism converted him to socialism.[14]

By the mid-Eighties, he returned to London. Burns was an active trade unionist and a keen orator, advocating universal adult suffrage, an eight-hour working day, legislative independence for Ireland, and the power of making war or peace vested solely in the democratic vote of the people. There were two significant contributions he made to the success of the Dock Strike.[15] One – a conspicuous figure now in his white straw hat and black beard – was his organization of processions through the City of London. Probably not since the reign of Mary Tudor had the Square Mile seen such an array of banners, with floats and carts like some Corpus Christi Miracle Play. Only instead of religious tableaux, here were coal-heavers with their baskets on poles, and the Social Democratic Federation – 'Justice not charity' the motto on their bright banners – and tens of thousands of followers. The second thing on which Burns insisted in his speeches was that workplaces be picketed and those who continued to work, the scabs, be verbally and physically abused. The intimidation was effective. Burns was later regarded as a renegade to the Labour movement, when in 1905 he accepted a seat in Sir Henry Campbell-Bannerman's Liberal Cabinet, but he has his place in the history books as the first working man to become a government minister. The docks directors and the City bosses, when they heard his speeches, did not see a future Cabinet minister and bookman – they saw a revolutionary.

If the directors had been callous enough to hold out until the winter they might have broken the strike. It was essential that the strikers should find a friend in the 'establishment' who would negotiate a settlement. Disraeli, if he witnessed the strike from the Empyrean, would have smiled to see who these workmen, many of them Irish, chose. It was the same man who had been the confidant of Charles Dilke, a go-between for Gladstone and the Irish bishops, a furious opponent of Bradlaugh, an unpopular advocate of Papal Infallibility – in short the cardinal with a finger in every pie – just like Disraeli's Cardinal Grandison – Henry Edward Manning. He it was, together with the MP Sydney Buxton, whom both sides – strikers and directors – felt they could trust. After five weeks out on strike, the men got their sixpence an hour (eightpence overtime) and the greatest port in the busiest and richest capital in the Empire was once more open, and operative. In unfurled silk which would not look out of place in a Catholic cathedral, the Amalgamated Society of Watermen and Lightermen (Greenwich branch) wove an image of Manning into their banner.[16]

It is remarkable that Manning – the old Harrovian Tory archdeacon of Chichester in his Anglican incarnation – should have evolved not merely into a prince of the Universal Church, but into an engaged prime social radical. Next to that other old Harrovian, Lord Shaftesbury, indeed, he stands out as one of the few of the great Victorian public figures to be aware of the true dimensions of the social problem. No doubt this was partly because, as he said to William Morris, he had upon him 'the burden of the poorest folk in London'[17] – the Irish refugees from the landlords' policy of coercion, who lived on casual labour when they could get it. Becoming a Catholic in England made Manning into a Radical – he confided in Dilke that if he was 'not Cardinal Archbishop he would stand for Westminster in the Radical interest'. Then again, the contradictions in his fascinating character are found in Dilke's adding, 'Radical though he be on social questions, he is a ferocious Jingo'.[18]

As a Catholic, he combined these qualities of triumphalism and social concern, being at one and the same time an extreme advocate of papal claims, while never losing sight of the primary evangelical commitment to the poor which lies at the heart of Christianity. His defence of the pope's claims not merely to Infallibility, but also to temporal power, endeared him to Pius IX, very naturally. The Holy Father on his deathbed said 'Addio, carissimo' to the English cardinal.[19] The new pope – Pecci – who was elected in 1878 and took the name of Leo XIII, was a stranger to him. He was rumoured to be more 'liberal' than his predecessor, which would not have been difficult. Politically, the great question facing the Papacy was whether it would admit that it had lost its temporal power, and accept the new kingdom of Italy. 'To the Italians it would seem that the Pope had abjured his principles, had abdicated his sovereignty. In Europe his reconciliation with the Revolution would be a triumph to the revolutionary party in every land.'[20] So the Holy See stood firm, refused to recognize the Italian king, and put Italian Catholics in the position of having to choose whether to accept the new realpolitik or be loyal to the Church. To vote in elections, or take posts as civil servants, automatically excommunicated them. Manning saw at once that this was a ridiculous state of affairs and immediately modified his 'ultramontane' or papal supremacist stance. Together with three other cardinals only, he urged the pope not to ban Catholics from voting in parliamentary elections, and to drop the dream of reclaiming his temporal power by force of arms. His voice at first went unheeded. Little by little, however, the pope began to show common sense in this respect, even going so far in 1901 as to write an encyclical (*Graves de communi*) which permitted the use of the phrase 'Christian democracy', though with the proviso that this had no political implications.[21]

Manning's change of heart about papal power shows his political mind on the move – as it was (though interestingly for this Jingo Englishman, it moved more slowly here) over the Irish question. He was eventually converted to Home Rule.[22] What is truly interesting is his identification of himself so firmly with a very minority and forward-looking group within the Catholic Church in Europe who – whatever the pope thought of democratic elections – thoroughly espoused the cause of working people.

Ignoring the question of whether the pope was 'right' or 'wrong' in his attacks upon the very concept of democracy, one can see, from a purely political viewpoint, that such a policy from the Vatican was going to be potentially disastrous in terms of holding up Church numbers. Anyone who wished to play a part in the newly emerging political systems of the continent would have to choose between their political rights and their religious duties. Many would abandon the Church because of this. Yet, leaving aside the question of the actual political institutions of parliaments, kingdoms and republics, there were many within the Catholic Church, as in the Anglican Church of F.D. Maurice and Charles Kingsley, who felt that to follow the Incarnate Carpenter of Nazareth, they could not but identify themselves with the poor. There was no single dominant group or organization who espoused such ideas, but in France among the more influential were the group who founded the Workingmen's Clubs in Paris after the Commune. They included aristocrats such as Count Albert de Mun (1841–1914) and Marquis René de La Tour du Pin (1834–1924), who devoted themselves to the social Catholic cause, and Léon Harmel (1829–1915), who turned his father's spinning-factory at Val-des-Bois near Rheims into a model Christian township, with each worker having his own house and garden, free medicine and partnership in the ownership and running of the firm. In 1885, he took a pilgrimage of 100 workers to Rome; in 1887, he took 1,800, and in 1889, 10,000 went.[23] Leo XIII, who was an intelligent man, could not fail to grasp what these enlightened Catholics were saying, decided to stand back from the arcane debates about Papal lands and to return to the fundamental implications of the social gospel. What had the Church, founded as Catholics believed by a carpenter who had commended the poor in spirit as blessed, and judged the pursuit of wealth to be vain – what had this Church to say to the world of Capitalism? In Belgium, Germany, France and England, that is, in the primary industrial nations, the question was of urgency, and to a congress in Liège in 1890 Manning wrote a letter, which was read out to the delegates, in which he proclaimed that 'To put labour and wages first and human or domestic life second is to invert the order of God and of nature.' He asserted the rights of trade unions, and the necessity for fair working hours.

These ideas were also to be found in the pope's encyclical of 1891, *Rerum novarum*. Whether or not Manning influenced this encyclical, or even had a hand in drafting all or part of it, will probably never be known.[24] Ben Tillett wrote to Manning on 9 June 1891:

> I have just been reading the Pope's letter – a very courageous one indeed, one that will test good Catholics much more effectively than any exhortation to religious worship. As you know, some of us would disagree very strongly with many of the strictures laid upon Socialists. These are minor matters. The Catholic sympathy abounds in generous strength. I hardly think our Protestant prelates would dare utter such wholesome doctrine.[25]

As if to emphasize the truth of what Tillett said, the Church of England, at roughly the time when *Rerum novarum* was being digested by the faithful, was witnessing the Alice-in-Wonderland spectacle of one of its more saintly High Church bishops – King of Lincoln – being placed on 'trial' at Lambeth by an unwilling archbishop of Canterbury, charged with such criminal offences as mixing wine and water in the chalice during the Communion Service and using the sign of the cross when blessing or absolving the people.[26] Improbable as Roman Catholic teaching was to many who had gut prejudices against the Papacy or visions of the Virgin, Manning had established that the Church of Rome was a serious institution engaged with the real-life struggles of men and women.

It was cavalier of Tillett to dismiss the pope's strictures on socialism as 'minor matters', for what *Rerum novarum* offers is an analysis of the Labour vs. Capital struggle which delicately detaches itself from the Marxist agenda. It foresees the possibility of state socialism being just as prejudicial to individual liberty as voracious capitalism. It asserts – is it the first major political tract of the nineteenth century to do so? – the notion of *human rights*.

> Rights must be held sacred wherever they exist . . . Where the protection of private rights is concerned, special regard . . . must be had for the poor and the weak. Rich people can use their wealth to protect themselves and have less need of the State's protection; but the mass of the poor have nothing of their own with which to defend themselves and have to depend above all on the protection of the state.[27]

The encyclical was inspirational to figures such as Hilaire Belloc, G.K. Chesterton and Eric Gill in the twentieth century, who drew from it the inference that socialism and capitalism were two sides of the same coin, both dedicated to depriving the individual of liberty. What was felt at its first publication was relief that after a generation of issuing denunciations of political liberalism, science and technology (the use of the electric light was condemned by the Vatican), while proclaiming more and more esoteric doctrines about the pope and about the Virgin Mary, the Church had returned to the harder task of applying the teachings of the Gospel to life in the complex and difficult world of urban capitalism.

That such ideas were reclaimed for European Catholicism was a key factor in its survival. If the Conservatives (theological and political) had had their way in this, as in most areas of Church teaching, Europeans would have been placed in a position, when democracies began to evolve in the twentieth century, of having to choose between their civic life and their faith.

In the Protestant world, and in England, such issues perhaps seem marginal. Of much greater impact, in terms both of intellectual developments in philosophical circles and of social theory as practised by politicians and others in the next generation, was the work of Thomas Hill Green (1836–82).

Green was preoccupied by many of the same concerns as Marx and John Stuart Mill. All three thinkers confronted the realities of nineteenth-century industrialist–capitalist market society, the divisions produced by market capitalism, the inequalities and injustices. But of the three philosophers, in the immediate English context, Green was much the most influential, as you can tell from reading Mrs Humphry Ward's novel about him. Green is Henry Grey in *Robert Elsmere*, one of the bestselling books of the century, about a young clergyman losing his faith in traditional Christianity but finding a new religion in Grey/Green's commitment to social justice for the poor. H.H. Asquith, the future Liberal prime minister, was only one of dozens of influential men and women whose world-view was fashioned by Green. You still read references to him in those journals sympathetic to social egalitarianism by those who see him as one of the key influences on the English Labour Party.

The product of Rugby and Jowett's Balliol, Green by dying young became a sort of liberal saint embodying the way a whole generation viewed the world. Given the division in Europe between Church and state, and given the influence exercised by Britain in the late nineteenth century (a cultural dominance comparable to the strength of the United States today), one sees the force and importance of Green's voice.

He differed from Marx both in his analysis of the capitalist horror-story and in his suggested remedy. 'The increased wealth of one man does not naturally mean the diminished wealth of another,' Green wrote;[28] and though he sometimes contradicted this view, he held to the principle that the market itself was legitimate so long as society was ordered on unselfish lines. Marx believed that one man's increased wealth *did* diminish the proletariat. Green even saw that 'there is nothing in the fact that their labour is hired in great masses by great capitalists to prevent them from being on a small scale capitalists themselves'.[29] Again, it is hard to envisage Marx finding this a desirable state of things.

Green wanted a fair and just distribution of wealth, and protection for the working classes from exploitation to enable them to lead good and dignified lives. He distanced himself not only from the materialism of Marx but from the modified Utilitarianism of Mill. Indeed, Green's whole metaphysic differed from Mill's, and he delivered some powerful arguments against the empiricism on which Mill's views were based.

Green was the inspiration for an entire generation of British and American philosophers known in their sphere as Idealists – not because they were 'idealistic' in the popular sense of the word but because of their theory of how human minds form their notions of truth and their impressions of the world. For the empiricist like Mill the mind which receives impressions of the world of nature is itself part of that world. But the empiricist can never explain the paradox of how a mind which is merely part of what it contemplates can be contemplating, among other things, itself. For T.H. Green, as for Kant, 'the understanding makes nature'.[30] Without the mind's activity, there would be no nature for us to contemplate. Green's greatest master was Hegel. There is a neatness about the fact that the great German metaphysician's influence should extend through his own country in the opening decades of the century and through the English-speaking world at its close. Marx came of age by wrestling with Hegel's theories of history. British Idealism in its glory years (1880–1930) grew out of redefinitions and re-explorations of Hegel's ethics and metaphysics.

Paradoxically, whereas the political influence of Hegel in Germany was intended to be, as it was in fact, conservative, in England, filtered through Green, it became an inspiration of political and social change. The growth of the Workers' Educational Association, of the college in Bristol which eventually became Bristol University, of 'missions' and 'settlements' in working-class districts of big industrial cities, carried on the work of earlier Christian socialists like Maurice without being either Christian or socialist. The impetus for women's education also owed much to Green, who was a member of the Council of the Association for the Higher Education of Women. If the political life of Victorian England had had to be worked out in Parliament, there might well have been a civil war or a revolution. In fact by means on the one hand of trade unions and on the other of independent movements in and for the working classes, change was effected without the need, as there might have been in a different culture, for the guillotine or the tumbril. The new religion was change itself, justice itself, fairness itself. T.H. Green was its prophet.[31]

37

The Scarlet Thread of Murder

Eighteenth-century London carried its poor in its midst. To walk with Garrick or Johnson through Covent Garden or down to Fleet Street would be to pass courts and alleys crammed with crime, poverty and disease, cheek by jowl with the houses of the rich. As Manning knew, surrounded by the poor of Westminster, there was still great poverty in central London. The Victorian Age, however, witnessed London being laid out along the social classifications which the capitalist revolution had created and enforced. The genteel squares of Belgravia and Mayfair were gated against the intrusion of undesirables. The world of shops and theatres, lights and delights, became for the rest of London the mythical 'West End'. To visit them was to go 'up West'. In turn, the villages and suburbs of an earlier age – Hoxton, Hackney, Shoreditch, Stepney, Bethnal Green – swarmed with overpopulation: the 'East End', no less mystic to the half-London who did not live there. This was the world which the Salvationists tried to win for God, and which the disciples of T.H. Green and Toynbee wanted for democracy: a hard, brick-built, low-lying, gin-soaked world out of whose gaslit music halls and fogbound alleys mythologies developed. Here Dan Leno and Marie Lloyd began their careers, here Jack the Ripper lurked, and from time to time Mr Sherlock Holmes emerged from a four-wheeler, sometimes heavily disguised.

The music halls developed out of pubs. By the 1850s, many taverns had their song-saloons – so popular that busybodydom required them to have a theatrical licence, which permitted the performance of popular music but forbade the playing of Shakespeare.[1] This was scarcely a hardship to the thirsty patrons of 'the halls', who did not go out in the evening with a burning desire to see *Measure for Measure*.

Mayhew believed that the theatres of the East End 'absorb numbers of the inhabitants, and by innocently amusing them, soften their manners and keep them out of mischief and harm's way'. He approved of the pyrotechnic displays at the Effingham Theatre in the Whitechapel Road – 'Great is the applause when gauzy nymphs rise like so many Aphrodites from the sea and sit down on apparent sunbeams midway between the stage and theatrical heaven.' (The theatre burnt down in 1879 and was rebuilt as a theatre for Yiddish plays that appealed to the huge new influx of refugees from Russia and Poland.)[2]

It was another matter at the 'Penny Gaffs', theatres which had a series of 'variety' turns, and where the audience was crammed with teenaged criminals picking pockets and undercover policemen trying to catch them doing so. The act which most revolted the normally unshockable Mayhew was performed by a fourteen-year-old boy, dancing 'with more energy than grace' and singing a song 'the whole point of which consisted in the mere utterance of some filthy word at the end of each stanza'. The audience loved it and cried for more, being rewarded with a song called 'Pine-apple Rock', with a rhyme which can easily be reconstructed. 'It was absolutely awful to behold the relish with which the young ones jumped to the hideous meaning of the verses.'[3]

It was to appeal to audiences with comparable tastes that the music halls evolved, though the best performers – from Marie Lloyd to Max Miller in the middle years of the twentieth century (the last great music-hall artist) – depended on double-entendre rather than the blatant crudity which so upset Mayhew.

Marie Lloyd was born as Matilda Alice Victoria Wood on 12 February 1870 at 36 Plumber Street in the slums of Hoxton. It was a large, poverty-stricken family. Her father, John Wood, made artificial flowers for an Italian who paid him 30 shillings a week, and he worked part-time as a waiter at the Royal Eagle – the tavern in Bethnal Green immortalized in 'Pop Goes the Weasel' ('Up and down the City Road, In and out the Eagle'). It was here when she was fourteen that Matilda Wood did a turn under the name Bella Delmare and won instant success. She went on to perform at the Falstaff Music Hall in Old Street, and when her talent was spotted by George Belmont, a music-hall impresario, she was taken on by a big music hall in Bermondsey. By the time she was sixteen she was on tour and earning £10 a week. Soon she was earning £600 a week.

She died in the year that T.S. Eliot published *The Waste Land*, 1922. 'Although I have always admired the genius of Marie Lloyd,' Eliot wrote, 'I do not think that I always appreciated its uniqueness; I certainly did not realize that her death would strike me as the important event it was. Marie Lloyd was the greatest Music Hall artist of her time in England; she was also the most popular.'[4]

She had a rough life. She was alcoholic. Her third husband, a jockey, beat her, and they were arrested when they tried to disembark at New York harbour posing as man and wife before they were actually married. Her life from the grinding poverty of its origins to the alcoholic pathos of its end had the carelessness for safety which is often the ingredient of an artist's career that distinguishes talent from genius. The capacity to let rip, to let go, must have been part of what enabled this weird-looking girl with buck teeth and thin hair to electrify an audience of cynical drunks from the moment she got up and sang 'The boy I love is up in the gallery'.

Apart from the release of risqué humour, she provided the audience with a reflection, an embodiment of their own hideous lives. It was humour based on staring into the abyss. Some of her most famous songs are about bankruptcy, drunkenness, dereliction. 'My old man said follow the van' (a twentieth-century, not a Victorian song) is about being evicted, piling one's few pathetic belongings on to a cart and getting drunk.

> My old man said follow the van
> And don't dilly-dally on the way.
> Off went the cart with me home packed in it,
> I followed on with me old cock linnet – but
> I dillied, I dallied, I dallied and I dillied,
> Lost me way and don't know where to roam.
> Who's going to put up the old iron bedstead
> If I can't find my way home?

Her wit was shown at its best in

> Outside the Cromwell Arms last Saturday night,
> I was one of the ruins that Cromwell knocked about a bit.

It was very much a humour for hard, cynical Londoners. She could 'bomb' in the provinces. In Ardwick, Manchester, she shouted, 'So this is Ardwick, eh? Well, to hell with the lot of you.' And to the good people of Sheffield, after a cool reception, she yelled, 'You don't like me, well I don't like you. And you know what you can do with your stainless knives and your scissors and your circular saws – you can shove 'm up your arse.'[5]

Dan Leno (1860–1904) – his real name was George Galvin – made his first stage appearance as an adult on 5 October 1885 at Forester's

Music Hall in Mile End – but he had been on the stage since he was three ('Little George, the Infant Wonder, Contortionist and Posturer'). His humour was much more fantastical than Marie Lloyd's. 'No one ever accused him of vulgarity.'[6] There is something almost Blakean about his mad song about a wasp who loved a hard-boiled egg –

> But not one word said the hard-boiled egg,
> The hard-boiled egg,
> The hard-boiled egg,
> And what a silly insect the wasp to beg
> For you can't get any sense out of a hard-boiled egg![7]

He was a legendary pantomime dame – hurling himself into the parts with quite literally manic energy. He went mad while playing Mother Goose. He was a broken and exhausted man at forty-three: 'the funniest man on earth' as it said on the posters. 'Ever seen his eyes?' asked Marie Lloyd. 'The saddest eyes in the whole world. That's why we all laughed at Danny. Because if we hadn't laughed, we should have cried ourselves sick. I believe that's what real comedy is, you know. It's almost like crying.'[8]

We can still hear Dan Leno on record – but the magic was to see him on stage. Max Beerbohm, when asked by foreign visitors to show them something inherently British, would take them first to see the Tower of London or Westminster Abbey – and then to a music hall to see 'the big booming Herbert Campbell, and his immortal, nimble little side-kick, Dan Leno'.[9]

Part of the attraction of music hall for the middle class was its sheer entertainment value. When one considers that there were no plays of any interest or quality written in English between the death of Sheridan and the emergence of Oscar Wilde (both Irish, note well) it is not surprising that many middle-class theatregoers flocked with rapture to Little Tich, Marie Lloyd or Dan Leno. They were superb performers, artists of first-rate quality. But for someone of the class of Max Beerbohm or T.S. Eliot to frequent the halls there was also an element of excitement – tasting a bit of rough. It was the secular equivalent of those who came out in their cabs and carriages to savour the exotic delights of ritualist worship in the 'slum' churches.

Those who penetrated the East End could discover that it was indeed one of the roughest and most exotic ports in the world, where a prodigious mixture of races and cultures could be glimpsed. In many streets in Whitechapel, since the recent influx of thousands of Russian and Polish Jews, English was not spoken at all. In Whitechapel and Commercial Roads' Jewish shops and kosher restaurants, Yiddish was spoken. Nearer the river in Limehouse and West India Dock Road, Chinese and Lascars could be seen in abundance. The American Daniel Kirwan, visiting Ratcliff, now in Stepney, was astounded by the White Swan public house. Known locally as 'Paddy's Goose', it was:

perhaps the most frightful hell-hole in London. The very sublimity of vice and degradation is here attained, and the noisy scraping of wheezy fiddles, and the brawls of intoxicated sailors are the only sounds heard within its walls. It is an ordinary dance house, with a bar and glasses, and a dirty floor on which scores of women of all countries and shades of colour can be found dancing with Danes, Americans, Swedes, Spaniards, Russians, Negroes, Chinese, Malays, Italians and Portuguese in one hell-medley of abomination.[10]

The enchantment of the alien, the half-thrilling terror of violence lurking in such 'hell-holes', the cheap excitement of knowing that such 'scores of women' are readily available, masculine self-hatred at the thought of prostitutes, transferring into hatred of the women themselves – all these factors are present in the pornographic fascination of the Jack the Ripper murders. There would seem to be no end to the appetite of so-called Ripperologists for more films, more books and more crazy theories about 'the autumn of terror' in 1888 when over ten weeks – from 31 August to 9 November – five women had their throats slit. In two cases, organs were removed from the victims' bodies with sufficient skill to suggest on the murderer's part an at least rudimentary knowledge of anatomy. The murders became increasingly savage, culminating with a blood-saturnalia of dismemberment on 9 November – the murder of Mary Jane Kelly. This was the only killing to occur indoors – the others took place in darkened alleys. All the victims – Mary Ann Nichols (42), Annie Chapman (47), Elizabeth Stride (45), Catherine Eddowes (43) and Mary Kelly (25) – had been married. Between them they had twenty-one children. They were all prostitutes.

This undoubtedly quickens the interest of those who are obsessed by these murders. Their imaginations running riot, the 'Ripperologists' have supposed that the women were killed by a Harley Street physician taking revenge for the death of a beloved son from syphilis, or for reasons of religious zeal. (Anti-semites can imagine that the women were killed by methods of kosher slaughter.) Conspiracy theorists imagine a royal murderer (the Duke of Clarence is the favourite) or a cabal organized by Lord Salisbury himself. But the key excitement of the unsolved crimes is the professional activity of the women themselves.

Part of the excitement stems from the cliché of the Victorian Age as being excessively puritanical or buttoned-up in relation to sex. For those who believe this, or who imagine that the Victorians were so prudish that they draped their chair-legs (whence stemmed *that* bizarre fiction?), a key text is the pseudonymous pornographic work *My Secret Life*, privately printed by Auguste Brancart of Brussels *circa* 1890. Far from lifting the lid on the actual behaviour of Victorian middle-class life, this crazy account of some 1,500 relations by a married man called Walter has all the hallmarks of porno-fantasy. It has lately been suggested that 'Walter' was Henry Spencer Ashbee,[11] bibliophile father of the Arts and Crafts designer and teacher Charles Ashbee. In a percipient review of the book which sets out this theory, Eric Korn said:

> *My Secret Life* . . . despite the often sprightly and inventive copulation, ultimately disgusts because of the power relations, not the sexual relations. Walter was a gentleman; in his pockets were shillings, and half-crowns, even the occasional guinea in cases of exceptionally obdurate virginity. All doors, all orifices were open to him, and if a little violence was needed too, his conscience was clear . . . 'Kto kovo?' asked Lenin in another context, 'Who does what, who is done to?'[12]

The gleeful way in which the murders are still made a subject of entertainment tells us more about the psychology of those who write or buy the books, or flock to the films, than about the nineteenth century.

The murders were never solved.[13] Those who imagine that the Ripper committed suicide, or that he was an alcoholic who killed while under the influence, and then gave up drinking, have as much claim to be believed as anyone.

The Whitechapel murders unfolded before the newspaper-reading public like a detective story of the grisliest kind, with the arrest and release of suspects, the letters to the police purporting to come from

'Jack' himself – ('I send you half the Kidne [*sic*] I took from one woman prarsarved [*sic*] it for you tother piece I fried and ate it was very nise [*sic*].' Everyone had a theory, everyone wanted to chip in with advice. It was left to the Queen in an angry communication to Lord Salisbury to state the most obvious fact of all, after the most disgusting of all the murders, Mary Kelly's. 'This new most ghastly murder shows the absolute necessity for some very decided action. All these courts must be lit, and our detectives improved. They are not what they should be.'[14]

The trouble was, that although the Whitechapel murders acquired instantaneous mythic status, the authorities relied on the services of real-life policemen, the equivalents of Lestrade and Gregson in the Sherlock Holmes stories. Holmes himself was required.* It was in fact one month before the first of the Whitechapel murders – in July 1888 – that *A Study in Scarlet*, the story in which the greatest detective of them all makes his début, was first published in book form, though its author, a young doctor called Arthur Conan Doyle (1859–1930), first published the tale the previous year in *Beeton's Christmas Annual*.[15]

Sherlock Holmes was very much a thinker of his time, his view of the nature of things absolutely in tune with the English Idealists F.H. Bradley and T.H. Green.

A logician could infer the possibility of an Atlantic or a Niagara without having seen or heard of one or the other. So all life is a great chain, the nature of which is known, whenever we are shown a single link of it. Like all other arts, the Science of Deduction and Analysis is one which can only be acquired by long and patient study, nor is life long enough to allow any mortal to attain the highest possible perfection in it.[16]

When common-sense Dr Watson reads this article in a magazine he exclaims, 'What ineffable twaddle!' He cannot believe, as the article

---

*In December 1965 the BBC broadcast 'The Case of the Unmentioned Case' by L.W. Bailey, which points out that when the entire police force was at its wits' end trying to solve the Whitechapel case, Holmes was not consulted. Inevitably, Bailey suggested that Holmes, with his rudimentary knowledge of anatomy and supposed misogyny, was the Ripper – a thesis which more than one listener was right to find 'shameful': the essence of Holmes's appeal consisting in his virtue. See Wilson & Odell, p. 191.

suggests, that 'By a man's finger-nails, by his coat-sleeve, by his boot, by his trouser-knees, by the callosities of his forefinger and thumb, by his expression, by his shirt-cuffs – by each of these things a man's calling is plainly revealed.'[17]

Needless to say, it transpires that the author of the article is the man with whom Watson is sharing lodgings at 221B Baker Street. He immediately demonstrates his skills by 'deducing' – from merely looking at him across the street – that a man on the pavement is a retired sergeant of the Marines. He has no sooner met Watson than he can *know*, by his supposedly scientific method, that he had been wounded in Afghanistan. In a later story, *The Sign of Four*, he enrages Watson by telling him that his brother was 'left with good prospects; but he threw away his chances, lived for some time in poverty with occasional short intervals of prosperity, and finally, taking to drink, he died'. All this is inferred by looking at the dead brother's gold watch and noticing its scuffed appearance and the pawnbroker's number scratched minutely on the case.

It seems entirely apt that by far the greatest Victorian of the later part of the Queen's reign should be a character in fiction. The triumph of the first story, *A Study in Scarlet*, partly derives from its clumsy construction. A murder story set in London, it is concerned with the Mormons, and its second half – a lengthy flashback explaining the crime – takes us away from Baker Street to the state of Utah and the country of the Saints. What reader of the story has not pined, as for a dear friend, during those American pages, and rejoiced when we return to the bachelor apartments and the great amateur detective?

Holmes evolves through several stories. In *A Study in Scarlet* we find him in a laboratory – he never seems to return to it in the *Strand Magazine* short stories which – reprinted as *The Adventures of Sherlock Holmes* in book form – are the best in the collection. Also in *A Study in Scarlet* Holmes does not wish to clutter his brain with general learning which does not relate to his profession. He says he is ignorant of the work of Carlyle (while going on to quote him) and, less probably, ignorant of the Copernican theory of astronomy. In later tales, Holmes has become a polymath. ('Breadth of view . . . is one of the essentials of our profession' – *The Valley of Fear*.) In *A Study in Scarlet* Watson dismisses the notion that Holmes was 'addicted to the use of some narcotic' because 'the temperance and cleanliness of his whole life'[18] forbade such a notion. In the later stories we discover that Holmes is a cocaine addict and frequents opium dens.

Yet in spite of all the inconsistencies, Holmes comes before us as totally real. T.S. Eliot said that 'when we talk of him we invariably fall into the fancy of his existence'.[19]

Much has been written about the evolution of Holmes in the mind of his creator. His deductive method owes a lot to similar tricks performed by the Edinburgh surgeon Joseph Bell when Doyle was a medical student; his relationship with Watson is partly derivative from Boswell and Johnson. But he is also archetypically of his time. Like the great scientists who turned their cleverness into technological miracles – telegraph, bicycles, electricity, telephones – Holmes marries intellectual skill with commonplace observation. When he has nothing to use his great mind upon he turns, decadent as the decade in which he became so prodigiously popular, to the syringe and the needle:

Hence the cocaine. I cannot live without brainwork. What else is there to live for? Stand at the window here. Was ever such a dreary, dismal, unprofitable world? See how the yellow fog swirls down the street and drifts across the dun-coloured houses. What could be more hopelessly prosaic and material? What is the use of having powers, Doctor, when one has no field upon which to exert them?[20]

Watson, like the empiricist philosopher Mill, never sees connections – or what philosophers call relations – unless they are externally explained. Holmes discovers the nature of reality by inductive methods which presuppose the idealist belief in 'internal relations'. He is the most modern of philosophers but – here again – operating in a wholly mundane and yet bizarre world: the fogbound courts and streets of London, where the actual Whitechapel killings had revealed 'the scarlet thread of murder running through the colourless skein of life'.[21]

38

The Fall of Parnell

Arthur Balfour, Lord Salisbury's clever nephew, succeeded Hicks Beach as Irish secretary in March 1887 and was immediately faced with the prospect of dealing with the so-called 'Plan of Campaign', which called on tenants all over Ireland to organize, and to treat with landlords as if they were a united body. Parnell privately disapproved of the Plan of Campaign. Important as the Land Issue was to him – the basic issue of how the Irish rural population could till the land, and eat, without being squeezed into unbearable poverty – he never lost sight of the larger political dream, from which agitation over Land Acts detracted. Balfour was his uncle's stooge, but he was also highly ambitious, and he was anxious to use the Irish situation to prove himself. A keen amateur philosopher, a bachelor who enjoyed being spanked by his friend Lady Elcho, he had been known at Cambridge by the nicknames 'Clara', 'Tiger Lily' and 'Pretty Fanny'. His emotional and inner life remain something of a mystery, the more so when we have read the story of his psychic involvement with Mary Catherine Lyttelton, to whom he was almost engaged when he was twenty-three, and who died on Palm Sunday 1885 in her twenty-fifth year.[1] For the next fifty-five years, Balfour would spend Palm Sunday with the friends he had in common with Mary Lyttelton (the Talbots). Spiritualists believe that Mary and Balfour's younger brother Frank (1851–82) made frequent attempts to communicate with the Tory statesman, often referring to Palms, or using Palm imagery in their language in commemoration of that dire Palm Sunday. The voluminous Spirit-speeches, made while the medium was in a state of trance, which record Mary Lyttelton's continued obsession with Balfour from Beyond, are kept at the Society for Psychical Research. 'Tell him he gives me joy,' she was saying to him, as a medium stroked his hand, as late as 1929.[2] In Ireland he was to be known simply as 'Bloody Balfour'.

On the one hand he allowed some concessions to the tenants, but on the other he brought in a new Crimes Act – the Criminal Law and Procedure Act, 1887 – which was much more drastic than any previous legislation. Boycotting, resistance to eviction, intimidation and conspiracy now carried much heavier penalties. Suspects – before they had committed any of these offences – could now be held and examined. Those accused could be moved away from their own districts for trial. Six months' hard labour was the maximum sentence.[3]

Salisbury wanted even tougher measures. Ireland was the test case, before the eyes of the world, of British competence to govern. If Britain could not rule Ireland, 'what right have we to go lecturing the Sultan as to the state of things in Armenia or in Macedonia?'[4]

'Loot, loot, pure loot, is the sacred course for which the Land League has summoned the malcontents to its standard,' Salisbury had written in the *Quarterly Review* in 1881. If the government surrendered to 'land hunger', why should not governments give way in the future to 'house hunger', 'consols hunger' or even 'silver plate hunger'? Salisbury was not himself a harsh landlord. When times were bad, he entirely remitted rents on his 20,000 acres, all of which were held in England. ('How pleasant it must be to have nothing but Consols,' he remarked to a friend.)[5] His opposition to the Irish and 'the amiable practice to which they were addicted of shooting people to whom they owe money' was deep, and his Irish policy drew on his wells of cynical pessimism. In 1872 he had written, 'the optimistic view of politics assumes that there must be some remedy for every political ill. But is not the other view barely possible? Is it not just conceivable that there is no remedy that we can apply to the Irish hatred for ourselves?'[6]

One remedy to mutual hatred is divorce, but for the Imperialist reasons already stated, Salisbury was unwilling to contemplate Home Rule. He was astute politically and could see that the Irish Party and the Irish 'question' possessed a vulnerable, not to say spurious, unity. Land agitation and individual cases of hardship were not the same as an ideal for political independence; Fenian nationalism had been different in texture from Parnell's Home Rule idea – and the differences between Parnell and some of his followers could be exploited. The era of 'Parnellism' in Irish politics was one in which issues were subsumed in one superbly attractive personality, Parnell himself, who by masterful political manoeuvre and charm, deployed in equal measures of skill, had managed to unite the various aspirant Irish nationalists and Irish liberals with the English Liberal Party, itself a coalition. Destroy Parnell, and the Tories would have managed in large measure to divide the enemy. It would not make the problem of Ireland go away but it would make it – which was Salisbury's ideal – utterly insoluble.

So, while Balfour with great parliamentary aplomb was seeing his contentious Crimes Bill through the Commons, *The Times* printed what purported to be the facsimiles of letters from Parnell condoning the Phoenix Park murders of Lord Frederick Cavendish and his secretary. The old slur – that by associating with Irish nationalism you were rubbing shoulders with murderers – was very much helped by *The Times* 'revelations'. Parnell immediately denounced them as a 'felonious and bare faced forgery'.[7] Salisbury and Balfour must have had their suspicions that this was the case, even if they did not know it for certain. Would so highly literate a man as Parnell spell the word as 'hesitency'? At the time, it suited them very well to believe so. The Crimes Bill became law – nicknamed the 'Jubilee Coercion Act' by its enemies. 'The hot weather has been too much for us,' Salisbury said. 'I wonder when these fiendish Irishmen will let me go.'

In September 1887, at the opening of the trial of William O'Brien, MP – this nationalist with strong links to the Irish in Chicago was being prosecuted under the new act for inciting tenants to resist landlords and to boycott those who moved into farms where these had been evicted – O'Brien's parliamentary colleague John Dillon, another nationalist, was addressing the crowd of 8,000 who had congregated at Mitchelstown, County Cork. A scuffle broke out, the police moved in, and as they were driven back by the crowds, a number of officers opened fire. One man was killed, several others injured.

Edward Carson (1854–1935), the thirty-three-year-old counsel for the Irish attorney general, told 'Pretty Fanny' Balfour, 'It was Mitchelstown that made us certain we had a man at last.'[8] Others were less impressed. A coroner's jury found wilful murder against the county inspector and five constables. The Queen's Bench in Dublin, five months later, quashed the verdict on technical grounds.[9] The lengths to which the Tory Unionists in government were prepared to go had been revealed. Gladstone, addressing a rally in England that Jubilee autumn, declared, 'I have said and say again, "Remember Mitchelstown!"' Salisbury did not mind. When he arrived in Oxford and found three-foot-high posters reading 'Lord Salisbury is coming. Remember Mitchelstown', he was perfectly happy that the people should do so. 'I was delighted to see you had run Wilfrid Blunt in,' he told Balfour after he had imprisoned this eccentric poet under the Crimes Act.[10] The year, he told his nephew, had 'enormously added to your reputation and influence'.

Unfortunately for Salisbury and Balfour, Parnell insisted on a Special Parliamentary Commission to look into *The Times* forgeries. He also took legal action against the newspaper for its articles 'Parnellism and

Crime'. He was vindicated. The letters were shown to be the work of a clever forger called Richard Pigott (not so clever as to be able to spell hesitancy), who admitted his crime in the witness box. Pigott's humiliation caused him to flee abroad, to Madrid. There he committed suicide.[11]

Parnell now, in the period of 1889–90, enjoyed unprecedented popularity and public support. His truthfulness had been proven by a Special Commission to Parliament. When he first appeared in the House after the collapse of Pigott, the entire Opposition, including Gladstone, rose to their feet and cheered for some minutes. He found himself a hero not only in Ireland but among the English public. Even in the Unionist press, it was said that if the Irish government – i.e. Dublin Castle, acting under directions from London – had wished to make the coercive system appear as odious as possible, they would act as they were acting.[12]

Yet Parnell's triumph was short-lived. On Christmas Eve 1889, Captain William O'Shea, the MP for Galway, filed for divorce, citing Parnell as co-respondent. The trial of the case came up nearly a year later, in November 1890, and though O'Shea clearly lied in pretending that his wife's relations with Parnell were very shocking to him, and that he had heard about them only shortly before filing for divorce, the central fact was not contested. Parnell and Mrs O'Shea were lovers.

Gladstone had known about it for years, and often used Mrs O'Shea as a go-between when negotiating with the Irish Party. Given the willingness of Salisbury's government to make political capital out of the Dilke divorce, and the Pigott forgeries, one does wonder whether they made it worth Captain O'Shea's while to destroy Parnell. After all, O'Shea had been totally complicit for ten years. Three of his wife's children were Parnell's.

There are many remarkable things about the whole story, which, because it has passed into legend, is difficult to deconstruct. For something approaching a year – from January to November 1890 – the Irish Party was in suspense, awaiting the outcome of the trial. Parnell assured his close supporter Michael Davitt that 'he would emerge without a stain on his reputation'.[13] Either this was a simple untruth, or we are to assume that Parnell meant he had not broken the code of a gentleman; he had not *deceived* O'Shea. The Press, in Ireland and England, was not silent, and for this whole period there was plenty of time for the implications of the story to sink in. Yet almost all Irish public bodies, all the MPs and the Catholic bishops remained loyal and expressed confidence in Parnell's leadership. When one considers how extremely puritanical the Irish were (until our own generation) about such matters, the loyalty, and the political maturity, thus demonstrated is all the more extraordinary.

The crisis came in the middle of November 1890, when Mrs O'Shea accepted in court that she had been unfaithful to her husband. The leader of a parliamentary party was now legally defined as an adulterer.

Politically speaking, what mattered was how many votes this would cost the cause of Home Rule. How many Liberal MPs would be moved to change sides over the Irish issue because of it? How many Irish MPs would feel tempted to form an anti-Parnellite faction? What would the electorate in the Irish constituencies feel about it all?

Cardinal Manning, less than a week after the O'Shea divorce proceedings, urged Gladstone to repudiate Parnell, and much more importantly he had advised the Irish bishops that Parnell could not survive politically, and that on their part, 'plain and prompt speech was safest'. 'We have been slow to act,' the archbishop of Dublin telegraphed to one of the Irish members, 'trusting that the party will act manfully.'

Yet although W.B. Yeats, in common with many Irishmen, believed that

> The Bishops and the Party
> That tragic story made . . .

this was not strictly true. At least in chronological terms, it was the English Liberals who at first made it clear that they would no longer continue supporting Parnell. It so happened that there was a Liberal convention meeting in Sheffield on 22 November, from which Harcourt reported back that the assembled Northern grocers and Methodistical aldermen with their silver watch-chains could not tolerate co-operation with Irish Home Rulers so long as they were led by an adulterer. Gladstone thereafter wrote a letter – which he subsequently had published – to John Morley conveying the views of the Liberal Party and saying that Parnell's continuation as leader would render Home Rule 'almost a nullity'. Davitt meanwhile was writing articles complaining about the silence of the Catholic bishops on the subject.

The real drama of the story began when Parliament reassembled and the Irish MPs met in Committee Room 15 to ratify Parnell's leadership for the next session. On all previous occasions this had been a mere formality. After an agonizing week, forty-five members withdrew from the Committee Room, leaving Parnell with twenty-eight followers. The Press Association summarized the situation with the words, 'the old Irish party no longer exists'.[14]

Almost as soon as the vote had gone against him, Parnell went over to Ireland to help one of his candidates fight the Kilkenny by-election. Parnell had a good candidate, and in one district of the constituency he was even supported by the parish priest, but he was beaten by two to one.

A little before the announcement of the election result, Morley, who had been visiting Ireland, called on Gladstone at Hawarden, finding the eighty-year-old recovering from a cold. He 'looked in his worsted jacket, and dark tippet over his shoulders, and with his white, deep-furrowed face, like some strange Ancient of Days. When he discovered from Morley that Parnell was still fighting on, he "flamed up with passionate vehemence" – "Are they mad, then? Are they clean demented?"'[15]

They continued to talk of Ireland, and then Gladstone asked if there was anything in history like the present distracted scenes in Ireland. Morley suggested Florence, Pisa or some other Italian city, with the French emperor at the gates. Gladstone came up with the siege of Jerusalem, with Titus and the legions marching on the city, and the Jews still fragmented into factions. Then they go into luncheon, and Morley says that Joseph de Maistre observed that in the innocent primitive ages, men died of diseases without names. Gladstone: 'Homer never mentions diseases at all.' Morley: 'Not many of them die a natural death in Homer.' Gladstone quotes the passage where Odysseus meets his mother among the shades, and Morley says that the Greek word *pothos* is 'such a tender word, and it is untranslatable'. Gladstone suggests *desiderium* and quotes from Horace:

> *Quis desiderio sit pudor aut modus*
> *Tam cari capitis . . .*[16]

– 'What restraint or limit should there be to grief for one so dear?'

Can one imagine any politician in the Western world today having such a conversation? They wander off into the library and a little later, Morley finds that the old man has turned up the passage in his 'worn old Odyssey'. 'Homer's fellows,' says the leader of the Liberal Party, 'would have cut a very different figure, and made short work in that committee room last week!'

Comparatively recent as it is, Gladstone himself seems as remote from our world as Homer's fellows.

Parnell was a brave man, but vanity played its part. He was thunderstruck by the defection of Irish MPs and fought two more gruelling by-elections, hoping to prove a point. He was humiliated on both occasions, at North Sligo in April and at Carlow in July. In June 1890 he married Katharine O'Shea, a step which placed him finally beyond the pale in the eyes of the Catholic bishops who had always been prepared to overlook his Protestantism and his unbelief. 'You cannot remain a Parnellite and remain a Catholic,'[17] a priest told his flock the following year in Meath, and the truth or otherwise of this contention exercised many an angry Irish household or bar in the years to come, as readers of Joyce's *Portrait of the Artist as a Young Man* will recollect.

Parnell himself was exhausted. On 27 September 1890 he addressed a meeting in the rain, while suffering from rheumatism. He came over to England gravely ill, joined his wife at Brighton and died in her arms on 6 October. Like Homer's fellows, he was already a figure in mythology, as Joyce showed – and Yeats, with his talk of

> None shared our guilt; nor did we play a part
> Upon a painted stage when we devoured his heart.[18]

To this day one has an overpowering sense, reading his story, that Parnell was a greater man than any of those who took part in the tragic drama of his downfall, a man of epic status, whose fall was not merely a private tragedy but also a great national calamity.

PART VI

The Eighteen-Nineties

39

The Victorian Way of Death

The English, who in our day are so diffident about funerals, positively revelled in the trappings of death during the nineteenth century; and the 1890s 'witnessed the golden age of the Victorian funeral'.[1] The surviving photographs remind us that the most elaborate ceremonials, of a kind which today would appear extravagant for the obsequies of a head of state, were matters of routine when burying a grocer or a doctor.[2] The hearse would be a glass coach groaning with flowers, but smothered in sable and crêpe. Four or six horses nodding with black plumes would lead the cortège, preceded by paid mutes who, swathed in black shawls and with drapes over their tall silk hats, make an alarming spectacle to the modern eye: medieval Spain could hardly produce images more macabre. Behind the coffin in their carriages would follow the mourners, in new-bought black clothes, bombazine and crêpe and tall silk hats and black gloves and bonnets – all a tribute to how much money the mourners had, and how highly they considered themselves to have climbed in the ladder-game class-system created by democratic capitalism. The more the funeral became a social status symbol, the more in turn it grew to be big business, with many undertakers in the larger cities becoming people of substance on the strength of it.

If private families went to such impressive lengths to ensure costly funerals for their loved ones, public figures could be sure of huge shows. The one which stayed in everyone's mind from the middle of the century was that of the Duke of Wellington. The funeral of Cardinal Manning, on Thursday 21 January 1892, attracted even larger crowds – possibly the largest ever to assemble for any such event in London. The greatest promoter of Roman Catholicism in Britain who has ever lived – the man who ensured that his religion would be followed and believed by millions, and respected by ten times that number – died before there was a cathedral for his branch of Christianity in London. Getting a cathedral built was precisely the sort of thing which brought out the worst – the Cardinal Grandison – in Manning. First he commissioned a relation by marriage, Henry Clutton, who spent six years designing a Gothic pile, only to realize that no money had been raised to pay for it. Then in the Eighties, a wealthy Yorkshire landlord, Sir Tatton Sykes, offered to pay for a cathedral if they employed Baron von Herstel as an architect. The baron died in 1884, and Manning thought no more of a cathedral – that was to be the concern of his successors, completed in the twentieth century.[3]

Manning's genius was human, organizational. He wasn't an intellectual. 'I habitually considered Manning's faculties of action, I mean in the management and government of men, to be far in advance of his faculties of thought,'[4] Gladstone wrote, somewhat loftily, of his old friend – but this should not imply that Manning's mind was not sharp and serviceable. He had the true statesman's faculty of quick adaptability – witness his immediate recognition, once the kingdom of Italy was created, that claims for the Temporal Power of the Papacy should be dropped. Always the clever Balliol man, he had in common with one of a later generation, Thomas Hill Green, the rare quality of applied intelligence – whether he was thinking about the personal and political implications of the Dilke case, or the solution to the Dock Strike. Another Balliol man, Hilaire Belloc (whose feminist Unitarian mother, Bessie Parkes, had been overwhelmed by Manning's personality, and like the women in *Lothair* became a Catholic in consequence), saw Manning as the greatest figure of his age.

> The poor of Jesus Christ whom no man hears
> Have waited on your vengeance much too long,[5]

Belloc wrote, in a poem about the London poor. It was these people that, without any desire to cut a figure for himself, Manning represented. He was sufficiently a gentleman to know that Roman Catholicism in England was utterly not the religion of gentlemen. To this degree, no one could have been less like Cardinal Grandison, and the snobbish fantasies which *Lothair* bred – most notably Waugh's *Brideshead Revisited* – would have disgusted Manning. If a member of his own class visited him in the early days of his Catholicism he would apologize for his clothes – the 'Roman Collar' now worn even by Protestant clergymen. But once he had lost his self-consciousness, he could make the joyful claim, 'If I had not become Catholic I could never have worked for the people of England, as in the last year they think I have worked for them. Anglicanism would have fettered me.'[6]

It was probably true that Manning was driven out of the Church of England by quasi-political factors. 'If Manning leaves us it will be because his trust in our being a true branch of the Church Catholic is killed – & this will mainly be the work of Lord J Russell,' Soapy Sam Wilberforce had written bitterly in October 1850.[7] What a world away that was from the urban, industrialized, politicized London of the 1890s which – on one level so surprisingly – had taken to its heart this etiolated, severe, early Victorian parson turned Roman prince and prelate. It was surely because people recognized that he was one of the few establishment figures who had dared to leave the establishment, and who was genuinely moved by principles to which they would have liked to aspire. 'Without God there is no law but the human will, which is *lawless*, & without law, no moral bonds or cohesion among men.' By arguing the case of the dockers with their employers (Manning said he had 'never in my life preached to so impenitent a congregation') he had shown in the concrete what was meant by his embracing as his political watchword the saying of Aquinas – *Reges propter regna, non regna propter reges.** No one else in the Victorian Age – not even Shaftesbury – had been in quite that position of Manning in the strike: actually being able to call individual rulers to account and bringing off victory, albeit modest victory, for the ruled.

So it was, after the solemn requiem at the Brompton Oratory, that pastiche of a Roman city church set down in the middle of Knightsbridge, attended by sixteen bishops, that they took their cardinal to be buried. Many Londoners had never seen such a sight – hundreds of priests, monks and friars in their medieval habits, singing their solemn Gregorian chant, set out in procession to Kensal Green cemetery. From the windows of shops selling the shades for electric lamps or the latest outfit for a cycling holiday, the chanting friars could be seen – just such figures as Gibbon had watched in the ruins of the Capitol a hundred years and more earlier. But these enchantments of the Middle Ages were accompanied by figures quite new in history: behind the Funeral Car were the National League, United Kingdom Alliance, Trades Unions of London, Dockers' Societies, Amalgamated Society of Stevedores, Federation of Trades and Labour Unions, Independent Order of Good Templars and Universal Mercy Band Movement. How strange they would have seemed to Manning's parishioners if they had appeared half a century earlier to greet him in his Protestant incarnation, and had appeared on the lawn of the

---

*Kings are for the realm's service, not vice versa.

archdeacon of Chichester at Lavington. Now they marched on, they the future, taking the old Victorian to his grave. And for every step of that four-mile journey, the pavements were thickly lined with crowds. At some points, they were so dense that the procession was halted.

It was twilight, on that dim January day, when they finally reached Kensal Green. The bishop of Birmingham said the final prayers, the acolytes held up their twinkling tapers, and the choir sang a Miserere, as they buried him in the Catholic plot, near Wiseman, and near that heroine of the Crimean War, Mary Seacole. As the candlelit procession dispersed, some mourners might have turned their eye to the huge expanse of Kensal Green Cemetery and thought perhaps how apt it was to bury Manning beside a burial-ground so much a creation of the swollen population of Victorian London* – and a plot, too, which is full of such a rich variety of his contemporaries.

There, among the merchants and self-made men of the age, is the solid grey mausoleum inscribed 'In Memory of His Royal Highness Augustus Frederick, Duke of Sussex, K.G.': the uncle who gave away the Queen in marriage. (He had requested to be buried in the new public cemetery because he had been so appalled by the slipshod funeral of his brother William IV at St George's Chapel, Windsor).[8] Here lies James Miranda Barry, the Inspector General of the Army Medical Department, who was found by those laying out his corpse in 1865 to be a woman.[9] Here lie Anthony Trollope and Wilkie Collins and William Makepeace Thackeray. Charles Blondin, the tight-rope walker, would in 1897 be destined to join Isambard Kingdom Brunel, who was buried here in 1859. Here is the resting place of Millais, Leigh Hunt, Mulready, Cruikshank. Feargus O'Connor, Chartist firebrand, John Murray, publisher, Robert Smirke, the architect of the British museum, and John Gibson, the sculptor, still lie here. It is rather a pity that Manning does not do so any more, but has been taken to lie in the twentieth-century Catholic cathedral among his comparatively undistinguished successors as archbishop of Westminster. Manning belongs in the rich variety of Victorian grandees and eccentrics, more than in the narrow confines of ecclesiasticism.

Kensal Green, the first public cemetery (as opposed to churchyard or church-owned burial-ground), was the inspiration of a barrister called

---

*The Catholic burying-ground, St Mary's, adjoins Kensal Green Cemetery proper.

G.F. Carden, who had been impressed by the new general cemeteries in Europe, especially Père Lachaise in Paris. Carden first attempted to take over Primrose Hill. He engaged Thomas Wilson to design a vast pyramid on the site, capable of housing 5 million bodies, but in the end the General Cemetery Company established itself at Kensal Green in 1831. There were soon public cemeteries in Norwood (1837), Highgate (1839), Nunhead, Abney Park and Brompton in 1840, Tower Hamlets in 1841. It was initially the custom to pay sums ranging from 1s. 6d. to 5s. to one's parish clergy in compensation for the funeral fee which would have been paid had the burial occurred on consecrated ground. The truth was, though, that the Malthusian principle operated in death as in life. There was simply no room for any more dead in the old burial grounds, and the new public cemeteries – which of course could provide interment for those who owed no loyalty to the established Church – soon filled up.

A very obvious solution lay to hand but there were objections – emotional, theological, and even legal – to the sensible idea that in an overcrowded world, riddled with disease, dead bodies should be consumed by fire, rather than buried in the earth.

Sir Henry Thompson (1820–1904) was one of the first to pioneer the idea of cremation as an alternative to burial, in an article in *The Contemporary Review* in January 1874. Thompson was a versatile man, an eminent surgeon at University College Hospital, London, learned and caring. His wide interests included an expertise in Nanking china. He also concerned himself with what we would call preventive medicine and with all the social aspects of the medical calling. The overcrowding of urban cemeteries was a major problem of town planners. Thompson in his *Contemporary Review* article reminded readers that it is a mistake to suppose that burial is the beginning of eternal rest. 'Rest! No, not for an instant! Never was there greater activity than at this moment exists in that still corpse. Already a thousand changes have commenced. Forces innumerable have attacked the dead . . . Nature's ceaseless agents [are] now at full work.' Thompson went into graphic detail about the putrescent decay of the body, and proposed the substitution of a furnace, cheap and hygienic. The cheapness hardly recommended itself to a generation addicted to advertising their social status by ostentatious obsequies. The fact that the body will in any event dissolve in the earth did not deter the Roman Catholic Church from teaching that cremation would somehow interfere with, if not actually prevent, the resurrection of the body.

(This doctrine was changed in 1963, when Catholics were for the first time allowed to be cremated.) While many other Christians shared the Catholic misgiving, the police feared that in – for example – the case of a poisoning, cremation would destroy vital forensic evidence. Thompson, undeterred, formed the Cremation Society with a number of friends, including Sir John Tenniel of *Punch*, the illustrator of *Alice*.

Though the habit of cremation was slow to be adopted, the notion of it, as the most efficient means of disposing of the dead, had certainly entered public consciousness. When the English cricket team lost heavily in the Test match against Australia in 1882, the result was not the Coffin of British Luck – but the Ashes. (The joke appeared first in *The Sporting Times* – 'In affectionate remembrance of English cricket, which died at the Oval, 29th August, 1882, deeply lamented by a large circle of sorrowing friends and acquaintances. RIP. NB The body will be cremated and the Ashes taken to Australia.')[10]

The Cremation Society applied for a site on which to erect the first furnace, and at length managed to find one next to the 'London Necropolis and National Mausoleum' at Woking, Surrey. (This had been designed as an absolutely splendid modern burial-ground, with a funeral railway, and a magnificently tomb-like Gothic station at Woking by Smirke, which never got built.)[11]

It remained an open question whether cremation was yet legal. When a Captain Hanham of Blandford, Dorset, cremated both his wife and mother (at their own request) in a privately constructed furnace, it was felt that the law had been infringed, but nothing was done about it by the then home secretary.[12]

It was a Welshman who, in 1884, was bold enough to take an action which, eventually, made clear what the law actually was. William Price, eighty-three years old, was an outspoken radical, a medical doctor, a fervent Welsh Nationalist and a Druid. When his five-month-old son – whom he had christened Jesu Grist (Jesus Christ) – died, Dr Price placed the infant in a barrel of petrol on a hillside at Llantrisant and ignited it.[13] He was prosecuted for the common law offence of burning, not burying, a body, and the case came before Mr Justice Stephen at the Glamorganshire Assizes, Cardiff, on Tuesday 12 February 1884.[14] The judge ruled that 'a person who burns instead of buries a dead body does not commit a criminal act unless he does it in such a manner as to amount to a public nuisance at common law'.[15]

Thereafter the way was open, and the Society carried out its first cremation at Woking in March 1885. There were only 3 that year, 10 in 1886, 104 in 1892. Even by 1914 there were just 1,222 cremations, 0.2 per cent of the 516,000 deaths that fateful year. The baleful Edwardian and Victorian legacy of the huge public cemetery is with us yet, and every large city in Britain has its miserable hinterland, now ruinous, bramble-grown and strewn with our own contemporary detritus, of mile on mile of damp vaults, sunken tombstones, chipped stone angels and illegible headstones, monuments to the forgotten Victorian millions.

Kensal Green, where Manning lay until his co-religionists disturbed his bones, and where so many of his celebrated contemporaries lie beneath the grass, is, by the standards of most public cemeteries, a model of beauty and decorum. When they buried Manning it must have still possessed real charm, when the rich were still extravagantly interred in the undecayed catacombs at six guineas each.[16] It was one of the sights of London. Those who went there as sightseers in the Nineties must have had a sense of palpable difference between themselves and the early Victorians. It is probably impossible to define precisely the spirit of any particular period. Generalizations about the 1890s abound – but who is to say that Oscar Wilde and Aubrey Beardsley are more 'typical' of the decade than the lower-middle-class Charles and Carrie Pooter satirized in *The Diary of a Nobody*? Is Cecil Rhodes a more archetypical Nineties man than David Lloyd George or Keir Hardie?

Recognizing the danger of generalization, however, one can discern in the last years of the nineteenth century ways in which the world seemed different to those with eyes to see it: and, which is rather different, trends in the 1890s which history was later to read as decisive. To define is perhaps more dangerous than to generalize – *A thought expressed is a lie* as Fedor Tyutchev wrote – but one can discover trends, or areas of understanding, in which the ethos of the 1890s may be seen as transitional, leaving behind the old Victorian world and looking ahead to the modern. Three such areas might be loosely grouped under the three headings of Metaphysics, English Domestic Politics and the World Order.

Metaphysics might seem an off-putting word, but one struggles to find a synonym for anything as *general* as the first of these categories which I wish to consider: namely the way that men and women now viewed the Nature of Things – what they thought this world was, who they were, what they were doing in it. We would be considering here a matter which is clearly all but impossible to define neatly: but without

545

an understanding of the metaphysic which guides (or does not guide) individuals and societies, there seems little point in trying to say anything about them at all. Without such a metaphysical under-standing, history would be a mere catalogue of *events*, or of the clothes worn on these occasions. To understand the words written or said by our ancestors, the shape of society which they created or accepted, the first task must be to understand how they saw reality itself. And the perception of reality during this era – the many perspectives of artists, poets, religions, philosophy – can be said to have shifted somewhat at the end of the nineteenth century.

Secondly, since our focus has been largely on Victorian Britain, no image of the 1890s would make sense unless it could examine the political situation in this period of transition. It is the beginning of the end for aristocratic government. The system which had delivered a succession of aristocratic prime ministers from Lord Liverpool to Lord Salisbury – and whose two great commoner prime ministers, Gladstone and Disraeli, lived the lives of landed aristocrats – was radically challenged by the sort of Liberalism represented by Chamberlain and Dilke on the one hand in the 1880s or the young David Lloyd George in the 1890s. But how much of the old aristocratic system would be obliterated in the process of change? How successful would the gradualist or Fabian socialists become in changing the structure of society altogether? Why would the revolutionary socialists succeed in some European countries but not in Britain? These are the questions which come to mind in the decade in which the forces of reaction seemed for the most part triumphant, and in which such events as the foundation of the Independent Labour Party at Bradford in 1893 – so momentous to the perspective of later generations – barely disturbs the prosperous surface of a political world still dominated by the aristocracy.

And they relate very closely to the third matter – world order, the shape of the late nineteenth-century, early twentieth-century world. The rival nationalisms of the European powers, which hindsight sees marching inexorably to the tragic calamity of the First World War, seemed to those engaged in much of the sabre-rattling like displays of power. The generals, monarchs, armament manufacturers and politicians who appeared to lesser mortals so powerful seem to hindsight as mighty as a child playing 'I'm the King of the Castle' on a hayrick with a can of petrol in one hand and a box of matches in the other. Much of that story lies outside the scope of this book, but what lies very much within it is the New Imperialism. After the Scramble for Africa, the expansion of the British Empire beyond India to Burma and Malaya and wider still to China, Papua, Polynesia, and the rush by the European countries to colonize the world, the Imperial idea became the central fact of the new world-order. As with aggressive nationalism in Europe itself, so here, hindsight can see the inescapable fragility of the Imperial idea, the shows of strength leading to inexorable disaster for many, if not all, concerned – governed and governors. That is not how it appeared at the time, even though the great Imperial War in South Africa in which Britain was engaged, as the Queen's reign drifted to its close, forced even the most devoted prophets of Imperialism to ask heart-searching questions about the future.

40

Appearance and Reality

One of the strangest spiritual Odysseys of the age was that of Annie Besant (1847–1933), the vicar's wife who was brave enough, aged twenty-seven, to run away from a cruel husband and a religion in which she no longer believed. She risked losing her children (though in the event, the deed of separation, dated 25 October 1873, gave her custody of her daughter Mabel). With atheism and political radicalism she espoused, as an ineluctable consequence, poverty and social ostracism.[1]

She became the friend and collaborator of Charles Bradlaugh, leader of the National Secular Society. As an advocate of birth control and a distributor of *The Fruits of Philosophy* (an inappropriately titled tract about how to limit procreation) she was arrested, tried and condemned, though on appeal she escaped imprisonment. But then she began to drift away from Bradlaugh's secular radicalism in favour of socialism. The arch-cad and con-artist Edward Aveling, medic, actor, Marxist, helped to effect this transition. She was rescued when he subsequently fell in love with Eleanor Marx, whose life he quite literally destroyed – luring her into a 'suicide pact' without keeping his side of the bargain. In the socialist circles of Aveling, Bernard Shaw and the rest, Annie flourished. She was immensely brave as an agitator, as we have seen in our account of 'Bloody Sunday' – November 1887 – and she was also a superb public speaker.[2] Something, however, was lacking. In W.T. Stead, of all people, she briefly found a father-figure. Atheism, she admitted, had brought peace from the torment of believing in an unjust God, but it left her 'without a Father'.[3]

Where would such a figure go? Beatrice Potter, after her marriage to Sidney Webb in 1892, was another woman of essentially religious disposition, who poured her longing for a 'cause' into socialism. She and her husband would be seen as key figures in the story of the British Labour Movement. Certainly, Shaw and the Webbs remained forever scornful of the direction in which Annie Besant chose, by contrast, to move, but in its way it was no less revealing, no less characteristic of its time.

In January 1889 Stead took her to meet the founder of the

Theosophical Society, Madame Blavatsky (1831–91), on one of the sage's visits to London. The obese, pop-eyed Russian aristocrat (naturalized American since 1878) talked 'easily and brilliantly' of her travels.[4] 'Nothing special to record, no word of occultism, nothing mysterious; a woman of the world chatting to her evening visitors.' But when they rose to go, Madame Blavatsky, with a 'yearning throb' in her voice, said, 'Oh my dear Mrs Besant if you would only come among us.' Annie felt an overwhelming urge to bend down and kiss Blavatsky, but she resisted, and made her *adieux*.[5] Within a few months, Annie Besant had found her vocation and her life's work. Although in April 1889 she accepted re-election as a member of the Fabian executive and was still aligning herself with such secular figures as Shaw and the Webbs, her eyes were now upon the distant horizons of the Orient. Like the soldier in Kipling's 'Mandalay', she could hear the temple bells a-calling. By the time she had attended the funeral of her old comrade Charles Bradlaugh she had put on Madame Blavatsky's ring – the symbol of esoteric power – and became one of the great prophets of Theosophy. (One of the young Indians she befriended and who attended Bradlaugh's funeral was Mohandas Karamchand Gandhi, who had visited Madame Blavatsky at Annie's house in St John's Wood.)[6]

Blavatsky has been much ridiculed, and her credentials are often questioned. She claimed that she had achieved enlightenment and initiation into the esoteric mysteries after seven years wandering alone in the Tibetan mountains. Even after the Younghusband expedition of 1903–4, Tibet remained closed to all but a very few travellers, so a white female traveller would, one would have supposed, have encountered some difficulties. As it happens, Blavatsky was so obese as to have difficulty climbing the stairs: another reason sceptics have cast doubt on her claims to have ascended Himalayan heights in quest of wisdom.

By pioneering, or inventing, Theosophy, however, Helena Blavatsky was giving shape and voice to a yearning which lies buried in many human souls, the notion or wish that all faith is really one. True, the nineteenth century was an era of faith quite as much as it was one of doubt. While sophisticates abandoned the old Bible, new bibles were in the making. An angel called Moroni directed Joseph Smith, a teen-aged labourer from New England, to find, in 1827, those Golden Plates which would contain the new gospel, the *Book of Mormon*. In 1875, Mary Baker Eddy (1821–1910) was to publish *Science and Health*, later named *Science and Health with Key to the Scriptures*, which, as the central document of the new religion of Christian Science, was in effect to be a further testament, assuring believers that disease and indeed evil itself were illusory. Blavatsky's new Scripture, *Isis Unveiled* (1877), was written by invisible Spirit hands. Half a million words long, it began by denouncing the scientific materialism of Darwin and Huxley, and went on to expound its key doctrine, namely that all wisdom is One, that science is not opposed to religion, and that religious differences are man-made. Anyone who has nursed the thought that 'deep down all religions are saying the same thing' is more than halfway towards Theosophy. It appealed, said Peter Washington somewhat dismissively in his *Madame Blavatsky's Baboon*, to:

> the world of autodidacts, penny newspapers, weekly encyclopedias, evening classes, public lectures, workers' educational institutes, debating unions, libraries of popular classics, socialist societies and art clubs – that bustling, earnest world where the readers of Ruskin and Edward Carpenter could improve themselves, where middle-class idealists could help them to do so, and where nudism and dietary reform linked arms with universal brotherhood and occult wisdom.[7]

Henry Olcott (*c*.1830–1907), Blavatsky's heavily bearded sidekick, was to be one of Annie's close theosophical allies. A farmer from Ohio, who had been a signals officer in the Union army, Olcott was of good New Jersey stock, claiming descent from the pilgrims. Whereas Blavatsky was visited by Hidden Masters from the ancient Egyptian dynasties of Luxor, Olcott's spiritual visitants came from India. A dark stranger from the Himalayas in an amber turban and white robes laid his hands on the colonel and told him he would do great work for humanity.[8] It was largely through Olcott that Annie Besant visited India – a revelation which changed her life – in 1893. And it is in the Indian context that one sees *some* of the appeal of Annie's new mystical creed for her old radical self. In Ceylon, the British officials regarded Theosophy as seditious. It questioned one of the very bases for a European presence there: namely the superiority of Christianity over Buddhism. Olcott and Blavatsky actually 'took pansil' – a form of Buddhist confirmation – in Colombo. Olcott wore sandals and dhoti. He identified with the Buddhist protests against Christian missions – 805 Christian schools against four Buddhist ones; Christian marriage the only legal form of marriage. In promotion of Buddhist parity with Christianity there was a cause which would certainly appeal to Annie Besant's rebellious heart. There is an Olcott Street in Colombo. In 1967 the Singhalese prime minister said that 'Colonel Olcott's visit to this country is a landmark in the history of Buddhism in Ceylon'.[9] At the very time in history when the white races were imposing Imperialism on Egypt and Asia, there is something gloriously subversive about those Westerners who succumbed to the Wisdom of the East, in however garbled or preposterous a form. The political implications of this were not lost on Gandhi, who welcomed Annie Besant's support for Indian nationalism even when he rejected her spiritual teachings. (She in turn deplored his *satyagraha* – soul-force – policies of resistance to the Raj, believing, by the closing decades of her life, that change would come to India by means of spiritual revival, not political agitation. Such was the revolution which had come about in thirty years in the heart of the heroine of Bloody Sunday.)

Annie Besant was an exotic, and if all her life showed was one woman's journey from socialism to theosophy, then she would hardly seem typical. But though her individual journey was distinctive, in many respects she was a mirror of her age – the wronged feminist of the Seventies, the political activist of the Eighties and, in the Nineties, the seeker after mystery, the grasper of some Greater Whole.

W.B. Yeats, who moved in some of the same circles as Annie Besant, has described in his unforgettable *Autobiographies* the liberating effects of what might seem – to a reader of our times – to be mumbo-jumbo. He too met Madame Blavatsky. And though he did not take her particularly seriously ('a sort of old Irish peasant woman with an air of humour and audacious power')[10] and was sceptical about her claims to be the mouthpiece of long-dead Indian or Egyptian 'masters', he by no means scorned the pursuit of 'psychical research and mystical philosophy'. He saw it directly as a reaction against his own father (a genial artist) and the generation who had believed in both John Stuart Mill and 'popular science'.[11] For Yeats it was an epiphany when he met, in the British Museum Reading Room, 'a man of thirty-six, or thirty-seven, in a brown velveteen coat, with a gaunt resolute face, and an athletic body, who seemed before I heard his name, or knew the nature of his studies, a figure of romance'. This was Liddell Mathers, author of *The Kabbala Unveiled*, who introduced Yeats in 1887 to a society called 'The Hermetic Students' – where, after his initiation in a Charlotte Street studio, the Irish poet met alchemists, necromancers, readers of Henri Bergson, symbolists, fantasists. The magic, and the wisdom of the East, and the Kabbalistic-mystery side of Yeats were all usable, as were the Irish politics and the friendships, in the fashioning of his mighty poetic achievement: he remakes them in his later verse, just as the Grecian goldsmiths in his Byzantium hammer 'gold and gold enamelling'.

> Civilisation is hooped together

he wrote in a poem published in 1935, but it is in one sense a manifesto for the 1890s.

> Civilisation is hooped together, brought
> Under a rule, under the semblance of peace
> By manifold illusion; but man's life is thought,
> And he, despite his terror, cannot cease
> Ravening through century after century,
> Ravening, raging, and uprooting that he may come
> Into the desolation of reality . . .[12]

The 1890s were apprentice years for Yeats. Though he played with Indian and Irish mythology, his symbolism really developed later. The decade was for him, as a poet, the years of lyric, of the Rhymers' Club, of those contemporaries whom he dubbed the 'tragic generation'. 'I have known twelve men who killed themselves,' Arthur Symons looked back from his middle-aged madness, reflecting on the decade of which he was the doyen. The writers and artists of the period lived hectically and recklessly. Ernest Dowson (1867–1900) (one of the best lyricists of them all – 'I cried for madder music and for stronger wine') died from consumption at thirty-two; Lionel Johnson (1867–1902), a dipsomaniac, died aged thirty-five from a stroke. John Davidson committed suicide at fifty-two; Oscar Wilde, disgraced and broken by prison and exile, died at forty-six; Aubrey Beardsley died at twenty-six. This is not to mention the minor figures of the Nineties literary scene: William Theodore Peters, actor and poet, who starved to death in Paris; Hubert Crankanthorpe, who threw himself in the Thames; Henry Harland, editor of *The Yellow Book*, who died of consumption aged forty-three, or Francis Thompson, who fled the Hound of Heaven 'down the nights and down the days' and who died of the same disease aged forty-eight. Charles Conder (1868–1909), water-colourist and rococo fan-painter, died in an asylum aged forty-one.

Arthur Symons might be said to have defined the Ethos of the Decadence when he came back from Paris and announced to his friends in the Rhymers' Club, 'We are concerned with nothing but impressions.'[13] Yeats provides many archetypical vignettes of the set. One of the most memorable is of Lionel Johnson in his rooms in Clifford's Inn: the walls covered with brown paper, the curtains (over door, window and book-case) grey corduroy; a portrait of Cardinal Newman hung on the walls and a religious painting by Simeon Solomon, a friend of the Swinburne–Rossetti circle until they rather priggishly dropped him after an incident in which he was arrested by the police for homosexual indecency. Yeats went to see Johnson at 5, but he never rose before 7 p.m., having his breakfast when others dined and spending the night reading theology, writing lyrics and – chiefly – drinking. 'As for living,' he said languidly, quoting from Villiers de l'Isle-Adam, 'our servants will do that for us.'

Johnson was as it happens a gentleman, but this absurd remark should not lead a later generation into supposing that the appeal of the Decadence was limited to those who could afford servants. What it offered was the capacity for self-reinvention, for making the world into anything you wanted it to be. For that reason it was actually of particular appeal to those whose incomes did not run to employing many servants, and whose outer lives were limited by the crushing restraints of petty bourgeois semi-poverty. It is no accident that Arthur Machen (1863–1947) or Frederick Rolfe (1860–1913) should have flourished at the same time as Mr Pooter. Their exotic sorties into the world of the Occult in Machen's case, and in Rolfe's into full-blown fantasies first about himself becoming pope (his novel *Hadrian the Seventh*, 1904, is very nearly a work of genius), then about pursuing boys in Venice (the posthumous *The Desire and Pursuit of the Whole*), are surely admirable protests against the dingy worlds which both men in fact inhabited. They were the camp equivalent of Kipling's 'British soldier' pining for the 'Burma girl' in Mandalay, sun-drenched or incense-drowned dreams to blot out the hell of suburban boredom. Rolfe's background – the son of a piano-maker, he became a teacher before beginning his extraordinary career as would-be priest, failed seminarian, con-man and sponger – more than justified his decision to transform himself into Baron Corvo, a distressed nobleman of the Holy Roman Empire.

Lionel Johnson drank, and kept himself locked in his nocturnal rooms, to escape those very demons who led Baron Corvo to the darkened *calle* of Venice in pursuit, not merely of the Whole, but of young gondoliers. The grandson of a baronet (General Sir Henry Johnson) and the son of an infantry officer, Captain William Johnson, the boy went to Winchester, and on to New College, Oxford. It was there that the insomnia began, and a doctor recommended alcohol as a palliative. And it was at Oxford that he fell under the influence of Walter Pater (1839–94), who had been a fellow of Brasenose since 1864.

Yeats tells us that 'if Rossetti was a subconscious influence, and perhaps the most powerful of all, we looked consciously to Pater for our philosophy'[14] – and this philosophy, in a few words, was *l'art pour l'art*. When he came to compile *The Oxford Book of Modern Verse* in 1936, Yeats began it with a passage of Pater's prose, which he divided into broken lines as if it were verse.

> She is older than the rocks among which she sits:
> Like the Vampire,
> She has been dead many times,
> And learned the secrets of the grave . . .[15]

Many who heard these words read aloud would not instantly, from the word-picture they create, form a picture of Leonardo da Vinci's *La Gioconda* in their minds. But for the generation who were young in the last quarter of the nineteenth century, Pater's *Studies in the History of the Renaissance* (1873), from which the Mona Lisa passage is taken, and his historical novel *Marius the Epicurean* (1885, set in the period of Marcus Aurelius) were revolutionary. They were the beginnings of the modern. They helped a whole generation to lose their faith in Bentham and Mill and Utilitarianism and to embrace the notion that Imagination fashions the world. As the more scornful and disapproving critics of Pater would insist, this would also suggest that morality, if adopted at all, was something we can make up as we go along. No wonder it appealed so strongly to the young. He saw religion as purely aesthetic, and aestheticism was his religion. No wonder those disciples who feared the consequences of this in their own lives, such as Lionel Johnson or the slightly older Gerard Manley Hopkins (1844–89), embraced the disciplines of a religious life. For those who drank Pater undiluted it could be heady stuff. Oscar Wilde (1854–1900) when he first met Yeats described Pater's *Renaissance* as 'My golden book; I never travel anywhere without it; but it is the very flower of decadence: the last trumpet should have sounded the moment it was written.'[16]

If Pater was the godfather of the Nineties, then undoubtedly its most precocious child and greatest visual genius was Aubrey Beardsley (1872–98), and *The Yellow Book*, the artistic quarterly which he helped to found with his friend Henry Harland, its Scripture. When he took a bundle of drawings to Burne-Jones's studio in Fulham, the older artist told Beardsley, then aged eighteen, 'Nature has given you every gift which is necessary to become a great artist. I *seldom* or never advise anyone to take up art as a profession, but in your case *I can do nothing else.*'[17] Whistler, whose relations with Beardsley were much edgier, made a generous admission in 1896 when he saw Beardsley's brilliantly clever illustrations to Pope's *Rape of the Lock* – 'Aubrey, I have made a very great mistake – you are a very great artist' – a tribute which reduced the consumptive (and not always sober) genius to tears.

Art historians can spot the influences on Beardsley's work – some William Morris here, some Japanese prints there. Beardsley's drawings, however, do not merely illustrate, they define their age, as with his design for a prospectus of *The Yellow Book*, showing an expensively dressed, semi-oriental courtesan perusing a brightly lit bookstall late at night while from within the shop the elderly pierrot gazes at her furiously, quizzically. Half the square is black; the whitened spaces, of books, shop window, lantern, seem shockingly bright. She is an emblem of new womanhood, and of erotic power. The candour with which Beardsley evokes erotic feeling in both sexes made his designs 'shocking' to his contemporaries: and it was partly on this shock value that his reputation rested. After he lost interest in *The Yellow Book* he started a new periodical called *The Savoy*, the prospectus for which depicted John Bull, emblem of bluff Englishry, with a notable erection. His illustrations for *Lysistrata*, with their fleshy-calved, full-breasted women whose pubic hair peeps from behind silks and feathers, capture the erotic power of the work they illustrate, and deliberately cock a snook at the suburbs.

But Beardsley is a much greater artist than these naughtinesses might imply. It is hard to think of any British artist who had a more certain sense of composition. Every small square and oblong is an innovation, an experiment in how to arrange black and white shapes. The draughtsmanship is impeccable. And, as is the case with all great art, no one who has imbibed these drawings is quite the same person as before. After Beardsley, no 'modern art' – not Picasso, not the Dadaists nor the Surrealists of the twentieth century – is a surprise. He has been there before. But he has also seen into the tired old soul of his age. The illustration of Juvenal's *Sixth Satire – Messalina Returning from the Bath* is an astonishing piece of work. A woman (or can we dispense with the indefinite article?) angry and sexually dissatisfied stomps upstairs after an unsatisfying quest for pleasure, her taut nipples bare, her hair loose over her shoulders. Her placing to the left of the picture, while the carefully drawn balustrades are all that occupy the right, is a good example of Beardsley's impeccable sense of space. But it is much, much more than a piece of book-illustration. When he was dying of consumption, the poor young man, who had converted from Anglo-Catholic to Roman Catholic piety, wrote to his publisher Smithers, 'Dear Friend, I implore you to destroy *all* copies of *Lysistrata* and bad drawings . . . By all that is holy *all* obscene drawings. In my death agony.'[18] One is grateful to Smithers, publisher to the Decadents, for ignoring this prayer. Perhaps in any case he realized, as we must do, for example, if we walk into an Arts and Crafts Nineties church such as Holy Trinity, Sloane Street, in Chelsea, that the religion of those times was more than a touch decadent, and the decadence of Beardsley's drawings more than a little religious.

One feels the same sentiments when leaving Beardsley's Bohemian world of Soho restaurants or the flats he shared with his sister Mabel, and turning to the country houses of the group known as the Souls.

Arthur Balfour, the languid nephew of Lord Salisbury, who would succeed as Conservative prime minister on 12 July 1902, felt within himself a superficiality, a frivolity against which he forced himself to guard. He told his niece Blanche Dugdale in the late 1920s that in his youth he had taken his philosophic writings and musings very seriously indeed. This activity 'was my great safeguard against the *feeling* of frivolity'.[19] Balfour's philosophy is not much read now, though the still popular C.S. Lewis provides what is in effect a *rechauffé* version of Balfour's *The Foundations of Belief* in his writings, especially in *Mere Christianity* and *Miracles*. Some of the more lightweight biographical coverage of Balfour and his circle has, by reading only one famous extract from that book, formed the impression that his philosophical position was one of despondency and unbelief, an impression confirmed by his confusingly titled book *A Defence of Philosophic Doubt*. But what Balfour took leave to doubt was not religion but the pretensions of scientific materialism. The 'famous passage', almost an anthology piece, from *The Foundations* describes the world as seen through the eyes not of Balfour himself but those of his philosophical opponents. So powerful is the period prose, however, that one cannot but recognize that it describes the night outside the country houses where Balfour spent his days, the cold windy chaos to which the world would return if all the things he cherished about that upper-class Tory intellectual world, including its Established Church, were removed.

A man – so far as natural science by itself is able to teach us, is no longer the final cause of the universe, the Heaven-descended heir of all the ages. His very existence is an accident, his story a brief and transitory episode in the life of one of the meanest of the planets. Of the combination of causes which first converted a dead organic compound into the living progenitors of humanity, science indeed, as yet knows nothing. It is enough that from such beginnings famine, disease, and mutual slaughter, fit nurses of the future lords of creation, have gradually evolved after infinite travail, a race with conscience enough to feel that it is vile, and intelligent enough to know that it is insignificant. We survey the past, and see that its history is of blood and tears, of helpless blundering, of wild revolt, of stupid acquiescence, of empty aspirations. We sound the future, and learn that after a period, long compared with the individual life, but short indeed compared with the divisions of time open to our investigation, the energies of our system will decay, the glory of the sun will be dimmed, and the earth, tideless and inert, will no longer tolerate the race which has for a moment disturbed its solitude. Man will go down into the pit, and all his thoughts will perish.[20]

For Pater, the natural response to the dark godless universe suggested by Victorian science was to live in myth, and in art. It is in the creation of art that humanity retains its dignity.[21] But for the nephew of Lord Salisbury, this was not quite enough: Balfour tried nobly to create an intellectual justification for *not* believing in the nihilism suggested by Darwin, *not* believing in a godless universe – and by implication, therefore, for accepting Church and State by Law, and by God, established. The atmosphere at Hatfield, during the lifetime of Balfour's uncle, the great prime minister, was distinctly pious. Gladstone liked the feeling in the chapel where Lord Salisbury prayed every day, saying it was 'hearty' – by which he meant full of felt piety, not in the modern sense alive with the noise of tambourines. One of

Balfour's biographers describes the 3rd Marquess's children as 'fanatical Anglicans'.[22]

Balfour, though a believer, could never be so described. His 'set' – nicknamed the Souls – had a different ethos altogether. They were aristocrats who deplored the philistinism of their kind. Mention has already been made of George Nathaniel Curzon's knowledge of languages, architecture and art in East and West – demonstrated with panache when he became viceroy of India. Other 'Souls' included Violet, Duchess of Rutland, who described herself in one word in her *Who's Who* entry as 'artist' – her sculpture of her nine-year-old son lying dead on his tomb at Haddon is testimony of how worthy she was of the name. Another was her lover Harry Cust, minor poet, dashingly handsome man of letters. Wilfrid Scawen Blunt was the oldest member of the circle, a man of enormous accomplishments and a scurrilous pen whose diaries continue to confuse historians with their questionable gossip about upper-class life. A keen Arabist (his wife painted him in Arab costume), he also espoused Irish nationalism (and was imprisoned for a while in consequence). His great house Clouds, now famous as a fashionable clinic – he commissioned Philip Webb to build it at a cost of £80,000 – was often so full of guests that Blunt camped in an Arab tent on the lawn. While the 'Crabbet Club' which Blunt had founded were staying, all twenty of them at once, his wife Lady Anne (Byron's granddaughter) asked guests to share, three to a room. It was a magnificent house – Webb's masterpiece, built of green sandstone, with interiors chiefly white, with here and there a splash of colour provided by Morris carpets or tapestry. Undoubtedly in some of its aspects it suggested the great house in *The Spoils of Poynton* to Henry James – himself an 'honorary Soul' – with Madeline Wyndham, Blunt's cousin by marriage, a part-model for Mrs Gereth. 'In all the great wainscotted house there was not an inch of pasted paper.'

Other 'Souls' houses included the manor house at Mells where the beautiful Frances Graham, subject of many a Burne-Jones canvas, had married the lord of the manor, John Horner. Mells was said to be the 'plum' pulled out by Jack Horner in the rhyme – formerly it was the summer residence of the abbots of Glastonbury. (The Horners had lived at Mells since the Reformation.) Then there was Stanway in Gloucestershire, the superb Jacobean house where Mary Wyndham became the chatelaine, marrying Hugo Charteris, Viscount Elcho, and conducting a lifelong *amitié amoureuse* with Balfour. Far less beautiful architecturally, but no less alive with bright conversation and clever

Souls, was Taplow Court near Maidenhead, where the ethereal, sad-faced Lady Desborough presided. 'Even breakfasts at Taplow were more lively than champagne dinners elsewhere.'

Though Burne-Jones was besotted with Frances Horner, Sargent was the painter who captured the essence of the Souls, as in his stupendous portrait of *The Wyndham Sisters* – Lady Elcho, Mrs Tennant and Mrs Adeane – of 1900. It depicts a world of immense privilege and lightheartedness, but one of dazzling talent too. Yeats, thinking of the rather comparable world of his aristocratic friends in Ireland, saw that country-house life did provide a very special opportunity for a very few clever, nice people to lead lives of the mind, and to be detached from *la vie quotidienne*. By so doing they did not produce works of philosophy to rival Plato or poetry to arouse envy in the shade of Alexander Pope, but it is hard to think of any way of life in any period of history which more deserves the epithet civilized. By destroying it, Yeats believed, his generation had destroyed something irrevocably good –

> O what if levelled lawns and gravelled ways
> Where slippered Contemplation finds his ease
> And Childhood a delight for every sense,
> But take our greatness with our violence?[23]

His Irish contemporary, Wilde, was often in, though not of, this set. Lady Desborough admired the way he would seek out the most prosaic person in the room and 'conjure him into being a wit'.[24] It is strange to think of him being the guest of Herbert Asquith – home secretary who for eight years was married to Margot Tennant, a great Soul.[25] At one moment, Asquith basks in Wilde's wit at his table. At the next, as home secretary, Asquith was ultimately responsible for prosecuting him on a criminal charge and sending him to prison.

Oscar Wilde, as Yeats reminds us, 'hated Bohemia'[26] and was happier in the houses of the rich. 'Olive Schreiner,' he once said to Yeats, 'is staying in the East End because that is the only place where people do not wear masks upon their faces, but I have told her that I live in the West End because nothing interests me but the mask.'[27]

What lay behind Wilde's mask is anybody's guess. (When Arthur Balfour once asked him his religion, he replied, 'I don't think I have any. I am an Irish Protestant.')[28] The mask itself, the persona presented to the world, was clear for all to see, which is why one takes with a pinch of salt the clever modern interpretations of the plays as metaphors for a hidden homosexual life – Bunburying being such a metaphor for example. What amazed Wilde's contemporaries was not furtiveness – which was alien to his nature – but his exhibitionistic candour. Frank Harris, hardly the most shockable of men, was astounded to overhear him describing the physical charms of Olympic athletes in ancient Greece to a pair of extremely suspect youths.[29] Curzon, who had been at Oxford with Wilde, was asked to play devil's advocate when Wilde attended the Crabbet Club in 1891. The custom, laboriously humorous, was that one member would propose a new member and then another would speak against; so Curzon was not being gratuitously offensive, simply playing the game. Nevertheless, as Wilfrid Scawen Blunt recollected, Curzon knew all Wilde's 'little weaknesses and did not spare him, playing with astonishing audacity and skill upon his reputation for sodomy and his treatment of the subject in *Dorian Gray*. Poor Oscar sat helplessly smiling, a fat mass, in his chair . . . What is really memorable about it all is that, when two years later he was arraigned in a real Court of Justice, Oscar's line of defence was precisely the same as that made in his impromptu speech that evening at the Crabbet.'[30]

In the final paragraph of *De Profundis*, the long, overwritten ietter penned by Oscar Wilde in Reading Gaol to Lord Alfred Douglas, Wilde gave utterance to some generalizations which were so wholly of their time that we could almost imagine finding them among the mystical writings of Blavatsky, the philosophical musings of the Idealists, or in the slightly precious letters exchanged by 'The Souls' – 'Time and space, succession and extension, are merely accidental conditions of Thought. The Imagination can transcend them, and move in a free sphere of ideal existences. Things, also, are in their essence what we choose to make them.' With what is a typical inversion of common-sense meaning, Wilde then makes a remarkable prophecy – 'What lies before me is my past. I have got to make the world look on it with different eyes, to make God look on it with different eyes.'

Leaving the Almighty out of consideration, we may say that Wilde has been remarkably successful in achieving his ambition. During his lifetime, he could be seen as a man of incomparable wit who had written some jolly plays and one masterpiece – *The Importance of Being Earnest*. The fairy stories, the creakingly obvious *Picture of Dorian Gray*, the unsuccessful lyrics, can surely only be savoured by the most enthusiastic devotees. As for his private life – he chose not to make it private. A case could be made out for the Victorians being more prudish than we are. An equally strong case could be made for their retaining what is necessary to be retained in order to lead a sane or civilized life: namely, a sense that while there are some things which one would say or do in private, they change their nature if made public. By so incomprehensibly choosing to make an exhibition of himself in court, Wilde made life measurably more uncomfortable for all the homosexuals in Britain, many of whom fled abroad after the second trial. On the day that Wilde was bound over at Great Marlborough Street Police Court, London was placarded with his name on news-stands. 'Well,' a friend remarked to him, 'you have got your name before the public at last.' 'Yes,' Wilde laughed. 'Nobody can pretend now not to have heard of it.'[31] He showed extraordinary courage, but the trials did not do much except create an impression in the public mind of a murky homosexual underworld in which fairly sordid things took place, often with boys who were legally minors.

Yet while the Victorians made the crude moral mistake of treating Wilde like a criminal, our generation has made the almost more mysterious mistake of seeing him as part martyr for sexual liberation, part great thinker.

What cannot be doubted is that Wilde's trial and conviction made a profound impact on his times. It did not necessarily change the way Victorians thought about homosexuals, or the Irish, or prisons, or prostitutes, or relations between the propertied and unpropertied classes. All these ideas have been put forward to attach significance to the Wilde trials, but this is to impose rational shape on something which at the time was upsetting in different ways. On the one hand it upset those, including Wilde's closest friends (and one can assume his wife), who had supposed him innocent of the charges. And on the other, it caused (and still causes, if one reads the transcripts of the trials) that generalized pain felt if one has been the unwilling witness of human beings behaving badly – a row in a restaurant, a brawl on the street corner outside one's window. Certainly, very few emerge well from the episode.

On 18 February 1895, the 8th Marquess of Queensberry, a choleric nobleman with only a slender hold on what others would consider sanity, called at the steps of Wilde's club, the Albemarle, and left a visiting card on which he had written, 'To Oscar Wilde posing as a Somdomite' (sic). The hall porter at the club read the words as 'ponce and Somdomite'.[32]

The behaviour was entirely characteristic of the Scarlet Marquis (as

Wilde called him). His elder son, Lord Drumlanrig, had become private secretary to Lord Rosebery, Gladstone's foreign secretary. In 1893 Rosebery suggested a promotion for the young man by making him a lord-in-waiting to the Queen, but this involved giving him an English peerage. Scottish peers elected from among their number those who could sit in the English House of Lords. When Drumlanrig got an English peerage, entitling him to sit there as of right, Queensberry was wild with rage. He had himself not been elected by his fellow peers, on the reasonable grounds that he refused as an atheist to take an oath to the Queen and had made a nuisance of himself, littering the red leather benches of the chamber with his atheistic pamphlets.

Furious at his son's promotion where he had failed, Queensberry also sniffed out a homosexual tinge to the relations between Drumlanrig and Rosebery. He pursued Rosebery to Homburg, where he had retreated on health grounds, offering to horsewhip the foreign secretary on the steps of his hotel. Perhaps to quieten the rumours, poor dim Drumlanrig proposed marriage to a general's daughter. This did nothing to appease Queensberry's wrath. 'It makes the institution of marriage ridiculous,' he spluttered. On 18 October 1894 Drumlanrig was found dead during a shooting party at Quantock Lodge in Somersetshire. He was lying with his head in a bramble bush and the double-barrelled gun lay on his chest. Though the doctor told the inquest that Drumlanrig had been shot through the mouth, the coroner decided that it was an 'accidental death', and that the gun had gone off while Drumlanrig was climbing the hedge to join his shooting chums.[33]

The death of this unfortunate young man removed a very considerable occasion of scandal from the public scene. Quite what Drumlanrig and Rosebery ever did when they were alone together we shall probably never know, but they were widely believed to have been lovers, and the belief is far from implausible, given the temperament of both men. Six months before the shooting, in March 1894, Gladstone had resigned as prime minister and Lord Rosebery had succeeded him. Even in today's relaxed and tolerant climate there would surely be misgivings about a prime minister who had promoted his apparently talentless and very young secretary to a peerage.

It is against the background of the scandal which never quite happened – Rosebery and Drumlanrig – that Queensberry was able to highlight the scandal which did, the unsuitable friendship of Drumlanrig's younger brother, Lord Alfred Douglas (1870–1945), and the famous playwright and aesthete, Oscar Wilde. The fateful pair met in 1891 when Lord Alfred (known as Bosie) was twenty-two and Wilde thirty-eight. Lionel Johnson brought the young man to tea at Wilde's house in Tite Street and the rapport was instantaneous, quickly developing into a mutual obsession. Letters, notes, presents of all kinds were soon being showered upon the young man.

In the long letter to Douglas sent from prison and entitled *De Profundis* by Wilde's friend Robert Ross,[34] Wilde makes it clear that even in the midst of the most besotted feelings of love for Bosie there was also deep boredom. The young man needed constant amusements – bicycling holidays, golfing holidays, treats, nights out. To a working artist, such distractions must have been torture. Great loves of this kind involve sexual feeling, but sex is not a big part of what is going on. Douglas afterwards said, 'I did with him and allowed him to do what was done among boys at Winchester [Douglas's school] and Oxford ... Sodomy never took place between us, nor was it attempted or dreamed of . . .' It would seem, though, that both men had a taste for going in search of the young male prostitutes who were so plentiful in Victorian London. Wilde's large income – over £3,000 p.a. by now – and lavishly generous nature involved many a hotel room or suite, or restaurant table, at which these young men would indulge in what seems to have been sordid, but fairly mild sexual activity for Bosie's amusement.[35] It would seem as if Wilde's part in these proceedings was largely, if not entirely, voyeuristic. Rumours circulated. Blackmailers stole some of Wilde's more extravagantly phrased letters to Douglas. The furious marquess left his card at Wilde's club.

It was then that Wilde made his incomprehensible mistake of suing Lord Queensberry for libel. One of the most popular dramatists of the age suing one of the most colourful noblemen! It was bound to attract the enormous attention which both men so mysteriously needed. Equally, by the time of the trial Queensberry's defence counsel, Edward Henry Carson (1854–1935), was bound to accumulate evidence which would reveal the nature of Wilde's life to the world. His love letters to Bosie would be read out in court; the rent-boys would be subpoenaed; no jury of the time would have found for the plaintiff in such a case. Moreover, when one remembers that all Carson had to prove was that Wilde was 'posing as a Somdomite', one might think that the plaintiff did the counsel for the defence's own work. Asking Wilde about Walter Grainger, Douglas's servant at Oxford, Carson said:

'Did you ever kiss him?'
'Oh, dear no! He was a peculiarly plain boy. He was,
    unfortunately, extremely ugly.'[36]

Wilde, in this first trial – the one in which he was suing Queensberry for libel – came up with lines which are quite as good as anything in his plays.

'Iced champagne is a favourite drink of mine – strongly
    against my doctor's order.'
Carson: 'Never mind your doctor's orders, sir!'
'I never do,' replied Wilde, sweetly, to roars of laughter
    from the gallery.[37]

When Wilde's libel case collapsed, as it inevitably did, it was only a matter of time before he himself was arrested for infringements of the Criminal Law Amendment Act (1885). The magistrates gave Wilde time to escape. The manager of the St James's Theatre, where *The Importance of Being Earnest* was still showing, urged him to go abroad. 'Everyone wants me to go abroad. I've just been abroad. One can't keep going abroad, unless one is a missionary, or, what comes to the same thing, a commercial traveller.'

Bosie even rounded on Shaw and Harris, both of whom urged flight – 'Your telling him to run away shows that you are no friend of Oscar's.'[38]

There are a number of explanations for his reckless decision to stay in England and stand trial. Likeliest, surely, is that Bosie wanted him to do so and – such is the madness of love – Wilde was in Bosie's thrall. He also surely knew that if he told the full truth in the witness box he would be acquitted, but he could only do so by admitting that he had witnessed various indecent acts, but performed few, if any. Indeed, the mad Marquess surely had a point when he said that 'I do not say you are it, but you look it, and you pose as it which is just as bad.' Wilde, who was sent to prison for two years' hard labour for being indecent, was actually much more accurately to be described as decent. The real reason this camp, sentimental man suffered was to protect his friend.

In 1889 there had been a police raid on a homosexual brothel at No. 19 Cleveland Street, north of Soho. Various grandees were implicated including the Earl of Euston, son of the Duke of Grafton, and Lord Arthur Somerset, an equerry to the Duke of Clarence (the Prince of

(*Above*) William Barnes, the parson-poet, at Winterborne Came Rectory, Dorset, with his family. Although it looks an idyllic scene, the closing decades of the 19th century saw an increase in rural poverty. (*Below*) Meanwhile the life of the urban poor was scarcely more enviable. This London slum was photographed in 1889.

The education of women was one of the great advances of the age. This picture, however, shows a cheerful male crowd gathering in Cambridge in 1897 when the University rejected the admission of women. Like the dummy female undergraduate on the bicycle, the fate of Cambridge women was in suspense until 1947, when they were at length allowed to take degrees.

Newspaper scandal for the late Victorians was what tragedy was to the ancient Greeks: human misery concocted for spectators. Among the more celebrated victims were (*above*) Oscar Wilde, seen here, paunchy and seedy after his release from gaol; (*above right*) Sir Charles Dilke, whose sexual appetites destroyed his political career – pictured here with his loyal wife; and (*right*) Charles Stewart Parnell, perhaps the greatest statesman of the age, who came so close to achieving Irish Home Rule, until his affair with Mrs O'Shea was exposed. Irish Peace was thereby scuppered for over a century.

Leisure activities and games began to have mass appeal. (*Left*) The races were as popular in 1860 as they are today. (*Middle*) The 1897 Cup Final between Aston Villa and Everton at Crystal Palace drew vast crowds. (*Bottom*) In India, tennis was as popular with Maharajahs as among the British.

(*Left*) The Queen in old age went very much her own way; to the disquiet of her courtiers she placed implicit trust in a mildly fraudulent character called Abdul Karim ('The Munshi') – 'Such a very excellent person.'

The Golden and Diamond Jubilees led to a revival of popularity for the monarchy.

(*Left*) The Victorian passion for fancy dress. Here Princess Beatrice poses as 'India', attended by her nieces Princess Louise of Wales (holding box) and Princess Alix of Hesse. Around them from left to right are Khairat Ali, Abdul Karim (the Munshi), Mohammed Bukhsh and Abdul Hussain.

(*Left*) At the Devonshire House Ball the Duke of Devonshire (Harty Tarty) dressed as the Emperor Charles V. (*Right*) Arthur Balfour, future prime minister, standing, came as a Gentleman of Holland, Mrs Grenfell came as Marie de' Medici and Sir W.V. Harcourt came as his ancestor the Lord Chancellor. The picture nicely demonstrates how the same families held power in England for hundreds of years.

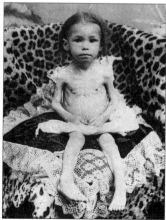

(*Above*) More aristocrats at play. Lord Edward Cecil as a boy with his siblings in Elizabethan dress at Hatfield House. He is a chubby little fellow. He would play a significant role in the Boer War when his father, 3rd Marquess of Salisbury, was prime minister.

Lord Edward as a child was considerably plumper than these Boer children, starving in a concentration camp, perhaps the least glorious of all Victorian inventions. Tens of thousands of women and children were moved from Boer farms to camps like these.

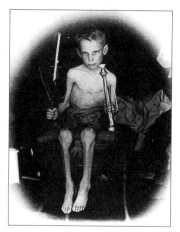

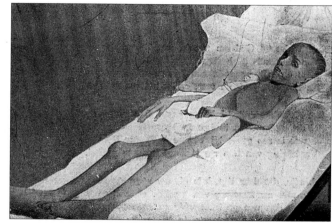

(*Left*) Marie Lloyd – toothy, bald but exuding energy and erotic appeal; she was perhaps the greatest of the music hall *artistes*.

(*Below*) The advent of the motor-car – even with a man with a red flag walking in front – heralded the end of the old world.

Wales's eldest son). Lord Salisbury met the courtier Sir Dighton Probyn VC at King's Cross station to tip him off that there was trouble afoot. Lord Arthur – son of the Duke of Beaufort – fled the country and eluded arrest.

It was a serious matter that the prime minister of the day should conspire to let a potential criminal escape justice, but Salisbury passed the whole matter off with aplomb in the House of Lords. He admitted to Parliament that he had met Sir Dighton Probyn 'for a casual interview for which I was in no way prepared, to which I did not attach the slightest degree of importance, and of which I took no notes whatever. The train started very soon afterwards.' He sat down amid the cheers of his fellow peers.

As the many public scandals of the nineteenth century show, the Victorians enjoyed such things as much as we do. But they were perhaps more conscious of their destructive effect.

The Irish people, many of them highly puritanical in private life, were prepared to overlook the scandal of Mrs O'Shea's divorce; it was the English puritans who initiated and confirmed the destruction of Parnell. There are some who to this day believe that the Wilde trials were likewise brought to pass to discredit yet another Irishman. All the evidence, though, is that Wilde destroyed himself. Many puritans then, and some now, must be shocked by the details of homosexual life which emerged in evidence during the trials – the stained sheets at the Savoy Hotel being the most distressing. But though for a modern reader of these transcripts Wilde might seem like a gay martyr, to the Victorians his real crime was appalling frankness. 'Things are in their essence what we choose to make them' – the lesson he tried in his long vituperative letter to Bosie to expound from the prison cell was not really a doctrine he preached. Without a measure of hypocrisy, a blurring of the edges between Appearance and Reality, societies cannot function.

It is not merely a moral affront to most twenty-first-century readers, it is wholly baffling, that our forebears – and right down to recent times – prosecuted men on grounds of erotic preference, and criminalized something which is mere temperament. It seemed that way to people at the time, too.

Oh who is that young sinner with the handcuffs on his wrists?
And what has he been after that they groan and shake their fists?
And wherefore is he wearing such a conscience-stricken air?

Oh they're taking him to prison for the colour of his hair.

Now 'tis oakum for his fingers and the treadmill for his feet
And the quarry-gang on Portland in the cold and in the heat,
And between his spells of labour in the time he has to spare
He can curse the God that made him for the colour of his hair.[39]

A.E. Housman (1859–1936) did not, of course, dare to publish these lines on the Wilde trial at the time. When his own first collection, *A Shropshire Lad*, was first published, in that golden age of lyric verse, all readers of the English language knew that a new star had risen in the firmament beside whom Symons and Johnson, Davidson and Francis Thompson, and all the other 'Nineties' poets would seem like pygmies.

Housman's poems are a manifesto, against 'nature, heartless, witless nature', and against 'the laws of God, the laws of man'.[40]

> The laws of God, the laws of man,
> He may keep that will and can;
> Not I: let God and man decree
> Laws for themselves and not for me.[41]

The perfectly formed, tautly contained lyrics are time-bombs of blasphemy and sexually frustrated torment; but – this is the point, not just of Housman but of the England that took him to its heart – they were deeply *conservative*. The yeomen and soldiers whom he hymns, who are the Shropshire equivalent of Hardy's fictional characters, are not being enlisted for Keir Hardie's labour movement. Housman sings of the misery of existence, the impossibility of expressing unmentionable feelings, but he does not therefore want to overthrow society.

> The street sounds to the soldiers' tread
> And out we troop to see:
> A single redcoat turns his head,
> He turns and looks at me.
>
> My man, from sky to sky's so far,
> We never crossed before;
> Such leagues apart the world's ends are,
> We're like to meet no more;

What thoughts at heart have you and I
We cannot stop to tell;
But dead or living, drunk or dry,
Soldier, I wish you well.[42]

The archbishop of Canterbury, Edward White Benson, and his wife Mary went to stay with the Gladstones at Hawarden in the autumn of 1896. And it was there, during the confession at the beginning of Morning Prayer in the parish church, that Archbishop Benson's breathing was heard to be stertorous and irregular. He was unconscious when they had begun on the Lord's Prayer. By the time he had been carried back to the house and laid on a sofa in that library where Gladstone had spent so many hours, reading Homer, Dante and theology, Archbishop Benson was dead. Later they dressed him in his robes – 'looking kingly and strong'.[43]

The Benson clan provide sure proof of how dangerous it would be to confuse Appearance and Reality when surveying the late Victorian scene. You could hardly hope to find a more 'establishment' figure than the archbishop – the Rugby master, made successively master of Wellington and first bishop of Truro before his translation to Canterbury. He is the pioneer of a certain sort of Anglican piety – he invented the festival of Nine Lessons and Carols at Christmas, one of the central national rituals of Britain, just as his son Arthur – Eton master, later master of Magdalene, Cambridge – was the author of another tradition: he wrote the words of unofficial national anthem, 'Land of Hope and Glory'. Yet the whole family was the reverse of 'conventional'. Fred – E.F. Benson – one of the six children of the archbishop, was an extraordinarily prolific comic novelist, satirizing the Souls in *Dodo*, anatomizing schoolboy homosexuality in *David Blaize* and creating a series of high camp masterpieces in the Mapp and Lucia stories. His many memoirs, which include *As We Were* and *Mother* – the latter an account of his mother's life from the death of the father until 1918 – give away more than the autobiographies of Arthur. But the whole fascination of Bensoniana is that much of the *stuff* tormenting them is unexamined and perhaps unanalysable. Edward White Benson, the future archbishop, proposed to Mary Sidgwick when she was twelve – she wrote in her diary on her wedding night, 'He restrained his passionate nature for seven years, and then got *me*! This unloving, childish, weak, unstable child! Ah God, pity him! . . . misery, knowing that I felt nothing of what I knew people ought to feel.'[44]

After the birth of their sixth child – Hugh – the Bensons in effect separated for a while, and Mary had a breakdown. When she recovered, it was to discover, as Fred says, that she, 'like all very intellectual women, formed strong emotional attachments to her own sex'. The daughter of the previous archbishop was Lucy Tait, a huge girl who dwarfed Mary, but happily shared not merely her household, but her bed. 'Lucy slept with my mother in the vast Victorian bed where her six children had been born in Wellington days.' Ethel Smyth was a great friend.[45]

Of the children, Martin died of a mystery illness aged seventeen. The death sent their father into a deep depression and probably caused him to lose his faith. Nellie died suddenly of diphtheria aged twenty-six. All suffered from the blackest depressions, only relieved by psychosomatic illnesses. Arthur kept copious diaries in which he confided his muted crushes on boys and young men and his professional grievances and rivalries, but his character is so repressed that you could not get anywhere near explaining it by labelling any supposed erotic preference. Sex would have been out of the question for such a figure, as for his depressive sister Maggie, or for brother Hugh – convert to Rome, friend of 'Baron Corvo' and author of lurid historical romances with such titles as 'Come Rack, come rope!'

It is strangely fitting that the germ of Henry James's *The Turn of the Screw* (published in 1898) was an anecdote told him by Archbishop Benson, about the 'spirits' of certain 'bad' servants, dead in the employ of the house, who were believed to have appeared with the design of 'getting hold of' the children. It is in many respects the most finished, the most suggestive and the most terrible of all James's shorter works. The ghostly Peter Quint, who 'did what he wished' not only with the governess but also with the children, is a terrifying emblem of forbidden, morbid sexuality.

Critics divide over this story. For Edmund Wilson, for example, the story is 'about' the governess's own sexual repression: the ghosts are mere hallucinations, the products of neurosis. One can be fairly certain that Henry James himself wanted to make his readers shiver with the sense that these apparitions were real: 'Only make the reader's general vision intense, I said to myself . . . and his own experience, his own imagination . . . will supply him quite sufficiently with all the particulars. Make him *think* the evil, make him think it for himself . . .'[46]

*

One could put this another way.

> My way of contact with Reality is through a limited aperture. For I cannot get at it directly except through the felt 'this', and our immediate interchange and transfluence takes place through one small opening. Everything beyond, though not less real, is an expansion of the common essence which we feel burningly in this one focus. And so, in the end, to know the Universe, we must fall back upon our personal experience and sensation.[47]

The words are those of F.H. Bradley (1846–1924), the weightiest and most influential of British philosophers of the period, who was in correspondence and dialogue with Henry James's philosopher-brother William, whose 'pragmatism' stood at variance with the 'idealism' of the British school. It is tempting to see *The Turn of the Screw* as a contribution to this discussion, since, fairly obviously, to equate the imagination of the governess with delusion, as Edmund Wilson does, is to lose not just the terror, but the very kernel of the story. Idealists did not deny the outward reality of things. They were setting out to demonstrate that, *pace* Locke, the human mind is not a blank on to which sensations are projected as magic lantern slides might be shown on a screen. Rather, the human mind – and more, our capacity to perceive – edits and to some degree *creates* what we see. The sense in which any statement or proposition can be wholly true; the degree to which any human mind can escape the subjective – these are the matters with which Idealism was engaged. The very basic question – is there any reliable criterion by which we may distinguish between the truth and falsehood of propositions? – must be primary. If no such criterion exists, then we might as well not open any book of mathematics, science or history. Most of us, even if philosophers, recognize that we can distinguish between statements we call true and statements we call false, but our metaphysical justification for doing so is more complex than might appear to the common-sense layman.

It would be quite beyond the scope of this book to enter into, still less to pronounce on, such high themes. But it will be obvious that they are of more than passing importance to non-philosophers. From a narrative point of view, the big story in the philosophical history of the 1890s is how G.E. Moore and Bertrand Russell broke with the Idealists and adopted the philosophy of 'realism': how they escaped what they termed a 'hot-house' and laid the foundations for the analytical school of philosophy.

When he was an undergraduate, Russell was told by his tutor, J.M.E. McTaggart, that Bradley's *Appearance and Reality* 'says everything that can be said on the subject of metaphysics'. By 1900, Russell had completely thrown off his belief in Idealism, and in *The Principles of Mathematics* he adopted what amounts to a Platonic-mystical belief in the reality or truth of mathematics independent, it would almost appear, from human minds.[48] Moore's influential and confidently titled article, 'The Refutation of Idealism', published in 1903, is 'widely believed to have given the *coup de grâce* to idealism'.[49]

In so far as Moore was the godfather, or rather non-God-father, to the Bloomsbury set, and Russell was an influential academic philosopher and a popular opinion-former and journalist for the second half of his long life, we can see that the abandonment by these two of the principles of the English Hegelians is of more than academic concern.

The Hegelians based their metaphysics on a conviction that Truth was a unity. They were, on the whole, non-theists but their lucubrations possessed a quasi-religious flavour, especially if you accept McTaggart's definition of religion as 'an emotion resting on a conviction of a harmony between ourselves and the universe at large'. It is easy to see from his many autobiographical writings that Russell found the notion of such a harmony comforting, but felt forced to reject it on intellectual grounds. There is therefore in his career a violent disjunction between the belief in vast impersonal realities – logical or mathematical truth – and the vacillations of his wholly irrational, often self-contradictory views on free love, the education of children, or war and peace. In 1897 he was candid enough to admit:

I am quite indifferent to the mass of human creatures; though I wish, as a purely intellectual problem, to discover some way in which they might all be happy. I wouldn't sacrifice myself to them, though their unhappiness, at moments, about once in three months, gives me a feeling of discomfort, and an intellectual desire to find a way out. I believe emotionally in Democracy, though I see no reason to do so.[50]

We have travelled as far as possible here from the socially engaged philosophy of T.H. Green, which in the twentieth century would have its followers in such influential figures as Collingwood.[51] By then,

Wittgenstein really *had* refuted Russell's ideas about the foundations of mathematics, and the analytical school with which Russell is sometimes associated was very much detached from him.

Russell was in every sense a Victorian. He was brought up by his grandparents, Lord and Lady John Russell. The Cabinet made the decision to invade the Crimea in Pembroke Lodge, the house where his grandparents were still living when Russell went to live there. This aristocratic child whose godfather was John Stuart Mill and who had dinner with Gladstone (one of the funniest episodes in his childhood) lived deep into the twentieth century as a controversialist, anti-war demonstrator and television pundit. 'Three passions, simple but overwhelmingly strong, have governed my life,' he claimed at the beginning of his autobiography: 'the longing for love, the search for knowledge, and unbearable pity for the suffering of mankind.'[52] By his own admission the pity was actually sporadic. His philosophical journey by the end of the 1890s made it seem pointless, even illogical. This detachment in Russell, so influential to the whole of the later generation, between the demands of the ethical, and of logical truth, is the true Decadence of the 1890s.

41

Utopia: The Decline of the Aristocracy

Utopia Limited opened at the Savoy Theatre on 7 October 1893 and ran for 245 performances. It marked the reconciliation of Gilbert and Sullivan after one of their celebrated tiffs. Perhaps the reason that it is not performed as often as some of their other operas is that Sullivan was not really on form: the music does not match the amusing plot, in which a South Sea island – Utopia – decides to improve itself by modelling its constitutional and political arrangements on 'a little group of isles beyond the wave'.

> O may we copy all her maxims wise,
> And imitate her virtues and her charities;
> And may we, by degrees, acclimatize
> Her Parliamentary peculiarities!
> By doing so, we shall, in course of time,
> Regenerate completely our entire land –
> Great Britain is that monarchy sublime,
> To which some add (but others do not) Ireland.[1]

The Utopians make themselves into a Limited Company, convinced by this commercial expedient that they will turn into a democracy. Merely by passing laws intended to make things happen, they believe that improvement is round the corner. They are a 'Despotism tempered by Dynamite' – on the first lapse by their ruler, he is denounced by two Wise Men and blown up by the Public Exploder. They do not realize that they have already achieved perfection, with no crime, no disease, and the jails let out 'as model lodgings for the working-classes': they are persuaded, as many another tried to persuade themself in 1893, that Britain's in these areas is an example to follow.[2]

The audiences of this satire would have returned to their suburban homes reminded that the late Victorian political scene was an extraordinary phenomenon. If Professor Bradley had been looking about for an example of the ambiguous relationship between Appearance and Reality, he might well have been satisfied by attending election meetings in the constituencies newly formed in 1884, or by going to the Houses of Parliament and asking whether the Honourable Members there – all men (as were the electorate) – offered a fair or realistic representation of the 38 million or so people in Ireland, England, Scotland and Wales.

The 1884 Reform Act had extended the possibilities of parliamentary democracy. The electorate was now enlarged to 5 million (or thereabouts), and included agricultural labourers and the urban working classes. Such was the cleverness with which Lord Salisbury had negotiated the borders of constituencies with the Liberals that this did not materially threaten his party's dominion over Parliament, nor his class's dominion over his party. The radicals and socialists made a little headway in the late Eighties, but the suburbs had been conquered by the Conservative Party. The split in the Liberal Party over Home Rule went very much in favour of the Unionists – as witnessed by the fact that when Gladstone resigned as prime minister in 1894 he was replaced by a Liberal Unionist, Lord Rosebery. Lord Salisbury formed a government in June the following year and the Conservatives remained in office for the next ten years.

While the Independent Labour Party, formed in 1893, raised many hopes, it did not do very well electorally. One of its founding fathers, Philip Snowden, believed that its formation was 'the most important political event of the nineteenth century'.[3] The three ILP candidates – John Burns, Keir Hardie and James Havelock Wilson – who won as independent socialists seats in the 1892 election lost them again as ILP candidates in 1895. That election saw Hardie himself, the leader of the ILP who had so movingly taken his seat in the Commons wearing his working clothes and his tweed cap and his boots, defeated by the Conservative at West Ham. The ILP fielded 28 candidates in that election, the Social Democratic Federation 4. They were all defeated.

Now, of course, the Labour Party would one day – after the disintegration of the Liberals during and after the First World War – become the equivalent party of the Left in British politics. Old ILP men like Ramsay MacDonald and Snowden would find themselves forming a Labour government in 1924, though by then neither of them retained any of his socialist ideas and Snowden, as chancellor of the Exchequer, was a tax-cutting Free Trader who had more in common with Thatcherite Conservatives of later times than with the tweed-capped, home-knitted leftist ideologues of the 1890s. The years in which MacDonald was prime minister were ones of excessive economic crisis and hardship, but they ended in spectacular failure, with the former illegitimate farm-labourer from the north-east of Scotland cutting unemployment benefit and forming a National Government with the Tories. While the beginnings of the ILP were important, then, some might question whether it was 'the most important political event' of a century which contained three very major reforms of parliamentary franchise; three major (and innumerable minor) wars; the extension of the British Empire to a position of previously unimaginable extent, scope and strength; and the beginning of the parliamentary career of David Lloyd George.

It was the failure of socialism to take hold in Britain which was really of significance. As for the strength of the aristocracy, or its apparent strength during the years of Lord Salisbury's premiership – this too is not all that it seems. Any simplistic, or blanket, explanation for the political climate in the 1890s is going to distort reality. Had England ceased, since the passing of the 1884 Reform Act, to be a country governed by the aristocracy? Was it now a true democracy? Were the poor, the working class and the lower middle class represented by the political system? And what had happened to the Liberal Party since the split over Home Rule?

Utopia, Limited or otherwise, Lord Salisbury's Britain certainly wasn't. Viewed in many lights it seems like a country in crisis: at the very least a *deluge* which that consummate Conservative was postponing until he had left the stage.

In *My Apprenticeship*, published in 1926, Beatrice Webb drew on the diaries and punctilious records which she kept in the last quarter of the nineteenth century to explain the question 'Why I became a Socialist'. Since, with her husband Sidney Webb, she was one of the greatest architects and prophets of the British Labour Movement, the question is broader than the merely personal. This was not just the question of how one clever, guilty rich young woman chose to become left-wing to appease feelings of awkwardness about her father's wealth. It was the exposition, by a deeply informed political intelligence, of the nature of the nineteenth-century problem, and the most plausible solution – as she came to see it. It is all the more interesting because of her character – its innate conservatism, its essentially religious bent, and its intense seriousness. This was the woman who in her youth had enjoyed the friendship of old Herbert Spencer and painfully discarded Christian belief, while remaining 'in search of a creed'; who had been painfully in love with Joseph

Chamberlain; and who, by her first-hand investigation of the lives of the poor with Charles Booth, had made herself one of the best-informed social observers in Europe.

Slowly, during the late 1880s, Beatrice (still Potter) had become involved with trade unions and with the Co-operative Movement (which had begun in 1844 in the small Lancashire town of Rochdale). The twenty-eight flannel weavers known as the Rochdale Pioneers pooled a proportion of their earnings to buy groceries at wholesale prices. The more people who joined the Co-operative the wider the range of goods offered and the lower the prices. This in turn developed into a nationwide English Co-operative Society, with department stores and simple banking arrangements for its members, and, since it was run on a non-profit-making basis, a dividend (or 'Divvy') handed back to members each year in proportion to their contribution.

For Beatrice Potter, the Co-operative Movement was not merely an ideal blueprint for the way that a Socialist Society could work. It had actually, as a matter of practical and observable fact, demonstrated an economic truth about value which significantly modified the previous theories accepted by Ricardo, or Marx. Their doctrine had been that Labour is the Source of Value. Versions of the Socialist Dream in England had revolved around the ideas of Robert Owen, that workers might have a 'self-governing workshop' in which they undid the prime injustice and evil of the capitalists. The Industrial Revolution removed from fourth-fifths of the population the tools of their trade and the product itself. Power looms ruined the home weavers. The 'self-governing workshop' would hand the joint ownership of the machines and the workshop to the workers.

As Beatrice Potter saw, however, there was a perversity about this, since it placed some mythic 'value' in the manufactured product itself rather than recognizing that things possess value only if people want them. What the Co-operative Movement had done was to treat all its members not as Nibelungs toiling to produce some supposed value, but as consumers. 'To organize industry from the consumption end, and to place it, from the start, upon the basis of "production for use" instead of "production for profit", under the control and direction not of the workers as producers, but of themselves as consumers, was the outstanding discovery and practical achievement of the Rochdale Pioneers.'[4]

If it had been possible to construct society as a whole on the model of the Co-operatives, using compulsory tax rather than voluntary contributions of 'Co-op' members, then there might be the means to alleviate poverty, and to provide public services.

'Man does not live by bread alone'; and without some 'socialism' – for instance, public education and public health, public parks and public provision for the aged and infirm, open to all and paid for out of rates and taxes, with the addition of some form of 'work or maintenance' for the involuntarily unemployed, even capitalist governments were reluctantly recognizing, though hardly fast enough to prevent race-deterioration, that the regime of private property could not withstand revolution.[5]

This, then, was her blueprint; and when she had abandoned her unfocused radicalism and joined herself quite definitely – and literally, by marriage – to Fabian socialism, she had not merely discovered her aim but agreed the best means of achieving it. By 1898 she and her husband had founded the London School of Economics as the seminary of the new creed. *The New Statesman and Nation* was its unfolding scripture, disseminated to 2,500 subscribers in the first issue, and soon to be much the most influential of all left-wing periodicals in the English language. Like the islanders in *Utopia Limited*, the Webbs were gradualists. They wished to substitute for the language, and tactics, of the wilder leftist revolutionaries a slow progress towards the Promised Land. But the end was the same – a capitalist jungle rescued from the cruel excesses of individualism by means of a slowly imposed collective medicine.

The Labour Movement's strength was not simply in its alliance between 'workers' and 'intellectuals'. Such supposed friendships were the commonplace of all continental revolutionary or democratic movements. What solidified the Labour Alliance in Britain was the perception that the underlying idea, the Co-operative Movement, derived from the working classes themselves. In its own 'personal myth', therefore, the Labour Party could not have been more different from Marxism. The communist faithful absorbed their wisdom from the sacred texts written by Marx and expounded by Engels. In the Fabian socialist movement Mrs Webb attributed her conversion to socialism to the Rochdale pioneers (though she did so with backhanded condescension, believing they did not realize the economic or political implications of what they had demonstrated).

It is not in a spirit of satire that one uses religious language to describe the early days of organized parliamentary socialism. The Independent Labour Party was founded in Bradford in 1893. Keir Hardie, who had won the parliamentary seat of West Ham, chaired the first conference and was elected its first leader. Shaw came up for the conference, to establish from the first the Fabians' condescending desire to take the thing over, and Engels sent his glad greetings. But the atmosphere of the conference and of many Labour meetings in the 1890s was that of the Chapel.

Bradford, one of the great wool towns of the North, was also one of the places where the mid-century Nonconformist revival had been strongest. Horton Lane Congregational Chapel towered like a great symbol in the town of Nonconformist strength.[6] It was known as the Temple of Nonconformity, many of the early mayors of Bradford, and most of the aldermen, coming from this congregation. By the 1890s, however, these middle-class worthies had moved to the suburbs, or to the more genteel dormitory towns of Ilkley and Harrogate.[7] Those who retained religion expressed their gentility by transferring their allegiance to the Church of England. The Cathedral of Nonconformity gradually declined until, by the end of the century, a local newspaper described its 'parlous state – no congregation to speak of, no Sunday school worth mentioning, no pastor'.[8]

The mayors and aldermen with their great silver 'Alberts' – watch-chains stretched over well-tailored worsted – the small businessmen, shopkeepers, manufacturers and traders were Gladstone's natural supporters, the creators of that political world whose 'prevalent tone . . . is one of surfeited, self-satisfied Liberalism. Local papers were busy celebrating the improvements in standards of life since the hungry forties, and recalling for the hundredth time the wisdom of the repeal of the Corn Laws.'[9]

The new Labour Party was never to appeal to such as these. For many of its adherents it satisfied the same religious hunger which in an earlier age had been appeased by the Congregationalists, Baptists and different varieties of Methodists. The atmosphere of the political meetings was revivalist, with new songs set to old tunes. Verses by J.L. Joynes, printed in the year of the ILP's foundation and entitled 'What, Ho! My Lads', proclaimed:

> In our Republic all shall share
> The right to work and play,
> The right to scoff at carking care,

> And drive despair away –
> Drive poverty away, my mates,
> With struggle, strain and strife:
> What use are Parliaments and States
> Without a happy life?

To the tune of 'The Union Jack' they sang 'The Starving Poor of Old England':

> Let them brag until in the face they are black
> That over oceans they hold their sway,
> Of the Flag of Old England, the Union Jack,
> About which I have something to say;
> 'Tis said that it floats o'er the free; but it waves
> Over thousands of hard-worked, ill-paid British slaves,
> Who are driven to pauper and suicide graves –
> The starving poor of Old England.

The message was not merely simple, but compelling – spelt out in *The Labour Annual* of 1894 (produced, at the cost of one shilling, for 'The Nationalist Socialist Federation' – of the Fabian Society, the ILP, the Labour Church, the SDF and 'all the Advanced Movements'): 'in a country where our accounts are so incredibly ill-balanced that out of a population of thirty-six millions, only one and a half-millions get above £3 each week and more than half of the total national income "belongs" to a very few *thousand* people'. Hardie himself made the same point in his 'chat with the Scotch miners on their strike' – 'Why have 50 Mineowners power to starve 70,000 miners into submission?'

In their electoral contests, the Labour candidates had two principal enemies. The first were the Liberals. For the first twenty or thirty years of its life, the Labour Party was unable to shift the perception that the best way to achieve radical change was through alliance with the Liberals. Many heroes of the early socialist cause, such as John Burns, supported a Lib–Lab alliance, partly because this appeared the only plausible way of achieving actual political power (as opposed to the inner satisfaction of striking heroic attitudes), and partly because they distrusted some of the left-wing extremists who gave support to the ILP. Versions of these two dilemmas would dog the Labour Party throughout its century or so of coherent history – before the arrival of 'New Labour'. It was always necessary, then, to persuade the electorate that the Liberals and the Tories elected to Parliament 'are rich men – landlords, employers and lawyers – and they are not Socialists. They are making wealth out of the present system, and so they want it to continue.'

John Morley received the deadliest verbal attacks from the socialists in his Newcastle-upon-Tyne constituency. Fred Hamill, from the Woolwich branch of Amalgamated Engineers, stood against him, and he identified the other great enemy against which the ILP contended: working-class scepticism or indifference. He told a Newcastle audience in 1893:

> Your greatest enemy is the poor, indolent, apathetic, indifferent, lazy, cowardly worker, who will not support those who are trying to do their very best to improve his condition and lift him from the gutter of despair. (Applause) The emancipation of Labour can be brought about, but only by *bona fide* Labour representation in the House of Commons, independent of any party, faction, clique or class. (Applause) Too long! too long have you, fellow-workers, been looked upon as mere human machines; as illustrated by the words of Sir Lyon Playfair, now a lord of the Upper House. He said, 'The children of the productive classes grow up stunted in form and of low productive value, because the State does not provide for conditions of healthy human development in crowded populations. If the babies were pigs, or oxen, or sheep, the Vice-President of the Council would be daily questioned in the House of Commons if any unusual mortality came amongst them, but being only human infants, no one thinks of their welfare. Beasts with a selling value are taken more care of than men in free countries.' Because this is true of England as she is today, we intend to replace it by real liberty, equality and economic freedom. And where is the man who can deny the necessity of an Independent Labour Party to achieve it?

No one would question the reality of the sufferings and injustices identified by the socialists. In trade unions and Co-operative Societies throughout Britain, working-class people joined the Movement, but never in the numbers that Fred Hamill and his comrades would have hoped. G.K. Chesterton, with his brilliant political reading of Dickens's *Great Expectations*, which was discussed in relation to Marx on page 335, had seen Joe Gargery, the patient poor man, and Trabb's boy, the perky tailor's assistant, as archetypal: 'The first is the poor man who

579

does not assert himself at all, and the second is the poor man who asserts himself entirely with the weapon of sarcasm.' Chesterton went on to say that this sarcasm was a real weapon – 'what guns and barricades were to the French populace, that chaff is to the English populace . . . It is the one way in which they can make a rich man feel uncomfortable, and they use it very justifiably for all it is worth. If they do not cut off the heads of tyrants at least they sometimes do their best to make the tyrants lose their heads.'

Trabb's boy is the assistant at the tailor's where Pip first goes to be measured for a suit of clothes when he comes into those Great Expectations which give the title to Dickens's greatest novel. Later, when he returns to the town, Trabb's boy pursues him down the street, first pretending to be overcome with terror at Pip's dignity. He then imitates Pip's walk. Altogether he refuses to be impressed by the pretensions of his supposed betters.

As it happens British politics was to be provided, in the 1890s and onwards, with the most wonderful Trabb's boy, though Chesterton would not have recognized him as such: one who could use comic sarcasm to an even greater effect than Disraeli. But this Welsh firebrand and comic genius, whom we shall encounter before this chapter is done, chose not to join the Labour Party.

The architect of that party, and its most outstanding political inspiration in its first twenty years, was James Keir Hardie (1856–1915). The illegitimate son of a Lanarkshire farm servant, he began work in a Glasgow printing works at the age of eight and became a coal miner at the age of ten. He was a working collier until he was twenty-three, and entered politics by becoming active in trade unionism. The Labour Party was always a marriage of contrarieties, and some of these oddities reflect the strangeness of Hardie's own character. He was always much more of a Bohemian than a stereotypical member of the working class, affecting a Sherlock Holmes-style deerstalker hat as often as the famed cloth cap which he wore for his first entry to the Commons. In summer months he defied convention yet further, and while other Honourable and Right Honourable members still wore their black frock-coats and stiff collars he wore a 'Japanese kaftan' (a kimono we must assume) and nothing on his feet. In this eccentricity of dress he rather resembled the Tory prime minister: not that Lord Salisbury wore a kaftan and sandals, but he was often swathed in loose tweed when other parliamentarians would have been wearing dark clothes.

Hardie's ideological credentials were as eclectic and perplexing as his clothes. Sometimes he claimed to be a disciple of Marx, discovering in the writings of the German revolutionary a quiet gradualism, a belief in socialism by degrees, which was surprising to doctrinaire Marxists. Having insisted with great bravery that the Labour Party must be Independent of even the most sympathetic Liberals, and having vilified and attacked such figures as Morley at the beginning of the Nineties, by the end of the decade he was making common cause with Morley and Lib–Labs over the issue of the Boer War. Having begun as an ardent trade union activist, he lost all sympathy with the unions and by the late Nineties he was referring to the hero of the Dockers' strike as 'that dirty little hypocrite' Ben Tillett. At times he seemed to speak as if socialism was Class War or it was nothing; at others, as if it was a creed to unite all classes behind a common cause. Certainly in the initial decade of his leadership the ILP lost members at an alarming rate. (10,720 members in 1895 had shrunk to 6,084 in 1900, and its appeal was increasingly to the middle classes.)

Yet the fact remains that Keir Hardie was there in the Palace of Westminster. The man who had worked down the pits for thirteen years was sitting on the green leather benches beside the (still overwhelmingly) upper-class Tory and Liberal MPs. Not until the Liberal landslide of 1906, when the Tories lost not merely seats but a hold on the political scene, could the Labour Party make a significant *parliamentary* advance. (In that election they won 29 seats and could begin to look like an alternative radical party when the Liberals disintegrated.) In the 1890s, Hardie was right to see that his role in the Commons was primarily a prophetic, symbolic one. Socialism is, as he observed, 'much more an affair of the heart than of the intellect'; and although with his thick bushy beard he bore a passing resemblance to Marx, he liked to reflect that long before he had heard of *The Communist Manifesto* he had learnt what *he* called socialism from the ballads of Robbie Burns, with their message of the brotherhood of man and their acerbic distrust of the rich or the 'unco guid'.

Hardie's finest moments in the Commons were in fact worthy of Robert Burns. In June 1894, in the Albion colliery at Cilfynydd in east Glamorgan, 251 men and boys were killed in an explosion. In the previous three years alone, over a thousand miners had lost their lives in explosions. The disaster in Cilfynydd coincided with the birth of the future Edward VIII – the son of the Duke and Duchess of York. The

House of Commons put down a motion to congratulate Her Royal Highness on the birth of her son. Hardie rose, after the various fawning compliments had fallen from the lips of other Honourables and Right Honourables, to say that, 'It is a matter of small concern to me whether the future ruler of the nation be the genuine article or a spurious imitation.' He then used his parliamentary privilege to allude to the frequent adulteries of the Prince of Wales and other members of the royal family. This same Prince of Wales – grandfather of the newborn baby – owned property in London 'which is made up of some of the vilest slums' and brought him in £60,000 a year. Moreover the 'fierce white light' which beat upon the Prince's private life could 'reveal things in his career it would be better to keep covered'. He then turned to the baby – a fact which that child, when he was in exile as the Duke of Windsor, recalled in his Memoirs – and said, 'From his childhood onwards, this boy will be surrounded by sycophants and flatterers by the score.' (Cries of 'Oh, oh'.) 'The government which could waste time in discussing so trivial an event, could not find time for a vote of condolence for the relatives of those who are lying stiff and stark in a Welsh valley.'

Hardie was much criticized for this speech. Even a sympathetic modern biographer says that his passion took control over his political instincts when he made it. But if passion cannot allow a politician to tell the truth, even in so unlikely a setting as the House of Commons, it is hard to know what the radical movement in British politics was for. Though many of his fellow MPs must have deplored his lack of manners, some of them must have heard in Hardie's accents the voice of the future, and wondered how long the aristocratic system, so undemocratic and so inequitable, could endure.[10] The Albion Colliery disaster paved the way for the very first Workmen's Compensation Act in 1897. This ended 'the doctrine of common employment' which had first been elaborated in 1837, the year of Victoria's accession, and which denied workpeople protection from negligent employers. In the year of the Diamond Jubilee this abuse was abolished. It is an eloquent example of 'Victorian values' at work: on the one hand, we see the cruelty of the capitalist system refusing what seems to us an obvious human right; on the other, the redeeming Victorian capacity for self-criticism and reform.

One of the more momentous surprises in *A la recherche du temps perdu*, Proust's masterly description of French aristocratic life from

1870 to 1919, is the fact that the Princesse de Guermantes in the final volume turns out to be none other than our old friend Madame Verdurin from the beginning of the story. The absurdly posturing social climber, with her '*petite bande*' of largely unimpressive friends, has become a high aristocrat. Victorian England could boast many such elevations and transformations, as we have already seen. The very class who had supposedly ousted the aristocracy from their seats of power by the Industrial Revolution and by the Reform Acts of 1832, 1867 and 1884 discovered, when they had made their millions, that there were few more agreeable things to do with them than to acquire lands, and having acquired lands to acquire the manners, daughters and titles of the old landed class. Between 1886 and 1914 two hundred and forty-six new titles were granted. Discounting those who were members of the royal family, or who were being promoted within the peerage, two hundred of these were entering the nobility for the first time and some seventy of these were new money made from business or industry. Lord Salisbury, who had fought so hard to defend the landed interest in 1866–7, quickly saw that this cause was lost, and that Conservatism henceforward was to be of a different complexion. In his first brief ministry he made a Burton brewer, Henry Allsopp, into the first Baron Hindlip. In his second administration he made a second Guinness peerage – that of Iveagh; the silk broker H.F. Eaton became Lord Cheylesmore and the wool-comber Samuel Cunliffe-Lister became Lord Masham.

In this Indian Summer of aristocratic life, then, in the thirty years before the outbreak of the First World War, the aristocracy could be said to have shown Darwinian skills at adapting and modifying itself to survive. In so doing they were able to bring money to prop up the system. Cunliffe-Lister's wool-combing, for example, enabled him to become a great Yorkshire landowner, with the purchase of the Swinton Park estate for £457,000 in 1882, and the Marquess of Ailesbury's estate in 1886, for £310,000. He owned some 34,000 acres by the time he established himself in his principal seat, Jervaulx Abbey.

The fact, however, that it was possible for industrialists and shipbuilders and brewers ('the beerage' they were snobbishly known in the Edwardian parliaments) to buy land was an indication that others had been forced by poverty to sell it.[11]

England had changed deeply and fundamentally since the Queen came to the throne, and the two doomed categories, sociologically and politically, were the old Whig aristocracy and the squires. The Whig idea – upheld by all the great aristocrats who supported the Reform Bill of 1832 – was that they governed *for* the People. The democratization of the representative system, albeit a very modified democratization, finished the notion of Whiggery. Because the voting systems introduced since 1884 are based on a 'first past the post' system, and because the electorate remained quite small, the new political castes could borrow from the Whigs the convenient cloak of being 'representative' when they least wished to consult the populace or its wishes. They do so even today. But the ethos of Whiggery, with its base in the educated aristocracy, was doomed by extending the franchise.

> Whigs did not believe in government *by* the people, whatever that might mean. They were an *élite* which upheld as its own by the right of heredity, tradition, rank, property and experience the prerogative of governing the country, dispensing patronage and regulating reform. At times of crisis they stood with 'the People' to detach it from 'the Populace', a distinction which assumed that the views of the Populace were of no importance, except as imparting the element of crisis to the national affairs. But if the People and the Populace were to become one and the same, if the mass was to preponderate on the ruins of the representation of interests and varied communities, Whiggery was doomed. For it was the one element in British politics so specialized that in a democratic climate it could exist only as a frail exotic.[12]

The Last of the Whigs was the Marquess of Hartington, Harty Tarty, who succeeded as the 8th Duke of Devonshire in December 1891. He was a spiritual exile in Gladstone's Liberal Party, and after the Home Rule split he joined Lord Salisbury's Cabinet as lord president of the Council. 'Villa Conservatism', however, was as remote from this man's world as had been the Liberalism of Northern mill-owners and chapel-ranters.[13] Lofty, forgetful – he once went to dine alone at the Turf Club forgetting he had invited the King to dine at his house – he said, 'I have six houses, and the only one I really enjoy is the house at Newmarket.'[14] His happiest appointment was as a steward of the Jockey Club and one of his proudest hours came in 1877, when his horse Belphoebe won the One Thousand Guineas (and a prodigious £4,750 in prize money).[15]

They were glory years for the Turf, with the Duke of Westminster's legendary Bend 'Or winning the Derby, and siring the almost no less brilliant Ormonde.* In 1892 the Duke of Devonshire married his mistress of thirty years, Louise, Duchess of Manchester (she was German – daughter of Count von Alten of Hanover). There had been no reigning Duchess of Devonshire since the celebrated Georgiana died in 1811. For the Queen's Diamond Jubilee in 1897 the Duke and Duchess gave a great ball in Devonshire House, in London: it was the most lavish and extraordinary of all the entertainments that year, in which the cream of the aristocracy and many members of the royal family came in court costumes of all times and countries.

The Duke himself was clad as the Emperor Charles V and the Duchess as Zenobia, Queen of Palmyra. The Prince of Wales – who himself attended in the costume of Grand Master of the Knights of Malta – lent the Duke the Collar and Badge of the Golden Fleece; Princess Henry of Pless came as the Queen of Sheba, her train borne by four negro boys; Jo Chamberlain came as Pitt the Younger and Mr Asquith, prophetically in some senses, came in the riding dress of a seventeenth-century Roundhead, while not actually claiming to be Oliver Cromwell. It would be during his premiership that the power of the House of Lords (after the prolonged constitutional crisis following the 1909 Budget) was critically curtailed. (The peers effectively thereby lost their power wholly to veto, rather than merely to check, legislation passed by the Commons.)

The photographs of the ball, perhaps because the costumes are studiedly obsolete, do look to the eyes of the twenty-first century like a doomed order: but – as with almost all impressions one might form of British political truth – it is only partly true. Apart from its colossal wealth, what impresses about the upper reaches of the British aristocracy is its immense staying-power. For almost the entire twentieth century, the hereditary peerage retained the power to sit in the Upper House of the British Parliament, legislators by right of birth. In no other European country would such an arrangement have been even a thinkable political proposition.

If the Whigs were the losers politically in the new order, they were not – many of them – the losers financially. The class which suffered the greatest loss of political and financial status was the squirearchy. The traditional Tories of the shires.

---

*Asked by a rich American visiting Eaton Hall if he could buy the champion, the Duke of Westminster replied, 'There is not enough money in the great American Republic to buy Bend 'Or.'[16]

'On a careful inquiry, it will be found that the coming in of American wheat has wrought a greater change in the composition of the British House of Commons than the first two Reform Acts,' wrote L.B. Namier in 1931.[17]

The squires in pre-industrial England were the effectual administrators of the country. Their lands provided employment for the agricultural labourers who made up the bulk of the population. Their pew in the parish church signified the indissoluble union between Church and state at a local level, just as their patronage of the living demonstrated in concrete form the Erastian character of that Church. The poacher who stole game or rabbits from the squire's land would find himself prosecuted before the local justice of the peace; and the justice of the peace was also the squire. The local government was conducted by unelected squires, and the seats in the Commons which were not occupied by aristocrats were occupied by this solid landed class. Their position was gravely jeopardized, however, with the passing of the Corn Laws and the crisis of agriculture, caused by the departure of men from the land and the decline both of rents and corn prices.

Disraeli extolled as the ideal type of legislator 'an English gentleman, born to business, managing his own estate, mixing with all classes of his fellow-men, now in the hunting-field, now in the railway-direction, unaffected, unostentatious, proud of his ancestors'. This London-born middle-class man of letters had a rich appreciation of the county families in his constituency, delighting in visiting 'the Pauncefort Duncombes of Brickhill Manor . . . Colonel Hanmer of Stockgrove Park, the Chesters of Chicheley, the Lovetts of Liscombe, the Dayrells of Lillingstone Dayrell and many more'. They were as he said, many of them 'greater men by a good deal than many German princes, and yet utterly unknown in London society'. Within half a century of Dizzy's death, none of the above-mentioned families appeared in Burke's *Landed Gentry*. Squires who had been in the same manor-houses for generations, often farming the same land from the time of the Norman Conquest to the time of Disraeli, found themselves facing ruin. The owner of 50,000 acres almost certainly owned London properties too, from which he derived rents; or coal mines; or he had interests in the City. The smaller squire, who owned 1,000 to 3,000 acres – owning together on average 12.4 per cent of the land in England in 1883 – could no longer make ends meet without selling his chief, sometimes his only, capital asset: the land itself.[18]

In 1882 Charles Milnes Gaskell analysed the plight of the squire for his readers in *The Nineteenth Century* – 'He has given up his deer, has dismissed his servants; he is advertising his house for a Grammar School or a Lunatic Asylum; he is making arrangements with little Premium for the sale of his ancestors, and with the nearest timber-merchant for that of his trees . . . He has made permanent reductions in three or four of his principal farms, and he has 800 acres on his hands.'[19]

As so often since in England, it was a Conservative government which delivered the *coup de grâce* to some venerable old aspect of national life.[20] Lord Salisbury appointed Charles Thomson Ritchie (1838–1906) as president of the Local Government Board, and he was the architect of the Local Government Act 1888. Ritchie, the fourth son of a Dundee merchant and jute-spinner, was himself a banker. He would rise to be chancellor of the Exchequer and home secretary. His Act was 'distasteful' to Salisbury, who did nothing to prevent it going through. Salisbury's were crocodile tears. In the end selfishness and greed overcame the attractive Anglican pessimism in this mixture of a man. The most important fact about the Cecils and the other great aristocrats was, after all, that they were richer than anyone else. It was quite natural that Salisbury should ditch the old Tory squirearchy and chum up with New Money. Britain was a rich man's club, sharing the 'business sense' of Birmingham radicals. Naturally it must be forced to 'modernize'. Sixty-two county councils were created. County boroughs and counties were divorced. The London County Council took over the administration of London. In the country, the squires were for the most part elected to the new councils, committees and boards set up by Ritchie's bureaucracy; but something had been lost. As Gladstone said, the public had confidence in the existing county authorities: their duties had not only been 'well discharged, but unselfishly, wisely and economically'. Ritchie took away from the quarter sessions and gave to the county councils the task of administering almost all the things which affected the lives of those living in the counties: finance, county buildings and bridges, the provision and management of lunatic asylums, the establishment and maintenance of reformatories and industrial schools, the diseases of animals acts, main roads, liquor licences, the police.

Henceforward, there was no particular reason for any local authority to be local. The squire, displaced economically from his land, was now politically redundant in his ancestral locality. Ritchie's legislation was both deeply bureaucratic and profoundly destabilizing. Manning thought it the most radical legislation since 1833, and it certainly put the seal on Old England. The country which had, in the Queen's girlhood, been a primarily rural community governed at local level paternalistically, at a national level aristocratically, was now an industrial country governed nationally by plutocrats, locally by bureaucrats.

Having lost rents and status and political power, the minor landowners were to be hit finally by the Liberal chancellor of the Exchequer, Sir William Harcourt (1827–1904), introducing death duties in his budget of 1894. For those whose wealth was primarily bound up in land, this measure more or less guaranteed that inherited estates would diminish, or be broken up.

All these measures, calculated to destroy the power and stability of the old landed class, were put in place when that class, and the aristocracy which largely depended upon it, were supposedly in power.

One should not, however, exaggerate the damage or suppose that it was all under way during the last ten years of the nineteenth century. In many places it needed the ravages of radical Liberal budgets in 1909 and 1910, and the First World War, to complete the revolution in English life which we have been describing. There was still a plenitude of squires in late Victorian England. In many parishes they were as old-fashioned and as all-pervasive as in the days of Colonel Sibthorp; and in the upper echelons of the squirearchy there were still some very rich men, such as the president of the Local Government Board in Salisbury's Third Cabinet, Henry Chaplin (1840–1923).[21] His sobriquet was 'the Squire' and Chaplin was 'a Squire of Squires'.[22]

When he came of age in 1862, Chaplin inherited an estate in Lincolnshire of 25,000 acres, as well as properties in Nottinghamshire and Yorkshire. His rent-roll was then £90,000 per annum. Thirty years later his seat, Blankney Hall, was up for sale. He was master of the Blankney hunt. His children 'in their infancy were taught to think, speak, and dream of hunting and riding almost like a religion. "The library of his daily use" constituted of the Bible, the Racing Calendar and the Parliamentary Guide.' He ate and drank on a prodigious scale and he was a generous host, keeping up – in the happy days before his financial troubles began – not merely Blankney but also a town house in Lincoln, Burghersh Chantry, where the hospitality was princely. This essentially eighteenth-century figure would have been at home in the pages of a novel by Fielding; he lived into the age of the motor-car. He detested these contraptions almost as much as he detested 'villa' or 'democratic' Conservatism, which he rightly saw as a contradiction in terms. Yet as president of the Local Government Board it was he who was responsible for the Act which relieved them from being preceded by a man with a red flag. During the bicycle craze of 1896, when many notable persons might be seen riding in Battersea Park, 'Mr Chaplin stood on the side-walk looking on.' He was to see worse things than motor-cars or bicycles. By the end of his life he had seen the class to which he belonged, and which had been ruined by death duties, low rents, agricultural depression and income tax, all but obliterated in the First World War; almost every village war memorial in England shows that the local aristocratic grandee and the local squire, or at least one of their sons, fell in France or Flanders. 'The War . . . changed the British aristocracy for ever . . . The belief . . . that proportionately more of their sons died than those of other classes was not just an arrogant illusion. It was true . . . Not since the Wars of the Roses had the English aristocracy suffered such losses as those which they endured during the Great War.'[23]

Even though Chaplin wore a frock-coat and a silk hat rather than a helmet and chain mail, he and his like probably had more in common with those who fought in the Wars of the Roses than those who came back from the trenches whistling Dixie music or expecting their wives to vote in democratic elections. Because the First World War was so overwhelmingly terrible, so destructive in its effects, we tend, with metaphors of Indian summers and long afternoons, to suppose that the *ancien régime* in England went on until the news came in 1914 of the assassination in Sarajevo. The fate of the Victorian squires reminds us that things were otherwise. The old order had changed irrevocably long before the death of the Queen. Tennyson, Chaplin's fellow man of Lincolnshire, returned in 'Locksley Hall Sixty Years After' to the fictitious Lincolnshire manor house which had been his theme in 1842. The trochaics of the young man's poem had lamented the loss of his beautiful cousin Amy to the local squire.[24]

As the husband is, the wife is; thou art mated with a clown.

Returning to Locksley as an old man, the poet sees this 'clown' as the embodiment of the good old ways, who

Served the poor, and built the cottage, raised the school,
and drained the fen.[25]

The poem is a hymn of hate to the modern world, seeing the country run down, the cities riddled with vice and injustice.

And the crowded couch of incest in the warrens of the poor.

He laments

Poor old Heraldry, poor old History, poor old Poetry, passing hence
In the common deluge drowning old political common-sense.[26]

It was indeed an age of commoners, and as if to prove it, on 4 May 1896 a young Irishman called Alfred Harmsworth (1865–1922) launched a new newspaper called *The Daily Mail*.[27] It was designed to encapsulate world news in bulletin form. The first issue sold 397,215 copies, so many more than predicted that it was necessary to hire the use of machinery from two evening newspapers to meet the demand. With his brilliant editor, Kennedy Jones, Harmsworth provided the public with an easily assimilable newspaper, with plenty of crime stories, football, racing and cricket. Lord Salisbury sent Harmsworth a congratulatory telegram, while famously sneering at the venture in private: Thackeray's *Pendennis*, said the prime minister, produced a newspaper 'by gentlemen for gentlemen'; the *Daily Mail* was 'a newspaper produced by office boys for office boys'.

Salisbury's acute political judgement would not have pursued 'villa Conservatism', against every aristocratic instinct, if he had not known that the new England had a very great number of office boys in it. They in turn had wives – leading Alfred Harmsworth to found the *Daily Mirror* in 1903, with an all-woman staff for an all-woman readership.

The Harmsworth family (Alfred's brother Harold was also a newspaper proprietor, buying the *Mirror* from Alfred, and for a while owning *The Times*) exemplifies the difficulty of defining the nature of social and political change in terms which would make sense to Karl Marx or to Sidney and Beatrice Webb. The aristocratic world, and its ethos of accepted deference, were done away with less by trade unions or striking dockers than by the acre upon acre, square mile upon square mile of perky, self-sufficient suburbanites who could happily get through life without once meeting a squire or a lord, still less having to doff their caps. Lenin's good old questions *Who? Whom?* came into play here. In the agricultural past, the peasantry or even the small yeomanry (the class from which the Harmsworths came) depended on landlords, just as urban proletarians depended on mill-owners and factory-owners. The Harmsworths had left Ireland, and the land, become merchants in a small way and taken up a shabby-genteel, hand-to-mouth London life, threatened by the constant spectre of bankruptcy (the father drank) but no longer specifically beholden to anyone. In short, Alfred Harmsworth (1865–1925, created Viscount Northcliffe 1918) and Harold (1869–1940, created Viscount Rothermere 1919) catered for Carrie and Charles Pooter, and moreover they drew attention to the fact that politicians now had to woo the petite bourgeoisie, not lord it over them.

Whereas a sentimental Ruskinian, or an old-fashioned Tory, might bemoan the modern, the Harmsworths celebrated and in some ways created it – from an imaginative point of view. The *Daily Mail* shared its proprietor's obsession with speed, expressed admiration for motor-bicycles, and was enthusiastic for 'automobilism'.[28]

On the one hand, the Harmsworths liked the idea of themselves as suburban men excitedly telling their hundreds of thousands of readers that the era of the Common Man had dawned. On the other, like so many newspaper proprietors since, they were megalomaniacs, power-crazed fanatics who in their furiously cruel behaviour to underlings and their bloated idea of themselves seemed like mini-dictators. The American war correspondent for the *New York Times* came upon Lord Northcliffe in 1919, shouting into a telephone, 'What have you done with the moon? . . . I said the moon – the moon. Someone has moved the moon . . . Well if it's moved again, whoever does it is fired.' It turned out that the weather report had been moved to a different page.[29]

In this new political world it did indeed feel as if someone had moved the moon. The balance of the electoral system, and the lack of cohesion or political sophistication, partly explained, perhaps, the reluctance of the urban working classes to rally in greater numbers to the Independent Labour Party. Many of them in any case were arch-Jingoes who preferred Lord Salisbury. The Whigs and the Tories of the old breed had both of them passed or were passing into oblivion. Except in Ireland, where the collapse of Parnell had badly weakened the cause of Home Rule, and the merest threat of its success had solidified Unionist opposition in the Protestant North, the political parties were losing touch with what could be seen as their natural constituencies. The field was open for a new type of politics altogether, based less upon identifiable interest and more on a kind of adaptable energy, prepared to ride the wave and watch the wind.

Surely much the most interesting political career, after Parnell's fall, is that of David Lloyd George (1863–1945), who would succeed Asquith as prime minister in 1916, and whose radical budgets when chancellor of the Exchequer – introducing welfare benefits, old age pensions and so on – did more for the working classes than Keir Hardie's rhetoric before the Labour Party had a chance of power or Ramsay MacDonald's incompetence after he'd been given that chance and squandered it.

Maynard Keynes's description of Lloyd George is that of a clever young man lampooning a wartime prime minister whose party broke into smithereens after the peace of 1918. It is well-known because it is so funny and so well-expressed; and it is only half-true – 'How can I convey to the reader, who does not know him, any just impression of this extraordinary figure of our time, this syren, this goat-footed bard, this half-human visitor to our age from the hag-ridden magic and enchanted woods of Celtic antiquity? . . . Lloyd George is rooted in nothing, he is void and without content; he lives and feeds on his immediate surroundings.'[30]

Lloyd George was not, in fact, rooted in nothing. He was rooted in something which was harder perhaps even for the economic genius of the great Keynes to fathom: namely, Victorian North Wales. In a sense, his political destiny was formed by Gladstone's obsessive mission to 'pacify Ireland', for it was the defection of so many English Liberals to the Unionist (and Imperialist) cause which forced Gladstonian Liberalism to the Celtic fringes of Britain, giving a prominence to Scots, Welsh and Irish which they might not have otherwise had. After Parnell, the Celtic fringes were not picturesque additions to a great metropolitan alliance between Whigs and Radicals: they were the Liberal heartlands. It was inevitable that Ireland should go its own way. In Scotland, radical opinion moved between the Liberal Party and the new-formed ILP – as to a slower degree it did in Wales. (Keir Hardie, after his defeat at West Ham, was adopted for the South Welsh mining constituency of Merthyr Tydfil.)

David Lloyd George, a Welsh-speaker and, in his earliest manifestations as a political being, to all intents a Welsh nationalist or at least a Welsh Home Ruler, belonged to a very different Wales from that of the pits and the valleys of the South. Though born and reared in poverty, he belonged to the tradition of teachers, preachers, dreamers and ranters who owe spiritual kinship to the Bards. Yet, such is the strangeness of David Lloyd George that he always transcended his background.

He was actually born in England – in Manchester, on 17 January 1863. His father had been a schoolmaster, a career he abandoned in favour of farming, but he died when his son was seventeen months old. Thereafter, David and his infant brother were brought up by his mother and Uncle Lloyd – their mother's brother, a shoemaker and pillar of the Baptist Chapel at Llanystumdwy.

Social class in Wales was not as crudely stratified as in industrial England. A clever, literate shoemaker was poor, but not the lowest of the low. The Idealist philosopher Sir Henry Jones (1852–1922) – Fellow of the British Academy, Companion of Honour, professor at Glasgow – was born the son of the village shoemaker at Llangernyw, Denbighshire, left school aged twelve, but grew up in a world which respected learning. Lloyd George received a good education at the local school – which was a Church school. In the early part of his political career, his preoccupation was the superficially parochial one of Church tithes. Since the (Anglican) Church in Wales was not (as the Irish one had been in 1859) disestablished, all local farmers and householders were obliged to pay a tenth of their income in tax to the parson. As in Ireland, so in Wales (where the majority of the population were Christians of a different complexion), the Established Church was deeply resented. The apparently small question of whether a shoemaker or a dairyman who attended the Baptist chapel should be made to pay money to the (Anglican) parson actually encapsulated the much bigger question of the powers of the state over the small nation and the small man.

In essence, surely, this is why Lloyd George never became a socialist. He saw the state as an enabler of private destinies, not as the paternalistic substitute for Church, mill-owner or landlord. When he was a well-established politician, in 1906, he told an audience in Birmingham that Joseph Chamberlain's Tariff Reform 'has focused the opera-glasses of the rich on the miseries of the poor. Once you do that, there is plenty of kindness in the human heart.'

Dickens could have said that: and Lloyd George has strong elements of the Dickensian in his nature – the hyper-energy, the tendency to fantasize, the essential benignity. He saw the great Liberal victory of

1906 as a chance to do the decent thing by the poor without the collectivist solutions of the Independent Labour Party:

> I have one word for the Liberals – I can tell them what will make this I.L.P. movement a great and sweeping force in this country – a force that will sweep away Liberalism, amongst other things. If at the end of an average term of office it were found that the present Parliament had done nothing to cope seriously with the social condition of the people, to remove the national degradation of slums and widespread poverty and destitution in a land glittering with wealth . . . then a real cry will arise in this land for a new party, and many of us here in this room [he spoke in Penrhyndeudrath] will join that cry.

That was the great Lloyd George who stood on the verge of becoming chancellor of the Exchequer, and eventually the prime minister. How utterly different from the world, social and political, in which the young Gladstone had come into prominence, was the self-driven early rise of David Lloyd George.

There is a marvellous photograph of Gladstone standing in the drizzle on the rocky slopes of Snowdon on 13 September 1892. The ostensible occasion of the Grand Old Man's visit was to open a footpath. In fact, it was to reassure his Welsh voters that over the vital issues of land (comparable, if less dire than in Ireland), tithes and independence of the Church, he was listening to them. Lloyd George's brother William was surprised by Gladstone's stockiness, and by his agility as he scrambled up the rocks to address the crowds. David Lloyd George, twenty-nine years old, was the MP for Caernarvon Boroughs, and met the G.O.M. at dinner the night before. He was thrilled by the deep vibrant tones of 'this great figure from a past world' – even when Gladstone spoke of such superficially prosaic subjects as corrugated-iron roofing.[31]

If Lloyd George saw an old man with a sonorous voice and silver hair, Gladstone would have seen an eager, humorous man with bright blue eyes, raven-dark hair, and with a beautiful musical voice. Gladstone would not have approved had he known not merely how attractive Lloyd George was to women, but how shamelessly this married father of – eventually – five (legitimate) children would exploit this appeal. (He once gave a private dinner in an hotel, in which the guest-list consisted of men usually supposed to be at enmity in the public political sphere. One of them, Sir Oswald Mosley, said, '"This will lift the roof if it gets out." Lloyd George replied, with his ineffable dimpling expression, "My dear boy, if everything I have done in this hotel during the last forty years had got out, you have no idea how many times I would have had to retire from politics."')[32]

From the very beginnings, Lloyd George had a Napoleonic confidence in his own destiny. At eighteen, three years before he so much as qualified as a solicitor, he made his first visit to London to take his Intermediate Law exams and visited a House of Commons which was empty – it being a Saturday. In his diary of 12 November 1881 he wrote, 'I will not say but that I eyed the assembly in a spirit similar to that in which William the Conqueror eyed England on his visit to Edward the Confessor, as the region of his future domain.'[33] His letter to the woman he would marry, Margaret Owen, written perhaps in 1886, is chilling in its candour. 'My supreme idea is to get on. To this idea I shall sacrifice everything – except I trust honesty. I am prepared to thrust even love itself under the wheels of my Juggernaut if it obstructs the way.' No one could say she had not been warned – though, poor woman, she could not have guessed how highly sexed he was, nor how unfaithful he was capable of being. Carlyle would have been shocked by Lloyd George's lapses from honesty and chastity, but he would surely, had he lived to witness it, been impressed by the way in which the small-town solicitor from Criccieth would emerge, with the apparent naturalness of a Muhammad, a Cromwell or a Frederick, as a Leader of the Leaderless. Knowing the extent of Lloyd George's virile energies it is hard not to think of them metaphorically when one considers the apparent flaccidity of Lord Rosebery and his Liberal Unionist followers in the Lords and Commons (though as a pawer of women under tablecloths and mauler of other men's wives, Herbert Asquith was more than a rival for the seer of Criccieth).

So long as his sphere was domestic politics, David Lloyd George could appear marginal. The Liberal Party was defeated in 1895 and would be out of office for a decade. Lord Salisbury and his government cared little for Welshmen and their local concerns. But it was as a spokesman on a much wider theme that Lloyd George was to rise to prominence.

In South Africa Britain had annexed the territory east of the Orange Free State known as Griqualand West, in order to secure the diamonds of Kimberley. Then gold was discovered in the Transvaal, on the Witwatersrand, and a group of foreigners (Uitlanders) were threatening the old-fashioned Bible-based way of life of the Boers. Paul

Kruger, the president of the Transvaal Republic, resisted the demands of the Uitlanders for political rights.

In December 1895 the young prime minister of the Cape, Cecil Rhodes, tried to engineer an uprising of the Uitlanders at Johannesburg, which would be joined by a flying column of Cape Chartered Company police, under the direction of his friend Dr Jameson. The new colonial secretary in Salisbury's government, Joseph Chamberlain, knew about this illegal, reckless scheme. The 'Jameson Raid', however, was an ignominious failure. Dr Jameson moved in too fast and had to be disowned; the Uitlanders did not rebel. Rhodes fell from power and the confidence he had tried to build up between Boers and British was destroyed.

The British Imperialists had been made a laughing-stock, and the rest of the world did not restrain its ridicule. A Welshman who had witnessed decades of English interference in his province (Welsh-speaking children were forced to carry a large letter W on their back in the schools where English was enforced) could not but be pleased. The Boers, Bible Protestants, hill farmers, were a more stolid lot than the Welsh, but there were obviously areas in common. 'In South Africa, a small republic, with an army the size of that of an ordinary German principality, has been able to defy the power of Great Britain,' Lloyd George could tell an audience at Penarth, on 28 November 1896. In the closing years of Queen Victoria's reign, all British eyes now turned towards South Africa.

42

The Boer War

During the First World War, Lord Baden-Powell, founder of the Boy Scout Movement, hero of the siege of Mafeking (14 October 1899–17 May 1900), peer of the realm and pillar of manly rectitude, was suffering badly from sleeplessness and headaches. He consulted a Harley Street physician, Dr F.D.S. Jackson, who suggested to him that he should keep a dream diary. Jackson was a medical doctor, not an analyst, but he clearly knew that the good Baden-Powell's troubles had an emotional origin.

On 3 April 1917 Baden-Powell dreamed that he was looking at a shop window in a small country town. Several men were standing beside him. 'One, on my left, whom I took to be a soldier without looking at him, pressed rather closely to me. As I turned away, suddenly I found his hand in my pocket . . . I thought of a ju-jitsu grip for holding him but finally put my arm around his neck to make it look as if we were good friends and yet to have a hold on him as we marched to the police station . . . Through his coat I could feel that he had little on under his coat and a sort of lump on his chest, and I felt great pity for him.'[1]

In 1919, two years after the birth of his third and last child, he began to sleep apart from his wife and his headaches vanished.

As an army officer – he left the army in 1910 – Baden-Powell had often had 'private chats' with his men, urging upon them the virtues of emotional and sexual restraint. For instance, in cases of bereavement, there was the hideous danger of tears. One highly suspect man in his regiment had made eye-contact with Baden-Powell. 'Something in the twinkle of his eye had pre-possessed me. I had a private talk with him, and from that day to this, he never gave a moment's trouble.' When this 'blackguard's' mother died, he came to Baden-Powell and wept. He 'sent him out with a "don't-be-a-fool" pat on the shoulder, but my right hand was richer for a hot and grimy tear-splash'.[2]

Cecil Rhodes (1853–1902) made no secret of preferring to surround himself with male servants and underlings. One secretary recalled that when Rhodes was prime minister of the Cape, 'he invariably called me into his office every afternoon to go through his private letters with him. I looked with the greatest pleasure to the half-hour or hour with him every afternoon. He was exceedingly kind and tender towards me. He made me draw up my chair quite close to him, and frequently placed his hand on my shoulder . . .' The closest of such relationships perhaps was that enjoyed between Rhodes and Neville Pickering, with whom Rhodes lived 'as a boy among boys' and at whose death he was desolated.[3]

To some minds, it would seem 'obvious' what was going on in the hearts of Baden-Powell or Cecil Rhodes. Frank Harris liked to gossip about Rhodes's 'erotic tendencies', claiming them to be 'worthy of Oscar Wilde', but nothing specific was ever substantiated, and even Harris had to admit that while enjoying repeating such rumours he did not actually believe them.

Of course in the manly world of the British Empire where soldiers and servants of all races and sizes were to be encountered across five continents, there were opportunities for all manner of behaviour. One of the biographers of Lord Kitchener, for example,[4] finds no evidence for his erotic preferences. Another book, dealing with Kitchener's relationship with Lord Curzon, contrasts his marked, if masochistic, fondness for women with Kitchener's allegedly different taste.[5] He quotes 'a lady who moved in the same social circles as he before the 1914–1918 war' who said that she had wanted to marry a young man. He told her he had no fondness for women, having been 'initiated' into a different practice by Lord Kitchener.

I wonder who this lady was. When I was a young man, Lady Diana Cooper, daughter of the Duchess of Rutland and Harry Cust, told me that she had been placed next to Mr Asquith at table. He had taken her hand and placed it inside his trousers under the tablecloth. When she complained to her mother, the Duchess allegedly replied that she could count herself lucky not to have attracted Lord Kitchener. When the great field marshal stayed in aristocratic houses, the well-informed young would ask servants to sleep across their bedroom threshold to impede his entrance. Rather than discriminating on grounds of sex, the hero of Omdurman had a compulsion – whether with men or women it did not matter – of a kind which Lord Queensberry had so unsuccessfully attempted to spell on that calling card left for Wilde at the Albemarle Club.

When Rhodes was the most famous British Imperialist, he would exclaim, 'I am a boy! Of course I shall never grow old.'[6]

It would be very easy to make sense of the Imperialists if we could attribute the whole phenomenon of the British Empire to repression of, or failure to understand, sexuality. How nearly one could argue that the careers of Rhodes, Kitchener, Baden-Powell and many another manly, knobbly-kneed son of Empire reached their zenith at the very moment Wilde confronted his nemesis. Empires are male phenomena. They presumably come about in conjunction with an excess of testosterone. The Emperor Claudius alone among the great Caesars excited derisive gossip to observe his unusual taste for women. All the others liked not merely men, but boys. The same could be said for the empires of Alexander the Great or the Ottomans at their apogee of strength. Nor need it be seen as accidental, at the time when the United States of America knows no rival as a global superpower, that it has witnessed the phenomenon of gay politics, the assertion that to discriminate against a man or woman on the grounds of sexual orientation is as wicked as to do so on grounds of race or class.

But here we enter into the whole difficulty of discussing the British Imperial past. Of course, it is easy for a modern person when revisiting the past to be quite certain of all the mistakes they made, and to be able, or think oneself able, to understand them better than they understand themselves. The repressive attitude to homosexuality, for instance, is bound to seem, to a later generation reared on therapy and 'talk cures' and letting everything out, to be tragic and unnecessary.

The first British soldier to rise from the ranks and become a senior officer was Sir Hector Macdonald (1853–1903). The youngest of five sons of a Scottish crofter, he enlisted in the Gordon Highlanders at seventeen. He fought as a common soldier in the Afghan War of 1879, earning the nickname 'Fighting Mac' on the march to Kabul with General Sir Frederick Sleigh Roberts (1832–1914). On his way home he fought in the First South African War and was present at the disastrous defeat at Majuba. Then in the late Eighties and early Nineties he took part with Kitchener in the reconquest of the Sudan, commanding a brigade and becoming very popular. He had 'a rare gift for handling troops'. By the time he returned to England, Fighting Mac was a popular hero, an aide-de-camp to Queen Victoria. During the Boer War he was a major-general, and given a knighthood. After the war he was posted to Ceylon, becoming the general in charge of the island, but a complaint – an 'opprobrious accusation' – was made against him. He set out for London to explain himself to the War Office, but never reached home. He shot himself in the Hotel Regina in Paris, at the age of forty-nine.[7]

Many of us would find this a much sadder story than that of the exhibitionistic Wilde. George V's innocent remark when told of someone's homosexuality ('I thought men like that shot themselves') was literally true.

Knowing as we do that the cult of Imperialist manliness was played out against a background of emotional repression might lead us to suppose that we would be closer to understanding the Imperialists if we were to 'out' as many as plausible as gays. Rudyard Kipling, for example, had thick moustaches and round spectacles; worn at the turn of the nineteenth and twentieth centuries they made him look like the 'gay clone' cohorts of the 1970s and 1980s. It is not surprising that he should have been claimed as a gay – conscious and crypto,[8] or unconscious.[9]

Most reviewers, and subsequent biographers, have pooh-poohed the notion of Kipling as a homosexual. In a sense it is a fruitless inquiry, since what is so difficult for a modern to come to terms with, in confronting the heyday of the British Empire, is what is obvious, not what is hidden. The unashamed and undiluted masculinity of this world needs 'explaining' to a generation where it seems desirable for both sexes to run the world. In the 1890s even the movement for women's suffrage went off the boil. Women as intelligent as Mrs Humphry Ward and Mrs Sidney Webb actually went public with their view that women should not be given the vote.

This was a world which was stiflingly, overpoweringly male. The army and navy, the civil service, the Houses of Parliament were all male. The Imperial adventurers who pushed back the frontiers of, and the local commissioners and governors who pacified and administered, the Empire were all male. It is an obvious fact, but it can hardly be overstated. Rather than thinking we have explained Kipling or Baden-Powell by uncovering homoeroticism in their psyche, we can, in our efforts to catch their accents and learn their language, only wonder at the maleness of their world. Kipling and Baden-Powell were friends. In the year of the siege of Mafeking, Kipling published his classic story of public-school life *Stalky and Co.* ('India's full of Stalkies – the Cheltenham and Haileybury and Marlborough chaps – that we don't know anything about and the surprises will begin when there is a really big row on.')[10] You can see in Kipling's story the origins of the Scout movement which Baden-Powell would start after the Boer War: 'In summer all right-minded boys built huts in the furze-hill behind the College – little lairs whittled out of the heart of the prickly bushes, full of stumps, odd root-ends and spikes.'[11] It is in a sense true that 'towards the end of the 1890s, Kipling invented Baden-Powell',[12] and certainly no surprise that Kipling wrote songs for the scout movement, most notably, 'All Patrols, Look Out'.

The Empire was the creation, in Kipling's devastatingly honest phrase, of 'flannelled fools at the wicket and muddied oafs at the goal', or to put it as politely as A.C. Benson (author of 'Land of Hope and Glory'), those 'well-groomed, well-mannered, rational manly boys all taking the same view of things, all doing the same things, smiling politely at the eccentricity of anyone who finds matter for serious interest in books, art or music'.[13]

Its philistine boyishness is part of the innocence of the British Imperial world, and part of the charm that those young enough to have no part in post-colonial guilt or angst can enjoy in the schoolboy yarns of G.A. Henty or, a little later, in the adventure stories of John Buchan.

Perhaps the most exciting, and at the same time definitive, ripping yarn in this genre was Rider Haggard's (1856–1925) *King Solomon's Mines* (1885). It is a classic quest-story. Allan Quatermain, the hero of several of Haggard's tales, is a big-game hunter and explorer in Africa. Page one promises a narrative of pure joy – 'I am laid up here at Durban with the pain in my left leg. Ever since that confounded lion got hold of me I have been liable to this trouble . . .' And no reader need fear that what is on offer is for girls or cissies – 'I can safely say that there is not a *petticoat* in the whole history.' In fact, once the adventure is under way and the Europeans, with the help of an old sixteenth-century map and letter left by a Portuguese explorer, have set out in search of the lost treasures of King Solomon, one of the party, rightly named Good, falls in love with an African woman. She conveniently dies, with the words, 'Say to my lord, Bongwan, that – I love him, and that I am glad to die because I know that he cannot cumber his life with such as I am, for the sun may not mate with darkness, nor the white with the black.'[14]

The African guide, Umbopa, turns out to be Ignosi, the true king of the Kukuana tribe, and he it is, after their hair-raising adventures, in which they see the remarkable mines and very nearly get trapped there forever among the frozen stalagmites, who delivers the damning verdict:

'Now do I learn,' said Ignosi bitterly, and with flashing eyes, 'that ye love the bright stones more than me, your friend. Ye have the stones; now ye would go to Natal and across the moving black water and sell them, and be rich, as it is the desire of a white man's heart to be. Cursed for your sake be the white stones, and cursed be he who seeks them. Death shall it be to him who sets foot in the place of Death to find them. I have spoken. White men, ye can go.'[15]

Writing about Haggard's mythopoetic masterpiece *She*, V.S. Pritchett coined a magnificent phrase. Whereas E.M. Forster had once spoken of the novelist sending down a bucket into the unconscious, Haggard, Pritchett said, 'installed a suction pump. He drained the whole reservoir of the public's desires.'[16] If this is true of the eternal woman – *She* Who Must Be Obeyed, which, while remaining a popular page-turner, comes close to being a great work of art and *is* a great work of myth-making – it is to a lesser extent true of *King Solomon's Mines*.

It was published when Haggard, the son of a Suffolk squire, was twenty-nine years old. It was the first popular novel in English to treat of Africa. The Scramble for Africa was in full swing and the Jingoistic public were thrilled by Haggard's story of a group of intrepid English gentlemen confronting the mysterious cultures of contemporary Africa and of lost antiquity. But it is not simply a tale of derring-do. Even though King Solomon's treasures remain sealed inside the mountain, Quatermain and his friends manage to scramble out with enough stones stuffed into their pockets to make them rich for life.

The novel nicely balances the heroism of the explorers, the avarice which prompted them to venture into the dark continent, and the piety they feel about the superiority of their own culture to that of the African. To this degree one sees why J.K. Stephen linked Haggard to the unofficial Laureate of Imperialism, looking forward to a time 'when the Rudyards cease from Kipling and the Haggards Ride no more'. Kipling spent more and more time in Africa – South Africa – and liked not merely the landscape and the climate but the attitude of the whites. He was to write 'Recessional', the great hymn for the Queen's Diamond Jubilee, and saw it as part of the British duty to subdue 'lesser breeds without the Law'. That was – to use another of his phrases which entered the language – 'the White Man's Burden'.

Many of Kipling's ideals – and those of his generation – were incarnate in a young man who had made himself a millionaire from diamonds. When Kipling was introduced to him, this pudgy mustachioed figure, prematurely aged, asked Kipling, 'What is your dream?' 'You are part of it,' Kipling replied.[17]

Cecil Rhodes, the son of a Hertfordshire parson, first sailed for Africa – the east coast – when he was seventeen, in 1870. It was in the fates that he would give his name to two great African countries, Northern and Southern Rhodesia (now Zambia and Zimbabwe). Whether he actually placed his hand on the map of Africa and said, 'That is my dream – all British'[18] – or in another version, 'all red'[19] – he certainly believed that in an ideal universe, Britain would hold dominion not merely over the Dark Continent, but over the world itself. In his 'Confession', written when he was a very young man, Rhodes even dreamed of the readmission of the United States to the Empire. True, 'without the low-class Irish and German emigrants' that great nation would be a greater asset. 'If we had retained America there would . . . be millions more of English living . . . Since we are the finest race in the world and that the more of the world we inhabit the better it is for the human race.'[20]

It is probably safe to say that there is no one alive on the planet who now thinks as Rhodes thought. Of course, there are those who, in an attempt to shock or amuse, might *pretend* to be British Imperialist, though with only a few outposts of rock in St Helena, Gibraltar or the Falkland Islands remaining of the Empire, it must be difficult, even as an affectation, to sustain the Rhodesian vision. Equally, there would be those, in far larger numbers, and not merely British or white, who might wish for a balanced view of the Empire. They might say, 'True, attitudes were expressed by the Empire-builders which shock a modern sensibility; and some unpleasant things happened; but the Empire brought good as well as bad to almost all the countries under its sway. There were countries which positively benefited from the educational system or the railway or the administrative skills into which they were initiated by the well-meaning British.' But while these views in themselves would be shocking to many of our contemporaries, they come nowhere near Rhodes's almost mystic sense that the British would inherit the Earth. Benson's great anthem, however, 'Wider still and wider, shall thy bounds be set! God who made thee mighty – make thee mightier yet!' – bellowed now with some irony at the Last Night of the Prom Concerts each year in the Albert Hall – was once sung seriously. It was a creed for two generations of Englishmen, and fashioned the foreign policy of British governments and the general attitude of the British public down until 1945.

Those who witnessed the demolition of the statue of Rhodes in the middle of Harare (formerly Salisbury, the capital of Southern

Rhodesia) in August 1980 saw something which in the Western world was comparable to the removal of the representations first of Stalin, next of Lenin in the old Soviet Union. To many a young Russian, it must seem hard to understand how the older generation were 'brainwashed' into admiring Lenin; it would be harder for him or her to see that by absorbing the new anti-communist ideology they had also submitted to a set of doctrines – for example that capitalism spells freedom – which might seem quaint to a later generation.

Likewise the post-colonial Britain is in a poor position to understand Rhodes and his generation, not least because though popular with the majority, he and his vision of Empire were deplored by some of his contemporaries. 'Rhodes had no principles whatever to give to the world. He had only a hasty but elaborate machinery for spreading the principles he had not got. What he called his ideals were the dregs of Darwinism which had already grown not only stagnant but poisonous' – G.K. Chesterton.[21] Beatrice Webb, though she believed war, when it came, inevitable, blamed it on 'the impossible combination in British policy of Gladstonian sentimental Christianity with the blackguardism of Rhodes and Jameson'.[22]

The diamonds which so fired Rider Haggard's imagination had begun to be discovered on Afrikaner farms in 1866. Between 1870 and 1880, gems of vast size and value had been found in the midst of country farmed for generations by Dutch settlers. Of course, ownership of the diamonds was contested, and of the land in which they were found. By 1870 5,000 diamond-seekers had arrived to look for jewels in the rivers. Cecil Rhodes arrived at the diggings in 1871, coming from his brother's cotton farm in Natal. Within months of establishing himself at the mine (named Kimberley after the British secretary of state for the colonies) Rhodes had gone into partnership with a man called Charles Rudd. In 1873 they had an ice-making machine in operation, in 1874 they imported heavy-duty pumping machinery from Britain, transporting it 600 miles by ox wagon from the Cape. They won the water-pumping contract for the whole mine. By 1887 Rhodes's De Beers Mining Company had full control of the large De Beers Mine, and he soon had control of the Kimberley mines too.

The pickings, or winnings, were prodigious. In 1886 there had been a rumour of gold, discovered along the ridge known by the Afrikaners as the Witwatersrand (white water ridge) near Pretoria. In fact the ore was low-grade, but the Kimberley diamond magnates could afford to invest in heavy machinery to mine at a depth of two and a half thousand feet where the best gold was found. Rhodes was there, forming the Consolidated Goldfields of South Africa in 1892.

Rhodes and Rudd wanted to exploit the gold potential in Matabeleland, and they approached King Lobengula with the so-called Rudd Concession. They agreed to pay the king and his heirs £100 per month, as well as 1,000 Martini-Henry breech-loading rifles and cartridges and a steamboat with guns, in effectual exchange for all the mineral wealth in his territory.

You can measure Rhodes's achievement by surveying the map of Southern Africa in 1870 and comparing it with the same in 1895, when he had annexed, with the blessing of the British government and Crown, Mashonaland, Matabeleland, all the territory which is now Zambia and Zimbabwe. He also notoriously had his eye on the Afrikaner territories in Bechuanaland, where the unsuccessful Jameson raid took place at the end of 1895. It was the beginning of the end for Rhodes – he was forced to resign as prime minister of the Cape. But in another sense, it did his career and reputation no harm at home. The public was openly pro-Jameson. The new colonial secretary, Joseph Chamberlain, encouraged Rhodes to create the new territories of Rhodesia and to move towards the dominance of South Africa as a whole. It is not surprising that the Boers, the descendants of those Dutch settlers who had first come to the Cape in 1652, should have viewed with dismay those they called outsiders or Uitlanders.

The Afrikaners, back in the 1830s, had made a mass exodus from the Cape Colony. About 10,000 of them had made their way to the Transvaal for an independent life. Those who had made the Great Trek were known as the Voortrekkers, the pioneers. One of these Voortrekkers, who had left the Cape Colony with his parents in 1835 when he was ten years old, was the formidable president of the Transvaal: Stephanus Johannes Paulus Kruger, a strange giant of a man who with his hooded eyes, his whiskers, his stoop and his air of religious melancholy bears in some photographs a striking resemblance to Lord Salisbury himself. Whereas Salisbury was a High Church Anglican, who irritated Archbishop Benson by his cynicism and flippancy, Kruger was a fervent adherent of the 'Doppers', the most uncompromising of the three South African Reformed Churches. He knew much of the Bible by heart and believed in the literal truth of its every word. The annexation of the Transvaal by the British in 1877 had been a bitter blow to him, and independence of them had been his long-cherished political ambition.

With the discovery of gold in the Witwatersrand, biblical images of blessing must have flickered through his mind; and when the little mining camp of Johannesburg sprang up into being a multinational town ('a kind of Dodge City on the veld') other biblical metaphors might have been supplied – of tribes inimical to the Lord being put to the sword, or consumed by divine wrath for their iniquity. For by 1898 the gold mines of the Transvaal were producing £15 million worth of gold each year. In 1899 this would be £20 million, with reserves conservatively estimated at £700 million. A British minister said it was 'the richest spot on earth'. In fifteen years, what had been a row of tents had become a city with 50,000 European inhabitants. Then the mines became organized. The gold rush died and an industrial pattern asserted itself. In the rich part of the town where the richer whites lived, there were broad gaslit pavements, big houses, theatres, hotels, nightclubs, brothels. In the poorer industrial hinterland 88,000 Africans lived in appalling conditions where typhoid and pneumonia were rife and home-made liquor, often literally deadly, was the only narcotic to numb the pain of existence. For all its mixture, Boer and Jew, black and brown, Johannesburg mysteriously felt British – both in its cruelly depressed slums, and in the street names of its salubrious quarters: Anderson Street and Commissioner Street.

No wonder Kruger and his government wished to deprive these invaders, these intruders, of as much as possible of their plunder by taxation: no wonder he wanted to withhold from them any political rights, such as a vote. And no wonder the British yearned to be the sole masters of the gold, as of the diamonds: the lords of a united South Africa under the British flag.

That is what the Boer War was about. The Jameson Raid of 1895 was a hasty, illegal operation for which the perpetrator received a token prison sentence in Holloway. But Rhodes and Jameson had only done with vulgar haste what Chamberlain – and Salisbury – wanted to do by negotiation or conquest: acquire Johannesburg. This is, as Rhodes wrote in a secret letter to Alfred Beit in 1895, 'the big idea which makes England dominant in Africa, in fact gives England the African continent'.[23]

Not many of Kipling's 'flannelled fools at the wicket' would have been students of contemporary philosophy; it is possible, nonetheless, to see the British Empire as yet another extension of the Idealist belief that if anything is real, then everything is one. Many Idealist philosophers were in fact keen defenders of the Imperial scheme.[24]

In the days when the British Empire was still growing, or when people could conceive of it coming into being in a fit of absence of mind,[25] then individual losses of face or territory in different parts of the globe could be shrugged off. Paradoxically, when the idea of Rhodes took hold – that Britain should rule not just some parts of the Earth, but the entire planet – then even the smallest rebellion here, military disaster there, could be seen as a threat to the whole. This perhaps explains in part, if anything can explain it, the growing ruthlessness of the British Imperial machine as it reached its zenith. Compare Gordon's campaign in Khartoum in 1884 and Kitchener's in 1898. Gladstone's government had sent Gordon to Khartoum not as a soldier but as a governor, with instructions to evacuate in the face of the Mahdi's insurgent popularity. Salisbury's Unionist government, with Chamberlain as colonial secretary, had very different ideas. So did Sir Herbert Kitchener (as he then was) who, against the advice of Lord Cromer, the consul-general in Cairo, wanted to reconquer the Sudan in the face of Dervish fighting against European forces.

Presumably if Kitchener's campaign in the Sudan happened today there would be an international tribunal and he would be summoned to The Hague to answer charges of war crimes and genocide. As far as the British public was concerned he was the gallant conqueror of Khartoum. The Dervishes fought with rifles and bayonets and spears. Kitchener's army had machine guns, which could explain the casualties. At the battle of Atbara Kitchener's force lost 125 white men, and 443 blacks. The Dervish Khalifa's army lost 2,000 dead, and a further 2,000 were taken prisoner.

> The coolness and pluck with which the enemy contained themselves during the bombardment proved that the Dervish was truly brave, not merely when fired with enthusiasm in a fanatical rush but when face to face with death, without hope of escaping or of killing his foe. Many unfortunate blacks were found chained by both hands and legs in the trenches, with a gun in their hands and with their faces to their foes – some with forked sticks behind their backs.

The second Sudan War was a *locus classicus* of the new Imperialism. No one doubted that the system of the Khalifa, based on slavery, was cruel. Few doubted that in the best of all possible worlds, the Dervishes would be converted to Western Liberal Agnosticism, with a devotion to Free Trade and Cricket. What was new was the preparedness not merely to fight, but to eliminate the enemies of the Empire. At the battle of Omdurman the Dervishes had two machine guns, Kitchener fifty-five. His forces were transported by steamer and railroad, which was just as well, since the boots issued were unwearable and had fallen to pieces on arrival. (Many British soldiers in Kitchener's army marched barefoot in this campaign.)[26] By the evening of 2 September 1898, Kitchener thanked 'the Lord of Hosts who had brought him victory at such small cost in British blood'. The casualties were 23 British dead, 434 wounded, and a staggering 11,000 dead Dervishes. A further 16,000 Dervishes, many of them wounded, were taken prisoner.[27]

Yet it would be a mistake to imagine that the Europeans had it all their own way, or even that in all their imperial wars they had all the technological superiority. Menelik's forces at Adowa in 1896 had overwhelmed 30,000 Italians, and were armed with more than 14,000 muzzle-loaders and similar rifles. The arms trade which made Armstrong and others into millionaires knew little of territorial restraint. By 1899 Paul Kruger's Boer Republic had an arsenal of 31 machine guns, 62,950 rifles, 6,000 revolvers and sufficient ammunition for a protracted campaign.

They would also be helped by another factor: the sheer incompetence of quartermasters, suppliers and others, the human capacity to make mistakes. Belloc was a master of the witty epigram – 'Whatever happens, we have got/The Maxim gun and they have not.' The truer picture of Imperial warfare is probably given by Sir Henry Newbolt with his 'The Gatling's jammed and the colonel dead' – see page 292.

Much of this bad luck and incompetence was on display in the opening months of the Boer War. So too was the resourcefulness of the Boers and the skill and courage with which they used their vast arsenal. So, ultimately, was that sheer ruthlessness which Kitchener had displayed at Omdurman.

In 1897, Chamberlain had appointed Sir Alfred Milner (1854–1925) as high commissioner for South Africa. He was a journalist – he had been a deputy editor to Stead and Morley on the *Pall Mall Gazette* – a barrister, a Liberal and a Balliol man. It would have been hard to find anyone with a mindset more different from Kruger's, who in an election of 1898 was returned as president of the Boer Republic with an overwhelming majority.

In the negotiations about the position of the Uitlanders which took place between Kruger and Milner, the Boer position hardened and the commissioner became increasingly exasperated. Every time Milner (on the Cabinet's instructions) made a minor concession to Kruger, the old man in his top hat upped the ante – for example by wishing to ban the immigration of Indians to Johannesburg. The dispute played out between the smooth, intelligent Milner and the stubborn, serious old Voortrekker was nominally concerned with the voting rights or residency permits of 'foreigners' in Johannesburg. It was really seen by everyone as something much bigger.

When Kruger had repelled the Jameson Raid, no less a person than the Kaiser, Wilhelm II, had cabled the Transvaal president on 3 January 1896: 'I sincerely congratulate you that, without appealing for the help of friendly Powers, you, with your people, by your energy against the armed hordes which as disturbers of the peace broke into your country, have succeeded in re-establishing peace and maintaining the independence of your country against attacks from without.'[28] When war eventually came, about 1,600 volunteers formed the 'foreign brigade' to help Kruger: Irish, Americans, Germans, Scandinavians, French, Dutch and Russians. (Among the European aristocrats were Count Sternberg and Prince Bagration of Tiflis, who was accompanied by two Cossack servants.)[29] The British, equally symbolically, drew on their Empire to supply them with troops – a Canadian regiment raised by Lord Strathcona, Australians, New Zealanders and Indians.[30] For this was to be a war which enabled other nations to deliver a verdict on the power of the British Empire.

That was why Milner believed that 'Krugerism' had to be checked. It was why he could stigmatize the prime minister of Natal (an English South African) as 'disloyal' for so much as sending a message of congratulation to Kruger on his re-election. It was why in a celebrated memo to the Westminster government, Milner flamboyantly said:

The case for intervention is overwhelming . . . The spectacle of thousands of British subjects kept permanently in the position of helots, constantly chafing under undoubted grievances, and calling vainly to Her Majesty's Government for redress, does steadily undermine the influence and reputation of Great Britain and the respect for the British Government within its own dominions.[31]

By September 1899 the garrison in South Africa was reinforced from 12,000 to 20,000 troops and war became inevitable. The Orange Free

State publicly allied itself with the Transvaal and war was declared on 11 October.

The Boers wore no uniform. An American newspaper correspondent, Howard Hillegas, commented:

> To call the Boer forces an army was to add unwarranted elasticity to the word, for it has but one quality in common with such armed forces as Americans or Europeans are accustomed to call by that name. The Boer army fought with guns and gunpowder, but it had no discipline, no drills, no forms, no standards, and not even a roll-call.

When one field cornet of the Kroonstad commando insisted on holding a morning roll-call and a rifle inspection, the men complained to a higher authority, and he was told to stop harassing them.[32]

In the initial stages of the war, though, the Boers had all the advantages. They were familiar with the country, which was certainly not true of the 20,000 British troops lately arrived in the Cape, or the 10,000 Indians drafted in.[33] They also, in the opening stages of the war, heavily outnumbered the British. They had 50,000 mounted infantry, and enough ammunition for 80,000. Their marksmen were extremely skilled and the Krupp guns they used were superior to British weapons.[34]

Initially, when they invaded Northern Natal, the Boers had great success. By the end of October, Joubert had outmanoeuvred Sir George White at the battle of Ladysmith, which was to be besieged until 28 February 1900. Kimberley, on the northernmost border of Cape Colony, the western border of the Free State, was also besieged, and so was Mafeking. Three important British forces were thereby immobilized and the Boers had the opportunity to press on through the Cape Colony and take Cape Town. Had they done so, they would have forced Britain to make terms. Instead, with their desire to capture Durban and give themselves a seaport, they made a tactical error which allowed the British time to land a formidable army at Cape Town at the end of October under Sir Redvers Buller as commander-in-chief.

Buller was a stupid man, and his initial actions led to heavy casualties. In December there was the 'Black Week' in which Lieutenant General Sir W.F. Gatacre was defeated at Stormberg; a day later on the 11th Lord Methuen was disastrously repulsed by Cronje at Magersfontein; and four days later Buller, advancing to relieve

Ladysmith, was defeated by Louis Botha at Colenso. The only son of Lord Roberts was killed in the action. Buller then lost his nerve. He signalled to White that Ladysmith should surrender and cabled the same to the Cabinet in London.

The Cabinet's response was to sack Buller and make Roberts commander-in-chief and Kitchener his chief of staff. Roberts was sixty-seven years old. Three years before he had retired from the Indian command. He and Kitchener landed at Cape Town on 10 January 1900.

Roberts gave categorical orders to Buller that he was to do nothing until they had arrived, but the ambitious Buller attempted one last chance of a victory which was his and his only. The disastrous battle of Spion Kop was fought on 24 January – witnessed by a twenty-four-year-old war correspondent called Winston S. Churchill. 1,200 men were killed or wounded, both sides fought with outstanding valour; it was one of the worst defeats inflicted on British troops since the Crimea. The next morning the Boers photographed the British dead on the battlefield and published the pictures all over the world. They caused uproar in England.

When Arthur Balfour referred to the disastrous setbacks, the Queen upbraided him with: 'Please understand that there is no one depressed in this house; we are not interested in the possibilities of defeat; they do not exist.'[35]

Under Roberts's command, the British army turned round the disastrous position into which Buller had led it. 1900 saw the relief of Ladysmith and Mafeking, the capture of Bloemfontein, Johannesburg and Pretoria and – by October 1900 – the formal annexation of the Transvaal. Roberts returned to England and Kitchener succeeded him as commander-in-chief on 29 November.

It might have been supposed that the war was all but over. Rather, it had eighteen terrible months to run, with the Boers fighting a resourceful guerrilla campaign and Kitchener responding with a dreadful ruthlessness. The first part of his strategy was to set up a line of prefabricated blockhouses – constructed out of stone, with corrugated iron roofs – from Kapmurden to Komatipoort, as lookout posts to defend the railway from commando attack. His second move was to clear the land. Women and children were to be separated from their menfolk and herded into concentration camps. Their farms were to be burned or blown up. Crops were to be burnt, livestock killed. Several million horses, cattle and sheep were shot. Barbed-wire fences totalling 3,000 miles were set up to corral the Boers into the camps, with a blockhouse to observe them every few hundred yards.

From then onwards in the war the function of the British army had become the collection of non-combatants and livestock. Lieutenant Colonel Allenby commanded 1,500 men at the beginning of 1901, one of eight columns 'driving' the Transvaal. At the end of three months, his 'bag' was 32 Boers killed, 36 captured, 154 surrendered; 5 guns; 118 wagons; 55 carts; 28,911 rounds of ammunition; 273 rifles; 904 horses; 87 mules; 485 trek oxen; 3,260 other cattle; and 12,380 sheep. He also imprisoned some 400 women and children.

The plight of those in the camps was brought to the public eye by Emily Hobhouse, who went to South Africa on behalf of the Women and Children's Distress Fund. While the military ran the camps (until November 1901) the death rate was 344 per 1,000, falling to 20 per 1,000 in May 1902. The families were deprived of clothes, bedding, cooking utensils, clean water and adequate medicine.[36] Children often had to lie on the bare earth exposed to unbearable heat. By October 1901, 80,000 Boers were living in these camps – a number which swelled to 117,871 in the eleventh month. 20,177 inmates died, most of them children.[37]

Kitchener appears to have been indifferent to the suffering he caused in South Africa. Like many who enjoy inflicting pain on their fellow men, or from whose natures compassion has been mysteriously excluded, he was a keen animal-lover. He had a pet bear in Cyprus. He instantaneously 'bonded' with horses and camels on campaign. His true mania, however, was for dogs. When he had finished tormenting the South Africans this cruel bugger – there is enough evidence, surely, to justify both the noun and the epithet – doted on four cocker spaniels named Shot, Bang, Miss and Damn. When he was in India he bought a house, something he had never done before: 'I need somewhere for my dogs to live.'[38]

No such shelter was offered by the field marshal to the Afrikaner women and children whom he had starved, or allowed to die of dysentery and typhoid, in the midday sun of the High Veld. The photographs of the children in those camps, skeletal as the inmates of Belsen,[39] are the silent footnote to the South African war. Six days after the peace was signed at Vereeniging on 31 May 1902 Kitchener was awarded £50,000 by Parliament. He was given the Order of Merit and created a viscount.

The Victorian age, haunted by the dire warnings of Malthus, had begun with the erection of workhouses on home territory. It ended with a war which was no more than a scramble for gold and diamonds. The war cost Great Britain £222 million. 5,774 British troops were killed, 22,829 wounded, and some 4,000 Boers died in battle. The war was hugely popular. The reliefs of Mafeking and Ladysmith were the occasions of wild public rejoicing. The songs of the war had an infectious music-hall brio. And Britain may be said to have won handsome returns on her expenditure. For her £222 million she had won control of the richest spot on Earth. Yet as in a morality tale, she had gained diamonds and gold and lost something in return. A people who built workhouses at the beginning of an era and concentration camps at the end might have gained the whole world, but they had lost honour, and soul.

43

Vale

Life at the court of Queen Victoria can never have been exciting, but as she entered the deeper, mistier recesses of old age, the tedium for her attendants was scarcely tolerable. At Osborne in the winters, there was so little to do that the equerries tried playing golf in the snow with red billiard balls: 'but the greens are of course useless. We share a great deal . . . We have had some good hockey.'[1]

There were moments of light relief, as when Hubert Parry came to be knighted. 'What a ripper he is,' observed Frederick Ponsonby.

> He told me that he had had a private rehearsal & had split his breeches in trying to kneel down in his velvet pants. Some of the others who came to be decorated were chattering with fear & one of them kept on repeating his name to me he was so frightened. H.P. however didn't care a d–n & roaring with laughter and telling stories before going in to the room where the Queen was . . . I was sorry that he wasn't going to stay & dine as I am sure that H.M. would be delighted with him.[2]

The numbers dining with the Queen were small: usually just Princess Beatrice, sometimes Princess Louise ('the petticoats' as the equerries dubbed them) and one or two courtiers. The old lady liked to eat off gold – even her eggcup at breakfast for the royal boiled egg was gold plate – and she maintained a Hanoverian level of greed. 'If she would follow a diet and live on Benger's [proprietary baby] Food and chicken all would be well,' opined her maid of honour Marie Mallet, 'but she clings to roast beef and ices! And what can you then expect? Sir James [Reid – the doctor] has at last persuaded her to try Bengers and she likes it and now to his horror, instead of substituting it for other foods she adds it to her already copious meals . . . And of course when she devours a huge chocolate ice followed by a couple of apricots, washed down with iced water as she did last night [25 July 1900] she ought to expect a dig from the indigestion fiend.'[3]

In this last phase of decrepitude her eyesight grew dim, and she became querulous about the darkened rooms (as they appeared to her) at Osborne, and the faintness of modern ink. She continued to be punctilious about overseeing the affairs of state and reading the boxes of state papers sent down by ministers. When she entered the very final stage, and was too ill to read them for just one week, Arthur Balfour 'was astounded at the accumulation of official boxes that had taken place during the last week and said it showed what a mass of routine work the Queen had to do'.[4]

She took a keen interest in the progress of the Boer War, and kept an album of photographs of all the officers killed: an agonizing task for the equerries who had to write to all the widows asking for these pictures. Having compiled it for a year she tired of it, saying it was too sad to look at.

Young Fritz Ponsonby was longing to go to South Africa and confided the fact to Princess Victoria (daughter of the Prince of Wales), who immediately told her mother, who told the Queen. 'HM was speechless and sent Mrs Grant flying to find out all about it. HM says you could have knocked her down with a feather and she says she will be jiggered if she'll allow it for a moment.'[5]

In fact, the last official engagement she performed was on Monday, 14 January 1901, when she received Lord Roberts on his return from South Africa. She was wheelchair-bound and very frail. She conferred on him an earldom, and since his only son had been killed in the war she allowed him the privilege of the title passing to his daughter. (The Queen herself had lost a beloved grandson in the fighting: Prince Christian Victor, Helena's boy, who died of enteric fever in Pretoria.) She also made 'Our Bobs' a Knight of the Garter.

Not long after this audience, she began to sink. On Wednesday 16th, for the first time in twenty years as her personal physician, Reid saw the Queen in bed: she remained there all day, only rising to dress at 6 p.m.[6] Over the next few days, Reid and the courtiers began to warn those most intimately connected with her that the Queen's life was coming to an end. The government needed to be told: no one could remember the procedures for summoning an Accession Council or for swearing in a new monarch. The bishop of Winchester, Randall Davidson, was summoned to the Queen's bedside. The Prince of Wales was telephoned at Marlborough House,[7] and set off for the Isle of Wight.

Much against the advice and wishes of 'the petticoats', the Kaiser in Berlin had been informed and had set off at once to see his grandmother. When he arrived at Osborne House, he said to the petticoats, 'My first wish is not to be in the light, and I will return to

London if you wish. I should like to see Grandmama before she dies, but if it is impossible, I should quite understand.'[8] Everyone was impressed by how well he behaved. She spent the last two and a half hours of her life leaning on the Kaiser's immobile arm, with Reid supporting her other side. She finally died at half-past six in the evening on 22 January 1901.

She died clutching a crucifix, but like so much else about Queen Victoria, her religion was *sui generis*. The 'Instructions', written out on 9 December 1897 and carried out by Reid to the letter,[9] insisted that she should be placed in her coffin with an array of trinkets worthy of an Egyptian pharaoh. Rings, bracelets, lockets, shawls, handkerchiefs and plaster casts of her favourites' hands were all placed in the casket. When all the royalties had come to pay their last respects to the body ('no smell')[10] and to look at that face – 'like a lovely marble statue, no sign of illness or age, and she looked *"the Queen"*'[11] – it was time for the doctor to cram more souvenirs into the casket – Prince Albert's dressing-gown: and in her left hand a photo of John Brown and a lock of his hair in tissue paper which the doctor tactfully covered with Queen Alexandra's floral tribute.[12] The new king kindly allowed the Munshi to come and look his last on the Empress of India, and finally two men came in and screwed down the coffin lid.[13]

To the end, she could indulge her love of clutter. The little body would now begin its stately journey to Windsor where – in accordance with her wishes – it was given a military funeral. Keir Hardie complained about this, and asked why the nation should have been obliged to take leave of its sovereign with guns and martial music and uniforms. This was to overlook the fact, which she never forgot, that underlying the consensus of constitutional monarchy there was relentless force. It had been prepared – though not used – early in her reign when she and her family were spirited out of London and sent to Osborne until the police and the military had subdued the Chartists. It had been used with ruthless efficacy late in the reign on 'Bloody Sunday'. The war in South Africa, still in progress as the Queen's military funeral took place, and as the cortège went to Paddington Station for its journey to the Mausoleum at Frogmore (where at last she would be reunited with the Prince Consort), reinforced the point that the genial power of the Victorian aristocracy, transforming itself slowly into parliamentary democracy, was underpinned by force. Ask – given the sickness and poverty of hundreds of thousands of Londoners on that cold February day, as the gun carriage bore the coffin through the silent streets – ask why they did not rebel, why they did not riot, why they did not behave like the Paris Commune of 1870 or the Bolsheviks of 1917. They had as much provocation, but part of the answer to the mystery of their submissiveness is supplied in those troops and those guns, following the procession. No one could doubt for a single second that at the first sign of trouble from the populace, pious old Salisbury and dear 'Old Bobs' – now an earl and KG – would turn the guns on the crowd, with all the confidence shown by the Chinese authorities eighty-eight years later in Tiananmen Square.

The other fact about the Victorians, however, which explains why the reign of the Queen ended in reverence and (domestically at least) peacefulness is more benign. From the first, the Victorians possessed the capacity for constructive self-criticism. Those who opposed the Boer War, or who had their doubts about this phase of the Imperial adventure, were not, as they would have been in a truly autocratic system, moved underground, silenced or imprisoned. The mercurial figure of Lloyd George made his career out of opposition to the war. 'The man who tries to make the flag an object of a single party is a greater traitor to that flag than any man who fires at it,'[14] said the great Welshman, replying to Tory accusations of treachery. All allowance should be made for Lloyd George's opportunism – not to say, in his later years at least, his downright dishonesty and corruption – but a country which enabled a man who grew up in a small shoemaker's cottage to rise in less than fifty years to be chancellor of the Exchequer was not a country which was entirely repressive. Against all the cruelty and the blunders – the workhouses, the oppression of Ireland, the blatant racism and butchery of the colonial wars – must be set a vast social (as well as technological) resourcefulness, a willingness to regroup and reorganize on behalf of the governing classes, which was guided by enlightened self-interest.

It is easy for those who come in after time to say what is wrong with a society, or a country, not their own. Those who have lived through a twentieth century whose wars slew and displaced tens of millions can easily, for some reason, turn a blind eye to the faults of their own generation and excoriate the Victorians, whose wars killed thousands. By the same token, life for a working-class Irish family in the slums of Liverpool in, let us say, 1880 may have been terrible; but it is only fair to add, terrible compared with what, and with whom? The nineteenth century was by many modern standards a cruel age. Those refugees, from Karl Marx to the Emperor Napoleon III, who fled to London from Europe suggest to us that with all its faults, Victorian England was more genial and tolerant than many other places at the same date. While we weep for Oscar Wilde developing an ear infection in Reading Gaol, we might pause to imagine how long he would have survived in a jail in Naples at the same date. The Victorian Age saw floggings of sailors and soldiers, it saw children working down the mines; it also saw these abuses, and hundreds like them, reformed and abolished.

At the beginning of the age, Dickens had likened Britannia to the old woman in the children's story who summoned the aid of all manner of farmyard creatures and characters to encourage her pig to leap over a stile. 'The national pig is not nearly over the stile yet; and the little old woman, Britannia hasn't got home tonight.' He spoke those words in 1855 'in this old country, with its seething hard-worked millions, its heavy taxes, its crowds of ignorant, its crowds of poor, its crowds of wicked'. Had he lived until 1901, would Dickens have thought the pig had got over the stile for the 'loyal, patient, willing-hearted English people',[15] or for their royal mistress of whom he spoke so loyally on that occasion?

The gun carriage making its way to Paddington Station across Hyde Park was followed by King Edward VII, Kaiser Wilhelm II, King George I of the Hellenes and King Carlos of Portugal. In the procession were Crown Princes of Romania, Greece, Denmark, Norway, Sweden and Siam. The Duke of Aosta represented the King of Italy, Grand Duke Michael Alexandrovitch the Tsar of Russia, and Archduke Franz Ferdinand the Emperor of Austria. Almost all these characters, in their uniforms and feathered hats, presided over countries where the poor were even more miserable than in Victorian England, where political dissent was vigorously denied, and where technological and social change had been slower than in England. Almost all of them (not the Scandinavians) oppressed minorities within their own borders and were cruel colonial masters to those in Africa and Asia whom they had subdued. The huge proportion of them would, during or after the First World War, be toppled by republican movements which were even less humanitarian, and even less efficient.

'Oh! Dearest George,' wrote the Queen's cousin, Princess Augusta of Strelitz, to the Duke of Cambridge, 'what a calamity! . . . anxiety terrible as to what poor England will have to go through *now*! God have mercy on us all.'[16] There were indeed terrible decades ahead – a First World War, decades of poverty and unrest, another war killing millions of Europeans, in addition to all the post-colonial problems visited upon the former dominions of the British Empire. Even so, one notices that through all these years of horror, the refugees were streaming towards London from Russia, Germany, Africa and Asia and not in the opposite direction. In fact, though dreadful mistakes were made by the Victorians, the comparative stability, comparative strength (military and political) and comparative benignity of England in the half-century after her death owed much to the Victorians. They even owed something to the tiny, round-faced woman trundling towards her last resting place with her coffin-load of mementoes.

'*Vale desideratissime*,' she had had inscribed over the doors of the Frogmore Mausoleum: 'Farewell, most beloved. Here at length I shall rest with thee, with thee in Christ I shall rise again.' That journey was hers, hers alone. Fascinating as it is to visit the mausoleum on open days, one always feels there something of an intruder. Let us, rather, take leave of 'the little old woman' before she leaves her island home for the great public funeral.

The gun carriage was drawn from Osborne House down York Avenue, East Cowes; the occupants of these villas, whose grandparents would not have had the vote, possessed not merely a share in parliamentary democracy but, in all probability, a savings account and a bicycle. The coffin was carried aboard the *Alberta* at Trinity Pier opposite the post office as a dull roll of forty drums rumbled. The royal family with their attendants boarded the royal yacht *Victoria and Albert* and set out, through the clear blue wintry air of the Solent, on the short sea-voyage to Portsmouth harbour. They sailed through an eight-mile-long allée of steel, in which the British fleet was joined by foreign warships, spaced at two and a half cable lengths, about 1,500 feet apart. They glided past *Australia*, between the *Camperdown* and the *Majestic*, the *Trafalgar*, the *Nile*, and the *Benbow*, the names of the ships recalling a vanished naval era, much at variance with the massy walls of gun-metal grey which they adorned. And here, still at peace with one another for another ominous thirteen years, were the *Dupuy de Lorne*, representing France, the *Dom Carlo I* from Portugal, the Japanese battleship *Hatsuse*, and four huge grey-masted ironclads flying the red, white and black German ensign, vastly overshadowing the others in strength and size.[17]

Notes

Unprinted sources are given in full, including the number of the manuscript and the folio number – e.g. Gladstone Papers, BL Add. MS 44790 f.177.

Notes on printed sources refer to the Bibliography. E.g. Litten (1991), p. 170 refers to Julian Litten's *The English Way of Death. The Common Funeral since 1450*. In cases where more than work by one author appears in the Bibliography, the reader should be guided by the date. E.g. Gash (1976) would refer to Norman Gash's *Peel*, published in 1976. Gash (1977) refers to *Politics in the Age of Peel*, 2nd edition, 1977.

In any case which could conceivably be confusing, the full title is cited. References to periodicals are self-explanatory. E.g. *The Law Journal*, 1884, can be found in any good reference library. References to signed articles in periodicals will, in general, be made to the author by name.

Thomas Curson Hansard was the printer of the Parliamentary Debates. This voluminous monument began as Cobbett's *Parliamentary History of England from the Norman Conquest to the Year 1803*, and was first published in October 1806 in thirty-one volumes. It continued as a record of Parliamentary Debates from 1812 onwards, *The Parliamentary Debates from the Year 1803 to the Present Time*, published under the Superintendence of T.C. Hansard in 1812. Thereafter the volumes are always popularly known simply as 'Hansard'. This series of forty-one volumes continues until February 1820. The next series, from 21 April 1820 to 23 July 1830, covers a further thirty-five volumes. Most of our period is covered in the Third Series, which extends to 5 August 1891. Reference in the notes is simply to Hansard, the number of a volume in Roman numerals and a column number in Arabic numerals. So 'Hansard, XXVI.3' would refer to Hansard's Parliamentary Debates, Third Series, volume XXVI, column 3. The date will only be added if it is considered of especial significance.

The Annual Register, now published by Keesing's Worldwide, began in 1759 (registering the year 1758) and was printed by R. and J.

Dodsley in Pall Mall. For most of our period, it was published by Rivingtons (taken over by Longmans, Green and Co., that great Victorian publisher, for the 1890 volume, published 1891). This invaluable survey has been consulted by me far more often than would be guessed at from the reference notes. It gave me my sense of pace, seeing the different events of each year so clearly spelled out side by side. References to it appear as *The Annual Register* followed by a year and a page number.

In referring to the works of the Victorians themselves, I have been conscious of the multiplicity of editions available to different readers. Sometimes a modern edition of a poet – most notably that of Tennyson by Christopher Ricks – is so good that it seems almost a necessity to consult that rather than an earlier version. Sometimes I refer to first editions, but more often simply to a volume which happens to be to hand. I try to guide the reader as carefully as I can by reference to chapter or section-numbers of books, as well as to the page numbers of the works cited. This is especially necessary in the case of the two giants. I refer to thirty-nine volumes of *The Works of John Ruskin*, edited by E.T. Cook and Alexander Wedderburn, because it is the standard edition to which all Ruskin scholars refer, and to the thirty volumes of the Edinburgh Edition of *The Complete Works of Thomas Carlyle*, published in New York in 1903 by Charles Scribner's Sons, because it happens to be the edition on my own shelves. (How we British visitors miss Scribner's beautiful shop in Fifth Avenue!)

1 The Little Old Woman Britannia

1 Cocks, p. 13.
2 Dickens, *Speeches*, ed. Fielding, p. 205.
3 Dorothy Thompson, p. 27.
4 Clapham, p. 53.
5 Paul Ehrlich's *The Population Bomb* takes the pessimistic Malthusian view; compare Julian Simon, *The Ultimate Resource*. Quoted Malthus, ed. Gilbert, 1993.
6 Quoted Anstruther (1984), p. 35.
7 Charles Shaw, p. 4.
8 Hansard, XXVI, p. 3.
9 Ruskin, *Modern Painters*, part vi, chapter 2, *Works*, vol. p. 215.
10 Jack Lindsay (1985), p. 124; James Hilton, *Turner A Life*, p. 269.
11 *The Times*, 17 October 1834.
12 Cocks, p. 16.

13 See Hastings, p. 77.
14 Clapham, p. 425.
15 Janet Browne, p. 398.
16 Froude (1882), I, p. 9.

2 Victoria's Inheritance

 1 Potts & Potts, *passim.*
 2 Woodham-Smith (1972), p. 139.
 3 David Cecil, p. 391.
 4 Woodham-Smith (1972), p. 140.
 5 Ibid., p. 141.
 6 Greville, IV, p. 32.
 7 David Cecil, p. 271.
 8 Ibid., p. 405.
 9 Woodham-Smith (1972), p. 146.
10 Victoria (1912), II, p. 144.
11 Anstruther (1984), p. 35.
12 David Roberts, pp. 97–107.
13 Andrew Roberts, pp. 10–11.
14 Dunn (1961), pp. 31, 39.
15 Clapham, pp. 388ff. The promotion of new railroad companies added over 1,000 miles to the potential railways of England in the year 1836/7.
16 Clapham, pp. 9, 19.
17 Ibid., p. 67.
18 Ibid., p. 28.
19 Ibid., p. 454.
20 Ibid., p. 456.

3 The Charter

 1 *The Lancet*, 7 November 1837.
 2 Durey, p. 7.
 3 *Quarterly Review*, November 1831.
 4 *The Lancet*, 23 December 1837, p. 459.
 5 Durey, p. 210.
 6 Douglas Browne, p. 83.
 7 Finer, p. 30.
 8 Halévy, p. 510.
 9 Philip Thurmond Smith, p. 18.
10 Ibid., p. 85.

11 Ibid., p. 44.
12 Ascoli, p. 83.
13 Woodward, p. 79.
14 Hansard, XCV, p. 988.
15 Hansard, XXXIX, pp. 68–71.
16 Gash (1927), p. 214.
17 Thomas Carlyle, *Chartism 1839* (Critical & Miscellaneous Essays, vol. IV, *Works*, vol. XXIX, p. 153).
18 McDonall, *Chartist and Republican Journal*, quoted in Slosson, p. 59.
19 Carlyle, op. cit., p. 159.
20 Dorothy Thompson, p. 58.
21 Woodward, p. 127.
22 Ibid., p. 130.
23 Quoted in Dorothy Thompson, p. 78.
24 *Northern Star*, 15 June 1839, quoted in Stedman Jones, p. 168.
25 Stedman Jones, p. 171.
26 Clapham, p. 191.
27 Ibid., p. 73.
28 Dorothy Thompson, p. 338.
29 Quoted in Stedman Jones, p. 104.
30 Slosson, p. 27.
31 Dorothy Thompson, p. 31.
32 Ibid., p. 17.

4 Typhoon Coming On

1   Hansard, XVII, p. 1341.
2   Ibid., p. 1345.
3   Macaulay, *Prose and Poetry*, p. 221.
4   Morley (1912), I, p. 78.
5   Alastair Hennessy, p. 40.
6   Darwin (1905), p. 512.
7   Woodward, p. 357.
8   Bethell, p. 329.
9   Quoted in Bethell, p. 345.
10 Ridley, p. 259.
11 See Hewison *et al.*, p. 71.
12 A.J. Newman, p. 102.
13 See Heuman, *Between Black and White. Race, Politics and the Free Coloureds in Jamaica, 1792–1865*.

14 Weintraub (1997), p. 65.

15 Netzer, p. 153.

16 Battiscombe (1974), p. 125.

17 Fulford (1949), p. 106.

18 Weintraub (1997), p. 60.

19 Ibid., p. 99.

5 The Age of Peel

1 Read, p. 61.

2 Keynes (1923), p. 7.

3 Quoted in Blake (1985), p. 18.

4 See ibid., p. 23, which quotes the view of Harold Perkin (1969).

5 Blake (1985), p. 13.

6 There are three superb historians of this for which I largely rely for what follows. Robert Blake (1985), Donald Read and Norman Gash (1976 & 1977).

7 Hastings, p. 104.

8 A.C. Benson (1899), I, p. 47.

9 Dunn (1961), p. 420.

10 For all previous see Anstruther (1963).

11 Disraeli (1980), p. 96.

12 Sheila M. Smith, Introduction to Disraeli (1982), p. xiii.

13 'A Letter to Sir Culling E. Smith, Bart., and J. Low, Esq., in Reply to Their Address and Letter from the Anti-Maynooth Committee by a Clergyman of the Church of England and Ireland', quoted Blake (1985), p. 81.

14 Read, p. 138.

15 Ibid., p. 139.

16 The Duke of Manchester, *Part of a Speech in the House of Lords.*

17 Quoted in Blake (1985), p. 52.

18 Gash (1977), p. 248.

19 See Macaulay, ed. Young, p. 636.

20 Ibid., p. 637.

21 Blake (1985), p. 59.

22 Woodward, p. 120.

23 Blake (1966), p. 191.

24 Clapham, p. 454.

25 Blake (1985), p. 67.

6 Famine in Ireland

1 See Col. Jas E. McGee, *'Thumping English Lies': Froude's Slanders on Ireland and Irishmen* (New York, 1872).
2 Froude (1872–4), p. 571.
3 Hoppen, p. 64.
4 Quoted in Gray, p. 76.
5 Quoted in Woodham-Smith (1962), p. 119.
6 Clapham, p. 391.
7 Quoted in Gray, p. 24.
8 Hoppen, p. 570.
9 Mokyr, p. 64.
10 Saville (1987), p. 46.
11 Dunn (1961), p. 69.
12 De Beaumont, quoted in Saville, p. 31.
13 Hoppen, p. 63.
14 Woodham-Smith (1962), p. 21.
15 Saville (1987), p. 6.
16 Percival, pp. 72–3.
17 Woodham-Smith (1962), p. 226.
18 Saville (1987), p. 16.
19 Woodham-Smith (1962), p. 167.
20 Berkeley, ed. Jessop, vol. 6, p. 243.
21 Woodham-Smith (1962), p. 165.
22 Ibid., p. 375.
23 Ibid., p. 409.

7 The Victorians in Italy

1 Morley (1912), I, p. 289.
2 Jenkins (1995), p. 93.
3 Dickens, *Pictures from Italy*, Fireside *Dickens*, p. 187.
4 Ruskin, *Praeterita*, II, *Works*, vol. 35, p. 51.
5 Quoted in Hilton (1985), p. 124.
6 Ibid., p. 29.
7 Hewson *et al.*, p. 144.
8 Browning, 'A Toccata of Galuppi's', *Poetical Works*, ed. Jack, p. 580.
9 Irvine & Honan, p. 139.
10 Karlin, p. 22.
11 Ibid., p. 47.
12 Chesterton (1943), p. 66.

13 Karlin, p. 169.
14 Korg, p. 84.
15 Ibid., p. 86.
16 Browning, ed. Jack, 'Old Pictures in Florence', p. 72.
17 Irvine & Honan, p. 86.
18 *De Vulgari Eloquentia.*
19 Browning, ed. Jack, *Sordello*, II, 570–3, p. 197.
20 Ibid., II. 583–5
21 Browning, ed. Jack, 'Bishop Blougram's Apology', p. 663.
22 Irvine & Honan, pp. 20–1.

8 Doubt

1   *The Leisure Hour*, September 1849.
2   Altick (1978), p. 318.
3   Ibid., p. 317.
4   Frederic Moore (1838).
5   *Eliza Cook's Journal (1850–3)*, p. 203.
6   *The Leisure Hour*, September 1849, p. 552.
7   *Eliza Cook's Journal*, p. 203.
8   Janet Browne, pp. 462–3.
9   James A. Secord, introduction to Robert Chambers (1994).
10 Robert Chambers, p. 468.
11 Anne Secord, 'Artisan Botany', in Jardine *et al.*, eds, p. 389.
12 De Beer, p. 32.
13 Ibid., p. 25.
14 Lyell, p. 407.
15 Robert Chambers, pp. 25–6.
16 Ibid., p. 157.
17 Quoted in de Beer, p. 12.
18 Robert Chambers, p. 231.
19 Janet Browne, p. 465.
20 Ibid., p. 466.
21 Disraeli, *Tancred*, 1847, quoted by Janet Browne, p. 463.
22 Alfred Tennyson, ed. Ricks, 'Locksley Hall', p. 688.
23 Ibid., p. 698.
24 Ibid., p. 859.
25 Ibid., 'In Memoriam A.H.H.', IX, ed. Ricks, p. 873.
26 Ibid., LV, p. 910.
27 Ibid., LVI, p. 911.
28 See Milton Malthauser, *Just Before Darwin*, Wesleyan University

Press, Middleton, Ct, 1954, p. 37.
29 Ibid., p. 36.
30 Robert Chambers, p. 203.
31 John Henry Newman (1974), p.107.

9 Mesmerism
1 See Appleyard, *Henry Francis Lyte*.
2 Quoted in Erikson, *Phrenology and Physical Anthropology*.
3 Ibid., p. 51.
4 See Storer, p. 7.
5 Darnton, p. 8.
6 Storer, p. 77.
7 Ibid., p. 29.
8 See Jonathan Miller, 'A Gower Street Scandal', pp. 183ff.
9 See Townshend, *Mesmerism Proved True*.
10 Kaplan, p. 9.
11 Ibid., p. 235. See also Crabtree, *From Mesmer to Freud*.
12 Townshend, *Mesmerism Proved True*.

10 John Stuart Mill's Boiled Egg
1 Packe, p. 55.
2 Ibid., p. 290.
3 Bertrand Russell (1946), p. 743.
4 Ibid., p. 742.
5 Ryan (1987) is the best introduction to J.S. Mill's philosophy.
6 See A.N. Wilson (1999), ch. 4, and Letwin, pp. 244–52.
7 Packe, p. 301.
8 Conrad Russell reminds us, though, of the interesting fact that Mill saw no logical connection between free market liberty and individual liberty. See C.D. Russell (1993).
9 From *Principles of Political Economy*, 1848, quoted by Kurer, p. 55.
10 Mill (1865), 6.10.3., pp. 913–14.

11 The Failed Revolution
1 Kurer, p. 31.
2 Quoted ibid., p. 28.
3 For the many significant textual and notional differences between the 1848 first edition (German) and the 1888 English version, see Fisher (1984).

4   Edwards, *Macaulay*, p. 41.
5   Macaulay, ed. Young, p. 431.
6   Quoted in Dorothy Thompson, *The Chartists*, p. 187.
7   Saville (1987), p. 81.
8   Ibid., p. 110.
9   Ibid., p. 112.
10 Stamp, pp. 84, 85.
11 Dorothy Thompson, pp. 341–68.
12 Woodward, p. 131. Fisher pp. 16, 96.

12 The Great Exhibition
1   Smith & Spear, p. 664.
2   Stanmore Papers, BL Add. MS 49,131, f. 73.
3   Ibid., f. 46.
4   Olive Anderson, p. 211.
5   John West (1971), but I owe the entire argument to Miles Taylor, 'The 1848 Revolutions'.
6   Auerbach, pp. 63, 64.
7   Lees-Milne, p. 131.
8   Ibid., p. 154.
9   Auerbach, p. 45.
10 Clapham, p. 536.
11 *DNB*, XV, p. 665.
12 Ridley, p. 379.
13 Woodward, p. 237.
14 Ridley, p. 287.
15 Lawrence, p. 92.
16 *DNB*, XV, p. 666.
17 Read, p. 285.
18 Arnould, *Memorial Lines on Sir Robert Peel*.
19 Bagehot, V, p. 216, 'Sir Robert Peel'.
20 Ibid., p. 218.
21 Woodward, p. 167.
22 Bird, p. 111.
23 Auerbach, p. 104.
24 Ibid., p. 106.
25 Bennett, p. 123.
26 Auerbach, p. 171.
27 *Geoffrey Madan's Notebooks, a Selection*, ed. J.A. Gere & John Sparrow, 1981.

28 G.O. Trevelyan, p. 359.

29 Chadwick (1966), p. 287.

30 Auerbach, p. 76.

31 Chadwick (1966), p. 291.

32 Ibid., p. 299.

33 Ward, p. 255.

34 Stanley (1844), II, p. 285.

35 Queen Victoria, *Letters*, ed. Benson, II, p. 281.

36 Chadwick (1966), p. 303.

37 John Ruskin, 'The Opening of the Crystal Palace Considered in some of its Relations to the Prospects of Art, 1854', quoted in Beaver, p. 59.

38 McKean, p. 45.

39 Auerbach, p. 148.

40 Longford (1972), p. 478.

41 Tennyson, 'Ode on the Death of the Duke of Wellington', *Poems*, ed. Ricks, p. 412.

42 Woodward, p. 249.

43 Eyck, p. 152.

44 Longford (1972), p. 484.

45 Marx, *Eighteenth Brumaire*, p. 116.

46 Ibid., p. 114.

47 Ibid., p. 117.

48 Kingsley (1984), p. 178.

49 Ibid., p. 179.

50 Ibid., p. 178.

51 By Father Herbert Kelly, quoted, approvingly, in Vidler (1966), pp. 10, 11.

52 Newman (1955), p. 29.

53 Fulford, ed. (1964), p. 210.

13 Marx – Ruskin – Pre-Raphaelites

1 Woodward, p. 144, and for most of supra.

2 Martineau (1855), p. 23.

3 Martineau (1844), p. 12.

4 Martineau (1853), p. 219.

5 Marx (1857), p. 289.

6 Ibid., p. 292.

7 Ibid., p. 247.

8 Mayhew (1967), III, p. 211.

9   Longford (1964), p. 372.
10   Quoted in Durey, p. 64.
11   *The Cambridge World History of Disease*, ed. Kiple, p. 648.
12   Ibid.
13   Mary Bennett, in Bowness, p. 163.
14   Hamlin, p. 333.
15   Carlyle, *Past and Present*, in *Works*, X, pp. 24, 31.
16   Ibid., p. 276.
17   Ibid., p. 271.
18   Ibid., p. 291.
19   Ibid., p. 136.
20   Marsh (1999), p. 119, Bowness, p. 86.
21   Burne-Jones, pp. 218–19.
22   Quoted in Marsh (1999), p. 202.
23   Ibid., p. 210.
24   Amor, p. 10.
25   Diana Holman Hunt, p. 69.
26   Ibid., p. 106.
27   Ibid., p. 52.
28   Creer, *Human Hair*, p. 82.
29   Ibid., p. 83.
30   Diana Holman Hunt, p. 106.
31   Hilton (1965), p. 156.
32   Ibid., p. 118.
33   Geoffrey Hill, *The Triumph of Love*, CXLVI, Penguin, 1998, p. 80.
34   Froude (1884), I, p. 97.
35   Haight, p. 101.
36   A.N. Wilson (1999), p. 176.
37   Fulford (1933), p. 293.
38   Battiscombe (1974), p. 207.
39   A.N. Wilson (1999), p. 101.
40   Roger Scruton, *A Short History of Modern Philosophy*, 1995, p. 175.
41   *DNB*, 1901–1911, p. 514.
42   Tennyson, 'To the Rev. F.D. Maurice', ed. Rix, p. 612.
43   Hewison *et al.*, p. 212.
44   Diana Holman Hunt, p. 165.
45   See Faber, pp. 306, 428.
46   Chesney, p. 7.

47 Ibid., p. 19.

14 The Crimean War

1 Soyer (1987), p. 142.
2 *DNB*, III, p. 831.
3 The above quotes from Seacole, pp. 90, 121.
4 Ibid., p. 137.
5 A.J.P. Taylor (1954), p. 81, characteristic of an English historian of a certain age, does not mention the Turkish casualties, which I have been unable to locate in any work of reference.
6 William Howard Russell (1995), p. 38.
7 Ibid., p. 50.
8 Ibid., p. 53.
9 Royle (1999), p. 130.
10 William Howard Russell (1995), p. 103.
11 Royle (1999), p. 269.
12 Ibid., p. 276.
13 Ibid., p. 290.
14 Quoted ibid., p. 126.
15 Tennyson, *Poems*, ed. Ricks, p. 1034.
16 Ibid., p. 1308.
17 A.J.P. Taylor (1954), p. 75.
18 Kinglake, I, p. 43.
19 Quoted in Royle, p. 62.
20 Olive Anderson, p. 76.
21 Marx, *Neue Oder-Zeitung*, 21 April 1855, reprinted in *The Russian Menace to Europe*, ed. Blackstock, 1953.
22 Marx, *The Eastern Question*, ed. A.M. & E. Aveling, p. 220.
23 Selina Hastings, *Evelyn Waugh*, p. 92.
24 Gladstone Papers, *BL* Add. MS 44,086.
25 Southgate, p. 375.
26 *DNB*, XV, p. 1013.
27 Quoted in Ridley, p. 433.
28 Southgate, p. 339.
29 Ibid., p. 428.
30 Olive Anderson, p. 109.
31 Ridley, p. 148.
32 Fitzroy, p. 65.
33 Apperson, p. 164.
34 Alford, p. 28.

35 Lawrence James (1981), p. 10.
36 Ibid., p. 136.
37 Ibid., p. 55.
38 Ibid., p. 73.
39 Ibid., p. 44.

15 India 1857–9
 1 Sen, p. 58.
 2 Ibid., p. 42.
 3 Hansard 1st series, XXVI, p. 164, 22 June 1813.
 4 Mill.
 5 Maclagan, p. 68.
 6 Ibid., p. 83.
 7 Chaudhuri, p. 116
 8 Eric Stokes (1986), p. 51.
 9 Hibbert (1978), p. 80.
10 Sen, p. 59.
11 Ibid., p. 61.
12 *Source material for a History of the Freedom Movement in India*, vol. II, 1885–1920, Bombay, 1958, p. 192.
13 Srivastava, p. 157.
14 Nanuk, 1858.
15 Smith & Spear, p. 668.
16 Quoted by Eric Stokes (1959), p. 3.
17 Hibbert (1978), p. 90.
18 Ibid., p. 111.
19 Lawrence James (1997), p. 287.
20 Rotton, p. 6.
21 Ibid., p. 86.
22 Ibid., p. 109.
23 Hibbert (1978), p. 173.
24 Having protested against his loss of privileges – permission to maintain his own army, for example, or exemption from the jurisdiction of civil courts – Nana Sahib bided his time, to all outward signs on cordial terms with the British authorities. Srivastava, p. 14.
25 Eric Stokes (1986), p. 53.
26 Ibid., p. 56.
27 Ibid., p. 80.
28 Quoted in P.J.O. Taylor (1996), p. 53.

29 Sen, pp. 147, 159.
30 Taylor (1992), p. 51.
31 Ibid., p. 81.
32 Ibid., pp. 6, 1.
33 Edward Thompson, p. 46.
34 Ibid., p. 48.
33 Sir J.W. Kaye, *A History of the Sepoy War*, II, quoted Edward Thompson, p. 70.
36 Coopland, p. 33.
37 Oldenburg, p. 3.
38 Ibid., p. 11.
39 Layard Papers, BL Add. MS 47,469, f. 98.
40 Hibbert (1978), p. 223.
41 JCP, *Siege of Lucknow by a Member of the Garrison*, p. 30.
42 Iddesleigh Papers, BL Add. MS 37,151, f. 6.
43 Hibbert (1978), p. 350.
44 Ibid., p. 424.
45 Quoted ibid., p. 244.
46 Ibid., p. 353.
47 *Illustrated London News*, 26 September 1857, No. 880, xxi, p. 305.
48 *Illustrated London News*, 9 October 1858.
49 Canning, quoted in Maclagan, p. 140.
50 Hibbert (1978), p. 366.
51 Ibid., p. 386.
52 Mitford, p. 195.
53 Ibid.
54 R.J. Moore, pp. 72–3.
55 Lawrence James (1997), p. 297.
56 Quoted ibid., p. 267.
57 Stokes (1986), p. 3.

16 Clinging to Life

1 Irvine, p. 64.
2. *DNB*, 1912–1921, p. 547.
3 Quoted Bowlby, p. 74.
4 Janet Browne, p. 447.
5 Irvine, p. 68.
6 Darwin (1951), p. 353.
7 A.N. Wilson (1999), pp. 250–1.

8   Bowlby, p. 355.

9   White & Gribbin, p. 30. See also Gribbin, *In the Beginning*.

10 Gilbert, p. 320.

11 Darwin (1951), p. 73.

12 Dennett, p. 21.

13 Darwin (1951), p. 72.

14 J.R. Moore, p. 82.

15 Behe, p. 22.

16 Hoppen, p. 200.

17 See Barzun, *Darwin, Marx, Wagner. Critique of a Heritage.*

18 Fulford (1949), p. 234.

19 Ibid., p. 242.

20 A.C. Benson (1899), I, p. 137.

21 Fulford (1949), p. 235.

22 Quoted ibid., p. 238.

23 Fulford, ed. (1964), p. 14.

24 Fulford (1949), p. 238.

25 Eyck, *The Prince Consort. A Political Biography*, especially pp. 66–100.

26 Ibid., p. 72.

27 Ibid., p. 89.

28 Ibid., p. 94.

29 Longford (1964), p. 398.

30 For a statement of the case on both sides see *The Schleswig-Holstein Question and its Place in History by Max Müller and the Danish View of the Schleswig-Holstein Question by Dr A.D. Jörgensen*, Spottiswoode & Co., 1897.

31 Longford (1964), p. 400.

32 Hoppen, p. 166.

33 Fulford (1949), p. 261.

34 Hibbert (2000), p. 185.

35 Fulford, ed. (1964), p. 144.

36 Ibid., p. 245.

37 ('I am sure you will be benefitting all Germany if they could be generally introduced') ibid., p. 171.

38 Ibid., p. 138.

39 Ibid.

40 Weintraub, p. 402.

41 Ibid., p. 407.

42 Ibid., p. 392.

43   Hibbert (2000), p. 279.
44   Fulford, ed. (1964), p. 171.
45   Hibbert (2000), p. 281.

17 *The Beloved* – Uncle Tom – and Governor Eyre

 1   Seton-Watson, p. 346.
 2   R. Arthur Arnold, p. 11.
 3   Ibid., p. 38.
 4   Alan Barker, p. 43.
 5   Pound, p. 210.
 6   Morley (1912), II, p. 77.
 7   Adams, II, pp. 304–5.
 8   Robert Blake (1966), p. 419.
 9   Gwendolen Cecil, I, p. 159.
10   Brian Jenkins, I, p. 70.
11   Arnold (1895), I, p. 245.
12   Brian Jenkins, II, p. 394.
13   Ibid., I, p. 235.
14   R. Arthur Arnold, p. 109.
15   Brian Jenkins, I, p. 761.
16   Ibid., p. 167.
17   *The Times*, 1 March 1862.
18   Craven, pp. 49–50.
19   Adams, II, p. 109.
20   Morley (1912), II, p. 55.
21   Robert Blake (1966), p. 579.
22   Morley (1912), II, p. 75.
23   Quoted Zinn, p. 205.
24   Devereux Jones, p. 275.
25   Sainsbury, pp. 196–7.
26   Marsh (1999), p. 292.
27   Brian Jenkins, II, p. 395.
28   Quoted ibid., p. 157.
29   Quoted Wilkinson Latham (1979), p. 91.
30   R. Arthur Arnold, p. 63.
31   Banks, p. 48.
32   Burn, p. 92.
33   H. Oliver Horne, p. 201.
34   See Banks, p. 35.
35   Ibid., p. 88.

36 Burn, p. 17.
37 Banks, p. 91.
38 Monypenny & Buckle, IV, p. 331.
39 *The Lancet*, 13 April 1861, p. 372.
40 *The Lancet*, 10 August 1861.
41 *The Times*, 15 April 1861.
42 *Illustrated London News*, 24 August 1861.
43 *Annual Register*, 1861, p. 149.
44 Gladstone Papers. BL Add. MS 44,407.
45 Semmel, p. 31.
46 Olivier, p. 125.
47 Charles Tennyson, p. 359.

18 The World of School

 1 *DNB*, XVIII, p. 947, John Andrew Hamilton, 'Edward George Geoffrey Smith Stanley, Fourteenth Earl of Derby'.
 2 Fulford, ed. (1977), p. 53.
 3 *DNB*, 1901–11, p. 559, Sidney James Law, Edward VII.
 4 Prothero, II, p. 69.
 5 *DNB*, 1901–11, p. 548.
 6 Hughes, *Tom Brown's Schooldays*, p. 164.
 7 Ibid., p. 175.
 8 Prothero, I, p. 47.
 9 *The Proceedings at the Installation of the Rt Hon. the Earl of Derby, Chancellor of the University of Oxford*, 1853.
10 *Debrett's Peerage and Baronetage* (1995), p. 1098.
11 Prothero, I, p. 41.
12 Ibid., I, p. 57.
13 Stanley (1900), p. 91.
14 Ibid., p. 124.
15 Stanley (1844), II, p. 285.
16 Ibid., II, p. 341.
17 Hoppen, p. 312.
18 Mack, p. 23.
19 Armytage, p. 128.
20 Hansard, 183, pp. 1925, 1926. 5 June 1866.
21 Mack, p. 32.
22 Kirk, p. 20.
23 Kirk, p. 24.
24 Ibid., p. 39.

25 Nick Davies, p. 102.

26 Armytage, p. 130.

27 Scrimgeour, p. 72.

28 Charlotte Brontë, *Jane Eyre*, p. 63.

29 Ibid., p. 32.

30 *DNB*, 1901–1911, Elizabeth Lee, 'Dorothea Beale', p. 116.

31 *The Public School Year Book*, Swann Sonnenschein & Co., 1889.

32 Scott, in Simon & Bradley (ed.), p. 49. Stanley (1844), I, p. 88.

33 Hughes, *Tom Brown's Schooldays*, p. 260.

34 Ibid.

35 Gathorne-Hardy, p. 87.

36 Hilton (2000), p. 135.

37 Scott, in Simon & Bradley, ed., p. 35.

38 *DNB*, XX, p. 160, 'Charles John Vaughan', by Charles Edwyn Vaughan.

39 Gibson (1978), p. 101.

40 Stanmore Papers, BL Add. MS 35,226.

19 Charles Kingsley and *The Water-Babies*

1 Rose G. Kingsley's introduction to *The Water-Babies*, 1908 edition, Dent.

2 Stanley (1875), p. 12.

3 *DNB*, Leslie Stephen, 'Charles Kingsley', p. 175.

4 Robert Bernard Martin, p. 258.

5 Chitty, p. 240.

6 Kingsley (1863), p. 88.

7 Ibid., p. 155.

8 Kendall, p. 137.

9 Ibid., p. 249.

10 Chitty, p. 57.

11 Ibid., p. 75.

12 Ibid., p. 88.

13 Ibid., p. 91.

14 Ibid., p. 58.

15 *Nunnery Life in the Church of England*, quoted in Walsh, p. 41.

16 Ibid., p. 117.

17 Ibid., p. 177.

18 Chitty, p. 236.

19 J.H. Newman (1955), p. 28.

20 Ward, II, p. 25.

21 Kendall, p. 135.
22 Ibid., p. 145.

20 *Goblin Market* and the Cause

1 Anthony Powell, *A Writer's Notebook*, 2000, p. 97.
2 *Macmillan's Magazine*, September 1863, p. 399.
3 Ray Strachey, pp. 35–40.
4 Quoted ibid., pp. 74–5.
5 Elizabeth Garrett, p. 6.
6 Butler, p. 82.
7 Dorothy Porter, in *Companion Encyclopedia of the History of Medicine*, p. 1248.
8 Kiple *et al.*, ed., p. 1268.
9 Elizabeth Garrett, p. 8.
10 Finnegan, p. 3.
11 Walkowitz, p. 70.
12 Soper, p. xii.
13 *The Lancet*, 6 July 1861.
14 Ibid., 17 July 1861.
15 Ray Strachey, p. 107.
16 Ibid.
17 Desmond MacCarthy, p. 78.
18 Weintraub, p. 103.
19 Marsh (1994), p. 220.
20 Ibid, p. 237.
21 Marsh (1999), p. 220.
22 Ibid., p. 241.
23 Ibid., pp. 374–9.
24 Davidoff, *Journal of Social History*, vol. 7, 1984, p. 410.
25 Ibid., p. 412.
26 Hudson, *Munby*, p. 18.
27 Ibid., p. 15.

21 Wonderland

1 Hudson, p. 3.
2 Hacking, p. 36.
3 Maurice, I, p. 226.
4 Gernsheim (1975), p. 35.
5 Bartram, p. 134.
6 Cohen, p. 170.

7   Quoted ibid., p. 101.
8   Ibid., p. 102.
9   Ruskin, *Praeterita*, III.31, *Work*, vol. 35, p. 471.
10 Ibid., p. 525.
11 Hilton (2000), p. 286.
12 Ibid., p. 140.
13 Ibid., p. 196.
14 Cohen, p. 77.
15 Ibid., p. 145.

22 Some Deaths

1   Brian Doyle (1968), p. 254.
2   Woodward, p. 179.
3   Robert Blake (1985), p. 98.
4   Ibid., p. 100.
5   Froude (1884), II, p. 312.
6   Ibid., II, p. 328.
7   Ibid., II, p. 13.
8   G.K. Chesterton, Introduction to *Great Expectations*, Everyman, 1907.
9   Gatrell, p. 295.
10 Quoted ibid., p. 296.
11 Ibid., p. 60.
12 Quoted ibid., p. 75.
13 Pope-Hennessy (1970), p. 329.
14 Ibid., p. 328.
15 *Annual Register*, 1868, p. 17.
16 Woodward, p. 360.
17 *Annual Register*, 1868, p. 64.
18 Ibid., p. 65.

23 Gladstone's First Premiership

1   See Milner, pp. 200–1.
2   Horne, p. 505. See also Michael Howard, *The Franco-Prussian War*.
3   Froude (1884), II, p. 427.
4   Ibid., p. 428.
5   Ensor, p. 6.
6   Fulford (1977), pp. 16–17.
7   Fulford (1971), p. 317.

8 Quoted by Swartz, p. 24.
9 Carlyle, XXX, p. 49.
10 Ibid., p. 58.
11 Ibid., p. 59.
12 Matthew, p. 133.
13 Shannon (1999), p. 62.
14 Ibid., p. 144.
15 Monypenny & Buckle, IV, p. 467.
16 Pattison, p. 114.
17 Faber, p. 134.
18 Ashton, p. 190.
19 Mander, p. 200.
20 Gordon, pp. 219–22.
21 Callender & Hinsley, p. 242. See also James P. Baxter, *The Introduction of the Ironclad Warship*, Harvard University Press, 1933; Stanley Sandler, 'The Emergence of the Modern Capital Ship', *Technology and Culture*, 11, no. 3 (1970), pp. 576–95; and Beeler, *British Naval Policy in the Gladstone–Disraeli Era, 1866–1880*.
22 Beeler, p. 76.
23 Matthew, pp. 168–74.
24 Cardwell, quoted in Spiers, p. 14.
25 Ibid., p. 4.
26 Morley (1912), II, p. 41.
27 Matthew, p. 235.
28 Spiers, pp. 2–24.
29 Skelley, p. 297.
30 Ibid., p. 290.
31 Ibid, p. 193.
32 Spiers, pp. 14 & 17.
33 Spiers, p. 15.
34 Jenkins, *Gladstone*, p. 344.
35 *DNB*, 1901–1911, Colonel E.M. Lloyd, 'George William Frederick Charles, Second Duke of Cambridge', p. 94.
36 Robert Blake (1993), p. 15.
37 G.M. Trevelyan, p. 69.
38 Shannon (1999), p. 92.
39 A.N. Wilson (1999), p. 198.
40 Hilton (2000), p. 409.
41 Ibid., p. 369.

42 Ibid., p. 368.
43 Ibid., p. 397.
44 Morley (1912), II, p. 226.
45 E.G. West, pp. 130–5.
46 Hinchliff, p. 97.

24 The Side of the Angels

1   Menzies, p. 34.
2   Lowder, p. 37.
3   Ibid., p. 38.
4   Menzies, p. 10.
5   Ibid., p. 33.
6   Ibid., p. 183.
7   Lowder, p. 33.
8   *DNB*, XIX, W.H. Fremantle, 'Archibald Campbell Tait', p. 292.
9   Lowder, pp. 214–15.
10 Monypenny & Buckle, V, p. 58.
11 Chadwick (1966), p. 321.
12 Fulford, ed. (1971), p. 161.
13 Fulford, ed. (1964), p. 173.
14 J.C. Colquhoun, ed., *Church Association Lectures*, Hatchards, 1869; Francis Close D.D. (Dean of Carlisle), *Anglican Ritualism Traced to Judaism*, Hatchards, 1873; W. Martin Brown, *The Pathway to Rome or Ritualism and its Remedy*, James Nisbet & Co, no date, etc.
15 E.A.T., p. 137.
16 Menzies, p. 17.
17 Quoted in *The Church Times*, 18 December 1987.
18 Chadwick (1970), pp. 318–19.
19 Hasler, p. 293.
20 *Oxford Dictionary of the Christian Church*, ed. F.L. Cross & E.P. Livingstone (1974), p. 1681.
21 Hasler, p. 130.
22 See Plummer, *Conversations with Dr Döllinger 1870–1890*.
23 Shannon (1999), p. 149.
24 J.H. Newman (1875), p. 66.
25 Darwin (1874), p. 619.
26 Ibid., p. 1171.
27 Ibid., p. 719.
28 Ibid., p. 45.

29 Alfred Tennyson, 'Locksley Hall, Sixty Years After', ed. Ricks, p. 1362.
30 C.A. Russell, p. 290.
31 Darwin (1874), p. 200.
32 *DNB*, XXI, Francis Legge, 'Samuel Wilberforce', p. 204.
33 J.R. Moore, pp. 60–65.
34 Clark, p. 171.
35 Ibid., p. 215.
36 Hoppen, p. 459.
37 Robert Blake (1966), p. 504.
38 Ibid., p. 505
39 Disraeli (1975), p. 26.
40 Ibid., p. 345.
41 Robert Blake (1966), p. 520.
42 Froude (1890), pp. 217–18.
43 Sykes (1982), p. 205.
44 Crook (1981), pp. 143–5.
45 Sykes (1985), pp. 289–91.
46 Ibid., pp. 272–3.
47 Girouard (1979), pp. 305ff.

25 The End of Lord Beaconsfield

1 Adelman, pp. 25–6.
2 Ensor, p. 26.
3 *Dizzi-Ben-Dizzi, or the Orphan of Baghdad … A lampoon on Benjamin Disraeli*, Weldon & Co., 1878, p. 50.
4 Politicus, p. 4.
5 Ibid., p. 12.
6 Ibid., p. 16.
7 Ibid.
8 Robert Blake (1966), p. 543.
9 Ibid., p. 542.
10 Ensor, p. 38, Robert Blake (1966), p. 582.
11 Rothschild, p. 47.
12 Ibid., p. 47.
13 Ibid., p. 46.
14 Robert Blake (1966), p. 581.
15 Ibid.
16 Ibid., p. 584.
17 Ibid., p. 587.

18   Pamuk, p. 123.

19   Ibid., p. 83.

20   Kasaba, p. 47.

21   Ibid., p. 48.

22   Mansel, p. 17.

23   Shaw & Shaw, pp. 77–9; 666–73.

24   Ibid., p. 158.

25   Macfie, pp. 35–6.

26   A.J.P. Taylor (1954), p. 233.

27   Shaw & Shaw, p. 162. William Miller, p. 366, places the Bulgarian casualties at 12,000 that summer.

28   Monypenny & Buckle, VI, p. 61.

29   Matthew (1995), p. 33.

30   Quoted in Shannon (1963) p. 47.

31   Quoted ibid., p. 66.

32   Quoted ibid., p. 65.

33   William Miller, p. 376.

34   Hoppen, p. 627.

35   Quoted in Robert Blake (1966), p. 613.

36   Dodwell, V, p. 418.

37   Headlam, p. 483.

38   Froude (1890), p. 251; Headlam, pp. 486–9.

39   Quoted in Robert Blake (1966), p. 610.

40   Quoted ibid., p. 612.

41   Quoted ibid., p. 607.

42   Cowen & Cowen, pp. xi ff.

43   Robert Blake (1966), p. 679.

44   Ibid., p. 646.

45   Ibid., p. 649.

46   Ibid., p. 566.

47   Quoted ibid., p. 712.

48   Morley (1912), II, p. 451.

49   *The Times*, 21 January 1905, p. 16.

50   *The Times*, 23 January 1905, p. 9.

51   Robert Blake (1966), p. 750.

52   Ibid., p. 765.

53   Haight, p. 533.

54   Ibid., pp. 470–3.

26 *The Devils* – Wagner – Dostoyevsky – Gilbert and Sullivan

1. Vamplew, p. 35.
2. Mason, p. 15.
3. Ibid., p. 25.
4. Ibid., p. 30.
5. Ibid., pp. 138–9.
6. Adburgham, p. 208 *passim*.
7. *Daniel Deronda*, Bk 1, xxiii, p. 218.
8. Ionides, p. 11. Frau Chariclea Dannreuther, the pianist's wife, was Luke Ionides's sister.
9. Haight, pp. 500–1.
10. Ionides, p. 29.
11. Haight, p. 457.
12. Henry James (1960), p. 42.
13. Quoted in James Pope-Hennessy, p. 338.
14. Bernard Shaw, p. 133.
15. Ibid., p. 1.
16. Ibid., p. 10.
17. Mosley (1956), p. 11.
18. MacCarthy, p. 372.
19. Bernard Shaw, p. 22.
20. Leatherbarrow, p. 10.
21. Seton-Watson, p. 428.
22. Leatherbarrow, p. 184.
23. Kermode, Introduction to *The Way We Live Now*, p. xxii.
24. Payne (1967), p. 384.
25. *The Complete Annotated Gilbert and Sullivan*, Oxford, 1996, ed. Ian Bradley, p. 43. Hereafter, Bradley.
26. Ibid., p. 3.
27. Jacobs, pp. 71, 106.
28. Bradley, p. 17.
29. Ibid., p. 639.
30. Ibid., p. 39.
31. Ibid., p. 111.
32. Ibid., p. 215.
33. Rothman & Rothman, ed. p. 29.
34. Olsen, p. 149.
35. Bradley, p. 485.
36. Merrill, p. 130.
37. Bradley, p. 137.

38 Padfield, p. 158.
39 Beeler, pp. 261, 266, 267.

27 Country Parishes – Kilvert – Barnes – Hardy
1 *Kilvert's Diary*, ed. Plomer, 1944, p. 119. Hereafter, Plomer.
2 Ibid., p. 318.
3 Ibid., p. 159.
4 Cobden, quoted in Woodward, p. 87.
5 Chambers & Mingay, p. 162.
6 Ensor, p. 115.
7 Ibid., p. 116.
8 Chambers & Mingay, p. 179.
9 Orwin & Whetham, p. 244.
10 Chambers & Mingay, p. 178.
11 Ibid., p. 182.
12 Ibid., p. 185.
13 Hoppen, p. 21.
14 Orwin & Whetham, p. 207.
15 George Edwards MP, *From Crow-Scaring to Westminster*, 1992, p. 22.
16 Orwin & Whetham, p. 216.
17 Chambers & Mingay, p. 188.
18 Ensor, p. 117.
19 Quoted in Chedzoy, p. 175. The photograph adjoins p. 87.
20 Hardy, 'The Last Signal (Oct. 11 1886). A Memory of William Barnes', quoted in Chedzoy, p. 177.
21 Stewart, p. 21.
22 The examples are quoted in Stewart, p. 26.
23 Seymour-Smith (1994), p. 20.
24 Ibid., p. 136.
25 Stewart, p. 45.
26 Seymour-Smith (1994), p. 422.
27 Stewart, p. 22.
28 Ibid.

28 A Crazy Decade
1 Jeffrey, p. 71.
2 All in Ford & Harrison.
3 See Calder-Marshall; Bertouch.
4 Russell & Goldfarb, p. 128.

5   Glendinning, ed., p. 10. See also Patterson, *100 Years of Spirit Photography*.
6   Dostoyevsky, II.i, p. 3.

29 The Plight of the Poor

1   Tolstoy, p. 15.
2   By his friend and English translator Aylmer Maude – ibid. (preface), p. ix.
3   See p. 394, where it is clear that Tolstoy is chiefly thinking of a back-to-the-land solution to the problems of urban poverty.
4   Henry James (1991), p. 124.
5   Ibid., p. viii.
6   Quoted Kynaston, p. 72.
7   Nightingale Papers LXIII, BL Add. MS 45,801.
8   Quoted Saville (1988), p. 9
9   Sims, p. 107.
10 Jay, p. 77.
11 Hoppen, pp. 70, 606.
12 Kynaston, p. 121.
13 MacCarthy, p. 466.
14 Ibid., p. 467.
15 Quoted Kynaston, p. 124.
16 Hoppen, p. 89, quoting Floud, Wachter & Gregory, *Height, Health, History*, Cambridge, 1990, p. 305.
17 Quoted MacCarthy, p. 466.
18 Ensor, p. 88.
19 Arnstein, p. 28.
20 Hoppen, p. 325.
21 Arnstein, p. 287.
22 Anne Taylor, p. 161.
23 Foster (1989), p. 428.

30 The Rise of Parnell

1   Neary, pp. 11, 12.
2   Ibid., pp. 11, 15.
3   Purcell, p. 13.
4   Andrew Roberts, p. 471.
5   Neary, p. 9.
6   Quoted Foster (1989), p. 386.
7   Kee, p. 370.

8   Ensor, p. 72.
9   Kee, pp. 75, 383.
10 Conor Cruise O'Brien, quoting Garrish (Chamberlain's biographer), p. 192.
11 Matthew, p. 231.
12 Ibid., p. 184.
13 Roy Jenkins (1958), p. 239.
14 Ibid., p. 356.
15 Ibid., p. 352.

31 The Fourth Estate – Gordon of Khartoum – The Maiden Tribute of Babylon

1   Hoppen, p. 633. See also Brown, *Victorian News and Newspapers*, and Alan J. Lee, *The Origins of the Popular Press 1855–1914*.
2   Roy Jenkins (1958), p. 139.
3   Ibid., p. 141.
4   F.W. Hirst in *DNB*, 1922–1930, p. 618.
5   Kingsmill, p. 174.
6   Quoted ibid., p. 171.
7   Ensor, p. 51.
8   *DNB*, XXII, p. 507.
9   Quoted in Pierce Jones, p. 17.
10 Farwell, p. 257.
11 Ibid., pp. 266–7.
12 Hoppen, p. 661; Farwell, p. 269.
13 Ensor, p. 80.
14 Hoppen, p. 660.
15 Zetland, p. 89.
16 Allen, p. 183.
17 Ibid., p. 189.
18 Ibid., p. 194.
19 Ibid., p. 195.
20 The idea began with W.S. Blunt in *Gordon at Khartoum* and is repeated in *Eminent Victorians* by Lytton Strachey and *After Puritanism* by Hugh Kingsmill.
21 Allen, p. 213.
22 Ibid., p. 215.
23 Ibid., p. 271.
24 See Douglas Johnson, 'The Death of Gordon. A Victorian Myth'.

25 Farwell, p. 294.
26 Lytton Strachey (1993), p. 301.
27 Carpenter, p. 22.
28 *Enthusiasm, Confidence, Determination*, p. 12.
29 Quoted *DNB*, VIII, p. 176.
30 Quoted Allen, p. 314.
31 Ensor, p. 83.
32 Fawcett & Turner, p. 40.
33 Butler, p. 99.
34 Ibid., p. 112.
35 Williamson, p. 80.
36 Pierce Jones, p. 26.
37 Quoted in Roy Jenkins (1958), p. 240.
38 Ibid., p. 241.
39 Coates, p. 11.
40 Ibid., p. 23.
41 Ibid., p. 50.
42 Ibid., pp. 112–13.

32 Politics of the Late 1880s
1   Roy Jenkins (1995), p. 560.
2   Hoppen, p. 265.
3   Ibid.
4   Quoted in A.N. Wilson (1984), p. 177.
5   Cannadine, pp. 184–5.
6   Crook (1999), p. 17.
7   Ensor, p. 87.
8   Beatrice Webb, *Diaries*, ed. MacKenzie & MacKenzie, I, p. 109.
9   Ibid., p. 265.
10 Ibid., p. 250.
11 Winston S. Churchill, p. 72.
12 Foster (1981), p. 270.
13 Ibid., p. 127.
14 Ibid., pp. 218–19.

33 Into Africa
1   *Annual Register*, 1885, p. 60.
2   Dawson, p. 441.
3   Ibid., p. 359.
4   Sundkler & Steed, p. 1007.

5   Pakenham (1991), p. xxiii.
6   Andrew Roberts, p. 518.
7   Hoppen, p. 664.
8   Pakenham (1991), p. 25.
9   Ibid., p. 17.
10 Ibid., p. 13.
11 Ibid., p. 22.
12 Ensor, p. 192.
13 Lawrence James (1994), p. 288.
14 Ibid.
15 Pakenham (1991), p. 413.
16 Stanmore Papers, BL Add. MS 49,242, f. 131, 132, 135, 123.
17 Pakenham (1991), p. 426.
18 Lugard, II, p. 355.
19 Lugard Diaries, III, p. 60.
20 Ibid., p. 61.
21 Ibid., p. 59.
22 Pakenham (1991), p. 429.
23 Lawrence James (1994), pp. 515–16.
24 Dilke Papers, BL Add. MS 43,915, f. 133.
25 Horrut, p. 36.

34 Kipling's India
1   Kubicek, pp. 247–58.
2   Field, 'Internal Combustion Engines', p. 164.
3   Field, 'Mechanical Road Vehicles', p. 427.
4   Mackechnie Jarvis, p. 217.
5   S.B. Hamilton, pp. 478–9.
6   Ibid., p. 476.
7   McLuhan, p. 90.
8   McGrath, p. 293.
9   Kipling (1990), 'McAndrew's Hymn', p. 98.
10 Ibid., p. 103.
11 Ibid., p. 338.
12 Raine, p. 1.
13 Kipling (1990), 'The White Man's Burden', p. 261.
14 Quoted Wurgaft, pp. 15–16.
15 Kipling (1890), p. 175.
16 Ibid., p. 177.
17 Ibid., p. 16.

18 Ibid., p. 23.
19 Smith & Spear, pp. 848–9.
20 Sarkar (1983), pp. 20–3.
21 Quoted ibid., p. 21.
22 R.J. Moore, p. 431.
23 Ibid., p. 432.
24 Quoted ibid., p. 435.
25 Quoted Metcalf, pp. 150–1.
26 R.J. Moore, p. 428.

35 Jubilee – and the Munshi
1   Fabb, p. 58.
2   Chapman & Raben. No pagination.
3   Ibid.
4   Andrew Roberts, p. 612.
5   Van der Kiste (1986), pp. 109–11.
6   Van der Kiste (1999), p. 36.
7   Ponsonby, p. 95.
8   Ibid.
9   Michaela Reid, p. 132.
10 Ibid., p. 128.
11 Ponsonby, pp. 13–15.
12 Longford (1961), p. 676.

36 The Dock Strike
1   Andrew Roberts, p. 462.
2   Mackenzie & Mackenzie, ed., *The Diary of Beatrice Webb*, vol. 1, p. 58.
3   Ibid., p. 150.
4   Andrew Roberts, p. 470.
5   Fiona MacCarthy, pp. 566–74; Mackail, p. 201; Ensor, pp. 180–1.
6   MacCarthy, p. 570.
7   Anne Taylor, p. 196.
8   Ibid., p. 197.
9   Quoted in Fiona MacCarthy, p. 573.
10 Webb, vol. 1, p. 290.
11 Anne Taylor, pp. 205–10.
12 H. Llewellyn Smith & Vaughan Nash, *The Story of the Dockers' Strike Told by Two East Londoners*, 1889, pp. 22–3.

13 Kent, p. 8.
14 Ibid., p. 13.
15 Ibid., p. 20.
16 Illustrated in Terry McCarthy, ed., facing p. 97.
17 Morris Papers, BL Add. MS 45,345, f. 49.
18 Roy Jenkins (1958), p. 109.
19 Purcell, II, p. 552.
20 Ibid., p. 314.
21 Vidler (1964), p. 158.
22 Purcell, II, p. 619.
23 Vidler (1964), pp. 120–5.
23 Sir Shane Leslie (1921) sees strong parallels between the encyclical and the cardinal's letter to Liège the previous year; others, such as Edward Norman (1984), dismiss the notion as unlikely.
25 Leslie, p. 165.
26 Chadwick (1970), p. 355.
27 Leo XIII, *Rerum novarum*, p. 21.
28 *Lectures on the Principles of Political Obligation*, in Green, II, p. 209.
29 Ibid., p. 215.
30 *Prolegomena to Ethics*, in Green, II, p. 19.
31 For all the above, see Tyler (1997), Richter (1983) and Greengarten (1981).

37 The Scarlet Thread of Murder

 1 A.E. Wilson, p. 212.
 2 Ibid., p. 201.
 3 Farson, p. 14.
 4 Ibid., p. 121.
 5 Ibid., p. 75.
 6 Brandreth, p. 47.
 7 Ibid., p. 55.
 8 Ibid., p. 46.
 9 Ibid., p. 31.
10 Farson, p. 31.
11 Ian Gibson, *The Erotomaniac*.
12 *TLS*, 9 March 2001.
13 A sensible account of the various theories is found in Wilson & Odell.
14 Quoted in Cullen, p. 151.

15 Doyle, *A Study in Scarlet*, ed. Edwards, p. xlvii.
16 Ibid., pp. 18–19.
17 Ibid., p. 19.
18 Ibid., p. 13.
19 Quoted in Doyle, *The Sign of Four*, ed. Lancelyn Green, p. xxxiii.
20 Ibid., p. 11.
21 Doyle, *A Study in Scarlet*, ed. Edwards, p. 40.

38 The Fall of Parnell
1   Jean Balfour, p. 85.
2   Ibid., p. 166.
3   Andrew Roberts, p. 445.
4   Quoted ibid., p. 261.
5   Quoted ibid., p. 258.
6   Quoted ibid., p. 123.
7   Conor Cruise O'Brien, p. 207.
8   Andrew Roberts, p. 447.
9   Ensor, p. 180.
10 Andrew Roberts, pp. 447–8.
11 Conor Cruise O'Brien, p. 232.
12 Morley (1912), III, p. 321.
13 Conor Cruise O'Brien, p. 279.
14 Ibid., p. 346.
15 Morley (1912), III, p. 340.
16 Ibid., p. 341.
17 Foster (1989), p. 424.
18 W.B. Yeats, 'Parnell's Funeral', p. 320.

39 The Victorian Way of Death
1   Litten, p. 170.
2   Ibid., p. 141. A photograph of 'the funeral of a London shopkeeper' seems to be half filling one side of Regent's Park.
3   Weinreb & Hibbert, p. 949.
4   Gladstone Papers, BL Add. MS 44,790, f. 177.
5   Quoted in A.N. Wilson (1984), p. 72.
6   Purcell, II, p. 801.
7   Croker Papers, Bodleian Library, MS Eng. Lett. 2.367, f. 215.
8   Fulford (1933), p. 294.
9   Weinreb & Hibbert, p. 131.
10 Stephen White, 'A burning issue', *New Law Journal*, 10 August

1990, p. 1145.

11 Curl, p. 142.

12 Jupp, p. 16.

13 Stephen White, p. 1157.

14 *The Law Journal*, June 1884, p. 141.

15 Ibid.

16 Curl, p. 70.

40 Appearance and Reality

1 Anne Taylor, pp. 60–1.

2 'The best female public speaker I ever heard' – eyewitness to author. Beatrice Webb said Annie's voice was 'neither female nor male but "the voice of a beautiful soul"' – Anne Taylor, p. 55.

3 Ibid., p. 199.

4 Ibid., p. 59.

5 Ibid., p. 240.

6 Ibid., p. 257.

7 Washington, p. 53.

8 Ibid., pp. 58–9.

9 Ibid., p. 67.

10 Yeats (1955), p. 173.

11 Ibid., p. 89.

12 'Meru', Yeats (1993), p. 289.

13 Yeats (1955), p. 167.

14 Ibid., p. 302.

15 Yeats, ed. (1936), p. 1.

16 Yeats (1955), p. 130.

17 Raby, p. 20.

18 Ibid., p. 105.

19 Quoted Mackay, p. 15.

20 Balfour, pp. 30–1.

21 Keefe & Keefe, p. 50.

22 Mackay, p. 14.

23 'Meditations in Time of Civil War', Yeats (1993), p. 201.

24 Abdy & Gere, p. 54.

25 Egremont (1977), pp. 185–6.

26 Yeats (1955), p. 165.

27 Ibid., p. 165.

28 Ellmann, p. 91.

29 Brian Roberts (1981), p. 156.

30 Quoted in Ellmann, p. 302.
31 Hyde, ed., p. 85.
32 Ellmann, p. 412.
33 Brian Roberts (1981), pp. 185–6.
34 Hart-Davis, ed., p. 423.
35 Hyde, ed., p. 65.
36 Ibid., p. 133.
37 Ibid., p. 129.
38 Ibid., p. 94.
39 A.E. Housman, *Collected Poems and Selected Prose*, ed. Christopher Ricks (1988), p. 67.
40 Ibid., p. 141.
41 Ibid., p. 109.
42 Ibid., p. 172.
43 A.C. Benson (1899), II, p. 77.
44 Masters, p. 21.
45 Askwith, p. 191.
46 Henry James, Preface to *The Turn of the Screw*, ed. Rahv (1989), p. 242.
47 Bradley, *Appearance and Reality*, p. 229.
48 Monk, p. 131.
49 Eames, p. 42.
50 Monk, p. 120.
51 See Quinton, pp. 200–1.
52 Bertrand Russell (1967), p. 1.

41 Utopia: The Decline of the Aristocracy
1 W.S. Gilbert, *Utopia Limited*, in Bradley, ed. (1996), p. 1079.
2 Ibid., p. 1077.
3 Ensor, p. 222.
4 Webb (1979), p. 381.
5 Ibid., p. 389.
6 Jowitt & Taylor, ed., p. 11.
7 Ibid., p. 12.
8 Ibid., p. 11.
9 Jowitt & Taylor, p. 108.
10 Morgan, p. 73. Most of the above is drawn from this source (pp. 55, 62, 71, 96).
11 F.M.L. Thompson, pp. 293–7.
12 Southgate, pp. 322–3.

13 Holland, II, p. 240.
14 Gervas Huxley, p. 177.
15 Ibid., p. 237.
16 Ibid., p. 178.
17 Cannadine, p. 182, quoting Lewis Namier, *Skyscrapers and Other Essays* (1931).
18 F.M.L. Thompson, p. 115.
19 Christie, p. 165.
20 Ensor, p. 203.
21 Ibid., p. 238.
22 Christie, p. 154.
23 Cannadine (1992), p. 35, quoting A. Lambert, *Unquiet Souls; The Indian Summer of the British Aristocracy* (1984).
24 Alfred Tennyson, 'Locksley Hall', ed. Ricks, p. 692.
25 Alfred Tennyson, 'Locksley Hall Sixty Years After', ibid., p. 1369.
26 Ibid., p. 1368.
27 S.J. Taylor, p. 31.
28 Ibid., p. 39.
29 Ibid., pp. 189–90.
30 Keynes (1933), pp. 36, 37.
31 Grigg (1973), pp. 124–5.
32 Mosley (1968), p. 244.
33 Grigg (1973), p. 44.

42 The Boer War
 1 Jeal, p. 102.
 2 Ibid., p. 100.
 3 Rotberg, pp. 404–5.
 4 Philip Warner, *Kitchener. The Man behind the Legend.*
 5 See Trevor Royle, *The Kitchener Enigma.*
 6 Rotberg, p. 64.
 7 Rowse, p. 219.
 8 Seymour-Smith (1989), *passim.*
 9 Angus Wilson, p. 17.
10 Kipling (1930), p. 271.
11 Ibid., pp. 1–2.
12 Brogan, p. 19.
13 A.C. Benson (1905), p. 164.
14 Haggard, p. 244.
15 Ibid., p. 265.

16 Pocock (1993), p. 245.
17 Lycett, p. 293.
18 *DNB*, 1901–11, p. 184.
19 Rotberg, p. 285.
20 Ibid., p. 102.
21 Chesterton (1913), p. 181.
22 Webb (1948), p. 190.
23 Pakenham (1991), p. 1.
24 See 'What Imperialism Means' by J.H. Muirhead in *The British Idealists*, ed. David Boucher, Cambridge University Press, 1997.
25 'We seem to have conquered and peopled half the world in a fit of absence of mind.' J.R. Seeley, *Expansion of England*, 1883.
26 Warner, p. 82.
27 Ibid., p. 98.
28 Quoted in Ensor, p. 211. Unless otherwise stated my chief sources for the following pages are Ensor, Le May, Pakenham and Emanoel Lee.
29 Emanoel Lee, p. 49.
30 Ibid., p. 57.
31 Quoted Le May, p. 107.
32 Ibid., p. 153.
33 Ensor, p. 251.
34 Ibid., p. 252.
35 Ibid., p. 254.
36 Le May, p. 119.
37 Warner, p. 124.
38 Ibid., p. 135.
39 See Emanoel Lee, p. 181.

43 *Vale*
 1 Arthur Bigge, writing to Arthur Ponsonby. Ponsonby Papers, MS Eng. Hist. c651, f. 43.
 2 Ibid., f.144b.
 3 Quoted by Hibbert (2000), p. 490.
 4 Ponsonby, p. 26.
 5 Ponsonby Papers, f. 207.
 6 Michaela Reid, p. 201.
 7 Ponsonby, p. 26.
 8 Ibid., p. 25.
 9 Michaela Reid, p. 215.

10 Ibid., p. 215.
11 Ibid.
12 Ibid., p. 217.
13 Grigg (1978), p. 270.
14 Ibid., p. 51.
15 Charles Dickens (1855), pp. 10–11.
16 Longford (1964), p. 562.
17 Packard, p. 241.

Bibliography

Abdy, Jane, and Charlotte Gere. *The Souls.* London: Sidgwick & Jackson, 1984.

Adams, Ephraim Douglass. *Great Britain and the American Civil War.* 2 vols. London: Longmans, Green, and Co., 1925.

Adburgham, Alison. *Shops and Shopping 1800–1914. Where and in What Manner the Well-Dressed Englishwoman Bought Her Clothes.* London: Barrie & Jenkins, 1989.

Adelman, Paul. *Gladstone, Disraeli and Later Victorian Politics.* 3rd ed. London: 1997.

Adrian, Arthur A. *Mark Lemon: First Editor of "Punch."* London: Oxford University Press, 1966.

Alcott, William A. *The Use of Tobacco, Its Physical, Intelectual, and Moral Effects on the Human System.* Boston: G. W. Light, 1844.

Alexander, Lt. Col. W. Gordon. *Recollection of a Highland Subaltern.* London: Edward Arnold, 1898.

Alexander, Ziggi, and Audrey Denjee. *Mary Seacole.* London: Brent Library Service, 1982.

Alford, B. W. E. *W. D. and H. O. Wills and the Development of the U.K. Tobacco Industry, 1786–1965.* London: Methuen, 1973.

Allan, Mea. *Palgrave of Arabia.* London: Macmillan, 1972.

Allen, Bernard M. *Gordon and the Sudan.* London: Macmillan and Co., 1931.

Altick, R. D. *The Shows of London.* Cambridge, Mass.: Belknap Press, 1978.

Amor, Anne Clark. *William Holman Hunt: The True Pre-Raphaelite.* London: Constable, 1989.

Anderson, Olive. *A Liberal State at War: English Politics and Economics during the Crimean War.* New York: St. Martin's Press, 1967.

Anderson, Robert. *The Potteries Martyrs.* Stoke-on-Trent: 1993.

Anstruther, Ian. *The Knight and the Umbrella.* London: Geoffrey Bles, 1963.

———. *The Scandal of Andover Workhouse.* London: Bles, 1984.

Apperson, G. L. *The Social History of Smoking.* London: M. Secker, 1914.

Appleyard, John. *Henry Francis Lyte M.A.* London: 1939.

Archives of the Independent Labour Party (held at London School of Economics). London: Harvester Press, 1984.

Armytage, W. H. G. *Four Hundred Years of English Education.* Cambridge: Cambridge University Press, 1970.

Arnold, Matthew. *Letters of Matthew Arnold: Collected and Arranged by George W. E. Russell.* 2 vols. London: 1895.

Arnould, Joseph. *Memorial Lines on Sir Robert Peel.* London: 1850.

Arnstein, Walter L. *The Bradlaugh Case: Atheism, Sex, and Politics among the Late Victorians.* 1965. Reprint. Columbia: University of Missouri Press, 1983.

Ascoli, David. *The Queen's Police: The Origins and Development of the Metropolitan Police, 1829–1979.* London: H. Hamilton, 1979.

Ashton, Rosemary. *G.H. Lewes: A Life.* Oxford: Clarendon Press, 1991.

Askwith, Betty. *Two Victorian Families.* London: Chatto and Windus, 1973.

Auerbach, J. A. *The Great Exhibition of 1851: A Nation on Display.* New Haven, Conn.: Yale University Press, 1999.

Ayres, Harry Morgan. *Carroll's Alice.* New York: Columbia University Press, 1936.

Bagehot, Walter. *The Works of Walter Bagehot, with Memoirs by R.H. Hutton.* Edited by Forest Morgan. 5 vols. Hartford, Conn.: Travelers Insurance Co., 1891.

Baker, Diane. *Workhouses in the Potteries.* Stoke-on-Trent: 1977.

Balfour, Arthur James. *The Foundations of Belief.* London: 1895.

Balfour, Jean. "The Palm Sunday Case." In *Proceedings of the Society for Psychical Research.* Vol. 52. February 1960: part 189.

Ball, Charles. *The History of the Indian Mutiny.* 2 vols. London: 1858.

Banks, J.A. *Prosperity and Parenthood: A Study of Family Planning Among the Victorian Middle Classes.* London: Routledge & Paul, 1954.

Barbay, James. *The Crimean War.* Harmondsworth: Puffin Books, 1975.

Barker, Alan. *The Civil War in America.* Garden City, N. Y.: Doubleday, 1961.

Barker, Felix. *Highgate Cemetery: Victorian Valhalla.* London: Friends of Highgate Cemetery, 1984.

Barrow, Logie, and Ian Bullock. *Democratic Ideas and the British Labour Movement 1880–1914.* Cambridge: Cambridge University Press, 1996.

Bartram, Michael. *La Fotografia e i preraffaelliti (The Pre-Raphaelite Camera).* Città del Vasto: Manifestazioni rossettiane 1982–1983 [1983]. London: Weidenfeld and Nicolson, 1985.

Barzun, Jacques. *Darwin, Marx, Wagner: Critique of a Heritage.* Boston: Little, Brown & Company, 1941.

Bassalle, George, et al., eds. *Victorian Science: A Self-Portrait from the Presidential Addresses of the British Association for the Advancement of Science.* New York: Doubleday, 1970.

Battiscombe, Georgina. *Shaftesbury: A Biography of the Seventh Earl.* London: Constable, 1974.

————. *Christina Rossetti: A Divided Life.* London: Constable, 1981.

Beale, Dorothea. *Work and Play in Girls' Schools.* London: 1898.

Beaver, Patrick. *The Crystal Palace: The Great Exhibition.* New Haven, Conn.: Yale University Press, 1999.

Beeler, John F. *British Naval Policy in the Gladstone-Disraeli Era, 1866–1880.* Stanford, Calif.: Stanford University Press, 1997.

Begg, Paul. *Jack the Ripper: The Uncensored Facts.* London: Robson Books, 1989.

Behe, Michael J. *Darwin's Black Box.* New York: Free Press, 1996.

Bell, H. C. F. *Life of Palmerston.* London: 1936.

Benians, E.A., et al., eds. *The Cambridge History of the British Empire.* Vol 3, *The Empire-Commonwealth, 1870–1919.* Cambridge: Cambridge University Press, 1959.

Bennett, J. A. *Science at the Great Exhibition*. London: 1983.

Benson, A. C. *The Life of Edward White Benson*. 2 vols. London: 1899.

————. *The Upton Letters*. London: Smith, Elder, & Co., 1905.

Benson, A. C., and Viscount Esher, eds. *The Letters of Queen Victoria*. 3 vols. London: J. Murray, 1907.

Benson, E. F. *Mother*. London: Hodder and Stoughton, 1925.

Berkeley, George. *The Works of George Berkeley*. Edited by T. E. Jessop. 6 vols. London: 1953.

Bertouch, Beatrice de, Baroness. *The Life of Father Ignatius, OSB: The Monk of Llanthony*. London: 1904.

Bethell, Leslie. *The Abolition of the Brazilian Slave Trade: Britain, Brazil and the Slave Trade Question, 1807–1869*. Cambridge: Cambridge University Press, 1970.

Bird, Anthony. *Paxton's Palace*. London: Cassell, 1976.

Blackburn, Douglas. *Thought-Reading, or Modern Mysteries Explained: Being Chapters on Thought-Reading, Occultism, Mesmerism, etc.* London: 1884.

Blake, Laurel, Aled Jones, and Lionel Madden, eds. *Investigating Victorian Journalism*. New York: St. Martin's Press, 1990.

Blake, Robert. *Disraeli*. London: Eyre & Spottiswoode, 1966.

————. "Disraeli and Gladstone: The Leslie Stephen Lecture, 1969." Cambridge: Cambridge University Press, 1969.

————. *The Conservative Party from Peel to Thatcher*. London: Methuen, 1985.

————. *Gladstone, Disraeli and Queen Victoria*. (Romanes Lecture.) Oxford: Oxford University Press, 1993.

Bowlby, John. *Charles Darwin: A New Life*. New York: W. W. Norton, 1991.

Bowness, Alan, ed. *The Pre-Raphaelites*. London: London Catalog of Tate Gallery Exhibition, 1989.

Bradley, F. H. *Appearance and Reality*. Oxford: Clarendon Press, 1893.

Bradley, Ian, ed., *The Complete Annotated Gilbert and Sullivan*. Oxford: Oxford University Press, 1996.

Brandreth, Gyles. *The Funniest Man on Earth: The Story of Dan Leno*. London: Hamilton, 1977.

Bridges, Yseult. *Saint—With Red Hands?* London: Jarrolds, 1954.

Brogan, Hugh. *Mowgli's Sons: Kipling and Baden-Powell's Scouts*. London: J. Cape, 1987.

Brontë, Charlotte. *Jane Eyre* (1847). Edited by Margaret Smith. Oxford: Oxford University Press, 1976.

Brooke-Shepherd, Gordon. *Royal Sunset: The Dynasties of Europe and the Great War*. Garden City, N.Y.: Doubleday, 1987.

Brown, Lucy. *Victorian News and Newspapers*. Oxford: Clarendon Press, 1985.

Browne, Douglas. *The Rise of Scotland Yard*. London: Harrap, 1956.

Browne, Janet. *Charles Darwin*. Vol. 1, *Voyaging*. London: J. Cape, 1995.

Browning, Robert. *Poetical Works, 1833–1864*. Edited by Ian Jack. Oxford: Oxford University Press, 1970.

Burn, William Lawrence. *The Age of Equipoise: A Study of the Mid-Victorian Generation*. London: 1964. New York: W. W. Norton, 1964.

Burne, Maj. Gen. Sir Owen Tudor, KCSI. *Clyde and Strathnairn*. Oxford: Clarendon Press, 1891.

Burne-Jones, Georgiana. *Memorials of Edward Burne-Jones*. 2 vols. London: Macmillan, 1904.

Butler, A. S. G. *Portrait of Josephine Butler*. London: Faber and Faber, 1954.

Butt, John, and Kathleen Tillotson,. *Dickens at Work*. London: Methuen, 1957.

Calder-Marshall, Arthur. *The Enthusiast: An Enquiry into the Life, Beliefs and Character of the Rev. Joseph Leycester Lyne, alias Father Ignatius*. London: Faber and Faber, 1962.

Callender, Sir Geoffrey, and F. H. Hinsley. *The Naval Side of British History*. London: Christophers, 1952.

Campbell, Sir George. *Memories of My Indian Career*. London: 1893.

Cannadine, David. *The Decline and Fall of the British Aristocracy*. Revised. New Haven, Conn.: Yale University Press, 1992.

Carlyle, Thomas. *The Complete Works*. 30 vols. New York: Charles Scribner, 1904.

Carpenter, William Boyd. *The Venture of Faith*. London: 1898.

———. *The Hidden Life: A Sermon Preached January 29th, 1899. In Commemoration of the Death of General Gordon*. London: 1899.

Carroll, Lewis. *The Annotated Alice*. Edited, with introduction and notes by Martin Gardner. New York: W. W. Norton, 1999.

Cecil, David. *Melbourne*. London: Constable, 1965.

Cecil, Lady Gwendolen. *Life of Robert Marquis of Salisbury*. 2 vols. London: Hodder & Stoughton, 1921.

Chadwick, Owen. *The Victorian Church*. 2 vols. London: A & C Black, 1966, 1970.

Chambers, J. D., and G. E. Mingay. *The Agricultural Revolution, 1750–1880*. London: Batsford, 1966.

Chambers, Robert. *Vestiges of the Natural History of Creation* (1844). Edited with introduction by James A. Secord. Chicago: Chicago University Press, 1994.

Chapman, Caroline, and Paul Raben. *Debrett's Queen Victoria's Jubilee, 1887 and 1897*. London: Debrett's Peerage Ltd., 1977.

Chaudhuri, S. B. "Civil Disturbances During the British Rule in India, 1757–1857." In *Bombay Governor Records: Source Material for a History of the Freedom Movement in India*. Vol. 1, *1818–1885*. Bombay: 1957.

———. *Theories of the Indian Mutiny (1857–9)*. Calcutta, India: The World Press Private, 1965.

Chedzoy, Alan. *William Barnes—A Life of the Dorset Poet*. London: 1985.

Chesney, Kellow. *Crimean War Reader*. London: F. Muller, 1960.

Chesterton, G. K. *Robert Browning*. London: Macmillan, 1903.

———. *G. F. Watts*. London: Duckworth, 1904.

————. *The Victorian Age in Literature*. London: Williams and Norgate, 1913.

Chinn, Carl. *Better Betting with a Decent Feller: Bookmaking, Betting and the British Working Class, 1750–1990*. New York: Harvester Wheatsheaf, 1991.

Chitty, Susan. *The Beast and the Monk: A Life of Charles Kingsley*. London: Mason/Charter, 1975.

Christie, O. F. *The Transition to Democracy, 1867–1914*. London: G. Routledge & Sons, 1934.

Churchill, Peregrine, and Julian Mitchell, eds. *Jennie: Lady Randolph Churchill, a Portrait with Letters*. London: Collins, 1974.

Churchill, Winston S. *My Early Life* (1930). London: 1989.

Clapham, J. H. *The Early Railway Age 1820–1850*. Cambridge: Cambridge University Presss, 1950.

Clark, Rufus W. *The Work of God in Great Britain under Messrs. Moody and Sanky 1873 to 1875*. New York: Harper & Brothers, 1875.

Clarke, A. K. *A History of the Cheltenham Ladies' College, 1853–1953*. London: Faber and Faber, 1954.

Coates, James. *Has W. T. Stead Returned?* London: L. N. Fowler & Co., 1913.

Cocks, Barnett. *Mid-Victorian Masterpiece*. London: Hutchinson, 1977.

Cohen, Morton. *Lewis Carroll: A Biography*. London: Random House, 1995.

Compton, Piers. *The Last Days of General Gordon*. London: Hale, 1974.

Coopland, Mrs. *A Lady's Escape from Gwalior*. London: 1859.

Cotton Minchin, J. G. *Our Public Schools: Their Influence on English History*. London: S. Sonnenschein & Co., 1901.

Cowen, Anne and Roger. *Victorian Jews Through British Eyes*. Oxford: Oxford University Press, 1986.

Cowling, Maurice. *1867 Disraeli, Gladstone and Revolution: The Passing of the Second Reform Bill*. Cambridge: Cambridge University Press, 1967.

————. *Religion and Public Debate in Modern England*. Cambridge: Cambridge University Press, 1980.

Crabtree, Adam. *From Mesmer to Freud: Magnetic Sleep and the Roots of Psychological Healing*. New Haven, Conn.: Yale University Press, 1993.

Craven, Margaret J. *The Effects of the American Civil War Upon the People of Bolton, Lancashire*. Lancashire, England: Chorley Day Training College, 1964.

Creer, Edwin. *A Popular Treatise on Human Hair*. London: 1865.

Crook, J. Mordaunt. *William Burges and the High Victorian Dream*. London: J. Murray, 1981.

————. *The Rise of the Nouveaux Riches*. London: J. Murray, 1999.

Crosby, Travis L. *The Two Mr. Gladstones*. New Haven, Conn.: Yale University Press, 1997.

Crowther, M. A. *The Workhouse System 1834–1929: The History of an English Social Institution*. London: Batsford Academic and Educational, 1981.

Cullen, Tom. *Autumn of Terror*. London: Bodley Head, 1965.

Cunningham, Suzanne. *Philosophy and the Darwinian Legacy*. Rochester, N.Y.: University of Rochester Press, 1996.

Curl, James Stevens. *A Celebration of Death: An Introduction to Some of the Buildings, Monuments and Settings of Funerary Architecture in the Western European Tradition.* London: Constable, 1980.

Darnton, Robert. *Mesmerism and the End of the Enlightenment in France.* Cambridge, Mass.: Harvard University Press, 1968.

Darwin, Charles, *The Origin of Species* (1859). London: Oxford University Press, 1951.

——. *The Descent of Man* (1871). London: J. Murray, 1874.

——. *The Voyage of a Naturalist.* London: Oxford University Press, 1905.

Davidoff, L. "Mastered for Life." In *Journal of Social History.* Vol. 7. 1984: 406–28.

Davies, Nick. *The School Report: Why Britain's Schools Are Failing.* London: Vintage, 2000.

Davis, Mary. *Comrade or Brother? A History of the British Labour Movement, 1789–1951.* Boulder, Colo.: Pluto Press.

Dawson, E. C. *James Hannington: First Bishop of East Equatorial Africa.* London: Seeley & Co., 1887.

de Beer, Gavin. Introduction to *Vestiges of Creation,* by Robert Chambers. Leicester and New York: 1969.

Dennett, Daniel C. *Darwin's Dangerous Idea.* New York: Simon & Schuster, 1995.

Depositions Taken at Cawnpore Under the Direction of Lieut.-Colonel [sic] G. W. Williams. Allahabad: 1858.

Desmond, Adrian, and James Moore. *Darwin.* London: Michael Joseph, 1991. New York: W. W. Norton, 1995.

Dickens, Charles. *Speech of Charles Dickens Esq. Delivered at the Meeting of the Administrative Reform Association at the Theatre Royal, Drury Lane, June 27, 1855.* London: 1855.

——. *The Works of Charles Dickens.* London: 1880.

——. *The Speeches of Charles Dickens,* Edited by K. J. Fielding. Atlantic Highlands, N.J.: Humanities Press International, 1988.

Disraeli, Benjamin. *Coningsby* (1844). Oxford: Oxford University Press, 1982.

——. *Sybil* (1845). Harmondsworth: Penguin, 1980.

——. *Lothair* (1870). Edited by Vernon Bogdanor. Oxford: Oxford University Press, 1975.

Dods, John Boree. *Six Lectures on the Philosophy of Mesmerism.* New York: Fowlers & Wells, 1854.

Dodwell, H. H., ed. *The Cambridge History of India.* Vol. 5, *British India 1497–1858.* Cambridge: Cambridge University Press, 1929.

—— ed. *The Cambridge History of India.* Vol. 6, *The Indian Empire 1858–1918.* Cambridge: Cambridge University Press, 1932.

Dostoyevsky, F. M. *The Devils.* Translated and edited by Michael R. Katz. Oxford: Oxford University Press, 1992.

Doyle, Arthur Conan. *The Sign of Four.* Edited by Roger Lancelyn Green. Oxford: Oxford University Press, 1993.

————. *A Study in Scarlet.* Edited by Owen Dudley Edwards. Oxford: Oxford University Press, 1993.

Doyle, Brian. *The Who's Who of Children's Literature.* Oxford: Oxford University Press, 1968.

Draper, Hal. *The Annotated Communist Manifesto.* Berkeley, Calif.: Center for Socialist History, 1984.

Dudley, Edwards Owen. *Macaulay.* New York: St. Martin's Press, 1988.

Dunbar, Janet. *The Early Victorian Woman: Some Aspects of Her Life.* London: Harrap, 1953.

Dunn, Waldo Hilary. *James Anthony Froude: A Biography (1818–1856).* Oxford: Oxford University Press, 1961.

————. *James Anthony Froude: A Biography (1857–1894).* Oxford: Oxford University Press, 1963.

Durant, John. *Darwinism and Divinity.* Oxford: B. Blackwell, 1985.

Durey, Michael. *The Return of the Plague: British Society and the Cholera 1831–2.* Dublin: Gill and Macmillan, 1979.

Dutt, Romesh (Ramesachandra Datta). *India in the Victorian Age.* London: K. Paul, Trench, Trübner, & Co., 1904.

Eames, Elizabeth Ramsden. *Bertrand Russell's Dialogue with his Contemporaries.* Carbondale and Edwardsville, Ill.: Southern Illinois University Press, 1969.

Edwardes, Michael. *A History of India.* Revised ed. London: New English Library, 1967.

Edwards, Owen Dudley. *Macaulay.* New York: St. Martin's Press, 1988.

Egremont, Max. *The Cousins: The Friendship, Opinions, and Activities of Wilfred Seawen Blunt and George Wyndham.* London: Collins, 1977.

————. *Balfour: A Life of Arthur James Balfour.* London: Collins, 1980.

Ehrlich, Paul. *The Population Bomb.* New York: Ballantine Books, 1968.

Eliot, George. *Daniel Deronda* (1877). Edited with introduction by Graham Handley. Oxford: Oxford University Press, 1988.

Ellmann, Richard. *Oscar Wilde.* London: H. Hamilton, 1987.

Encyclopedia Britannica. 13th ed. London and New York: 1926.

Ensor, R. C. K., *England, 1870–1914.* Oxford: Clarendon Press, 1936.

Erikson, Paul A. *Phrenology and Physical Anthropology: The George Combe Connection.* Nova Scotia: St. Mary's University, 1979.

Esher, Viscount. *The Girlhood of Queen Victoria.* London: J. Murray, 1912.

Evans, Martin Marix. *Encyclopedia of the Boer War.* Santa Barbara, Calif.: ABC-CLIO, 2000.

Eyck, Frank. *The Prince Consort: A Political Biography.* London: Chatto and Windus, 1959.

Fabb, John. *The Victorian and Edwardian Army from Old Photographs.* London: B. T. Batsford, 1975.

Faber, Geoffrey. *Oxford Apostles.* London: Faber and Faber, 1933.

Farrar, Frederic W. *St. Winifred's, or, the World of School.* New York: W. L. Allison Co., 1897.

Farson, Daniel. *Marie Lloyd and Music Hall.* London: Tom Stacey, 1972.

Farwell, Byron. *Queen Victoria's Little Wars.* London: Allen Lane, 1973. New York: W. W. Norton, 1985.

Fawcett, Millicent G. and E. M. Turner. *Josephine Butler.* London: Association for Moral & Social Hygiene, 1927.

Field, D. C. "Internal Combustion Engines," In *A History of Technology.* Vol. 5, *The Late Nineteenth Century.* Edited by Charles Joseph Singer et al. Oxford: Clarendon Press, 1958. Pp. 157–77.

———. "Mechanical Road Vehicles." In *A History of Technology.* Vol. 5, *The Late Nineteenth Century.* Edited by Charles Joseph Singer et al. Oxford: Clarendon Press, 1958. Pp. 414–38.

Finer, S. E. *The Life and Times of Sir Edwin Chadwick.* London: Methuen, 1952.

Finnegan, F. *Poverty and Prostitution.* Cambridge: Cambridge University Press, 1979.

Fitzroy, Almeric. *History of the Travellers' Club.* London: Travellers' Club, 1927.

Forbes, Duncan. "James Mill and India." In *Cambridge Journal.* Vol. 5. London: 1951–52.

Ford, Colin, and Brian Harrison. *A Hundred Years Ago: Britain in the 1880s in Words and Photographs.* Cambridge, Mass.: Harvard University Press, 1983.

Foster, R. F. *Lord Randolph Churchill: A Political Life.* Oxford: Clarendon Press, 1981.

———. *Modern Ireland 1600–1972.* New York: Penguin Books, 1989.

Froude, J. A. *The English in Ireland in the Eighteenth Century.* 3 vols. New York: Scribner, Armstrong, and Co.: 1873–74.

———. *The English in Ireland.* London: 1881.

———. *Thomas Carlyle: A History of the First Forty Years of his Life, 1795–1835.* 2 vols. London: Longmans, Green, and Co., 1882.

———. *Thomas Carlyle: A History of His Life in London, 1834–1881.* 2 vols. London: Longmans, Green., and Co., 1884.

———. *Lord Beaconsfield.* New York: Harper and Brothers, 1890.

Fulford, Roger. *Royal Dukes: The Father and Uncles of Queen Victoria.* London: Duckworth, 1933.

———. *The Prince Consort.* London: Macmillan, 1949.

Fulford, Roger, ed. *Dearest Child: Letters between Queen Victoria and the Crown Princess of Prussia, 1858–1861.* London: Evans Brothers, 1964.

———. ed., *Dearest Mama: Letters between Queen Victoria and the Crown Princess of Prussia, 1861–1864.* London: Evans Brothers, 1968.

———. ed., *Your Dear Letter: Private Correspondence of Queen Victoria and the Crown Princess of Prussia, 1865–1871.* New York: Scribner, 1971.

Fuller, Robert C. *Mesmerism and the American Cure of Souls.* Philadelphia, Pa.: University of Pennsylvannia Press, 1982.

Garrett, Elizabeth L.S.A. *An Enquiry into the Character of the Contagious Diseases Act.* Pamphlet, reprinted for the *Pall Mall Gazette.* London: 1870.

Garrett, Richard. *General Gordon.* London: Arthur Barker, 1974.

Gash, Norman. *Peel.* London: Longman, 1976.

———. *Politics in the Age of Peel.* 2nd ed. Hassocks, Sussex, England: Harvester Press, 1977. New York: W. W. Norton, 1971.

Gathorne-Hardy, Jonathan. *The Public School Phenomenon.* London: Penguin, 1979.

Gatrell, V. A. C. *The Hanging Tree: Execution and the English People, 1770–1868.* Oxford: Oxford University Press, 1994.

Gaunt, William. *The Pre-Raphaelite Tragedy* (1942). London: J. Cape, 1975.

Gernsheim, Helmut. *Julia Margaret Cameron.* London: Gordon Fraser, 1975.

———. Introduction to *Lewis Carroll, Victorian Photographer.* London: Thames and Hudson, 1980.

Gibson, Ian. *The English Vice: Beating, Sex, and Shame in Victorian England and After.* London: Duckworth, 1978.

———. *The Erotomaniac: The Secret Life of Henry Spencer Ashbee.* London: Faber and Faber, 2001.

Gilbert, Sir W. S. *The Savoy Operas.* London: Macmillan, 1926.

Girard, Louis, *Napoléon III.* Paris: Fayard, 1986.

Girouard, Mark. *Life in the English Country House.* New Haven, Conn.: Yale University Press, 1978.

———. *The Victorian Country House.* Revised. New Haven, Conn.: Yale University Press, 1979.

Gladstone, W. E., *The State in Its Relations with the Church.* London: 1838.

———. *The Church of England and Ritualism.* London: 1875.

———. *The Vatican Decrees in Their Bearing on Civil Allegiance.* New York: Harper, 1875.

Glendinning, Andrew, ed. *The Veil Lifted: Modern Developments in Spirit Photography.* London: 1894.

Glick, Thomas F., ed. *The Comparative Reception of Darwinism.* Chicago, Ill.: Chicago University Press, 1988.

Goodway, David. *London Chartism 1838–1848.* Cambridge: Cambridge University Press, 1982.

Goodwin, Jason. *Lords of the Horizons: A History of the Ottoman Empire.* New York: Henry Holt, 1999.

Gordon, Colin. *Beyond the Looking-Glass: Reflections of Alice and Her Family.* London: Hodder and Stoughton, 1982.

Gorham, D. *The Victorian Girl and the Feminine Ideal.* Bloomington, Ind.: Indiana Universtiy Press, 1982.

Graves, Richard Perceval. *A. E. Housman: The Scholar-Poet.* London: Routledge & K. Paul, 1979.

Gray, P. "Potatoes and Providence: British Government Responses to the Great Famine." In *Bullán: An Irish Studies Journal.* No. 1. London: 1994.

Green, Thomas Hill. *Works.* Edited by by R. L. Nettleship. 3 vols. London: Longmans, Green, and Co., 1885.

Greengarten, I. M., *Thomas Hill Green and the Development of Liberal-Democratic Thought*. Toronto: University of Toronto Press, 1981.

Gregorio, Mario A. D., and N. W. Gill, eds., *Charles Darwin's Marginalia*. Vol. I. New York: Garland, 1990.

Greville, Charles Cavendish Folke. *The Greville Memoirs, 1814–1860*. Edited by Lytton Strachey and Roger Fulford. 8 vols. London: Macmillan and Co., 1938.

Gribbin, John. *In the Beginning: The Birth of the Living Universe*. London: Penguin Books, 1993.

Griffin, Nicholas. *Russell's Idealist Apprenticeship*. Oxford: Clarendon Press, 1991.

Grigg, John. *The Young Lloyd George*. London: Eyre Methuen, 1973.

———. *Lloyd George: The People's Champion 1902–11*. London: Eyre Methuen, 1978.

Groom, Helen M. I. *With Havelock from Allahabad to Lucknow, 1857*. London: S. Low, Marston, 1894.

Gurd, Eric. *Prologue to Cigarettes*. London: issued by the Cartophilic Society of Great Britain, n.d.

Hacking, Juliet. *Princes of Victorian Bohemia*. Prestel, Munich, London, New York: National Portrait Gallery, 2000.

Haggard, H. Rider. *King Solomon's Mines* (1885). London: Macdonald, 1965.

Haight, Gordon S. *George Eliot*. Oxford: Clarendon Press, 1968.

Halévy, Elie. *The Growth of Philosophical Radicalism*. Boston: Little, Brown & Company, 1955.

Hamburger, Joseph. *Macaulay and the Whig Tradition*. Chicago, Ill.: University of Chicago Press, 1976.

Hamilton, James. *Turner: A Life*. London: 1977; Sceptre, 1998.

Hamilton, S. B. "Building Materials and Techniques." In *A History of Technology*. Vol. 5, *The Late Nineteenth Century*. Edited by Charles Joseph Singer et al. Oxford: Clarendon Press, 1958. Pp. 466–99.

Hamlin, Christopher. *Public Health and Social Justice in the Age of Chadwick, Britain 1850–1854*. Cambridge: Cambridge University Press, 1998.

Hannary, John. *The Camera Goes to War—Photographs from the Crimean War*. Edinburgh: Scottish Arts Council, 1974.

Hare, Augustus. *The Story of My Life*. 6 vols. London: 1885.

Hart-Davis, Rupert, ed. *The Letters of Oscar Wilde*. New York: Harcourt Brace, 1962.

Hasler, August Bernhard. *How the Pope Became Infallible*. New York: Doubleday & Co., 1981.

Hastings, Maurice. *Parliament House*. London: Architectural Press, 1950.

Hastings, Selina. *Evelyn Waugh: A Biography*. London: Sinclair-Stevenson, 1994.

Hayter, Althea. *A Sultry Month*. London: Faber and Faber, 1965.

Headlam, Cecil. "The Failure of Confederation, 1871–1881" (ch. 18). In *The Cambridge History of the British Empire*. Vol. 8, *South Africa, Rhodesia and the High Commission Territories*. Edited by Eric Walker. Cambridge: Cambridge University Press, 1963.

Hennessy, Alastair. "Penrhyn Castle." In *History Today*. Vol. 45(1). London: January 1995.

Hennessy, James Pope. *Anthony Trollope*. London: J. Cape, 1971.

Henty, G. A. *Through the Sikh War: A Tale of the Conquest of the Punjawb.* London: Blackie, 1894.

Heuman, Gad J. *Between Black and White: Race, Politics and the Free Coloreds in Jamaica 1792–1865.* Westport, Conn.: Greenwood Press.

Hewison, Robert, et al. *Ruskin, Turner and the Pre-Raphaelites.* London: Tate Gallery, 2000.

Hewitt, Margaret. *Wives and Mothers in Victorian Industry.* London: Rockcliff, 1958.

Hibbert, Christopher. *The Great Mutiny: India, 1857.* London: Allen Lane, 1978.

———. *Queen Victoria: A Personal History.* New York: Basic Books, 2000.

Hilton, Tim. *John Ruskin, The Early Years, 1819–1859.* New Haven, Conn.: Yale University Press, 1985.

———. *John Ruskin: The Later Years.* New Haven, Conn.: Yale University Press, 2000.

Hinchliff, Peter. *Benjamin Jowett and the Christian Religion.* Oxford: Clarendon Press, 1987.

Hinton, James. *Labour and Socialism.* Brighton, England: Wheatsheaf Books, 1983.

Hirst, F. W. "Viscount Morley of Blackburn." In *Dictionary of National Biography, 1922–1930.* London: Oxford University Press, n.d.

Holland, Bernard C. B. *The Life of Spencer Compton, Eighth Duke of Devonshire.* 2 vols. London: Longmans, Green, and Co., 1911.

Holloway, Richard. "Holiness Plus Laughter." In *Church Times*. 18 December 1987.

Hopkins, Pat, and Heather Dugmore. *The Boy: Baden-Powell and the Siege of Mafeking.* Rivonia, SA: Zebra Press, 1999.

Hoppen, K. Theodore. *Ireland Since 1800.* 2nd ed. New York: Longman, 1998.

———. *The Mid-Victorian Generation 1846–1886.* Oxford: Oxford University Press, 1998.

Horn, Pamela. *Pleasures and Pastimes in Victorian Britain.* Stroud: Sutton Publishing, 1999.

Horne, Alistair. *The Fall of Paris: The Siege and the Commune 1870–71.* New York: St. Martin's Press, 1966.

Horne, H. Oliver. *A History of Savings Banks.* London and New York: Oxford University Press, 1947.

Horrut, Claude. *Frederic Lugard et la Pensée Coloniale Britannique.* Bordeaux: Institut d'études politiques de Bordeaux, 1970.

House, Humphry. *The Dickens World.* London: Oxford University Press, 1941.

Housman, A. E. *A. E. Housman: Collected Poems and Selected Prose.* Edited by Christopher Ricks. London: Penguin, 1988.

Howard, Michael. *The Franco-Prussian War.* New York: Macmillan, 1961.

Hudson, Derek. *Munby, Man of Two Worlds*. London: J. Murray, 1972.

Hughes, Thomas. *Tom Brown's Schooldays* (1856). London: 1948.

Humpherys, Anne [*sic*]. *Travels into the Poor Man's Country: The Work of Henry Mayhew*. Athens, Ga.: University of Georgia, 1977.

Hunt, Diana Holman. *My Grandfather: His Wives and Loves*. London: H. Hamilton (1969), 1987. New York: W. W. Norton, 1969.

Hunt, Peter, ed. *Children's Literature: An Illustrated History*. Oxford: Oxford University Press, 1995.

Hunter Blair, the Right Rev. Sir David, Bt OSB. *John Patrick, Third Marquess of Bute K.T. (1847–1900)*. London: J. Murray, 1921.

Huntley, Eric. *Two Lives: Florence Nightingale and Mary Seacole*. London: Bogle L'Ouverture, 1993.

Huxley, Gervas. *Victorian Duke: The Life of Hugh Lupus Grosvenor, First Duke of Westminster*. Oxford: Oxford University Press, 1967.

Huxley, Julian Sorell. "Alfred Russel Wallace." In *Dictionary of National Biography, 1912–1921*. London: 1927.

Hyde, H. Montgomery, ed. *The Trials of Oscar Wilde*. London: William Hodge & Co., 1948.

Hylton, Peter. *Russell, Idealism and the Emergence of Analytic Philosophy*. Oxford: Clarendon Press, 1990.

Iliffe, John. *Africans: The History of a Continent*. Cambridge: Cambridge University Press, 1995.

Inglis, Hon. Julia Selina. *The Siege of Lucknow: A Diary*. London: James R. Osgood, McIlvane & Co., 1892.

Ionides, Luke. *Memories*. Paris: James R. Osgood, 1925.

Irvine, William. *Apes, Angels, and Victorians*. New York: McGraw-Hill, 1955.

Irvine, William, and Park Honan. *The Book, the Ring and the Poet*. London: Bodley Head, 1975.

Jacobs, Arthur. *Arthur Sullivan: A Victorian Musician*. Oxford: Oxford University Press, 1984.

Jamaica Addresses to His Excellency Edward John Eyre, Esquire, 1865. Kingston, Jamaica: M. De Cordova & Co. Printers, 1966.

James, David, Tony Jowitt, and Keith Laybourn, eds. *The Centennial History of the Independent Labour Party*. London: Ryburn Academic Publishing, 1993.

James, Henry. *English Hours*. Edited by A. L. Lowe. New York: Orion Press, 1960.

———. *The Princess Casamassima*. Introduction by Bernard Richards. London: Everyman's Library, 1991.

James, Lawrence. *Crimea 1854–56: The War with Russia from Contemporary Photographs*. New York: Van Nostrand Reinhold, 1981.

———. *The Rise and Fall of the British Empire*. London: Little, Brown & Co., 1994.

———. *Raj: The Making and Unmaking of British India*. New York: St. Martin's Press, 1998.

Jardine, N., J. A. Secord, and G. C. Sperry, eds. *Cultures of Natural History.* Cambridge: Cambridge University Press, 1996.

Jay, Richard. *Joseph Chamberlain: A Political Study.* Oxford: Clarendon Press, 1981.

JCP. *Siege of Lucknow by a Member of the Garrison, 1858* (no place of pub. or author).

Jeal, Tim. *Baden-Powell.* London: Hutchinson, 1989.

Jeffrey, Jan. *Photography: A Concise History.* London: Oxford University Press, 1981.

Jenkins, Brian. *Britain and the War for the Union.* 2 vols. Montreal: McGill-Queen's University Press, 1974–80.

Jenkins, Roy. *Sir Charles Dilke: A Victorian Tragedy.* London: Collins, 1958.

———. *Gladstone.* London: Macmillan, 1995.

Jenkins, T. A. *Disraeli and Victorian Conservatism.* New York: St Martin's Press, 1996.

Johnson, Douglas J. "The Death of Gordon: A Victorian Myth." In *Journal of Imperial and Commonwealth History.* 10 (1982): 285–310.

Johnson, Rev. Paul. *An Epitome in Verse of the Life of His Royal Highness the Late Prince Consort.* London: 1883.

Johnston, Valerie J. *Diet in Workhouses and Prisons, 1835–1895.* New York: Garland, 1985.

Jones, Kathleen. *Learning Not to Be First.* Adlestrop: Windrush Press, 1991.

Jones, Wilbur Devereux. *Lord Derby and Victorian Conservatism.* Oxford: B. Blackwell, 1956.

Jowitt, J. A., and R. K. S. Taylor, eds. *Bradford 1890–1914: The Cradle of the Independent Labour Party.* London: Bradford Centre Occasional Paper, October 1908.

Jupp, Peter. *From Dust to Ashes: The Replacement of Burial by Cremation in England, 1846–1967.* London: Congregational Memorial Hall Trust, 1978.

Kamm, Josephine. *Rapiers and Battleaxes: The Women's Movement and Its Aftermath.* Foreword by Mary Stocks. London: Allen and Unwin, 1966.

Kaplan, Fred. *Dickens and Mesmerism: The Hidden Springs of Fiction.* Princeton, N.J.: Princeton University Press, 1975.

Kapp, Yvonne. *Eleanor Marx.* Vol. 1. London: Lawrence & Wishart (1972), 1979.

———. *Eleanor Marx.* Vol. 2. London: Lawrence & Wishart (1976), 1979.

Karlin, Daniel. *The Courtship of Robert Browning and Elizabeth Barrett.* Oxford: Oxford University Press, 1987.

Kasaba, Resat. *The Ottoman Empire and the World Economy.* Albany, N.Y.: State University of New York, 1988.

Kaye, Sir John William. *A History of the Sepoy War.* 4 vols. London: 1864–80.

Kee, Robert. *The Laurel and the Ivy: The Story of Charles Stuart Parnell and Irish Nationalism.* London: H. Hamilton, 1993.

Keefe, Robert and Janice A. *Walter Pater and the Gods of Disorder.* Athens, Ohio: Ohio University Press, 1988.

Kendall, Guy. *Charles Kingsley and His Ideas*. London: Hutchinson & Co., 1947.

Kent, William. *John Burns: Labour's Lost Leader*. London: Williams & Norgate, 1950.

Keppel-Jones, Arthur. *Rhodes and Rhodesia*. Pietermaritzburg: University of Natal Press, 1983

Kermode, Frank. Introduction to *The Way We Live Now*, by Anthony Trollope. London: Penguin, 1994.

Kerr, Donald A. *Peel, Priest and Politics*. Oxford: Clarendon Press, 1982.

Keynes, J. M. *A Tract on Monetary Reform*. London: 1923.

———. *Essays in Biography*. London: 1933. New York: W. W. Norton, 1963.

King, Peter. *The Viceroy's Fall: How Kitchener Destroyed Curzon*. London: Sidgwick & Jackson, 1986.

Kinglake, Alexander William. *The Invasion of the Crimea*. 8 vols. London: 1863–87.

Kingsley, Charles. *The Water-Babies*. London: 1863.

———. *Alton Locke*. Edited with an introduction by Elizabeth A. Cripps. Oxford: Oxford University Press, 1983.

———. *Yeast*. London: Dover, 1984.

Kingsmill, Hugh. *After Puritanism*. London: Duckworth, 1929.

Kiple, Kenneth F., et al., eds. *The Cambridge World History of Human Disease*. Cambridge: Cambridge University Press, 1993.

Kipling, Rudyard. *Plain Tales from the Hills*. New York: F. F. Lowell & Co., 1890.

———. *Stalky and Co*. London: Macmillan, 1899.

———. *The Complete Verse*. With a foreword by M. M. Kaye. London: Kyle Cathie, 1990.

Kirk, K. E. *The Story of the Woodard Schools*. Revised. Abingdon-on-Thames: Abbey Press, 1952.

Klein, Viola. *The Feminine Character: History of an Ideology*. London: K. Paul, Trench, Trüber, 1946.

Korg, Jacob. *Browning and Italy*. Athens, Ohio: Ohio University Press, 1983.

Kruger, Rayne. *Good-bye Dolly Gray: The Story of the Boer War*. London: Cassell, 1959.

Kubicek, Robert. "British Expansion, Empire and Technological Change." In *The Oxford History of the British Empire*. Edited by André Porter. Oxford: Oxford University Press, 1999.

Kurer, Oskar. *John Stuart Mill: The Politics of Progress*. New York: Garland, 1991.

Kynaston, David. *King Labour*. London: Allen and Unwin, 1976.

Lawrence, T. E. *The Seven Pillars of Wisdom*. New York: G. H. Doran, 1926.

Leatherbarrow, W. J., ed. *Dostoevskii and Britain*. Oxford, England, and Providence, R.I.: Berg, 1995.

Lee, Alan J. *The Origins of the Popular Press, 1855–1914*. London: Croom Helm, 1976.

Lee, Emanoel. *To The Bitter End: A Photographic History of the Boer War, 1899–1902*. Harmondsworth, Middlesex, England, and New York: Viking, 1985.

Lees-Milne, J. *The Bachelor-Duke: A Life of William Spencer Cavendish, 6th Duke of Devonshire*. London: J. Murray, 1991.

Leithbridge, Robert. Introduction to *La Débâcle*, by Emile Zola. Oxford: Oxford University Press, 2000.

Le May, G. H. L. *The Afrikaners*. Oxford: Oxford University Press, 1995.

Leo XIII. *Rerum Novarum: Encyclical Letter on the Condition of the Working Classes*. London: Catholic Truth Society, 1983.

Leslie, Shane. *Henry Edward Manning: His Life and Labours*. London: Burns, Oates & Washburn, 1921.

Letwin, Shirley Robin. *The Pursuit of Certainty*. Cambridge: Cambridge University Press, 1965.

Lightman, Bernard, ed. *Victorian Science in Context*. Chicago, Ill.: University of Chicago Press, 1997.

Lindsay, Jack. *William Morris: His Life and Work*. London: Constable, 1975.

————. *Turner: The Man and his Art*. New York: F. Watts, 1985.

Litten, Julian. *The English Way of Death: The Common Funeral Since 1450*. London: R. Hale, 1991.

Lloyd, Arthur D. D. Bishop (Suffragan) of Thetford. *Enthusiasm, Confidence, Determination*. London: 1897.

London Physician, A. *Emotional Goodness or Moody and Sankey Reviewed*. London: Dean & Son, 1875.

Longford, Elizabeth. *Victoria R.I*. London: Weidenfeld and Nicolson, 1964.

————. *Wellington, Pillar of State*. London: Weidenfeld and Nicolson, 1972.

Longhurst, Arthur E. T. *The Diet of the European Soldier in India with the Effects of "Tobacco Smoking" Upon the Animal Economy*. Calcutta, India: R. C. Lepage & Co., 1862.

Lovett, William. *Chartism: A New Organization of the People, Written in Warwick Gaol*. London: 1841.

Lowder, C. F. *Twenty-One Years in St. George's Mission*. London: 1877.

Lugard, F. D. *The Rise of Our East African Empire* (1893). Reprint. 2 vols. London: Cass, 1968.

Lycett, Andrew. *Rudyard Kipling*. London: Weidenfeld and Nicolson, 1999.

Lyell, Charles. *The Geological Evidences of the Antiquity of Man*. London: J. Murray 1863.

Macaulay, Thomas Babington. *Prose and Poetry*. Selected by G. M. Young. London: R. Hart-Davis, 1952.

MacCarthy, Desmond. *Criticism*. London: Putnam, 1932.

MacCarthy, Fiona. *William Morris: A Life for Our Time*. London: Faber and Faber, 1994.

MacDonald, Robert. *Sons of the Empire: The Frontier and the Boy Scout Movement 1890–1918*. Toronto, Buffalo, London: University of Toronto Press, 1993.

Macfie, A. L. *The Eastern Question*. London: Longman, 1989.

Mack, Edward C. *Public Schools and British Opinion Since 1860*. New York: Columbia University Press, 1941.

Mackail, J. W. *The Life of William Morris* (1899). Oxford: Oxford University Press, 1950.

Mackay, Ruddock F. *Balfour: Intellectual Statesman*. Oxford: Oxford University Press, 1985.

Mackechnie Jarvis, C. "The Generation of Electricity." In *A History of Technology*. Vol. 5, *The Late Nineteenth Century*. Edited by Charles Joseph Singer et al. Oxford: Clarendon Press, 1958. Pp. 177–208.

MacKenzie, Norman and Jeanne, eds. *The Diary of Beatrice Webb*. Vol. 1, *Glitter Around and Darkness Within*, 1982; vol. 2, *All the Good Things of Life*, 1983. London: Virago Press, in association with London School of Economics and Political Science.

Maclagan, Michael. *Clemency Canning*. London: Macmillan, 1962.

McLuhan, Herbert Marshall. *Understanding Media: The Extensions of Man*. New York: McGraw-Hill, 1964.

Majeed, Javed. *Ungoverned Imaginings: James Mill's History of India and Orientalism*. Oxford: Oxford University Press, 1992.

Malthus, Thomas. *An Essay on the Principle of Population* (1806). Edited by Geoffrey Gilbert. Oxford: Oxford University Press, 1993.

Manchester, Duke of. *Part of a Speech in the House of Lords Against the Maynooth Grant*. London: 1845.

Mander, John. *Our German Cousins: Anglo-German Relations in the 19th and 20th Centuries*. London: J. Murray, 1974.

Mansel, Philip. *Sultans in Splendour*. London: André Deutsch, 1988.

Manton, J. *Elizabeth Garrett Anderson*. New York: Dutton, 1965.

Marsh, Jan. *Pre-Raphaelite Sisterhood*. New York: St. Martin's Press, 1985.

———. *Pre-Raphaelite Women: Images of Femininity in Pre-Raphaelite Art*. New York: Harmony Books, 1988.

———. *The Legend of Elizabeth Siddal*. London: Quartet Books, 1989.

———. *Christina Rossetti: A Literary Biography*. London: J. Cape, 1994.

———. *Dante Gabriel Rossetti*. London: Weidenfeld and Nicolson, 1999.

Martin, B. Kingsley. *The Triumph of Lord Palmerston: A Study of Public Opinion in England before the Crimean War*. London: G. Allen and Unwin, 1924.

Martin, Robert Bernard. *The Dust of Combat*. London: Faber and Faber, 1959.

Martineau, Harriet. *Life in the Sick-Room: Essays by an Invalid*. London: E. Moxon, 1844.

———. *Letters from Ireland*. Reprinted from *The Daily News*. London: J. Chapman, 1852.

———. *The Factory Controversy*. London: 1855.

Martyn, Edith How, and Mary Breed. *The Birth Control Movement in England*. London: J. Bale, Sons & Daniellson, 1930.

Marx, Karl. *The Eastern Question*. Edited by E. M. and E. Aveling. London: 1897.

———. *The Story of the Life of Lord Palmerston*. London: 1899.

———. *The Russian Menace to Europe: A Collection of Articles etc.* Edited by Paul W. Blackstock. Glencoe, Ill.: Free Press, 1953.

————. *Capital.* 2 vols. in one. London: Everyman, 1957.

————. *The Eighteenth Brumaire of Louis Bonaparte.* Moscow and London: 1984.

Marx, Karl, and Friedrich Engels. *The Communist Manifesto.* With an introduction by A. J. P. Taylor. Harmondsworth: Penguin, 1967.

Marx, Roland. *Jack l'Eventreur et les fantasmes Victoriens.* Paris: Editions Complexe, 1989.

Mason, Tony. *Association Football and English Society 1863–1915.* Brighton, Sussex: Harvester Press. Atlantic Highlands, N. J.: Humanities Press, n.d.

Masters, Brian. *The Life of E.F. Benson.* London: Chatto and Windus, 1991.

Matthew, H. C. G. *Gladstone 1809–1874.* Oxford: Oxford University Press, 1988.

————. *Gladstone 1875–1898.* Oxford: Oxford University Press, 1995.

Maurice, Frederick. *The Life of Frederick Denison Maurice Chiefly Told in His Own Letters.* 2 vols. London: Macmillan and Co., 1884.

Mayhew, Henry. *Mr and Mrs Sandboys and Family.* London: 1851.

————. *London Labour and the London Poor* (First ed., 1851; enlarged ed., 4 vols., 1861–62). New York: A. M. Kelley, 1967.

Mazlish, Bruce. *James and John Stuart Mill: Father and Son in the Nineteenth Century.* New York: Basic Books, 1975.

McCarthy, Terry, ed. *The Great Dock Strike, 1889.* London: Weidenfeld and Nicolson, in association with Transport and General Workers Union, 1988.

McClure, John A. *Kipling and Conrad: The Colonial Fiction.* Camridge, Mass.: Harvard University Press, 1981.

McCrum, Michael. *Thomas Arnold Headmaster.* Oxford: Oxford University Press, 1989.

McGee, J. A. *"Thumping English Lies": Froude's Slanders on Ireland and Irishmen.* New York: 1872.

McGrath, J. "Explosives." In *A History of Technology.* Vol. 5, *The Late Nineteenth Century.* Edited by Charles Joseph Singer et al. Oxford: Clarendon Press, 1958. Pp. 284–97.

McKean, John. *Crystal Palace: Joseph Paxton and Charles Fox.* London: Phaidon, 1994.

Menzies, Lucy. *Father Wainwright: A Record.* London: Longmans, 1947.

Merrill, Linda. *A Pot of Paint: Aesthetics on Trial in Whistler v. Ruskin.* Washington, D.C.: Smithsonian Institution Press, 1992.

Metcalf, Thomas R. *Ideologies of the Raj.* Cambridge: Cambridge University Press, 1994.

Meyrick, Frederick. *But Isn't Kingsley Right After All?* London: 1864.

Mill, J. S. *A System of Logic.* 4th ed. London: 1865.

————. *The Subjection of Women.* London: 1869.

Miller, Jonathan. "A Gower Street Scandal." In *Journal of the Royal College of Physicians of London.* Vol. 17. 1983.

Miller, Jonathan, and Borin Van Loon. *Darwin for Beginners.* London: Writers and Readers, 1982.

Miller, William. *The Ottoman Empire and its Successors*. Cambridge: Cambridge University Press, 1934.

Millhauser, Milton. *Just Before Darwin*. Middletown, Conn.: Wesleyan University Press, 1959.

Milner, John. *Art, War and Revolution in France 1870–1871*. New Haven, Conn.: Yale University Press, 2000.

Milton, Maj. Gen. Richard. *The Indian Mutiny: A Centenary History*. London: Hollis & Carter, 1957.

Mitford, Nancy, ed. *The Stanleys of Alderney: Their Letters between the Years 1851–1865*. London: Chapman and Hall, 1939.

Mokyr, J. *Why Ireland Starved*. London: Allen and Unwin, 1985.

Monk, Ray. *Bertrand Russell: The Spirit of Solitude*. London: J. Cape, 1996.

Monypenny, W. F., and George Earle Buckle. *The Life of Benjamin Disraeli, Earl of Beaconsfield*. 6 vols. London: J. Murray, 1910–20.

Moore, Frederic. *The Zoological Gardens: A Handbook for Visitors*. London: 1838.

Moore, J. R. *The Post Darwinian Controversies*. Cambridge: Cambridge University Press, 1979.

Moore, R. J. *Sir Charles Wood's Indian Policy, 1853–66*. Manchester, England: Manchester University Press, 1966.

Morgan, Kenneth. *Keir Hardie: Radical and Socialist*. London: Weidenfeld and Nicolson, 1975.

Morley, John. *The Life of Richard Cobden*. Chapman & Hall, 1882.

———. *The Life of William Ewart Gladstone* (1903). 3 vols. London: Macmillan, 1912.

Morris, James. *Heaven's Command: An Imperial Progress*. London: Faber and Faber, 1973.

Morris, William. *News from Nowhere*. London: Longmans, Green, and Co., 1896.

Mosley, Oswald Ernald Bart. *Wagner and Shaw: A Synthesis* (reprinted from *The European*). London: Sanctuary Press, 1956.

———. *My Life*. London: Nelson, 1968.

Muddock, J. E. *The Great White Hand, or the Tiger of Cawnpore*. London: 1896.

Müller, Max. *The Schleswig-Holstein Question and Its Place in History*, with Jörgensen, Dr. A. D., *The Danish View of the Schleswig-Holstein Question*. London: 1897.

Nanak, Chand. *Translation of a Narrative of Events at Cawnpore*. Allahabad: 1858.

Neary, Tom. *I Saw Our Lady*. Mayo, Ireland: Knock, Co., 1977.

Netzer, Hans Joiachim. *Albert von Sachsen-Coburg und Gotha. Ein Deutscher Prinz in England*. Munich: 1988.

Newbolt, Henry. *Selected Poems*. Edited by Patric Dickinson. London: Hodder & Stoughton, 1981.

Newman, A. J. *The Times Geography and History of Jamaica*. Kingston, Jamaica: 1935.

Newman, J. H. *A Letter to His Grace the Duke of Norfolk on the Occasion of Mr Gladstone's Recent Expostulation.* London: Pickering, 1875.

———. *Apologia Pro Vita Sua* (1864). London: Everyman, 1955. New York: W. W. Norton, 1968.

———. *An Essay on the Development of Christian Doctrine.* Harmondsworth: Penguin, 1974.

Newsome, David. *The Convert Cardinals.* London: J. Murray, 1993.

———. *The Victorian World Picture.* New Brunswick, N.J.: Rutgers University Press, 1997.

Nisbet, Hume. *The Queen's Desire.* London: F. W. White & Co., 1893.

Norman, E. R. *The English Catholic Church in the Nineteenth Century.* Oxford: Oxford University Press, 1984.

Norman, Colonel H. W. *A Lecture on the Relief of Lucknow.* London: Dalton and Lucy, 1867.

O'Brien, Conor Cruise. *Parnell and His Party, 1880–1890.* Oxford: Clarendon Press, 1957.

O'Brien, James Bronterre. "Ode to Lord Palmerston." London: 1856.

O'Malley, Ida B. *Women in Subjection.* London: Duckworth, 1933.

Oldenburg, Veena Talwar. *The Making of Colonial Lucknow 1856–1877.* Princeton, N.J.: Princeton University Press, 1984.

Olivier, Sydney. *The Myth of Governor Eyre.* London: Leonard and Virginia Woolf, 1933.

Olsen, Kirstin. *Chronology of Women's History.* Westport, Conn.: Greenwood Press, 1994.

Orwin, Christabel, and Edith H. Whetham. *History of British Agriculture.* London: Newton Abbot, 1964.

Packard, Jerrold M. *Farewell in Splendour.* Thrupp, Stroud, Gloucestershire: Sutton Pub., 2000.

Packe, Michael St. John. *The Life of John Stuart Mill.* London: Secker and Warburg, 1954.

Padfield, Peter. *Rule Britannia: The Victorian and Edwardian Navy.* London: Routledge & Kegan Paul, 1981.

Paffard, Mark. *Kipling's Indian Fiction.* New York: St. Martin's Press, 1989.

Page, Norman. *A Kipling Companion.* London: Palgrave Macmillan, 1984.

Pakenham, Thomas. *The Boer War.* New York: Random House, 1979.

———. *The Scramble for Africa, 1876–1912.* New York: Random House, 1991.

Paley, Bruce. *Jack the Ripper: The Simple Truth.* London: Headline, 1996.

Palgrave, William Gifford. *Essays on Eastern Questions.* London: 1872.

Pamuk, Sevket. *The Ottoman Empire and European Capitalism, 1820–1913.* Cambridge: Cambridge University Press, 1987.

Pares, Bernard. *A History of Russia.* London: J. Cape, 1955.

Parry, J. P. *Democracy and Religion: Gladstone and The Liberal Party, 1867–1875.* Cambridge: Cambridge University Press, 1986.

Patmore, Coventry. *The Angel in the House.* 3rd ed. Oxford: Oxford University Press, 1860.

Patterson, Major Tom. *100 Years of Spirit Photography.* London: Regency Press, 1965.

Pattison, Mark. *Memoirs* (1885). London: Fontwell, 1969.

Payne, Robert. *Dostoyevsky: A Human Portrait.* New York: Alfred A. Knopf, 1967.

———. *Marx.* W. H. Allen, 1968.

Pearson, Hesketh. *Gilbert and Sullivan.* London: H. Hamilton, 1935.

Percival, John. *The Great Famine: Ireland's Potato Famine, 1845–1851.* London: BBC Books, 1995.

Pereiro, James. *Cardinal Manning: An Intellectual Biography.* Oxford: Clarendon Press, 1988.

Perham, Margery, ed. *The Diaries of Lord Lugard.* 4 vols. London: Faber and Faber, 1959.

Perkin, Harold. *The Origins of Modern English Society 1780–1880.* London: Routledge and Paul, 1969.

Pierce Jones, Victor. *Saint or Sensationalist: The Story of W.T. Stead.* East Wittering, W. Sussex: Gooday Publishers, 1988.

Plomer, William, ed. *Kilvert's Diary, 1870–1879: Selections from the Diary of the Rev. Francis Kilvert.* London: J. Cape, 1944.

Plummer, Alfred. *Conversations with Dr Déllinger 1870–1890.* Edited by Robrecht Boudens. London: Leuven University Press, 1985.

Pocock, Tom. *Rider Haggard and the Lost Empire.* London: Weidenfeld and Nicolson, 1993.

Poe, Edgar Allan. *Mesmerism.* London: 1846.

Poirteir, Cathal, ed. *The Great Irish Famine.* Dublin: Mercier Press, 1995.

Politicus. *The Apparition of the Late Lord Derby to Lord Beaconsfield.* Manchester, England: Tubbs & Brook, 1879.

Pollock, John. *Shaftesbury: The Poor Man's Earl.* London: Hodder and Stoughton, 1985.

Ponsonby, Frederick (First Lord Sysonby). *Recollections of Three Reigns.* London: Eyre and Spottiswoode, 1951.

Pope-Hennessy, James. *Anthony Trollope.* London: J. Cape, 1971.

Pope-Hennessy, Una. *Canon Charles Kingsley: A Biography.* London: Chatto and Windus, 1948.

———. *Charles Dickens* (1945). Harmondsworth: Penguin, 1970.

Porter, Andrew, and Alaine Low, eds. *The Oxford History of the British Empire.* Vol. 3, *The Nineteenth Century.* Oxford: Oxford University Press, 1999.

Porter, Dorothy. "Public Health." In *Companion Encyclopedia of the History of Medicine.* Edited by W. F. Bynum and Roy Porter. London and New York: Routledge, 1993.

Potts, D. M. and W. T. W. *Queen Victoria's Gene: Haemophilia and the Royal Family.* Stroud: Sutton Publishers, 1999.

Poulton, Edward Bagnall. "Darwin." In *Encyclopedia Britannica.* 13th ed. New York and London: Encyclopedia Brittanica, 1926.

Pound, Ezra. *Selected Prose*. London: Faber and Faber, 1973. New York: W. W. Norton, 1973.

Prothero, Rowland. *The Life and Correspondence of Dean Stanley*. 2 vols. London: 1893.

Pudney, John. *Lewis Carroll and His World*. London: Thames and Hudson, 1976.

Purcell, Edmund Sheridan. *Life of Cardinal Manning*. 2 vols. London: Macmillan and Co., 1895.

Quinton, Anthony. *Thoughts and Thinkers*. New York: Holmes and Meier, 1982.

Raby, Peter. *Aubrey Beardsley and the Nineties*. London: Collins and Brown, 1998.

Rahv, Philip, ed. *The Great Short Novels of Henry James*. London: Robinson Publishing, 1989.

Raine, Craig, ed. *A Choice of Kipling's Prose*. London: Faber and Faber, 1987.

Read, Donald. *Peel and the Victorians*. Oxford: B. Blackwell, 1987.

Reboul, Marc. *Charles Kingsley, La formation d'une personnalité et son affirmation*. Paris: Presses Universitaires de France, 1973.

Reid, J. C. *The Mind and Art of Coventry Patmore*. London: Routledge and Paul, 1957.

Reid, Michaela. *Ask Sir James*. London: Hodder and Stoughton, 1987.

Rich, Norman. *Why the Crimean War? A Cautionary Tale*. Hanover, N.H.: Hanover University Press of New England, 1985.

Richter, Melvin. *The Politics of Conscience. T. H. Green and His Age*. Lanham, N.Y.: University Press of America, 1983.

Ridley, Jasper. *Lord Palmerston*. London: Constable, 1970.

Roberts, Andrew. *Salisbury: Victorian Titan*. London: Weidenfeld and Nicolson, 1999.

Roberts, Brian. *The Mad Bad Line*. London: H. Hamilton, 1981.

————. *Cecil Rhodes: Flawed Colossus*. London: H. Hamilton, 1987. New York: W. W. Norton, 1988.

Roberts, David. "How Cruel Was the Victorian Poor Law?" In *The Historical Journal*. 1963: 97–107.

Robertson Scott, J. W. *The Life and Death of a Newspaper*. London: 1952.

Robinson, Gertrude. *David Urquhart: Some Chapers in the Life of a Victorian Knight-Errant of Justice and Liberty*. Oxford: B. Blackwell, 1920.

Robinson, Jane. *Angels of Albion: Women of the Indian Mutiny*. London: Penguin, 1996.

Rotberg, Robert I., with Miles F. Shore. *The Founder: Cecil Rhodes and the Pursuit of Power*. New York: Oxford University Press, 1988.

Rothman, David J. and Sheila M., eds. *The Dangers of Education*. New York: Garland, 1987.

Rothschild, Lord. *"You Have It, Madam."* London: privately printed, 1980.

Rotton, John Edward Wharton. *The Chaplain's Narrative of the Siege of Delhi*. London: Smith, Elder, and Co., 1858.

Rowse, A. L. *Homosexuals in History: A Study of Ambivalence in Society, Literature and the Arts*. London: Weidenfeld and Nicolson, 1977.

Royle, Trevor. *The Kitchener Enigma*. London: M. Joseph, 1985.

————. *Crimea: The Great Crimean War, 1854–1856*. London: Little, Brown, 1999.

Ruskin, John. *The Works of John Ruskin*. Edited by E. T. Cook and Alexander Wedderburn. 39 vols. London: G. Allen, 1903–12.

Russell, Bertrand. *History of Western Philosophy, and Its Connection with Political and Social Circumstances from the Earliest Times to the Present Day*. London: G. Allen and Unwin, 1946.

————. *Autobiography*. Vol. 1. London: Allen and Unwin, 1967.

Russell, C. A. *Cross Currents: Interactions between Science and Faith*. Grand Rapids, Mich.: W. B. Eerdman's Publishing Co., 1985.

————. *John Stuart Mill: The Free Market and the State*. London: John Stuart Mill Institute, 1993.

Russell, M., and Clare R. Goldfarb. *Spiritualism and Nineteenth-Century Letters*. Cranburg, N.J.: Fairleigh Dickinson University Press, Associated University Presses, 1978.

Russell, William Howard. *My Indian Mutiny Diary*. London: Cassell, 1957.

————. *William Russell, Special Correspondent of The Times*. Edited by Roger Hudson. Introduction by Max Hastings. London: 1995.

Ryan, Alan. *The Philosophy of John Stuart Mill*. 2nd ed. Houdsmill, Basingstoke, Hampshire: Macmillan, 1987.

Ryan, Alan. ed. *Mill*. A Norton Critical Edition. New York: W. W. Norton, 1997.

Saintsbury, George. *The Earl of Derby*. New York: Harper and Brothers, 1892.

Sarkar, Sumit, *Modern India, 1885–1947*. 2 vols. Delhi: Macmillan, 1983. New York: St. Martin's Press, 1989.

Saunders, Christopher, and Iain R. Smith. "Southern Africa 1795–1910" (ch. 26). In *The Oxford History of the British Empire*. Vol. 3, *The Nineteenth Century*. Oxford: Oxford University Press, 1999.

Saville, John. *1848: The British State and the Chartist Movement*. Cambridge: Cambridge University Press, 1987.

————. *The Labour Movement in Britain: A Commentary*. London: 1988.

Scott, Patrick. "The School and the Novel. Tom Brown's Schooldays." In *The Victorian Public School*. Brian Simon and Ian Bradley. Dublin: Gill and Macmillan, 1975.

Scrimgeour, R. M., ed. *The North London Collegiate School 1850–1950*. London: Oxford University Press, 1950.

Seacole, Mary. *Wonderful Adventures of Mrs. Seacole in Many Lands* (1857). New York: Oxford University Press, 1988.

Semmel, Bernard. *The Governor Eyre Controversy*. London: MacGibbon & Kee, 1962.

Sen, Surendra Nath. *Eighteen Fifty-Seven*. Delhi, India: The Publications Division, Ministry of Information & Broadcasting, 1957.

Seton-Watson, Hugh. *The Russian Empire 1801–1917*. Oxford: Clarendon Press, 1967.

Seymour-Smith, Martin. *Rudyard Kipling*. London: MacDonald/Queen Anne Press, 1989.

———. *Hardy*. New York: St. Martin's Press, 1994.

Shannon, Richard. *Gladstone and the Bulgarian Agitation 1876*. London: Nelson, 1963.

———. *The Age of Disraeli, 1868–1881*. London: Longman, 1992.

———. *Gladstone: Heroic Minister 1865–1898*. London: Penguin, 1999.

Shaw, Bernard. *The Perfect Wagnerit: A Commentary on the Ring of the Nibelungs*. London: 1898.

Shaw, Charles. *When I Was a Child* (1903). London: Caliban Books, 1977.

Shaw, Stanford J. and Ezel Kural. *History of The Ottoman Empire and Modern Turkey*. Cambridge: Cambridge University Press, 1977.

Simon, Julian. *The Ultimate Resource*. Princeton, N.J.: Princeton University Press, 1981.

Sims, George R. *How the Poor Live*. London: 1883.

———. *Horrible London*. London: 1889.

Singer, Charles, et al., eds. *A History of Technology*. Vol. 5, *The Late Nineteenth Century*. Oxford: Clarendon Press, 1958.

Singh, Shailenda Dhari. *Novels on the Indian Mutiny*. New Delhi, India: Arnold-Heinemann, 1973.

Skelley, Alan Ramsay. *The Victorian Army at Home*. London and Montreal: McGill-Queen's University Press, 1977.

Skorupski, John. *John Stuart Mill*. London: Routledge, 1989.

Slosson, Preston William. *The Decline of the Chartist Movement*. New York: Columbia University Press, 1916.

Smiles, Samuel. *Self Help*. New York: Harper and Brothers, 1860.

Smith, Iain R. *The Origins of the South African War 1899–1902*. London: Longman, 1996.

Smith, Philip Thurmond. *Policing Victorian London*. Westport, Conn.: Greenwood Press, 1985.

Smith, Vincent A., and Percival Spear. *The Oxford History of India*. Oxford: Clarendon Press, 1958.

Soper, Kate. Introduction to *Enfranchisement of Women,* by Harriet Taylor Mill. London: Virago Press, 1983.

Source Material for a History of the Freedom Movement in India. Bombay, India: 1958.

Southgate, David. *The Passing of the Whigs, 1832–1886*. London: Macmillan, 1962.

Soyer, Alexis. *A Shilling Cookery for the People*. London: G. Routledge & Co., 1855.

———. *The Selected Soyer: The Writings of the Legendary Victorian Chef.* Compiled by Andrew Langley. London: 1987.

———. *A Culinary Campaign*. London: Southover Press, 1995.

Spiers, Edward M. *The Late Victorian Army*. Manchester, England: Manchester University Press, 1992.

Sprigge, T. L. S. *James and Bradley—American Truth and British Reality*. Chicago and La Salle, Ill.: Open Court, 1993.

Srivastava, M. P. *The Indian Mutiny 1857*. Allahabad: Chugh Publications, 1979.

Stamp, Gavin. *The Changing Metropolis: Earliest Photographs of London, 1839–1879*. Hammondsworth, Middlesex, England: Viking, 1984.

Stamp, Robert M. *Royal Rebels: Princess Louise and The Marquis of Lorne*. Toronto: Dundurn Press, 1988.

Stanford, Derek. *Introduction to the Nineties*. Austria: Institut für Anglistik und Amerikanistik, Universität Salzburg, 1987.

Stanley, Arthur Penrhyn. *Life and Correspondence of Thomas Arnold*. 2 vols. London: B. Fellows, 1844.

———. "Charles Kingsley: A Sermon Preached in Westminster Abbey on January 31st 1875." London: 1875.

———. *Historical Memorials of Canterbury Cathedral*. London: J. Murray, 1900.

Stansky, Peter. *Gladstone: A Progress in Politics*. New York: W. W. Norton, 1979.

———. *Redesigning the World: William Morris, the 1880s and the Arts and Crafts*. Princeton, N.J.: Princeton University Press, 1985.

Stedman Jones, Gareth. *Languages of Class*. Cambridge: Cambridge University Press, 1983.

Steele, David. *Lord Salisbury: A Political Biography*. London: U.C.L. Press, 1999.

Stevens Cox, J., ed. "Hair Care in Late Victorian and Edwardian Days." St. Peter Port, Guernsey, C.I., 1979.

Stewart, J. I. M. *Eight Modern Writers*. Oxford: Clarendon Press, 1963.

Stokes, Eric. *The English Utilitarians and India*. Oxford: Oxford University Press, 1959.

———. *The Peasant Armed: The Indian Revolt of 1857*. Oxford: Oxford University Press, 1986.

Stokes, John, ed. *Eleanor Marx, 1855–1898. Life, Work, Contacts*. Aldershot, England, and Burlington, Vt.: Ashgate, 2000.

Storer, Henry. *Mesmerism in Disease: A Few Plain Facts*. London: Baillère, 1845.

Strachey, Lytton. *Queen Victoria* (1921). Harmondsworth: Penguin, 1984.

———. *Eminent Victorians* (1918). London: Penguin, 1993.

Strachey, Ray. *"The Cause": A Short History of the Women's Movement in Great Britain*. London: G. Bell & Sons, 1928.

Stubbs, C. W. *Charles Kingsley and the Christian Socialist Movement*. London: Blackie, 1899.

Sturgis, Matthew. *Aubrey Beardsley: A Biography*. Woodstock, N.Y.: Overlook Press, 1999.

Sullivan, Zohreh T. *Narratives of Empire: The Fictions of Rudyard Kipling*. Cambridge: Cambridge University Press, 1993.

Sundkler, Bengt, and Christopher Steed, eds. *A History of the Church in Africa*. Cambridge: Cambridge University Press, 2000.

Swartz, Marvin. *The Politics of British Foreign Policy in the Era of Disraeli and Gladstone*. New York: St. Martin's Press, 1985.

Sykes, Christopher Simon. *Black Sheep*. London: Chatto and Windus, 1982.

———. *Private Palaces*. London: Chatto and Windus, 1985.

Taylor, A. J. P. *The Struggle for Mastery in Europe, 1848–1918*. Oxford: Clarendon Press, 1954.

———. *English History, 1914–1945*. Oxford: Clarendon Press, 1965.

Taylor, Anne. *Annie Besant: A Biography*. Oxford: Oxford University Press, 1992.

Taylor, Bernard. *Cruelly Murdered: Constant Kent and the Killing at Road Hill House*. London: Souvenir Press, 1979.

Taylor, D. J. *Thackeray*. London: Chatto and Windus, 1999.

Taylor, Lucy. *Sahib and Sepoy, or Saving an Empire*. London: 1897.

Taylor, Miles. "The 1848 Revolutions and the British Empire." In *Past and Present*. No. 166. February 2000: 146ff.

Taylor, Miles, ed., *The European Diaries of Richard Cobden, 1846–9*. Aldershot, England: Scholar Press, 1994.

Taylor, P. J. O. *A Companion to Vol. 1 Mutiny of 1857*. Delhi: Oxford University Press, 1996; *Chronicles of the Mutiny*. Delhi: Indus, 1992.

Taylor, S. J. *The Great Outsiders: Northcliffe, Rothermere and the Daily Mail*. London: Weidenfeld and Nicolson, 1996.

Tennyson, Alfred. *The Poems of Tennyson*. Edited by Christopher Ricks. Harlow: Longmans, 1969. New York: W. W. Norton, 1972.

Tennyson, Charles. *Alfred Tennyson*. New York: Macmillan, 1950.

Thomas, Donald. *Lewis Carroll: A Portrait with Background*. London: J. Murray, 1996.

Thompson, C. J. *A Handbook of Personal Hygiene*. London: 1894.

Thompson, Dorothy. *The Chartists: Popular Politics in the Industrial Revolution*. New York: Pantheon, 1984.

Thompson, Edward. *The Other Side of the Medal*. London: Leonard and Virginia Woolf at the Hogarth Press, 1925.

Thompson, E. P. *William Morris: Romantic to Revolutionary*. New York: Lawrence & Wishart, 1955.

Thompson, E. P., and Eileen Yeo, eds. *The Unknown Mayhew: Selections from the Morning Chronicle 1849–50*. London: Merlin Press, 1971.

Thompson, F. M. L. *English Landed Society in the Nineteenth Century*. London: Routledge and Kegan Paul, 1963.

Thompson, Paul. *The Work of William Morris*. Oxford: Oxford University Press, 1991.

Thornton, A. P. *The Imperial Idea and its Enemies: A Study in British Power*. London: Macmillan, 1959.

Tillotson, Kathleen. *Novels of the Eighteen-Forties*. Oxford: Oxford University Press, 1954.

Tolstoy, L. N. *What Then Must We Do?* (1886). Translated by Aylmer Maude. London and New York: Oxford University Press, 1925.

Towle, Eleanor A. *Alexander Heriot Mackonochie: A Memoir*. London: K. Paul, Trench, Trübner, & Co., 1890.

Townshend, Chauncy Hare. *Mesmerism Proved True and the Quarterly Review Reviewed*. London: 1854.

Traill, H. D. *Lord Cromer*. London: Bliss, Sands, 1897.

Trench, Maria. *Charles Lowder; A Biography, by the Author of the "Life of St. Teresa."* London: K. Paul, Trench, Trübner & Co., 1891.

Trevelyan, G. M. *Sir George Otto Trevelyan: A Memoir*. London: Longmans, Green, and Co. 1932.

Trevelyan, G. O. *The Life and Letters of Thomas Babington Macaulay*. London: Harper and Brothers, 1876.

Tsuzuki, Chushichi. *The Life of Eleanor Marx, 1855–1898: A Socialist Tragedy*. Oxford: Clarendon Press, 1967.

Tyerman, Christopher. *A History of Harrow School*. Oxford: Oxford University Press, 2000.

Tyler, Colin. *Thomas Hill Green (1836–1882) and the Philosophical Foundations of Politics*. Lewiston, N.Y.: Edwin Mellen Press, 1997.

Vamplew, Wray. *The Turf: A Social and Economic History of Horse Racing*. London: Allen Lane, 1976.

Van der Kiste, John. *Queen Victoria's Children*. London: Allen Sutton, 1986.

———. *Kaiser Wilhelm II*. London: Sutton Publishing, 1999.

Van Riper, A. Bowdoin. *Men Among the Mammoths*. Chicago, Ill.: University of Chicago Press, 1993.

Victoria, Queen. *The Letters of Queen Victoria*. Edited by A. C. Benson and Viscount Esher. London: J. Murray, 1907.

———. *The Girlhood of Queen Victoria*. Edited by Viscount Esher. 2 vols. London: J. Murray, 1912.

Vidler, Alec R. *F.D. Maurice and Company*. London: S.C.M. Press, 1966.

Vidler, Alec R., ed. *A Century of Social Catholicism, 1820–1920*. London: S.P.C.K., 1964.

Vox Clamantis. *A History of Ritualism*. London: Open Road Publishing Co., 1907.

Walkowitz, Judith R. *Prostitution and Victorian Society*. Cambridge: Cambridge University Press, 1980.

Wallace, Richard. *The Agony of Lewis Carroll*. Melrose, Mass.: Gemini Press, 1990.

Walsh, Walter. *The Secret History of the Oxford Movement*. London: Church Association, 1897.

Ward, Wilfrid. *The Life of John Henry, Cardinal Newman, Based on his Private Journals and Correspondence*. 2 vols. London: Longmans, Green, and Co., 1912.

Warner, Philip. *Kitchener: The Man behind the Legend*. New York: Atheneum, 1985.

Washington, Peter. *Madame Blavatsky's Baboon: Theosophy and the Emergence of the Western Guru*. London: Secker & Warburg, 1993.

Webb, Beatrice. *Our Partnership*. London and New York: Longmans, Green, and Co., 1948.

———. *My Apprenticeship* (1926). Cambridge: Cambridge University Press, 1979.

Weinreb, Ben, and Christopher Hibbert, eds. *The London Encyclopaedia*. London: Macmillan, 1983.

Weintraub, Stanley. *Four Rossettis*. New York: Weybright & Tatley, 1977.

———. *Uncrowned King: The Life of Prince Albert*. New York: Free Press, 1997.

Weldon's Christmas Annual. *Dizzi-Ben-Dizzi, or The Orphan of Baghdad*. London: 1878.

West, E. G. *Education and the State: A Study in Political Economy*. London: Institute of Economic Affairs, 1965.

West, John. *The History of Tasmania*. London: Argus and Robertson, in assocation with Royal Australia Historical Society (Sydney), 1971.

Wheen, Francis. *Karl Marx: A Life*. London: Fourth Estate, 1999. New York: W. W. Norton, 2000.

White, Michael, and John Gribbin. *Darwin: A Life in Science*. New York: Dutton, 1995.

White, Stephen. "A Burning Issue." In *New Law Journal*. 10 August 1990.

Whitehouse, J. Howard. *Vindication of Ruskin*. London: Allen and Unwin, 1950.

Whyte, F. W. "William Thomas Stead." In *Dictionary of National Biography, 1912–1921*. London: 1927.

Williams, George Walter. *Depositions Taken at Cawnpore under the Direction of Lieut. Colonel G. W. W. etc.* Allahabad(?): 1858.

Williamson, Joseph. *Josephine Butler: The Forgotten Saint*. London: Leighton Buzzard/ Faith Press, 1977.

Wilson, A. E. *East End Entertainment*. London: 1954.

Wilson, A. N. *Hilaire Belloc*. London: H. Hamilton, 1984.

———. *God's Funeral*. London: J. Murray, 1999. New York: W. W. Norton, 1999.

Wilson, Angus. *The Strange Ride of Rudyard Kipling: His Life and Works*. London: Secker & Warburg, 1977.

Wilson, Colin, and Robin Odell. *Jack the Ripper: Summing Up and Verdict*. New York: Bantam Press, 1987.

Winter, Barry. *The I.L.P. Past and Present*. London: 1993.

Wolfreys, Julian. *Being English*. Albany, N.Y.: State University of New York Press, 1994.

Woodham-Smith, Cecil. *The Great Hunger, Ireland 1845–9*. London: H. Hamilton, 1962.

———. *Queen Victoria: Her Life and Times*. London: H. Hamilton, 1972.

Woodward, E. L. *The Age of Reform, 1815–1870*. Revised. Oxford: Oxford University Press, 1949.

Worder, Nigel, *The Making of Modern South Africa: Conquest, Segregation and Apartheid*. Oxford: Clarendon Press, 1994.

Wordsworth, William. *The Prelude* (1850). Harmondsworth: Penguin, 1971.

Wright, Brian. *A Fire in the House* (pamphlet, no name of publisher, no date).

Wurgaft, Lewis D. *The Imperial Imagination: Magic and Myth in Kipling's India*. Middletown, Conn.: Wesleyan University Press, 1983.

Yeats, W. B. *Autobiography*. London: Macmillan, 1955.

————. *The Poems*. Revised. Edited by Richard J. Finneran. London: Macmillan, 1993.

Yeats, W. B., ed. *The Oxford Book of Modern Verse*. Oxford: Clarendon Press, 1936.

Young, G. M. *Portrait of an Age*. London: Oxford University Press, 1936.

Young, Robert M. *Darwin's Metaphor*. Cambridge: Cambridge University Press, 1985.

Zetland, Lawrence John Lumly Dundas, Second Marquis of. *Lord Cromer: Being the Authorized Life of Eveyln Baring, First Earl of Cromer by the Marquess of Zetland*. London: Hodder and Stoughton, 1932.

Zinn, Howard. *A People's History of the United States: 1492 to the Present*. Revised and updated. New York: Harper Perennial, 1995.

Periodicals Consulted

British Journal of the History of Science
Bullán, An Irish Studies Journal
Eliza Cook's Journal
Gentleman's Magazine
Hansard
Historical Journal
History Today
Illustrated London News
Jamaican Historical Review
Journal of Imperial and Commonwealth History
Journal of Social History
Journal of the History of Medicine and Allied Sciences
Journal of the Royal College of Physicians of London
Judy, or The London Serio-Comic Journal
Lancet
Law Journal
Leisure Hour
New Law Journal
Nineteenth Century
Notes and Queries
Pall Mall Gazette
Punch
Quarterly Review
The Spectator

The Times

Manuscript Collections
Reference to specific Manuscript numbers is in the notes. In the British Library I
    benefited from being able to read:
Balfour Papers (Additional MSS 49683–49962)
Burns Papers (Additional MSS 46286–94)
Dilke Papers (Additional MSS 43874–43967 and 49610–12)
Gladstone Papers (Additional MSS 44086–44835, 44900–1, 45724, 5644–53)
Iddlesleigh Papers (Additional MSS 50041)
Layard Papers (Additional MSS 38931–39164, 46153–70, 58223–33)
Morley Papers (Additional MSS 48218–48301)
Morris Papers (Additional MSS 45298–45337)
(Florence) Nightingale Papers (Additional MSS 43393–43403, 45750–45849,
    47714–47767, 68882–90)
Stanmore Papers (Additional MSS 49199–49285)

In the Bodleian Library, I consulted:

Benson Papers
Croker Papers
Ponsonby Papers

Index

Aberdeen, Lord   136, 146–7, 174,
    187
'Abide with Me' (Lyte)   103–4
Academic Institutions (Ireland) Act
    68–9
accents, regional   60
acquired characteristics and
    evolution   97
Adams, Charles Francis   251
adultery   234
Afghan War, Second   400–1, 405
Africa
    diplomatic and physical
        annexations by European
        nations   489
    European nationalisms and
        489
    moral imperatives in   489
    resistance to modern world in
        488
    roots of post-colonial problems
        in   489
    scientific curiosity in exploration
        of   488–9
    scramble for   486–92, 512, 602
    see also South Africa
African Lakes Company   490
Afrikaners   605
after-life, doubts about   99–100,
    235–6
Agnew, Joan   326
agricultural labourers   72
    in electorate   573
    wages of   79

agriculture
    crops in   72
    depression in   428
    economic state of   71–2
    summer of 1845, effect of
        72–3
    see also Corn Laws; Ireland;
        potato blight
Ahmed, Mohammed   467
Ailsbury, 4th Marquess of   381
Ainsworth, William Harrison   19
Albert Edward, Prince of Wales
    (Bertie)   241, 242
    adulteries of   503–4
    education of   273
    inclinations of   273
    marriage of   305
    in Mordaunt divorce case   360
    Thanksgiving Service for
        recovery of   360
    tour of the Levant by   274
    and Wagner   412
Albert of Saxe-Coburg, Prince   54
    accomplishments of   183,
        349–50
    allowance granted to   55
    Asia, involvement in   237–8
    background of   56
    character of   240
    characteristics of   54, 55–6,
        183
    consequences of death of   244
    decline and death of   243
    European influence of   237–40

and the Great Exhibition 130
later years of 236–7
meets Henry Cole 128
opposition to marriage of 54
paternity of 54–5
public activities 237
relationship with children
240–1, 274
see also Great Exhibition
Albion Colliery disaster 582
Albion Terrace drinking water
investigation 156–7
alcohol
and poverty 365
tax on 478
Alexander II, Tsar 187, 416–17
Alice, Princess 243
Alice's Adventures Underground
(Dodgson) 324
Alice's Adventures in Wonderland
(Dodgson) 324, 327, 330
Allingham, William 323
Althorp, Lord 39
Amalgamated Society of Watermen
and Lightermen 515
American civil war 251–2
British attitudes to 268
consequences of 256
Amphitheatre (Astley's) 65
Amritsar massacre 501
anarchism and socialism 445,
447
ancestors, search for common 97
Andersen, Hans Christian 330
Anderson, Elizabeth see Garrett
Angel in the House, The (Patmore)
305, 314–15
Anglican Church in Ireland 361
animal magnetism see
Mesmerism

anti-Catholicism 69, 141
Anti-Corn Law League 71
anti-Semitism see Disraeli;
Wagner
anti-socialism 20
Apologia pro Vita Sua (Newman)
303–4
Archer, Scott 200
aristocracy
adaptability of 583
in the army 356
and Darwinian competition
256–7
English views of 192
in government 39, 385
in parliament 481
strength of 573–4, 585
transformations to 583
in upper chamber 385
see also class system
'aristocratic settlement' 255,
256
Arkwright, Richard 249
armaments 352–3
see also gun
Armstrong, Eliza see Stead
Armstrong, Sir William 384
army
incompetence in 608
reform 354–9
system of purchase in 355,
357–9
and unemployment
demonstrations 509
Army Enlistment Act 356
Army Regulation Act 356
Arnold, Matthew 253
Arnold of Rugby, Dr Thomas
141, 276, 277, 278–9, 283,
287

art
  as response to materialism 557
  see also Beardsley; Brown;
    Hunt; Rossetti; Turner;
    Whistler
Arthur, Duke of Connaught 465
arts, flourishing of 410–24
Ashes, the 544
Ashley, Lord (Earl of Shaftesbury)
    41, 60, 61, 66, 151, 167–8,
    193, 486
Ashworth, Henry 60, 61
Asquith, Henry 559
atheism 96–7, 433
Athenaeum 457
Augustine of Hippo 229
Austen, Jane 60
Australia, Irish prisoners in 127
Austria 394
autodidacticism 95–6
Aveling, Edward 548
Awakening Conscience, The
    (Hunt) 161, 163, 164
Awkward Age, The (James) 459

Baden-Powell, Lord Robert 597
Bagehot, Walter 135–6
bakers, working conditions of
    154–5
Balaclava 175
Balfour, Arthur 439, 530–1, 556,
    558
Balkan crisis 394–401
  beginnings of 394–5
  Christian–Muslim conflicts in
    395–6
  Disraeli's view of 395
  Russian involvement in 395
ballot, secret 40, 43
Balmoral 56

Bank of England 117
banking crisis 77
banking families entering the
    peerage 482
banks, savings in 261
Baring, Major Evelyn 466, 468
Barker, John 410
Barnes, William 430
Barrett, Sir William 439
Barry, Charles 62–3
Bathers at Asnières (Seurat) 344
Bayne, Peter 190
Beach, Sir Michael Hicks 478
Beaconsfield, Lord *see* Disraeli
Beagle, HMS 15, 50
Beale, Dorothea 285, 286
Beardsley, Aubrey 552, 555–6
Beata Beatrix (Rosetti) 161
Bedchamber Crisis 53–4
Bell, Alexander Graham 494
Beloved, The (Rosetti) 247,
    257–8
Bengal army 203
  see also Indian Mutiny; sepoys
Benson, Edward White 237, 297,
    324, 567
Benson, E.F. 567
Benson family 567–8
Bentham, Jeremy 37–8, 75, 109,
    554
Benz, Karl 494
Berlin Memorandum 394
Bermuda 127
Besant, Annie 509, 510, 511,
    548–9, 551
'Beyond the Pale' (Kipling) 497–8
Bibighar massacre 212–13
Bills of Mortality 36
birth control 12, 548
Bismarck, Prince Otto von 403

black people, attitudes to 255–6, 271–2
Black Reconstruction (Du Bois) 256
Blackwell, Elizabeth 312
blasting gelatine 495
Blavatsky, Madame Helena 549–51
Bleak House (Dickens) 463
Bloody Sunday 509
Bloomsbury set 570
Blunt, Wilfred Scawen 558, 560
Boer War 597–613
  Boer army in 610
  concentration camps in 611–12
  help for Kruger in 609
  Kimberley, siege of 610
  Ladysmith, battle of 610, 611
  see also Kitchener
Bonaparte, Louis Napoleon 146
Book of Snobs (Thackeray) 94
books, cost of 19
Booth, Charles 442, 512
Booth, William 378
botanical, amateur 96
bourgeoisie 119–20, 132, 279
  see also middle class
Boycott, Captain 453
Bradlaugh, Charles 447–9, 484–5, 548, 549
Bradley, F.H. 569–70
bread, price of 71
Brett, Reggie 464–5
Bridgewater House 382
Bright, John 39, 71, 82–3, 127, 191, 252, 352, 466
Britain
  American view of 253

  and Europe compared in 1870s 343–5
  'at the heart of Europe' 238
British army *see* Crimean War
British Association for the Advancement of Science 377
British and Foreign Review 306
British Guiana, unrest in 126
'British hotel' in Balaclava 178
British Medical Association 309
British Museum 117
British West Indies 48
Broad Church 276, 293, 294, 313, 366
Brontë, Reverend Patrick 94, 285
Brontë sisters 286
brothels, state-registered 474
Brougham, Henry 38
Brown, Ford Madox 157, 159
Brown, John 504
Browning, Elizabeth Barrett 89
  birth of son to 89–90
Browning, Robert 86, 88–9, 139
  courtship of Elizabeth 89–90
  involvement with Italy 90
  oeuvre of 90–1
  religious views of 91–2
  and Wordsworth 131
Bryant & May match factory 511–12
Buccleuch, Duke of 128
Buckingham Palace 128
Buksh, Mahomet 505
Bulgarian Atrocities 395–8, 464
Bulgarian Horrors and the Question of the East, The (Gladstone) 397–8
Buller, Sir Redvers 466, 610–11

Burgess, George, murder of 264–6
Burne-Jones, Georgiana 160
Burne-Jones, Sir Edward Coley 422, 555
Burnes, Sir Alexander 124
Burns, John 513–14, 573
Buss, Frances Mary 284–6
Buss, R.W. 18
Butler, George 473
Butler, Josephine 309, 473–4
Butler, Samuel 224
Butler, William 466

Caldwell, Charles 105
Calne, borough of 39–40
Cambridge, Duke of 358, 360
Cameron, Julia Margaret 323
Campbell, Sir John 176
Canada, effect of Corn Laws on 126
Canning, Viscount 202, 215, 219, 221
Cape see Zulu War
Capital (Marx) 153–4
capitalism
  and adultery 235
  conquering the globe 127
  constraints on 119
  gone awry 417
  opposition to 151
capital punishment see executions
Captain Moonlight see Land League
Cardigan, Lord 182–3, 270
Cardwell, Edward 354, 355, 356–9
Carlyle, Jane Welsh 332–3
Carlyle, Thomas 158–9, 349, 431

background 16
and Condition of England question 53
death of wife, 332–3
on electoral reform 332
on Europe 345–6
intellectual characteristics of 17–18
and Jamaica riots 271
philosophy of 158–9
relationship with wife 333
religious beliefs of 17, 158
on 'rights of man' 41
social life of 333
view of Awakening Conscience 164
view of Light of the World 162
visit to France of 16
see also French Revolution; Past and Present
carriages 262
Carrington, Robert, 2nd Baron 381–2
Cartwright, Edmund 249
Catholic Church 101, 139
  and communism 372
  creation of hierarchy and bishoprics in 139
  and cremation 543–4
  and fascism 372
  political loyalty of 375
  and reaction 371–2
  resistance to new hierarchy in 140–1
  strengthening of, in Europe 139–40
  see also Mortara; Papal Infallibility; Pius IX
Catholic emancipation 59, 135

Catholic Emancipation Act 78,
140
Catholic families 140
Catholicism 63–5, 343, 372–5,
539, 540
see also anti-Catholicism;
Protestantism
cattle plague 428
Cause, the (college, education,
professional life) 318
Cavendish, Lord Frederick 453,
532
Cecil, Lord Robert 252
cemeteries 543
Cetewayo, Chief 401
Ceylon, unrest in 126
Chadwick, Edwin 37, 156–7
Chamberlain, Joseph 360, 363,
447, 456, 459, 461, 465, 479,
482–4, 508, 605
Chambers, Robert 95–7, 100,
227
Chand, Nanak 207
*Chaplain's Narrative of the Siege
of Delhi* (Rotton) 209–10
Chaplin, Henry 588–9
Chapman, John 167
Chapman and Hall 19
Charlotte, Princess 24
Charterhouse School 281
Chartist Land Plan 118
Chartists 39–47, 62
and Corn Laws 72
divisions in 42
individualism and 45
as libertarians 44
National Convention of 118
national petition of, rejection of
46
newspaper of 41
numbers of 119
Physical Force 118
as political reaction to social
control 44
reasons for failure of 113, 116
riots of 44, 115
Tories in 46
working class support for
113–14
see also Third Chartist Petition;
People's Charter
'Chatsworth Stove' 129
Chauduri, S.B. 202
Cheltenham Ladies College 286
Chesterton, G.K. 45, 579–80
childhood 260
child labour
agricultural 428
as chimney sweeps 299, 304
in cotton industry 250
minimum age of 153
mistreatment of 28–30
working hours of 41, 151–2
see also urban proletariat
children
adults seeing themselves as
330
expendability of 264
literature for 263
of the poor 264
see also prostitution
Children of the New Forest, The
(Marryat) 330
chloroform 156
cholera 34–6, 74
attitudes to 36
causes of 155–8
in Delhi siege 210
in Ireland 83
in Lucknow 216

responses of rich and poor to
36
see also Crimean War
Christ as man-god 162
Christian charity 22
Christian church, power of 227
Christianity
apparent, in Victorian England
169
conversion of India to 205
conversion of sepoys to 202
as mythology 167
see also religion
Christian 'martyrs' in Hercogovina
394
Christian morality 162
Christian opposition to capitalism
151
Christian Science 550
Christian Socialist Movement
149
Christmas card 128
Christmas Carol, A (Dickens) 22
Church of England
disestablishment of 371
High Church malcontents in
140
Churchill, Lord Randolph
484–5
Churchill, Winston Spencer 484
Church Missionary Society 487,
491
cigarette-makers 197–9
city life 131–2
City of London, commercial
development in 443
civil service 361
civil war, American *see* American
civil war
Clarendon, Lord 81

Clarendon Commission on public
schools 280–1, 282
class conflicts 115
see also working class
class system, Victorian 59, 192,
274
fluidity of 383–4
gulf created by 319–20
in *Savoy Operas* 420
and Women's Movement 312
see also aristocracy; middle
class
class views of revolution 119
Clergy Daughters' School,
Casterton 285
Clough, Arthur Hugh 103
coal mines 31, 45
coal production 15
Cobbett, William 32
Cobden, Richard 60, 61, 66,
71–2, 127, 128, 253, 352,
427
Cole, Henry 128–9
Coleridge, Samuel Taylor 349
colonies 48–57
attitudes towards 48
exploitation of, in Great
Exhibition 152–3
sexual appeal of expansion of
496
technological change in
annexation of 493
unrest in 124–4, 258
see also empire
commerce *see* trade
common land, enclosure of 31
communism 151, 343
Communist Manifesto, The
(Marx) 231
Comte, Auguste 110–11

Condition of England question
    53, 62
Conforth, Fanny 161
Congress of Berlin 403, 464
Congress of Vienna 48
Coningsby (Disraeli) 66
Conroy, Sir John 25, 26
Conservative Party 66–7, 331–2,
    404, 478, 479, 573
Constantinople as 'Key to India'
    395
constituencies, newly-formed
    572–3
Constitution, British 61
constitutional monarchy 59
consumers 575
Contagious Diseases Acts 308,
    369, 473–4
    repeal of 474, 476
    Royal Commission into working
        of 473
*Contributions to the Theory of
    Natural Selection* (Wallace)
    226
Co-operative Movement 575,
    579
Cope Bros 198
cordon sanitaire against cholera
    35
corn
    export from Ireland of 79
    import of cheap American 427
    tariffs on 427
    see also Corn Laws; maize
Corn Laws 19, 32, 45, 58, 62,
    71–3, 135, 355, 402
    effect on colonies 126
    repeal of 133, 427
    and squirearchy 586
    see also Free Trade

Corry, Montague 389
Corsica 69
cost of living 32
Cotton Famine 253–7
cotton goods 15, 513
cotton mills of Lancashire 253
cotton production in America
    249–50
cotton spinning machines 138
country parishes 425–33
Cowper, Lady 190
Cragside 384
Crawford, Donald 457–60
Crawford v. Crawford and Dilke
    457–8
Crawford, Virginia 457–60
creation, concept of 228
Creation, Special 229
cremation 543–5
Cremation Society 544–5
Crimean War 20, 175–200
    Alma River in 181
    as 'aristocratic sport' 191
    armaments in 181
    as armchair war 194
    Armenia, fighting in 187
    Balaclava campaign in 181–2
    British love of 186
    causes and motivations in 186
    Causeway Heights in 183
    cholera in 178–9, 180, 181
    command of 179–80
    dinner with Russians after
        Balaclava 195–7
    feeding of troops in 175–6
    'forgotten war' in 187
    and free market 194
    Heavy Brigade in 182
    Inkerman, battle of 183, 186
    Light Brigade in 182

military engagement in 179
mutual understanding in, lack of
 186
negotiated settlement to 186–7
numbers of troops in 181
organisation of expedition for
 178
origins of 172–4
and Palmerston 191, 192
photography in 199–200
reporting of 175, 180, 183–4
Russian artillery in 181–3
Russian cavalry in 182–3
Russophobia during 187
Sebastopol, siege of 181, 187
significance of 184
suffering of troops in 178
treatment of British wounded in
 175
Troop Horse Artillery in 182
see also Airey; Cardigan; Lucan;
 Nightingale; Nolan; Peace of
 Paris; Raglan; Russell;
 Seacole; Soyer
criminal code 38
Criminal Law Amendment Act
 448, 564
Criminal Law and Procedures Act
 530
Cruelly Murdered - Constance
 Kent (Taylor) 268
Crystal Palace 129–30, 144–5
in Sydenham 144
Cubitt, Thomas 128
Cumberland, Duke of 26
Curzon, Lord 500, 558, 560
Cyprus, occupation of 400, 405

Daily Chronicle 461
Daily Mail, The 590, 591

Daily Mirror 590
Daily News 337, 346, 355, 396,
 461
Daily Telegraph 411, 451, 461
Daimler, Gottlieb 494
Dale, R.W. 363
Dalhousie, Lord 202, 211, 215
 see also East India Company
Daniel Deronda (Eliot) 408, 410
Dannreuther, Chariclea 411
Dannreuther, Edward 411
Dante Alighieri 236, 371
Darwin, Charles 15, 98
autobiography of 15
background of 45, 50, 224,
 226, 283
character of 225, 226–7
development of theories of 15
nature of writing 231–2
on racial differences 375–6
reluctance to publish 226, 227
see also natural selection; Origin
 of Species
Darwin, Emma 226, 227
Darwin, Erasmus 97, 224
Darwinism see evolution
Das Kapital (Marx) 231
Das Leben Jesu (Strauss) 167
Das Wesen des Christenthums
 (Feuerbach) 167
David Copperfield (Dickens)
 335
Davidson, John 552
Davis, Jefferson 253
Davitt, Michael 452–3, 454
Death of Buckingham, The
 (Winfield) 322
death certificates see Bills of
 Mortality
death duties 588

'Death Song, A' (Morris) 510
Débâcle, La (Zola) 344
decadence 553
Delhi
  British reprisals in 214
  massacre 208–9
  siege of 210
democracy 67, 252–3, 271, 385,
  584
Democratic Federation 444–5
dependency-culture 12
depression see economic
  depression
De Profundis (Wilde) 560
Derby, Lord 146, 189–90, 271,
  273, 309, 331, 386–7, 395
Desborough, Lady 559
Descent of Man, The (Darwin)
  375
determinism 132
Devils, The (Dostoyevsky) 415,
  417, 447
Devonshire, 6th Duke of 129,
  383
Devonshire, 8th Duke of, see
  Hartington
Devonshire House 382–3
Dhondu Pant (Nana Sahib)
  211–12, 213
Dickens, Charles 16–23, 85
  background 16, 260, 283
  as benign force 22
  death of 335–6
  funeral of 336
  at Gad's Hill 21, 336
  nature of novels of 335
  at public executions 337
  sex in works of 334
  visit to Italy 85–6
  visit to Vesuvius 86

see also Bleak House; Christmas
  Carol; David Copperfield;
  Great Expectations; Little
  Dorrit; Oliver Twist; Pictures
  from Italy; Posthumous
  Papers of the Pickwick Club
Dilke, Sir Charles 360, 457, 461
Dillon, John 532
Disraeli, Benjamin 27, 28, 59,
  65–6, 98, 146, 252, 262–3,
  283, 331, 346, 368
  and anti-Semitism 402–3
  in Balkan Crisis 395–7,
  399–400
  characteristics of 379, 402
  comparison with Gladstone
  379–80
  at Congress of Berlin 403
  and Corn Laws 430
  death of 406–8
  as Earl of Beaconsfield 404
  loses election 404
  religious attitudes of 368
  on Schleswig-Holstein 348
  second cabinet of 386–91
  view of Jews 403
  on Zulus 402
divorce 234–5
Divorce Bill 306
docks
  procession of strikers 514
  stevedores in 513
  strike 508, 513–15
doctors
  attitudes to 37
  changing role of 309
Dodgson, Reverend Charles (Lewis
  Carroll) 324, 439
  contemporary allusions in work
  of 328

interpretations of works of
327–8
language-games in work of
328
refused by Alice Liddell 324
and Ruskin 327
sexual nature of 325, 327
sympathy with children of
328–9
Döllinger, Ignaz von 373
domestic violence 314
Dostoyevsky, Fyodor
Mikhailovich 415–17, 431
doubt, religious see religion
Douglas, Lord Alfred 562–4
Dowson, Ernest 552
Doyle, Arthur Conan 527
D'Oyly Carte, Richard 417, 418
drainage 156
Drew, Mary 361
drink see alcohol
drinking water 155–6
Drumlanrig, Lord 562
Du Bois, W.E.B. 256
Dudley, 1st Earl of 382
Dyer, General 501

East End of London 521, 524–5
Eastern Equatorial Africa 486
'Eastern Question' see Ottoman
Empire
East India Company 48, 207,
211, 218, 258
abolition and transfer to Queen
Victoria 218, 221
and Afghan Wars 124
expansion of forces of, in
North-West India 125
and greasing of Enfield rifle
cartridges 201–2

offices of 108–9
see also Indian Mutiny
East Lynne (Wood) 274
eccentricity in upper classes 381
Ecclesiastical Titles Act 142
economic depression 28–9, 254,
405, 480, 508, 573
see also unemployment
economic disparity 30, 41
economic expansion 15, 72
and territorial expansion 52,
148
economic hardship, extent of 113
economic policy 148
economic stability 58
Eddy, Mary Baker 549–50
Edinburgh Review 346
education
and army organisation 355
compulsory 284
Liberal reform of 362–4
religious liberty in 363
secular and uniform 363–4
universal 119, 364
as Victorian invention 282
for women 284, 421, 480
see also public schools; schools
Education Act 284, 363–4
Effingham Theatre 521
Eglinton, Lord, tournament of 65
Egypt 465
annexation of 466–7
expedition to 465–6
nationalism in 465
trade with 465
Eiffel, Gustave 494
Eiffel Tower 494
Eighteenth Brumaire of Louis
Bonaparte, The (Marx) 147
Elcho, Lady 559

electoral districts, equality of 43
electoral reform 330–1, 479
   Conservative Bill on 331
   Liberal Bill on 331
   see also Reform Acts; suffrage
electoral systems 42
Eliot, George *see* Evans, Marian
Elliotson, John 105, 106
Ellis, William 129, 130
emigration 428
empire
   definitions of 391
   effects of Free Trade on 126
   expansion of 124
   and imperial pomp 391
   wealth dependent on 351–2
   see also Afghanistan; Australia;
      Bermuda; British Guiana;
      Canada; colonies; Gambia;
      Gibraltar; Hong Kong;
      Indonesia; Jamaica; Norfolk
      Island; South Africa
empiricism 110
employment, rural 429
Endicott, Mary 484
Endymion (Disraeli) 407
Enfield rifle cartridge 201–2
Engels, Friedrich 114, 131–2
England, regions of 250–1
English Co-operative Society 575
*English in Ireland in the
   Eighteenth Century, The*
   (Froude) 74
Eric, or, Little by Little (Farrar)
   280, 288–9, 330
*Essay on the Development of
   Christian Doctrine, An*
   100–1
Essay on Population (Malthus)
   224

ethical truth, demonstrability of
   110–11
Ethics of the Dust, The (Ruskin)
   326
Eton, St Mary's College, abuse at
   29
Eton School 280, 283
   corporal punishment in 291
Etwall, Ralph 32–3
Europe
   Britain's relationship with 348
   decline of monarchies in 244
   revolutions in 123
   speculations on diplomacy in
      184–5
   see also Franco-Prussian War
Euston station 21
Evans, Marian (George Eliot)
   167, 168, 349, 408, 411, 412
   German language skills of 349
   and Wagner 412–13
evolution, theory of 15, 97, 98,
   100, 224–31, 376
   and acquired characteristics
      224
   Christian objections to 227,
      376
   Christians absorbing 377
   'Darwin or Christ' as
      consequence of 229
   and divorce 234–5
   impact on Victorian scientists
      232
   influence on current thought
      230–2
   perceived as picture of
      competitive world 226
   shaped by the times 225
   see also Darwin; *Origin of
      Species*; Wallace

examinations, public 284–5
Excursion, The (Wordsworth)
131
executions, public 336–8
of Irish bombers 339
Eyre, Governor Edward John 53,
269–72, 298

Faber, F.W. 140
Fabianism 511, 576
factories of Lancashire 253
Factory Act
of 1833, 1844 and 1847 153
of 1850 151
see also Ten Hours measure
Factory Controversy, The
(Martineau) 152
factory inspectors 152, 154
factory system 15, 20, 22, 248
factory workers' view of slavery
254
Falconet (Disraeli) 406
Falstaff Music Hall 522
fantasy, retreat into 322–9
Far From the Madding Crowd
(Hardy) 432
Farrar, Dean 280, 288, 289–90
feminism 307
Fenian movement 338–9, 452,
453, 531
bombing by 453
Fenton, Roger 199–200
Feuerbach, Ludwig Andreas 167
firefighting 13, 14
Fitzroy, Captain Robert 228
flagellation 291–2
Flashman 279
Florentine radicalism 90
fluidity of society 60–2
foot-and-mouth disease 428

football as British national game
409
Football Association 409
Football Association Cup 344
Fors Clavigera (Ruskin) 422
Forster, W.E. 363, 461
Fortnightly Review 462
Foundations of Belief, The
(Balfour) 556–7
Fox and Henderson 130
France
British attitudes to 16
invasion by, feared 16
nationalism and expansionism
of 351
see also French revolution
franchise *see* suffrage
Franchise Act 447
Francophobia 145
Franco-Prussian War 343–6, 354
Frederick William of Prussia,
Prince 238
free market
and Crimean War 194
liberty and enslavement in
132
Free Trade 19, 20, 58, 59, 62,
72, 111, 119, 352
discrediting of 428
effects of, on colonies 126, 127
and Irish Famine 81
terminology of 127
see also Corn Laws
Free Will 132
French revolution
inevitability of 17
perceived implications of
16–17
French Revolution, The (Carlyle)
16–18

French troops in Crimea 178,
179
Froude, James Anthony 30, 74,
103
fundamentalism, Christian 100,
171, 229
funerals 539–45
  as status symbol 539

Gallipoli landing 178
Galvin, George *see* Leno
Gambia 124
games ethos 292–3
Gangs Act 428–9
Garrett, Elizabeth 310–12, 321
gasworkers 512
gendarmerie, British 119
Gentle Art of Making Enemies,
  The (Whistler) 422
geologists 97, 100
  see also Principles of Geology
George, Henry 444
George III, King 24, 25
Germany 238
  comparative strength of 350–1
  influence of philosophy,
    literature and culture of
    348–50
  language of 348–9
  learning to live with 350
  potential domination of 350–1
  scientific education in 350
  see also Franco-Prussian War
Germinal (Zola) 442
Gibraltar 127
Gibson, Thomas Milner 128
Gilbert, William Schwenk
  418–24, 572
Gilbert and Sullivan operas
  417–24

Girdlestone, Canon 429
Girton College 285, 313, 421
Gladstone, Herbert 470
Gladstone, William Ewart 27–8,
  49, 128, 142, 146, 189, 234,
  386, 439, 464, 594
  on American civil war 251–2,
    346
  on aristocracy 356
  attitude to Franco-Prussian War
    346
  background 50, 94, 355
  in Balkan Crisis 396–400
  on Bismarck 347
  and Bradlaugh 449
  campaigning for second
    administration 404–5
  and Catholicism 372–5
  and Chamberlain 457
  as chancellor of the Exchequer
    194
  and Contagious Diseases Acts
    474
  contradictions of 250, 361
  and Dilke 457
  on disestablishment 371
  and Disraeli 379–80, 407
  and educational reforms 363–4
  and Egypt 465
  first administration of 343–64
  and Gordon 472
  and Home Rule for Ireland
    453–4, 455, 456, 479
  intellectual character of 348
  and Ireland 85, 101, 338–9,
    455, 456
  and Khartoum 469–70
  and occupation of Cyprus 400
  as orator 398
  and Parnell 533, 535

as product of public school 280
and prostitutes 356
psychosomatic illnesses of 397
religious attitudes of 70, 101,
347–8, 371, 398
resignation of 70
on rich and poor 444
and Ruskin 355, 360–2
second administration of 478
on slavery 255
third administration of 479
transformation of 85
visits Döllinger 373
visits Italy 84
visits Neapolitan prisons 85
visits Newcastle 251
voice of 251
on working class 443
see also army reform
Gloag, Robert Peacock 197
global policemen, British as see
intervention
Goblin Market (Rossetti) 305,
315–16, 330
Goethe, Johann Wolfgang von
349–50
Golden Bowl, The (James) 484
Gordon, General Charles George
467–72
character of 471
death of 470–1
as governor of the Congo
468–9
Gordon, George William
269–71, 499
Gordon's Last Stand (Joy) 470–1
Gosse, Edmund 430
Götterdämmerung (Wagner) 414
Gough, Lieutenant Sir Hugh 201,
204–5

government
as administration 385
aristocratic form of 385–6
class lines in 386
forms of 17–18
unaltered in Britain 385
Government of India Bill 221
Graham, Frances 558, 559
Graham, Sir James 76
Granville, Lord 130, 397
Great Exhibition of 1851
127–30, 136–9
admission charges to 137
appearance of displayed
artefacts 143–4
attendance 137–8
designs for exhibition halls for
129
internationalism of displays
142–3
machines displayed in 138
opening of 137–8
perspectives on 127–8, 12–43
Royal Commission on 128,
129
site for 129
see also Crystal Palace; Paxton;
Pugin
Great Expectations (Dickens)
127, 335, 579–80
Great Famine see Irish Famine
Great Uprising see Indian Mutiny
Green, Thomas Hill 519–20, 570
Greville, Charles 26
Grey, Lord 39
Grey, Sir George 117
growth see economy; population
Gubbins, Martin 216
gun, breech-loaded 384
'gunboat diplomacy' 133–5

Gurkhas 203
Gurney, Edmund 439

habeas corpus, suspension of
  309
haemophilia 24
Haggard, Rider 601
hair, import of 163
Hairdressers Journal, The 163
hairdressing 162–3
hair thieves 163
*Half a Century of the British
  Empire* (Martineau) 152
Hallam, Arthur 99
Hamilton, Sir William 349
Hannington, James 486–8
Harcourt, Sir William 588
Hardie, Keir 573, 577, 580–2
Hardy, Thomas 430–33
Hargreaves, James 249
Harmsworth, Alfred 590–1
Harney, George Julian 113, 114
Harrow School 290
Hartington, Lord (later 8th Duke
  of Devonshire) 397, 456,
  465, 468–9, 470, 584
Hastings, Warren 208
'Hawarden Kite' 455–6
Hegel, Georg Wilhelm Friedrich
  111, 349
Helmholtz, Hermann 494
Henry Esmond (Thackeray) 140,
  334
Henty, George Alfred 259–60
Hercegovina 394
heresy-hunting 169–70
Hertz, Heinrich 494
Hewitt, Major-General W.H.
  204, 205
Hicks, General William 467

High Church *see* Oxford
  Movement
Hignett Bros 198
Hill, Rowland 128
Hindu religion 201, 202
HMS *Devastation* 423
H.M.S. Pinafore (Gilbert and
  Sullivan) 422–3, 479
Hogarth, George 411
Holford, R.S. 382
holidays *see* leisure time
Holland, Henry Scott 370
Holmes, Sherlock 527–9
Holy Land 173
  see also Palestine
Home Rule for Ireland *see* Irish
  Home Rule
homosexuality 290, 448, 565,
  567
  and imperialism 597–600
  see also Drumlanrig; Wilde
Hong Kong 124
Hooker, Sir William Jackson
  229
Horner, John 558
horse racing 409, 584–5
housekeeping guidance 261–2
House of Lords, power of 585
houses of London 382–3
Houses of Parliament
  architectural style of 63–5
  composition of 62
  destruction by fire of 9–10,
    13–14, 35
  electric light in 494
  rebuilding of 14, 62
Housman, A.E. 566
Howick, Lord 49
Howley, Archbishop 26
Hueffer, Francis 412

Hughes, Thomas 276–7, 296,
    367
humanity, nature of 104
Hunt, William Holman 159, 162,
    165, 185
  visit to Palestine 171
Hutton, James 97
Huxley, T.H. 228, 376–7, 462
Hyndman, Henry 444

Idealism 520, 569–70, 606–7
Illustrated London News 142,
    145, 218
Imperial British East Africa
    Company 491
Imperial College of Science and
    Technology 144
imperialism 601, 607
  and homosexuality 597–600
  see also colonies
Independent Labour Party
    573–4, 577
India 493–501
  assumptions of racial superiority
    towards 209
  Blavatsky in 550
  divide and rule in 499
  education in 499–500
  Hindu–Mohammedan friction
    in 499
  land tenure in 202
  Liberal and Conservative
    approaches to 499–500
  mutual distrust in following
    mutiny 222
  perceptions of 258–9
  resistance to programmes of
    improvement in 221–2
  Russian invasion of 389
  as source of cholera 34

  see also East India Company;
    Indian Mutiny; sepoys; Suez
    Canal
Indian Mutiny 20, 126, 500
  British reprisals after 207,
    213–15
  civilian involvement in 206
  Delhi Declaration in 205–6
  as Independence Movement
    206
  Indian support for British
    during 207
  likelihood of success of
    220–19
  as 'mutiny' 206
  perceptions of 217–23
  reform of army after 500
  roots of 201–5
  scale of 206
  warnings of 204
  war of reprisal in 208
  see also Bengal army; Delhi;
    Enfield rifle; Gurkhas;
    Kanpur; Lucknow; Meerut;
    sepoys
Indian National Congress 500
Indian nationalism 500–1
Indian soldiers *see* sepoys
Indonesia 124
induction coil 494
industrial expansion 124
  and armaments 353
  see also economic expansion
    124
Industrial Revolution 61, 98–9
industrial workers 79
industry, rural 31
Infants' Custody Act 306
In Memoriam (Tennyson)
    99–100

intervention by British, global
52
'intuitionist' school of philosophy
110
Invasion of the Crimea (Kinglake)
186
investing 58
Invincibles 453
Iolanthe (Gilbert and Sullivan)
421
Ireland
agrarian society in, structure of
80
British army recruitment from
357
British economic interests in 80
cholera in 83
'conacre' portions of land in
79
crime figures for 78
education of Catholics in 78
emigration from 81
export to Canada of tenants
from 80–1
Fenianism in 127
government policies in 101
landlords in 78, 79
land ownership in 78, 111,
451
living conditions in 79, 451
population of 77
potato as exclusive diet in 78
poverty in 78–9, 452
Protestant Ascendancy in 78
protests at corn exports from
79–80
rent enforcement in 455–6
Republicanism in 127
tenant farmers in 77, 78, 79
transportation from 126–7

see also Home Rule; Irish
Famine; Irish nationalism;
Irish people; Irish question;
Land League; maize; Parnell
Irish Church Bill 361
Irish Coercion Bill 76
Irish Famine 62, 74–83, 185
British reaction to 82
chronology of 76
deaths from 77, 81
emigration during 80–1
force in suppression of protests
81–2
homicides during 83
relief by British government for
77
relief by British merchants for
82
religious interpretations of 76
responsibility for 74–5
trade in corn during 75
Irish Home Rule 453, 454, 456,
460, 480, 516, 531
Irish immigrants as Catholics 140
Irish Land Act 338, 361
Irish nationalism 70
Irish people, British attitudes to
69, 75–6
Irish question 62, 70, 449, 512,
516
as poverty question 460
iron production 15
Isis Unveiled (Blavatsky) 550
'Italian in England, The'
(Browning) 88
Italy, visitors to 84–92

Jack the Ripper 525, 526–7
Jamaica 48
English views of riots 270–1

government of 269
population of 269
response to riots 270
unrest in 126, 269–70
see also Eyre
Jamaica Committee 270, 298
James, Henry 413, 442, 459,
483–4, 568–9
Jameson Raid 596, 606, 609
Jane Eyre (Brontë) 285, 289
Jerome, Jennie 484
Jewel Cabinet 143
Jewish immigrants 525
Jews *see* Disraeli
Jex-Blake, Dr Sophia 312
jingoism 399–400
John Murray 98, 226, 397
John Player and Sons 198
Johnson, Lionel 552, 553–4
Johnson, Samuel 248
Jones, Ernest 116
Jordan, Dorothea 24
journalism
and modern journalism 476
as moral mirror to society 440
popular 461–4: origins of
463–4
Journalism, New 462–3
Jowett, Benjamin 83, 364
Jude the Obscure (Hardy) 432
'July monarchy' of Louis Philippe
114

Kabbala Unveiled, The (Mathers)
551
Kanpur
British reprisals at 214
importance of 211
on Independence Day 222–3
massacre 208, 210–12

see also Bibighar; Dhondu Pant
Karim, Abdul 505
Keble, John 101
Kennington model housing (Prince
Albert) 57
Kensal Green cemetery 542–3,
545
Kensington Ladies' Discussion
Society 313
Kensington museums 57
Kent, Constance, case of 266–7
Kent, Edward, Duke of 24
Khartoum *see* Sudan
Kibroth-Hathaavah 288
Kilvert, Reverend Francis, diaries
of 426
Kim (Kipling) 498
'King, The' (Kipling) 496
Kingdom of Christ (Maurice)
299
King Edward's School 63
Kinglake, Alexander William 186
Kingsley, Charles 45, 148–9,
270, 273, 295–304
character of 295, 296–7
funeral of 296
sexuality of 299–302
views of 297–9
King Solomon's Mines (Haggard)
601–2
Kipling, Rudyard 495–501,
600–1
Kitchener, Lord Horatio Herbert
598, 607, 611–12
Knock (Ireland), visions at 451
Kruger, Stephanus Johannes
Paulus 605–6, 608

Labouchere, Henry 66, 130, 448
Labour Annual, The 578

labour as form of wealth 42
Labour Party 194, 577
  see also Independent Labour
    Party
Lacaita, Joseph 85
Lamarck, Jean Chevalier de 97,
  224
Lamb, Charles 36
Lambert and Butler 198
La Mont, John 43
Lancet, The 35–6, 312
Land Acts 455, 530
Land League 452, 455, 531
land ownership 427, 583, 594
Lansdowne, Lord 190
Lascelles family 50
Last Conquest of Ireland
  (Perhaps) 1860, The (Mitchel)
  80
la Touche, Rose 325
Lawrence, Sir Henry 216–17
Layard, Sir Henry 191
learning see autodidacticism
Lectures on the History of the
  Turks (Newman) 180
Left, the 10
Leighton, Frederic 322
leisured activity 409
leisure time 409
Leno, Dan 523–4
Leopold of Saxe-Coburg, Prince
  54, 504
  Civil List pension 54
Leslie, Sir Shane 327
Lesseps, Ferdinand de 389
Lewes, George 349, 412
liberalism 362
Liberal Party 71, 75, 77, 336,
  379, 386, 404, 444, 479, 573
  education reform of 362

and Ireland 454, 478, 480
and Labour Party 578–9
and Parnell 534
Liberal Radicals 447, 508, 573
liberty
  Comte's championing of 110
  free market 111
  personal 38, 111
  and security 109, 134
Liddell, Alice 323–5, 352
Life and Labour of the People in
  London (Booth) 442, 512
light bulb 494
Light of the World, The (Hunt)
  159, 160, 163
Lincoln, Abraham and cotton
  embargo 254
Linton, W.J. 43
literacy 363
Little Dorrit (Dickens) 20, 335
liver-rot in sheep 428
Livingstone, David 488
Llanthony (Wales), visions at 451
Lloyd, Marie 522–3
Lloyd George, David 574, 592–5
Local Government Act 587
Local Government Board 345,
  587
Localisation Act 357
'Locksley Hall' (Tennyson) 99,
  589–90
Lodge, Sir Oliver 494
London
  conditions of poor in 442–3
  population of 443
  suburbs of 443, 573
London Docks 365–6
London Oratory 140
London School of Economics
  576

London School of Medicine for
Women 312, 421
*London and Westminster Review,
The* 109
London Working Men's
Association 42
Longhurst, Arthur E.J. 197–8
Lorne, Marquess of 503
'Lost Chord, The' (Sullivan)
418
Lothair (Disraeli) 379–81
Louise, Princess 503
Lovett, William 42–3, 46
Lowder, Charles 365, 369–70
Lowood School *see* Clergy
Daughters' School, Casterton
Lucan, Lord 181–3
Lucknow
descriptions of 215
on Independence Day 222–3
relief of 208, 217
siege of 204, 215–17
uprising in 204, 216–17
Lugard, Frederick 490–2
Lyell, Charles 96, 97–8, 128
Lysistrata 555
Lyte, Reverend H.F. 103–4
Lytton, Lord 400–1, 499

'McAndrew's Hymn' (Kipling)
495
Macaulay, Thomas Babington
66, 139
views on classes 115
views on Irish Catholicism of
70
MacDonald, George 169–70,
328
Macdonald, Sir Hector 599
machines *see* Great Exhibition

Macmillan's Magazine 295, 302,
305, 314, 319
Macnaghten, Sir William Hay
124
magistrates 44
Mayhew, Henry 521
Maillet, Benoît de 97
maize, import of 76–7
profits from 81
see also Irish Famine
Malthus, Daniel 11
Malthus, Reverend Thomas
11–12, 14, 75, 224, 225
Manchester, Duke of 69
Manchester Guardian 82
'Mandalay' (Kipling) 496
*Manifest der Kommunistischen
Partei* (Engels and Marx)
114
Manning, Cardinal Henry Edward
142, 458, 515–18, 534,
539–42, 545
Marconi, Gugliemo 494
Marius the Epicurean (Pater) 554
market economy 98–9
marriage 260–1
age of 324
and prostitution 310–11
published guidance on 261
Married Women's Property Act
248
Marshall and Snelgrove 410
Martineau, Harriet 152–3, 167,
168, 174, 250
Marx, Karl 61, 114, 335
on Aberdeen as Russian spy
187–8
burial of 510
on dangers of Pan-Slavism 187
on English Christianity 149

on European political structures
187
influence of 444
in Kentish Town 262
on Napoleon Bonaparte's coup
d'état, 147
Marxists 508
masculinity of Imperial life 600
masturbation 288–9
Matchmakers Union 511
match-manufacturers 154
Mathers, Liddell 551–2
Matrimonial Causes (or Divorce)
Bill 234
Maurice, F.D. 158, 169, 170,
187, 194, 284, 296, 323, 367,
405
Mayhew, Henry 145, 155
Maynooth, Royal College of St
Patrick at 67–70, 75–6, 338
Mayor of Casterbridge, The
(Hardy) 432
Mazzini, Giuseppe 89
Mearn, Andrew 442
medicine, women studying 312
Meerut uprising 204
see also Indian Mutiny
Melbourne, Lord 14, 26
attitudes to workhouses of
28–9
and Jamaica Assembly 53
relationship with Victoria 26–8
resignation of 53
Melbourne's government 48–9
Mendel, Gregor Johann 232
Mesmer, Franz Anton 105
Mesmerism 103–7
and Christ's miracles 106
metaphysics 570–1
Metropolitan Police Force 37

Middle Ages 185
middle classes
aspirations of 191–2
attitudes towards public schools
279
childhood in 260
definition of 281–2
schools founded for education
of 281–2
tax increases and support of
125
Middlemarch (Eliot) 344, 349
Midland Railway 129, 130
Mikado (Gilbert and Sullivan)
419
military resources 351, 354
see also armaments; army
Mill, James 37–8, 109, 202
Mill, John Stuart 37, 108–12,
554
background 108–9, 260
on capital punishment 337–8
influence of 109–10
on liberty 132
political views of 111–12
and women's suffrage 313
Millais, John Everett 159, 165–6
Miller, Annie 161, 162, 163
mills, factory 45
Milman, Reverend H.H. 12
Milner, Sir Alfred 608
Milton, John 229
mines, conditions in 151
Minton and Co. 128
*Missionary Travels and Researches
in South Africa* (Livingstone)
493
Mitchel, John 80
*Mode of Communication of
Cholera, On the* (Snow) 156

Modern Painters (Ruskin) 164–5
Montenegro 394–5
Moody, Dwight L. 377
Moore, G.E. 569
Morley, John 462, 534, 535, 579
Mormons 549–50
Morning Herald, The 258
Morning Post, The 461
Morris, William 164, 185, 262,
    414–15, 444–5, 509, 510
Mortara, Edgar 371–2
motor-vehicle 494
Mumler, W.H. 439
Munby, Arthur J., diaries of
    319–21
murder 521–9
music
    flourishing of 410–24
    philistine attitude of upper class
        to 410
music halls 521–4
Muslim religion 201
Mwanga of Uganda, King 486,
    491
My Apprenticeship (Webb) 574
Myers, Frederic W.H. 439
myth as response to materialism
    557

Nana Sahib *see* Dhondu Pant
Napier, Sir Charles 46, 66, 125
Napoleon III
    election of 113
    in England 344, 345
    declares war on Prussia 343
    in Palestine dispute 173
Narratives of Events at Cawnpore
    (Chand) 207
National Education League 363
National Secular Society 548

National Union of Gasworkers
    and General Labourers 512
natural calamities, rural 428
natural selection 15, 148
    Wallace and 228
    see also Darwin; evolutionary
        theory
navy, expansion of 423
Neapolitan prisons 85
Neill, Colonel James 214
Nemesis of Faith (Froude) 103
Newbolt, Henry 292
Newman, John Henry 100–1,
    101–2, 103, 140, 180, 283,
    302–4, 375
Newnham College 421
New Poor Laws of 1834 14, 32,
    41
New River Company 382
newspapers, cost of 19
New Statesman and Nation 576
Nicholas, Tsar 187
Nicholas Nickleby (Dickens) 289
Nicklin, Richard 199
Nightingale, Florence 52, 175, 177
    in Crimea 178
    founding school of nursing 284
    on the working class 443
Nobel, Alfred 495
Nolan, Captain 182
Nonconformism 377, 577
'No Popery' issue 139
Norfolk Island 127
Northcote, Sir Stafford 389
North-East England, prosperity in
    250
Northern Echo 464
Northern Star, The 41, 45
North London Collegiate School
    for Girls 284

Norton, Caroline 305–6, 314
Norton, Richard 305–6
nostalgia 21
Notes and Queries 457
nouveaux riches 383

O'Brien, James Bronterre 41–2
O'Brien, William 509, 532
O'Connell, Daniel 66
O'Connor, Feargus 42, 46, 118
Olcott, Henry 550
'Old Cumberland Beggar'
    (Wordsworth) 36
oligarchy of government 42–3
Oliver Twist (Dickens) 28, 29
Opera Comique Theatre 417
Oppenheimer, Henry 389
*Origin of Species by Means of
    Natural Selection, On the*
    (Darwin) 98, 224
  commercial success of 226
  Darwin's later modifications to
    224
  scientific objections to 232–3
Orthodox religion in Russia
    185, 415
Osborne House 56, 117, 128
O'Shea, Katharine, and Parnell
    460, 533
  English and Irish attitudes to
    565
Ottoman Empire
  cotton textiles manufacture in
    393
  decline of 391
  life in 392
  nationalist aspirations in
    391–2
  predatory attitude of Europe
    and Russia to 391–2

see also Turkey
Our Ladye of Llanthony 439
Our Mutual Friend (Dickens)
    155
Owen, Robert 42, 575
'Oxen, The' (Hardy) 433
Oxford Letters (Clough) 103
Oxford Movement 101, 366–7,
    370

Pacifico, Don 133–4
Painted Chamber 62
Palestine 171
  see also Holy Land
Palgrave, William Gifford 275
Pall Mall Gazette 459, 462, 463,
    464, 469, 472–6
Palmerston, Lord 39, 51–2, 66,
    117, 136, 189–90, 250
  approval of Bonaparte's coup
    d'état, 146
  on aristocracy 192
  character of 188–9, 191,
    192–3
  comparison with Churchill 189
  and Crimean War 194
  death of 330
  and Don Pacifico affair 133–5,
    146
  forms government 190
  on Free Trade 264
  and Matrimonial Causes Bill
    234
  political ambivalence of 193
  popularity of 193
  and Ten Hours Bill 193
  treatment of Irish tenants by
    51, 80, 193
  and Urquhart 188–9
  Victoria's objections to 190

view of American civil war 253
views of political change 192
Pandenanga, Ramchandra (Tatya
 Tope) 208, 211, 212,
 219–20, 223
Panopticon prisons 38
Papal Infallibility 372, 373
papal power and kingdom of Italy
 516
Paradise Lost (Milton) 229–30,
 279
Paradiso (Dante) 236
Parliament
 aristocracy in 481
 party system in 481
 payment for members of 43
 preserving the power of the rich
  481
 property qualification for
  membership of 43
 in *Savoy Operas* 420
 see also Houses of Parliament
parliamentary system, oligarchic
 20
Parnell, Charles Stewart 454–7
 adultery of 458, 533–5
 death of 536
 fall of 530–6, 565
 imprisonment of 455
 and leadership of Irish MPs
  534–5
 marriage to Katherine O'Shea
  536
 popularity of 533
 see also Home Rule
Parry, Sir Charles Hubert Hastings
 56, 410, 614
Past and Present (Carlyle) 158–9,
 185
Pater, Walter 554, 557

Patience (Gilbert and Sullivan)
 422
Patmore, Coventry 305, 314–15
Pattison, Mark 442, 462
paupers 29
 see also poverty; workhouses
Paxton, Joseph 129
Peace of Paris 186, 189
Peel, Janus 59
Peel, Sir Robert 27, 49, 53,
  58–73, 128
 as architect of new order 61
 assessments of 135–6
 characteristics of 58
 conservatism of 71
 and Corn Laws 72
 death of 133, 135
 on Don Pacifico affair 135
 economic views of 133
 and Free Trade 72
 parliamentary career of 58–9
 parliament of 66
 religious views of 76
 see also Maynooth
Penal Laws 78
Pendennis (Thackeray) 334
'Penny Gaffs' 522
Penny Post 128
People's Charter and National
 Petition 43–4
periodicals, importance of 19,
 462
Peterhouse, Cambridge 494
petite bourgeoisie 19–20
Peto, Samuel Morton 130
philistinism 410
Phoenix Park murders 532
photographs
 authenticity of 438
 of late Victorian era 437–8

of presentation of Third
Chartist Petition 118
photography 58, 197, 199–200,
437–8
and fantasy 323–4
phrenology 104–5
picketing
in dock strike 514
peaceful 444
*Pickwick Papers see Posthumous
Papers of the Pickwick Club*
Pictures from Italy (Dickens) 85
piece-rates 512
Pigott, Richard 533
Pius IX, Pope 139–40, 371–2
Plain Tales from the Hills
(Kipling) 497
Playfair, John 97
Podmore, Frank 439
police force 38–9
as arm of state 38
opposing cremation 544
preventive policing by 38
separating rich and poor 383
staffing of 39
strength of 119
at unemployment
demonstrations 509
see also gendarmerie
political career and divorce 460
political classes, control of
populace by 10–11
political map, difficulty of 20
political prisoners, transportation
of 126
political representation 194
political system, development of
546
political viewpoints, ambivalence
of 361

poor, the 28–9, 36
aspirations of 383
children of *see* children
education removed from 283–4
improving 335, 378
prostitution among 310–11
separated from the rich 383
urban 148
see also economic disparity;
poverty; rich; Salvation Army
Poor Law Amendments 29, 42
Poor Law Commission 31, 44
Poor Laws 12
see also New Poor Laws
population
growth of 11–12, 249
movement of, with
industrialisation 249
size of 351
'surplus' 12–13
*Population, Essay on the Principle
of* (Malthus) 11–12, 15
pornography 526
porphyria 25
Porter, Sir Joseph 422–3
Portrait of a Lady (James) 484
*Posthumous Papers of the
Pickwick Club* (Dickens) 16,
18–22
influence of 19
origins of 18
sales of 19
potato blight 74, 76, 78
see also Irish Famine
Potter, Beatrice 483, 548, 574–6
see also Webb
Potteries Political Union 44
poverty
and affluence in London 383,
521

and alcohol 365
and army recruitment 357
causes of 36
in Celtic fringes 429
and cholera 36
clergy embracing 366–8, 369
in London Docks 365
Malthus' views on 12
rural 32, 426–30
visibility of 30
see also economic depression;
    economic disparity;
    Ireland; paupers; urban
    poor; workhouses
Prelude, The (Wordsworth) 131,
    132–3, 159
Pre-Raphaelite, meaning of 162
Pre-Raphaelite Brotherhood 159,
    164, 322
Press 461–4
and army reform 355
conversions to Conservatism in
    461
'leaks' to 461–2
popular, as Victorian legacy
    461
power of 460
Pretorius, Andries 126
Preventive Policing (Chadwick)
    37
Prince of Wales 240, 241
Princess Casamassima, The
    (James) 442
Princess Ida (Gilbert and Sullivan)
    421
Principles of Geology (Lyell) 97,
    98, 104
Principles of Mathematics, The
    (Russell) 570
printing, steam 493

prisons 117
progress 94–5
property
    crimes against 38
    as qualification for suffrage
        10
proprietary boroughs 39
prosperity, feeling of 446
prostitution 308–11, 416
    child 472–5
    Christianity's effect on trade in
        367
    concept of 310–11
    perceptions of 473
    and poverty 365
    purchase of children for 474
protectionism 71–2
    see also Corn Laws
Protestant Ascendancy in Ireland
    78
Protestantism
    and Britishness 64
    see also Catholicism
Prussia 238–40
psychical research 551
Psychical Research, Society for
    439
public executions see executions,
    public
public health see cholera;
    Contagious Diseases Act;
    drainage; drinking water
public houses 525
public schools 278–82
    Clarendon Commission to
        investigate 280–1
    foundation of new 281, 286
    institutionalisation in 287–8
    middle-class attitudes towards
        279

poor scholars in 280–1, 283
teaching of science in 280
as vehicles of social engineering 281
Public Schools Act 280, 283–4
Public Worship Regulation Act 368, 369, 370, 371
martyrs of 369
Pugin, Augustus Welby Northmore 185
in Great Exhibition 138–9, 142
Houses of Parliament interior by 63–4
Punch 219, 411
Punjab, expansion in 203
Pusey, Edward Bouverie 103, 348
Puseyites 141, 267

Quakers 362
Quarterly Review 252
Queensbury, Marquess of 561–4
Queen's College, Harley Street 284

racial superiority, assumed 493
racing *see* horse racing
Radical Federation 509
Radicals 71, 360
Ragged Schools 167
Raglan, Lord 178, 182
railways
American 42
development of 21, 72
effect on communications 30
extent of 351
in India 220
and leisured activity 409
single gauge for 128

and travel speed 493
Raj, the 220, 498
see also India
Recluse, The (Wordsworth) 131
recruitment and depopulation 357
Red House (Webb) 262
Reform, Age of 10
Reform Act
of 1832 10, 20, 39–40, 48, 142
of 1867 20, 252, 312, 331–2, 386
of 1884 480, 573
effects of 39–40
reformatories 266
refugees, Britain as asylum for 123
relief funds 257
religion
and decadence 556
development of 100–1
as human construct 167
numbers leaving 103–4
unbelief in 168, 185
see also Christianity; country parishes; Orthodox religion
Religion of Humanity 110–11
religious liberty in education 363
religious prejudice and evolution 98
Renaissance and Special Creation 229
rentier interests 147–8
Representation of the People Act 479
republicans 360
see also Radicals
Return of the Native, The (Hardy) 432

revolution in Britain
  failed (presentation of Third
    Chartist Petition) 113–20
  lack of 27, 110, 113
  and nature of Victorians 120
  see also colonies
Reynolds' Newspaper 254
Rhodes, Cecil 596, 597–8, 603–5
rich, the
  pointlessness of lives of 417
  and poor, gulf between 441–50
Richter, Hans 412
Ring, The (Wagner) 414–15
Ring and the Book, The
  (Browning) 90
Ripon, Lord 499
Rise of Our East African Empire,
  The (Lugard) 491
Ritchie, Charles Thomson 587
ritualism in churches 370
Ritualist movement 366, 367,
  368–71
Roberts, Lord 611, 615
Roman Catholic Church see
  Catholic Church
Rorke's Drift 401
Rose and the Ring, The
  (Thackeray) 334
Rosebery, Lord 562
Rossetti, Christina 159, 305,
  315–16
  in Highgate penitentiary 315
Rossetti, Dante Gabriel 90,
  159–61, 185, 247, 257, 316
  marriage of 317
  retrieval of poems from tomb
    318
  women in paintings of 416
Rothschild, Lord Lionel 389
Rothschild, Nathaniel 389

rotten boroughs, abolition of 10
Rotton, Reverend John 209–10
Royal Albert Hall 144
royal family 117
Royal Holloway College 421
Royalty Theatre 418
Rudd Concession 605
Rugby School 276–9, 282, 283,
  286–7
Rural Rides (Cobbett) 32
Ruskin, Effie 166
Ruskin, John 64, 271
  and Alice Liddell 325
  baby language of 326
  divorce of 289
  and Dodgson 327
  and Gladstone 355, 360–2
  on Great Exhibition 143–4
  and Holman Hunt 165
  in later life 326
  and Millais 165–6
  political contradictions of
    361–2
  and Rose la Touche 325–6
  sued by Whistler 87, 422
  visit to Venice 87–8
  and Wordsworth 133
Russell, Bertrand 109, 569–71
Russell, Lord John 39, 40, 77,
  80, 116, 117, 118, 128, 146,
  190, 250, 330
  attitude to Irish Famine 83
  and Catholic church 141,
    142
  'Finality' speech of 40
  and franchise 261, 271
  view of American civil war 253
Russell, Scott 128
Russell, William Howard
  in America 247–8

in the Crimea 175, 179–81,
183–4, 187
in India 214, 215
as 'power without
responsibility' 187
Russia
corn exports to Europe from
427
diplomatic aims of 184
invasion of 180
and Ottoman Empire 391–3
pan-Slavic fervour in 392
religious piety in 186
see also Balkan Crisis; Crimean
War; Russo-Turkish War
Russo-Turkish War 399–400

'St John's Wood Clique' 322
St Stephen's Chapel 14
Salisbury, Lord 27, 29, 324, 345,
395, 399, 444, 487, 531, 532,
533, 565, 574, 587, 590
Salvation Army 378
Sanitary Acts 309
Sankey, Ira D. 377–8
Sargent, John Singer 559
saving 58
as basis of franchise 261
Savings Bank movement 261
Savoy, The 555
Savoy Operas, The (Gilbert and
Sullivan) 420–4
effect of 420, 422–4
Savoy Theatre 420
Scapegoat, The (Hunt) 171
schools 281
boarding 282
hierarchy of 281
homosexuality in 289–92
stories of 289

as waking nightmares 289
see also public schools; school
stories
science
exploration in spirit of 488
fascination of 105–7
in school education 280
scientific materialism 556–7
Scott, Charlotte 421
Scott, Sir Walter 36
Scutari hospitals 179
Seacole, Mary 176–8, 180
seasonal employment 512
Sebastopol 181
Second World War 186
Secret Ballot 361
sectarianism in England 445
self-criticism of Victorians 617
Self-help (Smiles) 191
sepoys 180
comparisons with British
workers 203
composition of 203
in Cyprus 400
imprisonment and release of
204
loyalty to East India Company
219
Meerut uprising of 201–5
pay of 125, 126
religious sensibilities of 126, 201
role of 20
transport of, and caste system
203
views of 202
see also Indian Mutiny
Serbia 394–5
servant class 318
Seurat, Georges 344
see also Crimean War

sexuality and religious symbolism
301–2
sexually transmitted diseases *see*
venereal diseases
Seymour, Robert 18
Shaftesbury, Earl of *see* Ashley
Shaw, Charles 12–13
Shaw, George Bernard 414, 475,
511, 577
Shaw, Norman 384
She (Haggard) 602
Sherer, J.W. 212–13
Sherman, General 247
Shooting Niagara: and After
(Carlyle) 332
shopping as leisured activity
409
Shropshire Lad, A (Housman)
566
Sibthorp, Colonel 66
Siddal, Elizabeth 159–61
Sidgwick, Henry 439
Sidgwick, Mary 567
Sikh wars 125
Sims, George 442
Sind, conquest of 125
Sketches by Boz (Dickens) 18,
335
*Slavers Throwing Overboard the
Dead and Dying* (Turner) 52
slavery 247
abolition of 48, 49, 268
in Africa 490
and American Constitution
249
in American cotton industry
249
attitudes to 20
economic difficulties more
important than 254

economic implications of 51,
248–9
increased by industrial
revolution 249
pre-Raphaelite views on 258
in West Indies 48
slaves
emancipated, fate of 53
insurance for, on slaving ships
52
ownership of 48
treatment of 50–1
Smiles, Samuel 191
Smith, Adam 132
Smith, Joseph 549
Smith, Reverend Sydney 70
Smith, W.H. 423, 424, 482, 485
smoking habits 197–9
Smyth, Colonel Carmichael 201,
204
Snow, Dr John 156–7
social climbers 94
social control 37–8
Social Democratic Federation
511
socialism 443, 548, 574
see also anti-socialism
Socialist League 445–6
social progress 111
society, Victorian *see* Victorian
society
Society of Arts 128
Society for the Encouragement of
Arts, Manufacture and
Commerce 128
Somerset, Lord Fitzroy 117
Somerset House 117
Sorcerer, The (Gilbert and
Sullivan) 417, 420
Souls, the 556–60

South Africa 124, 126
  Boers in 490
  diamonds in 595, 604
  gold in 595–6, 604–5, 606
  Johannesburg in 606
  see also Boer War; Kruger;
    Rhodes
Soyer, Alexis 175–6, 180, 195–6
  vegetable cakes of 175–6
Spectator, The 213, 462
Spencer, Herbert 94, 224
Spielmann, M.H. 219
spiritualism 439, 530
squirearchy 585–9
stagecoaches 21
Stalky and Co. (Kipling) 600
Standard, The 461
Stanford, Sir Charles Villiers 410
Stanley, Arthur Penrhyn 275,
    276–8, 290, 292–4, 367
Stanley, Henry Morton 488
Stanley, Lord 128, 134
  see also Derby
Stansfeld, James 476
state interference 75, 354–5
Stead, William Thomas 423,
    463–4, 468, 471, 472–3, 474,
    475–7, 510
  and Annie Besant 548
  death of 477
  and Eliza Armstrong fabrication
    475–6
steamships
  production of 15
  shallow-draft, in exploration of
    Africa 493
Stephen, Sir James Fitzjames 220,
    500
Stones of Venice, The (Ruskin)
    87

Stowe, Harriet Beecher 268
Strachey, Lytton 236
Strauss, David Friedrich 167
Struggle for Mastery in Europe,
    The (Taylor) 184
Strutt, Jedediah 482
Studies in the History of the
    Renaissance (Pater) 554
Study in Scarlet, A (Doyle) 527
Suárez, Francisco de 229
Sudan 465
  death of Gordon in 470
  defeat at Abu Klea 470
  difficulty of withdrawing
    garrison from Khartoum
    468
  expedition to Khartoum 469
  Kitchener in 607
  military decisions on 469–70
  rebellion of Mahdi in 467–72
  Second Sudan War 607–8
  siege of Khartoum 470
Suez Canal 388–90
  Dual Control of 465
  commercial interests in 465
  and India 390, 465
  see also Egypt
Suez Canal Company 389–90,
    405
suffrage
  in Chartism 43
  extent of 10, 39, 42, 43, 385,
    447, 478–9, 573
  see also electoral reform;
    Reform Acts
Sullivan, Arthur 418–24, 572
'survival of the fittest' see natural
    selection
Sussex, Duke of 168
Sutton Coldfield School 284

Swan, Joseph 494
Swan and Edgar 410
Sybil (Disraeli) 66
Symonds, John Addington
  290–1, 439
syphilis 309–310
  see also veneral diseases
System of Logic, A (Mill) 110
Swinburne, Algernon Charles
  291
Symons, Arthur 553
Szathmari, Carol Popp de 199

tailors, working conditions of
  155
Tait, Archibald Campbell 367–8
Tancred (Disraeli) 66
tariffs, lifting of 58
Tatya Tope *see* Pandenanga
taxation
  and Crimean War 194
  and middle class 125
Taylor, A.J.P. 184, 632
Taylor, Bernard 268
Taylor, Reverend W.F. 369
technological revolution 494–5
  and expansion of Empire 493,
  495
telegraphy, wireless 494
  in India 220, 493
telephone 494
'Telliamed' *see* Maillet
Temple, William 85
Ten Hours Act 119, 151, 193
Tennant, Margot 559
Tenniel, Sir John 219, 324
Tennyson, Alfred 99, 103, 170,
  181, 184, 271, 272, 439, 472
Tess of the D'Urbevilles (Hardy)
  432

Thackeray, William Makepeace
  94, 140, 256, 334, 336–7
Thames, stench of 155
Theological Essays (MacDonald)
  170
Theosophical Society 549
Third Chartist Petition,
  presentation of 116–20
Thompson, Sir Henry 543
*Thoughts on the Unity of the
  Human Species* (Caldwell)
  105
Through the Looking Glass
  (Dodgson) 324
'Thrown Away' (Kipling) 498
Tillett, Ben 518
Times, The 29, 30, 33, 136, 174,
  175, 180, 181, 186, 187, 191,
  192, 254, 287, 337, 355, 390,
  418, 429, 461, 462, 489, 531
'Toccata of Galuppi, A'
  (Browning) 88
Tolpuddle martyrs 28, 35
Tolstoy, Lev Nikolayevich 441–2
Tom Brown's Schooldays
  (Hughes) 276–7, 279,
  286–7, 289, 330
Topham, William 106
Tory Party 71, 386
Tower of London museum 65
Townshend, Reverend Chauncy
  Hare 106–7
Tractarians 101, 103
trade
  as basis of power 253
  cholera and 35
  compared with Germany
  351–2
  conditions of colonial peace for
  125

entering the peerage 482–3
epicentre 108
exploitation of Africa for 489
with Ottoman Empire 393
Trades Union Congress 444
trade unions 444, 511, 512, 575, 579
Trafalgar Square 508–9
transportation 126–7
Travellers' Club 62, 63
travel speed 493–4
treaty of Paris *see* Peace of Paris
Trevelyan, Charles Edward 80
Trevelyan, G.O. 360
Trial by Jury (Gilbert and Sullivan) 418, 420
Tristan und Isolde (Wagner) 235
Tristram, Canon H.B. 225
Trollope, Anthony 259, 413–14
Trustee Savings Banks 261
Turkey 172–4, 184
bankruptcy of 393–4
extravagance of sultans in 393–4
military strength of 399
Urquhart in 188
see also Balkan crisis; Ottoman Empire ; Russo-Turkish War
Turkish army in Crimean War 180–1
Turner, Joseph Mallord William 13–14, 52, 164
Turn of the Screw, The (James) 568–9

Uganda 486–7, 491
atrocities in 492
Ulster 454, 456
Uncle Tom's Cabin (Beecher Stowe) 258, 260, 268, 330
sales of 268
Under the Greenwood Tree (Hardy) 432
Underground Railway, London 453
unemployment 508, 512
Universities Terms Act 364
Unto this Last (Ruskin) 326
urban poor 367
urban proletariat 154
Urquhart, David 188
utilitarianism 37–8, 46, 405, 554
and liberty 132
Utopia, Limited (Gilbert and Sullivan) 572

Vaccination Act 309
Vanity Fair (Thackeray) 334
Varna, Crimea, destruction of stores in 179
Vatican Decrees and their Bearing on Civil Allegiance, The (Gladstone) 374
Vaticanism (Gladstone) 374
Vaughan, Charles John 290–1
venereal diseases 308–10
see also Contagious Diseases Act; prostitution
Venice 87–8
as emblem of Britain 88
Vestiges of the Natural History of Creation (Chambers) 95–8, 99, 104, 227
Victoire, Princess of Leiningen 24–6
Victoria, the Princess Royal (Vicky)
marriage of 238, 503
on Franco-Prussian War 346

relationship with parents
  240–1
Victoria, Queen
  accession of 14
  in Bedchamber Crisis 53–4
  behaviour of 241–3
  character of 240–2, 503
  characteristics of 26, 55, 56
  and Civil List 360, 503–4
  death of 615–16
  death of mother of 241–2
  delight in company of Indians
    219
  and Disraeli 403, 407
  dress at Jubilee 502
  as Empress of India 390–1
  funeral of 616–19
  and Gladstone 359
  Golden Jubilee of 502–7
  at the Great Exhibition 130
  and Indian servants 505–7
  'invisibility' of 360
  and John Brown 504
  last months of 614–15
  and Lord Cardigan 183
  marriage of 54–5
  morals of family of 503
  parentage of 24–5, 54
  political leanings of 57, 359
  relationship with children
    240–1
  relationship with Prince of
    Wales 274
  religious preferences of 506
  response to anti-Catholicism
    141
  response to Prussian victory
    345
  and Ritualists 368
  sexual life of 57
  unpopularity of 359
  wealth of see Civil List
  widowhood of 236
  see also royal family
Victoria and Albert Museum 144
Victorian society
  contact with today 352
  differences between early and
    late 545–7
  differences from modern
    307–8
  nature of 120
Vindication of the English
  Constitution (Disraeli) 67
'Vitae Lampada' (Newbolt) 292
Voltaire, François Marie Arouet
  de 97, 98
Voortrekkers 605
vote see suffrage
Voyage of the Beagle, The
  (Darwin) 227
Voyage of a Naturalist (Darwin)
  375

Wagner, Cosima 412–13
Wagner, Richard 235–6
  anti-Semitism of 412
  reaction to the Thames 413
  visits to London 411, 417
Wainwright, Lincoln Stanhope
    365, 366, 369, 370
Wakley, Thomas 35, 40, 66
Wales
  separatism in 452
  visions in 451–2
Wallace, Alfred Russel 95, 439
  background 224
  response to Origin of Species
    226
wallpaper manufacturers 154

Walpole, Sir Robert 60
Walter, John 33
wars of Victorian era 353–4
Water Babies, The (Kingsley) 295–304
as satire 299
water-borne diseases 155–7
Way We Live Now, The (Trollope) 413, 417
wealth, growth in 14, 446
Wealth of Nations (Smith) 132
Webb, Beatrice 511, 574–6
see also Potter
Webb, Philip 262, 558
Webb, Sidney 511
Wedgwood, Josiah 44–5, 50, 225
Weismann, August Friedrich Leopold 232
Wellington, Duke of 117, 130, 145–6, 539
West Indies, unrest in plantations of 126
Westmacott, Richard 128
Westminster, Duke of 584–5
Westminster Hall 14
Westminster Review, The 168, 174, 462
Westminster School, mistreatment at 30
What Maisie Knew (James) 459
What Then Must We Do? (Tolstoy) 442
wheat production 428
Whigs 67, 71, 331, 358, 386, 584
Whistler, James McNeill 87, 422, 555
Whitechapel murders *see* Jack the Ripper
Whitely, William 409–10

'White Man's Burden' (Kipling) 496–7
White Swan public house 525
Whitney, Eli 249
'Who? Who?' government 146
Wilberforce, Bishop Samuel 228, 366, 377, 380
Wilberforce, William 48, 49, 202
Wilde, Oscar 448, 552, 559–66
sues Lord Queensberry 563–4
Wild Woodbine cigarettes 199
Wilhelm II, Kaiser 503, 609, 615–16
William IV, King 14, 24–5
Wills, W.D. and H.O. 198
Wilson, Edmund 568
Wilson, James Havelock 573
Wilson, Reverend Cairns 285–6
Wilson, Thomas 543
Winchester School 283
Windsor 56
Winfield, David Wilkie 322
Winterhalter, Franz 145
Wiseman, Nicholas 139–42
Wolseley, General Sir Garnet Joseph 466, 470
women
ageing, in *Savoy Operas* 419
'delicacy' of 312
and divorce 234
education of *see* education
equality with men of 307
legal rights of 306
parental rights of 306
in parliament 481
property rights of 306
in rural labour gangs 429
status of 248
studying medicine 312

understanding of nineteenth
century, by twentieth 316
working hours of 41, 151–2
see also Divorce Bill; domestic
violence; feminism; Infants'
Custody Act; Women's
Suffrage
Women's Movement 310–13
as bourgeois movement 312
underpinning class system 313
Women's Suffrage 43, 110,
313–14
Wood, Mrs Henry 274
Wood, Sir Charles 77
Woodard, Reverend Nathaniel
281–3
woodland, stripping of 31
woollen goods 15
wool production 428
Wordsworth, William 36, 131
*see also Excursion, The;
Prelude, The; Recluse, The*
Work (Madox Brown) 157–8
Workers' Educational Association
520
workhouses 12–13, 28–9, 44,
75
Andover, scandal of 31–3
Eton 29
Fareham 30
see also economic depression;
poverty
working classes
childhood in 260
distrust of 511
Dostoyevsky on 416
in electorate 573
scepticism of 579, 591
sense of solidarity of 41
smoking and 198–9

socialism slow to appeal to
445
status of 248
support for Chartism 113–14
see also factory workers; servant
class
Working Men's College 158
see also Chartism; child labour;
Factory Acts; urban
proletariat
Workmen's Compensation Act
582
world order in early and late
Victorian era 546–7
wrought-iron 494
Wynfield, D.W. *see* Winfield
Wyse, Elizabeth 29

xenophobia during Great
Exhibition 143

Yeast (Kingsley) 148
Yeats, W.B. 551–2, 553, 559
Yellow Book, The (Beardsley)
555
Young England movement 65–6,
67–8

Zola, Emile 344, 442
Zoological Gardens (Regents Park)
93–4
*Zoönomia or the Laws of Organic
Life* (E. Darwin) 97, 224
zoos, attitudes to 93–4
Zoological Society 93, 94
Zulu War 401–2, 405